An Introduction to Irish Company Law
Third Edition

Gráinne Callanan

Gill & Macmillan

Gill & Macmillan Ltd
Hume Avenue
Park West
Dublin 12
with associated companies throughout the world
www.gillmacmillan.ie

978 07171 41999
Index compiled by Julitta Clancy
Print origination by Carole Lynch

The paper used in this book is made froom the wood pulp of
managed forests. For every tree felled, at least one tree
is planted, thereby renewing natural resources

TABLE OF CONTENTS

Preface		*iv*
Table of Cases		*vi*
Table of Statutes		*xvii*
Table of Articles of the Constitution of Ireland 1937		*xxvii*
Table of Statutory Instruments		*xxvii*
Table of EU Legislation		*xxviii*
Table of UK Legislation		*xxviii*
Chapter 1	The Development of Companies	1
Chapter 2	Company Law Enforcement, Compliance and Review	17
Chapter 3	Company Promotion and Formation	27
Chapter 4	The Memorandum of Association	42
Chapter 5	The Articles of Association	50
Chapter 6	The Consequences of Incorporation	59
Chapter 7	Contractual Capacity of the Company	75
Chapter 8	Company Securities	84
Chapter 9	Allotment of Shares	94
Chapter 10	Maintenance of Share Capital	111
Chapter 11	Loan Capital and Charges	124
Chapter 12	Membership	135
Chapter 13	Market Abuse	150
Chapter 14	Shareholders' Meetings	161
Chapter 15	Minority Protection	174
Chapter 16	Directors and Secretaries	188
Chapter 17	Directors' Powers and Authority	200
Chapter 18	Directors' Duties and Liabilities	207
Chapter 19	Restriction and Disqualification of Directors	231
Chapter 20	Accounts and Returns	246
Chapter 21	Auditors	264
Chapter 22	Investigation of Companies	275
Chapter 23	Reorganisation of Companies	286
Chapter 24	Receivers	298
Chapter 25	The Liquidation Process	315
Chapter 26	Asset Realisation and Distribution	333
Chapter 27	Court Protection	350
Appendix:	Table A, Companies Act, 1963	368
Index		400

PREFACE

The law relating to companies is vast and students are often confused by the complex web of rules and legal principles that govern the area. If the reasoning behind those principles is understood, the technical rules can be easier to understand. This book is designed to help students recognise and understand the basic rules and principles that govern company law.

Many of the principles of company law are intended to protect shareholders and creditors. The reason why these categories need protection is simple. First, companies are managed on a day-to-day basis by directors, and while the directors of small private companies are often the shareholders there is no legal requirement that this be the case. Therefore, shareholders are investing in a company that is often run by someone else — the board of directors — which makes decisions on their behalf. To prevent arbitrary use of the decision-making powers of the board, the law imposes a number of rules and obligations on directors.

Secondly, limited liability companies — with which this text concerns itself — enjoy a privilege granted by the State which other businesses do not enjoy, viz., the liability of their members is limited. In the event that the underlying business and ultimately the company fail, there is generally no recourse to the owners of that company. Bearing this in mind, along with the potential for abuse, legislation has attempted to protect creditors by imposing obligations on those natural personalities which are the face of the company and whose decisions can ultimately affect those who deal with the company.

Company law also takes into account the requirements of other players in a company's existence: promoters, directors, employees and auditors. Furthermore, the law provides detailed rules for those who may become involved with a company when it is in financial difficulty, such as examiners, liquidators and receivers.

Since the last edition of this book there have been a number of legislative developments in company law. The Companies (Auditing and Accounting) Act 2003 established the Irish Auditing and Accounting Supervisory Authority, an independent body primarily responsible for supervising the regulation of the accountancy bodies and promoting high professional standards in the auditing and accounting professions. The Investment Funds, Companies and Miscellaneous Provisions Act 2005 provides for the transposition of the European Union Directives on Market Abuse and Prospectuses into Irish company law. The Investment Funds, Companies and Miscellaneous Provisions Act 2006 increases the maximum number of members for private companies, increases the audit exemptions thresholds for private companies and introduces provisions to facilitate the implementation of the European Union Transparency Directive.

This text is aimed at students who are studying company law modules as part of their undergraduate studies, whether in the fields of business, banking and accountancy or otherwise. These students are generally required to have a thorough, though not overly academic, knowledge of the subject. Law undergraduates who wish to obtain a sound knowledge of the first principles of company law before engaging in the more advanced or specialist works would also benefit from the book.

I wish to express my gratitude to a number of people without whose support this text would not have been completed: my colleagues Dr Albert Keating, Dr John Ennis, Dr Michael Howlett, Brian Cantrell, Jason O'Riordan, Elliot Payne, Neil Van Dokkum and Walter O'Leary; former student John McNally; Emma Farrell and Marion O'Brien of Gill & Macmillan; Monica Mernagh, Ger Kehoe, Elizabeth Hudson, Martina Hudson and John Wolfe; and finally my parents, Philip and Ann Callanan, for the never-ending support they always maintain for the ventures of their seven children.

Gráinne Callanan
Waterford Institute of Technology
24 December 2006

DEDICATION

To Philip and Ann Callanan

Table of Cases

A & L Underwood Ltd v. Bank of Liverpool and Martins Ltd [1924] All ER 230 205
Adams v. Cape Industries [1990] Ch 433 . . . . 64–5, 67
Allen v. Gold Reefs of West Africa Ltd [1900] 1 Ch 656 . . . . 53, 171n
Allen v. Hyatt (1914) 30 TLR 444 214–15
Allied Irish Banks Ltd v. Ardmore Studios International, unreported, High Court,
    May 30, 1973 203–4
Allied Irish Coal Supplies Ltd v. Powell Duffryn International Fuels Ltd [1997]
    1 ILRM 306 (HC); [1998] 2 ILRM 61 (SC). 67
Aluminium Fabricators Ltd, In re [1984] ILRM 399 223
Aluminium Industrie Vaasen BV v. Romalpa Aluminium Ltd [1976] 2
    All ER 552 . . . . 131n, 314n
Amantiss Enterprises, In re [2000] 2 ILRM 177 41
American Express International Banking v. Hurley [1986] BCLC 52 . . . . 301, 305–6
Andrews v. Gas Meter Co. [1897] 1 Ch 361 . . . . 89n
Anglo-Irish Agencies Ltd v. Green [1960] All ER 244 . . . . 76n
Ansbacher (Cayman) Ltd and Others, In re, unreported, High Court, May 25, 2004 . . 282n, 284
Antigen Holdings Ltd, In re [2001] 4 IR 600 365
Arctic Engineering Ltd, In re (No. 2) [1986] BCLC 341 . . . . 243, 243n
Ardmore Studios (Ireland) Ltd v. Lynch [1965] IR 1 . . . . 300n, 313
Armagh Shoes Ltd, In re [1984] BCLC 405. . . . . 129n
Arulchelvan v. Wright, unreported, High Court, February 7, 1996 . . . . 135n, 167n
Ashbury Railway Carriage & Iron Co. v. Riche (1875) LR 7 HL 653 . . . . 8, 50n, 75n
Ashmark Ltd, In re (No. 1) [1990] ILRM 330 . . . . 336n
Aston Colour Print Ltd, In re, unreported, High Court, February 21, 1997. . . . . 195–6, 351n
Atlantic Magnetics Ltd, In re [1993] 2 IR 561 . . . . 350, 356, 362
Attorney General v. Great Eastern Railway (1880) 5 App Cas 473 HL 75n, 80n
Aveling Barford Ltd v. Perion Ltd [1989] BCLC 626 . . . . 145n

Bahia and San Francisco Railway, In re (1868) LR 3 QB 584. 141
Bailey Hay & Co. Ltd, In re [1971] 1 WLR 1357 172
Baillie v. Oriental Telephone & Electric Co. [1915] 1 Ch 503 . . . . 166, 178–9
Balkis Consolidated Co. v. Tomkinson [1893] AC 396 142–3
Banfi Ltd v. Moran, unreported, High Court, July 20, 2006 138
Bank of Cyprus (London) Ltd v. Gill [1980] 2 Lloyd's Reports 51 . . . . 307n
Bank of Ireland v. Rockfields [1979] 2 IR 21. 120
Barings plc, In re [1999] 1 BCLC 433 . . . . 234n
Barnett Hoares v. South London Tramways (1887) 18 QBD 815 197–8
Barrett v. Duckett & Others [1995] 1 BCLC 243. . . . . 180n
Beattie v. Beattie [1938] Ch 708. 56–7
Bede Steam Shipping Co. Ltd, In re [1917] 1 Ch 123 139
Bell Houses Ltd v. City Wall Properties Ltd [1966] 2 All ER 674. 77
Bellador Silk Ltd, In re [1965] 1 All ER 667 . . . . 182n
Birch v. Cropper, Re Bridgewater Navigation Co. (1889) 14 App Cas. 525 . . . . 86n
Bloomenthal v. Forde [1897] AC 156. 143

Table of Cases

Blue Arrow plc, In re [1987] BCLC 585 .... 184n
Bolands Ltd (in receivership) v. Ward & Others [1988] ILRM 382. .... 304n
Bond v. Barrow Haematite Steel Co. [1902] 1 Ch 353 .... 87, 148
Borland's Trustee v. Steel [1901] Ch 279 85
Bradford Banking Co. v. Briggs & Co. (1886) 12 App Cas 29 .... 145n
Bratton Seymour Service Co. Ltd v Oxborough [1992] BCLC 693 56
Brightlife Ltd, In re [1986] 3 All ER 673 130
Brook's Wharf Ltd v. Goodman Bros [1937] 1 KB 534. 70
Brown v. British Abrasive Wheel Co. [1919] 1 Ch 291 54
Buchanan Ltd v. McVey [1954] IR 89 172
Bugle Press Ltd, In re [1961] Ch 270 .... 68, 292n, 293n
Bula Ltd, In re [2002] 2 ILRM 513 306
Bula Ltd v. Tara Mines Ltd [1994] 1 ILRM 111. .... 281n
Bula Ltd v. Tara Mines Ltd [1987] IR 85 .... 62n
Bula Mines Ltd, In re, unreported, High Court, July 18, 1986, Supreme Court,
      May 13, 1988 .... 321n
Burland v. Earle [1902] AC 83 87
Bushell v Faith [1969] 1 All ER 1002 .... 51-2, 194
Byng v. London Life Association Ltd [1989] 1 All ER 560. .... 167n, 179

Cahill v. Grimes, In re CB Readymix Ltd, unreported, Supreme Court,
      March 1, 2002 .... 242, 244
Cane v. Jones [1981] 1 All ER 533. .... 172n
Caparo Industries plc v. Dickman [1990] 2 AC 605. 269
Caratal (New) Mines Ltd, In re [1902] 2 Ch 498 168-9
Carruth v. ICI [1937] AC 707 .... 163n
Carvill v. Irish Industrial Bank [1968] IR 325 .... 194, 194n
Casey v. Irish Intercontinental Bank [1979] IR 364. .... 305n, 307
Castigliones Will Trusts, In re [1958] Ch 549 114-15
Cautious Trading Ltd, In re; Director of Corporate Enforcement v. Forristal
      and Forristal, unreported, High Court, March 15, 2005 .... 241n
Cavan Crystal Group Ltd, In re, unreported, High Court, April 26, 1996 232-3
CH (Ireland), In re [1999] 4 IR 542 120
Charterbridge Corporation Ltd v. Lloyds Bank Ltd [1969] 2 All ER 1185 79
Charterhouse Investment Trust Ltd v. Tempest Diesels Ltd [1987] BCLC 7. 120
Cherby Ltd, In re; Kavanagh v. Cooke [2006] 1 ILRM 91 234
Chestvale Properties Ltd and Hoddle Investments Ltd v. Glackin [1993] 3 IR 35. .... 281n, 283n
Choppington Collieries v. Johnson [1944] 1 All ER 762 165
Churchill (Plymouth) Hotel Ltd, In re [1988] BCLC 341 .... 243n
City Car Sales Ltd (in receivership & liquidation), In re [1995] 1 ILRM 221 .... 300n
City Equitable Fire Insurance Co. Ltd, In re [1925] Ch 407 .... 226, 230
Cladrose Ltd, In re [1990] BCLC 204 239
Clare Textiles Ltd, In re [1993] 2 IR 213 .... 360-1, 366
Clark v. Workman [1920] 1 IR 107 .... 58n, 208, 210
Clawhammer Ltd, In re; Director of Corporate Enforcement v. McDonnell
      and Endicott, unreported, High Court, March 15, 2005. .... 241n, 244-5
Clemens v. Clemens Bros Ltd [1976] 2 All ER 268. .... 90-1, 210
Clifton Place Garage Ltd, In re [1970] Ch 477. 336-7

Coalport Building Co. Ltd v. Castle Contracts (Ireland) Ltd, unreported,
 High Court, January 19, 2004 . . . . 318n
Cockburn v. Newbridge Sanitary Steam Laundry Company [1915] 1 IR 237 178
Coleman v. Myers [1977] 2 NZLR 225 . . . . 150n, 214
Colonia Insurance (Ireland) Ltd, In re, unreported, High Court, March 15, 2005 289–90
Companiea de Electricidad de la Provincia de Buenos Aires Ltd [1978] 3 All ER 668 . . . . . 149n
Company, In re a [1985] 1 BCC 99 63
Company(No. 00789 of 1987), In re a [1990] BCLC 384 183
Company(No. 004475 of 1982), In re a [1983] 2 All ER 36 183
Cook v. Deeks [1916] 1 AC 554 179–80
Coombe Importers Ltd, In re, unreported, Supreme Court, June 22, 1995 366
Copp, Ex p. [1989] BCLC 12 . . . . 190n
Cork Electric Supply Co. Ltd v. Concannon [1923] IR 314 88
Corran Construction v. Bank of Ireland Finance Ltd [1976-77] ILRM 175 340
Cotman v. Brougham [1918] AC 514 76–7
Coubrough v. James Panton & Co. Ltd [1965] IR 272 193–4
Countyglen plc, In re [1995] 1 ILRM 213 . . . . 282n
Coyle v. O'Brien, unreported, High Court, July 14, 2003 . . . . 235n
Creation Printing Co. Ltd, In re [1978] ILRM 219 342
Cretanor Maritime Co. Ltd v. Irish Marine Management Ltd [1978] 3 All ER 164 . . . . 300n
Crindle Investments v. Wymes [1998] 2 ILRM 275; [1998] 4 IR 567 . . . . 180n, 183, 185
Crompton & Co. Ltd, In re [1914] 1 Ch 954 . . . . 126n
Cummins (M.J.), In re: Barton v Bank of Ireland [1939] IR 60 . . . . 78n

Dafen Tinplate Co. Ltd v Llanelly Steel Co. (1907) Ltd [1920] 2 Ch 124 54
Daimler v. Continental Tyre Co. [1916] 2 AC 307 69
Daniel Murphy Ltd, In re [1964] IR 1 342
Daniels v. Daniels [1978] Ch 406 180
Darby, In re: ex parte Brougham [1911] 1 KB 95 68
Dawson International plc v. Coats Paton plc [1989] BCLC 233 . . . . 211, 211n
Dawson Print Group Ltd, In re [1987] BCLC 601 . . . . 243, 243n
Debtor (No. 340 of 1992), In re a [1994] 2 BCLC 171 . . . . 318n
Derry v. Peek (1889) 14 App Cas 337 . . . . 109n
Destone Fabrics Ltd, In re [1941] Ch 319 . . . . 342n
DHN Food Distributors Ltd v. Tower Hamlet Borough Council [1976] 1 WLR 852 65
Director of Corporate Enforcement v. D'Arcy, unreported, High Court, October
 26, 2005 . . . . 241n, 242–3, 242n, 244
Don Bluth Entertainment Ltd, In re [1994] 3 IR 141 361
Don Bluth Entertainment Ltd, In re (No. 1), unreported, High Court, August 27, 1992 . . 351
Dorchester Finance Co. Ltd v. Stebbing (1989) BCLC 498 227
Dorman Long and Company Ltd, In re [1934] 1 Ch 635 . . . . 289n
Douglas Construction Services Ltd, In re [1988] BCLC 397 . . . . 17n
Dovey v. Cory [1901] 1 Ch 477 229
Dublin North Cily Milling Co. Ltd, In re [1909] 1 IR 179 208
Durham Fancy Goods Ltd v Michael Jackson (Fancy Goods) Ltd [1968] 2 QB 839 . . . . . 45, 70

Eccles Hall Ltd v. Bank of Nova Scotia, unreported, High Court, February 3, 1995 . . . 120n
Eddystone Marine Insurance Co., In re [1893] 3 Ch. 9 . . . . 99n

Table of Cases

Edenfell Holdings Ltd, In re [1999] 1 IR 443 ....307n
Edenpark Construction Ltd, In re [1994] 3 IR 126.........................362, 366
Edwards v. Halliwell [1950] 2 All ER 1064...................................176
Eisc Teoranta, In re [1991] ILRM 760 309
El Sombrero, In re [1958] 3 All ER 1..161
Eley v. Positive Government Life Assurance Co. (1876) 1 Ex D 21 ....57, 58
English & Scottish Mercantile Investment Co. Ltd v. Brunton [1892] 2 QB 700 ......127n
Erlanger v. New Sombrero Phosphate Co. (1878) 3 App Cas. 1218 ....28, 29
Ewing v Buttercup Margarine Co. Ltd [1917] 2 Ch 1 44
Exchange Banking Co., In re (1882) 21 Ch D 519.............................147–8

Fargo v. Godfrey [1986] BCLC 370 181
Farm Fresh Frozen Foods Ltd, In re [1980] ILRM 131 ....133n
Fennell v. Carolan & Cosgrave, In re CMC (Ireland) Ltd (in voluntary
    liquidation), unreported, High Court, March 4, 2005 236–7
Ferngara Associates Ltd, In re; Robinson v. Forrest, unreported, High Court,
    11 February, 1999 238
Firestone Tyre and Rubber Co. v. Llewellin [1957] 1 WLR 464 64
First City Corporation Ltd v. Downsview Nominees Ltd [1990] 3 NZLR 265 312
Fitzwilton plc, In re; Duggan v. Stoneworth Ltd [2000] 2 ILRM 263 ....293n
FLE Holdings Ltd, In re [1967] 1 WLR 1409 341
Fomento (Sterling Area) Ltd v Selsdon Fountain Pen Co. [1958] 1 All ER 11 ....267n
Foss v. Harbottle (1843) 2 Hare 261................................8, 150n, 175–81
Frederick Inns Ltd, In re [1991] ILRM 582 (HC); [1994] 1 ILRM 387
    (SC)...80–1, 80n, 82, 216
Freeman Lockyer v. Buckhurst Park Properties (Mangal) Ltd [1964] QB 480 .... 201, 202, 203
French's (Wine) Bar Ltd, In re [1987] BCLC 499 334
Fulham Football Club Ltd v. Cabra Estates plc [1994] 1 BCLC 363.................211
Fyffes plc v. DCC plc and Others, unreported, High Court, December 21,
    2005 ....66–7, 154–5, 189–90, 190n, 233n

Gasco Ltd, In re, unreported, High Court, February 5, 2001 234
Gee & Co. (Woolwich) Ltd, In re [1974] 1 All ER 1149........................149n
Geoghegan v. Institute of Chartered Accountants in Ireland [1995] 3 IR 86...........10n
Gerald Cooper Chemicals, In re [1978] 2 All ER 49 ....222n
German Date Coffee Co., In re [1882] 20 Ch D 169 ....46, 319
Gilford Motor Co. Ltd v. Horne [1933] Ch 939................................68
Gilligan v. Criminal Assets Bureau [1998] 3 IR 185 ....282n
Gilt Construction Ltd, In re [1994] 2 ILRM 456 331
GL Saunders Ltd (in liquidation), In re [1986] 1 WLR 215......................310n
Glackin v. Trustee Savings Banks [1993] 3 IR 55 282
Gluckstein v. Barnes [1900] AC 240 28–9
Gramophone & Typewriter Ltd v. Stanley [1904] 2 KB 89 CA...................200n
Gray v. McLoughlin; In re First Class Toy Traders Ltd, unreported,
    High Court, July 9, 2004..188–9, 233n
Green, In re [1949] 1 All ER 167 ....137n
Greendale Developments Ltd, In re (No. 1) [1997] 3 IR 540 ....315n
Greendale Developments Ltd, In re (No. 2) [1998] 1 IR 8 ..... 80, 145n, 172n, 173n, 213n

Greenhalgh v. Arderne Cinemas Ltd [1946] 1 All ER 512. 90
Greenhalgh v. Arderne Cinemas Ltd [1950] 2 All ER 1120 53
Greenore Trading Co. Ltd, In re [1980] ILRM 94 182–3
Griffin Hotel Co., In re [1940] Ch 87 130
Guinness plc v. Saunders [1988] 2 All ER 652. . . . . 217n
GWI Ltd, In re, unreported, High Court, November 10, 1987 339

H R Harmer Ltd, In re [1959] 1 WLR 62 . . . . 171n
Hafner, In re; Olhausen v. Powderley [1943] IR 426 . . . . 137–8, 208n
Halley v. Nolan, unreported, High Court, July 1, 2005 229
Halpin v. Cremin [1954] IR 19 . . . . 126n
Harlowe's Nominees Pty Ltd v. Woodside Oil Co. (1968) 121 CLR 483 . . . . 209n
Hartley Baird Ltd, In re [1954] Ch 143 167
Harvela Investments v. Royal Trust Company of Canada [1986] AC 139 102
Hayes Homes Ltd, In re, unreported, High Court, July 8, 2004. 331
Heaney v. Ireland [1996] 1 IR 580 . . . . 282n
Hedley Byrne v. Heller & Partners [1964] AC 465 . . . . 109n, 268, 269
Heffernan Kearns, In re (No. 2) [1993] 3 IR 191 224
Hellenic and General Trust, In re [1976] 1 WLR 123 288
Hely-Hutchinson v. Brayhead Ltd [1968] 1 QBD 549 202
Hickman v. Kent or Romney Marsh Sheepbreeders Association [1915] 1 Ch D 881 56
Higgins v. Stafford, In re Xnet Information Systems Ltd (in voluntary
    liquidation), unreported, October 10, 2006. 238–9
Hilder v. Dexter [1902] AC 474 100
HKN Invest OY v. Incotrade PVT Ltd & Others [1993] 3 IR 152 . . . . 31n, 32
HL Bolton (Engineering) Ltd v. TJ Graham & Sons Ltd [1957] 1 QB 159 . . . . 63n
Hogg v. Cramphorn [1966] 3 All ER 420. . . . . 208–9, 213
Holdair Ltd, In re [1994] 1 IR 416 . . . . 357, 360, 362
Holders Investment Trust Ltd, In re [1971] 1 WLR 583; [1971] 2 All ER 289 . . . 90, 113n, 172n
Holidair Ltd, In re [1994] 1 IR 481 129
Holland v. McGill, unreported, High Court, March 16, 1990 . . . . 196n
Hollicourt Contracts Ltd v. Bank of Ireland [2001] 2 WLR 290 335
Holohan v. Friends Provident and Century Life Office [1966] IR 1 . . . . 305n, 307
Home Treat Ltd, In re [1991] BCLC 705 . . . . 172n
Hopkins v Shannon Transport Systems Ltd, unreported, High Court, 10 January 1972 . . . 29
Horgan v. Murray [1998] 1 ILRM 110 . . . . 185n
Houghton & Co. v. Northard Lowe & Wills Ltd [1927] All ER 97 205
House of Fraser v. AGCE Investments Ltd [1987] AC 387 . . . . 90n
Howard Smith Ltd v. Ampol Petroleum Ltd [1974] AC 403 209
Howard v. Patent Ivory Manufacturing Co. [1883] 3 Ch D. 156 204
Hunting Lodges Ltd, In re [1985] ILRM 75. . . . . 222n, 223, 229, 241n
Hutton v. West Cork Railway Co. [1883] 23 Ch D 654 . . . . 80, 80n

Imperial Hotel (Cork) Ltd, In re [1950] IR 115 . . . . 88n
Industrial Development Consultants Ltd v. Cooley [1972] 2 All ER 162 212–13
Industrial Services Company (Dublin) Ltd, In re (No. 2), unreported, High
    Court, May 15, 2002. . . . . 336n, 337
Industrial Services Ltd, In re [2001] 2 IR 118 335

Table of Cases

International Sales & Agencies Ltd v. Marcus [1982] 3 All ER 551 78
Introductions Ltd v. National Provincial Bank [1968] 2 All ER 1221 77–8
IRC v. Crossman [1937] AC 26 .... 85n
Irish Oil and Cake Mills Ltd v. Donnelly, unreported, High Court, 27 March,
    1983 .... 301, 308
Irish Press v. Ingersoll Irish Publications Ltd, unreported, High Court,
    15 December 1993 185
Irish Press v. Ingersoll Irish Publications Ltd [1995] 2 IR 175; [1995] 2 ILRM 270 (SC) ... 185
Irish Rail Ltd v. Ireland and Others [1995] 2 ILRM 161 .... 62n
Irish Visiting Motorist's Bureau Ltd, In re, February 7, 1972 .... 182n
Irvine v. Union Bank of Australia (1877) 2 App Cas 366 204

Jackson v. Munster Bank Ltd, ex parte Dease (1885) 15 LR Ir 356 227–8
JEB Fasteners Ltd v. Marks, Bloom & Co. [1981] 3 All ER 289 268
Jermyn Turkish Baths Ltd, In re [1971] 1 WLR 1042 209
Jetmara Teo Ltd, In re [1992] 1 IR 147 364–5
Johnson & Co. (Builders) Ltd, In re [1955] 2 All ER 775 .... 313n
Jon Beauforte (London) Ltd, In re [1953] Ch 131 75–6
Jones v. Bellgrove Properties Ltd [1949] 2 All ER 198 .... 149n
Jones v. Lipman [1962] 1 All ER 442 67–8

Kavanagh v. Delaney [2005] 1 ILRM 34 .... 228, 233–4
Kaye v. Croydon Tramways Co. [1898] 1 Ch 358 165–6
Kaytech International plc, In re; Potier v. Secretary of State for Industry
    [1999] 2 BCLC 351; [1999] BCC 390 .... 189n
Keenan Bros Ltd, In re [1985] IR 401 128–9
Kelleher v. Continental Irish Meats, unreported, High Court, May 9, 1978 .... 340n
Kelly v. Haughey Boland & Co. [1989] ILRM 373 .... 268–9, 268n
Kelly's Carpetdrome Ltd, In re, unreported, High Court, July 1, 1983 222–3
Kelner v Baxter (1866) LR 2 CP174 31
Kilgobbin Mink and Stud Farm Ltd v. National Credit Company Ltd [1980] IR 175... 300n
Kinsella v. Russell Kinsella Property Ltd [1986] 4 NSWLR 722 215
Knocklofty House Hotel Ltd (in liquidation), In re, Ex tempore, unreported,
    High Court, April 5, 2005 235–6

La Moselle Clothing Ltd v. Souhali [1998] 2 ILRM 345.............. 231n, 233, 236
Lafayette Ltd, In re [1950] IR 100 .... 87n, 148n
Lagunas Nitrate Co. v. Lagunas Syndicate [1899] 2 Ch 392 .... 28n, 226–7
Lambert Jones Estates Ltd v. Donnelly, unreported, High Court, November 5, 1982... 307n
Land Credit Co. of Ireland v. Lord Fermoy (1870) LR 5 Ch App 763 .... 228n
Lascomme Ltd v. UDT [1994] 1 ILRM 227.................................... 303n
Lee & Co. (Dublin) Ltd v. Egan (Wholesale) Ltd, unreported, High Court,
    April 27, 1978 .... 58n
Lee v. Lee's Air Farming Ltd [1961] AC 12................................... 60–1
Leinster Contract Corporation, In re [1902] IR 349 99
Levin v. Clark [1962] NSWR 686.. 211
Lewis Merthyr Consolidated Collieries, In re [1939] 1 Ch 498.................. 310n
Lindholst & Co. A/S v Fowler [1988] BCLC 166 .... 45n

Lloyd v. Grace Smith & Co. [1911] 2 KB 489 143
Lo-Line Electric Motors Ltd, In re [1988] BCLC 698 . . . . 190n, 242
Lombard & Ulster Banking Ltd v. Amurec Ltd [1976-1977] ILRM 222 132
Lombard & Ulster Banking Ltd v. Bank of Ireland, unreported, High Court,
    June 2, 1987 121
Longman v. Bath Electric Tramways [1905] 1 Ch 646 140–1
Lyle & Scott Ltd v. Scott's Trustees [1959] AC 763 139
Lynrowan Enterprises Ltd, In re, unreported, High Court, July 31, 2002 . . . . 189n, 242n
Lyons and Others v. Curran [1993] ILRM 375 277–8

Macaura v. Northern Assurance Co. Ltd [1925] AC 619 . . . . 61, 62
McBirney & Co. Ltd, In re, unreported, High Court, July 2, 1992 . . . . 336n
MacDougall v. Gardiner (1875) 1 Ch D 13 . . . . 167n, 176
Mace Builders (Glasgow) Ltd v. Lunn [1987] BCLC 55 . . . . 342n
McGowan v. Gannon [1983] ILRM 516 . . . . 305n, 308
Madden v. Anglo-Irish Bank plc [2005] 1 ILRM 294 177–8
Mahoney v. East Holyford Mining Co. (1875) LR 7 HL 869 205–6
Majestic Recording Studios Ltd, In re (1988) 4 BCC 519 243
Manning Furniture Ltd, In re [1996] 1 ILRM 13 309–10
Mechanisations (Eaglecliffe) Ltd, In re [1964] 3 All ER 840 132–3
Mehigan v. Duignan [1997] 1 IR 340 248
Menier v. Hooper's Telegraph Works (1874) LR 9 Ch App 350 179
Metafile Ltd, In re, unreported, High Court, December 20, 2006 319–20
Mills v. Mills (1938) 60 CLR 150 209–10
Mont Clare Hotels Ltd, In re, unreported, High Court, December 2, 1986 . . . . 225n
Mooregate Mercantile Holdings Ltd, In re [1980] 1 All ER 40 . . . . 165, 167n
Morgan Crucible Co. plc v. Hill Samuel Co. Ltd [1991] Ch 295 269
Morris v. Kanssen [1946] AC 459 205
Moylan v. Irish Whiting Manufacturers Ltd, unreported, High Court, April 14, 1980 . . . . . 180n
Munster Bank, In re (Re Dillon's claim), (1886) 17 LR Ir 341 98
Murph's Restaurant Ltd, In re [1979] ILRM 141 . . . . 69, 182n, 186–7, 194n, 321

Nash v. Lancegaye Safty Glass (Ireland) Ltd (1958) 92 ILTR 11 209
National Irish Bank Ltd, In re, unreported, High Court, July 23, 2004 . . . . 283–4, 285
NEW-AD Advertising Company Ltd, In re, unreported, High Court, July 1, 1997 185
New British Iron Co., In re [1989] 1 Ch 324 57
Newcastle Timber Ltd, In re, unreported, High Court, October 16, 2001 243
Newdigate Colliery, In re (1912) 1 Ch 468 . . . . 314n
Newhart Developments v. Co-operative Commercial Bank [1978] QB 814 302–3
Newstead v. Frost [1980] 1 WLR 135 . . . . 77N
Northern Bank Finance Ltd v. Quinn & Achates Investments [1979] ILRM 221 . . . 81–2, 83
Northside Motors Co. Ltd, In re, unreported, High Court, July 24, 1985 121
Nurcombe v. Nurcombe [1984] BCLC 557 . . . . 181n

Ocean Coal Co. v. Powell Duffryn Steam Coal Co. [1932] 1 Ch 654 97
O'Ferral v. Coughlan and Others; in re 360 Atlantic (Ireland) Ltd, High Court, December 21,
    2004 . . . . 230n
O'Keefe v. An Bord Pleanala [1993] 1 IR 39 . . . . 283n

Table of Cases

Old Silkstone Collieries, In re [1954] 1 All ER 68 113–14
O'Neill v. Ryan & Ryanair Ltd [1993] ILRM 557 . . . . 61–2, 177
Ooregum Gold Mining Co. of India v. Roper [1892] AC 125 . . . . 98, 111n

Pageboy Couriers Ltd, In re [1983] ILRM 510 318
Panorama Developments (Guildford) Ltd v. Fidelis Furnishing Fabrics [1971] 2 QB 711 . . 198
Parke v. Daily News Ltd [1962] 2 All ER 929 . . . . 80, 178, 215
Parker & Cooper v. Reading [1926] Ch 975 172
Parkes v. Hong Kong & Shanghai Banking Corporation [1990] ILRM 341 216
Pavlides v. Jensen [1956] 2 All ER 518 180
Peat v. Gresham Trust [1934] AC 252 340
Pender v. Lushington [1877] LR 6 Ch D 70 . . . . 171, 176
Penrose v Martyr (1858) EB & E 499 45
Percival v. Wright [1902] 2 Ch 421 . . . . 150n
Percival v. Wright [1902] Ch 421 213–14
Pergamon Press Ltd, In re [1970] 3 All ER 589 . . . . 283n
Peso Silver Mines Ltd v. Cropper (1966) 58 DLR (2d) 1 213
Phonogram Ltd v Lane [1981] 3 All ER 182 . . . . 31, 32N
PMPA Garage (Longmile) Ltd, In re [1992] ILRM 337 . . . . 78, 79n
Popely v. Planarrive Ltd [1997] 1 BCLC 8 138
Power (John) & Sons Ltd, In re [1934] IR 412 . . . . 113n
Power Supermarkets Ltd v. Crumlin Investments Ltd and Dunnes Stores
    (Crumlin) Ltd, unreported, High Court, June 22, 1981 65–6
Power v. Sharpe Investments Ltd [1994] 1 BCLC 111 . . . . 343n
Probets v. Glackin [1993] 3 IR 134 . . . . 282n
Prudential Assurance Co. Ltd v. Newman Industries Ltd [1982] 1 All ER 354 177
Prudential Assurance Co. Ltd v. Newman Industries Ltd (No. 2) [1982] Ch 204 . . . . . . 180n
Pye Ireland Ltd, In re, unreported, High Court, November 12, 1984 288–9

Quigley v. Burke, unreported, Supreme Court, November 7, 1995 . . . . 281n
Quinn's Supermarket Ltd v. Attorney General [1972] IR 1 . . . . 62n

R. v. Harris [1970] 2 All ER 746 . . . . 282n
R. v. Morrissey [1997] 2 CR App Rep 426 . . . . 153n
R. v. Staines [1997] 2 CR App Rep 426 . . . . 151, 153n
Rafsanjan Pistachio Producers Co-operative v. Reiss [1990] BCLC 352 70
Ranks (Ireland) Ltd, In re [1988] ILRM 751 339
Rayfield v. Hands [1960] 1 Ch 1 57–8
Read v. Astoria Garage Streatham Ltd [1952] Ch 637 . . . . 194n
Redbreast Preserving Company (Ireland) Ltd, In re, 91 ILTR 12 . . . . 282n
Regal (Hastings) Ltd v. Gulliver [1967] 2 AC 134 . . . . 211–12, 213
Richborough Furniture Ltd, In re [1996] 1 BCLC 507; [1996] BCC 155 . . . . 189n
Rogers v. George Maloney (Authorised Officer) and the Director of Corporate Enforcement,
    unreported, High Court, December 21, 2005 281
Rolled Steel Products (Holdings) Ltd v. British Steel Corporation [1985] 3 All ER 52 . . . 79, 80n
Roper v Ward [1981] ILRM 408 50
Roundabout Ltd v. Beirne [1959] IR 423 61
Royal British Bank v. Turquand [1843-60] All ER 435 . . . . 83, 203–6

Ruben v. Great Fingall Consolidated [1906] AC 439 143
Ruby Property Co. Ltd et al. v. Kilty & Another, unreported, High Court, December 11,
    1995 . . . . 308n
Russell v Northern Bank Development Corporation [1992] 3 All Er 161 . . . . 51n

Salmon v. The Hamborough Co. (1671) 1 CH Cas 204 . . . . 1n
Salomon v. Salomon & Co. Ltd [1897] AC 22
    . . . . 8, 28, 59–60, 61, 62, 63, 99n, 350
Saltdean Estate Co. Ltd, in re [1968] 1 WLR 1844 . . . . 90n
Saul D Harrison & Sons plc, In re [1994] BCC 475 . . . . 184n
Saunders v. The United Kingdom (43/1994/490/572) 282n
Scottish Co-operative Wholesale Society Ltd v. Meyer [1959] AC 324 211
Scottish Insurance Corporation v. Wilsons and Clyde Coal Company [1949] AC 462 . . . 88n
Scottish Wholesale Co-operative Society Ltd v. Meyer [1959] AC 324 . . . . 182, 184–5
Secretary of State for Trade and Industry v. Baker [1999] 1 BCLC 433 . . . . 228n
Securities Trust Ltd v. Associated Properties Ltd and Others, unreported,
    High Court, November 19, 1980 . . . . 215n, 292n
Selangor United Rubber Estates Ltd v. Craddock & Others (No. 3) [1968]
    2 All ER 1073 . . . . 228n
Seluckwe Ltd, In re, unreported, High Court, December 20, 1991 . . . . 354, 365
Shannonside Holdings Ltd, In re, unreported, High Court, May 20, 1993 . . . 133, 161n, 173
Sharman (R W), In re [1957] 1 All ER 737 . . . . 321n
Shinrone Food Market Ltd, In re; Director of Corporate Enforcement v.
    Hoctor and Hoctor, unreported, High Court, March 15, 2005 . . . . 241n
Short v. Treasury Commissioners [1948] 1 KB 122 . . . . 85n
Shrinkpak Ltd, In re, unreported, High Court, December 20, 1989 320
Shuttleworth v. Cox Brothers & Co. (Maidenhead) Ltd [1927] 2 KB 9 54
Sidebottom v. Keeshaw, Leese & Co. [1920] 1 Ch 154 54
Siebe Gorman v. Barclay's Bank Ltd [1979] 2 Lloyd's Reports 142 . . . . 128n
Smith, Stone and Knight Ltd v. Birmingham Corporation [1939] 4 All ER 116 64
Smith & Fawcett Ltd, In re [1942] 1 All ER 452 . . . . 138, 207n, 208
Smiths Ltd v. Middleton [1979] 3 All ER 942 . . . . 308n
Smurfit Paribas Bank Ltd v. AAB Export Finance Ltd [1991] 2 IR 19 342–3
Southern Foundries (1926) Ltd v. Shirlaw [1940] AC 701 55
Sowman v. David Samuel Trust Ltd [1978] 1 All ER 616 . . . . 303n
Squash (Ireland) Ltd, In re, unreported, Supreme Court, February 8, 2001 235
Squash (Ireland) Ltd, In re [2001] 3 IR 35 233
Stafford v. Higgins and Others, Re Xnet Information Systems Ltd,
    unreported, High Court, May 6, 2004 . . . . 218n, 220–1
Standard Chartered Bank v. Walker [1982] 3 All ER 938 . . . . 305n
Station Motors v. AIB [1985] IR 756 341
Stewart's Supermarkets Ltd v. Secretary of State [1982] NI 286 62
Sugar Distributors Ltd, In re [1995] 2 IR 195; [1996] 1 ILRM 342 . . . . 95, 119n
Sussex Brick Co. In re [1961] Ch 289 292–3
Sutton's Hospital Case (1612) 10 Co. Rep. 7a 62n
Swabey v. Port Darwin Gold Mining Co. (1889) 1 Meg 385 57
Swaledale Cleaners Ltd, In re [1968] 1 WLR 1710 139
Sweeney v. Duggan [1997] 1 ILRM 211 61

Tailby v. Official Receiver (1883) 13 App Cas 523 . . . . 128n
Tangney v. Clarence Hotel Co. Ltd [1933] IR 51 139
TCB v. Gray [1986] 1 All ER 587 . . . . 73n
Teck Corporation Ltd v. Millar (1972) 33 DLR (3d) 288. . . . . 209n
Teleomatic Ltd, In re [1994] 1 BCLC 90 . . . . 133n
Tempany v. Royal Liver Trustees Ltd [1984] ILRM 273 338
Thames Ironworks Co. Ltd, In re [1912] WN 66 313–14
Thomas Gerrard & Sons Ltd, In re [1967] 2 All ER 525 . . . . 148, 267–8
Thorby v. Goldberg (1964) 112 CLR 597. 210–11
Tintin Exploration Syndicate v. Sandys (1947) 177 LT 412. . . . . 99n
Trevor v. Whitworth (1887) 12 App Cas 409 HL 114
Truck and Machinery Sales Ltd v. Marubeni Komatzo Ltd [1996] 1 IR 12 . . . . 318n
Tse Kwong Lam v. Wong Chit Sen [1983] 1 WLR 1349. 307
Tudor Grange Holdings Ltd v. Citibank NA [1991] 4 All ER 1 . . . . 303`
Tunstall v. Steigman [1962] 2 All ER 417 61
Turquand's case. *see* Royal British Bank v. Turquand . . . .
Tuskar Resources plc, In re [2001] 1 IR 668 . . . . 352n, 356
Twycross v. Grant [1877] 2 CPD 469. . . . . 27n

Ulster Factors Ltd v. Entoglen (in liquidation) and Moloney, unreported, High Court,
    February 21, 1997 202
Unisoft Group Ltd No. 30, In re [1994] 1 BCLC 609 . . . . 182n
United Bars Ltd v. Revenue Commissioners [1991] 1 IR 396 310
Usit World plc, In re, unreported, High Court, August 10, 2005 . . . . 233n

Van Hool McArdle Ltd v. Rohan Industrial Estates Ltd & Anon [1980] IR 137 . . . . 331n
Vehicle Buildings and Insulations Ltd, In re [1986] ILRM 239. . . . . 319n, 320–1
Vehicle Imports Ltd, In re, unreported, High Court, February 23, 2000 232

W & M Roith Ltd, In re [1967] WLR 432 . . . . 207, 215n
Walls v. Walls Holdings Ltd, unreported, High Court, November 5, 2004 293
Webb v. Earle (1875) LR 20 Eq 556. . . . . 87n
Welch v. Bowmaker (Ireland) Ltd and Bank of Ireland [1980] IR 251 125–6
Welton v. Saffery [1897] AC 299 . . . . 88n
Westbourne Galleries Ltd, In re [1973] AC 360; [1972] 2
    All ER 492 . . . . 184n, 186, 321n
Westwinds Holding Co. Ltd, In re, unreported, High Court, May 21, 1974 183–4
Wheatley v. Silkstone and Haigh Moor Coal Co. [1885] 29 Ch D 715 . . . . 126n
White Star Line, In re [1938] Ch 458. . . . . 99n
White v. Bristol Aeroplane Co. Ltd [1953] Ch 65 90
Will v. United Lankat Plantations [1914] AC 11 . . . . 87n
Williams Group (Tullamore) Ltd, In re [1985] IR 613. . . . . 183n, 184
Wilson v. Kelland [1910] 2 Ch 306 127
Wogan's (Drogheda) Ltd, In re (No. 1) [1993] 1 IR 157 . . . . 129, 352n
Wogan's (Drogheda) Ltd, In re (No.2), unreported, High Court, May 7, 1992 . . . . . 354, 355
Wogan's (Drogheda) Ltd, In re (No. 3), unreported, High Court, February 9, 1993 366
Wood v. Odessa Waterworks Company (1889) 42 Ch D 636. 149
Woodroffes (Musical Instruments) Ltd, In re [1985] BCLC 227 . . . . 126n

Worldport Ireland Ltd (in liquidation), In re, unreported, High Court,
    February 16, 2005 . . . . 190, 233, 334n, 335–6
Wragg Ltd, In re [1897] 1 Ch 796 99
Wymes v. Crowley, unreported, High Court, February 27, 1987 303

Yenidje Tobacco Co., In re [1916] 2 Ch 426 320
Yorkshire Woolcombers Association, In re [1903] 2 Ch 284 125

Table of Statutes

Bankruptcy Act 1988
  s. 3 . . . . 346n
  s. 136 (20) 346n
  sch.1, para. 24 346–7
Bubble Act 1720 2

Central Bank Act 1971
  s. 9 283
Chartered Companies Act 1837. 3
Companies Act 1900 3
Companies Act 1907 3
Companies Act 1959 4
Companies Act 1963 4
  s. 2 . . . . 188n
  s. 2 (1) 189
  s. 5 . . . . 11, 46n
  s. 6 42
  s. 6 (1) 46
  s. 6 (2) 47n
  s. 8 . . . . 81–2, 83
  s. 8 (1) 81–2, 83
  s. 8 (2). 82, 85n, 174n
  s. 10 . . . . 46n
  s. 10 (3) 47n, 84n
  s. 10 (7) 84n
  s. 10 (9) 49n
  s. 11 . . . . 50n
  s. 12 . . . . 50n
  s. 13 . . . . 42n
  s. 13 (2) 50n
  s. 14 50
  s. 15 51
  s. 18 (2) 34n
  s. 21 44
  s. 22 . . . . 44n
  s. 23 (1) 45n
  s. 23 (2) 44n
  s. 24 . . . . 43n
  s. 25. . . . . 39, 56–8, 85, 174
  s. 27 . . . . 47n, 55n, 85n
  s. 28 (3) 48n, 52n
  s. 29 . . . . 174n

  s. 31 . . . . 84n, 135n, 181n
  s. 31 (2) 95
  s. 33 (1) 11n
  s. 33 (1)(a) 137n
  s. 34 . . . . 11n
  s. 34 (1) 11n
  s. 36 70
  s. 37 (1) 31
  s. 37 (2) 31
  s. 55 . . . . 94n
  s. 57 (1) 110n
  s. 57 (2) 110n
  s. 58 (1) 96n
  s. 58 (1)(b) 98n
  s. 60. . . . . . 120–3, 175, 178, 182, 295
  s. 60 (1) 120
  s. 60 (2). 120, 121, 122
  s. 60 (2) (a). 121n
  s. 60 (2) (b). 121n
  s. 60 (2-11). 237n
  s. 60 (3) 122n
  s. 60 (4) 122n
  s. 60 (5) 122n, 344n
  s. 60 (6) 121n
  s. 60 (7) 121n
  s. 60 (8) 121n
  s. 60 (12)(a) 122n
  s. 60 (12)(b) 122n
  s. 60 (12)(c) 122n
  s. 60 (12)(d) 122n
  s. 60 (12)(e) 123n
  s. 60 (12)(f) 123n
  s. 60 (12)(g) 123n
  s. 60 (12)(h) 123n
  s. 60 (14) 120
  s. 60 (15) 120
  s. 60 (15A) 121n
  s. 62 . . . . 100n
  s. 65 115
  s. 68 112
  s. 70 (1) 112n
  s. 72. . . . . 47, 85, 115n, 146, 175

s. 72 (1) 112
s. 72 (2) 112
s. 73 . . . . 85n
s. 73 (1) 113n
s. 73 (2) 113n
s. 73 (3) 113n
s. 74 (1) 113n
s. 74 (2) 113n
s. 75 (1) 114n
s. 78 . . . . 89, 288
s. 78 (1) 89n
s. 78 (3) 90n
s. 79 . . . . 85, 137n
s. 81 137
s. 84 139
s. 85 (1) 140n
s. 86 . . . . 141n
s. 87 . . . . 142n
s. 88 143
s. 89 . . . . 95, 119
s. 93 . . . . 92n
s. 94 . . . . 92n
s. 98 . . . . 126, 308–10
s. 99 . . . . . . 93n, 132n, 133, 313n, 348
s. 99 (1) 131
s. 99 (2) 131–2
s. 99 (2A) 132n
s. 99 (2B) 132n
s. 100 (1) 131
s. 100 (3) 133n
s. 103 132
s. 104 . . . . 132n
s. 105 . . . . 134n
s. 106 (1) 133
s. 106 (2) 133n
s. 107 . . . . 305n
s. 109 . . . . 133n
s. 110 (1) 133n
s. 113 . . . . 73n
s. 114 (1) 45n
s. 114 (3) 45n
s. 114 (4) 45n, 70
s. 114 (5) 70
s. 115 . . . . 347n
s. 116 135–6

s. 117 . . . . 135n
s. 119 . . . . 136n
s. 122 (1) 136n
s. 122 (5) 136n
s. 123 136
s. 124 136
s. 125 . . . . 260, 262
s. 125 (2) 267n
s. 127 . . . . 259, 262
s. 127 (12) 267n
s. 128 (1) 261n
s. 131 . . . . 161n, 328n
s. 131 (2) 161n
s. 131 (3) 85n, 161n
s. 131-133 . . . . 174n
s. 132 . . . . 163n
s. 133 . . . . 85n, 163–4
s. 133 (2) 164n
s. 133 (3) 164n
s. 134 (a) 164
s. 134 (c) 167n
s. 134 (e) 168n
s. 135 (1) 161n
s. 136 . . . . 169n
s. 137 168
s. 139 . . . . 344n
s. 141 (1) 165
s. 141 (2) 164n
s. 141 (3) 168
s. 141 (5) 165n
s. 141 (8) 52, 121n, 172–3
s. 142 . . . . 164n, 166
s. 143 . . . . 52n, 72n, 170–1, 174n
s. 145 . . . . 169, 196
s. 146 . . . . 169n, 174n
s. 148 . . . . 162, 222n, 249
s. 148 (2) 250n
s. 148 (8) 249n
s. 149 . . . . 249, 250
s. 149 (1)(a) 251n
s. 149 (1)(b) 251
s. 149A 250
s. 150 . . . . 13n
s. 150 (10) 253n
s. 150A 253

s. 150B (1) 253n
s. 150B (2) 253–4
s. 150C (1) 252n
s. 151 (1) 252n
s. 151 (2)(a) 253n
s. 151 (2)(b) 253n
s. 151 (3) 252n
s. 153 (1) 253n
s. 153 (2) 253n
s. 154 .... 174n
s. 155 13–14
s. 155 (5) 15
s. 156 .... 249n
s. 158 162
s. 158 (1) 254–5
s. 158 (2) 256n
s. 159 (1) 85n, 259–60
s. 159 (4) 259n
s. 160 (1) 265n
s. 160 (2) 265n
s. 160 (3) 265n
s. 160 (5) 270n
s. 160 (5A) (a) 265n
s. 160 (5A) (a)(ii) 271n
s. 160 (7) 265n
s. 160 (8) 272n
s. 160 (9) 265
s. 161 (1)(a) 270n
s. 161 (2A) 271n
s. 161 (3) 270n
s. 161 (4) 270n
s. 162 (5) 191n
s. 163 162
s. 165-173 275
s. 174 188
s. 175 .... 197n
s. 176 .... 190n
s. 178 206
s. 178 (6) 90n
s. 180 192
s. 181 .... 193n
s. 182 .... 149, 193–4
s. 182 (7) 194
s. 183 .... 190n
s. 184 .... 231n

s. 187 294
s. 188 .... 294n
s. 190 (3) 338
s. 191 .... 251n, 254n
s. 191 (8) 258n
s. 193 (2) 256n
s. 193 (4) 256n
s. 194 .... 217–18, 220
s. 194 (1) 217
s. 195 198–9
s. 196 .... 192n
s. 200 230
s. 200 (2) 230n
s. 201 .... 288, 290, 291, 292
s. 201 (1) 286n
s. 201 (2) 287n
s. 201 (3) 287
s. 201 (7) 286n
s. 201-3 286–90
s. 202 287
s. 202 (10) 241
s. 203 289
s. 204 292–4
s. 204 (1) 292, 293, 294
s. 204 (2) 294
s. 204 (4) 294
s. 205 .... 55, 138n, 181–5, 210,
.... 215, 317, 321, 357–8
s. 205 (1) 181, 182–3
s. 205 (6) 181
s. 205 (10) 115
s. 208 .... 316n
s. 213 .... 170, 317–18
s. 213 (f) 46, 194
s. 213 (g) 321
s. 214 .... 224, 318
s. 214 (a) 355, 355n
s. 214 (b) 355, 355n
s. 215 .... 84n, 317
s. 217 .... 321n
s. 218 .... 323n, 334–6, 340n
s. 219 .... 323n
s. 220 .... 322n
s. 221 .... 322n
s. 222 .... 321n, 323n

s. 223 . . . . 322n
s. 224 . . . . 322n
s. 226 . . . . 321n
s. 227 (1) 322n
s. 228 (c). 326n
s. 228 (d) 322n
s. 228 (g) 322n
s. 229 . . . . 321n, 323n
s. 230 . . . . 324n, 333n
s. 231 324
s. 232 . . . . 323n
s. 234 (1) 324n
s. 234 (4) 325n
s. 235 . . . . 325n
s. 236 . . . . 325n
s. 238 . . . . 325n
s. 241 . . . . 325n
s. 242 . . . . 349n
s. 243 . . . . 325n
s. 244 . . . . 325n, 346
s. 245 . . . . 325n
s. 245A 325n
s. 246 . . . . 325n
s. 247 . . . . 21n, 325n
s. 249 . . . . 315, 325n
s. 251 (1) 326
s. 252 (1) 326n, 327n
s. 256 (1) 326n
s. 256 (2) 326n
s. 256 (2)(b) 327n
s. 256 (5) 327–8
s. 256 (8) 327n
s. 256 (9) 327n
s. 260 . . . . 286, 291
s. 260 (1) 291
s. 260 (2) 291
s. 260 (3) 291
s. 260 (4) 291
s. 261 328
s. 262 . . . . 330n
s. 263 . . . . 332n
s. 266 (1) 328n
s. 267 . . . . 328n
s. 268 . . . . 328n
s. 268 (2) 329n

s. 269 . . . . 329n
s. 271 . . . . 286, 291
s. 272 . . . . 330n
s. 273 . . . . 332n
s. 275 . . . . 345n
s. 275 (1)(b) 349n
s. 276 (1) 329–30
s. 276 (2) 349n
s. 276A 327n
s. 277 . . . . 328n
s. 278 (1) 327n
s. 280 . . . . 331, 333
s. 280 (2) 331n
s. 281 346
s. 282A 330n
s. 282B 330n
s. 282C 330n
s. 282D 331n
s. 283 348
s. 283 (1) 345
s. 283 (2) 149n, 348n
s. 285. . . . . 127n, 309, 347, 361
s. 285 (6) 347n
s. 285 (7) (a). 348n
s. 286 . . 216n, 303n, 313n, 333, 339–41
s. 286 (3) 340n
s. 288 . . . . 129, 131, 216n,
. . . . 313n, 333, 342–3
s. 289 343
s. 290 337–9
s. 290 (1) 338
s. 290 (5) 338n
s. 290 (9) 339n
s. 297 222–3
s. 297A 222, 223–4, 241
s. 297A (2) 224
s. 297A (3)(a) 224n
s. 297A (4) 224n
s. 297A (6) 224n
s. 298 . . . . 333n
s. 298 (1) 224–5
s. 299 . . . . 20, 23, 316n
s. 299 (1A) 24n
s. 299 (2) 311n
s. 299 (2A) 24n

s. 299 (5) 311n
s. 300 . . . . 315n
s. 300A 315n
s. 303 . . . . 323n
s. 310 . . . . 40n
s. 311 (1) 39n
s. 311 (3) 39n
s. 311 (6) 40n
s. 311 (8). 40n, 41, 41n
s. 313 . . . . 40n
s. 314 . . . . 299n
s. 315 (1) 299n
s. 315 (2) 299n
s. 315 (5) 299n
s. 316 . . . . 307n, 313n
s. 316 (1) 312, 312n
s. 316 (3) 313n
s. 316A 306–8
s. 316A (2)(a) 307n
s. 316A (2)(b) 307n
s. 316A (3)(a) 308n
s. 317 (1) 301n
s. 317 (2) 301n
s. 318 300
s. 319 . . . . 311n
s. 319 (1)(b) 302n
s. 320 302
s. 320 (5) 302n
s. 320A 302n
s. 321 . . . . 311n
s. 322A (1) 300n
s. 322A (2) 300n
s. 322B 303n
s. 322C (1) 300n
s. 322C (2) 300n
s. 323A 20n, 312n
s. 352 (1) 36n
s. 371 . . . . 20n, 175n
s. 377 (4) 10n
s. 379 (1) 63n
s. 383 . . . . 107n
s. 383 (1) 221
sch. 1 . . . . 42, 50
sch. 6 249

Companies Act 1990
. . . . 5, 15, 32, 67, 71, 151, 191,
. . . 197, 207, 216, 223, 308, 315, 317n
Part II 5n, 275
Part III 5n
Part IV 5n, 6, 295
Part V 6, 151, 152, 157
Part VII 12, 231, 239, 266
Part XI 115
s. 7 (1) 175n, 275
s. 7 (2) 275n
s. 7 (3) 275n
s. 8 . . . . 317n
s. 8 (1) 276
s. 8 (2)(a) 276n
s. 8 (2)(b) 276
s. 9 . . . . 276, 277, 278
s. 9 (1) 16n
s. 9 (2) 16n
s. 10 281–3
s. 10 (1) 281
s. 10 (6) 282
s. 11 (1) 283n
s. 11 (2) 283n
s. 12 . . . . 284, 285
s. 12 (1) 283n
s. 12 (1) (a). 283n
s. 12 (1) (b). 284n
s. 12 (2) 285n
s. 14 . . . . 21n, 277–8, 317n
s. 14 (2) 277
s. 14 (3) 277n
s. 14 (4) 277n
s. 15 . . . . 21n, 278
s. 16 278–9
s. 16 (1) 278n
s. 16 (2) 278n
s. 16 (3) 278n
s. 16 (5) 279
s. 16 (6) 279
s. 16 (6) (b). 278n
s. 16 (7) 279
s. 18 282
s. 19 . . . . 21n, 279–81
s. 19 (3) 280n

s. 19 (3) (b)..................280n
s. 19 (4) 280n
s. 19 (5) 280n
s. 19 (6) 281n
s. 19A.....................281n
s. 20 ....281n
s. 25 (2) (a).................219n
s. 25 (3) 219n
s. 26 217
s. 27 190
s. 27 (1) 189–90, 233n
s. 28 ....195n
s. 29 ....218, 308n
s. 29 (3) 218
s. 30 (1) 217
s. 30 (3A)..................217n
s. 31 ....219, 220–1
s. 31 (1) 219–21
s. 32 ....219n, 237n
s. 37 ....220n, 237n
s. 38 (1) 220n
s. 40 ....220n
s. 41 221
s. 41 (7) 221n
s. 41-45..............251n, 254n
s. 46 ....258n
s. 50 ....195n
s. 52 215
s. 53 (1) 216
s. 56 (1) 216n
s. 56 (7) 216n
s. 59 217
s. 60 (2) 217n
s. 60 (5) 217n
s. 63 ....251n, 254n
s. 64 (1) 216n
s. 66 (1) 216n
s. 91 ....217n, 295n
s. 98 ....174n
s. 107 151–2
s. 108 154
s. 108 (1) 151–2, 155
s. 108 (2) 152
s. 108 (3) 152–3
s. 108 (6) 153n

s. 108 (8) 153n
s. 108 (10) 153
s. 109 154
s. 109 (4) 154n
s. 110 154
s. 112 ....155n
s. 113 ....153n
s. 114 ....155n
s. 115 (3) 155n
s. 135 ....340n
s. 136 ....342n
s. 139 ....24n, 334
s. 140............16, 71, 333, 343
s. 140 (5) 15, 16
s. 141 ....16n, 71n, 343
s. 149 232
s. 150 .. 188, 218, 230, 231–8, 238, 316
s. 150 (1)..........231, 236, 237n
s. 150 (2) (a)...............232n
s. 150 (2) (c)...............232n
s. 150 (3)......12n, 197n, 237n, 239
s. 150 (4) 238n
s. 150 (4B) 231n
s. 152 238–9
s. 152 (1) 239
s. 153 (1) 239n
s. 154 ....231n
s. 159 ....239, 241
s. 160...23, 175, 241–2, 244, 245, 285
s. 160 (1) 240, 244
s. 160 (2) 244
s. 160 (2) (h)...............40
s. 160 (8) 244
s. 160 (9A) 243n
s. 161 (1) 245n
s. 163 (2) 245n
s. 171 ....307n
s. 172 306
s. 178 ....24n
s. 179 ....24n, 311n
s. 180 (2) 24n
s. 185 (1) 271n
s. 186 ....163, 270n, 271n
s. 187 273
s. 187 (1) 265, 272

s. 187 (2) 265–6
s. 187 (12) (a). 272n
s. 192 (6) 272n
s. 193 266
s. 193 (1) 256–7, 266n
s. 193 (2) 266n
s. 193 (3) 269n
s. 193 (4A) (a) 257n
s. 193 (4B) 257n
s. 193 (4C) (i). 257n
s. 193 (4C) (ii) 257n
s. 193 (4D) 257n
s. 193 (4D) (a) 258n
s. 193 (4E) 257n
s. 193 (5A) 267n
s. 193 (6) 266n
s. 194 . . . . 23n, 249n, 266n
s. 194 (2) 249n
s. 194 (3A) 249n
s. 194 (5) 24n, 267n
s. 197 . . . . 269n
s. 199 (3) 265
s. 202 . 72, 222n, 246–7, 248, 255, 344n
s. 202 (3) 247
s. 202 (10) 247
s. 203 247–8
s. 203 (1) 248n
s. 204 248
s. 205B 256
s. 205D 272
s. 205E 256
s. 207 117–18
s. 208 . . . . 118n
s. 209 (6) 118n
s. 211. . . . . 115, 118
s. 211 (3). 115n
s. 212 (1) (a). 115n
s. 212 (2) 116n
s. 212 (b) 116n
s. 213 . . . . 116n
s. 213 (3) 116n
s. 213 (5) 116n
s. 215 (1) 116n
s. 215 (2) 116n
s. 216 (2) 117n

s. 222 . . . . 119n
s. 224 . . . . 13n, 117n
s. 225 (1) 117n
s. 225 (2) 117n
s. 226 . . . . 119n
s. 229 . . . . 119n
s. 230 . . . . 120n
s. 232 (a). 115n
s. 236 197
s. 239 . . . . 7, 142
s. 243 22
s. 243 (1) 248n
s. 251 . . . . 224, 224n
Companies Acts 1963-2006 . . . 8, 10, 246
Companies (Amendment) Act 1977 . . 4
Companies (Amendment) Act 1982 . . 4
s. 12 . . . . 39n, 241
s. 12 (3) 41n
s. 12A 40n
s. 12A (3) 41n
s. 12B 40n
s. 12B (3) 41n
s. 12B (7) 41n
s. 12B(c). 41n
s. 12C 41n
Companies (Amendment) Act
1983 . . . . 4, 11, 99
s. 2 . . . . 11n
s. 5 (2) 12n
s. 5 (4) 34n
s. 6 . . . . 13n
s. 6 (1) 34
s. 6 (3) 34n
s. 6 (5) 34n
s. 6 (7) 34n
s. 6 (8) 35n
s. 8 . . . . 34n
s. 9 37
s. 10 37
s. 14 38
s. 15 . . . . 38, 115
s. 15 (2) 38n
s. 17 (3) 114n
s. 20 . . . . 94, 208n
s. 20 (3) 94

s. 20 (4) 94n
s. 20 (6) 94n
s. 21 . . . . 101n
s. 23 . . . . 96, 174n
s. 23 (1) (b). 97n
s. 23 (7) 96n
s. 23 (8) 97n
s. 23 (10) 97n
s. 23 (11) 97n
s. 24 . . . . 97n
s. 26 . . . . 98n
s. 26 (2) 99n
s. 27 98
s. 27 (1). 111n
s. 29 (1) 99n
s. 30 . . . . 29n, 99n
s. 30 (10) 29n
s. 31 . . . . 100n
s. 31 (3) 100n
s. 32 . . . . 30n, 100n
s. 32-36. . . . . 237n
s. 38 . . . . 89, 113n
s. 40 (1). 114, 163, 257
s. 41 115
s. 41 (3) 115n
s. 42 . . . . 114n
s. 42 (5) 114n
s. 42 (6) 114n
s. 44 . . . . 145n
s. 45 (1) 145n
s. 45 (2) 145–6
s. 45 (A) 146n
s. 46 (1) 146–7
s. 47 147
s. 49 147
s. 50 . . . . 147n
s. 51 (2) 146
s. 52 . . . . 38n, 47n
s. 52 (3) 85n
s. 53 . . . . 38n, 47n
s. 55 35
s. 56 43
sch.1, para. 10 . . . . 121n
sch.2 . . . . 42, 48n

Companies (Amendment) Act 1986
. . . . 5, 249, 250
s. 2 . . . . 250n
s. 3 (1) (b). 250n
s. 4 . . . . 250n
s. 7 . . . . 261, 262
s. 7 (1A) 261n
s. 7 (3) 261n
s. 8 . . . . 250n, 261n
s. 8 (2) 250n
s. 15 . . . . 258n
s. 16 . . . . 15n, 251n
s. 16 (1) 13n
s. 16 (1) (b). 14n, 15n
s. 16A 251n
s. 17 262
s. 17 (1) (d). 262n
s. 20 . . . . 146n
sch. 252
para. 26-28 . . . . 251n
para. 32A 251n
para. 36 . . . . 251n
para. 37 (2). 251n
para. 39 (5). 251n
para. 39 (6). 251n, 258n
para. 42 . . . . 251n
para. 46 . . . . 251n
Companies (Amendment) Act 1990
. . . . 5, 163, 182, 223, 286n, 287,
. . . . 290, 299, 315, 317n, 350–67
s. 2 (1) 355
s. 2 (2) 356
s. 3 . . . . 84n, 175n
s. 3 (1) 351–2
s. 3 (2) 352n
s. 3 (3) 352n
s. 3 (3A) 352n
s. 3 (3B) 353n
s. 3 (4) 352n
s. 3 (6) 304n, 355
s. 3A 354n
s. 3A (3) 354n
s. 3B 355n
s. 4 359
s. 4A 354–5

s. 5 357
s. 5 (2) (b). 304n
s. 5A 358n
s. 6 . . . . 304n
s. 6A (1) 310n
s. 7 359
s. 7 (5) 360
s. 8 359
s. 9 360
s. 10 . . . . 361, 362
s. 11 . . . . 360, 362
s. 12 (1) 356n
s. 13A 363
s. 18 (3) 357
s. 18 (4) 357
s. 21 . . . . 358n
s. 22 (5) 364
s. 23 . . . . 364n
s. 24 (3) 365n
s. 24 (4) 365n
s. 25 . . . . 365n
s. 25A 358
s. 26 . . . . 367n
s. 27 366
s. 29 . . . . 361, 362, 366
s. 29 (3) 346

Companies (Amendment) Act 1999
. . . . 6, 351, 353, 356, 362

Companies (Amendment) (No. 2) Act
1999 6
s. 32 258
s. 32 (1) (a). 258n
s. 32 (3) 258
s. 32A 259n
s. 33 (1) 259n
s. 33 (4) 259n
s. 33 (5) 259n
s. 34 . . . . 259, 271
s. 34 (1) (ii) 271n
s. 34 (3) (a). 271n
s. 35 . . . . 259n
s. 43 191
s. 43 (1) 33
s. 43 (15) 40n
s. 44 . . . . 33n, 191n

s. 45 (1) 191
s. 45 (8) 192n
s. 48 . . . . 40n
sch. 2 . . . . 258, 258n

Companies (Auditing and Accounting)
Act 2003 . . . . 7, 19, 246, 272
s. 8 . . . . 273n
s. 9 273
s. 10 . . . . 274n
s. 26 . . . . 260n
s. 26 (8) 260n
s. 26 (11) 260n
s. 42 256
s. 44 . . . . 272n
s. 45 256

Companies (Consolidation) Act 1908 . . 3

Company Law Enforcement Act 2001
. . . . 6, 18–21, 231, 275
Part 2 18
Part 7 25
s. 3 . . . . 19n
s. 7 18
s. 7 (5) 19n
s. 8 (1) 18n
s. 8 (3) 18n
s. 10 (2) 18n
s. 12 (1) 19
s. 12 (5) 19n
s. 12 (6) 20n
s. 13 (1) 21n
s. 15 21
s. 16 21–2
s. 55 . . . . 225n
s. 56. . . . . 20n, 24n, 231n, 235
s. 56 (1) 316n
s. 56 (2) 235n, 316n
s. 56 (3) 235n
s. 57 . . . . 20n
s. 57 (1) 332n
s. 58 . . . . 332n
s. 68 (1) 25n
s. 68 (2) 26n
s. 70 (1) 26n
s. 80 . . . . 36, 42, 50
s. 109 20

Competition Act 2002 295
Criminal Justice (Theft and Fraud
Offences) Act 2001 . . . . 24, 267
s. 73 . . . . 24n, 267n

Electoral Act 1997
s. 26 . . . . 255n

Finance Act 1986
s. 115 . . . . 124n, 129
Finance Act 1995
s. 174 . . . . 124n, 129n, 347n
Finance Act 1996
s. 112 . . . . 42n, 50n

Health, Safety and Welfare Act 2005 . . 72

Industrial and Provident Societies Acts
1893 to 1978 240
Investment Funds, Companies and
Miscellaneous Provisions Act 2005
. . . . 6, 7, 102, 106, 295
Part 5 . . . . 30n
s. 31 . . . . 151, 158
s. 32 . . . . 160n
s. 33 (1) 159n
s. 41 106–8
s. 42 (1) 107n
s. 42 (3) 108
s. 42 (6) 107n
s. 43 (a). 107n
s. 48 108
s. 49 . . . . 103n
s. 53 109–10
Investment Funds, Companies
and Miscellaneous Provisions Act
2006 . . . . 7, 273
s. 9 . . . . 258n
s. 12 . . . . 142n

Joint Stock Companies Act 1844 3
Joint Stock Companies Act 1856 3

Limited Liability Act 1855 . . . . . . 3, 72

Minimum Notice and Terms of
Employment Act 1973
s. 13 348

Prosecution of Offences Act 1974. . . 23
Protection of Employees (Employer's
Insolvency) Act 1984. . . . . 348n

Redundancy Payments Act 1967
s. 42 348
Registration of Business Names Act
1963 44
Royal Exchange and London Assurance
Corporation Act 1719. *see* Bubble Act
1720

Sale of Goods Act 1893
s. 17 . . . . 131n
s. 19 . . . . 131n
State Property Act 1954
s. 28 . . . . 39n
Stock Transfer Act 1963
s. 22 . . . . 140n

Takeover Panel Act 1997. 296
Taxes Consolidated Act 1997
s. 882 (3) 40
s. 1001 . . . . 124n, 129n, 347n
Trading Companies Act 1834 2

Unfair Dismissals Act 1977
s. 12 348

Table of Articles of the Constitution of Ireland 1937

Article
28 . . . . 10n
40 62
49.1.2 . . . . 10n

Table of Statutory Instruments

Companies Act 1990 (Uncertificated
  Securities) Regulations 1996 (SI
  68/1996) 141–2

European Communities (Branch
  Disclosures) Regulations 1993 (SI
  395/1993)
  reg. 14 36–7
European Communities (Companies)
  Regulations 1973 (SI 163/1973)
  reg. 4 (1) 35, 204n
  reg. 4 (2) 35n
  reg. 6 . . . . 81, 83, 203, 206
  reg. 6 (2) 206
European Communities (Companies:
  Group Accounts) Regulations 1992
  (SI 201/1992) 71, 252, 258
  reg. 4 (1) 14n
  reg. 5 . . . . 13n, 14, 15, 252
  reg. 5 (5) 253n
  reg. 7 . . . . 252n
  reg. 8 . . . . 252n
  reg. 33 (1) 15n
  reg. 35 (4) 15n
  reg. 36 . . . . 254n
  reg. 37 . . . . 255n
  sch.
    para. 15 . . . . 254n
    para. 16 . . . . 254n
    para. 17 . . . . 254n
    para. 18-22 . . . . 254n
    para. 26-28 . . . . 254n
    para. 32A 254n
    para. 36 . . . . 254n

    para. 37 (2) 254n
    para. 39 (5) 254n
    para. 46 . . . . 254n
European Communities (International
  Financial Reporting Standards and
  Miscellaneous Amendments)
  Regulations 2005 (SI 116/2005)
  . . . . 251, 253n, 257n
  art. 4 257
European Communities (Protection of
  Employees on Transfer of
  Undertakings) Regulations 2003
  (SI 131/2003) 313n
European Communities (Public Limited
  Companies Subsidiaries) Regulations
  1997 (SI 67/1997) 115
European Communities (Single-
  Member Private Limited
  Companies) Regulations 1994
  (SI 275/1994) 12, 162, 318n
  reg. 5 (1) 39n
  reg. 7 (1) 70n
  reg. 8 (1) 162n
  reg. 9 (1) 171n
  reg. 10 . . . . 166n
European Communities (Stock
  Exchange) Regulations 1984 (SI
  282/1984) 110
European Communities (Takeover Bids
  Directive 2004/25/EC) Regulations
  2006 (SI 255/2006) 292n, 296

Market Abuse (Directive 2003/6/EC)
  Regulations 2005 (SI 342/2005) . . .
  . . . . 7n, 151, 156–60
  Part 2 156
  Part 5 158
  Part 6 159
  reg. 2 (1). 157
  reg. 2 (2). 156–7
  reg. 2 (3). 157–8
  reg. 5. 156
  sch. 2 and 3 158

Prospectus (Directive 2003/71)
  Regulations 2005 (SI 324/2005)
  102–10

reg. 8. . . . . 103n
reg. 9. . . . . 104n
reg. 10. 104n
reg. 11. 104n
reg. 19. 105n
reg. 21. 105n
reg. 22. 105n
reg. 30. 105n
reg. 45. 106n

Rules of the Superior Courts 1986 (SI
  15/1986). 346
O. 74, r. 128 . . . . 346n

Table of EU Legislation

EU Directives
  77/91/EC (Second Directive on
    Company Law) 4
  78/660/EEC (Fourth Directive on
    Company Law) 5
  84/253/EEC (Eighth Directive on
    Company Law) 5
  92/101/EEC 115n
  2003/6/EC (Market Abuse
    Directive) 7n, 9
  2003/71/EC (Prospectus Directive)
    . . . . 9, 102–10
  2003/124/EC 151n
  2003/125/EC 151n
  2004/25/EC (Takeovers Directive)
    . . . . 9, 292, 292n, 296
  2004/72/EC 151n
  2004/109/EEC (Transparency
    Directive) 7, 9

EU Regulations
  4064/89/EEC (Merger Regulation)
    295
  1346/2000/EC (Insolvency
    Regulation) 9, 332n
    Art. 31. . . . . 316n
  1606/2002/EC (International
    Accounting Standards (IAS)
    Regulation) 9
  2273/2003/EC 151n, 295
  809/2004/EC (Prospectus
    Regulation)
    . . . . 30n, 105

Table of UK Legislation

Companies Act 1948 68   Insolvency Act 1986 130

CHAPTER ONE

THE DEVELOPMENT OF COMPANIES

Introduction

Prior to 1844, persons who associated for the purpose of carrying on business generally did so by way of a partnership arrangement. Although companies existed, they were rare and enjoyed only by the privileged. This was because incorporation was possible only by obtaining a charter from the Crown or by the authority of a special Act of Parliament. In the seventeenth century joint stock companies emerged. They possessed some of the characteristics of the modern company, in that the shares were transferable, the assets and liabilities of the company were separate from those of the members and the company could sue in its own name. The joint stock company was used to manage trade between Britain and initially the Near East. A more notable example was the British East India Company, which used the model to develop the tea trade between Britain and India.

However, the main advantage of the modern company — the limited liability of the members — was not enjoyed by these companies, even where they were incorporated by charter, because some charters expressly conferred a power on the company to make calls or 'leviations' on the members to meet the company's liabilities. If the company failed to make such calls, creditors could step in and recover the amounts due from the members.[1]

In the early eighteenth century, persons with common business objectives began associating together by forming companies based on contract. The contract would determine the rules regarding membership and share transfers. Rather than applying for a charter, which was an expensive and tedious procedure, some of these companies purchased charters from defunct companies. Representing themselves as having charter status, many of these 'companies' succeeded in raising funds from the public.

One of the more noted schemes was that of the South Sea Company. Formed in 1711, the company proposed a scheme whereby it would purchase the entire national debt (of £31 million) by either buying out the holders of the debt or offering them company shares in return for their holdings. On the basis of having an interest-bearing loan from the State, the company hoped to raise further monies to expand its trade, having been granted monopolies over English trade with South America. The company experienced difficulties for two reasons. First, it had paid an excessive price for the privilege of buying the national debt, and second, it was unable to expand its trade because Spain, which was still in

---

1 *Salmon v The Hamborough Co.* (1671) 1 CH Cas 204.

control of South American trading, created many obstacles to trade development. However, it was the institution of legal proceedings against the company's bankers, the Sword Blade Company, which had been operating under an obsolete charter, that caused panic among the South Sea investors. As a result, the value of the South Sea Company's shares plummeted. Because of the government's heavy involvement in the company and growing public disquiet about the fraudulent and speculative activities of company promoters in general, Parliament intervened with the passing of the Bubble Act 1720.

The Bubble Act 1720

At the height of the South Sea Bubble, England's Parliament passed an Act that severely restricted the formation of new corporations. The Bubble Act[2] sought to check the rise in company promotions by prohibiting the formation of joint stock companies, except those incorporated by statute or charter. The idea behind the Act was to restore security to commercial expansion and economic innovation. In an attempt to divert investment from other schemes into the South Sea Company, it was granted an exemption under the Act. If one of the Act's objectives was to save the South Sea Company, it failed in this respect. The loss of public confidence in joint stock companies caused by the Act, together with the events that had led to its introduction, caused a further downward spiral in the fortunes of the South Sea Company, which never fully recovered.

The Act did, however, exempt most partnerships from its effect, resulting in the emergence of a new form of company, which was based on a combination of the partnership and trust concepts. Using this device, the subscribers to these 'deed of settlement' companies would agree by deed to associate in an enterprise with a predetermined joint stock divided into shares. The deed usually provided for the vesting of the company's property in a board of trustees and the delegation of the management functions to a committee of directors. Like the joint stock company, the deed of settlement company was still treated as a partnership before the law and the liability of the members remained unlimited.

Nineteenth-Century Developments

In 1825 the Bubble Act was repealed and the Crown was given the power to grant charters that declared the extent of members' liability rather than exempting them totally from liability. Because applications for charters were still dealt with strictly, and as the statutory procedure remained expensive, most promoters continued to rely on the unincorporated association. In 1834 the Trading Companies Act was introduced. This gave the Crown the power to grant — by way of letters patent — the privileges of incorporation. This Act did not,

---

2 Officially titled the Royal Exchange and London Assurance Corporation Act 1719.

however, make provision for limiting the liability of members. In fact, it specifically provided that members were liable to the extent of a judgment against the company for up to three years after they had ceased to become members. This obvious disincentive to investors was rectified by the Chartered Companies Act 1837, which provided that limited liability could be conferred by letters patent to a specified amount per share.

In 1844 the Joint Stock Companies Act[3] introduced some of the features of modern company law. In particular, it provided for the following:

(a) the incorporation of companies by registration, which obviated the need for incorporation by Royal Charter, letters of patent or an authorising Act of Parliament;
(b) the registration as companies of all associations with more than twenty-five members or with freely transferable shares;
(c) the introduction of publicity requirements; and
(d) the establishment of the office of the Registrar of Companies in England and Ireland.

Despite these developments, it was not until the passing of the Limited Liability Act 1855 that members of companies could enjoy limited liability, upon compliance with certain conditions, including the use of the word 'limited' at the end of the company's name. The Joint Stock Companies Act 1856 relaxed many of the conditions for registration and introduced for the first time the requirement that registered companies provide a memorandum and articles of association.

Ireland's Independence

By the early twentieth century, several further pieces of legislation had been introduced which sought to amend, repeal or consolidate the legal framework governing companies. The Companies Acts of 1900 and 1907 were significant in that they not only recognised the small private company, but also exempted it from many of the statutory requirements regarding publicity. Following Ireland's Independence in 1921, little was done to amend the Companies (Consolidation) Act 1908, which remained the principal legislation governing companies in Ireland until 1963.[4] In 1951 a committee was established with the remit of investigating the entire area of company law.[5] Its findings were reported in 1958

---

3 William Gladstone, who had become the President of the Board of Trade, chaired the Parliamentary Committee on Joint Stock Companies, whose Report led to the introduction of the Act.
4 Although a Committee was appointed in 1927 to investigate the law relating to bankruptcy and the winding up of companies, no legislation was introduced following its Report.
5 Report of the Company Law Reform Committee (1958).

and although some of its recommendations were given legal effect in the Companies Act 1959, it was the Companies Act of 1963 ('the Principal Act') that embodied many of the Committee's recommendations.[6]

The Principal Act

The most significant changes effected by the Principal Act relate to the following:

(a) the requirement to maintain proper books of account by all companies;[7]
(b) the imposition of an obligation on all companies to present annual accounts to shareholders;[8]
(c) the introduction of measures designed to protect oppressed shareholders;[9]
(d) the imposition of penalties for fraudulent trading;[10]
(e) a relaxation of the common law doctrine of *ultra vires*, whereby third parties could, if certain conditions were satisfied, enforce transactions against the company which were outside its stated objects;[11]
(f) the requirement that auditors be professionally qualified;[12] and
(g) the requirement to maintain a register of directors' shareholdings.[13]

The Principal Act remains the cornerstone of modern Irish company law. However, given the number of amendments that have been made to it by successive pieces of legislation and statutory instruments, there is now an obvious need for consolidating legislation.

Subsequent Legislation

Between 1963 and 2006 successive Companies Acts were introduced as follows:

1. The Companies (Amendment) Act 1977 simplified procedures in relation to share transfers in public companies.
2. The Companies (Amendment) Act 1982 introduced relatively minor changes in respect of company registration and other miscellaneous matters.
3. The Companies (Amendment) Act 1983 gave effect to the Second EU Directive on Company Law which was mostly concerned with rules governing the formation and capital requirements of public companies.

---

6 The draftsmen of the Principal Act also embodied some of the recommendations of the 1962 Report of the Jenkins Committee in the UK, Report of the Company Law Committee (Cmnd.1749)
7 See Chapter 18.
8 Ibid.
9 See Chapter 14.
10 See Chapter 17.
11 See Chapter 7.
12 See Chapter 19.
13 See Chapter 17.

4. The Companies (Amendment) Act 1986 gave effect to the Fourth EU Directive on Company Law which primarily concerned publicity, disclosure and the accounts requirements of all companies.

[5] The Companies (Amendment) Act 1990 was introduced in response to the impending collapse of the Goodman Group of Companies (which would have had a disastrous effect on the Irish beef industry and the economy as a whole). The Act introduced into Irish law, for the first time, the concept of 'court protection' for companies which, although in financial difficulties, have a chance of survival if a rescue package can be organised. Under the Act the court, by appointing an examiner to formulate rescue proposals, can give the company a temporary reprieve from actions by creditors whose rights against the company are effectively 'frozen' for the duration of the court protection.[14]

6. The Companies Act 1990 is the most comprehensive piece of legislation introduced since the Principal Act. It was not hurried into law in the same manner as the Amendment Act of the same year. Rather, its passage was prolonged as successive governments between 1987 and 1990 exerted their influence upon its content by way of amendments before it finally became law on 22 December 1990. The Act, containing thirteen parts, introduced substantial changes to company law including, *inter alia*, the following:

   (a) the transfer of the power to appoint company inspectors from the Minister to the court;[15]

   (b) the imposition of further restrictions on transactions between companies and their directors;[16]

   (c) the introduction of disclosure requirements in relation to certain persons' interests in shares held in companies;[17]

   (d) the prohibition of insider dealing;[18]

   (e) the introduction of further legislative provisions in relation to liquidations and receivers;

   (f) the imposition of restriction provisions and improved disqualification provisions on company directors;[19]

   (g) the implementation of the European Union's Eighth Directive, which requires a minimum standard for persons who can be company auditors.[20]

---

14 See Chapter 27.

15 Part II of the Act. See Chapter 21.

16 Part III of the Act. See Chapter 17.

17 Part IV of the Act. See Chapter 17.

18 These provisions have since been repealed and replaced by a prohibition on market abuse which includes insider dealing. See Chapter 9.

19 See Chapter 21.

20 See Chapter 19.

7. The Companies (Amendment) Act 1999 was introduced to amend and extend Part IV (relating to disclosure of interests in shares) and Part V (relating to insider dealing) of the Companies Act 1990, in order to permit stabilising activities in relation to the issue or sale of securities and other related matters. The Act has been repealed in so far as it relates to securities traded on a regulated market following the introduction of the Investment Funds, Companies and Miscellaneous Act, 2005.

8. The Companies (Amendment) (No. 2) Act 1999 makes provisions for the following:
   (a) to exempt certain companies and partnerships from the requirement to have accounts audited;
   (b) to impose a requirement on Irish companies that they carry on an activity within the State;
   (c) to require, subject to certain exceptions, that one director of an Irish incorporated company be resident in the State;
   (d) to limit to 25 the number of directorships any person may have;
   (e) to provide increased powers to the registrar of companies in relation to the striking off of companies; and
   (f) to amend aspects of legislation relating to the court protection procedure.

9. The Company Law Enforcement Act 2001 was introduced following the recommendations of the Working Group on Company Law Compliance and Enforcement,[21] which were published in March 1999. The Working Group found that Irish company law was characterised by a culture of non-compliance, with many companies and officers failing to fulfil their obligations under the Companies Acts. The Group also found that, in overall terms, very few of the offences under the Companies Act were ever prosecuted. The primary recommendation of the Group was the establishment of an independent statutory officer who would have general responsibility for the enforcement of company law. This recommendation and several others made by the Working Group were given a legislative footing in the Company Law Enforcement Act. The main provisions of this Act relate to the following:
   (a) the establishment of the office of Director of Corporate Enforcement ('the Director');[22]
   (b) the transfer to the Director of many of the functions of the Minister relating to the investigation and enforcement of the Companies Acts;
   (c) the introduction of additional measures to improve compliance with company law and filing obligations;
   (d) the establishment of the Company Law Review Group as a statutory body;

---

21 Pn. 6697.
22 See Chapter 19.

   (e) the amendment of existing legislative provisions relating to accounts and audit;

   (f) the amendment of existing legislative provisions governing financial transactions between companies and their directors.

10. The Companies (Auditing and Accounting) Act 2003 was introduced following the recommendations of the Review Group on Auditing.[23] The Act establishes the Irish Auditing and Accounting Supervisory Authority, an independent body primarily responsible for supervising the regulation of the accountancy bodies and promoting high professional standards in the auditing and accounting professions.[24] Provision is also made for the mandatory establishment of audit committees for all public companies, and the responsibilities of such committees are listed. The Act introduces a new requirement for directors of public companies and certain private companies in respect of the preparation of compliance statements and the sanctions for non-compliance. This provision is one of the most controversial aspects of the Act and, as with many of the provisions of the Act, has yet to be commenced.

11. The Investment Funds, Companies and Miscellaneous Provisions Act 2005 provides *inter alia* for the transposition of EU Directives on Market Abuse[25] and Prospectuses[26] into Irish company law.

12. The Investment Funds, Companies and Miscellaneous Provisions Act 2006 provides *inter alia* for the following:

   (a) recognition of statutory declarations outside the State subject to certain conditions;

   (b) increasing the minimum membership of private companies to nintey-nine (excluding employees and ex employees);

   (c) permitting private companies to issue shares and debentures to qualified investors or to less than 100 persons provided certain conditions are satisfied and such issues will not constitute and offer to the public;

   (d) increasing the audit exemption thresholds for private companies (see Chapter 20);

   (e) amending the costs provisions in relation to applications for restriction and disqualification;

   (f) amending section 239 of the Companies Act 1990 to enable the Minister to make regulations in respect of the dematerialisation of securities of public companies;

---

23 The Report of the Review Group on Auditing (Pn.8683)
24 See Chapter 19.
25 Market Abuse Directive 2003/6/EC implemented by S.I. 342 of 2005 and the Investment Funds, Companies and Miscellaneous Act (the 2005 Act).
26 Prospectus Directive 2003/71/EC implemented by S.I.324 of 2005 and the 2005 Act.

    (g) restricting liability of guarantors where non-equity securities are solely involved;

    (h) minor changes in respect of prospectus and takeover rules;

    (i) the implementation of the Transparency Directive.[27]

While the Companies Acts 1963—2006 comprise the primary legislation governing companies in Ireland, a number of other statutes also impinge on companies. These include, *inter alia*, the Bankruptcy Acts, the Competition Acts, successive Finance Acts, Takeover and Merger legislation, Employment and Health and Safety legislation. Secondary legislation, particularly in the form of Ministerial Regulations, is also used to implement various company law matters arising from our membership of the European Union.

Other Sources of Law

While legislation is clearly the principal source of company law, it is not the only one. Indeed, the legal framework governing companies in Ireland is derived from several different sources, including common law and equity and the law of the European Union.

Common Law and Equity

Since the nineteenth century the courts have played an important role in the development of company law. Where legislation ends, case law begins; and this is as true of company law as it is of any other branch of the law. In interpreting legislative provisions and adjudicating disputes, judges have developed key principles that are still regarded as central to company law today. Principles of equity and common law have made a unique contribution to the jurisprudence of company law. The speeches of Lord Macnaghten and his fellow Lords in the case of *Salomon v Salomon*[28] are regularly cited in modern cases concerning the issue of a company's separate personality. The principle, in *Ashbury Railway Carriage & Iron Co. v Riche*,[29] that contracts entered into by a company for purposes other than those set out in its object clause are *ultra vires,* void and unenforceable remains intact today despite subsequent legislative provisions to temper the effect of this principle. The rule in *Foss v Harbottle*[30], which states that when a wrong is done to the company it is the company who is the proper plaintiff, is a fundamental rule of company law. The fiduciary duty of directors towards the company, originating in the courts of equity, remains the yardstick against which a director's action will be judged and upon which many statutory duties of directors are now based.[31]

---

27 Transparency Directive 2004/109/EEC.
28 [1897] AC 22. See Chapter 5.
29 (1875) LR 7 HL 653.
30 (1843) 2 Hare 261. See Chapter 14.
31 See Chapter 17.

The Law of the European Union

Accession to the European Union in 1973 created new legal obligations for the Irish State and its people. As part of the European Union's objective of creating a single market, a harmonisation process began which included *inter alia* the area of company law. To effect the harmonisation of company law a number of directives have been adopted by the European Council, some of which have been implemented in Ireland by way of the statutory reforms mentioned earlier. Other directives have been given the force of law by Ministerial Regulations and Statutory Instruments.

As part of the European Union Financial Services Action Plan (FSAP) further directives and regulations that affect companies, particularly those listed on regulated markets such as the Irish Stock Exchange, have been introduced. The implementation of these legislative initiatives has contributed in no small way to the existing body of Irish company law.

Recent developments include the Transparency Directive,[32] which aims to improve the information available to investors of listed companies; the Takeovers Directive,[33] which introduced certain common principles and a limited number of general requirements relating to takeovers of certain listed companies; the Prospectus Directive,[34] which provides rules relating to the issue of prospectuses for securities trading on a regulated market; and the Market Abuse Directive,[35] which prohibits insider dealing and market manipulation in relation to securities trading on a regulated market.

The EU also employs Regulations as a means of achieving the FSAP. Recent examples include the International Accounting Standards (IAS) Regulation,[36] which requires all companies listed on a regulated market to use International Accounting Standards[37] and the Insolvency Regulation,[38] which defines common rules on cross-border insolvency proceedings.

Types of Company

There are various means of categorising companies. They may be distinguished in terms of: the manner in which they are formed; the liability of their members; their public or private status; or their position within a group of companies.

---

32 Ibid., note 27.
33 Ibid., note 25.
34 Ibid., note 26.
35 Ibid., note 25.
36 Council Regulation 1606/2002.
37 See Chapter 18.
38 Council Regulation 1346/2000.

Formation

1. Chartered Corporations

As mentioned earlier chartered corporations were created by the assent of the British Crown, which by the grant of a charter or letters patent conferred the privilege of incorporation on a business entity. Many chartered bodies still exist in Ireland, including the Law Society of Ireland, Trinity College Dublin and the Bank of Ireland (which was established by public subscription under Royal Charter in 1783).[39] Since Ireland's Independence, the Executive has assumed the power to grant charters, although it has never done so.[40]

2. Statutory Companies

Statutory companies were granted their status by the authority of an Act of Parliament, and were usually conferred with special powers and monopolistic rights. Since Independence, most of these companies have been dissolved and their business undertakings transferred to new state bodies. However, several statutory companies have been established since 1921 whose objectives were considered to be of national importance, e.g. Aer Lingus, Aer Rianta, the Industrial Credit Company and the Agricultural Credit Company. Given the general prohibition by European Union law on giving state aid to companies, many statutory companies have now been privatised.

3. Registered Companies

The most common method of incorporation is by registration under the Companies Acts 1963–2006. Company legislation sets out the prescribed procedure that must be followed before registration can be effected by the registrar of companies. This procedure is considered further in Chapter 3.

Liability of Members

Companies formed by any of the above methods may also be categorised according to the potential liability of their members. In this regard the liability of the members of the company may be limited or unlimited.

1. Companies Limited by Shares

Where companies are formed to carry on a profit-making activity, it is usual that such companies will have shares. Accordingly, profits can be divided among

---

39 See *Geoghegan v Institute of Chartered Accountants in Ireland* [1995] 3 IR 86, where the Supreme Court rejected the plaintiff's contention that the charter of the defendant body had not survived the enactment and coming into operation of the Irish Free State and Bunreacht na hÉireann.
40 By virtue of Article 49.1.2. and 28 of Bunreacht na hÉireann and section 377(4) of the Principal Act.

members on the basis of their percentage holdings. In such companies the liability of the members to contribute to the assets of the company is limited to the amount, if any, unpaid on their shares.

2. Companies Limited by Guarantee

The liability of the members to contribute to the assets of the company in a winding up is limited to the amount specified in the guarantee. Such amounts will be stated in the memorandum of association. This form of company is usually used by charitable companies because, as there is no sharing of profits, the division of the undertaking into shares is not necessary.

3. Unlimited Companies

The liability of the members is unlimited and, in the event that the company is wound up, the members are liable to contribute to the assets of the company an amount sufficient for the payment of the company's debts and liabilities. It is for this reason that trading companies are rarely incorporated with unlimited liability. It is usual, although not necessary, for unlimited companies to have a share capital.

Public and Private Companies

Company law has always been based on the view that while the public company is the norm, the private company is the exception. This of course does not reflect the reality of modern business — there are far more private than public companies in Ireland. A private company is one with a share capital whose articles of association restrict the right to transfer its shares, limit the number of members to ninety-nine (excluding employees and ex-employees), and prohibit any invitation to the public to subscribe for its shares or debentures.[41] Where default is made in complying with any of these provisions, a private limited company does not lose its corporate existence, but it may forfeit many of the privileges and exemptions available to private companies.[42] The Companies (Amendment) Act 1983 (the 1983 Amendment Act) defines a public limited company as one which is not a private company and whose memorandum states that the company is a public limited company.[43]

However, the differences between private and public companies are more significant than these definitions would seem to suggest. Certain requirements of the Companies Acts vary depending on whether a company is private or public. The most important of these relate to the following.

---

41 Section 33 (1) of the Principal Act.
42 Section 34 of the Principal Act.
43 Section 2 of the 1983 Amendment Act.

1. Membership

Section 5 of the Principal Act fixes the minimum number of members for a private company at two, and at seven for all other companies. If the number of members in a company falls below the legal minimum and that company carries on business for more than six months while the number is so reduced, members who knew that it was carrying on business after the expiration of the six-month period may be severally liable for the debts of the company contracted during that time.

It should be noted that since the introduction of the European Communities (Single-Member Private Limited Companies) Regulations 1994[44] it is now possible to incorporate a single-member private limited company. Therefore, private companies limited by shares or by guarantee can be converted into single-member companies, thus avoiding any potential difficulties that might arise should their membership fall below two. Private unlimited companies continue to require two members. Although the maximum number of members for a private company is limited to ninety-nine (excluding employees and ex-employees), no such limit exists for public companies.

2. Capital

There is no minimum capital requirement for private companies. A private company limited by shares can be set up with as little as a €1 share. Public companies, on the other hand, are required to have a minimum share capital of £30,000 (€38,092), at least 25 per cent of which must be paid up.[45] However, if a company appoints a person who is restricted under Part VII of the Companies Act 1990 (the 1990 Act), that company must have a minimum share capital of £50,000 (€63,487) in the case of a private company and £250,000 (€317,435) in the case of a public company.[46]

The ability of a private company to raise finance by way of capital is restricted somewhat because it is prohibited from offering its shares or debentures to the public. A public company, on the other hand, may raise capital in this way but is subject to stringent rules.

Where new shares are being issued for cash consideration, companies must, as a general rule, offer them first to existing members. However, a private company may permanently exclude this rule by its articles of association. A public company can only do so for a period not exceeding five years, although this period can be extended for a further five years. Where shares are being issued for non-cash consideration, public limited companies are also subject to more stringent rules than private companies.[47]

---

44 SI 275/1994.
45 Section 5(2) of the 1983 Amendment Act.
46 Section 150(3) of the 1990 Act. See Chapter 19.
47 See Chapter 9.
48 See Chapter 20.

3. Accounts and Annual Returns

Small and medium-sized private companies are exempt from many of the provisions of the Companies Acts relating to the filing of accounts and annual returns. Furthermore, certain small private limited companies are exempt from the requirements to have their accounts audited.[48]

4. Commencement of Business

A private company can commence trading once the certificate of incorporation has been issued by the registrar of companies. Even where the certificate of incorporation has been issued to a public company, it can only trade if it obtains a 'trading certificate' from the registrar.[49] The certificate of trading will only be issued if the registrar is satisfied that the company has allotted at least £30,000 (€38,092) in share capital and that 25 per cent of it has been paid up. The promotion and formation of companies is considered further in Chapter 3.

Group Companies

1. Holding and Subsidiary Companies

The importance of the holding and subsidiary company relationship is recognised by a number of statutory provisions, including, *inter alia*, the following:

(a) a holding company must ordinarily prepare group accounts in which financial information pertaining to it and its subsidiaries is included;[50]
(b) at the end of each financial year, a holding company must generally include in its accounts, which are annexed to the annual return, information relating to the name and registered office of each subsidiary and various details relating to its shareholding in the subsidiary;[51] and
(c) a subsidiary company is only permitted to hold shares in its holding company in limited circumstances.[52]

A company is a holding company of another company if any of the following circumstances, prescribed by section 155 of the Principal Act, exist:

(a) it is a member of that company and controls the composition of its board of directors; or
(b) it holds more than half in nominal value of that company's equity share capital; or

---

49 Section 6 of the 1983 Amendment Act.
50 Section 150 of the Principal Act and Regulation 5 of the European Communities (Companies: Group Accounts) Regulations 1992: SI 201/1992.
51 Section 16(1) of the Companies (Amendment) Act 1986 (the 1986 Amendment Act).
52 Section 224 of the 1990 Act.

(c) it holds more that half in nominal value of the shares which carry voting rights; or

(d) the other company is a subsidiary of a subsidiary of the holding company.

On the basis of section 155 a holding company is essentially one which owns or controls other companies. Conversely a subsidiary is one which is owned or controlled by another company. A company may own one or more other companies which are its subsidiary's subsidiaries.

Where a parent company is required to prepare and present group accounts under Regulation 5 of the European Communities (Companies: Group Accounts) Regulations 1992, an undertaking[53] shall be deemed to be a subsidiary of another if, but only if:

(a) that other —
   (i)   holds a majority of the shareholders' or members' voting rights in the undertaking, or
   (ii) is a shareholder or member of it and controls the composition of its board of directors, or
   (iii) is a shareholder or member of it and controls alone, pursuant to an agreement with other shareholders or members, a majority of the shareholders' or members' voting rights; or

(b) that other has the right to exercise a dominant influence over it —
   (i)   by virtue of provisions contained in its memorandum or articles, or
   (ii) by virtue of a control contract; or

(c) that other has a participating interest in it and —
   (i)   that other actually exercises a dominant influence over it, or
   (ii) that other and the subsidiary undertaking are managed on a unified basis;
   (iii) that other and the subsidiary undertaking are managed on a unified basis, or

(d) the undertaking is a subsidiary of any undertaking which is that other's undertaking.[54]

The conditions prescribed above go beyond the normal 'ownership' and 'control' tests with the added circumstances of where one company is exercising or has the right to exercise a dominant position over the other company or where the companies are managed on a unified basis.

---

53 An 'undertaking' includes a corporate body for the purposes of the Regulation.
54 Regulation 4(1) of the European Communities (Companies: Group Accounts) Regulations 1992:SI 201/1992 (the 1992 Regulations).

2. Undertakings of Substantial Interest (Associated Companies)

An undertaking of substantial interest is one in which a company holds a qualifying capital interest equal to 20% or more in another undertaking.[55] A qualifying capital interest is one held by one undertaking in another on a long-term basis for the purpose of securing a contribution to that undertaking's own activities by the exercise of control or influence arising from or related to that interest.[56]

If an undertaking is a subsidiary, it will not be an associated undertaking.[57] Where a company has an interest in another company to the extent that the other company is an undertaking of substantial interest, a note must be included in the annual accounts of the company, which is annexed to the annual return, specifying the following details in relation to the undertaking of substantial interest: its registered office; the nature of its business; the identity of each class of shares; the percentage of the nominal value of the shares held in that class; the aggregate amount of the capital and reserves and profit and loss as at the end of the financial year of the undertaking of substantial interest.[58]

Where a company is required to prepare and present group accounts under Regulation 5 of the European Communities (Companies: Group Accounts) Regulations 1992[59] they are obliged to include various details including the amount of profit or loss attributable to each undertaking of substantial interest.[60]

3. Related Companies

The 1990 Act introduced the concept of a related company. By virtue of section 140(5) a company is related to another company if:

(a) that other company is its holding company or subsidiary; or
(b) more than half in nominal value of its equity share capital (as defined in section 155(5) of the Principal Act) is held by the other company and companies related to that other company (whether directly or indirectly, but other than in a fiduciary capacity); or
(c) more than half in nominal value of the equity share capital (as defined in section 155(5) of the Principal Act) of each of them is held by members of the other company (whether directly or indirectly, but other than in a fiduciary capacity); or

---

55 Section 16(1)(b) of the 1986 Amendment Act.
56 Regulation 35(4) of the 1992 Regulations.
57 Section 16(1)(b) of the 1986 Amendment Act.
58 Section 16 of the 1986 Amendment Act.
59 The obligation under Regulation 5 is limited to companies that have limited liability. There are exemptions from the obligation to prepare group accounts in the case of certain private companies who do not satisfy certain financial criteria and certain parent undertakings that are themselves subsidiaries.
60 Regulation 33(1) of the 1992 Regulations.

(d) that other company or a company or companies related to that other company together with a company or companies related to it are entitled to exercise or control the exercise of more than one half of the voting power at any general meeting of the company; or

(e) the businesses of the companies have been so carried on that the separate business of each company, or a substantial part thereof, is not readily identifiable; or

(f) if there is another company to which both companies are related.[61]

This definition of a related company clearly extends beyond the traditional view of group companies. Its relevance can be seen in various company law provisions. Under section 140 of the 1990 Act, companies may be liable to contribute to the assets of a related company in an insolvent winding up. Furthermore, the assets of related companies may be pooled in a winding-up situation.[62]

Where an inspector is appointed to investigate the affairs of a company he may, with the approval of the court, investigate the affairs of a related company.[63] In this regard a 'related company' is given a wider scope and includes not just those companies defined by section 140(5) of the 1990 Act but also those companies with which the company being investigated has a 'commercial relationship'.[64] A 'commercial relationship' exists where goods or services are sold or given by one party to another.

---

61 Section 140(5) of the 1990 Act.
62 Section 141 of the 1990 Act.
63 Section 9(1) of the 1990 Act.
64 Section 9(2) of the 1990 Act.

CHAPTER TWO

COMPANY LAW ENFORCEMENT, COMPLIANCE AND REVIEW

Introduction

Limited liability was instrumental in promoting the economic development of the late nineteenth and early twentieth centuries. Nonetheless the concept did not meet with universal approval. The *Law Times* described the concept as a 'Rogue's Charter' which would engender 'a mass of villainy.'[1] In an attempt to curb the potential for abusing the privilege of incorporation efforts are continuously made by the legislature through the imposition of numerous procedural, administrative and management duties on companies and their officers. These duties are considered to be a *quid pro quo* for the privilege of incorporation. Many of these duties are discussed in subsequent chapters. The courts are also active in this regard and several judicial principles have emerged that are aimed at protecting those who deal with companies.[2] As Harmon J. remarked:

> The purpose and great value of the investment in 1862 of the limited liability company was to enable entrepreneurs to take risks without bankrupting themselves. Down to that date persons had to trade on their personal liability. Thereafter, if they could get credit, they could trade with the protection of limited liability. That is a great privilege which has caused part of the great expansion of wealth in this country in the last hundred years. It is of course a privilege which must be exercised responsibly and cannot be abused, and if abused the courts must prevent those who abuse it from so doing in the future.[3]

Despite these statutory and judicial dictates, one concern which remained up until the turn of this century was the lack of compliance with company law and the ineffectual means of enforcement. Accordingly the Minister established the Working Group on Company Law Compliance and Enforcement in 1998 to conduct a comprehensive analysis of company law compliance and enforcement in Ireland. The terms of reference for the group included, *inter alia*, the following:

- a review of the compliance arrangements and enforcement regimes for company law;
- a consideration of the respective roles for the parties responsible for compliance and enforcement, particularly the courts, the Minister for

---

1 [1854] 24 Law Times 142.
2 Examples of judicial activism in this regard are evident in the development of fiduciary duties for directors discussed in Chapter 18 and the development of capital maintenance rules discussed in Chapter 10.
3 *Re Douglas Construction Services Ltd* [1988] BCLC 397 at 402.

Enterprise, Trade and Employment, the Director of Public Prosecutions and the registrar of companies;

• to identify and evaluate the legislative, organisational and resource issues affecting compliance and enforcement; and

• to examine and identify the resources and structures necessary to achieve a more frequent updating of companies legislation.

The Report of the Working Group[4] found that Irish company law was characterised by a 'culture of non-compliance' and a failure by companies and their officers to meet their obligations in respect of filing annual returns on time. The Report further found that the existing enforcement regime was ineffective, due primarily to a lack of resources and the absence of a dedicated agency dealing with breaches of company law. The Report distinguished between 'registration-type' and 'non-registration-type' offences.

With regard to the former the Report recommended that the registrar of companies be given increased powers, including the imposition of on-the-spot fines for non-compliance. With regard to non-registration-type offences the Report recommended the creation of an independent statutory officer — to be known as the Director of Corporate Enforcement — whose remit would include responsibility for the enforcement of company law. The Oireachtas incorporated many of the recommendations made in the report in the Company Law Enforcement Act 2001 (the 2001 Act).

The Director of Corporate Enforcement.

Part 2 of the 2001 Act created the Office of the Director of Corporate Enforcement. By virtue of Section 7 of the 2001 Act, the Director of Corporate Enforcement (the Director) shall be appointed by the Minister. The person appointed as the Director shall hold office for a period not exceeding five years, renewable for a further period of five years, and on such terms and conditions as the Minister, with the consent of the Minister for Finance, thinks fit.[5] The Director is not permitted to hold any other office or employment in respect if which payments are made.[6] A person cannot be appointed a Director, nor can a Director continue in office if he or she is nominated or appointed as a member of either House of the Oireachtas, the European Parliament or a Local Authority.[7] The Minister may appoint a person to be Acting Director in the following circumstances:

---

4 Report of the Working Group on Company Law Compliance and Enforcement 30 November 1998, (Pn 6697).
5 Section 8(1) of the 2001 Act.
6 Section 8(3) of the 2001 Act.
7 Section 10(2) of the 2001 Act.

(a) the Director is absent from duty or from the State;

(b) the Director is unable to perform the functions of Director;

(c) the Director is suspended from office; or

(d) where a vacancy arises in the office of Director.

The Acting Director can only be appointed for a maximum of six months during the vacancy in the office of Director.

Functions of the Director

The Director must perform the functions and duties conferred by the 2001 Act and any other legislation, and shall be assisted in the performance of those functions by the officers of the Director.[8] Officers include an officer of the Minister assigned to the Director, any member of An Gárda Síochána seconded to the Director and any person employed by the Minister or the Director under a contract for service or otherwise.[9] Section 12(1) specifies the functions of the Director as follows:

(a) to enforce the Companies Acts, including by the prosecution of offences by way of summary proceedings;

(b) to encourage compliance with the Companies Acts;

(c) to investigate instances of suspected offences under the Companies Acts;

(d) at his or her discretion, to refer cases to the Director of Public Prosecutions where he or she has reasonable grounds for believing that an indictable offence under the Companies Acts has been committed;

(e) to exercise, in so far as the Director feels it necessary or appropriate, a supervisory role over the activity of liquidators and receivers in the discharge of their functions under the Companies Acts;

(f) for the purpose of ensuring the effective application and enforcement of obligations, standards and procedures to which companies and their officers are subject, to perform such other functions in respect of any matters to which the Companies Acts relate as the Minister considers appropriate and may, by order, confer on the Director;

(g) to perform such other functions as may be assigned to him by, or under, the Companies Acts or any other Act; and

(h) to act, under the Companies (Auditing and Accounting) Act, 2003, as a member of the Irish Auditing Supervisory Authority and, if appointed under section 11 of that Act, as a director of the authority.

In performing his functions, the Director is independent in the performance of his or her functions.[10] The Director may perform his functions through or by an

---

8 Section 7(5) of the 2001 Act.

9 Section 3 of the 2001 Act.

10 Section 12(5) of the 2001 Act.

officer of the Director and such officer is, in performing those functions, subject to the directions of the Director only.[11]

The Powers of the Director

The Director is given extensive powers under the Companies Acts in order to carry out his statutory function. Section 109 of the 2001 Act provides that where the Director has reasonable grounds for believing that a person has committed an offence, he may, without instituting court proceedings, levy fines in respect of summary offences, under the Companies Acts. He may also prosecute summary offences in his own name.

The Director has the power to apply to the High Court for orders to restrict or disqualify company directors and other officers.[12] This power is intended to prevent unscrupulous persons from continuing to use the vehicle of limited liability where their past record demonstrates that they have acted irresponsibly, dishonestly, recklessly or unlawfully.

Liquidators are now obliged to report to the Director of Corporate Enforcement on the conduct of directors of insolvent companies in relation to the management of those companies.[13] Furthermore, section 299 of the Principal Act requires all liquidators to report to the Director if they suspect that an offence has been committed in relation to the company by a company officer (past or present), or by any of its members.

A significant power that the Director has been given is supervisory powers over the activities of receivers and liquidators. The Director can direct a receiver[14] and a liquidator[15] to produce their books. Liquidators and receivers play a key role in ensuring that the provisions of the Companies Acts are properly applied in company liquidations and receiverships and the Director is now responsible for ensuring that they meet their statutory obligations in this regard.

The Director has the power to apply to the High Court for injunctions restraining companies or their officers from continuing to breach the Companies Acts.[16] The Director can also seek an order for examination in a winding up and may apply to the court seeking any person who is being examined to pay any debts (if any) owed to the company, and to deliver up any property, books, money or papers to the company.

The Director has also been given certain investigative powers under the new Act, which includes the power to appoint inspectors to inspect suspected offences under the Companies Acts. The Director has even greater powers than

---

11 Section 12(6) of the 2001 Act.
12 See Chapter 19.
13 Section 56 of the 2001 Act.
14 Section 323A of the Principal Act.
15 Section 57 of the 2001 Act.
16 Section 371 of the Principal Act

an official liquidator. He can seek an order for civil arrest of contributories and officers who are absconding.[17] The Director has also the power to appoint one or more inspectors to investigate and report on the membership of any company.[18] The purpose of this investigation is to determine the true persons who are financially interested in the success or failure of the company or who are able to control or influence company decisions. This power should enable the Director to unveil some of the secrecy that surrounds nominee shareholdings. The Director also has the power to investigate a company's ownership without appointing an inspector.[19] The Director is empowered, without appointing an inspector, to require any person whom he has reason to believe to have, or to be able to obtain for him, information as to the ownership of shares or debentures, to supply that information to him.[20]

Any of the Director's powers may be delegated in writing by the Director with the exception of the power of delegation itself.[21] Where a person is affected by the exercise of any power delegated by the Director, the delegate officer shall produce the instrument of delegation for inspection. Any such delegation is revocable at will by the Director.

Indemnification

Section 15 relieves the Director, or office of the Director, from liability in damage for anything done in good faith by him in the performance of a statutory function.

Director's Report

Under section 16, the Director shall present a report to the Minister, within three months after the end of each year, about the performance of the Director's functions and other activities of the Director in that year. The Minister shall cause a copy of the report to be laid before the Dáil and Seanad within two months of receipt of the report. The Director's report shall include information about matters as the Minister may direct. In addition to this annual report, the Director must give any information about the performance of the Director's functions as the Minister may from time to time request. Where such a request is made, the Director must account to an appropriately established committee of either House of the Oireachtas. It should be noted that where the Director is presenting his report or complying with a ministerial request to supply information, the Director is not required to furnish any information or answer any questions that would, in

---

17 Section 247 of the Principal Act.
18 Section 14 of the 1990 Act. See Chapter 22.
19 Section 19 of the 1990 Act. See Chapter 22.
20 Section 15 of the 1990 Act. See Chapter 22.
21 Section 13(1) of the 2001 Act.

the opinion of the Director, prejudice the performance by the Director of his functions. Information obtained by virtue of the performance by the Director, an advisor to the Director, or officer or former officer of Director, or any other person, must not be disclosed except in accordance with the law, unless it is necessary to do so as part of the Director's investigative and enforcement functions. The 2005 Report of the Director of Corporate Enforcement (the ODCE Report 2005) demonstrates the increased benefit of an agency dedicated to ensuring compliance with company law and seeking redress where breaches occurred. Highlights of the Report include:

(a) the conviction of six individuals who had failed to abide by restriction orders;
(b) the initiation of a first prosecution under section 243 of the Companies Act 1990 arising from the use of a falsified document affecting or relating to the property or affairs of a company;
(c) the initiation of disqualification proceedings against nine former directors or senior managers of National Irish Bank Ltd as a consequence of the findings of the court-appointed inspectors;
(d) the imposition of disqualification periods on two directors of an insolvent building company arising from their misconduct in relation to the company's affairs; and
(e) the disqualification of ten directors who were directors of companies which had been struck off involuntarily by the registrar of companies and the companies in question had not discharged all their debts.

Removal of the Director

The Minister may at any time, for stated reasons, remove the Director from office. Where this occurs, the Minister must cause to be laid before the Dáil and the Seanad a statement of the reasons for the removal.

3. Other Enforcement and Compliance Agencies

The Companies Registration Office

The Companies Registration Office (CRO) is the authority for the incorporation of new companies and the registration of business names in the Republic of Ireland. The CRO is also responsible for the receipt and registration of post-incorporation documents, for enforcement of the filing requirements of companies and for the provision of information to the public. Where necessary the registrar can impose fines for late filing of certain returns and prosecute summary offences by non-compliant officers. One of the most far-reaching powers of the registrar, and one that is frequently exercised, is the power to strike companies from the register for various filing breaches.[22] The ODCE Report 2005 showed that the registrar of companies had struck 9,514 companies from the register for breach of company law filing obligations. The registrar of companies co-operates closely with the Director of Corporate Enforcement.

The Director of Public Prosecutions (DPP)

Prior to the appointment of the Director of Corporate Enforcement, responsibility for the enforcement of the criminal provisions of the Companies Acts vested with the DPP, the Minister for Enterprise, Trade and Employment, and the registrar of companies. The DPP, who functions under the Prosecutions of Offences Act 1974, has the right to prosecute on indictment any offences committed under the Companies Acts. Section 299 of the Principal Act provides for the reference to the DPP if, in the course of a winding up or receivership, it appears that any past or present officer or member of a company has been guilty of an offence. Section 160 of the 1990 Act gives the DPP power to apply to the court to disqualify persons from acting as directors, auditors, officers, receivers, liquidators or examiners, or from being involved directly or indirectly in the promotion, formation or management of any company.

Inspectors

The Companies Acts provide a number of means by which the ownership, control and the affairs of companies can be investigated to ensure compliance with company law and the general law. The findings of an inspector may be used as evidence in civil and criminal proceedings. Furthermore, in circumstances in which an inspector must prepare a report for the court, the court may, on receipt of the report, order the winding up of the company. The regulatory framework governing company investigations is described in Chapter 22.

Auditors

An auditor is an independent professional who is qualified to perform an audit.[23] In addition to the audit functions, auditors have a number of 'watch-dog' duties, which are aimed at ensuring compliance with company law. Where auditors form the opinion that the company is in breach of its obligation to maintain proper books of accounts, they must serve a notice of this opinion on the company. If the directors do not rectify this matter the auditors must notify the registrar of companies, who must then notify the Director of Corporate Enforcement.[24]

---

22 See Chapter 3.
23 See Chapter 21.
24 Section 194 of the 1990 Act.

Auditors are also required to report to the Director any indictable offences they believe have been carried out by the company or its officers, and the grounds for their opinion.[25] Auditors must also report to the Gardaí any suspected offence by a director under the Criminal Justice (Theft and Fraud Offences) Act 2001.[26] In the ODCE Report 2005 almost 83% of 2,373 reports and complaints received by the office of the Director were from auditors, signifying the importance of the role of auditor in ensuring compliance with company law.

Liquidators, Receivers and Examiners

Liquidators are appointed to wind up a company.[27] As part of their compliance and enforcement role liquidators are obliged to report to the Director on the conduct of directors of insolvent companies.[28] The ODCE Report 2005 demonstrates that during that year some 1,009 liquidators' reports were received.

Liquidators are also obliged to bring restriction applications against all directors of insolvent companies, unless the Director relieves them of this obligation. Where a liquidator, in a voluntary liquidation, believes that any past or present officers, or any member, or the company itself has been guilty of a criminal offence, the liquidator is obliged to report the matter to the Director and the DPP.[29] In the case of compulsory liquidations, where it appears to the court that any past or present officer, or any member, or the company itself has been guilty of a criminal offence, the court may instruct the liquidator to make a report to the Director and the DPP.[30]

A receiver is a person appointed by the court or a debenture holder to take control of certain assets of the company.[31] As part of his statutory duties a receiver is obliged, where it appears that any past or present officer, or any member of the company has been guilty of any offence in relation to the company that gives rise to criminal liability, to report the matter to the DPP.[32]

An examiner is appointed by the court to formulate proposals for the survival of insolvent companies.[33] Liquidators, receivers and examiners can apply to the court for the return of assets disposed of by the company if they consider that the effect of the disposal was to perpetrate a fraud on the company, its creditors or its members.[34]

---

25 Section 194(5) of the 1990 Act.
26 Section 73 of the Criminal Justice (Theft and Fraud Offences) Act, 2001.
27 See Chapters 25 and 26.
28 Section 56 of the 2001 Act.
29 Section 299(2A) of the Principal Act.
30 Section 299(1A) of the Principal Act.
31 See Chapter 24.
32 Section 179 of the 1990 Act.
33 See Chapter 27.
34 Sections 139 and 178 and 180(2) of the 1990 Act.

The Financial Regulator and The Irish Stock Exchange

The Irish Financial Services Regulatory Authority (the Finanical Regulator) is conferred with certain powers in relation to companies whose shares are offered to the public or admitted for trading on the Irish Stock Exchange. It is the competent authority for ensuring compliance with Prospectus Regulations[35] and the Market Abuse Regulations.[36]

The Irish Stock Exchange has been delegated certain functions in this regard. The Stock Exchange also plays a role in ensuring compliance with laws relating to the admission to and listing of public companies on the stock exchange. The ODCE Report 2005 indicates that the Irish Stock Exchange submitted thirteen reports of suspected breaches of the Companies Acts relating to missed notification deadlines involving share purchases or disposals by the directors of listed companies.

4. Company Law Review Group

The Company Law Review Group is an expert body with the responsibility for advising the Minister for Enterprise, Trade and Employment on the review and development of company law in Ireland. The Group was established on an informal basis for a number of years prior to 2001, but it was given statutory recognition by virtue of Part 7 of the 2001 Act. The 2001 Act sets out the functions and authority of the Group.

The primary functions[37] of the Review Group are to monitor, review and advise the Minister on matters concerning:

(a) the implementation of the Companies Acts;
(b) the amendment of the Companies Acts;
(c) the consolidation of the Companies Acts;
(d) the introduction of new legislation relating to the operation of companies and commercial practices in Ireland;
(e) the rules of the Superior Courts and case law judgments insofar as they relate to the Companies Acts;
(f) the approach to issues arising from the State's membership of the European Union insofar as they affect the operation of the Companies Acts,
(g) international developments in company law, insofar as they may provide lessons for improved State practice; and
(h) other related matters or issues, including issues submitted by the Minister to the Review Group for consideration.

---

35 See Chapter 9.
36 See Chapter 13.
37 Section 68(1) of the 2001 Act.

In advising the Minister the Review Group shall seek to promote enterprise, facilitate commerce, simplify the operation of the Companies Acts, enhance corporate governance and encourage commercial probity.[38]

The Minister shall, at least once in every two years, after consultation with the Review Group, determine the programme of work to be undertaken by the Review Group.[39] No later than three months after the end of each calendar year, the Review Group shall make a report to the Minister on its activities during that year and the Minister shall cause copies of the report to be laid before each House of the Oireachtas within a period of two months from the receipt of the report. The Review Group is presently focusing on a new consolidated Companies Bill, which is to replace the existing companies code.

---

38 Section 68(2) of the 2001 Act.
39 Section 70(1) of the 2001 Act.

CHAPTER THREE

COMPANY PROMOTION AND FORMATION

Promoters

Although the Companies Acts refer to 'promoters', no express definition is contained therein. The apparent inadvertence by the legislature to provide a general definition may stem from a reluctance to limit the range of persons to whom the law applies. The judiciary has not, however, shown the same reluctance, and the most noted definition is that of Cockburn C.J. who described a promoter as:

> ... one who undertakes to form a company with reference to a given project and to set it going and who takes the necessary steps to accomplish that purpose.[1]

Applying this description, promoters are said to be those persons who associate together to bring about the formation of a new company. This may involve the conversion of an existing business into a corporate form or the development of an entirely new business through the vehicle of a registered company. In either case, the promoters will usually arrange for some or all of the following:

1. the necessary business assets and personnel to enable the new business to function effectively;
2. the necessary capital, in the form of equity or loans, to finance the venture; and
3. completion of the statutory formalities necessary to form a company.

Although a promoter is a person who is engaged in the formation of a company, it should be noted that those who assist the promoter, by acting in a professional capacity, are not themselves promoters. Accordingly, neither the accountant who values the assets to be purchased by the company, nor indeed the solicitor who drafts the proposed constitutional documentation, is automatically deemed to be a promoter of the company. However, should they negotiate on behalf of the proposed company, or actively arrange the placement of the company's shares, or, indeed, arrange for somebody to become a director, they may be treated as promoters.

1. Fiduciary Duties of Promoters

While it may be difficult to identify precisely those persons who are considered company promoters, the same cannot be said of their duties. Promoters owe a

---

1 *Re Twycross v Grant* [1877] 2 CPD 469 at 541.

fiduciary duty to the company, which is essentially a duty of good faith. The extent of the duty owed will depend on the part played by the promoter in bringing about the company's formation. If the promoter stands to make a personal gain from his position, he must make a full and proper disclosure to an independent board of directors or to all existing members.[2] If he does not so disclose, and makes a secret profit, he must account to the company for this gain.

In *Erlanger v. New Sombrero Phosphate Co.*,[3] Erlanger, a banker, formed a company and arranged for the appointment of five directors. Prior to its incorporation he had acquired a lease of phosphate deposits in the West Indies, which was held for him in the name of a nominee. A subsequent board meeting of the company, the majority of which was 'controlled' by Erlanger, approved the purchase of the lease for a considerably greater sum. Shares in the company were then offered to the public but the offer made no disclosure of the promoter's profit. It was held that the contract should be rescinded on the grounds that there was no disclosure to an independent board of directors. As Lord Cairns stated:

> I do not say that the owner of property may not promote and form a joint stock company, and then sell his property to it, but I do say that if he does he is bound to take care that he sells it to a company through the medium of a board of directors who can and do exercise an independent and intelligent judgment on the transaction.[4]

This insistence that a promoter is under a duty to ensure the existence of an independent board has since been relaxed, and it is now accepted that disclosure to all the members and potential members, if any, will be adequate.[5]

It is not the profit made by the promoter that the law forbids; rather, it is the non-disclosure of it. Thus in the *Salomon* case[6] the sale of the assets to the company at an over-valued price was not struck down because all the members had agreed to it. However, if Salomon had promoted a public company which later invited offers for its shares to the public, disclosure to the existing members may not have been sufficient, as the case of *Gluckstein v. Barnes*[7] demonstrates. A syndicate had purchased the freehold of the Olympia Exhibition Hall in London for £140,000 from a company in financial difficulties. The hall was also the subject matter of a secured debenture issued by that company which was purchased by the syndicate at a price below par. The company's liquidator subsequently repaid the debenture at its par value, giving the promoters a profit of

---

2 In certain instances disclosure must also be made to potential members: see *Gluckstein v. Barnes* [1900] AC 240.

3 (1878) 3 App Cas 1218.

4 Ibid. at 1236.

5 *Salomon v. Salomon* [1897] AC 22 HL, *Lagunas Nitrate Co. v Lagunas Syndicate* [1899] 2 Ch 392.

6 [1897] AC 22 HL. See Chapter 6.

7 [1900] AC 240.

£20,000. The syndicate then promoted a new company to which it agreed to sell the Olympia for £180,000. The profit from the sale of the freehold was disclosed to the public, which was invited to subscribe for shares. However, the profit made on the debenture was only disclosed to the existing members of the company, who all happened to be members of the syndicate. It was held that the promoters were liable to account for the secret profit they had made on the undisclosed transaction.

2. Remedies for Breach of Promoters' Duties

When a promoter breaches his fiduciary duty, the remedy available to the company will depend on the nature of the breach. Where the breach is caused by the non-disclosure of the promoter's interest in a property contract, which is prejudicial to the company, as in the *Erlanger* case, the primary remedy is rescission of the contract. In *Hopkins v. Shannon Transport Systems Ltd*,[8] the plaintiff and a business associate promoted a company for the purpose of operating a ferry service across the River Shannon. They hoped to raise capital for their venture from share subscriptions and government grants. The promoters had also formed a partnership which, using some of the proceeds of the company's share subscription, purchased vessels that were subsequently sold to the company. Some of the investors were unaware of the promoters' interest in the contract. Later, when the government grants were not forthcoming, the plaintiff pulled out of the project. He then issued proceedings against the company for his share of the sums due to the partnership. The High Court held that the plaintiff as a promoter of the company was under a duty to disclose his gain to the subscribers, and, having breached this duty, the contract was voidable at the instance of the company.

The effect of an order for rescission is to restore the parties to their original position, thus eliminating the promoter's secret profit. However, restitution may not be granted if it is impossible to restore the parties to this position or where innocent third parties have acquired rights. In those circumstances the more suitable remedy would be for the company to retain the benefit of the contract and sue the promoter for breach of his duty to disclose.

3. Statutory Duties and Liabilities Relating to Promoters

In addition to the fiduciary duties imposed on promoters, there are a number of statutory provisions which regulate aspects of public companies' dealings in non-cash assets. Where a promoter is selling property to the company as consideration for its shares, the property must be valued by an independent expert.[9] Breach of this provision renders the promoter as the allottee liable to pay the company an amount equal to the face value of the shares.[10] Where a public

---

8 Unreported, High Court, 10 January 1972, noted in O'Dowd (1989) DULJ 120.
9 Section 30 of the 1983 Amendment Act.
10 Section 30(10) ibid.

company within two years of commencing business acquires an asset from a subscriber to its memorandum — in many cases the original subscribers will be company promoters — and the consideration for that acquisition amounts to one tenth or more of the nominal value of the company's issued capital, then that asset must also be independently valued, the terms of the sale must be approved by the company in general meeting and a copy of the agreement delivered to the registrar of companies.[11] Failure to comply with this obligation entitles the company to recover its consideration and the agreement, in so far as it has not been carried out, shall be void.

Where a company, established for less than five years, is issuing securities to the public, which requires a prospectus in relation to those securities,[12] the following details must be included in the share registration document:

1. personal details in relation to founder-promoters, including an indication of the principal activities performed by them outside the company, where these are significant with respect to that company;
2. any potential conflicts of interests between the duties owed by the company's founder-promoters to the company and any other duties the founder owes outside the company;[13] and
3. the amount of any remuneration paid including pension provisions, if any.

Breach of these provisions may render the promoter criminally and civilly liable.[14]

4. Pre-Incorporation Contracts

The exigencies of business may require promoters to grasp opportunities and enter into contracts on behalf of the venture being promoted. These contracts may be made either before or after the formalities for incorporation have been completed. If the company has already been incorporated, the normal rules of agency apply, and the promoter will act as the agent for the company. The difficulty arises when the proposed venture has not yet been incorporated. This is because the law of agency prevents a person from acting for a principal, if the principal does not exist. Neither could the company, once formed, ratify retrospectively the agent's agreement because ratification is only permitted if the principal itself could have entered into the contract at that time. Where a company

---

11 Section 32 ibid.
12 'Securities' includes shares which are or will be traded on a regulated market including the ISEQ.
13 Commission Regulation (EC) 809/2004 — The Prospectus Regulation.
14 Part 5 of the Investment Funds, Companies and Miscellaneous Act 2005. See Chapter 9 — Allotment of Shares.

has no legal existence, it has no capacity to contract. The difficulties facing promoters of 'yet to be formed' companies were clearly illustrated in *Kelner v. Baxter*.[15] In that case three promoters entered into a contract for the purchase of wine, which was signed by them 'on behalf of' a company which was not yet in existence. The company was subsequently formed but it went into liquidation before payment for the wine was made. It was held that as the contract was signed by persons who represented themselves as being agents for a principal that did not exist, the signatories were personally bound by the terms of the contract.

Section 37(1) of the Principal Act alleviates these difficulties by empowering a company to ratify pre-incorporation transactions and contracts entered into by the unincorporated company itself or by persons acting on its behalf. Although the section does not specify the manner in which the ratification may be authorised, it will usually be effected by the board of directors, which will normally be vested with the powers of managing the company under the articles of association. Where the articles do not so provide, ratification will be authorised by the company in general meeting. In the event that the company is wound up before the pre-incorporation contracts have been ratified, it has been held that a liquidator can ratify these contracts.[16]

Once the contract has been ratified by the company, section 37(1) further provides that the company shall be bound by the contract or transaction, and entitled to any benefits accruing thereon, in the same manner as if the company had been in existence at the date of and was a party to the contract or transaction. In the event that ratification does not occur, section 37(2) provides that any person who purported to act on behalf of, or in the name of, the company shall, in the absence of an express provision to the contrary, be personally bound by the contract or transaction. This is so even where the other party knew that the company was not yet formed.

In *Phonogram Ltd v. Lane*,[17] the defendant intended to form a company, Fragile Management, to manage a new pop group. Before the company was formed he entered into a contract with the plaintiff recording company whereby an advance payment would be made, but which was repayable if a recording contract was not agreed within one month. The contract was signed 'for and on behalf of Fragile Management Ltd'. The company was never formed, the recording contract was never made and the plaintiff sued for the return of the advance payment. Lane argued that the equivalent English provision only applied where the outsider did not know that the company had yet to be formed, and as the plaintiff knew that the company was not yet in existence he could not rely on the statutory protection. The Court of Appeal rejected this argument and held Lane liable.

---

15 (1866) LR 2 CP 174.

16 *HKN Invest OY v. Incotrade PVT Ltd & Others* [1993] 3 IR 152 at 161.

17 [1981] 3 All ER 182.

One way of avoiding these difficulties is to include a disclaimer of liability on the part of the promoter. However, while the contract may disclaim liability on the part of the promoter, it is unlikely that such a position would be acceptable to a third party. Furthermore, any disclaimer must be expressed in clear and unambiguous terms.[18]

If a promoter obtains payments under a pre-incorporation contract which is capable of being ratified by the company, those payments are held by the promoter as a trustee for the company. In *HKN Invest OY v. Incotrade PVT Ltd & Others*,[19] two foreign nationals set up a loan brokerage business in Ireland which defrauded a number of investors. In fleeing the jurisdiction, they left behind a sum of money in the personal account of one of the promoters. These monies represented commissions payable to the company, which were mostly pursuant to pre-incorporation contracts. No monies were paid from this account to the company after incorporation. The High Court held that the liquidator of the company was entitled to the commissions as they were being held by the promoters for the company under a constructive trust.

5. Preliminary Expenses of Promoters

Promoters' preliminary expenses are only payable if the company, once formed, ratifies the relevant contract. Where the promoter 'controls' the company he can cause it to ratify the contract, by ensuring that the memorandum and articles gives the directors the power to ratify pre-incorporation contracts, including his expenses, and that they do, in fact, ratify them. It is usual to include such provisions in the company's articles of association. Article 80 of Table A stipulates that the directors may pay all expenses incurred in promoting and registering the company.

6. Disqualification of Promoters

The provisions of the 1990 Act, relating to the restriction and disqualification of persons from acting as a director of a company, extend also to a prohibition on their acting as a promoter. (See Chapter 19, Restriction and Disqualification of Directors.)

Registration of New Companies

Before a company can be registered, the following documents must be delivered to the registrar of companies:

1. a memorandum of association in the prescribed form, signed by the subscribers, dated and witnessed;

---

18 *Phonogram Ltd v. Lane* [1981] 3 All ER 182 at 188.
19 [1993] 3 IR 152.

2. articles of association in the prescribed form, signed by the same subscribers, dated and witnessed (unless Table A is adopted);
3. form A1, which is a statement giving the following details:
   (a) the name of the company;
   (b) the registered office of the company;
   (c) the name, address and signature of the secretary;
   (d) particulars of the directors including their signatures;
   (e) a statutory declaration, by a solicitor engaged in the formation of the company or by a person named as a director or secretary of the company, that all the requirements of the Companies Acts in respect of registration have been complied with;
   (f) a statutory declaration that the company will carry on an activity within the State, the nature of that activity, the place within the State where it is proposed to carry on the activity, and the place, whether in the State or not, where the central administration of the company will normally be carried on; this declaration must be made by either a solicitor engaged in the formation of the company or by a person named as a director or secretary of the company;
   (g) a statement of capital, where the company is to have a share capital;
4. the appropriate registration fees and stamp duty.

Section 43(1) Companies (Amendment) (No.2) Act 1999 (the 1999 Amendment Act) requires that one director (not including an alternate director) of a company shall be resident in the State. This requirement will not apply if:

(a) the company holds a bond to the value of £20,000 (€25,395) to satisfy any failure by the company to pay fines or penalties under the Companies Acts and certain Taxes Acts; or
(b) the registrar has issued a certificate that the proposed company has a real and continuous link with one or more economic activities that are being carried on in the State.[20]

If the registrar is satisfied with the documentation, its contents, the company's name, the legality of the company's objects, and that the residency requirement is satisfied, he must register the company and issue a certificate of incorporation. The certificate of incorporation is analogous to a birth certificate and it will state the name of the company, the date it was incorporated and its registration number. The registration number is particularly important when identifying a company which has a similar name to another company. This will often be the case with companies in the same group. The company must publish a notice in the *CRO Gazette* that a certificate of incorporation has been issued.

---

20 Section 44 of the 1999 Amendment Act.

Effect of Registration

From the date of incorporation the company exists with perpetual succession, and is capable of exercising all the functions of an incorporated company.[21] It is also subject to all the statutory obligations which pertain to a company. The certificate of incorporation is conclusive evidence of the following:

(a) that the registration requirements of the Companies Acts have been complied with;
(b) that the association is a company authorised to be registered and is duly registered; and
(c) if the certificate contains a statement that a company is a public company, that the company is such a company.[22]

Commencement of Business

Once the certificate is issued, a private company can commence trading immediately. However, section 6(1) of the 1983 Amendment Act prohibits a public company from trading until it has been issued with an additional certificate of trading. In order to obtain this trading certificate the company must apply to the registrar of companies in the prescribed form. The application must be supported by a statutory declaration signed by a director or secretary of the company. This declaration must state:

(a) that the nominal share capital is not less than the authorised minimum;
(b) that the amount paid up on the allotted share capital is at least one-quarter of the nominal value and the entire premium, if any;
(c) details of the preliminary expenses involved in promoting the company, to whom they were paid, together with any other payments or benefits to the company's promoters.[23]

The registrar may accept the statutory declaration as sufficient evidence of the matters stated therein.[24] If a public company fails to obtain the trading certificate or does not re-register as a private company within twelve months, it may be struck off the register.[25] If a public company commences to trade without the appropriate certificate, the company and every officer in default is guilty of an offence and is liable to a fine.[26] Where a public limited company enters into a

---

21 Section 18(2) of the Principal Act.
22 Section 5(4) of the 1983 Amendment Act.
23 Section 6(3) of the 1983 Amendment Act.
24 Section 6(5) of the 1983 Amendment Act.
25 Section 8 of the 1983 Amendment Act..
26 Section 6(7) of the 1983 Amendment Act.

transaction without having obtained the appropriate trading certificate, the transaction is still enforceable by any other party. However, if the company fails to comply with its obligations within twenty-one days of being called upon to do so, the directors of the company shall be jointly and severally liable to indemnify any other party to the transaction who suffered any loss or damage by reason of the company's failure to comply with its obligations.[27] A private company converting to a public limited company is not required to cease trading pending receipt of a certificate of trading.

Notification in the *CRO Gazette*

Regulation 4(1) of the European Communities (Companies) Regulations 1973[28] requires all companies with limited liability to publish in the *CRO Gazette* notice of the delivery to, or the issue by, the registrar of companies the following documents and particulars:

(a) any certificate of incorporation of the company;
(b) the memorandum and articles of association, or the equivalent documents which constitute or define the constitution of the company, any amendments thereto and the text of the amended documents;
(c) any return relating to the company's register of directors or any notification of a change among its directors;
(d) any return relating to the persons, other than the board of directors, authorised to enter into transactions binding the company, or notification of a change among such persons;
(e) the annual return of the company;
(f) any notice of the situation of its registered office, or of any change therein;
(g) any copy of a winding-up order in respect of the company;
(h) any order for the dissolution of the company on a winding up; and
(i) any return by a liquidator of the final meeting of the company on a winding up.

All notices must be published within six weeks of the relevant delivery or issue.[29] Section 55 of the 1983 Amendment Act obliges public limited companies to publish in the *CRO Gazette* notice of delivery to the registrar of certain additional documents, including *inter alia* certain special resolutions, various experts' valuation reports, statutory declarations and other miscellaneous matters.

---

27 Section 6(8) of the 1983 Amendment Act.
28 SI 163/1973.
29 Regulation 4(2) of the European Communities (Companies) Regulations 1973.

Other Methods of Corporate Formation

Section 80 of the 2001 Act provides for the registration of reference memoranda and articles of association. This provision enables the registration of companies in an expeditious manner. Essentially, the registrar of companies may accept for registration a document containing standard form text from the objects clause of a memorandum of association or from articles of association and shall assign a reference number to each document so registered. Documents filed in this manner need not relate to a particular company or contain the registered number of a company.

When the memorandum or articles are subsequently registered they may contain a statement that they are to incorporate the text of a document already registered. Since January 2006 all former schemes that provide for registration within a given time period have been terminated and replaced with the CRODisk system using the reference memoranda and articles scheme provided for by section 80. The CRODisk system is an electronic company incorporation scheme designed to facilitate those presenters who require speedy company incorporation without the inconvenience of manually lodging the documents. Promoters who use this scheme must have a deposit account with the Companies Registration Office. Where the CRODisk system using the reference memoranda and articles is used by a company promoter, a certificate of incorporation will be issued within five working days. Since April 2006 anyone registering a company in the ordinary manner may also use the reference memoranda and articles scheme.

Registration of Foreign Companies

Companies may be incorporated outside the State but establish a place of business within the State. Within one month of the establishment of the place of business, the company must deliver to the registrar of companies the following documents:

(a) a certified copy of the company's constitutional documents which have been translated into English or Irish, where necessary;
(b) a certified list of the directors and secretary and the particulars relating to them;
(c) the names of at least one person who is resident in the State and is authorised to accept on behalf of the company service of process and any notices required to be served on the company; and
(d) the certified address of the company's principal place of business in the State.[30]

Companies incorporated outside the State but which only establish a branch within the State are subject to the requirements imposed by Regulation 14 of the

---

30 Section 352(1) of the Principal Act.

European Communities (Branch Disclosures) Regulation 1993.[31] These provisions impose similar registration requirements on foreign companies establishing a branch within the State. However, the requirements are more stringent for companies incorporated outside the European Union.

Re-registration of Companies

A company may convert from its original form during the course of its existence. Where the statutory requirements relating to re-registration have been satisfied, the registrar of companies will issue a new certificate of incorporation. The procedural requirements for re-registration vary depending on the existing form of the company and the proposed new form.

1. Private to Public Company

Sections 9 and 10 of the 1983 Amendment Act set out the prerequisites for converting from a private company to a public limited company. The first step is the passing of a special resolution to give effect to the change and to alter the memorandum and articles of association to reflect the form appropriate to a public company. An application is then made to the registrar of companies, in the prescribed form, together with the following:

(a) a printed copy of the altered memorandum and articles;
(b) a statement by the company's auditors to the effect that the company's net assets are not less that the aggregate of its called-up share capital and undistributable reserves;
(c) a copy of the balance sheet and an unqualified report by the auditors in relation to the balance sheet;
(d) a copy of a valuation report on any assets acquired for shares in the period between the balance sheet date and the passing of the special resolution, where applicable;
(e) a statutory declaration by a director or secretary that a special resolution has been passed, the statutory requirements have been satisfied, and that there has been no change (since the balance sheet date) in the financial position that has resulted in the amount of the company's net assets becoming less than the aggregate of its called-up share capital and undistributable reserves.

Assuming the registrar is satisfied that the application form and the ancillary documents are in order, he will issue a certificate of re-registration of the company as a public limited company. The certificate is conclusive evidence that all the statutory requirements have been complied with. A private company will

---

31 SI 395/1993.

not be re-registered as a public limited company unless, at the time the special resolution for its conversion was passed, it had satisfied the capital requirements imposed on such companies.

2. Public to Private Company

Sections 14–15 of the 1983 Amendment Act set out the procedure to be followed in order to re-register a public limited company as a private company. This procedure is similar to that mentioned above, but obviously the alterations to the company's memorandum and articles must reflect the proposed change in status. However, in this case dissenting members [32] may apply to the court to cancel the resolution purporting to make the alteration.[33] Where such an application is made, the company must notify the registrar, and the re-registration cannot be completed until confirmed by the court. The court, in considering such an application, may approve or cancel the resolution or may make such order as it sees fit, including an order that the company purchase the dissenting shareholders' shares in the company.

In certain circumstances, a public limited company may have no alternative but to re-register as a private company. Where a lawful reduction in capital brings the company's capital below the authorised minimum, the court will not confirm the reduction until the company has been re-registered as a private company.

3. Unlimited to Limited Company

An unlimited private company may convert to a limited company where the members agree by special resolution to a change in status and the resolution also sets out the necessary changes in the memorandum and articles of association.[34] The resolution must be delivered together with the prescribed application form to the registrar of companies.

4. Limited to Unlimited Company

A company formed with limited liability may re-register as an unlimited company.[35] The application in the prescribed form must be sent to the registrar together with evidence of the written consent of every member. The requirement to have the unanimous consent of the members is necessary because members of an unlimited company will be assuming full responsibility for the debts of the company.

---

32 Dissenting members must hold at least 5 per cent of the issued share capital or of any class of share capital; or in the case of a company with no share capital 5 per cent of its members.
33 Section 15(2) of the 1983 Amendment Act.
34 Section 53 of the 1983 Amendment Act.
35 Section 52 of the 1983 Amendment Act..

5. *Private to Single-Member Company*

A company may convert from a private limited company to a single-member company by reducing its members to one and by vesting all the company's shares in that sole member.[36] The conversion is then automatic, occurring by operation of the law. The company must however notify the registrar of the fact and date of conversion and the identity of the single member within twenty-eight days from the date of conversion. A private unlimited company may not convert to a single-member company in this manner. It is first required to convert to limited status.

6. *Single-Member to Private Company*

Where the members of a single-member company increase to more than one, it is automatically deemed to have converted to a private limited company. The company is obliged to notify the registrar within twenty-eight days of the conversion.

Company Dissolution and Restoration

A company continues to exist until the grant of corporate status has been revoked and the company is dissolved. Dissolution brings the separate personality of a company to an end. The section 25 contract[37] between the members and the company is terminated. The assets of the dissolved company are vested in the State.[38] A company will be dissolved when one of the following events occurs:

1. the court has made an order of dissolution following a compulsory liquidation;
2. three months, or such longer period as the court may direct, from the date of the submission of the liquidator's final report in a voluntary liquidation; and
3. the registrar has struck the company off the register for the following reasons:
   (i) failure to carry on business[39]; or
   (ii) failure to submit the annual return[40]; or
   (iii) where the company is being wound up and the registrar believes that no liquidator is acting, or the affairs of the company are fully wound up and the returns to be made by the liquidator have not been made for a period of six consecutive months;[41] or

---

36 Regulation 5(1) of the European Communities (Single-Member Private Limited Companies) Regulations 1994 SI 275/1994.
37 See Chapters 4 (The Memorandum of Association) and 5 (The Articles of Association).
38 Section 28 of the State Property Act 1954.
39 Section 311(1) of the Principal Act.
40 Section 12 of the Companies (Amendment) Act 1982 (the 1982 Amendment Act).
41 Section 311(3) of the Principal Act.

(iv) the registrar is satisfied that the company is in breach of the requirement that one director be resident in Ireland;[42] or

(v) where the registrar believes the company has no directors;[43] or

(vi) where the Revenue has given a notice to the registrar that a company has failed to deliver certain statements containing various particulars, as required by section 882 (3) of the Taxes Consolidation Act 1997;[44] or

(vii) the registrar has been formally requested by the company to strike the company's name from the register provided the company has no assets or outstanding liabilities, all outstanding annual returns have been filed, the Revenue Commissioners have no objections and an advertisement relating to the intended voluntary striking off has appeared in one daily newspaper.

The liability, if any, of every director, officer and member of the company will continue and may be enforced as if the company had not been dissolved.[45] Where a company is involuntarily struck off by the registrar of companies and the company has not paid all its debts, the directors of that company may face a disqualification order under section 160(2)(h) of the 1990 Act.[46]

The registrar of companies shall, after the expiration of twenty years from the dissolution of a company, send all the documents filed in connection with such company to the Public Record Office.[47]

Where a company has been dissolved, the court may within two years from the date of dissolution, on an application by a liquidator or any other interested party, declare the dissolution void.[48]

A company or any member or creditor thereof who feels aggrieved by the company having being struck off the register, may apply to the court within twenty years from the date of dissolution to have the company restored to the register.[49] The court, if satisfied that the company was trading at the time of the striking off or that it is just that the company be restored, may order the restoration of the company. The company will thereafter be deemed to have continued in existence as if its name had not been struck off and the court may make such an order and issue such directions as seem just for the placing of the company, and any other persons in the same position as nearly may be, as if the

---

42 Section 43(15) of the 1999 Amendment Act.

43 Section 48 of the 1999 Amendment Act.

44 Section 12A of the 1982 Amendment Act.

45 Section 311(6) of the Principal Act and section 12B of the 1982 Amendment Act.

46 See Chapter 19 – Restriction and Disqualification of Directors.

47 Section 313 of the Principal Act.

48 Section 310 of the Principal Act.

49 Section 311(8) of the Principal Act.

name of the company had not been struck off.[50] In *Re Amantiss Enterprises*[51] the High Court held that an order under section 311(8) had the effect of automatically validating retrospectively all acts done in the name or on behalf of the company while it was struck off the register.

Where a company has been struck off the register by the registrar of companies an application may also be made to the registrar by either a member or creditor to have a company restored to the register.[52] The application must be made within twelve months. Where the company has been struck off for more than twelve months, but for less than twenty years, the application must be made to the court to have the company restored to the register.[53]

---

50 Section 311(8) of the Principal Act. See also sections 12B(3) and 12B(7) of the
    1982 Amendment Act, which gives similar powers to the court to restore a company
    that was the subject of a striking off under section 12(3) or 12A(3) of the 1982
    Amendment Act.
51 [2000] 2 ILRM 177.
52 Section 12C of the 1982 Amendment Act.
53 Section 12B(c) of the 1982 Amendment Act.

CHAPTER FOUR

THE MEMORANDUM OF ASSOCIATION

Introduction

The memorandum and articles of association together form the constitution of the company. The memorandum contains provisions regulating the external activities of the company and the articles regulate its internal affairs. Together, they determine both the legal parameters within which the company and its agents must operate and the basis for the relationship between the company and its members and the members *inter se*.

The Memorandum of Association

The incorporation of a company cannot be effected without the registration of the memorandum.[1] The form of the memorandum for a private limited company must be in accordance with, or as near thereto as the circumstances permit, the forms set out in Tables B, C and D of the First Schedule to the Principal Act. In the case of public limited companies the forms are set out in the Second Schedule to the 1983 Amendment Act. The memorandum must be printed, or in a form pursuant to section 80 of the 2001 Act, signed and attested.[2] Once the format of the memorandum meets the statutory requirements, its contents are largely a matter for the company's promoters. However, section 6 of the Principal Act provides that the memorandum of all companies limited by shares must contain the following 'compulsory' clauses:

1. the name clause;
2. the objects clause;
3. the limited liability clause;
4. the authorised share capital clause; and
5. the association clause.[3]

---

1 Registration of the articles is not required because a company can adopt the model articles set out in the First Schedule of the Principal Act, as amended: section 13 of the Principal Act.

2 The requirement to have the memorandum stamped has been repealed by section 112 of the Finance Act 1996.

3 Although section 6 of the Principal Act does not specifically mention an association clause, every memorandum is required to have such a clause, often referred to as the un-numbered compulsory clause.

The memorandum of a company limited by guarantee is not required to have an authorised share capital clause. However, it must include a statement of the amount which each member agrees to contribute in the winding up of the company. An unlimited company is only required to include the names and objects clauses in its memorandum.

1. The Name Clause

Every company must have a name with which it may be identified. The name is necessary to enable proceedings to be taken on behalf of, or against, the company and to distinguish it from other companies and business entities. A person may apply to the registrar of companies to have a company name reserved in advance of registration of a company. Where the registrar makes a favourable determination in relation to the reserved name it will be reserved for a period of twenty-eight days. The registrar may extend this period on application. During the reserved period no other company will be incorporated with this name.

A private company, limited by shares or by guarantee, must end its name with the word 'limited', 'teoranta' or their respective abbreviations. In the case of a public limited company, the name must end with the words 'public limited company', 'cuideachta phoiblí theoranta' or their respective abbreviations. In certain cases, a limited company may obtain a dispensation from the registrar of companies to omit the word 'limited' from its name.[4] Such a dispensation may only be granted to a private company that is limited by shares and which satisfies the following conditions:

(a) the company is formed for the purpose of promoting commerce, art, science, religion, charity or any other useful object; and

(b) its memorandum or articles of association require its profits or other income to be applied to the promotion of its objects, prohibit the payment of dividends to its members, and require all the assets which would otherwise be available to its members to be transferred to another company that can satisfy these requirements.

The memorandum and articles of association of a company seeking a dispensation shall not be altered where such an alteration would cause the company to cease to comply with the statutory requirements for dispensation. A statutory declaration that the company has complied with the requirements for dispensation must be made by a director or secretary of the company and delivered to the registrar of companies. A company that is granted an exemption is still obliged to show on its letterheads and order forms the fact that it is a limited company.

---

4 Section 24 of the Principal Act.

Prohibition on the Use of Certain Names

As well as the above mentioned requirements, there are a number of statutory provisions which restrict the choice of company name. Section 56 of the 1983 Amendment Act makes it an offence to use the words 'public limited company' in a business name unless the company is in fact registered as a public limited company. More importantly, section 21 of the Principal Act provides that no name shall be registered which in the opinion of the registrar is undesirable. However, where the registrar refuses to register a name, an appeal may be made to the court.

The registrar of companies has issued informal guidelines as to the names that may be refused registration. These include:

(a) a name identical to one already on the register;
(b) a name which is offensive;
(c) a name that would suggest State sponsorship;
(d) a name which includes 'bank' or cognate words where a licence has not been obtained from the Central Bank;
(e) a name which includes 'insurance' or cognate words unless an appropriate licence has been granted by the Minister;
(f) a name which includes the words 'society' or 'co-op' or 'co-operative';
(g) a name which includes the word 'university' unless the Department of Education has granted permission for such usage; and
(h) a name that suggests specific funcions, e.g. holding company or group company.

Even if a name is registered, the registrar may, within six months after registration, compel a company to change its name if it is very similar to one already registered.[5] If the registrar so directs, the name must be changed within 6 weeks or such longer period as the registrar may allow. Even if the registrar makes no direction in this regard, the company may be directed by the court to change its name if it is found liable for the tort of passing off. Passing off involves the use of a business name or brand which is so similar to that of another business or brand that it creates confusion among the public. In *Ewing v. Buttercup Margarine Co. Ltd*,[6] the plaintiff, whose business was called 'The Buttercup Dairy Company', was successful in his attempt to prevent the defendant company from continuing to use its name because the public might think that the two businesses were connected.

A company may trade under a name that is different to its registered name. In such circumstances the trading name must be registered under the Registration of Business Names Act 1963.[7]

---

5 Section 23(2) of the Principal Act.
6 [1917] 2 Ch 1.
7 Section 22 of the Principal Act.

Display of Company Name

The company's name must be painted up or affixed to the outside of every office or place in which the business of the company is carried on, in a conspicuous position and in easily legible letters. The name must be engraved on the company's seal and must be mentioned on all the company's business letters, notices and official publications.[8] Failure to comply with these requirements may result in the company, and any person acting on its behalf, being liable to a fine. The company's name must also be placed on bills of exchange, cheques, orders for money and goods and receipts issued by the company. Where this does not occur, the company will be liable to a fine and the company officer who signed on its behalf shall be personally liable to the holder of a bill of exchange, promissory note or cheque or order for money or goods issued.[9]

In *Penrose v. Martyr*,[10] a bill was drawn on a private limited company which was described on the bill without the word 'limited' being mentioned. The bill was accepted by the company secretary. When it was later dishonoured, the company secretary was held personally liable for the amount of the bill because of the incorrect description of the company's name. Even if the error is caused by the holder of the instrument, the company's officers may still be liable as they ought to have ensured the accuracy of the name before signing it.[11] However, in certain circumstances the holder will be prevented from suing the officer who fails to correct the mistake. In *Durham Fancy Goods Ltd v. Michael Jackson (Fancy Goods) Ltd*,[12] a bill of exchange was drawn by the plaintiffs on the defendant company. The plaintiffs, in prescribing the form of words for the acceptance of the bill, had incorrectly described the defendant company's name. As the plaintiff had prepared both the bill and the form of acceptance, he was estopped from invoking the statutory liability of the signatory.

Change of Company Name

A company may change its name by passing a special resolution and obtaining the approval in writing of the registrar.[13] A new certificate of incorporation on change of name will be issued and the change comes into effect from the date the certificate is issued. The registered number of the company, which appears on the original certificate of incorporation, will be included on all subsequent certificates of incorporation issued on change of name. Where the company is

---

8 Section 114(1) of the Principal Act.

9 Section 114(3) and (4) of the Principal Act.

10 (1858) EB & E 499.

11 *Lindholst & Co. A/S v. Fowler* [1988] BCLC 166.

12 [1968] 2 QB 839.

13 Section 23(1) of the Principal Act.

changing from a public to a private company, or *vice versa*, the procedures for re-registering must be followed.[14]

2. The Objects Clause

Section 6(1) of the Principal Act requires every company to state its objects in the memorandum of association. As the objects clause will prescribe the permissible activities of the company, the promoters should carefully consider the anticipated activities. As persons can only associate to form a company with a lawful purpose, the objects cannot be illegal.[15] If a company cannot achieve the objects for which it was established, it may be wound up under section 213(f) of the Principal Act. In *Re German Date Coffee Co.*,[16] the company was formed for the sole purpose of acquiring a German patent under which to manufacture coffee from dates. The patent was not granted but the company continued to work the process by acquiring a Swedish patent. The members petitioned to have the company wound up on the grounds that it was no longer possible for the company to achieve its purpose. The court, in holding that the substratum of the company had failed, accepted the petition and ordered the company to be wound up. The inclusion of the objects clause in the memorandum is necessary for the following reasons:

(a) prospective investors will know what business the company is in;
(b) existing members can be assured that any plans to diversify into other activities will require an alteration of the objects clause which must be approved by the general meeting;
(c) creditors will be aware of what contracts are authorised and therefore enforceable against the company; and
(d) directors, as agents of the company, can be clear as to the type of transactions to which they can bind the company.

Where a company acts outside its objects, it is said to be acting *ultra vires*. An *ultra vires* transaction is void and can only be enforced by an outsider who either acted in good faith or was unaware of the *ultra vires* nature of the transaction. The doctrine of *ultra vires* and its effect on outsiders is considered in Chapter 7.

The objects clause may be altered by a special resolution of the company in general meeting. Holders of debentures secured by floating charges must be given notice of the meeting at which the proposed change is to be presented.[17] Any alteration must be made *bona fide* and in the best interests of the company. An application may be made to the court to have the alteration cancelled by the following:

---

14 See Chapter 3.
15 Section 5 of the Principal Act.
16 [1882] 20 Ch. 169.
17 Section 10 of the Principal Act.

(a) dissentient holders of at least 15 per cent in nominal value of the company's issued share capital or any class thereof; or
(b) in the case of a company with no share capital at least 15 per cent of the members; or
(c) holders of at least 15 per cent of the company's debentures secured by floating charges.[18]

The application must be made within twenty-one days from the date of the resolution purporting to alter the object. Where an application is made, the court may make an order cancelling the alteration or confirming it either wholly or in part, on such terms and conditions as it sees fit. It may also order the purchase of the interests of dissentient members. Where an application is made to the court, the alteration shall not take effect unless confirmed by the court. An alteration in the objects clause cannot have retrospective effect. Therefore, an *ultra vires* act cannot be subsequently ratified by the general meeting agreeing to alter the company's objects.

3. The Liability Clause

In the case of a company limited by shares or by guarantee, the memorandum must contain a statement that the liability of the members is limited.[19] The liability clause can only be altered to increase the members' liability to the company if every member agrees.[20] Where it is proposed to change a company's status from limited to unlimited liability, the consent of all members must also be obtained.[21] However, if an unlimited company is proposing to become a limited liability company, a special resolution will suffice.[22]

4. The Authorised Share Capital Clause

The capital clause must set out the total amount of the company's authorised share capital and the division thereof into shares of a fixed amount. It is important to remember that the authorised share capital will usually be far in excess of the amount of issued share capital. The authorised share capital clause may be altered, where the articles of association so provide, by an ordinary resolution of the company in general meeting. Where the alteration will have the effect of reducing the share capital of the company the procedure set out in section 72 of the Principal Act must be followed. (See Chapter 11, Loan Capital and Charges.)

---

18 Section 10(3) of the Principal Act.
19 Section 6(2) of the Principal Act.
20 Section 27 of the Principal Act.
21 Section 52 of the 1983 Act.
22 Section 53 of the 1983 Act.

5. *The Association Clause*

Every memorandum ends with a statement whereby the subscribers indicate their wish to form the company and their agreement to take the number of shares in the capital of the company which is set out opposite their names. Each subscriber must take at least one share. This statement is followed by the names, addresses and descriptions of the subscribers, the number of shares to be taken by each, and the signature of the subscriber and of a witness.

Additional Compulsory Clause in the Case of a PLC

In the case of a public limited company the memorandum must contain a statement that the company is a public company.[23]

The Non-Compulsory Clauses

It is rare in practice to include clauses other than the compulsory clauses in the memorandum of association. However, usually to protect the balance of power, the promoters and original subscribers may decide to 'entrench' certain provisions in the memorandum by declaring that they are unalterable. This has the same legal effect as an irrevocable agreement by the first and all future members that these provisions will always remain unalterable.[24] Therefore privileges bestowed on the first members, such as weighted voting rights or lifetime directorships, can be safeguarded from any future changes by new members or a new majority.

There is a general power to alter all other non-compulsory or non-entrenched clauses by special resolution,[25] subject to the following restrictions:

(a) dissentient shareholders may apply to the court to have any alteration cancelled;
(b) where a specific alteration procedure is prescribed by the articles it must be complied with;
(c) where the court has ordered the alteration of a clause in the memorandum, it cannot thereafter be altered by the company without the consent of the court;
(d) no alteration can increase the liability of a member in respect of shares already held, nor can a member be compelled to subscribe for additional shares without the member's consent in writing;
(e) any alteration which affects the rights attached to a class of shareholders will not be valid unless the correct variation procedure has been followed. (See Chapter 8, Company Securities.)

---

23 Second Schedule to the 1983 Amendment Act.
24 Section 28(3) of the Principal Act.
25 Section 28(3) of the Principal Act.

The company is required to deliver to the registrar a copy of the altered memorandum, together with a signed copy of the authorising resolution, within fifteen days of making the alteration.[26] Notice of the delivery of these particulars to the registrar must be made in the *CRO Gazette*.

---

26 Section 10(9) of the Principal Act.

CHAPTER FIVE

THE ARTICLES OF ASSOCIATION

Introduction

While the memorandum determines the relationship between the company and outsiders, the articles govern the internal dealings of the company, including *inter alia* the issue and transfer of shares, directors' powers, remuneration and removal, procedures at board meetings and general meetings, and the payment of dividends. Where there is a conflict between the articles and the memorandum of association, the latter prevails.[1] As Carroll J. stated in *Roper v. Ward*[2]

> In construing the articles I am guided by the principle that they are subordinated to and controlled by the memorandum of association which is the dominant document.

The memorandum and articles are commercial documents and as such they will be construed by the courts in such a manner to make them commercially workable.[3]

Every company must have articles of association. However, private companies limited by shares are not required to register articles.[4] Where they do not do so, the model articles (Table A), set out in the First Schedule to the Principal Act, will be deemed to be the articles of association of that company, in the same manner as if they had been duly registered.[5] Where a private company limited by shares voluntarily registers its own articles, the provisions of Table A will still apply unless they have been expressly excluded or modified by the company's own articles.[6]

The form of the articles is determined by section 14 of the Principal Act. It provides that the articles must be printed or in a form pursuant to section 80 of the 2001 Act, divided into paragraphs which are numbered consecutively, and signed by each subscriber to the memorandum in the presence of a witness who must attest the signature.[7] While the Companies Acts do not stipulate what the articles must contain,[8] Table A gives a clear impression of the particulars which would normally be provided in the articles.

---

1 *Ashbury Railway Carriage & Iron Co. v Riche* (1875) LR 7 HL 653.
2 [1981] ILRM 408 at 409
3 Ibid.
4 Section 11 of the Principal Act.
5 Section 13(2) of the Principal Act.
6 Section 13(2) of the Principal Act.
7 The requirement that the articles bear the stamp as if they were contained in a deed has been repealed by section 112 of the Finance Act 1996.
8 Certain information must be provided in the case of private companies limited by guarantee and unlimited companies — section 12 of the Principal Act.

In any case, there are a number of provisions in the Companies Acts that will permit certain matters only if the articles so permit, including, *inter alia*, the following:

(a) an alteration of the authorised share capital clause of the company by ordinary resolution;
(b) an increase in the company's share capital;
(c) a reduction in the company's share capital;[9]
(d) a purchase by a company of its own shares;[10]
(e) the issue of redeemable shares;[11]
(f) the holding of the annual general meeting outside the State;
(g) the signing by all the members of a written resolution as a valid substitute for a special resolution passed at a general meeting of the company.

Furthermore, where a company is listed on the Stock Exchange, the 'Listing Rules' regime dictates that such a company's articles contain provisions on such matters as transfer of securities, share certificates, dividends, accounts, notices, voting entitlements and proxies.

Alteration of the Articles

Section 15 of the Principal Act provides that a company may alter or add to its articles of association by passing a special resolution to that effect. Any attempt to deprive the company of this power, either by the articles themselves or by a shareholders' agreement, is void.[12]

However, it is possible to circumvent this rule by the use of certain devices. First, the articles may give additional or 'weighted' votes to a member where resolutions to alter the articles are proposed. In *Bushell v. Faith*,[13] the company was owned by three family members who were the company's only directors and who held equal shares. Each share carried one vote but the articles provided that in the event of a resolution being proposed for the removal of a director from office, the shares of that director-member would carry three votes per share. When it was proposed to remove one of the directors from office, he used his weighted votes to

---

9 A company cannot generally reduce its share capital. In exceptional cases it may do so subject to court approval.
10 A company cannot generally purchase its own shares. In exceptional cases it may do so subject to a number of conditions.
11 See Chapter 10 — Maintenance of Share Capital.
12 However, the shareholders may enter into an agreement among themselves as to how they will exercise their voting rights: see *Russell v. Northern Bank Development Corporation* [1992] 3 All ER 161. However, shareholder agreements are not binding on future members in the same way as the articles are.
13 [1969] 1 All ER 1002.

block the resolution. The House of Lords upheld the validity of the provision in the articles. A second method of preventing the alteration of the articles is to provide that, in the event of certain resolutions being proposed at a meeting, the quorum for that meeting must include a particular member. The member can then, by absenting himself, deny the meeting a quorum and prevent the resolution from being passed. Finally, the company may insert certain rules, which would normally be found in the articles of association, into the memorandum instead and declare them to be unalterable.[14]

When an alteration is made to the articles, a copy of the altered articles together with a signed copy of the authorising resolution must be delivered to the registrar within fifteen days.[15]

Informal Alteration of the Articles

An alteration may be effected without following the formalities of a special resolution. Both common law and statute recognise that informal agreements may have the same effect as a special resolution. In *Cane v. Jones*,[16] the shareholders entered into an oral agreement whereby the chairman was deprived of his casting vote at general meetings, a power which had been conferred on him by the articles. Later, when a dispute arose, one body of shareholders contended that the articles had not been altered, because a special resolution to that effect had not been passed. It was held that the 'assent principle', recognised by the common law, applied. The essence of this principle is that all members of a company can, by unanimous agreement, whether orally or in writing, whether formally or informally, take a binding decision on any matter which is *intra vires* the company. Accordingly, the alteration was held to be effective.[17]

Section 141(8) of the Principal Act provides that where a company is so authorised by its articles of association, a resolution in writing signed by all the company's members shall be as valid and effective as if the resolution had been passed at a general meeting of the company. This statutory provision differs from the common law rule in that it requires the consent of all the members in writing. It is not clear whether s.141(8) amends the common law principle or re-affirms it in part. In any case where an alteration of the articles is being proposed it would be more appropriate for the company to follow the statutory guidelines: the registrar of companies will require some evidence of approval by the company of the relevant alterations, whether in the form of special resolution of the general meeting or a written resolution of all the members.

---

14 Section 28(3) of the Principal Act.
15 Section 143 of the Principal Act.
16 [1981] 1 All ER 533.
17 See Chapter 14 for a fuller discussion of the 'assent principle'.

Restrictions on the Right to Alter the Articles

Whatever the form of agreement, a company does not have an unfettered right to alter the articles. This is because any alteration must be made *bona fide* and in the best interests of the company. It would appear from case-law on this particular point that once this test is satisfied the alteration is valid, despite any consequential detriment suffered by a minority of shareholders. This position was accepted by the Court of Appeal in *Allen v. Gold Reefs of West Africa Ltd.*[18] The articles provided that in the event that monies were owing to the company on unpaid or partly paid shares, a lien would attach to those particular shares. Following the death of a member, who owed the company certain amounts in relation to unpaid shares, the articles were altered. The effect of the alteration was such that the lien would extend to all shares, including fully paid shares, held by a member who owed monies on unpaid shares. The deceased member was the only holder of fully paid shares to which the lien would now apply. His executors argued that the alteration was discriminatory as it adversely affected only one member. The court, in rejecting this argument, held that as the alteration was for the benefit of the company as a whole it was valid. The court noted that the alteration applied to all members although in this particular instance only one happened to be affected.

1. The Bona Fide Test

When considering the best interests of the company as a whole, the courts may, depending on the circumstances, take into account the company itself or the general body of shareholders. In the *Allen* case the court clearly assessed the alteration in the context of the benefit to the company as a separate entity. In other circumstances the court has regard for the interests of the general body of shareholders. Thus in *Greenhalgh v. Arderne Cinemas Ltd*,[19] the articles included a pre-emption right which gave existing members the right of first refusal when shares were being sold. The majority of shareholders, who wished to sell their shares to an outsider, proposed a resolution to remove the pre-emption right from the articles. Greenhalgh, a minority shareholder, objected to the alteration on the grounds that it was sacrificing the rights of the minority against those of the majority. The court was not swayed by this argument and held the alteration was valid because all members, including Greenhalgh, would now be free to sell their shares. Evershed MR stated that as long as the majority honestly believed that the alteration would benefit the company as a whole, the court would not interfere with its decision.

When considering cases of this type, the courts must balance two conflicting claims. First, the majority is entitled to use its position to effect change, despite

---

18 [1900] 1 Ch 656.
19 [1950] 2 All ER 1120.

objections from the minority. Second, the minority must be protected from actions by the majority which are unfairly prejudicial to it. In *Shuttleworth v. Cox Brothers & Co. (Maidenhead) Ltd*,[20] the articles provided that five directors should be appointed for life unless one of six specified events occurred. One director failed on a number of occasions to account to the company for monies spent. This behaviour did not warrant his removal under the articles, so the company altered the articles to the effect that the other directors could resolve that a director be removed. The court held that the alteration was valid as it was *bona fide* and in the interests of the company as a whole. Similarly, in *Sidebottom v. Keeshaw, Leese & Co.*[21] the articles were altered to allow the directors to purchase the shares of any member who was competing with the company. A minority shareholder, who was in competition with the company, objected to the alteration on the grounds that it was an attempt by the majority to expel a minority. While the courts will normally scrutinise any alteration that is directed at a particular member, particularly in the context of expropriating that member, in this case the court was satisfied that there was no evidence of *male fides* on the part of the majority of the shareholders. Lord Sterndale MR suggested that the alteration was broadly for the benefit of the company in that it should not be obliged to have as a member persons competing with it and who could, through their membership, enable them to compete better. The alteration was therefore approved by the court.

However, in *Brown v. British Abrasive Wheel Co.*,[22] the majority did not persuade the court that the alteration was for the company's benefit. The company in question was in need of a capital injection. The majority agreed to provide the additional funds on condition that they could buy out the 2 per cent minority. The minority refused to sell and the majority caused the articles to be altered to enable them to acquire the minority shares compulsorily at a fair price. The minority's objection succeeded as the court held that the alteration was not an essential prerequisite to a capital injection, and was not therefore for the benefit of the company. A majority decision met with the same fate in *Dafen Tinplate Co. Ltd v. Llanelly Steel Co. (1907) Ltd.*[23] Here, a minority shareholder had transferred his custom from the company to a competitor. The majority altered the articles to provide for the compulsory acquisition of the minority's shares without specifying any grounds. The court accepted the plaintiff's contention that this new power had too wide a scope, and that the alteration was designed only to compel him to transfer his shares. Accordingly, the court refused to confirm the alteration.

---

20 [1927] 2 KB 9.
21 [1920] 1 Ch 154.
22 [1919] 1 Ch 291.
23 [1920] 2 Ch 124.

Whether the court is taking into account the interests of the company as a separate entity or the interests of the shareholders as a whole, it is clear from the aforementioned cases that the motivation behind the alteration can be a decisive factor in any determination.

2. Other Limitations

The power to alter the articles is subject to further limitations:

(a) the articles cannot be altered where the alteration is contrary to the memorandum of association, the Companies Acts or the general law;
(b) an alteration which requires a member to subscribe for additional shares or accept increased liability in respect of his shares will not be valid unless that member has given his consent;[24]
(c) where an alteration purports to vary the rights attached to a class of shares, it may only be made if the consent of that class has been obtained;
(d) where the court has altered the articles the company may not thereafter purport to make an inconsistent alteration without the court's consent.

An example of where the courts may make an alteration to a company's articles is where a successful application for relief is made by a member of the company on the grounds of oppression under section 205 of the Principal Act.[25]

The Effect of an Alteration on Outsiders

An alteration of the articles is valid even if it causes a breach of a contract with an outsider. Although the outsider cannot obtain an injunction to prevent the alteration, the company may be liable in damages for breach of contract. In *Southern Foundries (1926) Ltd v. Shirlaw*,[26] the respondent had been appointed managing director for a period of ten years. The articles provided that the managing director's appointment would automatically cease if he should cease to be a director. As part of a merger agreement with the Federated Industries Group, the members of the company agreed to alter the articles to the effect that Federated Industries would have the power to remove directors of group companies. This power was invoked to remove Shirlaw. As a result he ceased to be managing director even though the ten-year period had not expired. Shirlaw's claim for breach of contract succeeded because it was held that his service contract included an implied condition that the company would not do anything that would make it impossible for him to continue as managing director.

---

24 Section 27 of the Principal Act.
25 See Chapter 15 — Minority Protection.
26 [1940] AC 701.

The Contractual Nature of the Memorandum and Articles

By virtue of section 25 of the Principal Act, the memorandum and articles of association, once registered, bind the company and the members to the provisions thereof, in the same manner as if they had been respectively signed and sealed by each member. The effect of this statutory provision is that the provisions of the memorandum and articles become a legally enforceable contract which bind the company to the members, the members to the company and the members *inter se*. Unlike normal contracts, the members of a company who are bound under the section 25 statutory contract may not even know they are party to a contract. Furthermore, the terms of the contract can be altered without the consent of all the members (or parties to the contract).[27]

Although the 'section 25 contract' applies to both the memorandum and articles most of the litigation in this area relates to the articles of association. In *Hickman v. Kent or Romney Marsh Sheepbreeders Association*,[28] the plaintiff was in dispute with the company which had threatened to expel him from its membership. The articles provided that disputes between the company and its members should be submitted to arbitration. The plaintiff, in breach of the articles, began an action in court against the company. The court held that the plaintiff was bound by the provisions of the articles and the proceedings were stayed pending the outcome of arbitration.

It is important to note that the 'section 25 contract' applies only to rights and obligations affecting members in their capacity as members. As Steyn L J., in the case of *Bratton Seymour Service Co. Ltd v. Oxborough*,[29] observed:

> It is binding only in so far as it affects the rights and obligations between the company and the members acting in their capacity as members. If it contains provisions conferring rights and obligations on outsiders, then those provisions do not bite as part of the contract between the company and the members, even if the outsider is coincidentally a member.

Accordingly, directors and creditors who are enforcing their rights against the company cannot rely on the articles just because they also happen to be members. This position was clearly illustrated in *Beattie v. Beattie*,[30] which also concerned an arbitration clause in the articles. The company had commenced proceedings against the managing director, who was also a member, to recover monies improperly paid to him. The managing director applied to have the action stayed on the grounds that the dispute should first be put to arbitration as provided for by the articles. The court rejected this claim because the dispute

27 Once the statutory formalities for altering the memorandum and articles are followed.
28 [1915] 1 Ch D 881.
29 [1992] BCLC 693.
30 [1938] Ch 708.

related to obligations of the managing director in his position as managing director and did not concern his rights as a member.

Similarly, in *Eley v. Positive Government Life Assurance Co.*,[31] the plaintiff — a solicitor — had, when drafting the original articles of association, included a provision that the company would always employ him as a solicitor. He subsequently became a member of the company. When his services as a solicitor were no longer retained by the company, he sued it for breach of the 'section 25 contract'. It was held that Eley's claim under the articles could not succeed as it was asserted as an outsider (i.e. a solicitor) and not as a member of the company. On this basis, it is clear that the memorandum and articles define the position of the shareholder as shareholder and do not bind him in his capacity as an individual. Similarly, the provisions of the memorandum and articles that do not concern membership of the company are not contractually enforceable as part of the contract formed between the member of the company and the company as a separate person.

However, in certain circumstances an outsider may rely on the articles to infer a term or condition into a separate contract with the company. In *Re New British Iron Co.*,[32] the articles provided for directors' remuneration of £1,000 and the directors had accepted office on this basis. The company went into liquidation before any remuneration had been paid. It was held that the relevant provisions in the articles were also implied terms of the service contract between the directors and the company. The directors were therefore entitled to recover the arrears of remuneration. So even though the directors could not rely on section 25, they were permitted to rely on some of the articles as implied terms of their own separate contracts with the company. Where provisions of the articles are incorporated whether expressly or impliedly in the terms and conditions of a contract, those provisions may still be altered but not so as to affect an accrued right by an outsider. In *Swabey v. Port Darwin Gold Mining Co.*,[33] the articles provided for directors' fees of £200 per annum. This provision was incorporated into a service contract with a director. An alteration was made to reduce the amount retrospectively to £60 per annum. It was held that the articles could not be altered retrospectively to deprive a director of his right to fees already owed, and the alteration could only take effect prospectively. Lord Esher declared that 'the articles do not themselves form a contract, but from them you get the terms upon which the directors are serving.' Directors who are relying on the articles as an implied term of their own contracts should be conscious of the fact that the articles may be altered, which could affect their future rights.

Although section 25 does not specifically refer to a contractual relationship between the members *inter se*, this is in fact the legal position. In *Rayfield v.*

---

31 (1876) 1 Ex D 21.
32 [1989] 1 Ch 324.
33 (1889) 1 Meg 385.

Hands,[34] the articles provided that every member who wished to transfer shares should inform the directors who would take them at a fair value. The directors refused to buy the shares of the plaintiff and denied that the members could enforce the obligation under the articles. The court accepted the plaintiff's contention that there was a contract between the members and the member-directors to which the directors were bound. Vaissey J. interpreted the reference to 'directors' in the articles as a reference to a class of members who were directors and that, accordingly, the article had contractual effect. He granted the plaintiff an order requiring the directors to take the shares.The outcome of this case is arguably inconsistent with the *Eley* case as the articles imposed the obligation to buy the shares on the directors, who are not party to the section 25 contract. However, it can probably be reconciled with *Eley* on the basis that the court held the contract to be enforceable against the directors in their capacity as members. Of course, the question remains whether or not such a provision could be enforceable against a director who was not a member of the company. In any case the principle is that the memorandum and articles of association bind the members *inter se* and this has long been the accepted position in Ireland.[35]

---

34 [1960] 1 Ch 1.
35 *Clark v. Workman* [1920] 1 IR 107 per Ross J. and *Lee & Co. (Dublin) Ltd v. Egan (Wholesale) Ltd,* Unreported, High Court, Kenny J., April 27, 1978.

CHAPTER SIX

THE CONSEQUENCES OF INCORPORATION

Introduction

Once registered, and the 'certificate of incorporation' issued, a company has a legal existence separate and distinct from its members. As a separate legal entity the company is conferred with rights and is subject to duties and obligations. It can sue to have these rights enforced, and similarly it can be sued. It can own property in its own right and its existence will continue perpetually, irrespective of a change in its ownership, until the grant of incorporation has been revoked. The implications of the company's separate legal status were demonstrated in the case of *Salomon v. Salomon & Co. Ltd.*[1]

Salomon's Case

Salomon, a sole trader, sold his boot manufacturing business to a newly incorporated company. The business was sold to the company for £39,000, of which it was agreed that Salomon would be given cash, £10,000 in secured debentures issued by the company and 20,000 £1 shares in the company. To satisfy the statutory requirements that private companies could only be incorporated with seven members,[2] six members of Salomon's family were each given one share. These shares were held on trust for Salomon himself. Soon after incorporation the company suffered financial difficulties. In an attempt to keep the company going, Salomon sold his debenture, at a discount, for £5,000 and put this amount together with his other cash into the company. His rescue attempt proved futile and the company ultimately collapsed. The new debenture holder, a Mr Broderip, sought to realise his security by claiming against the company's assets. If his claim succeeded there would be nothing left over for the unsecured creditors. The liquidator of the company contended that the debenture, which had been issued to Salomon, was invalid because Salomon and the company were in fact the same entity and a person could not owe money to himself. The fact that there were other shareholders was irrelevant, as they were merely 'puppets' acting on Salomon's instructions. It was further argued that even if the company and Salomon were technically separate entities, the company was acting as the agent of Salomon who was the real owner of the business. These arguments

---

1 [1897] AC 22.
2 In 1907 the requirement to have two members of a private company was introduced. In 1994 this minimum was reduced to one member in the case of a private limited company. In the case of private unlimited companies the minimum number of members remains at two.

persuaded the Court of Appeal, which held that Salomon was still effectively a sole trader because the other shareholders were not independent of his control. He could not therefore enjoy the privileges of incorporation just because he had satisfied the machinery of incorporation.

However, the House of Lords reversed the decision of the Court of Appeal and held in favour of Salomon. Its opinion centred on the fact that once a company is registered it acquires a legal personality of its own which is separate from that of its owner. Furthermore, as the Companies Acts did not require shareholders to be independent of each other, the court would not read such a requirement into them. Accordingly, the company's liabilities were its own and not the responsibility of the company's principal shareholder. It followed that the secured debenture holder had a prior claim to the company's assets. In the famous speech of Lord Macnaghten it was observed that:

> . . . the company is at law a different person altogether from the subscribers to the Memorandum; and, although it may be that after incorporation the business is precisely the same as it was before, and the same persons are managers, and the same hands receive the profits, the company is not in law the agent of the subscribers or a trustee for them. Nor are the subscribers, as members, liable in any shape or form, except to the extent and in the manner provided by the Act.[3]

The legal effect of incorporation was thus made clear in the *Salomon* case. A business might have the same premises, plant, machinery, staff, management, employees, creditors and customers. However, once this business is transferred to a company a legal transformation takes place even if in practice nothing appears different. This business is no longer owned by a natural person but by a legal person. Anyone seeking legal redress as a result of the actions or failures of the company cannot have recourse to the company's owners — the shareholders — and must instead seek redress from the company itself.

The Separate Legal Personality Applied

The decision in the *Salomon* case gave judicial recognition to the principle that once the statutory formalities have been complied with, a 'veil of incorporation' is placed over the company. This veil distinguishes the company from its members and in doing so separates their respective obligations. The effect of the decision in *Salomon*'s case can be seen in *Lee v. Lee's Air Farming Ltd.*[4] Lee, who held the beneficial interest in the shares of the defendant company, was also its governing director and employed by the company as a pilot. When he was killed, while in the course of carrying on the company's business, his wife claimed compensation under the Worker's Compensation Act. The Court of Appeal of New Zealand held that the widow was not entitled to compensation since Lee as

---

3 [1897] AC 22 at 51.
4 [1961] AC 12.

owner and governing director of the company could not also be its worker. The Privy Council rejected this decision and held that by law, Lee and his company were separate persons and having been hired by the company as a pilot, he had become a worker within the meaning of the Act. Similarly, in *Tunstall v. Steigman*[5] a landlord attempted to avoid granting a statutory tenancy to the plaintiff on the grounds that the tenant wished to use the premises for extending her business practice. The landlord's claim failed on the basis that the business was in fact being carried out by a company in which the plaintiff was the principal shareholder.

The principles laid down in the *Salomon* case have been applied on numerous occasions by the Irish courts. In *Roundabout Ltd v. Beirne*[6] the employees of a public house, in a dispute with the owners, placed a picket at the owners' premises. The owners later transferred the pub to a company and the court ordered the picket to be lifted since there was no trade dispute between the workers and the new owner, despite the fact that ownership of the company was vested in the original owners of the pub. In the case of *Sweeney v. Duggan*[7] the plaintiff was employed by a company and was injured at work. The company went into liquidation before any compensation could be paid. The plaintiff sued the defendant, who owned and managed the company, on the grounds *inter alia* that he should have made sure that the company was insured. The Supreme Court held that the defendant was not liable to pay the company's obligations to the plaintiff.

It does not always work to the member's benefit to be treated as a separate entity from the company. Sometimes the 'veil of incorporation' will have a 'boomerang' effect on the member, as the following case illustrates. In *Macaura v. Northern Assurance Co. Ltd*,[8] the plaintiff sold his timber business to a company which he owned. The timber was subsequently destroyed and the plaintiff claimed under his own personal insurance policy. The insurers refused to pay on the grounds that the plaintiff had no insurable interest in the timber, as it belonged to the company. The House of Lords, applying the principle laid down in the *Salomon* case, held that the company and the plaintiff were two separate persons and as the company owned the timber, the plaintiff had no insurable interest in it. Accordingly, the insurance company was not liable. Similarly, in *O'Neill v. Ryan & Ryanair Ltd*,[9] the plaintiff alleged that breaches of competition law by the first defendant had diminished the value of his shares in the second defendant. The Supreme Court rejected his claim on the basis that

---

5 [1962] 2 All ER 417.
6 [1959] IR 423.
7 [1997] 1 ILRM 211.
8 [1925] AC 619.
9 [1993] ILRM 557.

if the alleged actions caused a loss to the company, a claim for compensation was payable to the company and not to an individual shareholder.

Segregation of Ownership

One of the consequences of a company having a separate legal personality, which went to the core of *Salomon*'s case, is that a company owns its property, assets and undertaking and does not hold them as agent or trustee for the members. Accordingly, the rights and obligations incidental to that property are the company's alone and not those of the company's owners. In the *Macaura* case it was held that only the company could have an insurable interest in its own property. Similarly, in *Stewarts Supermarkets Ltd v. Secretary of State*,[10] it was held that a parent company was not entitled to compensation under a statutory compensation scheme because damage was caused to the property of its subsidiary company which was a separate legal entity.

Suing and Being Sued

Another consequence of a company's separate legal personality is that it is conferred with rights which are enforceable by way of litigation. A company's contractual capacity is determined by the objects clause of the memorandum of association and, providing it acts within its capacity and satisfies the legal requirements for a valid contract, it can sue to have its contractual rights enforced. Similarly, a company can sue for torts committed against it, although certain torts, such as trespass to the person, cannot be committed against a corporation. What is less certain is whether or not a company has rights which are protected by the Constitution. It would seem that many of the personal rights afforded to citizens under Article 40 of Bunreacht na hÉireann do not ordinarily apply to companies.[11] However, it has been suggested that companies may be considered as citizens for the purpose of protecting their property rights.[12] Furthermore, a company is entitled to access to the courts in the same manner as natural persons.[13]

As well as having rights, a company has corresponding legal obligations which must be fulfilled. It must comply with its contractual and tortious obligations in the same manner as a legal person. However, a company's liability in crime is not as straightforward. First, companies have no physical manifestation and cannot therefore be prosecuted for crimes, such as rape and assault, which require a physical act. Second, a company has no mind of its own and is merely 'invisible, immortal and rests only in intendment and consideration of the law'.[14] Therefore, proving intent or *mens rea* on the part of a company is

---

10 [1982] NI 286.
11 *Quinn's Supermarket Ltd v. Attorney General* [1972] IR 1.
12 *Irish Rail Ltd v. Ireland and Others* [1995] 2 ILRM 161.
13 *Bula Ltd v. Tara Mines Ltd* [1987] IR 85.
14 Case of Sutton's Hospital (1612) 10 Co. Rep. 7a.

usually not possible, although in certain circumstances the intent or *mens rea* of the perpetrator may be attributed to the company.[15] There is no such difficulty in prosecuting a company for crimes which do not require a physical act or a *mens rea* on the part of the offender. When it comes to the matter of punishment, the most appropriate form for a company is the imposition of a fine or an order of sequestration because, naturally, a company cannot be imprisoned.

In order to commence any action against a company, it is necessary to serve it with the proceedings. The appropriate documents may be served at either the registered office of the company[16] or with an agent who has agreed to be served on the company's behalf.

Piercing the Corporate Veil

In the *Salomon* case it was argued that as the business had been over-valued, the company should have a right to rescind the sale. Although the court recognised that the value of the business was extravagant, the House of Lords suggested that the amount merely represented the 'sanguine expectations of a fond owner' rather that an attempt to perpetrate a fraud. However, Lord Halsbury did suggest that the privilege of incorporation could only be availed of as long as 'there was no fraud and no agency and if the company was a real one and not a fiction or a myth'.[17] Where any of these circumstances occur the court will strip away the veil of incorporation surrounding the company. In doing so, the corporate personality remains intact but the members, and in extreme cases the directors, are held responsible for obligations which would ordinarily be the responsibility of the company. The courts have not defined the circumstances which will cause it to disregard the separate legal personality of the company. However, in *Re a Company*[18] it was suggested that the court 'will use its power to pierce the corporate veil if it is necessary to achieve justice irrespective of the legal efficacy of the corporate structure'. In any case the courts have identified a company by its members in the following circumstances:

(a) where an agency relationship existed between the company and its members;
(b) where the relationship between companies in the same group is so intertwined that they should be treated as a single economic entity;
(c) where the company is being used to avoid existing legal obligations;
(d) where the company is being used to perpetrate a fraud or an injustice;
(e) to establish the true residency of the company; and
(f) where the company is in reality a 'quasi-partnership'.

---

15 *HL Bolton (Engineering) Ltd v. TJ Graham & Sons Ltd* [1957] 1QB 159.
16 Section 379(1) of the Principal Act.
17 [1897] AC 22 and 23.
18 [1985] 1 BCC 99.

Agency

The court has shown a willingness to lift the veil when the company is acting as the agent of another party, particularly when that party is the parent company. This is clearly illustrated by the case of *Smith, Stone and Knight Ltd v. Birmingham Corporation.*[19] There, the plaintiff's subsidiary carried out a waste business on land owned by the plaintiff. The land was subject to a compulsory acquisition order by the corporation, and the plaintiff claimed for losses suffered. The defendants argued that the plaintiff as a separate company was not carrying out any business and was not entitled to compensation. In determining whether an agency relationship existed, the court considered that the following questions should be addressed.

(a) Were the profits of the subsidiary treated as the profits of the parent company?
(b) Was the management of the subsidiary appointed by the parent company?
(c) Was the parent company the 'heads and brains' of the subsidiary?
(d) Did the parent company govern the operation of the subsidiary?
(e) Were the profits of the subsidiaries the result of the skill and direction of the parent company?
(f) Was the parent company in 'effectual and constant' control?

Having answered these questions in the affirmative, the court held that the subsidiary was acting as an agent for the parent company. Accordingly, the plaintiff company was entitled to the compensation claim. An agency relationship was also found to have existed in *Firestone Tyre and Rubber Co. v. Llewellin.*[20] There, an American company formed a subsidiary in the United Kingdom for the purpose of manufacturing tyres and distributing them to the company's customers in the European market. The American company obtained the orders, and the agreement with the UK company was such that the latter, having received its costs and a 5 per cent commission, the UK company would transfer the balance of the selling price to the American company. When the American company was assessed for UK tax on its profits, it claimed that it was a separate entity from the UK company. The court held that the subsidiary had acted as the agent of the American company, which was liable for UK tax.

However, the mere fact that companies are part of the same group will not automatically create an inference that an agency relationship exists between them. This is so even where the corporate structures are established purely to enable one company to avoid any prospective liabilities. In *Adams v. Cape Industries*[21] the English-based defendant was a large multinational company

---

19 [1939] 4 All ER 116.
20 [1957] 1 WLR 464.
21 [1990] Ch 433.

engaged in the asbestos business. One of its former subsidiaries had been liquidated following a settlement for injuries suffered by its workers and its operations transferred to a company named CPC. CPC, though not a subsidiary of Cape Industries, was set up with the latter's financial assistance and received instructions from it through an agent. The workers at CPC's plant obtained judgment against Cape in the US and sought to have that judgment enforced in the English courts. In order to succeed they had to demonstrate that Cape had been carrying on business in the US either by itself or through an agent. The court accepted that CPC had been set up as part of an overall group arrangement to reduce the appearance of Cape's involvement in the US, while at the same time enabling Cape asbestos to continue to be sold there. Despite this, the Court of Appeal held that Cape had no presence in the US, with the deciding factor being that CPC was independently owned and was not a subsidiary of Cape.

Single Economic Entity

In certain circumstances the courts will ignore the separate legal personality of one or more group companies where the relationship between these companies justifies treating them as a 'single economic entity'. *DHN Food Distributors Ltd v. Tower Hamlet Borough Council*[22] involved a similar claim for compensation as in the *Smith* case mentioned above. Here the plaintiff had two subsidiaries, one of which owned the landed property interests of the group. The plaintiff was the trading company and occupied the subsidiary's land for its business activities. When the land was compulsorily acquired, the Lands Tribunal claimed that the subsidiary was not entitled to compensation as it had no business to lose. Furthermore, the plaintiff was only entitled to a negligible amount of compensation for the loss of a revocable licence. Lord Denning advocated the view that where subsidiaries are bound hand and foot to the parent company, they should not be treated as separate entities where this would deprive them of compensation which is justly payable. The court rejected the Land Tribunal's claim and treated the companies as a single economic unit. Accordingly, the plaintiff's compensation claim succeeded.

The 'single economic entity' test was approved in Ireland in the case of *Power Supermarkets Ltd v. Crumlin Investments Ltd and Dunnes Stores (Crumlin) Ltd*.[23] The first defendant developed a shopping centre and leased a unit to the plaintiff. One of the terms of the lease included a covenant by the lessor that no other lease would be granted to another tenant in the grocery or food business. The shopping centre was not a great success and the first defendant was acquired by Cornelscourt Shopping Centre Ltd, a company owned by the Dunnes Stores Group. The purchaser then caused the first defendant to

22 [1976] 1 WLR 852.
23 Unreported, High Court, Costello J., June 22, 1981.

convey a freehold unit to the second defendant, Dunnes Stores (Crumlin) Ltd, which would enable the Dunnes Group to operate a supermarket in the centre. The plaintiff objected to the introduction of a trading rival. In treating the defendants as a 'single entity', Costello J. observed:

> that a court may, if the justice of the case so requires, treat two or more related companies as a single entity so that the business notionally carried on by one will be regarded as the business of the group or another member of the group if this conforms to the economic and commercial realities of the situation. It would, in my view, be very hard to find a clearer case than the present one for the application of this principle.

Accordingly, the court held that the second defendant was bound by the restrictive covenant even though it was not a contractual party to it.

The single entity argument persuaded the court to pierce the corporate veil in *Fyffes plc v. DCC plc and Others*[24], the first civil case for insider dealing in Ireland. Insider dealing, which is prohibited by law, arises where a person who is connected with a company and who is in possession of price-sensitive information that is not available to the public, deals in those shares with a view to securing a profit or gain.

In this case one of the defendants, Mr Flavin, was chief executive of DCC and a director of its subsidiary, S&L Ltd. These companies had acquired a shareholding in Fyffes in the 1980s and Mr Flavin had become a director of Fyffes. In 1995 DCC and S&L sold their shares in Fyffes to Lotus Green Ltd, a subsidiary of DCC. While the purchase price was paid by Lotus Green, the legal title was not transferred, and DCC and S&L remained the registered owner of the shares while Lotus Green retained beneficial ownership. By early 2000, shares in Fyffes were trading at a near all-time high. However, in January 2000 monthly management accounts that were circulated to the directors of Fyffes, including Mr Flavin, identified some difficulties in trading volumes. In February 2000 Lotus Green sold a substantial number of shares in Fyffes, making a profit of €85 million. In the same month Mr Flavin resigned as a director of Fyffes. In January 2002 Fyffes initiated a civil action for insider dealing and for the recovery of the profits made. In order to tie the 'dealing' by Lotus Green to the 'price-sensitive' information held by Mr Flavin, the plaintiff argued *inter alia* that it was just and reasonable that the actions of Lotus Green in respect of the shares be treated in law as the actions of DCC or S&L. The court concluded that Lotus Green, DCC and S&L should be treated as a single entity if, as regards the holding and disposal of the shares, there was a factual identification of the acts of Lotus Green and DCC and S&L. On the facts the court was satisfied that there was such a factual identification in that Mr Flavin made the agreements that formed the basis of the share sales and he did so as agent of DCC, the three corporate defendants dealt in the shares in consequence and in implementation of those

---

24 Unreported, High Court, Laffoy J., December 21, 2005.

agreements and the profit in question arose from those agreements. Furthermore, the court was satisfied that not treating the corporate defendants as a 'single entity' for the purpose of the share sale would allow the DCC Group to evade its obligations under company law. It should be noted that while the plaintiff succeeded in having the respondents treated as one entity for the purposes of the dealing in the shares it failed to establish the other requirements necessary to satisfy the court that such dealing was unlawful within the meaning of insider dealing provisions of the Companies Act 1990.

It should be observed that the courts will only ignore the strict veil that surrounds a company, even when it is part of a group of companies. In *Adams v. Cape Industries*,[25] it was suggested that in the context of group companies the court did not accept that:

> . . . as a matter of law the court is entitled to lift the corporate veil as against the defendant company which is a member of a corporate group, merely because the corporate structure has been used so as to ensure that the legal liability (if any) in respect of particular future activities of the group . . . will fall on another member of the group rather than the defendant company. Whether or not this is desirable, the right to use a corporate structure in this manner is inherent in our corporate law.[26]

In the Irish case of *Allied Irish Coal Supplies Ltd v. Powell Duffryn International Fuels Ltd*[27] the Supreme Court refused to join a parent company to an action being taken against its subsidiary company just because of the relationship between them. The court held that a subsidiary could be dependent on its parent company as regards control, finance and operations and that this did not prevent it from being a separate legal entity. According to the court, the concept of limited liability was to enable some part of a person's affairs to be placed in a separate compartment.

Avoidance of Legal Obligations

In *Cape Industries* the court recognised that corporate structures are put in place to avoid potential liabilities. Indeed, it is suggested that the very use of the privilege of incorporation is motivated by a desire to reduce the potential liability for the owner should things go wrong. Similarly, the taxation concessions which are available to companies encourage their formation. However, the courts will not countenance the use of the statutory privilege as a device for avoiding existing obligations. In such circumstances the courts are willing to cast aside the veil of incorporation to examine what lies behind it. In *Jones v. Lipman*,[28] the defendant entered into an agreement to sell his house to Jones. Thereafter he changed his

---

25 [1990] Ch 433.
26 Ibid. at 544 D, E.
27 [1997] 1 ILRM 306 (High Court); [1998] 2 ILRM 61 (Supreme Court).
28 [1962] 1 All ER 442.

mind, and to avoid the contract he acquired a company and transferred the house to it. The court held that the company was a mere 'device' and 'sham' created for the sole purpose of avoiding contractual obligations. Accordingly, the company was held bound by the defendant's obligations and an order of specific performance was granted in favour of the plaintiff. In *Gilford Motor Co. Ltd v. Horne*,[29] the court also set aside the veil where a company was being used to avoid a contractual obligation. There, the defendant had, while in the employ of the plaintiff, signed a restraint of trade agreement whereby he agreed that on leaving his employment, he would not set up a business in opposition to the plaintiff for a period of six years. Within a few weeks of his leaving his employment, his wife and son formed a company in competition with the plaintiff. Although the defendant had no shares and was not a director, the company acted on his instructions. The court held that the corporate entity was merely a 'mask', used to enable Horne to engage in business which he was contractually prevented from doing as a natural person. An injunction was granted against Horne and the company from continuing the business in competition with the plaintiff.

Fraud or Injustices

The courts will not allow the corporate personality to be used as an engine for 'fraud' or to cause an obvious injustice. The latter point was made clear in the case of *Re Bugle Press Ltd*.[30] The majority shareholders, holding 90 per cent of the issued share capital, wished to acquire the remaining 10 per cent held by a third shareholder. They formed a company which made a take-over bid, and having successfully obtained the 90 per cent shareholding it sought to enforce its right under section 209 of the UK Companies Act 1948 to acquire the minority's stake compulsorily. The minority successfully applied to the court for relief. The court viewed the transaction as one designed for the sole purpose of expropriating a minority, which is an act forbidden by company law unless permitted specifically by the articles.

Fraud was the rationale behind the court's decision to sweep aside the corporate veil in *Re Darby: ex parte Brougham*.[31] Darby and Gyde, two undischarged bankrupts, registered a company in the Channel Islands. This company then established a company in the United Kingdom and financed it by issuing debentures. The amount raised on foot of the debentures was paid to the Channel Islands company and distributed among the two bankrupts. When the UK company failed, the liquidator claimed in Darby's bankruptcy for the secret profits he had made. The court allowed the liquidator's claim, holding that Darby could not use the Channel Island company as a cloak for his fraudulent activities.

---

29 [1933] Ch 939.
30 [1961] Ch 270.
31 [1911] 1 KB 95.

Residency

The court will often be called upon to look behind the veil of incorporation to establish the true residence of the company. This usually, but not always, occurs in relation to establishing tax liabilities. In *Daimler v. Continental Tyre Co.*,[32] the defendant owed monies to the plaintiff, a British-registered company, whose directors and shareholders were German. Under wartime laws, trading with the enemy was forbidden. The House of Lords looked beyond the corporate personality to those who controlled the company and concluded that the defendant was not obliged to pay the 'debt', as to do so would constitute trading with the enemy.

Quasi-Partnerships

In certain circumstances the courts look beyond the technicalities of the company's legal existence, and in doing so recognise the commercial reality of the relationship between the company, its directors and its members. Where that relationship is more akin to a partnership, whose existence is dependent upon a degree of trust and communication between the partners, and the relationship breaks down, the company may be wound up by analogy with the dissolution of a partnership. In *Re Murph's Restaurant Ltd*[33] the company was formed by two brothers and a friend who each held equal shares in the company and were all directors. The business prospered and the friend ultimately gave up his job to work full-time in the business. The business expanded from Dublin to Cork, and it was the Cork branch that was run by the friend. The two brothers expanded their business horizons and purchased a hotel in Cork which, unknown to the friend, was partly financed by money from the company. Eventually, the two brothers decided to part company from the friend, and they notified him of a meeting at which they intended to remove him from office. The friend petitioned to have the company wound up on the 'just and equitable' ground. The court held that the company had been formed and operated on a 'quasi-partnership' basis which required a degree of trust and confidence between the members. As the relationship of trust and confidence had been destroyed by the acts of the brothers, an order for the compulsory winding up of the company was made.

Statutory Provisions

There are several provisions in the Companies Acts and other legislation that impose obligations on companies in relation to administrative and other matters. Where there is a default in complying with these requirements it is often the case that the company's officers (including directors and secretaries) will be held responsible and sanctioned accordingly. Furthermore, where directors of a

---

32 [1916] 2 AC 307.
33 [1979] ILRM 141.

company engage in certain activities such as fraudulent or reckless trading they will be held personally liable for some or all of the company's debts. The Companies Acts also ignore the separate legal personality of a company for the purposes of preparing group accounts, and may do so in the winding up of related companies and when appointing inspectors to investigate the affairs of a company. The following are examples of where statute ignores the separate legal existence of a company.

Insufficient Membership

Section 36 of the Principal Act provides that where the number of members is reduced below the minimum required by law and the company continues to carry on business for more than six months with this reduced number, all members who knew of the deficit will be severally liable for any debts incurred by the company after the expiry of this period. It was held in *Brook's Wharf Ltd v. Goodman Bros*[34] that if a member incurs liability under the section, he is entitled to be indemnified by the company. It should be noted that since October 1994, with the advent of one-member companies, this provision no longer applies to private limited companies.[35]

Failure to State the Company's Name Correctly

Under section 114(4) of the Principal Act, if an officer of the company signs on the company's behalf a bill of exchange, promissory note, endorsement, cheque or order for money or goods, without the company's name being mentioned thereon, he will be liable to a fine. More importantly, if the company fails to pay the signatory shall be personally liable to the holder of the relevant instrument for the amount thereof. In *Rafsanjan Pistachio Producers Co-operative v. Reiss*,[36] the defendant director had signed cheques on the company's behalf in favour of the plaintiff. No mention of the company's name was ascribed thereon and when they were subsequently dishonoured by the company, the defendant was held personally liable for the amount unpaid. In *Durham Fancy Goods Ltd v. Michael Jackson (Fancy Goods) Ltd*,[37] it was held that the abbreviation of 'Michael' to 'M' in describing the name of the company on a bill of exchange and the form of acceptance was a misdescription and a breach of the section. However, as the plaintiff had been responsible for the misdescription and had represented that it would treat the acceptance as regular, it was estopped from enforcing the liability.

Section 114(5) of the Principal Act provides, however, that where 'Ltd' is used for 'Limited', 'Teo' for 'Teoranta', 'plc' for 'public limited company' or 'cpt' for 'cuideachta phoibli theoranta', no liability will be incurred under the section.

---

34 [1937] I KB 534.
35 Regulation 7(1) of the European Communities (Single-Member Private Limited Companies) Regulations 1994 SI 275/1994.
36 [1990] BCLC 352.
37 [1968] 2 QB 839.

Accounts of Group Companies

In recognition of the phenomenon of the increasing number of groups of companies, legislative provisions have been introduced to reflect the overall group position and in certain instances, where the commercial realities of the situation so dictate, to treat some or all of the companies in a group as one entity. Accordingly, the European Communities (Companies: Group Accounts) Regulations 1992[38] require group accounts to be in the form of a consolidated balance sheet and a consolidated profit and loss. It is important to observe that ownership is not a necessary requisite to satisfying a group relationship: rather, the emphasis is on the control exercised by one company over another.

The Winding up of Related Companies

Under section 140 of the 1990 Act, a company may be required to contribute to the debts of related companies. The extent of a company's control over the management of the related company will be a significant factor in determining what, if any, liability should be attributed to the company. Furthermore, the court may also order that where a company is being wound up, the assets of a related company which is also being wound up should be pooled between the creditors of both companies.[39]

Investigation of Companies

Under the company investigation provisions of the 1990 Act, inspectors appointed by the court to investigate the affairs of a company may, subject to court approval, extend the investigation to companies related to that company. For this purpose a related company includes companies with which the original company has a 'commercial relationship'. Furthermore, where the Director of Corporate Enforcement appoints an inspector to investigate share membership in a company, the inspector may further investigate the ownership of any companies that own shares in that company.[40]

Liability of Directors and Other Officers

As a company is an artificial person it requires natural persons to act on its behalf. Accordingly many of the obligations imposed on companies by the Companies Acts and other legislation must be carried out by the officers of those companies. If the company breaches these obligations the directors may be held responsible in addition to the company itself. There are several statutory provisions that attach liability to the company officers (including directors and secretaries) including, *inter alia*, the following:

---

38 SI 201/1992.
39 Section 141 of the 1990 Act.
40 See Chapter 22 — Investigation of Companies.

(a) Section 202 of the 1990 Act requires companies to maintain proper books of accounts. The onus is on the directors of the company to ensure that this requirement is satisfied. Breach of this statutory duty may give rise to civil and criminal sanctions being imposed on directors;[41]

(a) Companies are required to register certain resolutions and with the registrar of companies.[42] Failure to comply renders every officer in default guilty of an offence and liable to a fine;

(c) Companies are required to maintain certain registers, including a register of members, a register of directors and secretaries, a register of debenture holders and a register of directors' contracts. Failure to comply with these obligations renders the directors in default liable;

(d) All companies are obliged to file an annual return with the registrar of companies. Failure to do so renders every officer in default liable to an offence;

(e) Under the Health Safety & Welfare Act, 2005 directors can be held liable, both civilly and criminally, for breach of a company's obligations under the Act.

Other Consequences of Incorporation

1. Limited Liability

All companies are liable without limit for their debts and liabilities. As long as assets are available, a company is obliged to pay its debts. However, a company, like a natural person, may not have sufficient assets to meet its debts and it is at this point that the concept of limited liability is important. Since the Limited Liability Act 1855, if a company is formed on the basis of limited liability its members are not liable to contribute to the assets of the company, except to the extent agreed. Typically, in the case of a company limited by shares, the liability of its members will be limited to the amount unpaid on those shares, if any. In the case of a company limited by guarantee, the memorandum of association will determine the amount that each member is liable to contribute. Where a company has unlimited status, its members will be liable to contribute to the assets of the company to the extent required to pay all of the company's liabilities.

2. Perpetual Succession

A company's life begins with the process of incorporation. It does not therefore have a natural birth, nor does it suffer a natural death. Its existence is perpetual and is not dependent upon the life of its members or directors. They may come and

---

41 See Chapter 20 — Accounts and Returns.
42 Section 143 of the Principal Act.

go, but the company continues until such time as it is dissolved or struck from the register.

3. Transferable Shares

The member's interest in the company is a form of property which is measured in shares. These shares are freely transferable, subject to any restrictions imposed by the memorandum and articles of association. (See Chapter 8, Company Securities.)

4. Floating Charge

Companies can raise capital in the form of loans by granting by way of security a floating charge over some or all of their assets. This form of security is peculiar to companies,[43] and its advantage lies in the fact that the company can still deal with the assets charged in the ordinary course of its business. (See Chapter 11, Loan Capital and Charges.)

5. Tax Concessions

Companies can avail of the tax advantages afforded by various pieces of taxation legislation. A company's liability to taxation on its profits takes the form of corporation tax, which is usually at a rate below the prevailing income tax rates for individuals.

6. Board of Directors

Unlike natural persons, who can act on their own behalf, a company has no physical manifestation. Accordingly it relies on natural persons to act on its behalf. The law requires all companies to have at least two directors, but companies may decide to have more than the legal minimum. The company usually authorises the board of directors to manage the company.[44] Irrespective of the powers given to the directors by the company itself, companies' legislation confers most of the statutory obligations relating to companies on the officers (which includes directors) or indeed the directors themselves.

7. Registered Office

All companies are required to have a registered office and details of same must be included in the Form A1 when a company is applying for registration.[45] Any change in the registered office must be notified to the registrar within fourteen

---

43 Although in theory a floating charge can be given by an individual, as in *TCB v. Gray* [1986] 1 All ER 587.

44 By virtue of the articles of association.

45 Section 113 of the Principal Act.

days of the change. The registered office must be an actual physical location and not a post office box number. All correspondence from the Companies Registration Office and all formal legal notices are addressed to the registered office of the company. Furthermore, where members of the company or, indeed, the public are permitted by law to inspect various statutory registers, these registers must be maintained and available for inspection at the company's registered office.

CHAPTER SEVEN

CONTRACTUAL CAPACITY OF THE COMPANY

Introduction

As mentioned in Chapter 4, a company's contractual capacity is restricted in so far as it can only enter into contracts that are within the objects clause of the memorandum. If a company acts outside its stated objects the transaction is said to be *ultra vires*. At common law, an *ultra vires* transaction is void and unenforceable.[1] The effect of the common law position regarding *ultra vires* was exacerbated by the fact that pre-twentieth-century legislation permitted the company to alter the objects clause only in limited circumstances and subject to the approval of the court. Furthermore, even where the general meeting was in a position to alter the objects, its effect could not operate retrospectively to validate an *ultra vires* act.[2]

The strict application of the *ultra vires* rule often caused hardship for innocent third parties acting *bona fide*, who found themselves unable to enforce a contract against the company. This hardship was compounded by the doctrine of constructive notice, which dictates that a person who deals with a company is deemed to have notice of the contents of the company's public documents. Apply both doctrines to an innocent third party and the result could not be any more severe, as the case of *Re Jon Beauforte (London) Ltd* demonstrates.[3] Here the company was established as a costumier and gown manufacturer. Without altering its objects it had engaged for several years in the business of veneer panel manufacturing. When the company failed, the liquidator disallowed a claim by a supplier of heating fuel. In fact, all but one of the creditors' claims was disallowed. The supplier argued unsuccessfully that the heating fuel could be needed for any of the company's businesses. It was held that the supplier had actual notice of the business being undertaken because it was specified on the company's headed paper. The supplier was also deemed to have constructive notice that the business was not within the company's objects, because the memorandum, which was available for public inspection, did not contain such an object. Accordingly, the contract, in furtherance of an *ultra vires* activity, was void and unenforceable. As the contract could not be enforced, the only other remedy available to the supplier was the equitable remedy of tracing, which

---

1 *Ashbury Railway Carriage & Iron Co. v. Riche* (1875) LR 7 HL 653.
2 *Attorney General v. Great Eastern Railway* (1880) 5 App Cas 473 HL. Although companies can now alter the objects by passing a special resolution, the position remains that an alteration cannot retrospectively validate an *ultra vires* transaction.
3 [1953] Ch 131.

would have been difficult to achieve, not least because the heating fuel had probably, like his chances of being paid, gone up in smoke!

Action, Judicial Reaction and Counteraction

In order to circumvent the effects of the *ultra vires* rule, the legal draftsmen departed from the model memoranda set out in the Companies Acts by registering memoranda containing a multiplicity of objects and powers. The courts responded to such initiatives by construing objects clauses strictly, and in so doing drew a distinction between the objects of the company and its powers. According to the court, the powers contained in the memorandum could only be used in furtherance of the company's main objects. Therefore, if the 'main objects' had been specified in the first few paragraphs of the objects clause, and there followed subsequent paragraphs containing wider powers, those powers could only be exercised in so far as they achieved the 'main' objects of the company.[4] Where, for example, a company's main object was to build houses, which was followed by the power to borrow money and give security, those powers could only be exercised where they were in furtherance of the company's building object.

The draftsmen responded to this 'main objects' rule by using the following devices:

1. the independent objects clause; and
2. the 'bell houses' clause.

1. The Independent Objects Clause

Memoranda were drafted whereby the 'objects clause' would end with a statement to the effect that each object and power should be <u>treated independently</u> and not as ancillary or subordinate to the others. In other words, each object and power was a main object. The intended effect of this practice was to prevent any single object being impugned on the application of the 'main objects' test. The 'independent objects clauses' proved successful as the House of Lords, however reluctantly, upheld their validity. In *Cotman v. Brougham*,[5] the first paragraph of the objects clauses authorised the company to own and work rubber plantations. Several other paragraphs empowered the company to engage in other activities including holding and dealing in securities. The final paragraph specified that all clauses should be construed as independent substantive clauses. The company underwrote an issue of shares of an oil company, and this transaction was subsequently challenged on *ultra vires* grounds. The presence of the 'independent objects clause' was held by the court to have ensured the *intra vires* nature of the transaction. This was so despite the fact, which was acknowledged by the court in

4 See *Anglo-Irish Agencies Ltd v. Green* [1960] All ER 244.
5 [1918] AC 514.

the *Cotman* case, that such clauses defeated the legislative requirement that a company's business activities should be transparent.

2. The 'Bell Houses' Clause

The second device used to circumvent the 'main object' rule is what is often referred to as the Bell Houses clause. This clause gives a company the capacity to enter into any contract which the directors believe would benefit the company. The effect of such a device was such that the company's objects could in practice be open-ended, depending on the opinion of the directors. In *Bell Houses Ltd v. City Wall Properties Ltd*,[6] the company's objects clause specified that the business of the company was the building and development of housing estates. However, the memorandum also empowered the directors to pursue any trade or business which could, in their opinion, be advantageously carried on by the company in connection with its business. The objects also contained an 'independent objects clause'. The company, in the course of its business dealings, had made a number of useful contacts. One of these was with a group of Swiss bankers who wished to loan money for the purpose of property development. The company agreed, in return for a commission, to introduce the defendant to the Swiss bankers. The defendant later refused to pay the commission and argued that the agreement was *ultra vires* the company and void. The court held that as a result of the discretionary power given to the directors, the objects of the company were limited only by the directors' subjective opinion. As the directors genuinely believed that 'mortgage broking' could be advantageously carried on as ancillary to the general business of the company, the agreement was *intra vires*, valid and enforceable.[7]

The use of both these devices — the independent objects clause and the Bell Houses clause — had the effect of reducing the value of the objects clause which was, after all, intended to protect members as well as creditors who entered into an *intra vires* transaction with the company. The modern objects clause of most private companies contains an independent objects clause and many small private companies also use a Bell Houses-type clause.

Objects v. Powers

Despite judicial acceptance of the above mentioned devices, their validity was subject to one important proviso — that regardless of what the memorandum might say, it is not possible to elevate what is by its nature a power, subordinate to a main object, into an independent object. In *Introductions Ltd v. National Provincial Bank*,[8] the company was incorporated with the object of providing

---

6 [1966] 2 All ER 674.

7 See also *Newstead v. Frost* [1980] 1 WLR 135.

8 [1968] 2 All ER 1221.

foreign visitors with accommodation and entertainment but it later devoted itself totally to the business of pig breeding. It borrowed money to finance this activity and granted a debenture to secure its borrowings. The objects clause included an express power to borrow and contained an 'independent objects clause'. The bank interpreted the memorandum as meaning that the company had the power to borrow for any purpose. When the company went into liquidation the bank sought to realise its security. The court held that borrowing as an activity was not an end in itself; rather, it was a means of achieving the company's objects. As the borrowing in question was not in furtherance of an *intra vires* activity, the entire transaction was *ultra vires* the company. Accordingly, the bank could not enforce its debenture or claim in the liquidation.[9]

According to the Court of Appeal in the *Introductions* case, ancillary powers are subject to an implied limitation in that they are exercisable only in furtherance of a stated object. In *International Sales & Agencies Ltd v. Marcus*,[10] the defendant was a licensed moneylender who made personal loans of £30,000 to F, a major shareholder in the plaintiff company. When the shareholder became ill, he told the defendants that in the event of his death his friend M would see that the loans were repaid. M was also a shareholder and director of the plaintiff company. F died insolvent and M arranged for the £30,000 to be repaid by drawing cheques on the plaintiff company's bank account. When M died, F's beneficiaries, who were now shareholders in the plaintiff company, caused the company to bring proceedings against the defendant to recover the £30,000 on the grounds that this money was paid over in respect of the obligations of F, and not the company, and therefore no benefit accrued to the company. It was held that the plaintiff company was entitled to the return of the £30,000. Although the company had the power to issue cheques, this power was not independent and could only be exercised to further the objects of the company. The payment was therefore *ultra vires* the company's objects and void.

Whether or not the exercise of a power is in furtherance of the company's objects is a matter for the court. In *Re PMPA Garage (Longmile) Ltd*,[11] certain group companies had issued guarantees in favour of another group company. The question arose as to whether the giving of guarantees for associate companies could be said to be in furtherance of the objects of the guarantor company. Although the directors had not considered the business interests of the guarantor companies, it was held that the advancement of the interests of one group company would necessarily involve a recognition that the other interests of the group should be protected. Accordingly, the exercise of the ancillary power to issue guarantees was justifiable and the guarantees were declared enforceable.

---

9 See also *Re M.J. Cummins: Barton v. Bank of Ireland* [1939] IR 60.
10 [1982] 3 All ER 551.
11 [1992] ILRM 337.

In the *Introductions* case it was held that the exercise of ancillary powers, which were themselves *intra vires* the company, for an *ultra vires* purpose rendered the exercise of the power itself *ultra vires* the company. This aspect of the decision has been criticised [12] for its failure to draw a clear distinction between transactions which are *ultra vires* the company and those which are *intra vires* the company but if exercised for an improper purpose, such as an illegal or *ultra vires* activity, are an abuse of directors' powers. The English Court of Appeal made this distinction in *Rolled Steel Products (Holdings) Ltd v. British Steel Corporation.*[13] There, the only two directors of the plaintiff company caused the company to issue a guarantee, which was counter-covered by a charge, in respect of the obligations of a company owned by one of the directors. The plaintiff company had an express power to give guarantees for customers and others who had dealings with the company on such terms 'as may seem expedient'. The memorandum of association also contained an independent objects clause. The court held that the giving of guarantees was an ancillary power, and the relevant paragraph in the memorandum should be construed in such a manner that the company could only give a guarantee in furtherance of the company's objects. The court went on to hold that the power to give the guarantee was within the capacity of the company and this was not altered by the fact that the actual exercise of the power was in furtherance of an unauthorised purpose. It was not therefore appropriate to impugn the transaction on *ultra vires* grounds. Rather, any challenge should be based on the directors' lack of authority, if any.[14]

Express and Implied Powers

Once a power is exercised in pursuance of the company's objects, its validity will not be questioned just because a benefit has not accrued to the company. In *Charterbridge Corporation Ltd v. Lloyds Bank Ltd,*[15] a company issued a guarantee and supporting charge in respect of obligations of an associated company. The company had an express power to guarantee the debts of persons with whom the company dealt or who had a business in which the company was interested. It was argued that as the granting of the guarantee conferred no benefit on the company it was *ultra vires* and invalid. Although the court held on the facts that the directors had grounds for believing the company did benefit from supporting an associated company, it nevertheless concluded that an express power is not limited to transactions which benefit the company.[16] On this basis it

---

12 *Gower's Principles of Modern Company Law,* Sweet & Maxwell (6th edition) 1997, p. 205; and Courtney, *The Law of Private Companies*, Butterworths 1994, par 6.069.
13 [1985] 3 All ER 52.
14 See Chapter 17, Directors' Powers and Authority.
15 [1969] 2 All ER 1185.
16 See also *Re PMPA Garage (Longmile) Ltd* [1992] ILRM 337.

would seem that express powers to give gifts and political donations are permitted even though they confer no benefit on the company, provided the company was solvent at the time.[17] The solvency requirement stems from the fact that once a company is insolvent the interests of the company are displaced by the interests of the general body of creditors, and any gratuitous application of company funds would be in effect a fraud on the creditors.[18]

The courts have even gone so far as to imply powers to the company where their exercise would be incidental to or consequential upon a company's objects.[19] However, it is settled law that an implied power will not be read into the memorandum unless it benefits the company and is being exercised for a purpose which is incidental to the company's business. In *Hutton v. West Cork Railway Co.*[20] a general meeting of the company had passed a resolution to pay compensation to officials for their loss of employment. The payments were successfully challenged as being *ultra vires* the company. In a frequently cited passage Bowen LJ. stated

> The law does not say that there are no cakes and ale, but that there are to be no cakes and ale except such as are required for the benefit of the company.

Similarly, in *Parke v. Daily News Ltd*,[21] when the company's main business was sold, a decision was made to advance gratuitous payments to the employees who were being let go. The payments were successfully challenged on the basis that the express powers did not permit such a payment. Furthermore, the court refused to imply such a power to the company, as the dissipation of the company's assets in such a manner did not benefit the company. There has been some suggestion that the courts no longer require that a benefit to the company accrues before a power will be implied.[22] However, the Irish courts have continued to insist that powers will not be implied unless they benefit the company. In *Re Greendale Developments Ltd*[23] the court struck down payments made to members on the grounds that in the absence of an express authorisation by the memorandum and articles of association a benefit must have accrued to the company. As no such benefit did accrue to the company the court refused to imply the power to make such payments and held that they were *ultra vires*. Similarly, in *Re Frederick Inns Ltd*,[24] Lardner J. in the High Court struck down excess payments to the

---

17 See the judgment of Bowen J. in *Hutton v. West Cork Railway Co.* (1883) 23 Ch D 654, and *Re Frederick Inns Ltd* [1991] ILRM 582 (High Court) and [1994] ILRM 387 (Supreme Court).

18 See judgment of Blayney J. in *Re Frederick Inns Ltd* [1994] ILRM 387 at 397.

19 *Attorney General v. Great Eastern Railway* (1880) 5 App Cas 473.

20 [1883] 23 Ch D 654.

21 [1962] 2 All ER 929.

22 *Rolled Steel Products (Holdings) Ltd. v British Steel Corporation* [1985] 3 All ER 52.

23 [1998] 1 IR 8.

24 [1991] ILRM 582.

Revenue as *ultra vires* on the ground, *inter alia*, that there was no evidence of any benefit accruing to the company.

Statutory Reform

The effect of the *ultra vires* rule on outsiders has been tempered by the introduction of two legislative provisions:
1. Section 8 of the Principal Act; and
2. Regulation 6 of the European Communities (Companies) Regulations 1973.[25]

1. Section 8 of the Principal Act

Section 8(1) of the Principal Act provides that any act or thing done by the company, shall, notwithstanding that the company had no power to do such act or thing, be effective in favour of any person relying on such act or thing provided two tests are satisfied. First, the person relying on the act is not shown to have been *'actually aware'* at the time when he so relied thereon, that such an act or thing was not within the powers of the company. Second, that the act or transaction would otherwise have been *'lawfully and effectively'* done. If the person dealing with the company can satisfy this two-pronged test then he can effectively render enforceable an *ultra vires* transaction. If the person cannot satisfy the tests then the common law position prevails, viz. the transaction being *ultra vires* is void and unenforceable.

The 'Actually Aware' Test

In order to enforce an *ultra vires* transaction against the company, the third party must not have been 'actually aware' of the *ultra vires* nature of the transaction. The term 'actually aware' has been construed quite narrowly by the courts as the case of *Northern Bank Finance Limited v Quinn & Achates Investments*[26] indicates. Quinn had borrowed £145,000 which was secured by the guarantee of an unlimited company, Achates Investments, of which he was the main shareholder. This guarantee was supported by a first legal mortgage on 56 acres of prime land in Co. Meath. The resolution was passed on 30 November 1973 and guarantee was executed on 30 November 1973. The mortgage supporting the guarantee was executed on 13 December 1973. When there was default in repayment the bank sued Quinn and the company and obtained judgment against them. It then sought an order that the mortgage was well charged on the land. Quinn's liability was not disputed. It was submitted on behalf of the company that the guarantee was *ultra vires* the objects and consequently void. The bank argued that it was protected by section 8(1) of the Principal Act. The Court heard

---

25 SI 163/1973.
26 [1979] ILRM 221.

evidence from the solicitor for the bank that although he read the Memorandum and Articles of the company he did not consciously advert to the fact that the act was *ultra vires*. The Court declared that in such circumstances a person who has read the memorandum and articles is deemed to be actually aware of its contents. Accordingly, the bank was deemed to be 'actually aware' and could not rely on section 8. The guarantee was declared void and unenforceable for being *ultra vires*.

On the basis of the judgment in this case, if a party is shown to have been 'actually aware' of the contents of the memorandum but has failed to understand them he cannot avail of the protection afforded by section 8(1).

The 'Lawfully and Effectively' Test

Even where the third party is shown not to have been 'actually aware' he will not be in a position to rely on section 8(1) if the act in question, notwithstanding the fact that it is *ultra vires*, is otherwise not 'lawfully and effectively' done. This aspect of section 8(1) arose in *Re Frederick Inns Ltd*.[27] There, £2.8 million was owed to the Revenue on behalf of four companies in the Belton group. The group sold four pubs, which were each company's main asset, and applied the proceeds to the Revenue to discharge their taxation obligations. The Revenue used the funds to maximise their preferential status. The liquidator argued, *inter alia*, that the payments, in the form of gratuitous payments to the Revenue, were *ultra vires*. The court agreed with the liquidator that when a company is insolvent it is beyond its powers to alienate or transfer its property or make a gift to a third party out of its assets, even if expressly empowered to do so by the memorandum. To do so would be in disregard of the interests of the creditors which could not be lawful. Accordingly, Lardner J. held that the payments by the four companies were not 'lawfully and effectively' done within the meaning of section 8(1).

Liability of Directors

If an *ultra vires* transaction is enforced against the company, any director or officer of the company who was responsible for the *ultra vires* act shall be liable to the company for any loss or damage suffered by the company in consequence thereof.

Rights of Members and Debenture Holders

Section 8(2) of the Principal Act provides that a member or debenture holder may apply to court for an injunction restraining the company from doing any act which is *ultra vires*.

---

27 [1994] 1 ILRM 582.

2. *Regulation 6*

Regulation 6 of the European Communities (Companies) Regulations 1973 [28] provides that if a person deals with a company in good faith, any transaction entered into by an organ of the company, being its board of directors or any person authorised to bind the company, shall be deemed to be within the capacity of the company and any limitation of the powers of that board or person, whether imposed by the memorandum or articles, may not be relied upon as against any person so dealing with the company.

Regulation 6 supplements section 8 of the Principal Act by providing an additional defence to third parties who deal with the company. However, the requirement to show that the person acted in 'good faith' is probably more onerous than the test of 'actually aware' imposed by section 8. On the basis of the judgment in the *Northern Bank Finance* case, it would seem that if the bank had not read the memorandum at all, rather than reading it incorrectly, it could have been protected by section 8(1) of the Principal Act. It is doubtful whether such inaction would protect a person invoking Regulation 6, as the refusal to read a document for fear of what may be found therein is unlikely to constitute a *bona fide* action for the purposes of Regulation 6. Nevertheless, there is a presumption that the person was acting in good faith and, accordingly, in order to prevent a person invoking Regulation 6 the applicant must prove that he was not so acting.

Regulation 6 applies only to limited companies. Presumably it was not raised in the *Northern Bank* case because the company in that case was not a limited company. In protecting outsiders who deal with not just the company but also its authorised agents, Regulation 6 has also limited the effect of the rule in the *Turquand* case, which is considered in Chapter 17.

---

28 SI 163/1973.

CHAPTER EIGHT

COMPANY SECURITIES

Introduction

Company securities fall into two main categories: shares and debentures. The most significant difference between the two is that a shareholder is a member[1] and owner of the company whereas a debenture holder is a creditor of the company. This difference in status is reflected in the legal rights conferred on the holders of each, which include, *inter alia,* the following:

(a) in contrast with the shareholder, who as an owner has an interest in the company, the debenture holder as a creditor has rights against the company;
(b) shareholders' rights are mostly determined by the company's articles of association and the Companies Acts whereas the debenture deed will set out the contractual rights of the debenture holder;
(c) the return on investment is measured in terms of a dividend for shareholders and interest payments for debenture holders. Dividends are only payable from distributable profits, whereas the company is contractually bound to pay interest on debentures even where profits have not been made;
(d) debenture holders can, by securing their debt, elevate themselves in the insolvency queue to a position ahead of all shareholders and some other creditors. A shareholder cannot legally contract out of his place in the insolvency queue. Even if the debenture is unsecured, the debenture holders will always be paid before the shareholders in a winding up.

In reality the distinction between the two may not be as obvious. This is because the debenture may give the holder contractual rights similar to those of shareholders, including the right to appoint a director and attend and vote at general meetings. The Companies Acts also recognise the economic reality of both shareholders and debenture holders having a vested interest in the company, by affording them similar rights in respect of the following:

(a) applying to court to have an alteration of objects clause cancelled;[2]
(b) petitioning the court to have the company wound up;[3]
(c) petitioning the court to have an examiner appointed;[4]

---

1 Technically speaking a shareholder only becomes a member on being registered in the Register of Members: Section 31 of the Principal Act.
2 Section 10(3) and (7) of the Principal Act.
3 Section 215 of the Principal Act.
4 Section 3 of the Companies (Amendment) Act 1990.

(d) applying to the court for an injunction restraining the company from acting *ultra vires*;[5]

(e) receiving a copy of the balance sheet and directors' and auditors' report which are to be laid before the annual general meeting of the company;[6] and

(f) the right to object to a proposed reduction of capital under section 72 of the Principal Act.[7]

The Legal Nature Of Shares

In *Borland's Trustee v. Steel*,[8] Farwell J. described a share as:

> the interest of a shareholder in the company measured by a sum of money, for the purpose of liability in the first place, and of interest in the second, but also consisting of a series of mutual covenants entered into by the shareholders *inter se*.[9]

As the definition suggests, a member is under a liability to the company to the extent that he must pay for his shares but he is also conferred with a bundle of rights, interests and obligations, which can be summarised as follows:

(a) those determined by the articles of association, which are capable of being enforced under section 25 of the Principal Act;[10]

(b) those determined by statute, which in many instances cannot be abridged by the company's regulations.[11]

It should be noted that while a share confers an interest in the company itself, it does not confer an interest in the property or undertaking of the company.[12]

Section 79 of the Principal Act describes a share as personal property which is transferable in the manner prescribed by the articles. A share is an intangible interest distinguishable from a share certificate, which is the document evidencing *prima facie* title to the shares. As an intangible interest, a share is a chose in action which gives the holder the right to take legal action to protect his interest therein.

---

5 Section 8(2) of the Principal Act.

6 Section 159(1) of the Principal Act.

7 Section 73 of the Principal Act.

8 [1901] Ch 279.

9 See also *IRC v. Crossman* [1937] AC 26.

10 See Chapter 5.

11 Any member can prevent re-registration of a limited company as an unlimited company: section 52(3) of the Companies (Amendment) Act 1983. Any member can apply to the Minister to have an AGM called: section 131(3) of the Principal Act. A member cannot be compelled by an alteration of the articles to subscribe for additional shares or to accept liability in respect of those shares: section 27 of the Principal Act. A member is entitled to minimum notice of general meetings: section 133 of the Principal Act.

12 *Short v. Treasury Commissioners* [1948] 1 KB 122.

Classes of Shares

Unless the articles of association expressly provide otherwise, it is presumed that all shares confer the same rights and impose the same liabilities on their holders.[13] Shareholders' rights are normally categorised in terms of the following:

(a) the right to attend and vote at meetings;
(b) the payment of dividends; and
(c) the return of capital and any surplus on a winding up of the company.

The presumption of equality may be modified by dividing shares into different classes and attaching to those classes different rights. The power to create different classes of shares and to confer on each class different rights may be provided for in the memorandum of association. However, in practice it is usually dealt with in the articles of association. Although companies do not normally complicate their capital structures by creating several different classes of shares, it is not uncommon to find at least two classes of capital to which different rights attach. Table A authorises the company, by ordinary resolution, to issue shares with 'preferred, deferred or other special rights'.[14] Accordingly, the three main classes of shares which are recognised by Table A are:

1. ordinary shares;
2. preference shares; and
3. deferred shares.

1. Ordinary Shares

Ordinary shares are those which do not confer on the holder any preferential entitlements. The holders of these shares bear the true burden of the company's fortunes, as the return on their investment is dependent upon the company's financial position. Where losses are incurred or the company is wound up because of its insolvency, the financial entitlements of the ordinary shareholders are postponed to those of the creditors and possibly those of the preference shareholders.

2. Preference Shares

Preference shares are those shares which carry preferential financial entitlements, usually in respect of dividends and return of capital. Preference shares are usually issued to attract investment in the company. Once preference shares are issued, it is usually presumed that the holder is entitled to a fixed dividend ahead of any other shareholders' entitlement in this regard. All other entitlements are conditional upon the terms of the preference share issue. Furthermore, no issue may offer preferential entitlements unless so authorised by

---

13 *Birch v. Cropper, Re Bridgewater Navigation Co.* (1889) 14 App Cas 525.
14 Model Article 2.

the articles of association. The rights of preference shareholders will now be considered in terms of:

(a) dividend entitlements;
(b) return of capital and surplus; and
(c) voting rights.

Dividend entitlements

Although preference shareholders have a priority right to receive dividends, this right cannot be invoked to compel a company to pay dividends. This is because dividends can only be paid where distributable profits are available from which they can be paid. Even where these profits are available the directors may refuse to declare a dividend, and cannot be compelled to do so because, as the court observed in *Burland v. Earle*:

> Their Lordships are not aware of any principle which compels a joint stock company while a going concern to divide the whole of its profits among its shareholders.[15]

Rather, it is a matter for the directors to decide whether or not dividends will be declared. In *Bond v. Barrow Haematite Steel Co.*[16] the company had available reserves of £240,000 but the directors did not declare a dividend. The plaintiff, a preference shareholder, argued that the dividend should have been paid given the availability of the reserves. The company claimed that it had decided to retain the reserves to make good losses arising from the disposal of current assets and a diminution of the value of the company's fixed assets. The court held that it would not interfere with the directors' discretion in relation to the declaration of dividends. However, there is nothing to prevent the articles of association from conferring an automatic right to receive a dividend, irrespective of whether or not one has been declared.[17] Such a right could only be invoked if there are distributable profits.

Where dividends are not declared, the preference shareholder is entitled to have the arrears paid the next time dividends are declared. This is because preference shares are presumed to be cumulative unless the contrary is stated in the articles of association. Where preference shares are not issued with cumulative rights, this must be made clear. A statement to the effect that dividends will only be payable 'out of the profits made by the company in that particular year' will be sufficient to make the shares non-cumulative.[18]

Once the preference shareholder has received his dividend he is not entitled to any further share in the distributable profits unless expressly provided for in the articles of association.[19]

---

15 [1902] AC 83 at 95.
16 [1902] 1 Ch 353.
17 *Re Lafayette Ltd* [1950] IR 100.
18 *Webb v. Earle* (1875) LR 20 Eq 556.
19 *Will v. United Lankat Plantations* [1914] AC 11.

Where the company is wound up the entitlement to arrears of dividends ceases unless they were already declared, but unpaid, before the company was wound up. Alternatively, the articles may provide that the arrears are to be paid before any capital or surplus is paid to the other members.[20] However, it should be noted that if a company is insolvent dividends owing to members will not be deemed to be a debt of the company. Therefore, members will not be categorised as creditors for the purposes of the dividends owing. Accordingly, when wound up, the non-member creditors will be paid before any arrears of dividends are paid to preference shareholders.[21]

Return of capital and surplus

In the absence of an express provision to the contrary in the articles, preference shareholders are not automatically entitled to the return of capital in priority to the ordinary shareholders in a winding up.[22] However, where they are entitled to a return of capital this does not necessarily exhaust their rights in this regard, and they may also be entitled to a share in the surplus assets in a winding-up situation. In *Cork Electric Supply Co. Ltd v. Concannon*,[23] the articles of association gave the preference shareholders preferred rights as to dividends and to the return of capital. When the company was being wound up because its assets had been compulsorily acquired by the newly established Electric Supply Board, the company sought directions from the court as to whether the entitlement to priority as to a return of capital exhausted the preference shareholders' rights in this regard. If such was the case it would have the effect of excluding them from participating in the surplus assets which were available. As the articles contained no limitation on the right to participate, the Supreme Court held that the preference shareholders were entitled in the same manner as the ordinary shareholders to a share in the surplus assets.[24] The decision was based on the construction of the company's articles, in particular the fact that the article providing for the dividend priority was qualified by the words 'and no such further dividend', which was regarded as an exhaustive right. No such qualification was applied to the priority right to a return of capital, which implied that this right was not exhaustive.

Voting rights

It is normal for the articles of association to restrict the voting rights of preference shareholders. However, in the absence of such provisions, the presumption of

---

20 *Re Imperial Hotel (Cork) Ltd* [1950] IR 115.
21 Section 207(1)(g) of the Principal Act.
22 *Welton v Saffery* [1897] AC 299.
23 [1932] IR 314.
24 The English courts take the position that once the articles specify an entitlement to a particular right, that entitlement is exhaustive. See *Scottish Insurance Corporation v. Wilsons and Clyde Coal Company* [1949] AC 462.

equality remains and all shareholders are entitled to equal voting rights in respect of their shares.

3. Deferred Shares

In the past it was not uncommon for the company to allot deferred or founder shares to the founders of the company. These shares carried special rights such as the right to receive a fixed dividend. However, these rights were deferred in priority to the ordinary shares. Deferred shares are rarely, if ever, issued nowadays.

Variation of Class Rights

If the articles of association attach different rights to different classes of shares, those rights can be altered by special resolution subject to the normal rules regarding the alteration of the articles.[25] However, the articles, or indeed the memorandum, may specify that a special voting procedure must be followed where such an alteration is being made. Section 78 of the Principal Act acknowledges the company's right to alter the articles to this effect, and it provides that where such a procedure is specified and complied with, the rights of different classes of shareholders can lawfully be varied. Although the Principal Act was silent as to whether the rights of class shareholders could be varied if no such provision was made in the memorandum or articles of association, this has been rectified by section 38 of the 1983 Amendment Act, which broadly provides that:

(a) where the rights attached to a class are determined otherwise than by the memorandum of association and no variation procedure is specified in the articles, the rights can only be varied with the written consent of 75 per cent of the class members or by a special resolution of that class; or
(b) where the memorandum of association determines the rights but the articles do not stipulate a variation procedure, the rights can only be varied with the consent of all the shareholders and not just the shareholders of that particular class.

Companies usually provide for their own variation rules, and Table A sets out a similar procedure to that mentioned in (a) above (Model Article 3).

Irrespective of the procedure followed, dissentient shareholders, holding at least 10 per cent of the shares of a class, may apply to the court to have the alteration cancelled.[26] If such an application is made within twenty-eight days of the authorising decision or resolution, the variation will not take effect until the court has confirmed it. The court will either confirm or reject the variation. It

---

25 *Andrews v. Gas Meter Co.* [1897] 1 Ch 361.
26 Section 78(1) of the Principal Act.

must confirm the variation unless it is satisfied that having regard to the circumstances, the variation would be unfairly prejudicial to the class represented by the applicant.[27] In *Re Holders Investment Trust Ltd*,[28] a proposal by the company to repay the 5 per cent preference shareholders by giving them unsecured loan stock was approved by the trustees who held 90 per cent of the shares of that class. The preference shareholders had a prior right to repayment of the capital ahead of the ordinary shareholders. The trustees who also held the majority of the ordinary shares would obviously benefit from the change. It was held that the resolution of the class meeting was invalid because the trustees acted in their interests as ordinary shareholders and not in the interests of the preference shareholders.

There are no statutory guidelines as to what will actually constitute a variation of class rights.[29] A decision that adversely affects a particular class does not necessarily amount to a variation of rights. A distinction is drawn between a decision that affects the rights themselves and one that merely affects the enjoyment of those rights. In *Greenhalgh v. Arderne Cinemas*,[30] the company had two classes of ordinary shares, 50p shares and 10p shares. Each share carried one vote. A resolution was passed to subdivide the 50p shares into five 10p shares, with the result that the holders of the original 50p shares now had five votes instead of one. The subdivision had the effect of diluting the voting strength of the existing 10p shareholders. Nevertheless, the court held that the rights of the original 10p shareholders had not been varied.

Similarly, in *White v. Bristol Aeroplane Co. Ltd*,[31] the issue of bonus preference shares to ordinary shareholders was held not to be a variation of class rights, even though the allotment had the effect of reducing the existing preference shareholders' percentage holdings.[32]

It is important to remember that any alteration of the articles must be carried out *bona fide* and in the best interests of the company, and any attempt to oppress a minority shareholder under the guise of a genuine alteration will be struck down by the court as invalid. Thus in *Clemens v. Clemens Bros. Ltd*,[33] the plaintiff held 45 per cent of the issued shares and her aunt held the remaining 55 per cent. The aunt's shares were used to secure the passing of a resolution to issue new shares to directors and employees. The intended effect of the resolution was to reduce the plaintiff's shareholding to below 25 per cent, which would deprive

---

27 Section 78(3) of the Principal Act.
28 [1971] 1 WLR 583.
29 Section 178(6) of the Principal Act provides that a variation included an abrogation.
30 [1946] 1 All ER 512.
31 [1953] Ch 65.
32 See also *Re Saltdean Estate Co. Ltd* [1968] 1 WLR 1844 and *House of Fraser v. AGCE Investments Ltd* [1987] AC 387.
33 [1976] 2 All ER 268.

her of the right to block special resolutions. The court set aside the resolution on the ground that it was oppressive to the plaintiff since it was designed to reduce her control over the company.

Other Categories of Shares

In addition to the three classes of shares mentioned above, ordinary and preference shares may be further described in terms of the following:

(a) redeemable shares are shares which must be bought back by the company after the expiry of a fixed period of time, which is usually set out in the articles of association;
(b) treasury shares are those shares that have been redeemed and having been so redeemed are retained by the company;
(c) bonus shares are shares that are issued by way of a bonus issue such as when the company capitalises profits by paying up bonus shares and issuing them to existing members in the same manner as it would pay dividends.

Legal Nature of Debentures

In its most basic form, a debenture is simply a written statement acknowledging indebtedness. The modern debenture is more likely to be a complex and formal legal document incorporating, *inter alia*, provisions for the following:

(a) an undertaking to repay the debt, subject to the terms and conditions agreed;
(b) the giving of security for the indebtedness, in such form as agreed;
(c) the events of default that will trigger the enforcement of the security; and
(d) the methods of enforcing the security.

Where the borrower defaults, the debenture holder may sue to recover the amount owing. Where the debenture is secured, which is normally the case, the debenture holder may enforce his security in the manner provided under the debenture. The enforcement of security is considered further in Chapter 24.

1. Types of Debentures

Debentures may be classified differently, but such classification only reflects the manner in which the debentures have been issued as opposed to the rights attaching to each category. This is because the rights of debenture holders are found in the underlying terms of the contract, which vary according to the bargaining position of the company and the creditor. Debentures are usually categorised as follows.

(a) Single debentures: this most common form of debenture is issued under a contractual instrument between the company and a single creditor, whereby the debenture is usually secured by a charge over some or all of the company's assets and undertaking;

(b) Series of debentures: the company may have more than one creditor, each providing a portion of an overall global loan facility. In such a case, it is usual to issue debentures as a series. As well as the standard conditions, it is normal to include in the debenture a provision for its transferability together with a *pari passu* clause whereby each debenture holder will rank equally in terms of repayment. This *pari passu* condition is essential to ensure equality between the lenders, irrespective of which loan was drawn first, or to whom the first debenture was issued.

(c) Debenture stock: it is not uncommon for public companies to raise loan capital by the issue of debenture stock to the public. The company raises a global loan which is subject to certain conditions including *inter alia* provisions for the payment of interest and the repayment of principal. Each subscriber will be issued a debenture stock certificate recording the amount and conditions of the loan. Debenture stock certificates are usually transferable.

2. The Debenture Trust Deed

Where companies are issuing a series of debentures or debenture stock, the potential subscribers may be numerous. Rather than negotiating with each subscriber individually, a trust deed is executed by the company under which a trustee is appointed to represent the debenture holders and enforce their rights. The trustee is normally vested with powers to enforce the security, if any, and to appoint a receiver. Although ordinarily appointed by the company itself, the trustee's duty is towards the debenture holder and any contractual term relieving the trustee from liability for a breach of trust is void.[34]

3. The Issue and Transfer of Debentures

Debentures are issued in the same manner as shares. Public companies can offer debentures to the public by means of a prospectus.[35] Debentures may be redeemable after a fixed period of time or they may be irredeemable.[36] They may also be convertible, which gives the holder a right to convert the debentures into shares. A debenture is transferable in the manner provided by the debenture itself. However, the company may not register a transfer of debentures unless a proper instrument of transfer has been delivered to the company. The transfer is usually in the same form as those used for share transfers.

---

34 Section 93 of the Principal Act.
35 See Chapter 9.
36 Section 94 of the Principal Act authorises the issue of irredeemable debentures.

4. Register of Debentures

Where the debenture is secured by way of a charge, the charge must be officially registered with the Registrar of Companies.[37] Furthermore, section 91 of the Principal Act requires a company to maintain a register of debenture holders and enter therein the names and addresses of the debenture holders and the amount of debentures held by each of them. However, neither debentures which do not form part of a series ranking pari-passu nor debentures which are transferable by delivery are required to be maintained in the register. The register must ordinarily be kept at the registered office of the company and be available for inspection by the registered holder of the debentures, the shareholders and any other interested person.

---

37 Section 99 of the Principal Act. See Chapter 11.

CHAPTER NINE

ALLOTMENT OF SHARES

Introduction

The process by which new shares are issued and allotted by a company is subject to a number of restrictions. Some of these are prescribed by the Companies Acts and others are set out in the company's articles of association. Because public companies are permitted to issue new shares to the public they are also subject to additional requirements and restrictions in this regard. These rules will now be considered under the following headings:

(a) allotment of shares generally; and
(b) allotment of shares to the public.

Allotment of Shares Generally

Prior to 1983 the authority to allot shares was usually considered to be within the remit of the directors, as a power delegated to them by the articles of association. This authority is now restricted by section 20 of the 1983 Amendment Act. It provides that the directors shall not exercise any powers of allotting shares unless so authorised by the company in general meeting or by the company's articles. Where the authorisation is granted by the general meeting, a copy of the authorising resolution must be delivered to the registrar of companies within fifteen days of it being passed.[1] Furthermore, notice of the delivery of the resolution to the registrar must be published in the *CRO Gazette*.[2] The authorisation to the directors, whatever its form, must state the maximum number of shares to be allotted and the date upon which the authority will expire.[3] The authority cannot be granted for an indefinite period because section 20(3) of the 1983 Act stipulates that the authority must not exceed five years from the date of incorporation or the date of the resolution. Even where the authority is vested in the directors, it may be revoked, varied or renewed for a further five years by an ordinary resolution of the company.[4] Although an allotment in contravention of section 20 will usually be valid, any director who knowingly and wilfully contravened the section will be guilty of an offence and liable to a fine.

---

1 Section 20(6) of the 1983 Amendment Act.
2 Section 55 of the 1983 Amendment Act.
3 Section 20(3) of the 1983 Amendment Act.
4 Section 20(4) of the 1983 Amendment Act.

Section 89 of the Principal Act empowers the court to validate an otherwise invalid issue of shares if the court is satisfied that it would be just and equitable to do so. Conversely, it will not validate the issue if it is not so satisfied. This provision was considered in the case of *Re Sugar Distributors Ltd.*[5] Here, the company's secretary prepared minutes which recorded that the requisite general meeting and board meeting had been held and resolutions had been passed thereat to enable the company to issue and allot additional shares to a majority corporate shareholder. In fact, the meeting of the shareholders to pass the resolution had never taken place, nor had the board meeting at which the decision to allot the shares was purportedly taken. The secretary had taken the decision on foot of instructions from the majority shareholder to issue new preference shares in order that both companies might avail of tax concessions. When an inspector was subsequently appointed to the company he found that the correct procedures had not been followed in issuing the preference shares. The company brought an application for an order under section 89 that the allotment was valid. Keane J. held that the object of the application was to enable the company to gain a tax advantage rather than to validate a defective title to shares already issued. Such an objective, he observed, was never contemplated by the section 89 procedure which gave the court a discretionary power that would only be exercised where it considered it just and equitable to do so. Accordingly, the court would not permit it to be used for such a purpose.

1. The Allotment Process

The allotment of shares is primarily governed by principles of contract law. Allotment occurs when an application for newly issued shares has been accepted by the directors and the acceptance has been notified to the applicant. Private companies typically expedite the allotment process by the straightforward issuance of a share certificate. Public companies usually adopt a more formal approach which commences with the issuance of a letter of allotment. This letter of allotment may contain a form of renunciation which allows the allottee to renounce the allotment in favour of another person. The allottee, provided he does not renounce, will then return the allotment letter together with an application for the registration of the shares in his name. On receipt of this the company will enter the name in the register of members and issue a share certificate.

By virtue of section 31(2) of the Principal Act, once the name of a person is entered in the register, that person becomes a member of the company. If, having issued a letter of allotment, a company fails to register the name, the person concerned may sue to enforce his contractual entitlement to have his name so registered.

---

5 [1995] 2 IR 195, [1996] 1 ILRM 342.

Where new shares have been allotted, the company is required, within one month, to make a return to the registrar of companies detailing the following:

(a) the number and nominal value of the shares comprised in the allotment;
(b) the names and addresses of the allottees; and
(c) the amount, if any, paid or due and payable on each share or in the case of shares allotted for non-cash consideration, details of the appropriate contract and consideration.[6]

If default is made in complying with this section, every officer of the company who is in default shall be guilty of an offence and liable to a fine.

2. Pre-emption Rights of Existing Shareholders

Where a company proposes to allot shares wholly for cash, the shares must first be offered to existing members in proportion to their respective holdings.[7] Not all members are entitled to a pre-emption right. Section 23 of the 1983 Amendment Act limits the right to those members who hold shares which do not confer any priority preference as to a dividend payment or a return of capital in a winding-up. This effectively removes all preference shareholders from the enjoyment of the statutory pre-emption right.

The right of first refusal only applies where an allotment of 'equity securities' is proposed. Equity securities are essentially all shares other than the following:

(a) shares, including preference shares, which confer restricted rights in respect to dividends or capital distributions;[8]
(b) shares allotted under an employee share scheme — this is an important exception as otherwise these schemes would become impossible to work if all existing shareholders were entitled to a right of first refusal;
(c) shares allotted for consideration otherwise than in cash — therefore where it is proposed to allot shares as consideration for the acquisition of a business undertaking, there is no requirement to make an offer to existing shareholders on the same terms.

Where such an allotment of equity securities is proposed, the offer must be served in the same manner as a notice of a general meeting.[9] It must specify a period of not less than twenty-one days during which the offer may be accepted,

---

6 Section 58(1) of the Principal Act.
7 Section 23 of the 1983 Amendment Act.
8 A restriction on voting rights is, therefore, irrelevant for the purpose of defining equity securities.
9 Section 23(7) of the 1983 Amendment Act.

and the offer may not be withdrawn before the expiry of this period.[10] Where an offer has been made, the directors shall not allot those securities to any other person until the offer has expired or has been rejected.[11]

A member cannot exercise a pre-emption right on only part of the offer. He either accepts the offer in full or rejects the offer. In *Ocean Coal Co. v. Powell Duffryn Steam Coal Co.*,[12] the plaintiff and defendant each held equal shares in the company. The articles provided that where a member wished to transfer his shares to outsiders, he must first offer them to existing shareholders at the same price. The defendant wished to sell his shares but the plaintiff only wished to purchase enough of them to ensure that he would retain control of the company. It was held that his pre-emption right did not entitle him to any portion of the shares offered. Accordingly the plaintiff was obliged to purchase all the shares or reject the offer.

The statutory pre-emption right of members may in the case of private companies be permanently excluded by the memorandum or articles of association.[13] Indeed, all companies may, where the directors of the company are authorised to allot shares, exclude the right in any of the following ways:

(a) directors may be given power under the articles or by a special resolution to disapply the pre-emption right or modify it to the extent permitted by that resolution; and

(b) directors may, by special resolution, be given the power to exclude or modify the right in relation to a particular allotment.[14] Where such a resolution is proposed, it must be recommended by the directors and the notice of the meeting must contain an explanation from the directors as to the reasons for their recommendation, the amount to be paid as consideration for the shares and the directors' justification for that amount.

However, the directors' power to disapply the pre-emptive right will cease when their authority to allot has been revoked or has expired. In any case, a company may provide in its memorandum or articles for its own pre-emption scheme which may even give entitlements to preference shareholders.

Failure to comply with the statutory requirements will not invalidate the allotment. However, it will render the company, and any officer who knowingly authorised or permitted the contravention, liable to compensate the members to whom the offer ought to have been made, subject to a two-year statutory limit on the right to claim such compensation.[15]

---

10 Section 23(8) of the 1983 Amendment Act.
11 Section 23(1)(b) of the 1983 Amendment Act.
12 [1932] 1 Ch 654.
13 Section 23(10) of the 1983 Amendment Act.
14 Section 24 of the 1983 Amendment Act.
15 Section 23(11) of the 1983 Amendment Act.

3. Consideration for the Allotment of Shares

Generally, all shares must be allotted with a nominal or par value. This value will be determined by the capital clause in the memorandum of association, which specifies the authorised share capital, the number of shares into which it is divided and the amount of each share. The nominal value will rarely reflect the market value of the company's shares, which will vary depending on the company's fortunes. Section 27 of the 1983 Amendment Act requires that when a company is allotting shares it must obtain, in money or money's worth, consideration of a value at least equal to the nominal value of the shares. This statutory prohibition on allotting shares at a discount reflects the common law position illustrated by the case of *Ooregum Gold Mining Co. of India v. Roper*.[16] In this case the market value of the company's shares had fallen below the nominal value. In an attempt to raise much-needed capital the company resolved at a general meeting to allot preference shares, a portion of which was deemed as having been paid. A shareholder successfully challenged the allotment on the ground that the company could not allot shares at a discount.

Consideration need not be paid in full at the time of allotment. However, a public company may not allot shares unless they are paid up to the extent of one quarter of the nominal value in addition to the whole, if any, of the share premium. Where the full amount of a share is not payable and has in fact not been paid, the holder of the share, even if not the original allottee, remains liable for the unpaid amounts until such time as they are called in by the company or a liquidator. In *Re Munster Bank (Re Dillon's claim)*[17] a bank manager, as part of a security arrangement with a customer, became the registered holder of partly paid-up shares previously held by the customer. It was held that he was personally obliged to pay for the outstanding amounts due on the shares when a call was subsequently made.

Non-cash consideration

When shares are allotted for non-cash consideration, different rules apply depending on the company's status. In the case of a private company the statutory dictates are few and relate to notification and delivery requirements.[18] Although the 1983 Act acknowledges the right of private companies to allot shares for non-cash consideration, including goodwill and services, it does not prescribe any preconditions for such an allotment.[19] In the absence of such provisions the general principles of contract law apply. Accordingly, the courts will not inquire into the adequacy of consideration provided it is real and not

---

16 [1892] AC 125.
17 (1886) 17 LR Ir 341.
18 Section 58(1)(b) of the Principal Act.
19 Section 26.

tainted by fraud or dishonesty. Thus in *Re Wragg Ltd*,[20] two former business associates sold their business undertaking to a newly incorporated company in which they were the shareholders. The consideration price of £46,300 was paid by the allotment of £20,000 in shares and the balance in cash and debentures. When the company was subsequently wound up, the liquidator contended that the business had been over-valued to the extent of £18,000 and that the company should be entitled to recover the excess amount from the shareholders. Although the court accepted that shares could not be issued at a discount, it held that a company was entitled to put its own value on the worth of property and pay for it in fully paid shares. As there was no element of dishonesty and the shareholders had agreed to the purchase price, the court would not interfere in the arrangement. Accordingly, the liquidator's claim failed.[21] Similarly, in *Re Leinster Contract Corporation*,[22] the court refused to set aside an allotment just because the consideration, which was in the form of patents, ultimately proved worthless. However, where there is evidence of bad faith or dishonesty, the allotment may be invalidated.[23] Furthermore, where consideration is past or illusory the allotment will fail on the basis of principles of contract law.[24]

In the case of public companies the statutory rules demand a more stringent approach. First, a public company is barred from accepting, in consideration for its shares, an undertaking for future services.[25] Second, it may not allot shares in consideration for any undertaking which will not be performed until after five years from the date of the allotment.[26] Contravention of these requirements will render the holder of the shares liable to pay an amount equal to the nominal value together with any premium and interest that applies. If an undertaking ought to have been performed within five years from the date of the allotment but is not, the allottee or the holder of the shares, if he had notice of the contravention, becomes immediately liable to pay for his shares in cash. Third, to avoid the difficulties inherent in establishing the adequacy of consideration, the 1983 Amendment Act requires that where non-cash consideration is being obtained, it must be independently valued; except in the case of a take-over bid where the consideration involves a share exchange.[27] The valuation report must be made to the company, within the six months prior to the allotment, by an independent person qualified to be an auditor of the company. The expert is entitled to require

---

20 [1897] 1 Ch 796.
21 See also *Salomon v. Salomon* [1897] AC 22.
22 [1902] IR 349.
23 *Tintin Exploration Syndicate v. Sandys* (1947) 177 LT 412.
24 *Re White Star Line* [1938] Ch 458 and *Re Eddystone Marine Insurance Co.* [1893] 3 Ch 9.
25 Section 26(2) of the 1983 Amendment Act.
26 Section 29(1) of the 1983 Amendment Act.
27 Section 30 of the 1983 Amendment Act.

from the company's officers such information and explanations as he thinks necessary to enable him to carry out the valuation and make the report.[28] He is also entitled, where he believes it necessary, to obtain a further report from another expert, such as a valuer. Any person who knowingly or recklessly makes a statement, as to a material particular, which is misleading, false or deceptive will be guilty of an offence.[29] The expert's report must contain the following information:

(a) the nominal value of the shares to be wholly or partly paid for by the consideration in question;
(b) the amount of any premium payable on those shares;
(c) the description of any premium payable on those shares;
(d) the extent to which the nominal value of the shares and any premium are to be treated as paid up by the consideration or by cash.

The company must, on receipt of the expert's report, send a copy to the allottee and the registrar of companies. Finally, a public company may not, within two years of receiving its trading certificate, receive a transfer of a non-cash asset from a subscriber to the memorandum, where the consideration to be given is equal to or greater than one-tenth of the nominal value of the company's share capital issued at that time, other than those assets normally acquired in the ordinary course of business, unless it has been independently valued and it has been agreed by the company by way of ordinary resolution.[30]

4. Share Premium

Where companies allot shares for a consideration greater than their nominal value, the excess amount must be credited to a share premium account.[31] Where non-cash consideration is obtained the same obligation is imposed, although a relief is provided where merger accounting principles apply. There is no obligation on directors to obtain the best possible price or a premium when allotting shares to members. However, where the allotment is to non-members, it was suggested in *Hilder v. Dexter*[32] that in exercising their powers in the best interests of the company, directors may be obliged to obtain a premium for the company. Although the share premium account is a reserve separate from the share capital account, for the purpose of capital maintenance rules they are treated similarly. Accordingly, the share premium account can only be applied in the following ways:

---

28 Section 31 of the 1983 Amendment Act.
29 Section 31(3) of the 1983 Amendment Act.
30 Section 32 of the 1983 Amendment Act.
31 Section 62 of the Principal Act.
32 [1902] AC 474.

(a) where a return to members is authorised by the reduction of capital rules in the Companies Act; or
(b) for the payment of bonus shares; or
(c) for writing off a company's preliminary expenses or the expenses of, or the commissions paid or discount allowed on, any issue of the company's shares; or
(d) in providing for any premium payable on the redemption of redeemable preference shares or debentures of the company. (See Chapter 10, Maintenance of Capital.)

Allotment of Shares to the Public

Private companies are by their nature restricted from raising equity capital.[33] By contrast, public companies may raise capital by offering their shares or debentures to the public. Although a public company may sell its shares directly to the public, it is usual for such a company to be *floated* on the Stock Exchange, through which medium it can trade its shares. An issue of shares to the public may be achieved by any of the following methods.

1. Issuing and Allotting Shares Directly

An offer is made directly through the issue of a prospectus (or offering document), which invites the public to subscribe for shares. The prospectus (or offering document) will be published through any of the acceptable means of publication under Irish prospectus law and the prospective investor applies for shares on foot of same.

2. Selling Shares through an Intermediary

In this instance the company sells all the securities on issue to an intermediary, usually an issuing house, whose business is that of corporate finance. The issuing house offers the shares to the public at a higher price than it paid for them. This method of issue is advantageous to a company for two reasons. First, the company is relieved of the responsibility of selling the shares. Second, the endorsement of the new issue by a reputable issuing house is bound to create public interest and confidence in the issue. In certain instances securities are issued in large quantities to a number of financial institutions or clients of the issuing house. The placement is generally effected by the issuing house by way of private negotiations. The prospectus rules will apply even if an intermediary is used, unless the issue of shares is excluded — see 'The Prospectus Rules', below).

---

33 Section 21 of the 1983 Amendment Act.

3. A Rights Issue

The company may wish to raise fresh capital without either offering the shares to the public at large or availing of a placing. In these circumstances, it may decide to raise the necessary funds by allotting shares to the existing shareholders, who are given the right to apply for a given number of new shares in proportion to their existing holdings. A rights issue is usually made renounceable. A prospectus will be required unless the share issue is one excluded under the prospectus rules.

4. By Tender

Shares may be offered by tender, i.e. a minimum price is fixed below which the shares will not be allotted and bids are invited. The shares will then normally be allotted to the highest bidder. A tender may not be submitted by way of a referential bid. In *Harvela Investments v. Royal Trust Company of Canada*[34] the company invited purchasers to submit sealed bids for shares. One of the bids stated that the bidder would pay a certain amount over any other offer received by the company. The House of Lords held that such bids were unacceptable as one bidder could not lose and the others could not win. This method of allotting shares is not used very often.

The Prospectus Rules

1. Regulatory Framework

The Prospectus Directive[35] was implemented into Irish law on 1 July 2005 as part of the European Union Financial Services Plan. The Directive was given effect in Ireland by the Prospectus Regulations 2005[36] and the Investment Funds, Companies and Miscellaneous Provisions Act 2005 (the 2005 Act). This Directive and its implementing measures (herein referred to as the Prospectus Rules) overhaul the law in relation to the public offer of securities[37] and their admission on a regulated market. The Prospectus Rules provide for the following:

(a) the requirement to produce a prospectus whenever securities are offered to the public or admitted to trading on a regulated market;
(b) the format and content of prospectuses;
(c) a process of prior approval of prospectuses; and

---

34 [1986] AC 139.
35 Directive 2003/71/EC.
36 Prospectus (Directive 2003/71/EC) Regulations, 2005: SI 324/2005.
37 The term 'securities' is given a much broader meaning than heretofore, when 'securities' were defined as shares and debentures. Under the new rules 'securities' means any transferable securities, equity and non-equity, with the exception of money market instruments having a maturity of less than twelve months.

(d) the recognition of approved prospectuses in all other member states of the EU and the European Economic Area.

2. Application of the Prospectus Rules

The rules apply in relation to the public offer of securities or their admission to a regulated market. Heretofore, what constituted an offer of securities to the public was not always clear. The Prospectus Rules now provide that an 'offer of securities to the public' or 'public offer' means a communication to persons in any form and by any means, presenting sufficient information on the terms of the offer and the securities to be offered, so as to enable an investor to decide to purchase or subscribe for those securities, or apply to purchase or subscribe for those securities, which includes the placing of securities through financial intermediaries.

Securities admitted to trading on a regulated market are also subject to the Prospectus Rules. In an Irish context a 'regulated market' includes the official listing of the Irish Stock Exchange (the ISEQ). The Irish Stock Exchange has recently established the Irish Enterprise Exchange (IEX), which is not a regulated market for the purpose of the Prospectus Rules. This market is designed to suit small to mid-sized companies.

Certain securities are deemed to be outside the ambit of the Prospectus Rules.[38] The most significant in terms of equity securities is the issue of such securities where the offer expressly limits the amount of the total consideration payable to €2,500,000 calculated over a twelve-month period. However, such issues are subject to the rules regarding local offers.[39] Essentially, in the case of local offers the offering document must contain a number of 'health warnings', including a statement to the effect that it has not been prepared or reviewed by any regulatory authority; warnings regarding reliance on past and simulated performance as a guide to future performance; warnings regarding investments, income and exchange rate (if any) fluctuations. The offering document must be forwarded to the registrar of companies before it can be issued by the company.

3. Excluded Offers

The obligation to publish a prospectus will not apply to an offer of securities in the State that falls into one or more of the following categories:

(a) An offer of securities addressed solely to qualified investors. Qualified investors are essentially those who are authorised or regulated to operate in the financial markets, companies whose object is solely to invest in securities, certain state or supranational authorities, large entities and certain

---

38 Regulation 8 of the Prospectus Regulations.
39 Section 49 of the 2005 Act.

SMEs registered in Ireland provided they are registered with the Central Bank.

(b) An offer of securities addressed to fewer than 100 persons, other than qualified investors.

(c) An offer of securities addressed to investors where the minimum consideration payable by each investor is €50,000, for each separate offer.

(d) An offer of securities whose denomination per unit amounts to at least €50,000.

(e) An offer of securities where the offer expressly limits the amount of the total consideration for the offer to less than €100,000. In calculating the €100,000 threshold, all offers of securities of the same type by the same issuer and made within the previous twelve months are taken into account.[40]

The obligation to publish a prospectus will not apply to: *offers of securities to the public* where the securities are issued in substitution for shares of the same class already issued provided there is no increase in share capital; securities offered in connection with a merger or takeover which involves a share exchange, provided the Financial Regulator is satisfied that a document is available containing information equivalent to that of a prospectus; bonus issues and scrip dividends, provided that a document is available containing information relating to the number and nature of the shares and the reasons for and details of the offer; and certain securities offered under employee share schemes, provided the issuer has securities already trading on a regulated market and provided a document is available containing information relating to the number and nature of the shares and the reasons for and details of the offer.[41]

The obligation to publish a prospectus will not apply to: *the admission to trading in the State* where the shares represent, over a period of twelve months, less than 10 per cent of the number of shares already admitted to trading on the same regulated market; shares issued in substitution for shares of the same class already admitted to trading, provided there is no increase in share capital; securities offered in connection with a merger or takeover that involves a share exchange, provided the Financial Regulator is satisfied that a document is available containing information equivalent to that of a prospectus; bonus issues and employee share schemes, provided the shares are of the same class as the shares already admitted to trading on the same regulated market, and scrip dividends, provided in these cases that a document is available containing information relating to the number and nature of the shares and the reasons for and details of the offer; and securities that are already trading on another regulated market, provided certain conditions have been satisfied.[42]

---

40 Regulation 9 of the Prospectus Regulations.
41 Regulation 10 of the Prospectus Regulations.
42 Regulation 11 of the Prospectus Regulations.

4. Content and Format of the Prospectus

The content of the prospectus is determined by the Prospectus Regulation of 2004.[43] This regulation provides for a variety of schedules and 'building blocks' by way of annexes to the regulations. Each annex provides a list of the information required to be included in the prospectus depending on the different type of securities being issued. In any case, all prospectuses must contain all information that, according to the particular nature of the issuer and the securities in question, is necessary to enable investors to make an informed assessment of the assets and liabilities, financial position, profit and loss, prospects of the issuer and of any guarantor and the rights attaching to the securities in question.[44]

All prospectuses should contain a summary that conveys the essential characteristics and risks associated with the issuer, any guarantor and the securities. The summary should also contain a warning that the summary should only be read as an introduction to the prospectus and any decision to invest should be based on consideration of the prospectus as a whole.[45]

The prospectus may be drawn up as a single document or by way of separate documents. Where it is drawn up by way of separate documents, the documents must be divided into a registration document, a securities note (both of which must contain the information required by the Prospectus Regulation) and a summary.[46]

5. Approval of the Prospectus

Every prospectus is required to be approved in advance of publication by the competent authority of the Home Member State. In the case of Ireland, the designated competent authority is the Irish Financial Services Regulatory Authority (the Financial Regulator), which has delegated the function of scrutinising prospectuses to the Irish Stock Exchange. However, final approval of the prospectus remains with the Financial Regulator. Once a prospectus is approved it is valid for twelve months after its publication.[47]

6. Publication of the Prospectus

Once the prospectus is approved and filed with the Financial Regulator and the registrar of companies (where the issuer is a company) it must be made available to the public by being published in any of the following ways:

(a) insertion in one or more newspapers widely circulated in the Member State in which the offer or admission to trading is made;

---

43 Commission Regulation (EC) 809/2004.
44 Regulation 19 of the Prospectus Regulations.
45 Regulation 21 of the Prospectus Regulations.
46 Regulation 22 of the Prospectus Regulations.
47 Regulation 30 of the Prospectus Regulations.

(b) in printed form and available free of charge to the public at the Irish Stock Exchange (or such other regulated market) or the registered office of the issuer, as the case may be;

(c) in electronic form on the issuer's website (and the website of a financial intermediary that is placing or selling the securities) or the website of the Irish Stock Exchange (or such other regulated market), as the case may be;

(d) in electronic form on the website of the relevant competent authority provided it provides such a service. The Financial Regulator offers this service.[48]

Issuers of equity securities who publish their prospectus using the method described in (a) or (b) above must also publish in electronic format on their website (and the website of any financial intermediary which is placing or selling the securities). The issuer must also publish a notice stating how the prospectus has been made available and where it can be obtained.

7. The Prospectus Passport

Once the prospectus has been approved by the IFSRA it can be used as a prospectus in any or all of the other members of the EU without the requirement of further approval by the competent authorities in those States. However, the competent authority of those member states must be notified where an offer or admission is to be made.

8. Annual Information Document

Issuers of securities admitted to trading on a regulated market are required to file an annual information document with the competent authority. This document is to contain or refer to all information the issuer has disclosed to the public over the preceding twelve months in any jurisdiction in compliance with the obligations of those jurisdictions' securities laws.

9. Breach of the Prospectus Rules

Breach of any of the above provisions will render the person responsible liable to an offence.

10. Liability for Mis-statements in a Prospectus

The 2005 Act provides for civil and criminal liability of persons responsible for producing a prospectus. Section 41 of the 2005 Act provides that a person who acquires securities on the faith of a prospectus may claim compensation for any loss or damage sustained as a result of any untrue statements included in the prospectus or by reason of any omission of information that ought to have been

---

48 Regulation 45 of the Prospectus Regulations.

included in the prospectus. The following persons[49] are liable to pay such compensation:

(a) the issuer who has issued the prospectus or on whose behalf the prospectus has been issued;
(b) the offeror of securities to which the prospectus relates;
(c) every person who has sought the admission of the securities on a regulated market;
(d) the guarantor of the issue of securities;
(e) every person who is a director of the issuer at the time of the issue of the prospectus;
(f) every person who has authorised themselves to be named and is named in the prospectus as a director of the issuer or as having agreed to become such a director of the issuer;
(g) every person being a promoter of the issuer;
(h) every person who has authorised the issue of the prospectus other than the competent authority.

Where the consent of an expert is required for the issue of a prospectus and such consent has been given, that expert will not be liable as a person who has authorised the issue of the prospectus except in respect of an untrue personal statement purporting to be made by him as an expert.[50] An expert who has given his consent to the inclusion of the statement which proves to be untrue may also escape liability if he can demonstrate that:

(a) he (or she) withdrew his consent in writing before publication of the prospectus; or
(b) after the publication but before the acquisition of securities he became aware of the untrue statement and withdrew his consent in writing and gave reasonable public notice of his withdrawal and the reason therefor; or
(c) that being competent to make the statement he had reasonable grounds for believing it to be true.[51]

---

49 In the case of prospectuses issued solely in respect of non-equity securities the number of persons who are liable is limited to the offeror or any person who has sought the admission of the securities to which the prospectus relates trading on a regulated market and the guarantor (if any) unless the prospectus expressly provides otherwise or that such person has been convicted on indictment of any offence created by Irish prospectus law — Section 43(a) of the 2005 Act. In this regard section 383(3) of the Principal Act, which requires directors and the secretary of a company to ensure that the requirements of the Companies Acts are complied with, will not apply if such would impose a liability under section 41 of the 2005 Act.
50 Section 42(1) of the 2005 Act.
51 Section 42(6) of the 2005 Act.

A person will not be liable under section 41 solely on the basis of a summary of a prospectus, including any translation thereof, unless it is misleading, inaccurate or inconsistent when read together with other parts of the prospectus. Section 42(3) of the 2005 Act provides additional defences in the following circumstances:

(a) the person concerned withdrew his consent in writing to acting as director before the prospectus was issued and it was issued without his authority or consent; or

(b) the prospectus was issued without the person's knowledge or consent and on becoming aware of it that person gave reasonable public notice that it was issued without his knowledge or consent; or

(c) after the issue of the prospectus and before the acquisition of securities thereunder, the person concerned, on becoming aware of any untrue statements therein or omission of material information required to be contained therein, withdrew in writing his consent thereto and gave reasonable public notice of their withdrawal and the reason therefor;

(d) in relation to any untrue statement, not purporting to be made by an expert or made in an public official document, or any omission from the prospectus, the person concerned had reasonable grounds to believe the statement was true or that the omission was properly omitted; or

(e) in relation to any untrue statement purported to be made by an expert, the person reasonably believed that expert to be competent to make it and had given his consent, and had not withdrawn his consent before the publication of the prospectus;

(f) in relation to any untrue statement purporting to be a statement made by an official person there was reasonable grounds for believing it was true.

Criminal liability arises under section 48 of the 2005 Act. Where a prospectus includes an untrue statement or omits any information required by the EU prospectus rules any person who authorised the issue of the prospectus shall on summary conviction be liable to imprisonment for a term not exceeding twelve months or a fine not exceeding €5,000, or to both. In respect of an indictable conviction the person concerned may be liable to imprisonment for a term not exceeding five years, or to a fine not exceeding €1,000,000, or to both. The person may escape liability if he can demonstrate that, in the case of an untrue statement, it was immaterial or that he believed on reasonable grounds up to the time of the issue of the prospectus that the statement was true or that he ought to be reasonably excused. In the case of an omission of information, the person may escape liability if he can demonstrate that the omission was immaterial, that he had no knowledge of it or that the omission ought to be reasonably excused.

10. Other Remedies for Mis-statements in Prospectuses

If a prospectus is misleading, the remedies of rescission or damages are also available to a subscriber for securities. An allottee may be entitled to rescind the contract if he can demonstrate that: the prospectus included a material false statement of fact; it was issued by or on behalf of the company; the person was one of the persons to whom the prospectus was addressed; and the false statement induced him to subscribe for shares. However, the right to rescind will not be available if the allottee discovers the true facts and then by his conduct affirms the contract. This is so even if this was not his intention. Therefore, his right to rescind may be lost if he, having discovered the true facts, exercises any of his rights as a member, including selling shares and receiving dividends. As the right to rescind is an equitable remedy, it will also be lost in the following circumstances:

(a) if, on discovering the truth, he fails to rescind promptly;
(b) if it is no longer possible to restore both parties to their pre-contractual position;
(c) if, in seeking the equitable remedy, he does not come to the courts 'with clean hands'.

Damages may also be recovered for negligent misrepresentation.[52] To succeed in such an action the plaintiff must demonstrate that there was a sufficient degree of proximity between the defendant and the plaintiff; the person who made the statement did so in a professional capacity which made it reasonably foreseeable that the plaintiff would rely on what he said; and the plaintiff did rely on what was said and in doing so suffered a loss which was reasonably foreseeable.[53]

The remedy of damages for deceit or fraud is also available but it is rarely successful as the allottee has to prove that the false statement was made knowingly, without belief in its truth or with reckless carelessness as to whether the statement was true or false.[54] The action for deceit will be brought against those responsible for the issue of a prospectus with intent to defraud, including the directors, the issuing house and the company.

11. Allotment on foot of Prospectus

Section 53 of the Principal Act provides that where a prospectus states the minimum amount that, in the opinion of the directors, must be raised from an issue of shares and that no allotment shall be made of any of those shares unless that minimum amount has been subscribed and the sum payable on application

---

52 *Hedley Byrne v. Heller & Partners* [1964] AC 465.
53 Ibid.
54 *Derry v. Peek* (1889) 14 App Cas 337.

for the amount so stated has been paid up, then no allotment shall be made unless that minimum amount has been subscribed and the sum so payable has been paid up. Where a prospectus states that an application has been made for permission to have the shares traded on a stock exchange or a regulated market, any allotment made on an application under such a prospectus shall be void if the permission has not been applied for within three days of the issue of the prospectus or if the permission has not been granted within six weeks from the date of the closing of the subscription lists.[55] Where the permission has not been applied for or has not been granted the company shall repay all money received from the applicants on foot of the prospectus.[56]

The Irish Stock Exchange Requirements

Where, as is usual, the shares are the subject of a flotation, the issue must also comply with the requirements of the Stock Exchange. While it is possible to invite the public to subscribe for shares and debentures without seeking Stock Exchange approval, this is uncommon, for two reasons. First, unless shares are dealt with on the Stock Exchange, they will have little attraction for the investor. Second, where an offer is made or a placement effected with the assistance of an issuing house, there will usually be an insistence that the Stock Exchange requirements are met in so far as they are applicable. The minimum requirements laid down by the Stock Exchange in this regard have been given the force of law by the European Communities (Stock Exchange) Regulations 1984.[57] Where a company seeks an official listing on a listed market in Ireland, it must also produce listing particulars and comply with the Listing Rules of the Stock Exchange. The Listing Rules provide for the conditions for admission to listing, the requirements of sponsors, listing applications and continuing obligation requirements for all companies whose shares are traded on the Irish Stock Exchange. If the listing rules are contravened by the issuer it may be liable to censure and in certain cases the Stock Exchange may suspend or cancel the listing of the issuer's securities, or any class thereof. If contravention of the listing rules is due to a failure of all or any of the issuer's directors to discharge their responsibilities under they may also be subject to censure. Further, in the case of wilful or persistent failure by a director to discharge his responsibilities following such a censure, the Stock Exchange may state publicly that in its opinion the retention of office by the director is prejudicial to the interests of investors. If the director remains in office following such a statement the issuer's securities may be suspended or cancelled.

---

55 Section 57(1) of the Principal Act.
56 Section 57(2) of the Principal Act.
57 SI 282/1984.

CHAPTER TEN

MAINTENANCE OF SHARE CAPITAL

Introduction

A company will raise its capital from members in the form of equity and from creditors in the form of loan capital. It relies on this capital to expand its business. Without it, the coffers of the company will run dry and the business will stagnate. The extent of the company's share capital is a primary indicator of the company's credit worthiness. If the company's owners are not prepared to invest more than the legal minimum, which can be as little as €1 in the case of a single-member private limited company, what message does that send to prospective creditors of the company? The law jealously guards the capital base of the company and will not permit indiscriminate accretions from that base except in the most limited of circumstances. Before considering the legal provisions relating to the maintenance of share capital, it is appropriate at this stage to distinguish between a company's authorised share capital and its issued share capital.

1. Authorised Share Capital

In the case of a company with a share capital, the capital clause must state the amount of the share capital with which the company proposes to be registered and the division of that share capital into shares of fixed amounts. This 'authorised' share capital is itself of little significance because it represents merely a notional amount, which the company may issue without having to go through the formalities of increasing the capital. It is not unusual to find grossly undercapitalised companies with an authorised share capital of millions.

2. Issued Share Capital

Issued share capital is the nominal value of the shares which have been allotted and issued to members and for which they have paid or have agreed to pay. In practice it is usual to pay the full price on shares shortly after they have been issued, although on occasion prospective investors may be encouraged to take up a new issue on the basis that payment will be by way of instalments. In any case, it is the issued share capital of the company that reflects the true level of capitalisation, and it is this capital base that the law regards as next to sacrosanct, so much so that as far back as 1892 it was a judicial decision, as opposed to a legislative one, which prohibited the issuance of a company's shares at a discount.[1] Fortunately this rule is now enshrined in legislation.[2]

---

1 *Ooregum Gold Mining Co. v. Roper* [1892] AC 125. See Chapter 9.
2 Section 27(1) of the 1983 Amendment Act.

Alteration of Share Capital

Section 68 of the Principal Act provides that a company, if authorised to do so by its articles, may in general meeting alter its existing share capital in any of the following ways:

(a) increase its share capital by new shares of such amount agreed by the company;

(b) consolidate and divide all or any of its share capital into shares of a larger amount than its existing shares;

(c) convert its paid-up shares, if any, into stock, and reconvert that stock into paid-up shares of any denominations;

(d) subdivide any or all of its shares into shares of a smaller amount, provided that in the subdivision the proportion between the amount paid and the amount, if any, unpaid on each reduced share shall be the same as it was in the case of the share from which the reduced share is derived;

(e) cancel shares which have not been taken or agreed to be taken by any person and diminish the amount of its share capital by the amount of the shares so cancelled.

1. Increase in Share Capital

A company may resolve, if so authorised by its articles of association, to increase the amount of its authorised share capital. Table A only requires the passing of an ordinary resolution to effect such a change. Within one month of making any increase above the registered capital, the company must deliver to the registrar notice of the increase and the registrar must record the increase.[3] Obviously, where a change is being made to the memorandum of association to reflect the increased capital a copy of the altered memorandum must also be sent to the registrar.

2. Reduction of Share Capital

Section 72(1) of the Principal Act contains an express prohibition on the reduction of share capital by a limited company. However, the general prohibition is subject to a number of exceptions and section 72(2) provides that, subject to confirmation by the court, a company may by special resolution, where the articles of association so permit (Table A does so permit), reduce its share capital by any of the following means:

(a) extinguish or reduce the liability on partly paid shares;

(b) cancel any paid-up share capital which is lost or is no longer represented by available assets;

---

3 Section 70(1) of the Principal Act.

(c) pay off any paid-up share capital which is in excess of the needs of the company.

When the company passes the resolution to reduce its share capital it must then apply to the court for a confirmation of the reduction.[4] When the company petitions the court to confirm the reduction, the procedure to be followed will vary depending on the potential effect of the reduction on the company's ability to pay its debts. In certain circumstances the reduction will not be confirmed unless the creditors have agreed to it, or they have had their debts discharged or secured.[5] Those circumstances are where the reduction involves:

(a) a diminution of liability in respect of unpaid share capital; or
(b) the payment to shareholders of any paid-up share capital; or
(c) any other reduction where the court so directs.

The court may decide that these provisions will not apply as regards any class or classes of creditors.[6]

Once the court is satisfied that every creditor has either consented to the reduction or has had their debt discharged or secured it may make the order confirming the reduction on such terms and conditions as it thinks fit.[7] The court in making such an order may authorise the company to be re-registered as another form of company without it having passed a special resolution. The court may also specify the change to be made to the company's memorandum and articles of association. The court may also order the company to add the words 'and reduced', or the Irish equivalent, to its name or to publish the reasons for the reduction.[8]

Even if the statutory formalities have been satisfied, the court will not sanction the reduction unless the majority shareholders in authorising the reduction were exercising their powers in good faith.[9] Similarly, the reduction must be equitable between the various classes of shareholders involved.[10]

Where the reduction involves a variation of class rights the consent of the class must be obtained.[11] In *Re Old Silkstone Collieries*[12] the company purported to repay part of its capital and in doing so agreed that the preference shareholders would obtain a priority claim in the final distribution of any surplus assets. When the second reduction of share capital was proposed which would have the effect

---

4 Section 73(1) of the Principal Act.
5 Section 73(2) of the Principal Act.
6 Section 73(3) of the Principal Act.
7 Section 74(1) of the Principal Act.
8 Section 74(2) of the Principal Act
9 *Re John Power & Sons Ltd* [1934] IR 412.
10 *Re Holders Investment Trust* [1971] 2 All ER 289.
11 Section 38 of the 1983 Amendment Act. See variation of class rights in Chapter 8.
12 [1954] 1 All ER 68.

of repaying the preference shareholders, they objected on the basis that the total repayment would prevent them from obtaining their interest in the remaining assets. It was held that this was a variation of class rights and since the necessary consent of the class had not been obtained the reduction would not be approved.

Where a reduction is approved a copy of the court order confirming the reduction and of a court-approved minute showing the altered share capital must be delivered to the registrar of companies who must then register the order and minute.[13] The registrar will then issue a certificate of registration which is conclusive evidence that all the requirements of the Act relating to the reduction have been complied with and that the share capital of the company is such as is stated in the minute. On registration the resolution for reducing the share capital takes effect. Where the reduction brings the allotted share capital of the company below the authorised minimum, it must be re-registered as another form of company.[14]

As well as the formal methods described above, the capital of a company may be reduced without the need for court confirmation. Shares may be forfeited or surrendered for non-payment of a call, provided the articles of association so authorise. The court is also empowered under certain provisions of the Companies Acts to order a company to purchase the shares of its members.

3. Loss of Capital

When a company incurs trading losses the capital base of the company will be diminished. Such an occurrence is involuntary and cannot therefore be the subject of any legislative prohibition. However, section 40(1) of the 1983 Amendment Act requires that where the net assets of the company fall below half or less of the company's called-up share capital, the directors must convene an extraordinary general meeting of the company, for the purpose of considering what measures, if any, should be taken to deal with the situation. The meeting must be held not later than twenty-eight days from the date on which such a situation became known to any director.

4. Purchase by a Company of its Own Shares

As far back as 1887 the House of Lords held in *Trevor v. Whitworth*[15] that a company could not purchase its own shares because this would cause a reduction of capital. This common law prohibition did not apply where the shares were given to a company by way of a gift and held by a nominee.[16] Thus in *Re*

---

13 Section 75(1) of the Principal Act.
14 Section 17(3) of the 1983 Amendment Act.
15 (1887) 12 App Cas 409 HL.
16 Section 42 of the 1983 Amendment Act extends the prohibition to the purchase of shares by a nominee of a company. Section 42(5) and (6) does provide for exceptions to this rule in limited circumstances.

Castigliones Will Trusts[17] a will provided that 1,000 fully paid-up shares were to be held in trust for the testator's son, but in the event that his son died without issue, the shares were to be transferred to the company. Following the death of the son the gift to the company was upheld provided the shares were transferred to a nominee for the company.

The modern statutory prohibition on a limited company purchasing its own shares is found in section 41 of the 1983 Amendment Act.[18] If a company purports to do so, the transaction is void and the company and every officer in default is guilty of an offence.[19] Despite the general prohibition, there are statutory exceptions:

(a) the acquisition of fully paid shares otherwise than for valuable consideration;
(b) the redemption of shares in pursuance of section 65 of the Principal Act or the redemption or purchase of shares in pursuance of Part XI of the 1990 Act;
(c) the purchase of shares in pursuance of a court order under section 15 of the 1983 Amendment Act or under section 205(10) of the Principal Act;
(d) the forfeiture or the acceptance of shares surrendered in lieu of forfeiture.

Despite the general prohibition contained in section 41, section 211 of the 1990 Act permits a company, if so authorised by its articles of association, to purchase its own shares subject to certain conditions, which also attach to the redemption of shares (discussed below). However, the purchase must not cause the nominal value of the non-redeemable share capital to be reduced below one-tenth of the total issued share capital.[20] Public limited companies which purchase their own shares must also comply with the additional requirements of the European Communities (Public Limited Companies Subsidiaries) Regulations 1997.[21]

The rules in relation to a purchase differ depending on whether the company is buying the shares in a market or off-market purchase.

Off-Market Purchases

An off-market purchase is one where the shares are purchased otherwise than on a recognised Stock Exchange or are purchased on a Stock Exchange but are not subject to a marketing arrangement on that Stock Exchange.[22] Shares are subject

---

17 [1958] Ch 549.
18 As amended by section 232(a) of the 1990 Act. A similar statutory prohibition had appeared in section 72 of the Principal Act along with the prohibition on reducing capital, but that part of the section was repealed by section 231(2) of the Companies Act 1990.
19 Section 41(3) of the 1983 Amendment Act.
20 Section 211(3) of the 1990 Act.
21 SI 67/1997, which gives effect to Council Directive 92/101/EEC, which amends the Second Company Directive.
22 Section 212(1)(a) of the 1990 Act.

to a marketing arrangement if they are listed on the Stock Exchange or the company has been afforded ongoing dealing facilities on the Stock Exchange.[23] A company can only buy its own shares off-market in pursuance of an authorised contract, the terms of which have been approved in advance by a special resolution of the company.[24] Such a resolution will not be effective if:

(a) the seller, where he is a member of the company, carries the vote by exercising his voting right over those shares which are the subject of the resolution;[25] or
(b) a copy of the proposed contract, or a memorandum of its details where the contract is not in writing, is not available for inspection at the company's registered office for twenty-one days before the meeting at which the authorising resolution is to be passed and at the meeting itself.[26]

Contingent Purchase Contracts

A contingent purchase contract is one whereby the company may at some future time become entitled to, or obliged to, purchase its own shares. Such a purchase can only occur on a contingent basis, if the contract has been approved in advance and the off-market purchase rules have been observed.

Market Purchases

A market purchase is one where the shares are purchased on a recognised Stock Exchange and are subject to a marketing arrangement.[27] The conditions attached to market purchases are less onerous than those attached to off-market purchases. A company can only buy its shares in a market purchase if it has been authorised in advance by an ordinary resolution of the company in general meeting.[28] There is no requirement that the contract itself must be authorised. The authority must, however, specify the maximum number of shares which may be acquired and the minimum prices which must be paid for the shares. A printed copy of the resolution must be forwarded to the registrar of companies.[29]

Where a public company proposes to make either a market or a non-market purchase, the authorisation by the general meeting must specify the date on which the authority is to expire, which must not exceed eighteen months after the date on which the resolution granting the authority is passed.[30] In the event that

---

23 Section 212(2) of the 1990 Act.
24 Section 213 of the 1990 Act.
25 Section 213(3) of the 1990 Act.
26 Section 213(5) of the 1990 Act.
27 Section 212(b) of the 1990 Act.
28 Section 215(1) of the 1990 Act.
29 Section 215(2) of the 1990 Act.
30 Section 216(1) of the 1990 Act.

the contract to purchase the shares was concluded before the authority expired, and the authority had provided for such an exigency, the contract may be executed wholly or partly after the expiry date.[31]

Purchase by subsidiary of shares in its holding company.

A company may acquire and hold shares in a company which is its holding company subject to the following provisions:[32]

(a) the consideration for this purchase is provided out of the profits of the subsidiary available for distribution;
(b) from the time of the acquisition, and while the subsidiary holds the shares, the profits of the subsidiary available for distribution shall be restricted by a sum equal to the total cost of the shares acquired, the shares are treated for consolidating accounting purposes as treasury shares and the subsidiary shall not exercise any voting rights in respect of those shares;
(c) the contract for the acquisition of the shares is authorised in advance by the subsidiary and the holding company.

If a company has acquired shares in its holding company and is wound up within six months of such an acquisition, and is unable to pay its debts, the court may declare that the directors of the company shall be jointly and severally liable to repay to the company the amount paid for the shares.[33] The court may relieve any persons from personal liability if they believed on reasonable grounds that the purchase was in the best interests of the company.[34]

5. Redemption of Shares

Section 207 of the 1990 Act empowers any company, where the articles so authorise, to issue redeemable shares and redeem them accordingly. Redeemable shares can only be issued provided that at least 10 per cent of the nominal value of the issued shares is non-redeemable and the terms of any redemption offer provide for payment on redemption. Once issued, the shares can only be redeemed in the manner provided for by the articles and where each of the following conditions is satisfied:

(a) the shares must be fully paid;
(b) the redemption can only be made out of the profits available for distribution or, in the case of a proposed cancellation of the shares, on redemption out of the proceeds of a fresh issue of redeemable shares.

---

31 Section 216(2) of the 1990 Act.
32 Section 224 of the 1990 Act.
33 Section 225(1) of the 1990 Act.
34 Section 225(2) of the 1990 Act.

Cancellation on Redemption

Redeemed shares may be cancelled on redemption. Where they are cancelled on redemption the company's issued share capital can be reduced by the nominal value of the shares redeemed.[35] However, an amount equal to the nominal value of the shares redeemed or, if there has been an issue made to fund the redemption and the value of the new shares is less than the value of the redeemed shares, the difference in value between the shares redeemed and the new shares issued for the purpose of the redemption, must be transferred to the fund called the Capital Redemption Reserve Fund. Accordingly, the company's former capital is not reduced, as one type of capital is substituted for another. This fund, like the share premium account, is treated in the same manner as paid-up capital but it may be applied in paying up bonus issues, thus converting it to share capital. When shares are redeemed from a fresh issue of shares they must be cancelled on redemption.

Treasury Shares

If shares are not cancelled on redemption or if a company purchases its own shares under section 211 of the 1990 Act, they may be retained by the company as treasury shares. Treasury shares are of little use as they do not confer any of the typical rights of a shareholder on the company that now holds them. The company cannot vote using those shares, it cannot receive dividends on the basis of those shares and they confer no rights in a winding up. The value of treasury shares cannot exceed 10 per cent of the nominal value of the issued share capital. Shares which have been retained as treasury shares can be re-issued provided certain conditions are complied with.[36]

Redemption at a Premium

If the shares are being repaid at a premium, then the premium can only be paid out of distributable profits[37] unless the redemption is being paid for out of the proceeds of a fresh issue of shares for that purpose, and in that case the premium can only be paid up to an amount equal to the lesser of:

(a) the aggregate of the premiums received by the company on the issue of the shares being redeemed; or

(b) the current amount in the company's share premium account including the amount transferred to that account in respect of premiums on the newly issued shares.

---

35 Section 208 of the 1990 Act.
36 Section 209(6) of the 1990 Act.
37 See Chapter 12.

Notification to the Registrar

Where a company has purchased shares or redeemed shares in the manner described above, it must, within twenty-eight days after delivery to the company of those shares, deliver to the registrar for registration a return in the prescribed form that states, with respect to shares of each class purchased, the number and nominal value of those shares and the date on which they were delivered to the company.[38] A copy of the purchase contract must also be kept at the company's registered office for ten years.[39]

Section 89 Validation

Where a company has acquired shares by redemption or purchase and those shares were invalidly acquired, the court may, under section 89 of the Principal Act, declare the acquisition valid if it considers it just and equitable to do so.[40] The court will not make such a declaration in relation to redeemable shares in the following circumstances:

(a) where they are redeemed otherwise than out of profits available for distribution; or

(b) where the premium payable on redemption, if any, is paid for otherwise than out of profits available for distribution; or

(c) where the premium payable on the redemption of shares issued at a premium is made out of a fresh issue of shares and exceeds the lessor of either the aggregate premiums received by the company on the issue of the shares redeemed, or the current amount of the company's share premium account; or

(d) if a special resolution authorising the issue has not been passed.

Furthermore, the court in granting relief, under section 89, may direct that the company and its officers are not relieved of liability in relation to the purchase by a company of its own shares.

Duty to Notify the Stock Exchange

Where a company has dealing facilities or a recognised stock exchange and its shares have been purchased in the manner described above, it must notify the Stock Exchange which may publish information received by it.[41] In certain

---

38 Section 226 of the 1990 Act provides that public limited companies must comply with further notification requirements in this regard.

39 Section 222 of the 1990 Act.

40 See Chapter 9 and *Re Sugar Distributors Ltd* [1995] 2 IR 195.

41 Section 229 of the 1990 Act.

instances, the Stock Exchange must notify the Director of Corporate Enforcement of unlawful purchases which come to its attention.[42]

6. Financial Assistance for Purchasing Shares

The general prohibition on a company giving financial assistance to enable a third party to purchase its shares is found in section 60(1) of the Principal Act. For the purpose of the section, the prohibition applies to financial assistance given directly or indirectly, whether by way of a loan, a guarantee or the provision of security. The prohibition extends to the giving of financial assistance by a company for the purposes of purchasing shares in that company's holding company. Although section 60 gives an indication of the matters that will constitute financial assistance, this list is not exhaustive. In *Charterhouse Investment Trust Ltd v. Tempest Diesels Ltd,*[43] Hoffman J. stated:

> the words have no technical meaning and their frame of reference is in my judgment the language of ordinary commerce. One must examine the commercial realities of the transaction and decide whether it can possibly be described as the giving of financial assistance by the company.[44]

The commercial reality test was applied by the High Court in *Re CH (Ireland) (in liquidation).*[45] It found that a circuitous set of transactions entered into by a number of parties, which began with the deposit by CHI of certain monies and ended with the purchase by another company of shares in CHI, was the giving of financial assistance within the meaning of section 60. Section 60(14) declares that any transaction in breach of the section is voidable at the instance of the company against any person who had notice of the facts constituting a breach. In *Bank of Ireland v. Rockfields,*[46] the Supreme Court held that 'notice' for the purpose of the subsection meant 'actual' rather than constructive notice.[47] A sanction is also imposed by section 60(15) of the Principal Act, which provides that every officer in default is liable to a fine or imprisonment, or to both.

Because the giving of financial assistance may in certain circumstances be unobjectionable, section 60 provides for a number of exceptions to the general rule. The principal exception is contained in section 60(2), which only applies to private companies.[48] Under this subsection the prohibition on a company providing financial assistance for the purchase of its own shares will not apply if

---

42 Section 230 of the 1990 Act.
43 [1987] BCLC 7.
44 Ibid. at 10.
45 [1999] 4 IR 542.
46 [1979] 2 IR 21.
47 See also *Eccles Hall Ltd v. Bank of Nova Scotia,* Unreported, High Court, Murphy J., February 3, 1995.
48 Section 60(15A) of the Principal Act as inserted by para. 10 of the First Schedule of the 1983 Amendment Act excluded this right from public limited companies.

the following conditions are satisfied. First, an authorising special resolution must be passed by the members in general meeting and second, a statutory declaration of solvency must be sworn by the directors of the company. In *Re Northside Motors Co. Ltd,*[49] Eddison owned half the shares in the plaintiff company in advance of the purchase. Wishing to acquire the remainder, the defendant advanced finance to another company which was owned by Eddison. The security for the loan was a guarantee from the plaintiff company. When the bank became aware that the procedures under section 60(2) had not been observed, it demanded that the company pass the appropriate resolution and that the directors make the necessary statutory declaration of solvency. The company acquiesced with the bank's request. Some time later the company honoured its commitments under the guarantee. When it was subsequently wound up, the liquidator sought the recovery of the money paid out under the guarantee. Costello J. held that the company had given financial assistance within the meaning of section 60 and the resolution and statutory declaration could not retrospectively validate the breach.

The special resolution must be passed within twelve months prior to the financial assistance being provided.[50] Every member of the company, notwithstanding any provisions in the articles to the contrary, must be given notice of the meeting at which the special resolution will be proposed.[51] The notice must be accompanied by a copy of the statutory declaration by the directors.[52] In the event that the members do not unanimously vote in favour of the resolution, the assistance must not be provided for at least thirty days to enable dissenting shareholders, holding at least 10 per cent of the nominal value of the company's issued share capital, to apply to the court for the cancellation of the special resolution.[53] In the event that such an application is made within twenty-eight days from the date of passing of the resolution, the special resolution will have no effect until confirmed by the court.[54] In *Lombard & Ulster Banking Ltd v Bank of Ireland*[55], it was held that an informal agreement by all the shareholders would not be an appropriate substitute for a special resolution authorising the giving of financial assistance. Therefore a subsequent verification of those acts could not substitute for the formal procedure required under section 60. However, section 60 has since been amended and provides that a resolution in writing signed by all the members shall be as valid as a special resolution passed at a duly convened meeting.[56]

---

49 Unreported, High Court, Costello J., July 24, 1985.
50 Section 60(2)(a) of the Principal Act.
51 Section 60(6) of the Principal Act.
52 Section 60(2)(b) of the Principal Act.
53 Section 60(7) of the Principal Act.
54 Section 60(8) of the Principal Act.
55 Unreported, High Court, Costello J., June 2, 1987.
56 Applying section 141(8) relating to informal resolutions to section 60.

The statutory declaration of solvency must be sworn by the directors of the company not more than twenty-four days before the meeting at which the special resolution is proposed.[57] The declaration must state the following:

(a) the form which the assistance is to take;
(b) the persons to whom such assistance is to be given;
(c) the purpose for which the company intends those persons to use such assistance;
(d) that the declarants, having made a full enquiry into the affairs of the company, have formed the opinion that the company, having given the financial assistance, will be able to pay its debts as they become due.[58]

A copy of the statutory declaration must be sent to the registrar of companies within 21 days after the date on which the financial assistance was given. Where any director makes the statutory declaration without having reasonable grounds for their opinion as to the solvency of the company, the penalties are severe. Such directors will be liable to a fine or imprisonment or both.[59] In the event that a company is wound up within twelve months after the making of the statutory declaration and its debts are not paid within the twelve months from the commencement of the winding up, it shall be presumed, until the contrary is shown, that the director did not have reasonable grounds for his opinion. Of course, this presumption may be rebutted.

Transactions which are not prohibited

The prohibition contained in section 60 does not apply to any of the following transactions:

(a) the payment by a company of a dividend properly declared;[60]
(b) the discharge of a liability lawfully incurred by the company;[61]
(c) the provision of finance or security for the purpose of refinancing a loan that had been made under the authority of a special resolution in accordance with the exception provided for by s.160(2);[62]
(d) lending in the ordinary course of business;[63]
(e) the provision of money for the purchase of, or subscription for, fully paid shares in the company or its holding company where such is for the benefit

---

57 Section 60(3) of the Principal Act.
58 Section 60(4) of the Principal Act.
59 Section 60(5) of the Principal Act.
60 Section 60(12)(a) of the Principal Act.
61 Section 60(12)(b) of the Principal Act.
62 Section 60(12)(c) of the Principal Act.
63 Section 60(12)(d) of the Principal Act.

of employees or former employees (including salaried directors or former salaried directors) of the company or its subsidiaries;[64]

(f) the giving of loans to persons, other than directors, *bona fide* in the employment of the company to enable those persons to purchase or subscribe for fully paid shares in the company or its holding company;[65]

(g) the making or giving by a company of one of more representations, warranties or indemnities to a person who has purchased or subscribed or proposes to purchase or subscribe for shares in the company or its holding company for the purposes of that purchase or subscription;[66]

(h) the payment of fees and expenses of the advisers of any subscriber for shares in the company or its holding company where those fees and expenses are incurred in connection with that subscription;[67]

(i) the incurring of expenses in relation to the preparation and publication of a prospectus or for the purpose of facilitating the admission of shares of the company or its holding company on a regulated market or other securities market, or for the purpose of ensuring compliance with takeover rules and related matters.

These exemptions apply to both private and public companies. However, in the case of those loans mentioned in (d), (e) or (f) above a public company can only give financial assistance where the company's net assets are not thereby reduced and if so reduced provided the financial assistance is given out of profits available for distribution.

---

64 Section 60(12)(e) of the Principal Act.
65 Section 60(12)(f) of the Principal Act.
66 Section 60(12)(g) of the Principal Act.
67 Section 60(12)(h) of the Principal Act.

CHAPTER ELEVEN

LOAN CAPITAL AND CHARGES

Introduction

The company's capacity to borrow will be determined by the objects clause of the memorandum. In the absence of an express power, a trading company is assumed to have an implied power to borrow for a purpose incidental to that trade.[1] If a company has an express or implied power to borrow, it will also have an implied power to give security for those borrowings. While the company is usually conferred with unlimited borrowing powers, it is normal, and obligatory in the case of listed companies, to impose restrictions on the amount that directors can borrow on the company's behalf. Article 79, Table A, confers an express authority on directors to borrow and to secure those borrowings by way of mortgage or charge. However, where limits are imposed on the amount that can be borrowed, these can only be exceeded with the prior sanction of the general meeting.

When a company borrows money it will often be required to provide security for the repayment of the amounts borrowed. Usually the company will issue debentures which are secured by a charge over some or all of the company's assets. From the lender's point of view a charge is an attractive form of security for the following reasons:

(a) the secured creditor may obtain a measure of control over the business of the debtor by the imposition of certain restrictive conditions and events of default in the loan and security documentation;

(b) in the event that the company defaults, the secured creditor will generally have a right of enforcement;

(c) in the event that the company becomes insolvent, a secured creditor will enjoy a priority over an unsecured creditor as to repayment;

(d) if the charge is fixed the charge holder will generally have a priority over the preferential creditors.[2]

Charges may be categorised in terms of either fixed charges or floating charges. However, it is not uncommon for security arrangements to incorporate both types of charge.

---

1 See Chapter 7.

2 However, fixed charges over book debts may be subordinated to certain preferential creditors: see section 115 of the Finance Act 1986 as amended by section 174 of the Finance Act 1995, now section 1001 of the Taxes Consolidated Act 1997.

Fixed Charges

A fixed charge is so called because it is essentially a charge on identifiable property. It attaches, from the moment of its creation, to the property in question. Accordingly, provided the charge is properly registered, the holder has an immediate security over the property.

If the company disposes of the asset which is the subject matter of the charge, it must either repay the loan amount out of the proceeds of the sale before legal ownership is transferred, or pass the asset over to the purchaser still subject to the charge. The latter would be a most unusual occurrence. Therefore a fixed charge is best suited to long-term assets that do not change frequently. Otherwise, every time a charged asset is disposed of the company would need to obtain the consent of the charge holder and draw up and register the appropriate deeds of release and memoranda of satisfaction. Furthermore, any new asset acquired would then have to be charged to replace the old security. The expenses involved in such a process would be prohibitive.

Floating Charges

A floating charge is a charge on the property of a company which is constantly changing, for example the stock-in-trade of a business or the assets or undertaking for the time being of a company. The advantage of this form of security is that it allows companies which do not have a solid asset base, in the form of identifiable long-term assets, to raise debt capital on the back of stock-in-trade, raw materials and work-in-progress. The nature of the floating charge was described by Romer LJ. in the case of *Re Yorkshire Woolcombers Association*[3] as:

(a) a charge on a class of assets of a company present and future;
(b) which class is, in the ordinary course of the company's business, changing from time to time; and
(c) until the holder enforces the charge, the company may carry on business and deal with the assets charged.

Although all three characteristics are usually essential, it would appear from one Irish decision that this is not necessarily the case. In *Welch v. Bowmaker (Ireland) Ltd and Bank of Ireland*,[4] a debenture was issued in favour of Bowmaker which created a specific charge over three of four parcels of land owned by the company, together with a floating charge over its other assets. The terms of the debenture included a 'negative pledge' clause whereby the company pledged not to create any other security over the property which would take priority over the existing charge. One month later the company deposited the title deeds of the fourth parcel of land as security with the Bank of Ireland, which was

---

3 [1903] 2 Ch 284 at 295.
4 [1980] IR 251.

unaware of the terms of the debenture. The company subsequently failed. The court held that a floating charge had been created over the fourth parcel of land and that the fixed charge created by deposit of deeds in favour of the Bank of Ireland took priority. Therefore, although it is unusual to create a floating charge over land, it was held possible to do so.

Crystallisation of the Floating Charge

Up until the point when the holder enforces the security, the floating charge 'hovers' over the assets in question, thus allowing the company to retain autonomy over, and continue to deal with, those assets. Once the security is enforced, the floating charge is said to crystallise. This does not involve any physical change in the nature of the assets — rather it is a process by which the floating charge is converted into a fixed charge on the occurrence of certain events. It has traditionally been accepted that one of the following events will trigger the crystallisation of a floating charge:

(a) the company ceases to trade, usually by the intervention of the debenture-holder;[5]
(b) the appointment of a receiver;[6]
(c) the liquidation of the company.[7]

When crystallisation occurs the charge is no longer said to be hovering, as it now attaches to the assets. From that point the company is no longer free to deal with those assets without the permission of the charge holder. Generally, the holder of the floating charge will appoint a receiver to collect and realise the assets. However, the receiver must first account to the preferential creditors for the amounts owed by the company.[8] This provision is necessary to safeguard the company from pre-emptive actions by floating charge holders who attempt to realise their security at a time which maximises their position but not that of the company or the other creditors. By virtue of section 98, a receiver will therefore be required to pay off the preferential creditors before he can apply any of the proceeds in discharge of the floating charge holders' debts.[9]

1. The Floating Charge as a Primary Security

While the floating charge was at its inception an adequate solution to the need for secured debt-capital, it has one major flaw, which is its susceptibility to having its priority postponed to subsequent fixed charges over the company's property [10] or to

---

5 *Re Woodroffes (Musical Instruments) Ltd* [1985] BCLC 227.
6 *Halpin v. Cremin* [1954] IR 19.
7 *Re Crompton & Co. Ltd* [1914] 1 Ch 954.
8 Section 98 of the Principal Act.
9 See Chapter 24 – Receivers.
10 *Wheatley v. Silkstone and Haigh Moor Coal Co.* [1885] 29 Ch D 715.

an increasing number of statutorily preferred creditors.[11] Furthermore, if a company is wound up before a floating charge is realised, the costs of the liquidation must be paid from the assets of the company in priority to all claims, including floating charges.[12] Taken together, these priority positions could represent a substantial erosion in the assets that would otherwise be available to the floating charge holder.

2. Negative Pledge Clauses

One technique employed to protect the holder of the floating charge against any subsequent security interest was the insertion of a clause — referred to as a 'negative pledge' clause — into the charge. The effect of such a clause is that the company is restricted from creating any further security interests which would have priority over the floating charge. The clause, which now appears in most standard charges, merely attempts to limit the authority of the company to issue any further security over the assets in question. If the company subsequently breaches the pledge and grants a fixed charge over the assets in question, that holder of the fixed charge will enjoy a priority position over the floating charge holder. This is because even though the holder of the fixed charge is deemed to have constructive knowledge of the existence of the floating charge, he is not deemed to have knowledge of the contents of that charge and therefore will not have knowledge of the 'negative pledge' made by the company.

In *Wilson v. Kelland*[13] the company had issued a floating charge to a creditor which incorporated a negative pledge clause. The company later, in breach of the negative pledge, granted a fixed charge over the same assets. The fixed charge holder had not made a search in the Companies Office and was unaware of the existence of the previous charge. It was argued that the fixed charge holder had constructive notice of the floating charge and its contents. The court accepted that the holder of the fixed charge had constructive notice of the floating charge, but he was not deemed to have notice of the negative pledge clause as this information was not required by law to be registered. The only way the floating charge holder will retain a priority position is to prove that the fixed charge holder had actual knowledge of the 'negative pledge' clause.[14] If the floating charge holder cannot prove this actual knowledge, then the only other recourse available is to sue the company for breach of contract. As the company is likely to be insolvent at that stage, any damages payable for the breach will form only part of the unsecured claims. On this basis the use of the negative pledge clauses in charges can be viewed as a source of comfort only.

---

11 Section 285 of the Principal Act: see Chapter 26.
12 See Chapter 26 with respect to the distribution of assets in a winding up.
13 [1910] 2 Ch 306.
14 *English & Scottish Mercantile Investment Co. Ltd v. Brunton* [1892] 2 QB 700.

3. Other Devices

The continued deterioration of the floating charge holder's position has forced creditors to take account of the risks involved in employing a floating charge as the primary security. The alternative solution of relying on non-security devices such as 'retention of title' clauses is not an option available to a lending bank which is supplying loans rather than goods. The solutions which have been developed to circumvent the diminishing effect of the floating charge have been twofold. First, attempts were made to revert to the pre-1880 method of employing the fixed charge. The difficulty here was that while the fixed charge was readily acceptable when it related to land and buildings, when it came to extending it to include revolving assets, particularly book debts, controversy arose. The other solution was to stipulate in the debenture that a floating charge would automatically crystallise on the occurrence of a specified event or events of default, thus converting it to a fixed charge without any action needed on the part of the charge holder.

Fixed Charges over Book Debts

The ability of a creditor to create a floating charge over future book debts received judicial support as far back as 1883.[15] However, it is only in the past thirty years that the position with respect to taking fixed security over such assets has been addressed, although some confusion stills surrounds the issue. Traditionally, it was considered impossible to take a fixed charge over assets, such as book debts, which are by their very nature changing from day to day. It is for this reason that it was always considered more appropriate to take a floating charge over such assets. However, in the English decision of *Siebe Gorman v. Barclay's Bank Ltd*[16] the validity of a fixed charge over book debts was upheld. The charge in question provided that the proceeds of the book debts should be placed into a specially designated bank account, withdrawals from which were permitted only with the consent of the charge holder. It was this element of 'control', a necessary feature of the fixed charge, that persuaded the court that the charge was fixed.

The first Irish case which addressed the issue was *Re Keenan Bros Ltd.*[17] Here, the charge was taken over the company's book debts, the proceeds of which were lodged to a bank account under the terms of the debenture. The charge also provided that withdrawals could not be made from that account without the consent of the charge holder. When the company was subsequently wound up, the Revenue Commissioners argued that, despite the description of the charge, it was in substance a floating charge because the bank, while retaining control over the

---

15 *Tailby v. Official Receiver* (1883) 13 App Cas 523.
16 [1979] 2 Lloyd's Reports 142.
17 [1985] IR 401.

asset, continually gave the company permission to withdraw monies from that account. According to the Revenue, this continued use by the company of the assets charged was a feature of a floating charge and not a fixed charge. Although the Supreme Court accepted the validity of the substance over form argument, it concluded that the charge in question was a fixed charge. The court was persuaded that an essential feature of a fixed charge — its immediate attachment to the assets — was a feature of the charge in question because the company was only permitted to deal with the assets charged to the extent permitted by the charge holder. Furthermore, the charged assets were so withdrawn from their ordinary trade use by putting them in the 'control' of the debenture holder that the charge constituted a fixed charge. On the basis of the decision in *Re Keenan Bros*[18] it seemed that a necessary requisite of a fixed charge over book debts was that the book debts, having been collected, should be paid into a designated bank account. This would seem to be the only method of maintaining control over the assets by the charge holder. However, in *Re Wogan's (Drogheda) Ltd*[19] this requirement appeared to be disregarded by Finlay CJ. who held that any delay or suspension in the operation of the proceeds account should not deprive a lender of his rights under a fixed charge. Rather, it was sufficient that the charge gave the holder the right to designate a proceeds account which he would control. Such a liberal approach was not accepted by the Supreme Court in *Re Holidair Ltd*.[20] The charge in question was described as a fixed charge and provided that the debenture-holder could designate a bank account into which the proceeds of book debts were to be paid. The charge did not restrict the company from using the proceeds of the book debts in the ordinary course of business. Accordingly the Supreme Court held that despite its description, the charge satisfied the criteria of a floating charge.

The advantage of obtaining a fixed charge over book debts has been eroded to some degree by the enactment of section 115 of the Finance Act 1986, as amended.[21] The effect of this section is that the holder of a fixed charge over book debts will be primarily liable for certain VAT and PAYE amounts owed by the company which issued the charge unless certain qualifications arise. However, the charge over book debts is still used by lenders for practical as well as legal reasons. First, it gives lenders control over the assets charged. Second, as the proceeds are lodged to the bank account, the charge holder can see the weekly income stream building up. This gives a very accurate insight into the business of the company which the normal creditor is not privy to. Finally, a fixed charge over book debts cannot be avoided by a liquidator under section 288 of the Principal Act. (See Chapter 25, The Liquidation Process.)

---

18 See also *Re Armagh Shoes Ltd* [1984] BCLC 405.
19 [1993] 1 IR 157.
20 [1994] 1 IR 481.
21 Section 174 of the 1995 Finance Act. See section 1001 Taxes Consolidated Act 1997.

Automatic Crystallisation Clauses

There has been considerable controversy in recent years about the validity of what are termed 'automatic crystallisation' clauses in a debenture. These clauses effectively crystallise the floating charge in an event other than the cessation of trade, the appointment of a receiver and the winding up of a company. In *Re Griffin Hotel Co.*[22] it was held that if a floating charge crystallised before a winding up had commenced, it would not lose its priority to preferential creditors in the event that the liquidator was subsequently appointed. In other words, if the debenture contains provisions which trigger the automatic crystallisation of a floating charge upon the happening of an event, other than those events which cause a floating charge to crystallise at law, does that floating charge become a fixed charge for the purposes of the insolvency queue? The idea behind the automatic crystallisation clauses is that the floating charge is crystallised without the appointment of a receiver. Therefore, the obligation to pay preferential creditors before the floating charge holder which is imposed on a receiver by section 98 of the Principal Act has no application if a receiver has not been appointed. In *Re Brightlife Ltd*,[23] Hoffman J. held that the appointment of a receiver, liquidator or the cessation of business was not an exhaustive list of the events which cause a floating charge to crystallise, and he could not see any reason why parties could not contract their own terms into the debenture or charge.

The public policy arguments against validating such crystallisation clauses are twofold. First, no other party would have notice of the crystallising events, and second, and more importantly, the party would not be aware that the floating charge has in fact crystallised. In the UK the legislature has intervened with the introduction of the 1986 Insolvency Act. It provides that once a charge is created as a floating charge it will always be considered a floating charge for the purpose of establishing its place in the insolvency queue. The issue has yet to be determined in Ireland, but Keane J. has stated extra-judicially[24] that such clauses are unlikely to be accepted in Ireland for the policy reasons mentioned above.

4. Other Disadvantages of Floating Charges

The other disadvantages of the floating charge can be summarised as follows.

(a) A floating charge is in effect a charge over future assets as it does not create immediate rights over identifiable assets. By contrast, a fixed charge is usually a more satisfactory form of security since it confers immediate rights over specific assets. If a creditor has obtained a fixed charge over a building, a quick visit will ensure that the building exists. Of course, the sensible fixed

---

22 [1940] Ch 87.
23 [1986] 3 All ER 673.
24 Keane, *Company Law* (4th edn), Tottel Publishing 2006.

charge holder will ensure that the building is insured and insist on seeing a copy of the insurance certificate. On the other hand, even if the holder of a floating charge inspects the charged assets he will know that those assets will not necessarily be available to him if at some future date he is required to realise his security. As the company is free to deal with them, the holder of a floating charge cannot be certain, until the company fails, which assets will actually form part of his security.

(b) Even when the floating charge crystallises, there is no guarantee that the assets, which fit the generic description of those charged, are in fact subject to the security. A supplier, who in normal circumstances would be an unsecured creditor of the company, may have sold goods only on condition that he is to retain legal ownership until he has been paid. The validity of these 'reservation or retention of title' clauses was recognised as far back as 1893.[25] The proliferation of 'retention of title' clauses clearly causes a problem for the floating charge holder because he is faced with a competing and superior claim, in the form of a supplier, to some of the assets in the company's possession. This problem is exacerbated by the fact that accounting practices dictate that assets, subject to retention of title clauses, should still appear on the buyer's balance sheet. This gives rise to an increased difficulty on the part of the floating charge holder to ascertain, at any particular time, the true worth of his security.

(c) A floating charge, unlike a fixed charge, created in the twelve months (or two years where it is in favour of a connected person) prior to the commencement of a winding up will be avoided by a liquidator under section 288 of the Principal Act as amended, unless certain conditions prevailed at the time. Essentially, if money was paid or goods or services supplied at the time of or subsequently to the creation of the charge and in consideration of the charge, it will not be impugned. Nor will the charge be avoided if it can be shown that the company was solvent immediately after the giving of the charge. The purpose of this statutory provision is to prevent creditors who realise that the insolvent company is on the brink of liquidation from obtaining a priority position by taking security over the company's remaining unencumbered assets which would otherwise have been available for the unsecured creditors.[26]

Registration of Charges

Section 99(1) of the Principal Act requires almost every type of charge to be registered with the registrar of companies within twenty-one days of its creation. Section 100(1) of the Principal Act places the onus of registration on the company which creates the charge. Section 99(2) sets out the types of charge that must be

---

25 Sections 17 and 19 of the Sale of Goods Act 1893. See *Aluminium Industrie Vaassen BV v. Romalpa Aluminium Ltd* [1976] 2 All ER 552.
26 See Chapter 26 for a detailed account of section 288.

registered.[27] It is open to the Minister to alter this list by statutory instrument.[28] The requirement that all charges are registered ensures that creditors can discover the extent to which the assets of a company are used to fund its borrowings. Indeed, this information is equally informative for the members of a company. Having imposed a duty on companies to register their charges, section 103 of the Principal Act imposes an obligation on the registrar of companies to keep, in respect of all companies, a register of charges.

A charge is registered by delivery to the registrar of companies, in the prescribed form, particulars of the charge including, *inter alia,* the following:

(a) the date the charge was created;
(b) the amount of the debt to which the charge applies;
(c) the property to which the charge applies;
(d) the person entitled to it.

If the registrar is satisfied with the particulars, he will issue a certificate of registration to the effect that the charge has been registered in accordance with section 99. The registrar's certificate is conclusive that the charge has been duly registered.[29]

This is so even if the charge had been incorrectly dated. In *Lombard & Ulster Banking Ltd v. Amurec Ltd*,[30] the defendant company issued an undated mortgage over a ballroom premises to the plaintiff bank in November 1972 together with a commitment to provide the appropriate stamping fee. In March 1974, when the stamping fee had not been provided, the bank, using its own funds, had the mortgage stamped and lodged in the Companies Registry Office. The Registrar issued the certificate of registration which certified that the charge was created in March 1974. When the defendant company was subsequently wound up, the liquidator argued that the charge was void because it had not been registered within twenty-one days of its creation. The court held that the certificate of registration was conclusive proof that the registration requirements had been complied with and the charge was valid. Even where other registered particulars are incorrect, such as the amount of the debt to which the charge applies, this will not invalidate the certificate of registration. This is because the court is only giving effect to the document creating the charge and not to the particulars contained in the certificate of registration In *Re Mechanisations (Eaglecliffe) Ltd*,[31] the certificate of registration mis-stated an amount of £18,000 as the debt

---

27 Not all charges are registrable: those that arise by operation of law, for example a banker's lien, do not fall into the category of charges required to be registered under section 99 of the Principal Act.
28 Section 99(2A) and (2B) of the Principal Act.
29 Section 104 of the Principal Act.
30 [1976–1977] ILRM 222.
31 [1964] 3 All ER 840.

to which the charge applied. In fact, the charge also applied to further unspecified amounts owing to the creditor in respect of any goods supplied. When the company was subsequently liquidated the charge holder claimed an amount of £23,000. The liquidator argued that the maximum entitlement was the amount specified in the certificate of registration. The court held that the charge covered the extra sums owing to the creditor, and the fact that incorrect particulars were registered did not affect the creditor's entitlement. This decision has been followed in Ireland in *Re Shannonside Holdings Ltd.*[32]

If the charge is not registered within the specific time frame it becomes void against the liquidator and any creditor of the company. In such a circumstance the loan which has been secured by the charge becomes immediately repayable. If the charge holder demands repayment and the company is not in a position to oblige, the charge holder has the same rights against the company as any unsecured creditor. He may petition the court to have the company wound up.

It is possible to apply to the court for an order to extend the time for registration. Under section 106(1) of the Principal Act the court may order that the time for registration be extended provided it is satisfied that:

(a) the omission was accidental; or
(b) the omission is not of a nature to prejudice the position of the company's creditors or shareholders; or
(c) it is just and equitable to grant such relief.

The court will usually grant such an order unless there is evidence of *male fides* on the part of the applicant.[33] However, it is unlikely to grant the extension where no useful purpose will be served by such an order.[34]

If the company fails to register the charge under section 99 the company and every officer of the company who is in default shall be guilty of an offence.[35] Where the court grants relief under sestion 106(1) it may have the effect, if the court so directs, of relieving the company or its officers of any such liability.[36]

The Register of Charges

Every company is obliged to keep at its registered office a copy of every instrument which creates a registrable charge.[37] Copies of such instruments must be available for inspection by any of the company's creditors or members for at least two hours per working day.[38]

---

32 Unreported, High Court, Costello J., May 20, 1993.
33 *Re Teleomatic Ltd* [1994] 1 BCLC 90.
34 *Re Farm Fresh Frozen Foods Ltd* [1980] ILRM 131.
35 Section 100(3) of the Principal Act.
36 Section 106(2) of the Principal Act.
37 Section 109 of the Principal Act.
38 Section 110(1) of the Principal Act.

Satisfaction of the Charge

When a charge is satisfied, a memorandum of satisfaction of charge, in the prescribed form, should be delivered to the registrar of companies. Once the registrar is satisfied that the debt has been paid in whole or in part and that all or part of the assets or undertaking charged have been released from the charge, he may then enter on the register a memorandum of satisfaction in whole or in part.[39]

---

39 Section 105 of the Principal Act.

CHAPTER TWELVE

MEMBERSHIP

Introduction

Because ownership and control of the company are often separated — a phenomenon more applicable to public companies and large private companies than small private companies — a number of problems arise. These problems range from the loss by the company's primary organ — the general meeting — of its decision-making powers to the potential abuse by the company's officers of their day-to-day control and management of the company's business and undertaking. Both common law and statute have long recognised these problems of corporate governance and have attempted to eliminate them by a series of provisions which make the controllers more accountable to the shareholders while at the same time protecting the position of the shareholder, even where his interest in the company is a minority one. In this and subsequent chapters the position of shareholders and their rights, duties and obligations are discussed.

The Register of Members

Before persons are entitled to any rights in relation to their shares, their name must be entered on the register of members.[1] Section 116 of the Principal Act requires every company to keep a register of members, which must contain the following particulars:

(a) the names, addresses and occupations of the members and, in the case of a company having a share capital, a statement of the shares held by each member, the number of each share (where the shares are numbered) and the amount paid or considered as paid on the shares of each member;
(b) the date at which each person was entered in the register as a member;
(c) the date at which any person ceased to be a member.

The register must be kept within the state at the company's registered office or such other place if work is being done on it. If it is kept anywhere other than the registered office, the registrar of companies must be notified of its location. Where a company has more than fifty members, an index of members must also be maintained unless the register itself is in the form of an index.[2] The register of

---

1 Section 31 of the Principal Act. See *Arulchelvan v. Wright*, Unreported, High Court, Carroll J., February 7, 1996, where the beneficiary of a deceased member's shares was held not to have the right to attend and form part of the quorum at an extraordinary general meeting.
2 Section 117 of the Principal Act.

members must be available for inspection free of charge by members and, subject to a nominal fee, by non-members for at least two hours every business day.[3] Requested copies of the register or a part thereof must be provided within ten days subject to a scrivenery charge. The register may be closed for up to thirty days in each year provided that the closure is advertised.

The register may be rectified by the company where any error or omission has occurred.[4] However, any rectification may not adversely affect any person unless he agrees to the rectification. Notice of any rectification must be sent to the registrar within twenty-one days where any such error or omission appears on any document already sent to him.

The court is also given the power to order the rectification of the register on an application by any aggrieved person, member of the company or the company itself.[5] The court may make such an order where:

(a) the name of any person is, without sufficient cause, entered into or omitted from the register, in contravention of section 116; or
(b) default is made in entering on the register the fact of any person having ceased to be a member within the period fixed by section 116.

In considering whether to make an order under the section the court may decide on any question relating to the title to the shares. If any order for rectification is made, the court may direct that compensation be paid by the company for any loss suffered by the aggrieved party.

Section 123 of the Principal Act provides that the register of members shall not be concerned with any trust arrangements relating to shares. Therefore the company will usually only have to deal with those rights pertaining to the registered owner of the shares irrespective of any underlying arrangements between the registered owner and another party.[6]

Section 124 of the Principal Act provides that the register of members shall be *prima facie* evidence of any matters directed or authorised by the Companies Acts to be inserted therein. It is not conclusive evidence and therefore persons who become aware of inaccuracies may apply for rectifications. However, an application for rectification must be made promptly on discovering the error or omission or a person may be estopped from denying the accuracy of its contents.

---

3 Section 119 of the Principal Act
4 Section 122(5) of the Principal Act.
5 Section 122(1) of the Principal Act.
6 There are exceptional circumstances whereby a company must take account of such underlying arrangements, for example where it receives a 'stop notice' from a third party holding shares as security: see 'Shares as Security for a Loan' later in this chapter.

Transfer of Shares

Shares are by their nature the transferable personal property of the company member.[7] However, the right to transfer shares is not absolute and may be restricted by the articles of association or the Companies Acts. Indeed, private companies are obliged to include restrictions on the transfer of shares in their articles of association.[8] This is usually achieved by the inclusion of a pre-emption clause which gives existing shareholders a right of first refusal to shares being sold by other members or to new shares being issued by the company and a clause empowering directors to refuse to register a transfer.

1. Restrictions on Transfers

A transfer of shares will not occur by operation of the law. A formal transfer must be completed. Section 81 of the Principal Act prohibits a company from registering a transfer of shares unless a proper instrument of transfer has been delivered to the company. Furthermore, the transfer must also be executed by the transferor.[9] Although Table A also requires that the instrument of transfer be executed by the transferee, companies usually dispense with this requirement in their own articles of association. Until a share transfer is registered, the transferor remains the holder of the shares. However, he holds them as nominee for the transferee who holds an equitable interest in those shares (Article 22; Table A).

2. Directors' Powers to Refuse Registration

Because a transferee has no legal right to the shares until his name has been entered in the register of members, it is imperative that his name be so registered as soon as possible. However, he is not automatically entitled to have his name registered because the directors may only register shares in the manner permitted by the articles of association.

Table A empowers directors to refuse to register a transfer of shares. In the case of a public company this power is limited to a right to refuse a transfer of unpaid shares, but in the case of private companies the power is not so restricted. Instead, under Article 3 of Part II of Table A directors may, in their absolute discretion, and without assigning any reason therefor, decline to register any transfer of any share, whether or not it is a fully paid share. Where the articles provide such a wide power to directors, it will be difficult to challenge any decision arising thereon.

However, the power must, as with all directors' powers, be exercised in good faith and for a proper purpose. In *Re Hafner*,[10] the directors exercised their

---

7 Section 79 of the Principal Act.
8 Section 33(1)(a) of the Principal Act.
9 *Re Green* [1949] 1 All ER 167.
10 [1943] IR 426.

powers under a Table A type article and refused to register the plaintiff as a member of the company. The plaintiff produced evidence that the directors' powers were exercised for the improper purpose of preventing him from asking questions about exorbitant payments being made to the directors. The directors, during the course of the proceedings, argued that they were not required to give reasons for their decision but the court held that once improper motivations were established the directors were estopped from relying on this right. Accordingly, the court drew an inference from the directors' silence that the allegations were well founded and the directors' decision was invalidated.

In the recent Irish case of *Banfi Ltd v. Moran*[11] the company in question had adopted Table A, which allowed the directors to refuse to register a transfer of shares without assigning any reason therefor. Rather than staying silent on the matter the directors claimed they had refused to register the transfer because the applicant had not engaged in certain communications with the board, which caused it to conclude that it would not be in the interests of the company to have the plaintiff as a member. The applicant asserted that the refusal to register the transfer was to prevent him pursuing section 205 proceedings against two of the directors.[12] The court was inclined to the view that this was the real reason for the refusal to register the plaintiff. The court concluded that the directors were motivated by self interest and had not acted *bona fide* in the interests of the company. The court ordered the rectification of the register to provide for registration of the plaintiff's shares.

In *Popely v Planarrive Ltd*[13] the directors exercised their discretion under Table A and refused to register the shares in the plaintiff's name. Evidence was provided that the plaintiff was not an ideal character to control the company, as many of his former actions were detrimental to the company. The court held that the board had, in refusing to register the plaintiff, acted in good faith and in the best interests of the company.

However, the court will presume that the directors have acted in good faith and the onus is on the plaintiff to prove otherwise. In *Re Smith & Fawcett Ltd*,[14] the directors refused to register a transfer of the shares of a deceased director but agreed that they would register a transfer of part of the shareholding if the transferor agreed to sell the balance to the surviving director at a fixed price. This decision was later justified as being in the company's best interests in that it ensured that the existing management remained in control. The court held that there was insufficient evidence of bad faith on the director's behalf and refused to invalidate the decision.[15]

---

11 Unreported, High Court, Laffoy J., July 20, 2006.
12 See Chapter 15 — Minority Protection
13 [1997] 1 BCLC 8.
14 [1942] 1 All ER 452.
15 Nowadays such a decision might constitute oppression under section 205 of the Principal Act: see Chapter 15.

Where the articles contain restrictions other than those provided for in Table A, the extent of the restriction is solely a matter of construction by the courts who tend, where the language is uncertain or ambiguous, to lean in favour of the shareholders' freedom to transfer. However, the courts will not defeat the obvious purpose of the restriction, as the case of *Lyle & Scott Ltd v. Scott's Trustees*[16] demonstrates. The company's articles conferred a pre-emption right on the other shareholders when any shareholder was 'desirous of transferring his ordinary shares'. Some of the existing shareholders attempted to avoid the articles by selling the beneficial interest in their shares to a prospective take-over bidder who would use his proxy cards to vote on their behalf. The court held that the articles must be construed to include a restriction on the transfer of the beneficial interest and not just a restriction on the process of having the transfer registered.

Where the directors are only entitled to reject a transfer on specified grounds, reliance on other grounds will invalidate the decision. In *Re Bede Steam Shipping Co. Ltd,*[17] the directors were authorised to refuse transfers if they were of the opinion that it was in the company's best interests that the transferee would not become a member. The directors refused to register transfers of shares on the stated ground that it was prejudicial to the company to have its issued share capital fragmented. The court held that the decision was invalid as it was not within the reasons prescribed by the articles of association. In *Tangney v. Clarence Hotel Co. Ltd*[18] a similar provision was contained in the articles. Accordingly, the directors refused to register a transfer to a person on the grounds that it was not in the company's interest to have him admitted to its membership. In fact, the transferee was already a member of the company and the court held that the directors could therefore not invoke this ground in refusing the transfer.

Directors must exercise their power to refuse to register a transfer within a reasonable period. In *Re Swaledale Cleaners Ltd,*[19] due to technical difficulties in holding a board meeting, the directors took over four months to exercise their power of refusal. The court held that the delay was unreasonable and the transfer should, accordingly, be registered. In any case section 84 of the Principal Act requires a company to notify the transferee of a refusal to transfer the shares within two months from the date the transfer is lodged. As a result of this provision, the maximum reasonable period is two months. If a director fails to notify the transferor within that period he can be compelled to register the transfer.

---

16 [1959] AC 763.
17 [1917] 1 Ch 123.
18 [1933] IR 51.
19 [1968] 1 WLR 1710.

3. The Transfer Procedure

In practice, the transfer of fully paid shares is effected by the use of the standard stock transfer form.[20] The transfer form is signed by the transferor and given to the transferee together with the share certificate. The transferee sends the transfer form, which must be stamped for the purposes of stamp duty,[21] to the company directors who must only register the transfer in accordance with the provisions of the articles of association. Once registered, the old share certificate is cancelled and a new one is issued to the transferee.

This procedure may not be possible where only part of the shares comprised in the share certificate are being transferred. This is because it would be unwise to hand over the share certificate when the transferor wishes to retain some of the shares. Similarly, it would be unfair to the transferee to pay for his shares if the transferor retained the certificate. In such a situation a certification of transfer must take place, which involves the following procedure:

(a) the transferor executes the transfer and sends it, together with the share certificate, to the company;
(b) the company retains the share certificate, endorses the transfer form with the words 'certificate lodged' and returns it to the transferor;
(c) the transferor delivers the transfer to the transferee who stamps it and presents it to the company; and
(d) the company then issues two new share certificates, one representing the amount of shares transferred to the transferee and the other representing those shares retained by the transferor.

A certification of transfer by the company estops it from denying the truth of the essential facts stated therein. Furthermore, the certification is a representation by the company to any person acting on the faith of the certification, that documents have been produced to the company which on the face of them show a *prima facie* title to the shares comprised in the instrument of transfer.[22] However, it is not a representation that he has in fact title to them. A person who accepts a certified transfer may claim damages from the company if it did not retain the share certificate or indeed if it certified the transfer without ever having received the certificate. However, in order to succeed in such a claim the person must show that he relied on the certification of transfer. In *Longman v. Bath Electric Tramways*,[23] the company mistakenly sent the share certificate together with the certification of transfer to the transferor. The transferor proceeded to deposit the share certificate with the plaintiff as security for a loan. The plaintiff later claimed that he was entitled to the shares.

---

20 As permitted by section 22 of the Stock Transfer Act 1963.
21 Normally 1 per cent *ad valorem* on the consideration paid on the shares.
22 Section 85(1) of the Principal Act.
23 [1905] 1 Ch 646.

The plaintiff's claim failed as he never knew of the existence of the certification of the transfer and had not relied upon it in his dealings with the transferor.

Every company must, within two months of a valid transfer of any shares lodged with the company, complete and have ready for delivery the certificates of all shares.[24]

4. Forged Transfers

Where a company registers a transfer made on foot of a forged transfer form and a stolen share certificate, the consequences are as follows:

1. the original transferor can have his name restored to the register of members because a forged document is a nullity which cannot deprive him of his title to the shares — this is so even if he failed to reply to a notice from the company advising him of the transfer;
2. the person who lodged the forged transfer cannot rely on the share certificate and he is further liable to indemnify the company for any loss it may have suffered from having to pay compensation — this is so even if he did not know of the forgery;
3. where a third party takes the transfer of the 'forged' shares in good faith and for value, the company is estopped from denying the title to the new transferee. If this person suffers a loss as a result of the restoration of the true owner to the register, the company must compensate him for this loss.

In *Re Bahia and San Francisco Railway*,[25] the holder of shares deposited his share certificate with a broker. The broker forged the holder's signature and transferred the shares to X. X then presented the share certificate and transfer to the company. Before registering the transfer to X the company notified the original holder. As he did not respond, X was duly registered as the holder. X subsequently sold his shares to Y who was then registered as the new holder. When the forgery was discovered the court held that the original holder should be restored to the register and that Y was entitled to damages from the company. Furthermore, X, although unaware of the forgery, had presented the forged transfer and was held liable to indemnify the company for its liability to Y.

5. Automated Transfers

The Companies Act 1990 (Uncertificated Securities) Regulations 1996[26] introduced provisions for the automated transfer of company securities. As the process is intended to be paperless, the regulations provide that instead of a share

---

24 Section 86 of the Principal Act.
25 (1868) LR 3 QB 584.
26 SI 68/1996.

certificate the buyer will receive an 'uncertified unit'. The regulations further provide for the transfer and registration of these units.

6. Dematerialisation of Shares of Public Limited Companies

Section 239 of the 1990 Act[27] allows the Minister to provide by regulations for the introduction of mandatory dematerialisation of securities of listed or unlisted public limited companies. Dematerialisation is an electronic system to replace paper share certificates and stock transfer forms. These will be replaced by a paper shareholder statement and shareholder reference number. As yet no regulations have been made in this regard but the proposed dematerialisation process is considered a matter of priority in order for the Irish equities market to respond to international developments and maintain its competitiveness. The removal of share certificates will have a number of advantages including, *inter alia*, the following:

(a) facilitating trading efficiency by investors;
(b) enhancing the international competitiveness of Ireland for securities trading; and
(c) reducing the current costs associated with the cumbersome process of managing paper-based transactions.

Transmission of Shares

Transmission of shares occurs by operation of law. This will occur in any of the following circumstances:

(a) where a member dies his shares will automatically vest in his personal representative who may be registered as the member or may transfer the shares without becoming a member;
(b) where shares are held jointly, the surviving owner becomes the registered owner on the death of the other;
(c) on the bankruptcy of a member, the beneficial ownership (not the legal ownership) passes to the official assignee.

Share Certificates

Although the share certificate is not a document of title, it is *prima facie* evidence of title.[28] A share certificate is a formal statement by the company, under seal, stating that the person named holds the shares specified and the extent to which the specified shares are paid up. The company may be estopped from denying any aspect of this statement if a third party relies on it to his detriment. In *Balkis Consolidated Co. v. Tomkinson*[29] P, who had no title to the shares, sold them to T

---

27 As amended by section 12 of the Investment Funds, Companies and Miscellaneous Provisions Act 2006.
28 Section 87 of the Principal Act.
29 [1893] AC 396.

and induced the company by fraud to issue a new share certificate to T. T later resold the shares but on discovering the original fraud, the company refused to register the transfer to the new purchaser on the ground that T had no title to the shares. In order to satisfy the claims of those to whom he had sold the shares, T purchased additional shares and brought an action against the company to recover the price paid for those shares. His action succeeded because he had changed his position in reliance on the share certificate. Similarly, in *Bloomenthal v. Forde*,[30] the company, in consideration of obtaining a loan from B, issued him a share certificate in which the shares were described as fully paid. When the company went into liquidation, the liquidator claimed from B the unpaid amount on his shares. It was held that the company was estopped from denying that the shares were fully paid. Accordingly, the liquidator's claim failed.

It has been held that the company may be able to deny the effect of the certificate where it was issued by a person who was not authorised by the company to do so. In *Ruben v. Great Fingall Consolidated*,[31] the company secretary had forged a director's signature on a share certificate which was issued to the plaintiff. The court held that the company could deny the correctness of the certificate as it had not been issued by an authorised person and, accordingly, was not issued by the company. However, the basis of this decision was rejected in *Lloyd v. Grace Smith & Co.*[32] Here the House of Lords held that if an agent commits a fraud while acting or purporting to act in the course of the business which he is authorised, or held out as authorised, to transact on account of his principal, the principal, although innocent of the fraud, is liable for the fraud of the agent whether the fraud results in a benefit to the principal or not.

Share Warrants

By virtue of section 88 of the Principal Act, a public company may issue share warrants where so authorised by the articles of association. A share warrant is a negotiable instrument which entitles the bearer of the warrant to the shares in question. An instrument of transfer is therefore not required as the title can be passed by simple delivery. Share warrants are rarely used in this jurisdiction.

Shares as Security for a Loan

Shares may be used as security for borrowings. Where a legal mortgage is taken over the shares, the shares are transferred to the mortgagee who is registered as a member. The mortgagee will usually undertake to re-transfer the shares when the loan has been repaid. A lender may prefer not to take a legal mortgage for the following reasons:

---

30 [1897] AC 156.
31 [1906] AC 439.
32 [1911] 2 KB 489.

(a) stamp duty is payable on each transfer; and

(b) if the shares are not fully paid, the mortgagee is liable to pay the calls while his name is on the register.

Alternatively, a lender may take an equitable mortgage, which is evidenced by a simple deposit of the share certificate and a blank transfer form with the lender. If the borrower defaults, the lender has an implied power to fill in his name on the blank transfer form and then dispose of the shares. The disadvantage of the equitable mortgage is that the borrower's name remains on the register. The borrower may falsely claim that his certificate has been lost and may obtain a new certificate. The mortgagee may protect himself by serving a 'stop notice' on the company, which has the effect of compelling the company to notify him if any attempt is made to transfer the shares.

Calls

A call is a demand by the company for money due on shares. Unless shares are fully paid, the holder, who need not be the original allottee, is liable to pay the balance when called upon by the company. The procedure for making calls is usually contained in the articles of association. Table A makes the following provisions in this regard:

(a) the power to make calls is vested in the directors;

(b) no call shall exceed one-quarter of the nominal value of the share;

(c) members must be given at least fourteen days' notice of the time and place of payment;

(d) a call is deemed to be made when the directors' resolution is passed;

(e) the joint holders of shares shall be jointly and severally liable to pay all calls in respect thereof;

(f) the directors may, on the issue of shares, differentiate between the holders as to the amount of calls to be paid and the time of payment;

(g) directors may, if they think fit, receive advance payments for calls.

Non-payment of calls

Table A provides for interest to be paid, from the date the call was due, at a rate of 5 per cent. However, the directors may waive payment of interest wholly or in part. Table A also provides that a member's shares may be forfeited for non-payment of a call. Where the directors propose to forfeit the member's shares, they must first serve a notice calling for the payment of the sum due within fourteen days of the date of the notice. Where the member does not comply with the terms of the notice, the directors may then resolve to forfeit the shares. The shareholder ceases to be a member on the forfeiture of his shares but he remains liable for all amounts owing to the company at the date of forfeiture. Forfeited shares may be re-issued or cancelled. To avoid a forfeiture, shareholders may decide to surrender their shares and this is permitted by the Companies Acts as an authorised reduction of capital.

Liens

It is usual for the articles to give the company a lien on a member's shares for non-payment of calls. A public company's articles can only create a lien on partly paid shares or in the ordinary course of the company's business.[33] The lien gives the company a first claim on the shares unless it has notice of some pre-existing claim such as an equitable mortgage.[34]

Dividends

A dividend represents the cash return to a shareholder whereas a debenture holder is paid interest. A dividend is a proportion of the distributable profits of the company. It may be a fixed annual percentage, as in the case of preference shares, or it may be variable depending on the fortunes of the company during a particular period. But because a dividend is only payable from the distributable profits of the company, it follows that if no profits are made, or if no profits are available for distribution, no dividend will be declared. At the outset it should be noted that the rules regarding the payment of dividends are incorporated into the general rules regarding the making of distributions, which cover a much wider range of transactions.[35]

Distributable Profits

Dividends may only be paid out of the company's profits that are available for distribution.[36] The reasoning behind this requirement is to ensure that the capital of the company is not eroded by distributions to members.[37] Central to an understanding of a company's ability to pay dividends are the definitions of 'profits' and 'distributions'.

1. Profits

Section 45(2) of the 1983 Act defines profits available for distribution as the company's accumulated realised profits, so far as they have not previously been distributed or capitalised, less its accumulated, realised losses, so far as they have

---

33 Section 44 of the 1983 Amendment Act.
34 *Bradford Banking Co. v. Briggs & Co.* (1886) 12 App Cas 29.
35 See *Aveling Barford Ltd v. Perion Ltd* [1989] BCLC 626 and *Re Greendale Developments Ltd* [1998] 1 IR 8.
36 Section 45(1) of the 1983 Amendment Act.
37 See Chapter 10.

not been previously written off in a reduction or reorganisation of capital. Under this definition dividends can only be made where there has been a surplus of profits for the current and past years, in so far as they have not already been distributed, over losses for those years, in so far as they have not already been written off. For the accountant the concept of 'realised profits' poses no great difficulty. For those who are not familiar with accounting, the matter is more complex. In general terms a 'realised profit' is a tangible profit as opposed to an artificial profit. Where for example a company makes a profit from a sale of goods, having deducted the cost of the goods sold and any other deductions required by accounting practices, this will constitute a tangible or realised profit. On the other hand, an unrealised profit would arise where, for example, a company revalues one of its buildings at a greater value than it had previously been shown in the company's audited balance sheet.

Accumulated realised losses include *inter alia* such things as a debit balance on a profit and loss account and amounts written off in respect of the depreciation of assets. Furthermore, except in limited circumstances, where development costs are shown as an asset in the company's accounts, those amounts shall be treated as a realised loss.[38]

2. *Distributions*

Section 51(2) of the 1983 Amendment Act defines a distribution as every description of a distribution of a company's assets to its members, whether in cash or otherwise, except those distributions made for the following:

(a) the issue of fully or partly paid-up bonus shares;
(b) the redemption or purchase of shares where authorised under the Companies Acts;
(c) the reduction of share capital by extinguishing or reducing the liability of any of the members on any of their shares as authorised under section 72 of the Principal Act; and
(d) a distribution of assets to members of the company on its winding up.

Additional Restrictions for Public Limited Companies

A public limited company is subject to further limitations in that section 46(1) of the 1983 Amendment Act provides that it can only make a distribution where:

(a) its net assets are not less than the aggregate of its called-up share capital and its undistributable reserves;
(b) the distribution does not result in its net assets falling below that aggregate.

---

38 Section 45(A) of the 1983 Amendment Act.

For the purposes of section 46(1) the undistributable reserves of a public limited company are the following:

(a) the share premium account;
(b) the capital redemption reserve;
(c) the amount by which the company's accumulated unrealised profits, so far as they have not previously been utilised by any capitalisation, exceed its accumulated unrealised losses, so far as they have not already been written off in a reduction or reorganisation of the company's capital;
(d) any other reserve which the company is prohibited from distributing by the law or the company's memorandum or articles of association.

Where a public company is an investment company, section 47 of the 1983 Amendment Act provides that it may make a distribution from its accumulated realised revenue profits, so far as they have not already been distributed or capitalised, less its accumulated revenue losses, whether they are realised or unrealised, and in so far as they have not already been written off in relation to a reduction or reorganisation of capital if:

(a) the amount of its assets is at least equal to one and a half times the aggregate of its liabilities; and
(b) the distribution does not reduce its assets to less than one and a half times its liabilities.

It is clear that section 47 makes special provision for investment companies because it draws a distinction between revenue profits and capital profits. Furthermore, the distribution can only be made after realised and unrealised losses have been deducted from the company's profits.

General Provisions for all Companies

Section 49 of the 1983 Amendment Act sets out the requirements in relation to the relevant accounts which must be used before a decision, in relation to whether a distribution should be made and the amount of such a distribution, should be made.

Consequences of Making an Unlawful Distribution

A member who receives a dividend payment, knowing at the time that it amounted to an unlawful distribution, is obliged to repay the amount he received.[39] Furthermore, directors may also be held liable for breach of their duties. In *Re Exchange Banking Co.*[40] the directors for several years laid before

---

39 Section 50 of the 1983 Amendment Act.
40 (1882) 21 Ch D 519.

the meeting accounts which, as the directors knew, inaccurately stated the position with respect to certain assets. In reliance on those accounts the shareholders passed resolutions to declare dividends out of the profits shown in the accounts. The truth of the matter was that the company had made losses. The company ultimately failed and the liquidator successfully claimed from the directors the amount which they had knowingly paid by way of dividend.

It is not only directors who may be held liable. In *Re Thomas Gerrard & Sons Ltd*[41] the managing director falsified accounts by including non-existent stock. As a result of the overstated profits, additional taxes were paid by the company and dividends were declared that otherwise would not have been. The auditors became suspicious when they discovered that invoices relating to the stock had been altered. Rather than investigate the matter, they accepted the managing director's explanation. The auditors were held liable to the company for the amounts paid by way of dividends and excess taxes.

Declaration of Dividends

Even when distributable profits are available for distribution there is no mandatory requirement on companies to pay dividends. In *Bond v. Barrow Haematite Steel Co.*[42] the company had available reserves of £240,000 but the directors did not declare a dividend. The plaintiff, a preference shareholder, argued that the dividend should have been paid given the availability of the reserves. The company claimed that it had decided to retain the reserves to make good losses arising from the disposal of current assets and a diminution of the value of the company's fixed assets. The court held that it would not interfere with the directors' discretion in relation to the declaration of dividends. However, there is nothing to prevent the articles of association conferring an automatic right to receive a dividend, irrespective of whether or not one has been declared.[43]

The power to declare a dividend is given in the articles of association. Table A makes the following provisions in this regard:

(a) the company in general meeting may declare dividends but no dividend may exceed the amount recommended by the directors;
(b) the directors may declare such interim dividends as they consider justifiable;
(c) dividends are normally payable on the paid-up amount of the share capital;
(d) a dividend must be paid in cash unless the contrary is specified in the company's regulations;
(e) if shares are held jointly, the dividend is payable to the first named joint holder on the register.

---

41 [1967] 2 All ER 525.
42 [1902] 1 Ch 353.
43 *Re Lafayette Ltd* [1950] IR 100.

Since the recommendation of the general meeting must not exceed the amount recommended by the directors, it is the directors who in effect have the last say as to when a dividend is to be declared and how much will be paid. The shareholders cannot force the directors to recommend a dividend. However, the directors will be conscious of the general meeting's power to remove them under section 182 of the Principal Act. Furthermore, the company may alter the articles to provide for alternative rules relating to the declaration of dividends.

Dividend Payments

Although dividends are generally payable in cash, the articles may permit a company to pay them by way of non-cash assets such as shares or debentures. Indeed, many public companies now give their shareholders the option of taking shares in the company in lieu of cash dividends — a scrip dividend. In any case, Table A provides that dividends may be payable by way of cheque. Where the articles are silent on the manner in which dividends must be paid, then payment must be in the form of cash. In *Wood v. Odessa Waterworks Company*,[44] the articles authorised the company to declare a dividend to be paid to shareholders. It did not specify the form of payment. The general meeting resolved that the dividends should be declared in the form of debentures on which the company would pay interest pending the redemption of the debentures. A shareholder sued the company, claiming that the articles required payment to be in cash. The court upheld the claim and an injunction was issued preventing the company from paying the dividend otherwise than in cash.

Limitation Period for Claims

Where a dividend has been declared, it then becomes a debt owing to the shareholder who may sue to enforce his right to the dividend. The time limit for bringing an action against the company for unpaid dividends is twelve years from the date of declaration or the declared date of the payment, whichever is the later. A balance sheet duly signed by the directors has been held to have constituted a written acknowledgment of the debt due by the company.[45] The articles may provide for the forfeiture of dividends that are not claimed within a lesser period of time. Where the company is wound up, any unclaimed dividends are subject to a six-year limitation period unless the articles of the company provide otherwise.[46]

---

44 (1889) 42 Ch D 636.
45 *Jones v. Bellgrove Properties Ltd* [1949] 2 All ER 198 and *Re Gee & Co. (Woolwich) Ltd* [1974] 1 All ER 1149, but cf. *Re Companiea de Electricidad de la Provincia de Buenos Aires Ltd* [1978] 3 All ER 668.
46 Section 283(2) of the Principal Act.

CHAPTER THIRTEEN

MARKET ABUSE

Introduction

Economic analysis of publicly quoted companies rests largely on the hypothesis that the market for shares and securities is efficient. This hypothesis, referred to as the 'efficient market hypothesis', suggests that share prices correctly reflect all public information available about those shares. According to the theory, it is only unforeseen new information that affects share prices. If information is the key to turning a profit or avoiding a loss, then clearly those with undisclosed price-sensitive information can use it to their advantage when buying or selling shares. Company directors and officers are in an ideal position to acquire knowledge about their company's affairs before it becomes publicly available and to use this information to make a personal profit.

The law recognises this potential abuse by imposing a fiduciary duty on directors, which prohibits their using company information to make a personal gain. More important, since the wrong is done to the company, it is given a cause of action to reclaim any profits made by directors in such circumstances. Furthermore, the statutory obligations imposed on directors and companies enable members and other persons to ascertain the true extent of the directors' involvement in the company.[1] Equity's insistence that directors should not use their position to further their personal interests will be considered in Chapter 18.

However, the available remedies are rarely invoked, for a number of reasons. First, the members have ordinarily no right against the directors whose duties are owed to the company,[2] although in exceptional cases a duty to the shareholders may be said to exist, where directors have put themselves in a special position vis-à-vis their dealings with them.[3] Accordingly, any action against the directors must be taken by the company which, as the beneficiary of the duty, is the only proper claimant for the available relief.[4] The difficulty lies in the fact that such a decision must be taken by the board of directors, which is unlikely to cause the company to sue one of their own. Therefore it is only in the most unusual circumstances, such as when a company is taken over or wound up, that it will take action against the errant directors.

Insider dealing and market manipulation are objectionable not just because of the potential wrong done to the company itself, but also because they affect the integrity of the securities market. Market integrity is essential for the proper

---

1 See Chapter 18 — Directors' Duties and Liabilities.
2 *Percival v. Wright* [1902] 2 CH 421.
3 *Coleman v. Meyers* [1977] 2 NZLR 225 (considered in Chapter 18).
4 *Foss v. Harbottle* (1843) 2 Hare 261.

functioning of the securities markets and the protection of investors. Insider dealing and market manipulation are an obstacle to this. As Bingham CJ. observed in *R v. Staines*[5]:

> The integrity of the market depends on equality of knowledge, since fair operation of the market is jeopardised if those who are 'in the know' (often called 'market insiders') can exploit information for their personal advantage which they have obtained in the course of their professional activities when such information is unavailable to others.

Legislative Framework

Part V of the Companies Act 1990 (the 1990 Act) was the first attempt by the legislature to tackle insider dealing. Its provisions have since been repealed by section 31 of the Investment Funds, Companies and Miscellaneous Provisions Act, 2005 (the 2005 Act) which, together with Market Abuse (Directive 2003/6/EC) Regulations 2005,[6] now regulate market abuse in Ireland. However, the commencement order for section 31 only applies the new provisions to companies whose securities are listed on a regulated market.[7]

Accordingly, there exists in Ireland a two-tiered framework: the 1990 Act, which continues to apply to a limited number of listed companies that are not trading on a regulated market (such as the IEX market[8]); and the 2005 provisions, which apply to companies trading on a regulated market (such as the ISEQ). As the list of companies applying for admission to the IEX is growing it is important to consider the 1990 provisions in addition to the new regime.

1. The 1990 Provisions

General Prohibition

Section 108(1) of the 1990 Act makes it unlawful for a person who is, or at any time in the preceding six months was, connected with a company to deal in its securities if that person is in possession of price-sensitive information that is not generally available. Furthermore, the prohibition applies only where the purpose of the transaction is to secure a profit or gain for the person involved.

The prohibition applies to 'dealing', which is defined in section 107 as the acquiring, disposing of, subscribing for or underwriting the securities; or making

---

5 [1997] 2 CR App Rep 426.
6 Which implement the Market Abuse Regulation (2273/2003) and the supplemental Commission Directives (2003/124/EC, 2003/125/EC and 2004/72/EC).
7 The Official Listing of the Irish Stock Exchange (ISEQ) is a regulated market but the IEX which was created in 2005 is not a regulated market. Therefore the provisions of Part V of the 1990 Act will still apply to companies whose securities are traded on the IEX.
8 An increasing number of small companies are applying for admission to the IEX.

or offering to make, or inducing or attempting to induce a person to make or offer to make, an agreement:

(a) for or relating to acquiring, disposing of, subscribing for or underwriting the securities; or

(b) the purpose or purported purpose of which is to secure a profit or gain to a person who acquires, disposes of, subscribes for or underwrites the securities or to any of the parties to the agreement in relation to the securities.

For the purposes of Part V of the Act 'securities' means:

(a) shares, debentures or other debt securities, issued or proposed to be issued, in the State and for which dealing facilities are, or are to be, provided by a recognised Stock Exchange; and

(b) any right, option or obligation in respect of any such shares, debentures or other debt securities referred to in paragraph (a); and

(c) any right, option or obligation in respect of any index relating to any such shares, debentures, or other debt securities referred to in paragraph (a); or

(d) such interests as may be prescribed.

Section 108(2) extends the basic prohibition on insider dealing to prevent a person who is, or at any time in the preceding six months has been, connected with the company dealing in securities of any other company, if the information relates to a transaction between the two companies. This prohibition applies even where the transactions were, but are no longer, contemplated. A person is connected if he is:

(a) an officer, which includes directors (and shadow directors), secretaries, employees, liquidators, examiners, auditors and receivers, of that company or a related company;

(b) a shareholder in that company or in a related company; or

(c) occupying a position which may reasonably be expected to give him access to inside information by virtue of his professional, business or other relationship with the company or a related company or by his being an officer of a substantial shareholder in that company or a related company.

Prohibition Imposed on 'Tippees'

Section 108(3) makes it unlawful for a person to deal in securities if he has received price-sensitive information from another person, often referred to as a 'tipper', and is, or ought reasonably to be, aware of the facts and circumstances that preclude the tipper from dealing in those securities. Where a person is prohibited from dealing in securities in any of the above-mentioned ways, it is also unlawful for him to cause or procure any other person to deal in those securities.

Indeed, the mere communication of price-sensitive information is unlawful if that person knows or ought reasonably to know that the recipient will use it for the purpose of dealing or causing or procuring another person to deal in those securities. It would appear to be irrelevant that the information communicated does not identify the individual company whose securities are the subject of the insider dealing. What is relevant is the fact that the information is sufficient to enable the recipient to identify the company whose securities are involved, even where further investigation is necessary to discover that identification.[9]

Dealing by Companies

A company is generally prohibited from dealing in securities when one of its officers is so prohibited.[10] However, the prohibition will not apply where a decision to deal is taken, on the company's behalf, by a person other than the officer concerned. To secure this derogation, the company must have written arrangements in place, referred to in the financial services industry as 'Chinese walls', which ensure that no information or advice relating to the transaction is given to that person and no information or advice was in fact given.

Supposing a financial services company had both a dealing division and a mergers and acquisitions division. If the latter is aware of price-sensitive information relating to a particular company's securities, such as a proposed merger, the dealing division can still deal in those securities, provided that a formal system is in place which ensures that the price-sensitive information remains within the mergers division.

A company is further exempted in circumstances where the price-sensitive information is itself the fact that the company proposes to deal in the securities in question.[11]

Section 108(10) provides an additional exemption where notice is given to the Stock Exchange of the person's intention to deal and the Stock Exchange publishes this notice. However, in such a circumstance, the dealing must take place within a specified 'window period' beginning seven days after the publication of the company's interim or final results, as the case may be, and ending fourteen days after the relevant publication.

Dealing by Others

Dealing on behalf of another person, where the dealer has reasonable cause to believe or to conclude that the deal is contrary to section 108, is prohibited and a person found guilty of dealing in this manner shall be guilty of an offence.[12]

---

9 *R v Staines, R v Morrissey* [1997] 2 CR App Rep 426.
10 Section 108(6) of the 1990 Act.
11 Section 108(8) of the 1990 Act.
12 Section 113 of the 1990 Act.

Exemptions from the Prohibition

Section 110 sets out what could be regarded as further exemptions from the provisions contained in section 108. The prohibition will not apply to persons who:

(a) acquire securities under a will or on the intestacy of another person; or
(b) acquire securities in a company pursuant to an employee profit-share scheme, provided that all the employees of the company are offered the opportunity to acquire the securities on the same terms, the company has approved the terms of the scheme in general meeting, and the approval of the Revenue Commissioners is obtained;
(c) acquire a right to shares in a company under a scheme approved by the Revenue Commissioners for the purposes of the Tax Acts and the Capital Gain Tax Acts;
(d) enter into, in good faith, any of the following transactions:
  (i) the acquisition by a director of a share qualification under section 180 of the Principal Act;
  (ii) a transaction pursuant to obligations in an underwriting agreement;
  (iii) a transaction by a personal representative of a deceased person, a trustee, or liquidator, receiver or examiner in the performance of the functions of his office; or
  (iv) a transaction by way of or arising out of a security interest taken over the securities or the documents of title to securities.

Civil Liability for Unlawful Dealing

Civil liability for insider dealing is imposed by section 109. The liability is twofold. First, the person is liable to compensate any other party to the transaction who sustained a loss.[13] The compensation will be the difference between the price of the securities at the time of the transaction and the price at which they would have been dealt in if the information had been generally available. Because of the difficulty in matching up sales and purchases, it will not be an easy task to prove a loss, particularly where the transaction involved securities bought or sold through stockbrokers. Second, the person is liable to account to the company whose securities were unlawfully dealt for any profit which accrued to him.

The only civil case ever taken for insider dealing under these provisions was the much publicised case of *Fyffes plc v DCC plc. and others*.[14] The plaintiff alleged that the defendants were in breach of the insider dealing provisions when

---

13 Subject to a two-year limitation period: Section 109(4) of the 1990 Act.
14 Unreported, High Court, Laffoy J., December 21, 2005.

they dealt (by selling) the plaintiff's shares at a time when they were in possession of price-sensitive information. This price-sensitive information was alleged to be contained in management accounts that indicated some financial difficulties facing the company. This information was circulated to the plaintiff's directors, one of whom was a defendant in the proceedings. The plaintiff succeeded in establishing that the shares were dealt within the meaning of section 108(1). However, they failed to demonstrate that defendants were in possession of information that would have affected the price of the shares had it been available to the public. Accordingly the action failed.

Criminal Liability for Unlawful Dealing

A person who deals, on his own or on some other person's behalf, in securities when prohibited from so doing shall be guilty of an offence. The guilty person is liable on summary conviction to a term of imprisonment not exceeding twelve months or a fine not exceeding €12,697, or to both, and on indictment to imprisonment for a term of imprisonment not exceeding ten years or a fine not exceeding €253,948, or to both.[15] Furthermore, a person convicted of an offence is prohibited from any dealing for twelve months from the date of conviction.[16]

Enforcement of the Provisions

The duty of policing the 1990 provisions rests with the Stock Exchange. Where it appears to the Stock Exchange or any of its members that an offence has been committed, the Director of Corporate Enforcement (the Director) must be notified. The Director must also be furnished with such information and be given access to such facilities for inspecting and taking copies of any documents in the possession of, or under the control of, the Stock Exchange, as he so requires. If it appears to a court that an offence has been committed which has not been reported to the Director, the court may direct the Stock Exchange to make such a report.[17] If the Director, on receipt of a report, has reasonable grounds for believing that an offence has been committed and he either initiates proceedings in respect of that offence or refers the matter to the Director of Public Prosecutions (DPP) who himself institutes proceedings in respect of that offence, the Stock Exchange and every officer of the company whose securities are concerned, or such other person as may have relevant information, must give all assistance in connection with the proceedings as can reasonably be given.

---

15 Section 114 of the 1990 Act.
16 Section 112 of the 1990 Act.
17 Section 115(3) of the 1990 Act.

2. The 2005 Provisions

General Prohibition of Market Abuse

Part 2 of the 1995 Regulations contains the general prohibition against market abuse, which comprises both insider dealing and market manipulation.

Regulation 5 provides that a person who possesses inside information shall not use that information by acquiring or disposing of, or by trying to acquire or dispose of, financial instruments (including shares) to which that information relates. The prohibition applies to any person who possesses the inside information concerned by virtue of the person's membership of the administrative, management or supervisory bodies of the issuer of the financial instrument or by virtue of the person holding shares in the issuer or by virtue of the person having access to the information through the exercise of the person's employment, profession or duties, or by virtue of the person's criminal activities, or any other person who possesses the inside information concerned while the person knows, or ought to have known, that it is inside information.

Furthermore, a person shall not disclose inside information to any other person unless such disclosure is made in the normal course of the exercise of the first-mentioned person's employment, profession or duties, or recommend or induce another person, on the basis of inside information, to acquire or dispose of financial instruments to which that information relates. According to Regulation 2(2) 'inside information' means, *inter alia*:

> information of a precise nature relating directly or indirectly to one or more issuers of financial instruments or to one or more financial instruments which has not been made public and which, if it were made public, would be likely to have a significant effect on the price of those financial instruments or on the price of related financial instruments.

Regulation 2(2) further provides that 'information of a precise nature' means information that

(a) indicates:
    (i)   a set of circumstances which exists or may reasonably be expected to come into existence; or
    (ii)   an event which has occurred or may reasonably be expected to occur; or
(b) is specific enough to enable a conclusion to be drawn as to the possible effect of that set of circumstances or event, as the case may be, on the prices of financial instruments or related derivative financial instruments.

'Information which, if it were made public, would be likely to have a significant effect on the prices of financial instruments or related derivative financial instruments' means information that a reasonable investor would be likely to use as part of the basis of the investor's investment decisions, and includes cognate expressions.

From these definitions it is clear that the Regulations provide far more guidance as to what constitutes inside information than the provisions of Part V of the Companies Act 1990.

The concept of market manipulation is new in Ireland. Regulation 2(1) defines 'market manipulation' as:

(a) transactions or orders to trade —
  (i) which give, or are likely to give false or misleading signals as to the supply of, demand for or price of financial instruments; or
  (ii) which secure, by a person, or persons acting in collaboration, the price of one or several financial instruments at an abnormal or artificial level, unless the person who entered into the transactions or issued the orders to trade establishes that the person's reasons for so doing are legitimate and the transactions or orders to trade, as the case may be, conform to accepted market practices on the regulated market concerned,
(b) transactions or orders to trade which employ fictitious devices or any other form of deception or contrivance; or
(c) dissemination of information through the media, including the Internet, or by any other means, which gives, or is likely to give, false or misleading signals as to financial instruments, including the dissemination of rumours and false or misleading news, where the person who made the dissemination knew, or ought to have known, that the information was false or misleading.

Regulation 2(3) provides some guidance as to the types of conduct that would constitute market manipulation. The list is a guidance only and is not intended to be exhaustive:

(a) conduct aimed at securing a dominant position over the supply or demand for a financial instrument which has the effect of fixing, either directly or indirectly, purchase or sale prices or creating other unfair trading conditions;
(b) buying or selling financial instruments at the close of the market with the effect of misleading investors acting on the basis of closing prices;
(c) taking advantage of occasional or regular access to the traditional or electronic media (including the Internet) by voicing an opinion about a financial instrument (or its issuer) while previously having taken positions on that instrument and profiting subsequently from the impact of opinions voiced on the price of that instrument, without having simultaneously disclosed that conflict of interest to the public in a proper and effective way.

Schedules 2 and 3 of the Regulations also set out the type of signals that could constitute market manipulation. The combination of Regulation 2(3) and the schedule therefore provide a comprehensive picture of the types of behaviour that will either constitute or indicate market manipulation.

Certain actions are exempted from the general prohibition where they are taken in conformity with takeover rules and buy-back or stabilisation measures. The Regulations impose disclosure and notification requirements on the relevant issuer, those acting on behalf of or for the account of the issuer and those involved in the management of such issuers.

Recommendations

The Regulations impose a general obligation on any person who produces or disseminates recommendations in relation to any financial instruments to take reasonable care to ensure that the recommendations are fairly presented, and to disclose any interests in or conflicts of interest concerning the financial instruments and issuer to which any such recommendation relates. To this end the Regulations are specific as to the matters which must be contained when presenting a recommendation.

The Competent Authority

The Central Bank and Financial Services Authority of Ireland (the Bank) is designated as the single administrative competent authority. The Financial Regulator has been delegated this function by the Bank. Part 5 of the Regulations and the section 31 of the 2005 Act set out the rights, powers and obligations of the Bank in terms of enforcement of the market abuse provisions including, *inter alia*, the following:

1. the power to appoint an assessor to conduct an assessment as to whether a contravention has occurred;
2. the power to require witnesses to appear and give evidence;
3. the right to refer a question of law for determination by the High Court;
4. the obligation to issue the assessee with any adverse assessments and advise the assessee of its right to appeal against the assessment;
5. the power to impose sanctions subject to a right of appeal to the High Court;
6. the right to apply to the court for an order confirming the adverse assessment;
7. the obligation to make rules to secure that the provisions of Irish market abuse law are complied with.

Obligations Imposed on Market Operators

Apart from the prohibition on insider dealing and market manipulation, the Regulations also contain a number of 'commands' that have a support function. These commands primarily provide for the fair, fast and complete disclosure of information by various participants in the financial world, ranging from news about issuers, securities ownership and transactions by insiders to the publication of investment recommendations. In addition, professional market operators such as securities institutions and issuing institutions are obliged to contribute to maintaining market integrity in different ways, from structuring their operations such that market manipulation practices are prevented, and detected, transparency of transactions is ensured and the requirement to report on a regular basis is met.

Offences

Part 6 of the Regulations contains provisions regarding the offences for breach of the insider dealing and market manipulation provisions, breach of the notification and disclosure provisions, breach of the recommendation provisions, obstruction of an authorised officer, failure to comply with a request or requirement of an authorised officer and giving false or misleading information in relation to a material particular. Summary proceedings may be brought by the Financial Regulator.

Civil and Criminal Liability.

If a person contravenes the market abuse rules he may be liable:

(a) to compensate any other party to the transaction concerned who was not in possession of the relevant information for any loss sustained by that party by reason of any difference between the price at which the financial instruments concerned were acquired or disposed of and the price at which they would have been likely to have been acquired or disposed of in such a transaction at the time when the first-mentioned transaction took place if that information had been generally available; and

(b) to account to the body corporate or other legal entity that issued the financial instruments concerned for any profit accruing to the first-mentioned person from acquiring or disposing of those instruments.[18]

---

18 Section 33(1) of the 2005 Act.

A person who is guilty of an offence under the market abuse rules shall, in respect of a summary conviction for an offence, be liable, on conviction on indictment, to a fine not exceeding €10,000,000 or imprisonment for a term not exceeding ten years, or to both.[19]

---

19 Section 32 of the 2005 Act.

CHAPTER FOURTEEN

SHAREHOLDERS' MEETINGS

Types of Meeting

1. Annual General Meeting

The first Annual General Meeting (AGM) of a company must be held within eighteen months of incorporation. Thereafter the AGM must be held every year with not more than fifteen months elapsing between each meeting.[1] A newly formed company need not hold an AGM in the year of incorporation or the following year, provided an AGM is held within eighteen months of incorporation.[2]

Unless otherwise provided by the articles, the AGM must be held within the State.[3] If default is made in holding the AGM within the prescribed time, the Director of Corporate Enforcement (the Director) may, on the application of any member of the company, call a meeting or direct that one be held.[4] He may also issue such directions as he thinks expedient for the holding of the meeting, including fixing the meeting's quorum at one member. A meeting called by the Director will be deemed to be the AGM if held in the year in which the default in holding the meeting occurred. Otherwise it will be deemed to be the AGM only if the company so resolves. A copy of such an authorising resolution must be forwarded to the registrar within fifteen days of its being passed. Default in complying with the requirement to hold an AGM will render every director who is knowingly and wilfully guilty of the default — or, in the case of default by the company, every officer in default — liable to a fine.

Where it is impractical to call a meeting in the manner normally followed, or to conduct a meeting in the manner prescribed by the articles, the court may, on the application of a member or director of the company, order that a meeting be called, held and conducted in such manner as it thinks fit.[5] In *Re El Sombrero*,[6] the applicant held 90 per cent of the shares in a private company but was not a director. The rest of the shares were held equally between two other persons who were the company's directors. The applicant convened a meeting with the stated object of removing the directors. The articles fixed the quorum at two persons and, as the directors did not attend, the meeting was denied a quorum. An application was made to the court,

---

1 Section 131 of the Principal Act.
2 Section 131(2) of the Principal Act.
3 Even where articles do provide that meetings should be held in the State, if all the members agree to hold it outside the State the meeting will be valid: *Re Shannonside Holdings Ltd*, Unreported, High Court, Costello J., May 20, 1993.
4 Section 131(3) of the Principal Act.
5 Section 135(1) of the Principal Act.
6 [1958] 3 All ER 1.

which directed that a meeting be held with a quorum of one member, thus allowing the applicant member his statutory right to remove a director.

The Business of the AGM

The articles of association determine for the most part the business of the AGM. However, section 148 of the Principal Act makes it incumbent on the directors to lay before the AGM a profit and loss account (or income and expenditure account in the case of a company not trading for profit) and a balance sheet. Furthermore, section 158 of the Principal Act requires that a report of the directors, concerning the state of the company's affairs, should be attached to the balance sheet. Section 163 of the Principal Act requires the auditors of the company to make a report to the members on the accounts examined by them, and this report must be read at the AGM. Group accounts must also be laid before the meeting in the case of parent companies.

Article 53 of Table A provides that the following matters be considered as the ordinary business of the AGM:

(a) the declaration of a dividend;
(b) the consideration of the accounts and balance sheet;
(c) the consideration of the directors' and auditors' report;
(d) the election of directors in the place of those retiring;
(e) the reappointment and remuneration of the auditor.

All other business is deemed by Table A to be the special business of the meeting.

Single-Member Companies

Since the coming into force of the European Communities (Single Member Private Limited Companies) Regulations 1994 (the 1994 Regulations), the above provisions relating to the AGM are no longer mandatory for all companies. Instead, single-member companies may dispense with holding an AGM if the sole member so decides.[7] Alternatively, the sole member or the auditors of a single-member company may, by notice to the company not later than three months before the end of the year, require the holding of an AGM in that year. Rather than laying the accounts and reports before the AGM, it is sufficient to have sent the accounts and reports to the sole member at least twenty-one days before the date of the AGM.

2. Extraordinary General Meetings

Any meeting which is not an AGM is an Extraordinary General Meeting (EGM). Table A provides that the directors may convene an EGM whenever they think

---

7 Section 8(1) of the 1994 Regulations SI 275/1994.

fit. Section 40(1) of the 1983 Amendment Act requires directors to convene an EGM when it becomes known to them that the net assets of the company have fallen to half or less of the company's called-up share capital. A company auditor who gives reasons for his resignation in his written notice may also requisition a meeting under section 186 of the 1990 Act. Members are also given a statutory right to requisition an EGM.[8] The members' requisition must satisfy each of the following criteria:

(a) it must be supported by members holding at least one-tenth of the paid-up share capital in the case of a company having a share capital, or, in the case of a company having no share capital, by members holding at least one-tenth of the total voting rights;
(b) it must state the objects of the meeting;
(c) it must be signed by all the requisitionists; and
(d) it must be deposited at the registered office of the company.

Presuming compliance with the statutory formalities, the directors must within twenty-one days from the date of deposit of the requisition convene a meeting to be held within two months. Failing this, either all the requisitionists or those representing more than half of their total voting rights may do so, provided that the meeting shall be held within three months. The company must repay any reasonable expenses incurred by the requisitionists in convening such a meeting. The company can recover any such payments by retaining any sums due by the company to the defaulting directors, by way of fees or remuneration.

3. Class Meetings

Meetings of the holders of different classes of shares are usually convened when it is necessary to obtain approval from that class. Class approval is prescribed by the Companies Acts in a number of situations including, *inter alia*, a proposed variation or abrogation of class rights or a proposal for a scheme of arrangement under the Companies (Amendment) Act 1990 (the 1990 Amendment Act). Although class meetings may be held at the same time as general meetings, it has been suggested that where there is likely to be intimidation by non-class members, the class members may seek to have a separate meeting.[9]

Notice of Meetings

The Companies Acts and the articles of association provide for different notice requirements depending on the type of meeting and the nature of the business to be transacted thereat. Under section 133 of the Principal Act, every member is

---

8 Section 132 of the Principal Act.
9 *Carruth v. ICI* [1937] AC 707.

entitled to twenty-one days' written notice of the AGM. All other meetings require seven days' notice in the case of a private company and fourteen days' notice in the case of a public company.[10] These notice periods may be waived, provided that the auditors and all the members entitled to attend and vote are in agreement.[11] If a special resolution is proposed at any meeting, the twenty-one-day notice period is required unless 90 per cent of the members entitled to attend and vote agree otherwise.[12] On account of this rule where a resolution requiring a minimum of twenty-one days' notice is proposed, the shorter notice periods may become irrelevant. The company's articles may provide for longer periods of notice, although Table A adopts the statutory notice periods.

1. Table A Requirements

Section 134(a) of the Principal Act requires notice to be served on every member, subject to any contrary provisions in the articles. The provisions of Table A that apply to notices of meetings are as follows:

(a) notice must be given to every member, those persons to whom shares have devolved by reasons of being a personal representative or the official assignee in bankruptcy of a member or deceased member and the auditor of the company;

(b) notice may be given to the joint holders of a share by giving the notice to the first named holder in the register of shares;

(c) notice may be given either personally or by post — if the notice is properly addressed and stamped the addressee is deemed to have received it twenty-four hours after posting;

(d) notice must be clear notice, in that the day of serving the notice and the day for which the notice is given are not counted in calculating the notice period;

(e) accidental failure to give notice of a meeting, or non-receipt of a notice by any person entitled to receive notice, will not invalidate the proceedings at the meeting.

A member may give notice to the company of his intention to propose a resolution to remove a director, or remove or appoint an auditor, or to fill a casual vacancy in the office of auditor. Where such a resolution is proposed the company must be given extended notice of twenty-eight days.[13] However, if the company, on receipt of such a notice, calls the meeting for a date less than twenty-eight days after receiving the notice, the notice is deemed to have been properly given.

---

10 Section 133(2) of the Principal Act.
11 Section 133(3) of the Principal Act.
12 Section 141(2) of the Principal Act.
13 Section 142 of the Principal Act. Members may not waive the extended notice requirements.

2. Form and Content of Notice

The notice convening an AGM must be in writing and in accordance with the provisions of the articles. The form of the notice will depend on the business being proposed at the meeting. Table A requires that the notice specify the place, the day and the hour of the meeting. It would appear that where ordinary business is being conducted, it is not necessary to give specific details in the notice of the meeting. This would seem to be the case even where an ordinary resolution is required. In *Choppington Collieries v. Johnson*,[14] a notice for an AGM specified the election of directors as ordinary business of the meeting. At the meeting a member proposed a resolution to elect new directors in place of those who were retiring. The chairman refused to accept the resolution on the basis that no notice had been given of the member's resolution. The court held that the member's resolution constituted the ordinary business of the meeting and therefore no notice of it was required.

Table A requires that where special business is to be transacted, the notice of the meeting should include the general nature of that business. Where that special business requires a special resolution to be moved, section 141(1) of the Principal Act provides that the notice should also specify the intention to propose a special resolution. The wording of the resolution contained in the notice must be precise and if an amendment to the terms of a resolution is later proposed at the meeting, it cannot be carried unless a majority agree and provided the terms of the resolution as amended are still such that adequate notice of the intention to pass the same can be deemed to have been given.[15] Typographical changes are usually acceptable, but even the most insignificant amendments to the substantive content may invalidate the resolution. In *Re Mooregate Mercantile Holdings Ltd*,[16] notices were issued of a resolution to cancel the entire share premium account of £1,356,900 which had been lost. On discovering that the share premium account stood at £321 more than the notice specified, the chairman proposed to amend the resolution to one reducing the share premium account to £321, and the resolution was carried. The resolution was held to be invalid as it was not the same as that which the notice had described.

It is also necessary to disclose all material information relevant to the proposed resolution in the relevant notice, even when it does not form part of the text of the resolution. In *Kaye v. Croydon Tramways Co.*,[17] the notice set out a resolution which if approved would involve the sale of the company's business. It did not, however, make any disclosure of an agreement to pay the directors compensation if the sale proceeded. It was held that the notice did not properly disclose the nature of the business being transacted at the meeting, and the

---

14 [1944] 1 All ER 762.
15 Section 141(5) of the Principal Act.
16 [1980] 1 All ER 40.
17 [1898] 1 Ch 358.

authorising resolution was therefore invalid. Similarly in *Baillie v. Oriental Telephone & Electric Co.*,[18] a special resolution was proposed and subsequently accepted, whose effect was to give retrospective approval to the payment of increased directors' remuneration. Although the notice and the accompanying circular had set out the text of the resolution and the reasons for it, it was silent on the matter of the sizeable amounts already paid to the directors. The resolution was held to be invalid as the notice did not give sufficient information concerning the transaction.

Where a company has been given extended notice of a resolution under section 142 of the Principal Act, it must give notice to the members of the resolution at the same time and in the same manner as it gives notice of the meeting to which the resolution is proposed. If this is impracticable, it must give notice in the manner provided by the articles not less than twenty-one days before the meeting. It is usual to do so by way of an advertisement in a newspaper circulating in the district in which the registered office is situated. The company must also send a copy of the proposed resolution to the director or auditor who is the subject of the resolution.

Proceedings at General Meetings

In order to be valid, a meeting must be properly convened by notice, a quorum must be present and the meeting must be presided over by a chairman. Furthermore, all resolutions must be passed in accordance with the requirements of the Companies Acts and the articles of association.

1. The Quorum

A quorum is the minimum number of persons whose presence is necessary before a meeting can be held. At common law, one person cannot constitute a meeting, even if he holds proxies for other members. However, there are now exceptions to that rule and a single person may constitute a quorum for any of the following meetings:

(a) class meetings where all the shares in that class are held by one member; or
(b) meetings called by the Director or the court where the quorum has been fixed at one person; or
(c) meetings of single-member companies;[19] or
(d) creditors' meetings if there is only one creditor; or
(e) an adjourned meeting.

In the case of all other meetings, unless the articles otherwise provide, the quorum is fixed at three members for a public company and two for a private

---

18 [1915] 1 Ch 503.
19 Regulation 10 of the European Communities (Single-Member Private Limited Companies) Regulations 1994: SI 275 of 1994.

company.[20] Table A provides that no business shall be transacted at any general meeting unless a quorum is present when the meeting proceeds to business. A similar type of article was the subject of judicial construction in *Re Hartley Baird Ltd.*[21] The company's articles fixed the quorum at ten members, who were present when the meeting began. During the course of the meeting, and before all decisions had been taken, some members left, causing the number remaining to fall below ten. It was held that once the meeting was quorate when it proceeded, it was not necessary that the quorum remained until all the business had been conducted. However, if the number of members at the meeting falls below two, except in those cases provided for by law, the common law principle is that a meeting no longer exists and any purported resolutions will be invalid.

Only members can constitute a meeting. As membership is dependent on entry to the register of members, a person who is the beneficiary of a deceased member's shares but has not procured registration of those shares in their own name cannot form part of the quorum for the purposes of the statutory requirement.[22]

Table A provides that if within half an hour from the time fixed for the meeting a quorum is not present, the meeting, if convened by the members, shall be dissolved. In any other case the meeting shall stand adjourned to the same day of the following week, at the same time and place, or to such other day, time and place as may be determined by the directors. Table A further provides that if at the adjourned meeting a quorum is not present within half an hour, the members present shall constitute the quorum.

2. Chairman

The meeting must be presided over by a chairman. The company's articles will determine who the chairman will be. Table A provides that the chairman of the board of directors or, failing him, another director nominated by the directors shall be the presiding chairman. Where no director is present and willing to act as chairman, the members may elect a chairman. The chairman's duties include the following:

(a) conducting the meeting in accordance with the Companies Acts and the articles;
(b) preserving the order of a meeting and adjourning it where necessary;[23]
(c) deciding on matters relating to motions and amendments;[24]
(d) demanding a poll, if appropriate;[25] and
(e) declaring the result of a poll.

---

20 Section 134(c) of the Principal Act.
21 [1954] Ch 143.
22 *Arulchelvan v. Wright,* Unreported, High Court, Carroll J., February 7, 1996.
23 *Byng v. London Life Association Ltd* [1989] 1 All ER 560.
24 See *Re Moorgate Mercantile Holdings Ltd* [1980] 1 All ER 40.
25 See *MacDougall v. Gardiner* (1875) 1 Ch D 13.

3. *Voting and Polls*

Unless the articles provide otherwise, voting in the first instance is decided on a show of hands. This is the position adopted by Table A, which also provides that a poll may be demanded before or on the declaration of the result of the show of hands. Section 137 of the Principal Act makes void any provision contained in a company's articles which would have the effect of:

(a) excluding the right to demand a poll on any question other than –
    (i) the election of the chairman; or
    (ii) the adjournment of the meeting; and
(b) requiring more persons to demand a poll than any of the following –
    (i) five or more members having a right to vote;
    (ii) members representing 10 per cent of the voting rights;
    (iii) members holding 10 per cent of the paid-up capital who are entitled to vote.

Table A provides that in addition to those categories mentioned in (b) above, the chairman of the meeting may also demand a poll.

Although voting by a show of hands has the advantage of saving time, a poll is more effective because it allows shareholders to exercise their voting rights in proportion to their shares in the company and it gives members who are unable to attend the opportunity to influence the decision-making by authorising a proxy to attend and vote on their behalf.

Unless the articles provide otherwise, the voting rights in a poll are determined as follows:

(a) in the case of a company having a share capital, one vote per share or one vote per €12.70 of stock; and
(b) in any other case, one vote per member.[26]

The procedure for taking a poll is governed by the articles, but it is usual to ask members and proxies to sign voting cards or lists. The votes are then checked against the register of members and the result is declared.

If a poll is not demanded the chairman will decide the outcome by counting the show of hands. Section 141(3) of the Principal Act provides that a declaration by the chairman that the resolution is carried is conclusive evidence of the fact of the number or proportion of the votes recorded in favour of or against the resolution. Table A goes further than the statutory provision by requiring that a record of the result be entered in a book containing the minutes of the proceedings of the meeting. It is possible to challenge the chairman's declaration on the grounds that it was blatantly wrong. In *Re Caratal (New) Mines Ltd*,[27] a

---

26 Section 134(e) of the Principal Act.
27 [1902] 2 Ch 498.

special resolution was proposed and put to the vote on a show of hands. The chairman counted the raised hands and declared that six were for the proposal and twenty-three were against it. He further declared that as a result of the 200 proxy votes the resolution was carried. The declaration was successfully challenged in court on the basis that the proxies could not be used for a vote by a show of hands.

The articles usually provide the chairman with a casting vote, although he is not obliged to exercise it. If he is not already a shareholder in the company, this will be his only vote.

4. *Proxies*

Members entitled to attend and vote at meetings have a right to appoint one 'proxy' to attend, speak and vote on their behalf.[28] However, unless the articles otherwise provide, the right to appoint a proxy shall not apply in the case of a company not having a share capital. Every notice calling a meeting must state that the member has the right to appoint a proxy and the proxy does not need to be a member of the company.

The articles may require that the instrument appointing the proxy shall only be valid if received in advance of the meeting, but the articles cannot fix a longer interval than 48 hours before the meeting for the receipt of same. Where the directors are authorised to issue 'proxy cards' at the company's expense, they must issue them either to all members or to none. However, this does not apply if a member requests in writing a proxy form and such forms are available on request in writing for all members. The form that the instrument appointing a proxy must take is detailed in Table A. It must be in writing, under the hand of the appointer or, if the appointer is a corporation, under the company seal or the hand of an authorised signatory.

5. *Minutes*

Section 145 of the Principal Act requires every company to keep minutes of all proceedings at general meetings. Any such minutes, if purported to be signed by the chairman of the meeting at which the proceedings were held or by the chairman of the next meeting, shall be evidence of the proceedings. Furthermore, unless the contrary is proved, the meeting is presumed to have been duly held and all appointments of directors or liquidators are deemed to be valid. The books containing the minutes must be kept at the registered office and be open to inspection by any member without charge for at least two hours per day.[29] A company shall, if required by the Director, produce to the Director the books containing such minutes.

---

28 Section 136 of the Principal Act.
29 Section 146 of the Principal Act.

6. Decision Making by Shareholders

Decisions taken by the company in general meeting are in the form of ordinary resolutions and special resolutions.

Ordinary Resolutions

Ordinary resolutions are those that are approved by a simple majority of members, present in person or by proxy, who are entitled to attend and vote. An ordinary resolution is the type used whenever the provisions of the Companies Acts or the articles of the company do not require a special resolution. The rules regarding notice of resolutions must be complied with in order to ensure their validity.

Special Resolutions

Special resolutions are those that are passed by at least a 75 per cent majority of members, present in person or by proxy, who are entitled to attend and vote. A special resolution is required by statute when certain decisions are being made, including *inter alia* decisions to:

(a) alter the name and objects clause of the memorandum of association;
(b) alter the articles of association;
(c) reduce the share capital of the company;
(d) wind up the company voluntarily, unless the company is insolvent;
(e) present a petition for a compulsory winding-up order, where the company is the petitioner under section 213 of the Principal Act;
(f) to approve the giving of financial assistance for the acquisition of shares in a private company;
(g) to approve the purchase by a company of its own shares in an off-market purchase.

Notification to the Registrar

Section143 of the Principal Act requires the following resolutions to be notified to the registrar of companies:

(a) special resolutions;
(b) unanimous resolutions which, had they not been unanimous, could not have been passed other than by special resolution;
(c) resolutions agreed unanimously by a class of members which, had they not been so agreed, could not have been passed other than by a particular majority or in a particular manner;
(d) all resolutions which bind the members of a particular class though not agreed to by all those members;
(e) resolutions increasing the share capital of a company;
(f) resolutions that a company be wound up voluntarily.

The registrar must be notified within fifteen days from the date of passing of the resolution. Furthermore, a copy of these resolutions must be made available for a nominal fee to a member on request. Where articles have been registered, a copy of every such resolution must be embodied in or annexed to all articles thereafter issued.

Default in complying with these provisions does not render them invalid. Rather, the company and every officer in default shall be liable to a fine.

Decisions of Single-Member Companies

In the case of single-member companies, there is no requirement to pass resolutions. Instead of a resolution, a written decision notified to the company will suffice.[30] However, the sole member cannot use this power to remove an auditor of the company.

7. Shareholders' Discretion in Decision-making

Assuming the procedure for voting and taking decisions complies with the law, the question arises as to whether shareholders may vote as they please. In Chapter 18, we see where directors who are in a fiduciary position towards the company cannot put themselves into a conflict between personal interests and duty to the company. A member, on the other hand, owes no such fiduciary duty and need not avoid a conflict between their own interests and those of the company. In *Pender v Lushington*,[31] Jessel M.R. observed: 'a man may be actuated in giving his vote by interests entirely adverse to the interests of the company as a whole ... but he cannot be restrained from giving his vote in what way he pleases.' These comments restate what the courts and indeed company legislation have always recognised, namely, the principle of majority rule. However, this rule is not absolute and is subject to limitations discussed in the next chapter, in the context of minority shareholder protection. Furthermore, while an individual shareholder may vote as he pleases, certain decisions taken by the company in the general meeting of the shareholders collectively must be taken *bona fide* and in the best interests of the company including *inter alia* the following:

(a) where the members are exercising their statutory power to alter the articles of association;[32]
(b) where directors are being appointed, such appointments must be for the benefit of the company as a whole, and not for an ulterior motive;[33]

---

30 Regulation 9(1) of the European Communities (Single-Member Private Limited Companies) Regulations 1994.
31 [1877] LR 6 ChD 70.
32 *Re Allen v Gold Reefs of West Africa Ltd.* [1900] 1 Ch 656, discussed in Chapter 5.
33 *Re H.R. Harmer Ltd.* [1959] 1 WLR 62.

(c) at a class meeting where the power of a majority must be exercised for the purpose of benefiting the class as a whole, and not the individual majority shareholder.[34]

8. Company Decisions Taken Informally

The common law recognised that a unanimous decision taken by shareholders in an informal manner was a valid and effective method of adopting a resolution.[35] In *Parker & Cooper v. Reading*,[36] the directors had issued a debenture on behalf of the company, which for technical reasons was invalid. All the shareholders had over a period of time discussed the transaction and had acquiesced in it, though not through the medium of a formal resolution. The liquidator of the company later sought to repudiate the transaction. The court held that as all the shareholders had agreed to the transaction, it was valid, irrespective of the fact that no meeting had been held. The legal principles applicable to such a decision were summarised by Kingsmill Moore J. in the Irish case of *Buchanan Ltd v. McVey*[37] as follows:

> If all the corporators agree to a certain course then, however informal the manner of their agreement, it is an act of the company and binds the company subject to only two prerequisites . . . The two necessary prerequisites are (1) that the transaction to which the corporators agree should be *intra vires* the company; and (2) that the transaction should be honest.[38]

The 'assent principle' may also apply to decisions where every member had the opportunity to state their objections but did not do so. In *Re Bailey Hay & Co. Ltd*,[39] a notice of a meeting to consider a resolution to wind up the company had been given which was one day short of the notice required by law. All five shareholders attended, two voted for the resolution, three abstained and the resolution was carried. Some time later, in an attempt to undermine the liquidation process, it was claimed that the authorising resolution was invalid because of the defective notice. This argument was rejected by the court on the grounds, *inter alia*, that by not attempting to stop the winding up by voting against it, all members had agreed to it.[40]

The assent principle has been given a statutory footing by virtue of section 141(8) of the Principal Act. This provides that where a company is so authorised

---

34 *Re Holders Investment Trust Ltd.* [1971] 1 WLR 583.
35 See *Cane v. Jones* [1981] 1 All ER 533.
36 [1926] Ch 975.
37 [1954] IR 89.
38 Restated with approval in *Re Greendale Developments Ltd (in Liquidation)* [1998] 1 IR 8.
39 [1971] 1 WLR 1357.
40 See also *Re Home Treat Ltd* [1991] BCLC 705.

by its articles, a resolution in writing signed by all the company's members shall be as valid and effective as if the resolution had been passed at a general meeting of the company, and if described as such shall be deemed to be such. This statutory provision is more rigorous than the common law 'assent principle' because it requires the agreement to be in writing. Whether or not section 141(8) overrides the common law position remains to be seen. However, one High Court judge has suggested that in the absence of an express agreement, the circumstances may imply that an agreement was in fact reached.[41] This would seem to suggest that the statutory provision supplements rather than replaces the common law rule.

---

41 Per Costello J. in *Re Shannonside Holdings Ltd,* Unreported, High Court, May 20, 1993. See also Supreme Court in *Re Greendale Developments Ltd (in Liquidation)* [1998] 1 IR 8.

CHAPTER FIFTEEN

MINORITY PROTECTION

Introduction

As discussed in the previous chapter, minority shareholders generally have to accept the decisions made by the majority of shareholders. However, while company law accepts the principle of majority rule, this principle is not absolute. It is tempered by statutory provisions and legal principles that have been developed to protect the minority shareholder. In previous chapters we have seen examples of this protection. In Chapter 8 we discussed the rules required where class rights are being varied. The rights of shareholders vis-à-vis their 'section 25 contract' were described in Chapter 5. The Companies Acts also confer specific rights on individual or minority shareholders, many of which cannot be abridged by the articles of association, including, *inter alia*, the right:

(a) to receive a copy of the memorandum and articles of association;[1]
(b) to apply to the court for an injunction restraining the company from acting ultra vires;[2]
(c) to receive notice of general meetings;[3]
(d) to receive copies of certain resolutions of the general meetings including, *inter alia*, special resolutions, resolutions increasing the share capital of the company and resolutions attaching rights or restrictions to any shares;[4]
(e) to receive copies of any minutes of proceedings are general meetings;[5]
(f) to receive copies of the latest balance sheet of any of the company's subsidiaries;[6]
(g) to inspect various registers of the companies including *inter alia* the register of directors and secretaries and the register of directors' shareholdings;
(h) to exercise their pre-emption rights, when applicable, on the issue of new shares by the company;[7]
(i) to apply to the court for a disclosure order in relation to shareholdings in a private company;[8]

---

1 Section 29 of the Principal Act.
2 Section 8(2) of the Principal Act (see Chapter 7).
3 Sections 131–133 of the Principal Act (see Chapter 14).
4 Section 143 of the Principal Act.
5 Section 146 of the Principal Act.
6 Section 154 of the Principal Act.
7 Section 23 of the 1983 Amendment Act.
8 Section 98 of the 1990 Act.

(j) to apply to the court for a disqualification order against any officer of the company under section160 of the 1990 Act;[9]

(k) to object to an alteration of the memorandum and articles of association;[10]

(l) to object to a reduction in capital by the company under section 72 of the Principal Act;[11]

(m) to object to the giving of financial assistance by a company to purchase shares in the company under section 60 of the Principal Act;[12]

(n) to petition the court to have an examiner appointed;[13]

(o) to apply to the court to have an inspector appointed to investigate the affairs of a company;[14] and

(p) to apply to the court to have the company wound up.[15]

In addition to any personal rights a member may have under the articles of association or under any statutory provisions, members also have a role in ensuring that the company and its officers comply with their legal obligations. Accordingly, any member has a right to issue a notice to the company or any officer requiring it or him to comply with any provision of the Companies Acts. If the company fails to make good any default within fourteen days after the service of the notice the member may apply to the court for an order directing that the company or the officer make good any default.[16]

The Rule in *Foss v. Harbottle*

If a wrong is done to a company, it follows from its separate legal personality that the proper plaintiff in any subsequent action is the company itself. The agency to decide on such a course will be the board of directors or, failing this, the company in general meeting. This rule of company law was established in *Foss v. Harbottle*.[17]

Here, the defendant directors had sold land to the company at an exorbitant price. Two shareholders took an action against them to make good the loss caused to the company. The action failed on the grounds that the wrongs committed were against the company, so any action against the wrongdoers ought to be taken by the company and not by the individual shareholders. As Wigham VC observed:

> It was not, nor could it successfully be argued that it was a matter of course for any individual members of a corporation thus to assume to themselves the right of suing

---

9 See Chapter 19.

10 See Chapters 4 and 5.

11 See Chapter 10.

12 Ibid.

13 Section 3 of the 1990 Amendment Act.

14 Section 7(1) of the 1990 Act.

15 Discussed later in this chapter.

16 Section 371 of the Principal Act.

17 (1843) 2 Hare 261.

in the name of the corporation. In law, the corporation and the aggregate members of the corporation are not the same thing . . .[18]

The rule in *Foss v. Harbottle* is a logical extension of the separate legal personality doctrine. It preserves the principle of majority decision-making, it prevents a multiplicity of actions by aggrieved shareholders and it deters futile actions by shareholders against irregularities and wrongdoings which are capable of being ratified by the general meeting.

Personal Rights of Shareholders

The rule does not, however, prevent individual members from bringing actions to defend their own personal interests. What constitutes a personal wrong to a member, as opposed to a wrong to a company, will not always be obvious. In *MacDougall v. Gardiner*[19] the chairman of the company, in breach of the articles of association, refused a request by some shareholders that a poll be held on the question of whether or not a general meeting should be adjourned. The plaintiff sought a declaration that the chairman's action was improper. The declaration was refused on the grounds that the 'irregularity' in the internal procedures of the company was one which could have been ratified by the majority. The case has been criticised, but since then there has been a growing acceptance by the courts that the failure to comply with the terms of the articles may be an infringement of the 'personal' rights of a shareholder. In *Pender v. Lushington*[20] the court was persuaded by such an argument. The plaintiffs had proposed a resolution but the chairman, in breach of the articles, refused to count the votes attaching to the plaintiffs' nominee shares and the resolution was not carried. The plaintiffs successfully applied for an injunction against the directors who proposed acting on the basis that the resolution had not been passed. The court held that, as a shareholder, the plaintiffs were entitled to have their votes recorded, and failing this they had a right to sue.

Similarly, in *Edwards v. Halliwell*[21] the court held that a breach of the internal procedures as set out by the articles of association was a breach of a member's personal rights. The case concerned a trade union, whose rules provided that no increase could be placed on membership subscriptions unless approved by two-thirds of a ballot of members. A decision was taken to increase the subscriptions without holding a ballot. The court held that the rule in *Foss v. Harbottle* had no application to the case, as the decision to increase the subscriptions constituted a wrong done to the members and not to the union.

---

18 Ibid at 490.
19 (1875) 1 Ch D 13.
20 [1877] LR 6 Ch D 7.
21 [1950] 2 All ER 1064.

A distinction should be made between a shareholder suffering a personal wrong and a shareholder suffering a reflective loss. A reflective loss is one suffered by a shareholder following a breach of duty owed to the company which causes a diminution of the company's assets and a consequential diminution of the value of the company's shares. In such circumstances, a shareholder is prevented from bringing a personal action to recover the damages for the loss in the value of his shares. The company's assets (and the corresponding value of the shares) could be restored if the company brings a successful action against the wrongdoers to make good any loss. In *Prudential Assurance Co Ltd v. Newman Industries Ltd*[22] proceedings were brought by Prudential, a minority shareholder in Newman, against the directors of the company. It was alleged that the directors' fraudulent actions had caused a loss to the company, which in turn led to a reduction in the value of Prudential's shareholding by affecting the price of the shares. The Court of Appeal held that it was not possible for a shareholder to bring a personal claim against a wrongdoer to the company in respect of the decreased value of his shareholding. The court observed:

> A personal action would subvert the rule in *Foss v. Harbottle* and that rule is not merely a tiresome procedural obstacle placed in the path of a shareholder by a legalistic judiciary. The rule is the consequence of the fact that a corporation is a separate legal entity. Other consequences are limited liability and limited rights. The company is liable for its contracts and torts; the shareholder has no such liability. The company acquires causes of action for breaches of contract and for torts which damage the company. No cause of action vests in the shareholder. When the shareholder acquires a share he accepts the fact that the value of his investment follows the fortunes of the company and that he can only exercise his influence over the fortunes of the company by the exercise of his voting rights in general meeting. The law confers on him the right to ensure that the company observes the limitations of its memorandum of association and the right to ensure that other shareholders observe the rule, imposed upon them by the articles of association.

The Irish courts have also accepted the rule against reflective loss. In *O'Neill v. Ryan & Ryanair*[23] a former shareholder and chief executive of Ryanair claimed damages in respect of the reduction in value of his shareholding as a result of alleged breaches of EU competition law which caused damage to the company. Applying the principles laid down in *Prudential,* the Supreme Court held that the plaintiff had no right of personal action in respect of the resulting reduction in the value of his shareholding. Similarly, in the recent case of *Madden v. Anglo Irish Bank plc*[24] the plaintiff, a substantial shareholder and a creditor of a construction company which was in liquidation claimed damages for an alleged breach of section 60 of the Companies Act 1963 in relation to an agreement

---

22 [1982] 1 All ER 354
23 [1993] ILRM 557
24 [2005] 1 ILRM 294

whereby the company agreed to accept liability for another party's debts and to grant a secured debenture to the bank. The plaintiff also contended that the agreement was also *ultra vires* the company. The defendant bank sought to have the claim struck out on the basis that it fell within the rule against recovery for reflective loss. The Supreme Court dismissed the claim on the grounds that it was reflective of the loss suffered by the company and held that the plaintiff could not maintain an action which was for the company or someone acting in its place, such as a liquidator, to maintain.

Exceptions to the Rule in *Foss v. Harbottle*

It has always been recognised that exceptions to the rule in *Foss v. Harbottle* may be permitted. In *Foss v. Harbottle* itself Wigham VC alluded to this possibility, but the facts did not justify an exception being made. It is now accepted that the following circumstances justify a departure from the rule. Essentially these circumstances relate to circumstances that cannot be ratified by the majority.

1. Where the transaction is illegal or *ultra vires* the company. In *Cockburn v. Newbridge Sanitary Steam Laundry Company*,[25] the company's managing director had paid bribes to officials in the War Office in order to obtain contracts for the company. Two of the company's shareholders instituted proceedings to compel the managing director to repay the bribe amounts to the company. The managing director's defence, that any cause of action ought to be by the company and not the shareholders, failed. The court, in holding for the plaintiffs, stated that acts which are beyond the powers of the company may be challenged by a shareholder. Similarly, in *Parke v. Daily News Ltd*,[26] a minority shareholder successfully claimed that gratuitous payments made to employees of the company were *ultra vires*. In any case, section 8(2) of the Principal Act specifically provides that a member may apply to court for an order restraining the company from carrying out *ultra vires* acts.

2. Where a special resolution ought to have been passed and this was not in fact done or it was done in breach of procedure. In *Baillie v Oriental Telephone and Electric Co. Ltd*[27] the directors of the Oriental were also directors of a subsidiary company owned by Oriental. The directors, in exercise of the voting powers of the Oriental in the subsidiary company, obtained the passing of resolutions whereby the articles of association of the subsidiary company were altered so as to increase the fixed remuneration of the directors and also to give them a percentage of the net profits. Some years

---

25 [1915] 1 IR 237.
26 [1962] 2 All ER 929.
27 [1915] 1 Ch 503.

later the auditors of Oriental drew attention to the fact that the receipt by the directors of remuneration in the capacity of directors of the subsidiary company ought to be sanctioned by the shareholders. An extraordinary general meeting of the shareholders of Oriental was then convened by the directors with the object of passing special resolutions for the purpose, *inter alia*, of ratifying what had been done by the directors and authorising them to retain all remuneration received by them. The notice convening the meeting was accompanied by a circular. The notice set out the proposed resolutions, but neither the notice nor the circular gave particulars as to the amount — which was substantial – of the remuneration that had been received by the directors in respect of the subsidiary company. The resolutions were passed by the requisite majority and subsequently confirmed. A shareholder took an action on behalf of all the shareholders for a declaration that the resolutions were not binding on the ground of insufficient notice of the meeting at which they were passed, and for an injunction to restrain the company and the directors from acting upon them. The court held that the rule in *Foss v. Harbottle* had no application and that the action was maintainable; that the notice did not give a sufficiently full and frank disclosure to the shareholders of the facts upon which they were asked to vote; and that the resolutions were invalid and not binding upon the company. Similarly, In *Byng v. London Life Association*,[28] a member succeeded in obtaining a declaration that a purported meeting and special resolutions were void because the correct procedure for adjourning the meeting had not been followed.

3. Where there is a 'fraud on the minority' by the majority of shareholders. Fraud in this context has been described as a 'notoriously vague concept'.[29] However, an indication of the type of behaviour that constitutes a 'fraud on the minority' can be gleaned from the case law dealing with this matter. In *Menier v. Hooper's Telegraph Works*[30] the company directors settled an action by the company on terms that were favourable to the majority shareholders but not to the company itself. The general meeting then purported to ratify the directors' action by way of resolution. The minority shareholders succeeded in an action claiming that the resolution was invalid and that any benefits made by the majority shareholders should be returned to the company. A more extreme example of fraud on a minority can be seen in the case of *Cook v. Deeks*.[31] Directors of the company had diverted profitable contracts away from the company to themselves. The minority shareholders sought an order directing that the directors account to the

---

28 [1989] 1 All ER 560.
29 Report of the Company Law Committee (the Jenkins Committee) (1962) (Cmnd. 1749).
30 (1874) LR 9 Ch App 350.
31 [1916] 1 AC 554.

company for the profits they made. Although a general meeting had purported to ratify the wrong done by the directors, this was held to be ineffective as it constituted a 'fraud on the minority'. Similarly, in *Daniels v. Daniels*[32] two directors who were also the majority shareholders had caused the company to sell land to themselves at an undervalue. Although no fraud was alleged, the court held that the transactions should be set aside on the grounds that the directors' negligence had benefited themselves at the expense of the company. However, if the negligent act of the directors did not benefit themselves, then their actions may be capable of ratification, as occurred in *Pavlides v. Jensen*.[33] The plaintiff, a minority shareholder, claimed that the directors had negligently sold the company's principal asset, a mine, to a third party at a gross undervalue. The action was dismissed on the grounds that the controlling shareholders who were represented by the directors had not benefited and accordingly the transaction was ratifiable by the general meeting.

4.   Where the justice of the case requires an exception to be made. In *Foss v Harbottle* Wigram VC. stated:

> If a case should arise of injury to a corporation by some of its members, for which no adequate remedy remained, except that of a suit by individual corporators in their private character, and asking in such character the protection of those rights to which in their corporate character they were entitled, I cannot but think that ... the claims of justice would be found superior to any difficulties arising out of technical rules respecting the mode in which corporations are required to sue.

Although the courts have on occasion made reference to this ground,[34] we still await a definitive pronouncement as in each of the relevant cases the courts were not required to rely on this exception. Therefore any comments either approving or discounting this ground can only be regarded as *obiter*.

It should be noted that a shareholder will not be entitled to bring a derivative action on behalf of a company unless that shareholder is acting *bona fide* for the benefit of the company in respect of wrongs done to that company.[35] Furthermore, the courts will not countenance a derivative action if the applicant shareholder has an ulterior motive. As Lawton LJ. stated:

> It is pertinent to remember, however, that a minority shareholder's action in form is nothing more than a procedural device for enabling the court to do justice to a

---

32   [1978] Ch 406.
33   [1956] 2 All ER 518.
34   *O'Neill v. Ryan* [1993] ILRM 557; *Crindle Investments v. Wymes* [1998] 4 IR 567; *Prudential Assurance Co. Ltd v. Newman Industries Ltd* (No. 2) [1982] Ch 204; and *Moylan v. Irish Whiting Manufacturers Ltd*, Unreported, High Court, Hamilton J., April 14, 1980.
35   *Barrett v. Duckett & Others* [1995] 1 BCLC 243.

company controlled by miscreant directors or shareholders. Since the procedural device has evolved so that justice can be done for the benefit of the company, whoever comes forward to start the proceedings must be doing so for the benefit of the company and not for some other purpose. It follows that the court has to satisfy itself that the person coming forward is a proper person to do so.[36]

Finally, if another adequate remedy is available the court will not allow the derivative action to succeed. In *Fargo v. Godfrey*[37] a minority shareholder brought a derivative action on behalf of the company alleging that the other shareholder and directors had diverted assets and business opportunities belonging to the company for their own personal use. By the time the plaintiff had issued the writ a liquidator had been appointed over the company. In striking out the writ the Court of Appeal held that once a liquidator is appointed the situation changes because neither the board nor the general meeting can control any longer the activities of the company.

Rather than pursuing a derivative action based on an exception to the rule in *Foss v. Harbottle*, the aggrieved shareholder may opt instead for the statutory remedy afforded by section 205 of the Principal Act.

Section 205 of the Principal Act

Section 205(1) of the Principal Act provides that:

> Any member of a company who complains that the affairs of the company are being conducted or that the powers of the directors of the company are being exercised in a manner oppressive to him or any of the members (including himself) or in disregard of his or their interests as members, may apply to the court for an order under this section.

Presenting the Petition

Section 205(1) specifically gives members the *locus standi* in regard to petitioning the court for a remedy. However, the definition of 'member' for the purposes of section 205 is much broader than the normal definition attributable to a member.[38] Section 205(6) gives the personal representative of a person who at the date of his death was a member of a company, or any trustee of, or person beneficially interested in, the shares of a company by virtue of the will or intestacy of the deceased, the right to apply for an order under section 205(1).

A member's right to petition the court is not dependent on his showing that the oppressive conduct affected him only in his capacity as a member.[39] The 1990

---

36 *Nurcombe v. Nurcombe* [1984] BCLC 557 at 562.

37 [1986] BCLC 370.

38 By virtue of section 31 of the Principal Act a person will not become a member until his name has been registered in the register of members.

39 In *Re Murph's Restaurant Ltd* [1979] ILRM 141. But see *Re Unisoft Group Ltd No. 30* [1994] 1 BCLC 609 where Harman J. took the contrary view that the shareholder must be affected *qua* shareholder.

Amendment Act has introduced some limitation on the discretion of a member to bring an action under section 205. It provides that complaints concerning the conduct of the affairs of the company while it is under the protection of the court shall not constitute the basis for the making of an order for relief under section 205.

All petitions must be presented for the genuine purpose of obtaining the relief claimed and not for any collateral purpose; otherwise, the petitioner will be abusing the process of the court.[40]

Oppression

What will constitute oppressive behaviour within the meaning of section 205(1) will be determined by an objective judgment based on the facts. It is irrelevant that no evidence of *male fides* on the part of the 'oppressor' can be found.[41] In *Scottish Wholesale Co-operative Society Ltd v. Meyer*[42] a subsidiary company was formed by a co-operative society in which the plaintiff became a minority shareholder. When the majority no longer required the plaintiff as a shareholder it sought to purchase the minority shareholding. The plaintiff refused to sell its shares and the co-operative transferred the subsidiary's business to itself. Without a business, the subsidiary was worthless. The plaintiff petitioned the court under the UK equivalent of section 205(1). The Court of Appeal held that the actions of the majority shareholder were oppressive as it had exercised its majority power in a manner which was 'burdensome, harsh and wrongful'.

This definition was accepted by Keane J. in *Re Greenore Trading Co. Ltd*[43] The plaintiff and two other shareholders, B and V, each held one third of the issued share capital of the company. Later B agreed to sell his shares to V for a consideration which represented, *inter alia*, £14,500 payable by the company as compensation for B's loss of office. The plaintiff sought relief under section 205, claiming that V's control over the company was being used in an oppressive manner. Keane J. held that the payment of £14,500 either represented an unauthorised payment of company monies, which had not been approved by the company in general meeting, or it represented the giving of financial assistance by the company to purchase its shares, which is contrary to section 60 of the Principal Act.[44] In either scenario the payment was unlawful and a misapplication of the company's monies for the purpose of giving V an increased shareholding. Accordingly, he granted the relief sought and made an order that the plaintiff's shares be purchased by V.

Although the behaviour in this case was deemed to be 'unlawful', this is not a

---

40 *Re Bellador Silk Ltd* [1965] 1 All ER 667.
41 *Re Irish Visiting Motorist's Bureau Ltd*, Unreported, High Court, Kenny J., February 7, 1972.
42 [1959] AC 324.
43 [1980] ILRM 94.
44 See Chapter 10.

requisite to an order under section 205. In *Re a Company* (No. 00789 of 1987),[45] the court held that continuous failure to hold AGMs and lay accounts before the members was conduct unfairly prejudicial to the interests of the members.

Repudiation of an agreement may also constitute 'oppression' within the meaning of section 205(1). In *Irish Press plc v. Ingersoll Irish Publications Ltd*[46] Barron J. held that the failure to operate a management agreement between the petitioner and respondents amounted to a repudiation of the agreement which was oppressive behaviour within the meaning of the Act. Accordingly, the respondent was ordered to sell its shares in the company to the petitioner. Similarly, in *Crindle Investments v. Wymes*[47] the Supreme Court considered a failure by the majority shareholders to accept offers of a compromise in relation to legal proceedings to be oppressive conduct within the meaning of section 205(1).

It would seem that the oppressive conduct does not necessarily have to be continuous. In *Re Westwinds Holding Co. Ltd*[48] Kenny J. held that a sale of lands by a company at an undervalue was a sufficient act of oppression to invoke section 205.[49]

However, it would seem that section 205(1) cannot be invoked on the basis of a mere possibility of oppression. In *Re a Company* (No. 004475 of 1982)[50] a majority of shareholders had indicated their wish to acquire a wine bar using company funds. A petition by a minority shareholder failed on the ground that it was premature to bring such an action before any final decision to proceed with the purchase was actually taken.

Disregarding Members' Interests

Even where no oppressive conduct is said to exist, section 205 may still be invoked where the petitioner can demonstrate that the affairs of the company or the powers of the directors are being conducted in disregard of the member's interests. In *Re a Company*[51] the court held that the continuous failure of the directors to hold annual general meetings and lay accounts before the members was conduct unfairly prejudicial to the interests of the members. In *Re Westwinds Holding Co. Ltd*. Kenny J. considered that the directors had not only exercised their powers in an oppressive way but also in 'disregard of the interests of the members of the company'.

However, it would seem that the phrase 'in disregard of the interests of a member' covers more than just the legal rights of the member.

---

45 [1990] BCLC 384.
46 Unreported, High Court, Barron J., December 16, 1993.
47 [1998] 2 ILRM 275.
48 Unreported, High Court, Kenny J., May 21, 1974.
49 In *Re Williams Group (Tullamore) Ltd* [1985] IR 613 Barrington J. also accepted that a single act was sufficient for a member to petition the court under section 205.
50 [1983] 2 All ER 36.
51 (No. 00789 of 1987) [1990] BCLC 384.

In *Re Williams Group Tullamore Ltd*[52] the company's articles of association provided that as long as there were preference shareholders the ordinary shareholders could not attend and vote at general meetings. The articles further provided that the preference shareholders received a fixed dividend which they duly did on an annual basis. The ordinary shareholders on the other hand fared much better, as they received substantial dividends. The preference shareholders, obviously tired of this imbalance, proposed a special resolution whereby a new class of share would be issued which would qualify for a dividend payment over and above the existing preference shareholder's dividend. Despite the fact that the new issue would be distributed to all shareholders, the effect of the proposal would be to distribute profits of the company to the preference shareholders which otherwise would have been available to ordinary shareholders under the original distribution scheme. Even though the correct procedures were followed and the proposal was put forward in good faith, Barrington J. held that the resolutions were in disregard of the ordinary shareholders' interests. This case gives some indication of the Irish courts' recognition that a member may have a 'legitimate expectation' that the status quo is maintained, a certain course of action followed or indeed that he will share in the management and profits of the company.[53]

Courts' Discretionary Powers under Section 205

If the court is satisfied that the claim is well founded it may, with a view to bringing to an end the matters complained of, make any order it deems fit, including the following:

(a) direct or prohibit any act; or
(b) cancel or vary any transaction; or
(c) provide for the future regulation of the conduct of the company; or
(d) order the purchase of the shares of any member by the other members or by the company itself.

In the *Scottish Wholesale* case the Court of Appeal ordered that the co-operative purchase the plaintiff's shares at the value they would have had if the business of the company had not been transferred. Similarly, in the Irish case of *Re NEW-AD Advertising Company Limited*[54] the court ordered the oppressor, a majority shareholder, to purchase the shares of the minority at a value that they would have been at but for the oppressive conduct. Even where the oppressor is

---

52 [1985] IR 613.
53 *Re Westbourne Galleries Ltd* [1973] AC 360 (discussed below), *Re Blue Arrow plc* [1987] BCLC 585 and *Re Saul D Harrison & Sons plc* [1994] BCC 475.
54 Unreported, High Court, Costello P., July 1, 1997.

in discussion with the petitioner with a view to acquiring the petitioner's shares at a fair value, this will not prevent a petition being presented.[55] Furthermore, the court may even order the respondent to sell his shares to the petitioner.[56] In the *Crindle* case the court ordered that the minority shareholder should be in control of negotiations which were to be conducted in relation to certain legal proceedings to which the company was a party. However, it stopped short of ordering the majority shareholders to join in an acceptance of an offer to compromise the proceedings in their own personal capacity.

While the remedy under section 205 is discretionary, it would appear that the court will not consider damages as an appropriate remedy under section 205. In *Irish Press v. Ingersoll*[57] Barron J. in the High Court awarded damages for the oppressive conduct. However, the Supreme Court[58] reversed the decision on the following grounds:

(a) the award of damages could not achieve the objective of section 205 which was to bring the oppression complained of to an end;

(b) awarding damages was a common law remedy and was not appropriate for actions under section 205; and

(c) if damages could have been awarded the legislature would have made such a provision in section 205.

Petition by Member to Wind Up the Company

Another remedy available to a shareholder is the radical step of applying to the court to have the company wound up. Ever since 1848 the courts have been empowered to order that a company be wound up on 'just and equitable grounds'.[59] Examples are where the raison d'être of the company has gone, where a majority has defrauded the company and where there was a complete deadlock in its affairs. The case-law has set out the following basic principles:

(a) a complaint does not have to be brought within any fixed set of categories or situations in order for it to afford grounds for ordering a winding up;

(b) the section is not confined to circumstances which affect the petitioner *qua* member — while he must be a member, the circumstances may relate to his relationship with the company or the other shareholders as an employee, a director or a creditor;

---

55 *Horgan v, Murray*, [1998] 1 ILRM 110.

56 *Irish Press plc v. Ingersoll Irish Publications Ltd*, Unreported, High Court, Barron J., 15 December 1993.

57 Ibid.

58 *Irish Press plc v. Ingersoll Irish Publications Ltd* [1995] 2 IR 175; [1995] 2 ILRM 270.

59 The modern provision is found in section 213 of the Principal Act (see Chapter 25).

(c) the action complained of, even though consistent with the company's own regulations, may be outside what can fairly be regarded as having been in the contemplation of the parties when they become members of the company, and the fact that such an action is within the powers of the company will not necessarily be an answer to a claim for winding up.

Where the company has been formed and is being operated in a manner similar to a partnership, and the relationship of trust and mutual confidence has broken down, the court may also make an order on the just and equitable ground. In *Re Westbourne Galleries Ltd*,[60] E and N had carried on business together for over twenty years. They had done so originally as business partners and subsequently as equal shareholders and joint directors of a company. Eventually they agreed to bring N's son into the business, and he was given 100 shares from each of them and appointed to the board. Following a disagreement between the original shareholders, the father and son used their majority at a general meeting to oust E from the board. E petitioned the court to have the company wound up on the 'just and equitable' ground. Despite the fact that the shareholders had exercised a statutory power, the court, in allowing the petition, held that it was not equitable to insist on legal rights as the company had been set up on the understanding that the business relationship would remain the same.

The breakdown of the 'quasi-partnership' relationship was accepted as a 'just and equitable reason' to wind up the company in the Irish case of *Re Murph's Restaurant Ltd*.[61] The company was formed by two brothers and a friend. One brother and the friend each invested £800 and also advanced £400 each on behalf of the other brother so that they would all be equal 'partners' in the business. They were each directors of the company. The business prospered and the friend ultimately gave up his job to work full-time in the business. The business expanded from Dublin to Cork, and it was the Cork branch that was run by the friend. While the business was well run and organised, the same could not be said of the company's administrative affairs. No general meetings were held, no accounts were maintained, but the directors took great care to draw equal amounts in drawings from the company. The two brothers expanded their business horizons and purchased a hotel in Cork which, unknown to the friend, was partly financed by money from the company. Eventually, the two brothers decided to 'break' from the friend, and they notified him of a meeting at which they intended to remove him from office. The friend petitioned to have the company wound up on the 'just and equitable' ground. The court held that the company had been formed and operated on a 'quasi-partnership' basis

---

60 [1972] 2 All ER 492.
61 [1979] ILRM 141.

which required a degree of trust and confidence between the members. As Gannon J. stated:

> a limited company is more than a mere legal entity . . . behind it or amongst it there are individuals with rights, expectations and obligations *inter se* which are not necessarily submerged in the corporate structure.

As the trust and confidence had been destroyed by the acts of the brothers, an order for the compulsory winding up of the company was made.

CHAPTER SIXTEEN

DIRECTORS AND SECRETARIES

Introduction

Companies, as artificial persons, cannot manage themselves. Therefore, the articles of association usually provide for the delegation of management powers to a board of directors. Directors, as agents of the company, can bind the company without incurring personal liability. They also have extensive power in relation to the day-to-day control of the company's business undertaking and its assets. The potential for abuse is obvious. The means of preventing this abuse is more complicated. Equitable principles, common law rules and statutory obligations are interwoven to form an intricate legal framework within which directors must operate. This is considered further in Chapter 18 and subsequent chapters.

Section 174 of the Principal Act requires every company to have at least two directors, who, together with the secretary of the company, are its officers.[1] Although there is no comprehensive definition, the Principal Act describes a director as 'any person who occupies the position of director by whatever name called'.[2] It is therefore the function rather than the title that will determine whether or not a person is in fact a director. Accordingly, persons who are not formally appointed as directors may be deemed directors. These *de facto* directors are subject to the same statutory duties as formally appointed or *de jure* directors.

De Facto Directors

A *de facto* director is a person who acts as a director without having been properly appointed to, or eligible for, office. In *Gray v. McLoughlin; Re First Class Toy Traders Ltd*[3] the official liquidator made an application for an order of restriction under section 150 of the Companies Act 1990 against three respondents. The first two respondents were appointed and acted as directors of the company until the date of commencement of the winding up. The third respondent, T, was not formally appointed as director, but the liquidator submitted that he was a *de facto* director of the company within the twelve months before the commencement of the winding up. It was accepted by the liquidator that the onus was on him to establish that T was a *de facto* director and it was further accepted that the court must decide the issue on the balance of probabilities. The court was referred to a number of authorities in Ireland and in England and Wales in relation to establishing whether a person is or is not a *de*

---

1 Even single-member companies by law require two directors.
2 Section 2 of the Principal Act.
3 Unreported, High Court, Finlay Geoghegan J., July 9, 2004.

facto director.[4] The court accepted that the crucial test was whether the individual had assumed the status and functions of a company director so as to make himself responsible as if he were a *de jure* director. Adopting this approach, the court considered that T was as a matter of probability a *de facto* director for the following reasons:

1. The *de jure* directors considered him to have acted as a director; and
2. T accepted that he agreed to the description of finance director for his position; and
3. T met regularly with the other directors at what have been categorised as board meetings; and
4. T was an authorised signatory for the purposes of company cheques; and
5. T appears to have had full information about the affairs of the company and he controlled the availability of financial information; and
6. T accepted that he had responsibility for the financial function of the company; and
7. T's involvement in the control and supervision of the affairs of the company went beyond the financial function: he appears to have had a role in the negotiation of property matters and in dealings with the principal supplier.

On the basis of the above the court concluded that T had assumed the status and function of a director and was accordingly a director within the meaning of section 2(1) of the Companies Act 1963.

Shadow Directors

The legal responsibilities of company directors are burdensome and in certain circumstances directors can be held responsible for the debts of the company. In the past, persons tried to avoid these responsibilities, and the potential for liability, by acting as directors without accepting formal appointment. Section 27(1) of the 1990 Act defines these shadow directors as: 'the persons in accordance with whose directions and instructions the directors of a company are accustomed to act, other than in a professional capacity'.

2005 — In *Fyffes plc v DCC plc and Others*[5], the High Court considered the matters that must be taken into account in establishing whether a person is a shadow director. The court held that it is implicit that the 'directions or instructions' must have an imperative quality. Furthermore, just because there is consideration by *(unimportant)*

---

4 *Re Lynrowan Enterprises*, Unreported, High Court, O'Neill J., July 31 2002; *Re Richborough Furniture Ltd*, [1996] 1 BCLC 507, [1996] BCC 155; *Re Kaytech International plc*, Potier v Secretary of State for Industry [1999] 2 BCLC 351, [1999] BCC 390.

5 Unreported, High Court, Laffoy J., December 21, 2005.

Development Capital Corporation Limited

the board interposed between the direction or instruction or imperative advice, it does not mean that the act of the board is not to be taken into account in applying section 27, if the board acts in accordance with the direction, instruction or imperative advice. Finally, the court concluded that the use of the expression 'accustomed' indicated that there was no requirement that the board should always act on the directions and instructions for a shadow directorship to exist.

Although exceptions are made for persons who advise directors in a professional capacity, it has been suggested that in certain circumstances even banks could be shadow directors, where many features of the company's business are being run on their instructions, for example where a debenture sets out in detail how the business is to be run.[6] In *Re Worldport Ireland Limited (in liquidation)*[7] the High Court held that a body corporate could be a shadow director for the purposes of the obligations imposed on directors under the Companies Acts.

The difference between a *de facto* and a shadow director is that the former has openly acted as if he had been validly appointed, whether or not there are other properly appointed directors, whereas the definition of shadow director 'presupposes that there is a board of directors who acts in accordance with instructions from someone else, the *éminence grise* or shadow director.'[8]

Executive and Non-Executive Directors

Executive directors are those who are involved in the day-to-day running of the company. They will often have a contract of employment with the company. Non-executive directors are not actively involved in the day-to-day running of the company. They are usually appointed because of some expertise in a particular area and generally only attend board meetings or meetings where their expertise is required. Both executive and non-executive directors owe the same duties to the company. However, the duty of care owed by non-executive directors may vary depending on their experience, knowledge and function. This distinction is discussed later in the chapter.

1. Directors' Qualifications

No formal qualifications attach to the position of director. However, the Companies Acts restrict the following persons from becoming directors:

(a) a body corporate;[9]
(b) an undischarged bankrupt;[10]

---

6 *Ex p Copp* [1989] BCLC 12.
7 Unreported, High Court, O'Leary J., February 16, 2005. See also *Fyffes v. DCC plc and Others*, Unreported, High Court, Laffoy J., December 21, 2005.
8 *Re Lo-Line Electrical Motors Ltd* [1988] BCLC 698.
9 Section 176 of the Principal Act.
10 Section 183 of the Principal Act.

(c) an auditor appointed to that company, its holding company or subsidiary;[11]
(d) a person who is restricted under the Companies Act 1990, unless the company of which he is to be a director meets certain capital requirements; and
(e) a person disqualified under the Companies Act 1990.

2. Residency Requirement

Section 43 of the 1999 Amendment Act introduces a new restriction in relation to the parties who may act as a director of a company by requiring that at least one director must be resident in the State. This provision was introduced to avoid the possibility that non-resident directors could avoid any sanctions imposed upon them for breaches of the Companies Acts or certain taxation legislation. A company does not have to comply with this requirement if it satisfies one of two conditions. First, the company may enter into a €25,395 bond securing the payment of any fine that could be imposed by the Companies Acts or certain Tax Acts. Second, it can obtain a certificate from the registrar of companies stating that a company has a real and continuous link with one or more economic activities that are being carried on in the State.[12] If a company breaches the provisions of section 43, the company and every officer of the company will be guilty of an offence.[13]

If a person ceases to be a director of a company and he is a resident in the State or he knows that no other director is resident in the State he must notify the registrar within 14 days. If the director fails to comply with this notification requirement he shall be jointly and severally liable with the company for any fine or penalty imposed. The registrar may prosecute summarily for breach of this provision.

3. Mimimum number of directorships

Section 45(1) of the 1999 Amendment Act stipulates that a person cannot, at a particular time, be a director (including shadow director) of more than twenty-five companies. In reckoning the number of companies directorships in the following companies will not be taken into account:

(a) public companies; or
(b) companies that have been granted a certificate by the registrar to the effect that they have a real and continuous connection with one or more economic activities that are being carried on in the State.

---

11 Section 162(5) of the Principal Act. as amended by section 6 of the Companies (Amendment) Act 1982.
12 Section 44 of the 1999 Amendment Act.
13 Section 44 of the 1999 Act.

An appointment as a director of a company in breach of the maximum directorships provisions shall be void. If a person becomes or remains a director or shadow director of one or more companies, he or she shall be guilty of an offence.[14] The registrar may prosecute summarily for this offence.

4. Share qualifications

Directors are not required to be members of the company unless the articles of association provide otherwise.[15] Where the articles require directors to hold a minimum number of qualifying shares, section 180 of the Principal Act provides as follows:

(a) the share qualification must be obtained within two months after the director's appointment, or such shorter time as may be fixed by the articles;
(b) if the share qualification is not obtained within the specified time, or the director ceases to hold his qualification, he must vacate his office immediately;
(c) in the event that the office is vacated because of failure to obtain or hold the necessary qualification shares, that person cannot be re-appointed as director of the same company until the qualification shares have been obtained.

5. Publicity

Generally speaking, all business letters on which the company's name appears, and which are sent by the company to any person, must state in legible characters the following particulars in relation to each director:

(a) his present Christian name, or the initials thereof, and present surname; and
(b) any former Christian names and surnames; and
(c) his nationality, if not Irish.[16]

6. Appointment

The first directors of the company are those named in the documents delivered to the registrar before incorporation. All subsequent appointments are governed by the articles of association. The usual method of appointment is by the company in general meeting. Where non-directors are proposing the appointment of a person as a director, other than a retiring director, Table A requires that notice should be sent to the company's registered office between twenty-one and three days before the meeting. When the appointment of directors is proposed at a

---

14 Section 45(8) of the 1999 Amendment Act.
15 Table A does not require directors to hold qualification shares.
16 Section 196 of the Principal Act.

general meeting a separate resolution should be proposed for the election of each director, unless the members unanimously agree to waive this rule.[17]

7. Alternate Directors

The articles of a private company may permit a director to assign or transfer his office to another person, subject to the approval of a special resolution of the general meeting. Where the articles permit retiring directors to nominate replacements, no such approval is required. Casual vacancies may arise due to the death or resignation of a director. Where this occurs, Table A empowers the board of directors to fill such vacancies and appoint additional directors, provided the maximum number specified in the articles is not exceeded. Persons appointed in this manner by the board hold office until the next Annual General Meeting, at which time they will be eligible for re-election.

8. Vacation of and Removal from Office

Table A sets out the rules relating to the retirement and rotation of directors as follows:

(a) at the first AGM all directors must retire and thereafter on an annual basis one-third of the directors must retire;
(b) those retiring shall be those longest in office since the last election — retiring directors are eligible for re-election;
(c) a director offering himself for re-election shall be deemed to be re-elected unless the meeting decides otherwise;
(d) directors co-opted by the board of directors must stand for re-election at the next AGM — such persons do not count in determining the one-third to retire for rotation;
(e) managing directors are not subject to retirement by rotation and do not count in the determination of the one-third to retire by rotation.

A director may vacate his office by resignation or by not offering himself for re-election.

Section 182 of the Principal Act gives the members the power to dismiss or remove a director by passing an ordinary resolution. Directors of private limited companies, appointed for life by the memorandum and articles of association, can only be removed if the correct procedure for the alteration of the constitutional documents is followed. In *Coubrough v. James Panton & Co. Ltd*,[18] the removal of a director by the passing of an ordinary resolution was declared invalid, because the articles had required the passing of a special

---

17 Section 181 of the Principal Act.
18 [1965] IR 272.

resolution for such an action. Where a resolution to remove a director is proposed, the Principal Act requires the following procedures to be followed:

(a) extended notice of twenty-eight days must be given to all members, and on receipt of such a notice the company must send a copy to the director concerned;
(b) on receipt of written representations, relating to the proposed resolution, by the director, the company must, unless the court otherwise orders, notify members of such representations;
(c) if the company fails to notify the members of such representations, either because they were received too late or because of the company's default, the director may require that the representations be read at the meeting — in any case, the director may speak on the resolution at the meeting.

The company may be deterred from exercising its power to remove a director for various reasons. First, section 182(7) of the Principal Act provides that a director who is removed under the section will not be deprived of compensation or damages to which he is entitled. Such an entitlement may exist where a director has a separate contract of employment. In *Carvill v. Irish Industrial Bank*,[19] a managing director was held to be entitled to one year's notice, and having been removed without notice he was awarded damages in lieu thereof. Second, where the articles provide weighted voting rights to members, the company may be precluded from generating sufficient support for a resolution to remove a director, as occurred in *Bushell v. Faith* (considered already in Chapter 5). Finally, any attempt to remove a director for improper reasons may give rise to an action by a director who is also a member of the company, and may result in the court making an order for the winding up of the company under section 213(f) of the Principal Act.[20]

9. Remuneration

Table A provides that the company in general meeting shall determine the remuneration and expenses of the directors. Directors, particularly executive directors, who do not have a substantial interest in the company, would be advised to negotiate a separate contract for services or contract of employment with the company. In some circumstances the courts have inferred the existence of such a contract.[21]

In any case, contracts of employment entered into between a company and a director for a term exceeding five years and which cannot be terminated by

---

19 [1968] IR 325.
20 *Re Murph's Restaurant* [1979] ILRM 141. See Chapter 15.
21 *Carvill v. Irish Industrial Bank Ltd* [1968] IR 325. Cf. *Read v. Astoria Garage Streatham Ltd* [1952] Ch 637.

notice, or which can only be terminated in specific circumstances, must be approved by the shareholders in general meeting.[22] A written memorandum of the agreement, including the term specifying its length, must be available for inspection by the members at the registered office for a period of not less than fifteen days prior to the meeting and at the meeting itself.

The company must keep a register of directors' contracts of service or, where the contract is not in writing, a memorandum of the details.[23] The requirement to keep records of directors' service contracts does not apply in the following circumstances:

(a) where the director concerned is working outside the State; and
(b) where the contract will expire in less than three years; and
(c) where the contract can be terminated within three years without payment of compensation.

10. Directors' Meetings

General

Unless otherwise provided in the articles, directors' powers are conferred collectively. In order to exercise these powers, there must be agreement among the directors. The formal manner of achieving such agreement is by a resolution of a properly constituted board meeting. However, Table A recognises the validity of decisions made informally, provided that an appropriate resolution is signed by all the directors.

The courts have accepted that board meetings may be held on an informal basis, but the directors must at least appreciate that they are in fact attending a meeting. In *Re Aston Colour Print Ltd*,[24] a meeting took place of some of the company's shareholders, two of its directors and the company's accountant to assess the failing fortunes of the company. The meeting was chaired by a non-director. The discussions focused on the option of appointing an examiner, but no formal resolution was put to the meeting in this regard. Following the meeting the accountant, who believed a decision had been made, initiated the petition process which culminated in an interim examiner being appointed. Later, it transpired that not everyone in attendance believed such a decision had been made, including one of the directors whose name appeared on the petition. The question arose as to whether a meeting had been held and whether a resolution to petition for the appointment of an examiner had been passed. The court concluded that a board meeting had not been validly held for the following reasons:

22 Section 28 of the 1990 Act.
23 Section 50 of the 1990 Act.
24 Unreported, High Court, Kelly J., February 21, 1997.

(a) the directors did not appreciate that they were attending a board meeting;
(b) despite the presence of two directors, the meeting was chaired by a shareholder;
(c) the chairman was unsure as to the nature of the meeting because he believed he was presiding over a general meeting of the shareholders which had subsequently become a board meeting.

With respect to the validity of the 'informal resolution', the court made it clear that where the solemn and important decision is being taken to petition the court to appoint an examiner, every care must be taken to ensure that the will of the board is clear. As it was not clear from the circumstances, the court held that no such decision had been made.

Proceedings at Directors' Meetings

The articles usually govern the proceedings of directors' meetings. Table A makes the following provisions in this regard.

(a) Questions arising shall be decided by a majority of votes. Where there is an equal vote, the chairman shall have a second or casting vote.
(b) A director may requisition a meeting of the directors and the secretary must then summon such a meeting.
(c) Directors must be given advance notice of meetings. Although the model articles are silent as to the amount of notice required, it has been held that such notice must be reasonable.[25]
(d) If the directors so resolve, it shall not be necessary to give notice of a meeting to any director normally resident in the State, but for the time being absent from the State.
(e) Unless otherwise agreed by the directors, the quorum necessary for the transaction of the business of the meeting is two. In the event that the number of directors falls below the quorum required by the articles, the continuing director may act only for the purpose of increasing the number of directors to satisfy the quorum or for the purpose of summoning a general meeting.
(f) The directors may elect a chairman of their meetings. If no such chairman is elected or if the chairman is absent from any meeting, the directors may choose an alternative chairman.
(g) The director may not generally vote in respect of any contract in which he is an interested party.

Section 145 of the Principal Act requires minutes to be kept of the proceedings of board meetings. When signed by the chairman, those minutes are *prima facie* evidence of the proceedings.

---

25 *Per* Murphy J. in *Holland v. McGill*, Unreported, High Court, March 16, 1990.

The Company Secretary

Every company must have a secretary, who may be one of the directors of the company.[26] Although there are no requisite qualifications for appointment of a person as secretary to a private limited company, section 236 of the 1990 Act imposes a duty on directors of a public limited company to take all reasonable steps to ensure that the secretary has the necessary knowledge and experience to discharge the functions of secretary and who is qualified by reason of:

(a) being secretary to the company at the time of coming into force of the section; or
(b) having been a secretary of a company for three of the five years prior to appointment; or
(c) being a member of a relevant professional body recognised by the appropriate Minister; or
(d) being a person who by reason of his having held any other position or having been a member of any other body appears to the directors to be capable of discharging the functions of the secretary.

Persons restricted or disqualified under the 1990 Act cannot act as a secretary of a company except in limited circumstances.[27]

1. Functions and Duties

The function of the company secretary is mostly administrative. Such a role is reflected by the Companies Acts, which impose very few duties that are exclusive to the secretary. These duties include signing the annual return, completing application forms to the Registrar where a company is converting to another type of company and compiling a statement of affairs on the appointment of a receiver or liquidator. The remaining administrative functions are allocated to the company itself, but are generally carried out by either the secretary or a director. These include maintaining the statutory registers, calling meetings of the board of directors and keeping records of their minutes, and arranging for the filing of various returns and notifications to the registrar of companies.

2. The Secretary's Power

The traditional view of the company secretary's role was described by Esher MR in *Barnett Hoares v. South London Tramways*,[28] when he observed that

---

26 Section 175 of the Principal Act.
27 Restricted persons may act as a secretary of an adequately capitalised company as described in section 150(3) of the 1990 Act.
28 (1887) 18 QBD 815.

> A secretary is a mere servant; his position is to do what he is told, and no person can assume that he has any authority to represent anything at all.

The imposition by statute of more onerous administrative functions on the company, which are often delegated to the company secretary, has been met by a corresponding recognition by the judiciary of the importance of the company secretary. As the chief administrative officer of the company, it is apposite that the secretary has apparent authority to make contracts, relating to his functions, on behalf of the company. This position was accepted in *Panorama Developments (Guildford) Ltd v. Fidelis Furnishing Fabrics*.[29] There a company secretary had hired cars, representing that they were for company purposes. The cars were then used for his personal use. The company refused to pay, claiming that the secretary did not have the authority to enter into such a contract. The court rejected this argument and held that the secretary did have apparent authority to make contracts relating to the administrative side of the business, which included contracts of this type. Lord Denning MR declared:

> Times have changed. A company secretary is a much more important person nowadays than he was in 1887. He is an officer of the company with extensive duties and responsibilities . . . He is certainly entitled to sign contracts connected with the administrative side of the company's affairs.

However, the court did suggest that had the contract related to the commercial side of the business, it might not treat the secretary as having such authority to bind the company. Therefore, the secretary has apparent authority to bind the company in administrative matters, but has no such authority in matters of an executive nature. However, it may be possible, if the articles do not provide otherwise, for the board expressly to delegate an executive function to the secretary and give him actual authority.

Register of Directors and Secretaries

Section 195 of the Principal Act requires every company to keep at its registered office a register of its directors and secretary which must contain the following details relating to each director:

(a) the forename, surname and any other names;
(b) the date of birth;
(c) the usual residential address;
(d) nationality;
(e) business occupation, if any;
(f) particulars of other directorships of other corporate bodies.

---

29 [1971] 2 QB 711.

In relation to the secretary, the register must contain the following details:

(a) in the case of an individual, his name, former names and his usual residential address;
(b) in the case of a body corporate, its name and registered address.

Any change in the details contained in the register must be notified to the registrar of companies within fourteen days of the change. Section 195 also imposes a duty on the directors and secretary to give information to the company in writing in order that it may comply with its requirements under the Act.

The register must be kept open for inspection for not less than two hours per working day.

CHAPTER SEVENTEEN

DIRECTORS' POWERS AND AUTHORITY

Actual Authority of Directors

The actual authority of an agent is the authority which the principal, either expressly or impliedly, agrees he shall have. In the case of company directors, their express authority will be determined primarily by the articles of association. While the authority of the company is, in the first instance, vested in the members, Article 80 of Table A provides that the business of the company shall be managed by the directors. The power to manage is conferred upon the board of directors acting collectively and not on individual directors. While Article 80 may seem to give directors very wide powers, the law confers many duties upon them in order to limit the abuse of those powers. These limitations are discussed in Chapter 18. Of course, a company does not have to adopt Article 80 and may accordingly limit the authority of directors. However, where the company adopts the model articles, the members cannot thereafter interfere with the director's power to manage the company without first altering the articles of association.[1]

In addition to the general power of management, Table A also contains articles delegating specific powers to the directors including *inter alia* the following:

(a) the power to borrow money and give security for such borrowings (Article 79);
(b) to allot un-issued shares (Article 5);
(c) to make calls on shares (Article 15);
(d) to decline to register share transfers (Article 3 Part II);
(e) to convene an EGM whenever they think fit (Article 50).

Article 110 Table A provides that the board can appoint a managing director from among their number and, under Article 112, they many confer on him any of the powers exercisable by them together. Where a company has adopted Articles 80, 110 and 112, the potential actual authority of the managing director is as extensive as that of the board of directors itself.

The express authority of individual directors and the company secretary is minimal under Table A. However, where a director is an 'executive director' or employed by the company, their actual authority may be greatly increased by the terms of their contract of employment. As Article 81 of Table A allows the directors to delegate their powers, the individual directors may be conferred with additional powers by the board itself. However, even if no actual authority exists,

---

1 *Re Gramophone & Typewriter Ltd v. Stanley* [1904] 2KB 89 CA.

the company may still be bound where the director, as agent for the company, acts within his implied or apparent authority.

Implied actual authority is based on the idea that if the principal appoints an agent to act in a particular capacity, the agent has the implied authority to do what is necessary to achieve those acts. Where, for example, a director is given the express authority to hire employees, then it is assumed, unless the contrary is expressly provided, that he has the implied authority to advertise vacancies and interview the candidates.

Ostensible Authority of Directors

The ostensible authority of an agent is that authority which his principal represents, to the party dealing with the agent, that he has given to the agent. If a company holds out a person as having a certain authority, when in fact he does not so have, the company will be estopped from denying this authority. The leading case is *Freeman Lockyer v. Buckhurst Park Properties (Mangal) Ltd.*[2] The defendant company carried on the business of property developers. The articles of association provided that the directors could appoint a managing director, but this was never done. One of the directors, to the knowledge of the board, but without its express authority, acted as if he were managing director in relation to finding a purchaser for an estate of land and in engaging a firm of architects and surveyors to prepare plans, draw up boundaries and apply for planning permission for the estate. The company later refused to pay the fee of the architects and surveyors on the grounds that the director did not have the authority to enter into the contract. The court held that the company was liable to pay the fees because the board had by its acquiescence represented that he was the managing director who had, by virtue of the usual authority of a managing director, the power to bind the company. In considering whether a contract could be enforced against a company on the basis of the ostensible authority of the company's agent, Diplock LJ. laid down four conditions, all of which must be proved by the claimant:

(a) a representation was made to him that the agent had the authority to enter into a contract, of the kind sought to be enforced, on behalf of the company;
(b) the representation was made to him by a person or persons who had 'actual' authority to manage the business of the company;
(c) he was induced to enter into the contract by such representations; and
(d) there is nothing in the company's memorandum or articles which deprived the company of the capacity to enter into that contract or to delegate the authority to enter into that contract to the agent.

The representation need not have been expressly made by the person with authority. Rather, the courts will infer from the conduct of that person whether or

---

2 [1964] QB 480.

not in fact a representation was impliedly made. In *Hely-Hutchinson v. Brayhead Ltd*,[3] the chairman of the board acted as the managing director of the company. Although the articles permitted the appointment of a managing director, the board never in fact appointed anyone to the position. As part of a complicated series of transactions between the defendant company and the plaintiff's company, the chairman of the defendant company purported, on the company's behalf, to indemnify the plaintiff against personal guarantees he had given to, and in respect of, the obligations of the plaintiff's company. When the company became insolvent, the plaintiff honoured his commitments under the guarantee. Later, the defendant company refused to indemnify him on the grounds that the chairman did not have the authority to sign the letters of indemnity on the company's behalf. The Court of Appeal held that the chairman had the appropriate authority and, accordingly, the company was bound by the letters of indemnity.

The conditions laid down by Diplock LJ. in *Freeman* were applied by Laffoy J. in the case of *Ulster Factors Ltd v. Entoglen (in liquidation) and Moloney*.[4] The plaintiff company had entered into a debt-factoring agreement whereby the debts of the defendant company were assigned to the plaintiff which, having deducted a factoring fee, would make the balance available for 'draw-down' by the defendant. The agreement stipulated that the defendant would advise the plaintiff as to which of its officers could authorise a draw-down instruction. The agreement further provided that the funds would, on draw-down by the defendant, be payable to the defendant company or the third parties specified by the defendant company. No formal notification of the authorised signatories was made to the company, although it was agreed orally that draw-down instructions would be authorised by either a director or secretary of the company. All but three draw-downs involved payments to the company itself and were authorised by one officer. The other three draw-downs were effected by payments to third parties. Two of those draw-downs were authorised by two officers of the defendant company in line with a decision of the board to that effect. The board's decision had not been notified to the company. The remaining draw-down instruction, the subject of the dispute, to pay a firm of solicitors £37,000 was signed by only one officer. The board, on being informed of the payment, did not query it until six months later. When the defendant company later became insolvent, the liquidator claimed that the payment to the firm of solicitors was unauthorised and that £37,000 should be deducted from the amount owed by the defendant to the plaintiff. The plaintiff successfully invoked the doctrine of ostensible authority. The court was satisfied that:

(a) there was a tacit representation that an individual director had the authority to draw down funds to both the company and third parties;

---

3 [1968] 1 QBD 549.
4 Unreported, High Court, Laffoy J., February 21,1997.

(b) the board had the authority to make the representation as it had been given the powers to manage the company by the articles of association;
(c) the plaintiff relied on the representations; and
(d) the company had not been deprived by the memorandum or articles of association from requesting funds to be paid to third parties.

In each of the above cases, the person making the representation had the capacity to 'hold out' the agent as having the relevant authority. This capacity is usually determined by the articles of association. Even if the outsider is not aware of the contents of the articles, under the doctrine of constructive notice he is deemed to be so aware. Therefore, if the representative has not the authority to 'hold out' the agent, the outsider cannot satisfy the conditions laid down in the *Freeman* case. However, the effect of the doctrine of constructive notice has been mitigated by the rule in the *Turquand* case and Regulation 6 of the European Communities (Companies) Regulations 1973.[5]

The Rule in Turquand's Case

The articles of association may reserve to the company in general meeting or to the board of directors itself the power to impose restrictions on directors. Under the rule in *Turquand*'s case the outsider is entitled to assume that the internal requirements have been complied with. In *Royal British Bank v. Turquand*,[6] the company's articles provided that directors could only borrow amounts authorised by the company in general meeting. Although a resolution was passed, it did not specify the amount. Unaware of the defect, the directors borrowed £2,000 and issued a bond as security. When the bearer of the bond later sought to enforce the bond, the company argued that the bank was deemed to be aware of the articles' requirement that borrowings must be sanctioned by the general meeting. The court rejected this argument and held that although the bank was deemed to be aware of the contents of the articles, it was entitled to infer that the internal formalities had been completed. The rationale for the rule in *Turquand*'s case is straightforward. The act which satisfies the requirements imposed by the articles may not be a matter of public record and therefore the outsider cannot be deemed to be aware that the internal requirements have or have not been satisfied.

The rule in *Turquand*'s case was applied in the Irish case of *Allied Irish Banks Ltd v. Ardmore Studios International*.[7] There, a bank had notice of the company's articles of association which required a quorum of two directors. The bank received a copy of a board resolution signed by two of the three directors authorising the loan from the bank. However, the resolution was defective because the third director had not been given notice of the meeting. The High

---

5 SI 163/1973: see Chapter 6.
6 [1843–60] All ER 435.
7 Unreported, High Court, Finlay J., May 30, 1973.

Court held that the invalid procedure was an irregularity in the internal management of the company. Applying the rule in the *Turquand* case, the bank was entitled to assume that internal procedures were complied with and the company was bound by the loan agreement.

The rule in the *Turquand* case will not apply where the outsider is actually aware that the director has no authority. In *Howard v. Patent Ivory Manufacturing Co.*,[8] the directors required the authority of the general meeting in order to borrow amounts over £1,000. Without this authority the directors borrowed £3,500 secured by debentures. As the bank was aware that the general meeting had not authorised the borrowing, the court held that the company was only liable to the extent of the authorised borrowings of £1,000.

The rule will not protect outsiders where the authorising act is one which must be filed in the companies registry office.[9] This is because the outsider, in such a case, is deemed to have notice of all public documents which have been filed. In *Irvine v. Union Bank of Australia*,[10] the company's articles required a special resolution of the members to authorise borrowings in excess of a specified amount. In breach of this requirement, the directors borrowed money from the bank. It was held that the bank could not recover the unauthorised amount because it had constructive notice that a special resolution had not been passed. This was so because it had not been filed in the companies registry office.

In addition to the memorandum and articles and special resolutions, outsiders are deemed to be aware of the following documents:

(a) certificate of incorporation and certificate of change of name;
(b) alterations to the memorandum and articles of association;
(c) returns relating to directors and changes in directors;
(d) any decision which authorises non-board members to enter into transactions on behalf of the company;
(e) annual returns;
(f) notice of the registered office;
(g) winding-up orders;
(h) orders for the dissolution of the company;
(i) returns by the liquidator relating to the final meeting on winding up.[11]

Notice of the delivery of the above documents to the Registrar of Companies must be published in the *CRO Gazette* within six weeks of the relevant delivery. A person is deemed to have notice of the documents from the sixteenth day after the date of publication in the *CRO Gazette*. Where the notice of delivery has not been published, an outsider will not be deemed to be aware of their contents

---

8 [1883] 3 Ch D 156.

9 For example, a special resolution.

10 (1877) 2 App Cas 366, Privy Council.

11 Regulation 4(1) of the 1973 Regulations.

unless the evidence shows that they were actually aware. Therefore, the filing with the registrar of companies will not itself be sufficient to put a person on notice.

Even where an outsider is not actually aware or deemed to be aware of the irregularity he may be obliged, where the circumstances suggest, to make such further enquiries as to satisfy himself that the purported agent has the power which he represents himself as having. In *A & L Underwood Ltd v. Bank of Liverpool and Martins Ltd*,[12] the bank paid cheques into the account of the director. The cheques were payable to the company but endorsed on behalf of the company by the same director. The bank was held liable to the receiver of the company. It could not rely on the rule in *Turquand*'s case as the circumstances were so suspicious that the bank should have made further enquiries with respect to the director's actions. Similarly, in *Houghton & Co. v. Northard Lowe & Wills Ltd*,[13] the defendant company's director purported to assign to the plaintiffs the right to receive and sell goods owned by the company as security for a loan. It was held that the transaction was so unusual that the plaintiff was put on enquiry and was not entitled to assume that the director had authority. As he made no such enquiry, the company was not bound by the contract.

Finally, the rule in *Turquand*'s case will not apply where the 'outsider' is also an 'insider', such as a director or other officer of the company. In *Morris v. Kanssen*,[14] K and C were first directors of a company. A dispute arose between them as C forged an entry in the board minutes to record the appointment of S as a director. C and S later co-opted M on to the board and the three of them purported to allot shares to themselves. M was aware of a dispute between C and K concerning the legality of certain transactions, but made no further enquiry. K later claimed that the allotment was invalid as S and M were not directors and had no power to allot shares. It was held that S could not rely on *Turquand*'s case because his 'appointment', on foot of a forgery, was no appointment at all. M could not rely on the rule because as an insider with access to the records he could have made further enquiries.

However, where outsiders are dealing with persons purporting to act as directors they may assume that, if those persons are capable of being appointed as directors, they have in fact been so appointed. In *Mahoney v. East Holyford Mining Co.*,[15] a bank had received a board resolution from a person describing himself as the company secretary, which instructed the bank to honour company cheques signed by any two directors and the secretary. The bank paid on foot of a number of these cheques. It was later discovered that the persons acting as the secretary and directors were not formally appointed to those positions. However, they were the original subscribers to the memorandum and articles and could have appointed themselves, and indeed had intended to. It was held that as the

---

12 [1924] All ER 230.
13 [1927] All ER 97.
14 [1946] AC 459.
15 (1875) LR 7 HL 869.

bank had no means of discovering the non-appointment they could assume that proper appointments had been made.

Section 178 of the Principal Act protects outsiders who deal with directors even where their appointment is defective. However, the statutory protection has no application where there has been no appointment at all.

The 1973 Regulations

Regulation 6 of the European Communities (Companies) Regulations 1973 modifies the doctrine of constructive notice by increasing the protection afforded to outsiders who deal with limited liability companies. The regulation provides that all transactions are deemed to be within the capacity of the company, the board or the authorised person where the outsider was acting in good faith. Furthermore, Regulation 6(2) provides that a person will be presumed to have acted in good faith unless otherwise proven. As a result of the regulation, the rule in *Turquand*'s case is no longer of direct relevance where the outsider is dealing with the board or an authorised person. It remains relevant, however, where an outsider is dealing with an officer or an agent not authorised by the board.

CHAPTER EIGHTEEN

Directors' Duties and Liabilities

Introduction

Table A provides that the directors may exercise all the powers of the company that are not otherwise required, either by the articles or the Companies Acts, to be exercised by the general meeting. This day-to-day control of the company's assets creates a potential for the abuse of directors' powers. In an attempt to curb such abuse, the law has developed a number of duties which must be followed by directors. Legislative provisions, particularly under the 1990 Act, have significantly expanded these duties, many of which are based on principles originally developed by the courts. For the purposes of this chapter, these duties will be considered under the following categories:

1. Fiduciary duties;
2. Statutory duties; and
3. Duties of care and competence.

Fiduciary Duties

First and foremost, a director is in a fiduciary position. Fiduciaries are those who have been entrusted with powers for the benefit of others, but who in the exercise of those powers are not subject to the direct and immediate control of those others. Directors are fiduciaries because in general they are in day-to-day control, without interference, of the company's assets and business undertakings. As fiduciaries, directors must exercise their powers *bona fide* in what they honestly believe to be the best interests of the company.[1] The test is multi-faceted. A claim of honesty will not be sufficient in defending the propriety of a director's decision, if the best interests of the company were not considered. In *Re W & M Roith Ltd*[2] the controlling shareholder and director of the company wished to make provision for his wife in the event of his death. He entered into a service agreement with the company whereby if he died his wife would receive a widow's pension for life. When the company ultimately failed, the administrators of his estate sought to prove for the amount owing under the pension. It was held that the agreement was for the benefit of the widow and as no thought was given to the interests of the company, the agreement was not binding on the company.

---

1 *Re Smith & Fawcett Ltd* [1942] 1 All ER 452.
2 [1967] WLR 432.

It is for those who claim that directors have exercised their powers in bad faith to produce evidence of this fact.

As Lord Greene MR. stated in *Re Smith & Fawcett Ltd.*[3], directors 'must exercise their discretion *bona fide* in what they consider not what the court may consider to be in the best interests of the company'. The test is therefore a subjective one and the court will not substitute its own view for that of the directors. The burden of proving the *male fides* of a director is particularly difficult given that directors are not required to give any reasons for their decisions. As Meredith MR. observed in *Re Dublin North City Milling Co. Ltd*:

> I think the law is wise in refusing to compel directors to disclose their reasons ... the law allows the directors to hold their tongues. It allows them to say that everything was done honestly and *bona fide* in the interests of their company ... and according to my view I have no power to make them say more.[4]

Although directors cannot be compelled to give reasons for their decisions, their silence may lead to an inference of bad faith. In *Clark v. Workman*[5] Ross J. held that on the basis of the director's failure to refute the allegations of impropriety made by the plaintiff, an inference of bad faith could be made. In determining the fiduciary duties of directors the courts have developed a number of principles. Directors must exercise their powers for a proper purpose; they must not fetter their discretion when deciding how to act; and they must not put themselves in a position whereby their own personal interests and those of the company conflict.

The Duty to use their Powers for a Proper Purpose

Directors are conferred with a number of discretionary powers, the use of which can have far-reaching effect. The powers must be exercised not only in furtherance of the company's objects, but also for a proper purpose. In ascertaining the purpose of a particular transaction, a difficulty may arise that has multiple consequences. In such a case, it is the substantial purpose of the transaction that will determine whether the powers have been exercised properly. If the directors can establish that they honestly believed the action was for the greater good of the company, they will have fulfilled their duty even though the outcome may be beneficial or indeed detrimental to some shareholders.

Most litigation concerning the misuse of directors' powers arises in relation to their power to allot shares.[6] In *Hogg v. Cramphorn*[7] the directors, in order to

---

3 Ibid.

4 [1909] 1 IR 179 at 184. See similar comments made by Black J. in *Re Hafner: Olhausen v. Powderley* [1943] IR 426.

5 [1920] 1 IR 107.

6 It should be noted that directors' power to allot shares has been restricted by Section 20 of the 1983 Amendment Act: see Chapter 9.

7 [1966] 3 All ER 420.

prevent a takeover bid they believed would be detrimental to the interests of the company, issued shares to the trustees of the employees' pension fund. The shares were paid for by a loan advanced by the company to the trustees. Although the court recognised that the directors were acting *bona fide*, the issue of shares to forestall a takeover bid was considered in breach of the directors' fiduciary duties and the allotment was thus invalid. Similarly, in *Nash v. Lancegaye Safety Glass (Ireland) Ltd*,[8] an allotment of preference shares, which was made to ensure that the company would be controlled by a director's family, was set aside on the grounds that it was an improper use of the directors' powers.

In *Howard Smith Ltd v. Ampol Petroleum Ltd*,[9] the majority shareholders intended to reject a takeover bid for the company. The directors honestly believed that the proposed takeover was in the company's best interest because the bidder was expected to inject additional capital into the company. The directors allotted new shares to the bidder, which had the effect of diluting the existing majority's stake and ensuring the takeover would succeed. Although the directors were not motivated by self-interest, the decision to allot the additional shares was successfully challenged. The court held that its primary purpose was to reduce the majority to a minority position and that this was an improper exercise of their powers. Interestingly, the court rejected the argument that the only proper purpose for which the power to allot shares could be exercised was to raise new capital when the company required it. Accordingly, it has been accepted that the issue of shares to a larger company to secure the financial stability of the company and to ensure its future trading activities was a proper exercise of the directors' power, even though the effect was to frustrate a takeover bid.[10] The issue of shares, as part of a joint-venture agreement relating to the exploitation of mineral rights owned by the company, has also been upheld, despite the fact that the issue had the effect of reducing a majority to a minority position.[11]

Even if the directors themselves benefit from a transaction, this will not automatically give rise to an inference of improper motives. In *Re Jermyn Turkish Baths Ltd*[12] an allotment of shares to a director that gave her a majority stake in the company was upheld because it formed part of rescue proposals for the failing company, and was therefore in its best interests. In *Mills v. Mills*[13] the company's board decided to capitalise profits by way of a bonus issue of shares rather than distributing them by way of dividend. The decision, which had the incidental effect of increasing the managing director's voting power, survived judicial scrutiny because the dominant purpose was to retain the profits for the

---

8 (1958) 92 ILTR 11.
9 [1974] AC 403 HL.
10 *Harlowe's Nominees Pty Ltd v. Woodside Oil Co.* (1968) 121 CLR 483, Aust. HC.
11 *Teck Corporation Ltd v. Millar* (1972) 33 DLR (3d) 288, BC Sup. Ct.
12 [1971] 1 WLR 1042.
13 (1938) 60 CLR 150.

company's business. Speaking for the Australian High Court, Latham CJ. suggested that directors:

> are not required by law to live in an unreal region of detached altruism and to act in a vague mood of ideal abstraction from obvious facts which must be present to the mind of any honest and intelligent man when he exercises his power as a director.[14]

The rules governing minority protection may overlap with cases concerning directors' abuse of power. In *Clemens v. Clemens Bros Ltd*[15] it was held that an allotment of shares for the purpose of reducing a member's stake might constitute oppression. This would entitle the member to bring an action against the directors under section 205 of the Principal Act.[16]

The Duty not to Fetter their Discretion

Directors must keep their discretion unfettered by outside influences, notwithstanding the *bona fides* of their intentions. They cannot therefore, as a general rule, contract with third parties as to how they will vote at board meetings. The case of *Clark v. Workman*[17] illustrates this point. The chairman of the board of directors had promised an outsider that he would use his influence to obtain approval from the board for the transfer of company shares from a majority shareholder to the outsider. The chairman then used his casting vote to secure board approval for the transfer. The plaintiff shareholders argued that the board did not have sufficient time to consider the matter and that the director was in breach of his duty by fettering his discretion to act in the best interests of the company. The court held that the actions of the director were such as to disqualify him from acting *bona fide* in the interests of the company.

However, if directors have entered into a contract that is in the best interests of the company, and committed to take further action at a board meeting to give effect to that contract it is not regarded as an improper fetter on their discretion. In *Thorby v. Goldberg*[18] the directors of a company agreed with third parties, as part of a reorganisation of the company, to alter the articles of association to provide for the issue of new shares. The argument that such an agreement was illegal as a fetter on the directors' discretion was rejected by the Australian High Court. As Kitto J. observed:

> There are many kinds of transaction in which the proper time for the exercise of the directors' discretion is the time of the negotiation of a contract and not the time at which the contract is to be performed ... If at the former time they are *bona fide* of the opinion that it is in the best interests of the company that the transaction should

---

14 Ibid. at 164.
15 [1976] 2 All ER 268.
16 See Chapter 15 — Minority Protection.
17 [1920] 1 IR 107.
18 (1964) 112 CLR 597.

be entered into and carried into effect, I can see no reason in law why they should not bind themselves to do whatever under the transaction is to be done by the board.[19]

A similar view was taken in the Scottish case of *Dawson International plc v. Coats Paton plc*.[20] Here, the plaintiff company had made a takeover bid for the defendant company. The directors of both companies entered into an agreement whereby the directors of the defendant company agreed not to co-operate with any other bidder and to recommend the plaintiff's bid to the general meeting. The defendant subsequently announced that it would be taken over by a rival bidder. The court held that the agreement between the plaintiff and the defendant was enforceable, because it was made in the best interests of the company. In the case of *Fulham Football Club Ltd v. Cabra Estates plc*[21] the English Court of Appeal endorsed the principle that, provided the fetter on the discretion of the directors is not improper, it will not necessarily amount to a breach of their fiduciary duties.

There may be circumstances in which a director is appointed to serve the interests of someone other than the company. Sometimes directors are appointed purely to represent a shareholder or creditor of the company. The terms of appointment of these directors, referred to as nominee directors, will usually determine the way in which they will cast their votes. In *Scottish Co-operative Wholesale Society Ltd v. Meyer*[22] it was suggested that nominees are not totally absolved from their duties to act in the best interests of the company even though this may place them in an impossible position.

However, in the Australian case of *Levin v. Clark*[23] commercial reality prevailed. The court held that the company, in accepting the appointment of a nominee to protect the interests of a financial institution, had waived its right to the loyalty of that nominee.

The Duty to Avoid a Conflict of Interest

Directors, as agents for the company, must not put themselves into a position whereby their personal interests and those of the company are in conflict. One of the leading cases concerning a director's duty to avoid a conflict of interest situation is *Regal (Hastings) Ltd v. Gulliver*[24] The plaintiff company had established a subsidiary company to acquire the lease of two cinemas. The subsidiary company had an authorised share capital of 5,000 £1 ordinary shares. The owner of the cinemas agreed to grant the lease on condition that the 5,000

---

19 Ibid., 605.
20 [1989] BCLC 233.
21 [1994] 1 BCLC 363.
22 [1959] AC 324.
23 [1962] NSWR 686.
24 [1967] 2 AC 134. See also *Dawson International plc v. Coats Paton plc* [1989] BCLC 233.

shares in the subsidiary company were subscribed for. The plaintiff company lacked the resources to acquire all the shares, so it was agreed that the company's directors would purchase 3,000 shares. When the plaintiff company and the subsidiary were subsequently sold, the directors made a substantial profit from their holdings in the subsidiary. The new owners of the plaintiff company caused the company to bring an action against the ex-directors to account for the profit they made from their office. The court held that the liability of a fiduciary 'in no way depends on fraud, or absence of *bona fides*'.[25] Despite the absence of *male fides* on the directors' part, they had made a profit from their position and were therefore obliged to account to the company.

The decision in *Regal* seems harsh when one considers that the directors were acting honestly and for the benefit of the company. However, the fact that they benefited personally from the transaction resulted in a conflict of interest. In holding that the directors were in breach of their fiduciary duty, the court endorsed the strict rule of equity that a person in a position of trust cannot benefit from that position, even if he acts honestly for the benefit of the company. It was, however, suggested in *Regal* that had the shareholders, either prospectively or retrospectively, ratified the directors' breach of duty, the outcome would have been different.[26]

The courts have imposed liability on directors to account to the company for profits they made from personally obtained information, if the company itself could have used that information. In *Industrial Development Consultants Ltd v. Cooley*[27] the defendant was the managing director of the plaintiff company, which was in the construction consulting business. He tried, unsuccessfully as it transpired, to obtain on behalf of the company a contract with the Gas Board. However, because of his own extensive experience in the gas industry, the Gas Board did offer him the contract in his personal capacity. He accepted, and resigned from the plaintiff company on the grounds that he was ill. Fearing the onset of a breakdown, the chairman released him immediately. The company later sought to make him account for the profit he had made. The defendant argued that the information concerning the contract had come to him in his personal capacity and not as a director of the company. In response to this, Roskill J. stated:

> The defendant had one capacity and one capacity only in which he was carrying on business at the time. That capacity was as managing director of the plaintiffs. Information which came to him ... was information which it was his duty to pass on ... because between himself and the plaintiffs a fiduciary relationship existed.[28]

---

25 [1967] 2 AC 134n at 144.
26 [1967] 2 AC 134n at 150.
27 [1972] 2 All ER 162.
28 Ibid. at 173.

Given the absence of good faith in the manner in which the defendant resigned, and having failed in his duty to disclose the relevant information to the company, he was in breach of his fiduciary duty and had to account for his profits.

There is some suggestion that the courts are now developing a more benign approach towards directors' liability to account for profits made. In *Peso Silver Mines Ltd v. Cropper*[29] the defendant was managing director of the plaintiff company. An opportunity to acquire prospecting claims had been presented to the company's board but was declined, mainly due to lack of finances. The defendant, together with two other directors, formed a syndicate and acquired the claims. The plaintiff company was later acquired and proceedings were instituted against the director to account for the profits he had made. The Supreme Court of Canada rejected the claim and held that where the board of directors rejects a business opportunity, individual directors are thereafter free to take up the opportunity and retain any resulting profits.

Ratifying Directors' Breaches

The general meeting may in certain circumstances ratify breaches of directors' duties. In *Hogg v. Cramphorn*,[30] Buckley J. held that, despite the improper use by the directors of their power to allot shares, the directors' actions could have been endorsed by the general meeting. He allowed the matter to stand until the general meeting was given an opportunity to consider the matter, at which point the breach was ultimately ratified. In *Regal Hastings*[31] Lord Russell suggested that had the directors sought the approval of the general meeting, either prospectively or retrospectively, they could have retained their profits. In a decision by the Supreme Court concerning misfeasance proceedings taken by a liquidator against the directors, it was made clear that a company can only ratify transactions involving the directors where the company itself benefited from the transaction.[32]

To Whom are the Duties Owed?

The fiduciary duties of directors are owed to the company as a whole and not to the individual shareholders. The case of *Percival v. Wright*[33] aptly supports this viewpoint. The plaintiffs offered to sell their shares to the defendants, who were directors of the company. The offer was accepted and the directors purchased the shares at £12.50. Unknown to the plaintiffs, the directors had also been in discussions with a third party concerning the sale of the company for a price representing an amount greater than that paid to the plaintiffs. Although the takeover

---

29 (1966) 58 DLR (2d) 1.
30 [1966] 3 All ER 420.
31 [1942] 1 ALL ER 378.
32 *Re Greendale Developments Ltd (in liquidation)* [1998] 1 IR 8.
33 [1902] Ch 421.

did not proceed, the plaintiffs claimed that the defendants had breached their fiduciary duty in not disclosing this information, and sought to have the transfer set aside. The court, rejecting the plaintiffs' submission, held that the directors owed a fiduciary duty to the company alone and not to any individual member.

Although this decision has been subjected to much criticism,[34] it can be defended on the basis that it was the plaintiffs who had in fact approached the directors. While it is clear that the duties are owed to the company, those duties may be extended in certain circumstances to include:

(a) individual shareholders;
(b) employees; and
(c) creditors.

Individual Shareholders

Although directors' duties are owed to the company and not to the individual shareholders, each case turns on its own facts, and if directors put themselves in a position whereby they have undertaken to act on behalf of the shareholders, the courts will impute a fiduciary relationship. Such was the position taken in the New Zealand case of *Coleman v. Myers*.[35] The defendants, a father and son, were directors and shareholders of a small family company. Using another company which they controlled, they successfully made a bid for enough shares in the 'family' company to enable them to force a compulsory acquisition of the remaining shares. Because the other shareholders had at all times looked to them for business advice and the defendants had suppressed information regarding the true value of the shares, the court held that the directors did owe a fiduciary duty to the plaintiffs, as shareholders. As Woodhouse J. stated:

> It is ... an area of the law where the courts can and should find some practical means of giving effect to sensible and fair principles of commercial morality in the cases that come before them; and while it may not be possible to lay down any general test as to when the fiduciary duty will arise for a company director or to prescribe the exact conduct which will always discharge it when it does, there are nevertheless some factors that will usually have an influence upon a decision one way or the other. They include, I think, dependence upon information and advice, the existence of a relationship of confidence, the significance of some particular transaction for the parties and, of course, the extent of any positive action taken by or on behalf of the director of directors to promote it.

The decision in *Coleman* echoes the view expressed by the Judicial Committee of the Privy Council in the earlier case of *Allen v. Hyatt*.[36] The appellants, who were

---

34 The Reports of the Cohen Committee (Cmnd 6659) and the Jenkins Committee (Cmnd 1749).
35 [1977] 2 NZLR 225.
36 (1914) 30 TLR 444.

the directors of the company, were in the process of negotiating a merger with another company. They obtained options to purchase the shares of the respondents at par value, by representing that the options were needed to enable the directors to negotiate on behalf of the shareholders. They did not disclose that when the merger was finalised the shares could be sold at 7 per cent above par. The directors exercised their options and resold the shares at a profit. It was held that the appellants had become the agents of the respondents on making the representations and were therefore obliged to account for the profit they had made. It would appear from *obiter* remarks made in one Irish decision that a similar approach may be adopted in this jurisdiction, particularly where insufficient or inaccurate information concerning a proposed takeover is given to shareholders.[37]

It should be noted that section 205 of the Principal Act gives a statutory remedy to shareholders where the affairs of the company are being conducted in a manner oppressive to them.[38]

Employees

It has long been accepted that directors do not owe a fiduciary duty to employees. This was made clear in *Parke v. Daily News Ltd*,[39] where an agreement by the company to make *ex gratia* payments to employees was struck down by the court on the ground that it did not confer any financial benefit on the company. However, section 52 of the 1990 Act now requires directors to have regard to the interests of employees when considering the interests of the company. While this provision gives greater flexibility to directors when considering the interests of employees, it remains the position that the duty is owed to the company and is therefore enforceable only by an action of the company.

Creditors

It is settled law that directors do not owe a fiduciary duty to creditors when the company is solvent. However, recent decisions of the Irish courts have endorsed the view taken in other jurisdictions[40] that, where the company is insolvent, the members' interests are subordinated to the interests of debenture holders and other creditors. In *Kinsella v. Russell Kinsella Property Ltd*, Street CJ. observed that:

> ... where a company is insolvent the interests of the creditors intrude. They become prospectively entitled through the mechanism of liquidation, to displace the power of shareholders and the directors to deal with the company's assets.[41]

---

37 *Per* McWilliam J. in *Securities Trust Ltd v. Associated Properties Ltd and Others*, Unreported, High Court, November 19, 1980.
38 See Chapter 15.
39 [1962] 2 All ER 929. See also *Re W & M Roith Ltd* [1967] WLR 432.
40 Most notably in Australia and New Zealand.
41 [1986] 4 NSWLR 722 at 730.

This passage was cited with approval by Blayney J. in the Irish case of *Parkes v. Hong Kong & Shanghai Banking Corporation.*[42] Here it was held that the disposition of company assets by a director of an insolvent company was a breach of the director's duty to the creditors of the company. In the case of *Re Frederick Inns Ltd*[43] a similar line of reasoning was adopted by both the High Court and the Supreme Court.

There are a number of statutory provisions designed to protect the creditors of companies which are insolvent or on the verge of insolvency.[44] Furthermore, directors who do not consider the interests of creditors while the company is insolvent may face an action for fraudulent or reckless trading — see 'Statutory Duties', below.

Statutory Duties

In an attempt to prevent directors from abusing their position and to create some level of transparency in relation to transactions between the company and its directors, a number of statutory provisions were introduced by the 1990 Act to reinforce the fiduciary duties of directors. Some of these provisions have the effect of amending previous statutory requirements while others create new obligations.

Interest and Dealings in Shares

The 1990 Act significantly increases the obligations both on directors, who must disclose their interests and dealings in company securities, and on companies, which must maintain a register of such interests. Section 53(1) of the 1990 Act requires directors, shadow directors and the company secretary to disclose any legal and beneficial interests in the company's securities, held either by themselves or their families.[45] On becoming a director or secretary the existence of any such interest must be notified within five days of becoming aware of it.[46] Where a director or secretary ceases to be interested in the company's securities, he must notify the company within five days. If any person fails to comply with these obligations they will be guilty of an offence.[47] Furthermore, the Director of Corporate Enforcement may, where he suspects a contravention of these provisions have occurred, appoint an inspector to carry out such investigations as are necessary to establish whether or not a contravention has occurred.[48]

---

42 [1990] ILRM 341.
43 [1990] ILRM 592 (High Court) and [1994] 1 ILRM 387 (Supreme Court).
44 Sections 286 and 288 of the Principal Act — see Chapter 26.
45 Spouses and children are included by virtue of section 64(1) of the 1990 Act.
46 Section 56(1) of the 1990 Act.
47 Section 56(7) of the 1990 Act.
48 Section 66(1) of the 1990 Act.

As with all individuals, if a director or secretary acquires or disposes of shares, which brings his interest in the company above or below 5 per cent in nominal value of the 'relevant nominal capital'[49] of a public limited company, he must disclose this fact to the company.[50]

Section 59 of the 1990 Act requires a company, on receipt of the relevant information, to keep a register of those interests and any changes thereto, all of which must be entered within three days.[51] The register must be maintained in the same place as the register of members.[52]

Section 30(1) of the 1990 Act makes it an offence for a director who deals in options to buy or sell certain shares in, or debentures of, the company or associated companies. This provision does not prevent directors acquiring a right to shares in a company pursuant to a scheme approved by the Revenue Commissioners.[53]

Substantial Property Transactions

Section 194(1) of the Principal Act imposes a statutory duty on directors to disclose to the board of directors the fact and the nature of any interest, whether directly or indirectly, in a contract or proposed contract with the company. Where a contract is made between the company and a 'connected person', the director is deemed to be interested in that contract. Section 26 of the 1990 Act provides that a person is a connected person if, but only if, he is:

(a) that director's spouse, parent, brother, sister or child;
(b) a person acting in his capacity as the trustee of any trust, the principal beneficiaries of which are the director, his spouse, or any of his children or any body corporate which he controls;
(c) a partner of that director; or
(d) a company controlled by that director.

The disclosure must be made to the board at the meeting at which the question of entering into the contract is first proposed or at the next meeting of the directors held after the director became interested. It is not sufficient that the disclosure is made to a sub-committee of the board: it must be made to a properly convened meeting of the board of directors.[54] Failure to comply with the requirements of section 194 renders a director liable to a fine. Furthermore,

---

49 'Relevant nominal capital' means the issued share capital of a class carrying voting rights at general meetings.
50 Where the plc is listed on the Stock Exchange, supplemental notification is required. Section 91 of the 1990 Act.
51 Section 60(2) of the 1990 Act.
52 Section 60(5) of the 1990 Act.
53 Section 30(3A) of the 1990 Act.
54 *Guinness plc v. Saunders* [1988] 2 ALL ER 652.

breach of section 194 could be a contributing factor in the making of a restriction order by the court under section 150 of the 1990 Act.[55]

Acquisition of Non-Cash Assets

In addition to the disclosure requirements described above, the Companies Acts impose restrictions on the kinds of transaction that may be entered into between the company and its directors. Section 29 of the 1990 Act provides that a company shall not enter into any arrangement:

(a) whereby a director of the company or its holding company or a person connected with such a director acquires or is to acquire one or more non-cash assets of the requisite value from the company; or
(b) whereby the company acquires or is to acquire one or more non-cash assets of requisite value from such a director or a person so connected;

unless the arrangement is first approved by a resolution of the company in general meeting and, if the director or connected person is a director of its holding company or a person connected with such a director, by a resolution of that holding company.

A non-cash asset of a requisite value is one whose value is greater than £50,000 (€63,487) or whose value is more than 10 per cent of the company's net assets, whichever is the lesser. In any case the provisions do not apply to an amount less than £1,000 (€1,269).

Section 29(3) broadly provides that where a company enters into a transaction in contravention of the section, the arrangement is voidable at the instance of the company unless:

(a) restitution of any money or assets, the subject of the arrangement, is no longer possible;
(b) rights acquired *bona fide* and for value by innocent third parties who are not a party to the arrangement would be affected by the avoidance of the transaction; and
(c) the arrangement is, within a reasonable period of time, affirmed by the company in general meeting.

Where the arrangement is entered into in breach of the provisions, the director involved is liable to account to the company for any gain he makes on the transaction, and to indemnify it against any loss.

---

55 *Stafford v. Higgins and Others, Re Xnet Information Systems Ltd (in voluntary liquidation)*, Unreported, High Court, Finlay Geoghegan J., May 6, 2004. See Chapter 19 — Restriction and Disqualification of Directors.

Prohibited Transactions

Section 31(1) of the 1990 Act provides that, subject to certain exceptions, a company is prohibited from entering into any transactions for the provision of:

(a) loans or quasi-loans[56] to a director of the company or its holding company or to a person connected with such a director;
(b) credit transactions[57] as creditor for such a director or a person so prohibited;
(c) guarantees or other security in connection with a loan, quasi-loan or credit transaction made by any other person for such a director or a person so connected.

Where the directors of a company become aware, or ought reasonably to become aware, that there exists a section 31 situation, it shall be the duty of the company, its directors and any persons for whom the arrangements were made, to amend, within two months, the terms of the arrangements concerned, so that the total amount outstanding falls within the permitted levels. The Act provides for exemptions to the general prohibition in the following circumstances.

(a) where the value of the arrangement and aggregate arrangements entered into by the company is less than 10 per cent of the company's relevant assets. For the purposes of the section, 'relevant assets' is defined as the value of the net assets of the company with reference to the accounts, which have been prepared and laid in accordance with the requirements of section 148 of the Principal Act, in respect of the last preceding financial year when such accounts were laid. Where no accounts have been prepared and laid under that section, the relevant assets will be the amount of the company's called-up share capital.[58] It should be noted that this exemption applies only to loans, quasi-loans and credit transactions and has no application to guarantees or the provision of security; or
(b) where, in the case of a guarantee or the giving of security in connection with a loan, quasi-loan or credit transaction by a person for a director of the company or holding company, the transaction is made under the authority of

---

56 A quasi-loan is defined by section 25(2)(a) as a transaction whereby one party agrees to pay a sum for another or agrees to reimburse expenditure incurred by another person on terms that the borrower will reimburse the creditor or in circumstances giving rise to a liability on the borrower to reimburse the creditor.

57 Section 25(3) defines a credit transaction as one where the creditor supplies any goods or sells any land under a hire purchase agreement or conditional sale agreement; or leases or licenses the use of land or hires goods in return for periodical payments; or otherwise disposes of land or supplies goods or services on the undertaking that payment is deferred.

58 Section 32 of the 1990 Act.

a special resolution of the company, passed not more than twelve months previously, before which the company has forwarded, with each notice of the meeting at which the special resolution is to be considered, a statutory declaration by the directors in the prescribed form accompanied by an independent report, by a person qualified to be an auditor of the company, stating that the statutory declaration is reasonable; or

(c) where a company makes a loan or quasi-loan to, or gives a guarantee or other security on behalf of, or enters into a credit transaction as creditor for, any company which is its holding company, subsidiary or a subsidiary of its holding company; or

(c) where a company provides any of its directors with funds to meet vouched expenditure properly incurred, or to be incurred, by them for the purposes of the company or to enable them to properly perform their duties as officers of the company, or doing anything to enable any of its directors to avoid incurring such expenditure. Where a company enters into such a transaction, any liability falling on any person from such a transaction must be discharged by him within six months. Failing this the person shall be guilty of an offence;[59]

(e) where such loans, quasi-loans and credit transactions are entered into in the ordinary course of the company's business and the value of the transaction, and the terms on which it is entered into, is not greater than that which the company ordinarily offers, or is reasonable to expect the company to have offered.

Transactions falling within section 31 are deemed to be transaction in which a director is interested and are subject to the section 194 disclosure rules. Where a prohibited transaction is entered into, it is voidable at the instance of the company provided however that rescission is possible, the company has been indemnified against any loss and innocent third party rights are not affected.[60] Any officer of the company who authorises a prohibited transaction may be guilty of a criminal offence where they know, or have reasonable cause to believe, that the company was contravening section 31.[61]

A director who breaches section 31 may be restricted if the company is subsequently wound up without being able to pay its debts. In *Stafford v. Higgins and Others*[62] two directors had obtained, on behalf of the company, a business development loan. The company loaned these funds to the directors, who used it

---

59 Section 37 of the 1990 Act.

60 Section 38(1) of the 1990 Act.

61 Section 40 of the 1990 Act.

62 *Re Xnet Information Systems Ltd (in voluntary liquidation)*, Unreported, High Court, Finlay Geoghegan J., May 6, 2004. See Chapter 19: Restriction and Disqualification of Directors.

to purchase premises. The premises were then leased to the company. The other directors of the company appeared to have knowledge of the purchase and the rent to be paid by the company, but the lease had not been approved by the board. The other directors became aware of the manner in which the premises were purchased and raised an objection at the board meeting. On discovering that the loan was unlawful, the company demanded repayment. The directors were not able to repay the money and the company was subsequently wound up. The liquidator took the view that the loans given by the company to the directors contributed to the demise of the company. The court was satisfied that, in entering into significant financial transactions between the company and themselves without obtaining approval from the board and in breach of their disclosure requirements under section 194 and in breach of the prohibition of loans to directors under section 31, the directors did not act responsibly and restriction orders were granted against the two directors.

Other Contracts

Section 41 of the 1990 Act provides that all loan and loan-type transactions between the company and its directors, shadow directors and connected persons must be disclosed in the company accounts.[63] Section 41 further requires all companies to disclose in their annual accounts contracts, transactions and arrangements in which any director, or director of a holding company, has a material interest.[64]

In the foregoing paragraphs and previous chapters, mention has been made of many of the statutory duties owed by directors and the sanctions that may be imposed if these duties are breached. These duties are prescribed to limit the potential for abuse by directors. By virtue of section 383(1) of the Principal Act, where any provision of the Companies Acts that provides that an officer of a company who is in default shall be liable to a fine or penalty, an officer for the purposes of those provisions means an officer who authorises or permits the relevant default.

Furthermore, section 383(3) pf the Principal Act categorically states that it is the duty of each director and secretary of a company to ensure that the requirements of the Companies Acts are complied with. In subsequent chapters the following statutory duties and liabilities will be outlined in detail:

---

63 Exemptions are available in the case of licensed banks and their holding companies or where the loan or loan type transaction, or the aggregate thereof, is for an amount not greater than £2,500 (€3,174) and represents an amount less than the company's relevant assets.

64 Certain transactions are not required to be disclosed: Section 41(7) of the 1990 Act.

(a) the duty to keep proper books of account and prepare the annual financial statements of the company;[65]
(b) the duty to lay before the annual general meeting of the annual accounts;[66]
(c) the duties of directors in relation to the re-organisation of the company;[67]
(d) the duty to co-operate in investigation, examinership, receivership and liquidation procedures under the Companies Acts;[68]
(e) the duty to co-operate with the Director of Corporate Enforcement;
(g) the duty to co-operate with inspectors appointed by the court or the Director of Corporate Enforcement; [69]

When a company becomes insolvent, the normal day-to-day activities and duties, while continuing, are displaced to some degree by the duty owed to the company's creditors. That this is the case is reflected by several statutory provisions, in particular those dealing with:

1. fraudulent trading;
2. reckless trading; and
3. misfeasance.

1. Fraudulent Trading

Under section 297 and 297A of the Principal Act a person is trading fraudulently if he is knowingly a party to the carrying on of the business of the company with intent to defraud creditors of the company or creditors of any other person or for any fraudulent purpose. The sanctions are both civil and criminal. On summary conviction the penalty is imprisonment for twelve months or a fine not exceeding £1,000 (€1,269), or both. On indictment, the penalty is a term of imprisonment not exceeding seven years or a fine not exceeding £50,000 (€63,487), or both. If the civil sanction is imposed the person may be held personally responsible for the debts of the company. The section is not restricted to directors or officers of the company but can apply to any person who is party to the fraudulent activities.[70]

Before a person can be found guilty of fraudulent trading it must be proved that the person was *knowingly* a party to the fraudulent carrying on of the company's business and did so with *intent*. The use of the double-subjective test of '*knowingly*' and '*with intent*' makes the standard a difficult one for a liquidator to prove. In *Re Kelly's Carpetdrome Ltd*,[71] the first Irish case dealing with section

---

65 Section 202 of the 1990 Act. See Chapter 20.
66 Section 148 of the Principal Act: see Chapter 20.
67 See Chapter 23.
68 See Chapters 24—27.
69 See Chapter 22.
70 *Re Hunting Lodges Ltd* [1985] ILRM 75 and *Re Gerald Cooper Chemicals* [1978] 2 All ER 49.
71 Unreported, High Court, Costello J., July 1, 1983.

297, debts were incurred by the company at a time when it failed to keep proper books of account. The evidence also showed that some of the company's records were actually destroyed. Certain of the company's assets were transferred to other connected companies in an attempt to hive off the company's only valuable assets. On the basis of the evidence before him, Costello J. ordered that personal liability for the debts of the company should be imposed on the defendants.

In *Re Aluminium Fabricators Ltd*,[72] two sets of books of account were maintained by the company. One was for the benefit of the controllers of the company and the other for the benefit of the Revenue Commissioners. The intention and effect of this was to allow the controllers to siphon off company assets for their own benefit. Obviously such activities do not impinge on creditors provided they continue to be paid. However, once the company went into insolvent winding up, it was clear that such actions had a detrimental effect on the creditors. O'Hanlon J. in the High Court held those responsible to be personally liable for the debts of the company.

It is not necessary that the fraudulent trading continues over a period of time. In *Re Hunting Lodges Ltd*,[73] a single act was held to constitute fraudulent trading. The act involved the sale, at an undervalue, of the 'Durty Nellies' public house, which was the company's principal asset. The company sold the pub but disguised the true price of the sale by paying a substantial part of the consideration in an under-the-counter payment to one of the directors. In addition, £160,000 was paid by the purchaser to the controllers. This single fraudulent act was held to constitute the carrying on of the company's business in a fraudulent manner. Interestingly, in this case it was not only the directors and shareholders but also the purchaser who were held liable, as the purchaser had received a 'kickback' of some of his purchase price for co-operating with the fraudulent transaction.

Because of the difficulties involved in proving that a person acted knowingly and with intent, it was only in the most blatant cases of fraud that an action would be taken by a liquidator, who would be conscious of the legal costs involved in any unsuccessful litigation. Accordingly, it was recognised that there was an obvious need for the introduction of a new measure which would not impose such a burden on liquidators. The legislative response to this need came in the form of the reckless trading provisions of the Companies Act 1990.

2. Reckless Trading

Section 297A of the Principal Act provides that if, in the course of a winding up of a company or in the course of proceedings under the Companies (Amendment) Act 1990, it appears that any person while an officer of the company is *knowingly* a party to the carrying on of business in a reckless manner, the court may, on the application of the receiver, examiner or liquidator or any other creditor or

---

72 [1984] ILRM 399.
73 [1985] ILRM 75.

contributory of the company,[74] declare that such person shall be personally liable without limitation of liability for some or all of the debts of the company.

Even where it cannot be shown that a person was 'knowingly' a party — the difficult subjective test — to the carrying on of business in a reckless manner, he may be deemed to have acted recklessly.

Section 297A(2) provides that a person is deemed to have been knowingly a party to reckless trading if either of two circumstances arise. First, that the person was party to the carrying on of such business which, in his experience and given his knowledge and skill, he ought to have known would cause loss to the creditors. This introduces an objective test based on the experience, knowledge and skill of the officer. Second, the person is deemed to have traded recklessly if he was a party to the contracting of a debt by the company and did not honestly believe, on reasonable grounds, that the company would be able to pay the debt when it fell due for payment, as well as all its other debts. If this circumstance arises the court must take into account whether the creditor in question was, at the time the debt was incurred, aware of the company's financial state of affairs and, being so aware, assented to the incurring of the debt.[75]

Liability will only be imposed under section 297A if the requirements of section 214 of the Principal Act have been satisfied.[76] These requirements are that:

(a) the company is unable to pay its debts within twenty-one days of a demand;
(b) an execution on the company has been returned unsatisfied; or
(c) it is proved to the court that the company is unable to pay its debts.

It should be observed that the section, unlike the fraudulent trading provision, applies only to officers of the company and not to other persons. An officer who acted honestly and responsibly in relation to the conduct of the affairs of the company may be relieved from liability on such terms as the court thinks fit.[77] This defence was successfully invoked in *Re Heffernan Kearns (No. 2).*[78]

3. Misfeasance

Section 298(1) of the Principal Act provides that where, in the course of a winding up or on an application under section 251 of the Companies Act 1990[79],

---

74 A creditor or contributory of the company can only make an application under the section if he suffered loss or damage as a result of the director carrying on business in a reckless manner.

75 Section 297A(4) of the Principal Act.

76 Section 297A(3)(a) of the Principal Act.

77 Section 297A(6) of the Principal Act.

78 [1993] 3 IR 191.

79 Section 251 of the 1990 Act provides a mechanism whereby many of the provisions of the Companies Acts that apply when a company is in liquidation will also apply where an insolvent company has not been formally wound up because of the insufficiency of its assets.

it appears that any person who has taken part in the formation or promotion of the company, or any past or present officer, liquidator, receiver or examiner of the company, has misapplied or retained or become liable or accountable for any money or property of the company or has been guilty of any misfeasance or other breach of duty or trust in relation to the company, the court may compel that person:

(a) to repay or restore the money or property; or
(b) to contribute such sums to the assets of the company by way of compensation in respect of the misapplication, retainer, misfeasance or other breach of duty or trust as the court thinks just.

What constitutes misfeasance is a matter for the court. It has been held that an act of negligence or an error of judgement will not necessarily amount to a misfeasance.[80]

Securing the Assets of Directors

The court may on the application of a company, director, member, liquidator, receiver, creditor or the Director of Corporate Enforcement order a director not to remove his assets from the State if the court is satisfied that the applicant has a substantive civil cause of action or the right to seek a declaration of personal liability or claim for damages against a director and there are grounds for believing that the respondent may remove those assets.[81]

Duties of Care and Competence

The fiduciary duties imposed on directors require them to keep the best interests of the company to the fore when they are making decisions. They further prevent them from abusing their powers and diverting company resources for their own personal gain. The statutory requirements reinforce these duties in many ways and have been developed to protect those who transact with the company, including, *inter alia*, shareholders and creditors. Otherwise, relatively few legal restraints are placed on directors' freedom to manage the assets and undertaking of the company. While directors may be held negligent for corporate mismanagement, the reported cases are few, leading one commentator to suggest that:

> the search for cases in which directors have been held liable for negligence uncomplicated by self-dealing is a search for a very small number of needles in a very large haystack.[82]

---

80 See *Re Mont Clare Hotels Ltd.*, Unreported, High Court, Costello J., December 2, 1986.
81 Section 55 of the 2001 Act.
82 Bishop (1968) 77 Yale LJ 1078 at 1099.

The reasons why negligence actions are not pursued against inept directors are understandable. First, the board of directors is unlikely to bring an action against one of its own members. Second, liquidators are always mindful that the pool of assets available to creditors would be depleted by unsuccessful litigation — furthermore, even if the liquidator is successful, the courts can relieve a director from liability if he acted honestly and reasonably. Third, even if litigation was initiated, judges have traditionally shown a marked reluctance to condemn business decisions made without the benefit of hindsight. Finally, a problem arises in establishing a standard of care and skill for a range of persons who may have a common title but whose knowledge, experience and business acumen will vary significantly.

The leading authority on the duty of care owed by company directors is the judgment of Romer LJ. in *Re City Equitable Fire Insurance Co. Ltd.*[83] The chairman of an insurance company had misappropriated sums of company money. He concealed his dishonesty by juggling short-term investments at financial year-ends. The other directors left the investment business of the company in the hands of the chairman and never queried the accounts. Although concerned about certain long-term investments, they left this matter to the general manager, who was instructed by the chairman. The company ultimately failed as a result of the misapplication of investments. The liquidator sued the other directors for negligence. The directors were held to be negligent but escaped liability because the company's articles of association exonerated directors from liability for negligence unless it was wilful. The case is important because of the three propositions put forward by Romer LJ. concerning the skill and diligence that must be exercised and the level of delegation that may be exercised by directors.

Skill

A director, while owing a duty of care to the company, need not exhibit in the performance of his duties a greater degree of skill than may reasonably be expected from a person of his knowledge and experience. The test is largely subjective, in that the reasonable person will be judged on the basis of that particular individual's knowledge and expertise. The formulation of the director's duty in these terms would seem to impose little or no duty on the unskilled and unqualified director, who can make business decisions, however ill-advised, safe in the knowledge that ignorance is bliss. In these cases it would seem that only acts of gross negligence will give rise to liability. In *Lagunas Nitrate Co. v. Lagunas Syndicate*[84] the directors of the company had overvalued a mining business that the company was purchasing. The court refused to hold them liable for negligence. As Lindley MR. stated:

---

83 [1925] Ch 407.
84 [1899] 2 Ch 392.

The amount of care to be taken is difficult to define; but it is plain that directors are not liable for all the mistakes they may make, although if they had taken more care they might have avoided them ... Their negligence must not be the omission to take all possible care; it is much more blameable than that; it must be in a business sense culpable and gross.

However, the director who has, or purports to have, a particular skill will be required to use that skill. Failure to do so may render the director, whether executive or non-executive, liable for negligence. In *Dorchester Finance Co. Ltd v. Stebbing*[85] the three defendants were all directors of a licensed moneylending company. Stebbing was an executive director and the other two were non-executive directors. Each of them had either an accountancy qualification or extensive accounting experience. No board meetings were ever held, and the non-executive directors left the management of the company's affairs to Stebbing, often leaving blank cheques for him to complete at a later date. Stebbing used some of these cheques for transactions outside the terms of the moneylending licence, which subsequently proved to be irrecoverable. The company issued proceedings against all three directors for negligence. The court held that had the directors exercised their skills the loss in question would not have arisen. Furthermore, these skills must be exercised by all directors, not just executive directors. Accordingly, all three were held liable.

Diligence

The second proposition put forward by Romer LJ. relates to the degree of diligence required by directors. He suggested that a director is:

not bound to give continuous attention to the affairs of his company. His duties are of an intermittent nature to be performed at periodical board meetings, and at meetings of any committee of the board upon which he happens to be placed. He is not, however, bound to attend all such meetings, though he ought to attend, whenever, in the circumstances, he is reasonably able to do so.

What will constitute reasonable attendance is not clear from the above passage. What is clear, however, is that failure to attend meetings, having been put on notice of irregular decision-making, may render a director liable in negligence. In *Jackson v. Munster Bank Ltd ex parte Dease*[86] Dease was a director of a bank with branches in Cork and Dublin. He regularly attended Dublin board meetings, which concerned the Dublin branch, but rarely attended the Cork board meetings. In his absence, the Cork directors approved unauthorised loans to themselves, many of which were irrecoverable. Although Dease was advised of these irregular dealings in February 1883, he took no action to investigate them. He was successfully sued for breach of duty. The court accepted that Dease could

---

85 (1989) BCLC 498.
86 (1885) 15 LR Ir 356.

be excused from attending all the Cork meetings because of his heavy schedule in Dublin. However, once he was put on notice of the fraudulent misappropriation of the property of the bank, it was his duty to attend those meetings and enquire into the matter. Because he had not done so, he was held liable for the losses incurred by the bank as a result of the improper loans made after February 1883.

The mere attendance at meetings is not enough to discharge the duty of care and diligence. Directors who attend but fall asleep or allow themselves to be distracted cannot escape liability by claiming that they took no part in or were unaware of the decisions being made at that meeting.[87] Similarly, the director who rubber-stamps a recommendation by the chairman is in a riskier position than the person who does not attend at all.[88]

The degree of diligence required of directors goes beyond attendance and participation at meetings. All directors, irrespective of their status, are under an obligation, both collectively and individually, to acquire and maintain a sufficient knowledge and understanding of the company's business to enable them properly to discharge their duties as directors.[89] This is the case irrespective of whether a person is an executive or non-executive director.

In *Kavanagh v. Delaney and Others*,[90] the liquidator brought an application for restriction against four directors of an insolvent company, three of whom were non-executive directors of the company. All the non-executive directors stated that they relied on the executive director to provide them with financial information in relation to the company. The evidence suggested that there were no board meetings — formal or informal — during the final two years of the company's trading. The court observed that it was a fact of commercial life that persons are appointed as non-executive directors to act alongside executive directors. It was further noted that it was common sense that the duties and responsibilities of executive and non-executive directors may differ. A non-executive director may be invited to join the board to bring a range of skills and it is appropriate to consider the discharge of their duties in relation to their particular skills and their agreed role on the board. Nonetheless the court accepted that all directors, irrespective of their status, are under a duty to discharge the minimum obligation of informing themselves about the company's affairs and joining with their co-directors in supervising and controlling such affairs. As this duty was not adequately discharged, the court was satisfied that the non-executive directors had not acted responsibly and restriction orders were granted against them.

---

87 *Land Credit Co. of Ireland v. Lord Fermoy* (1870) LR 5 Ch App 763.
88 *Selangor United Rubber Estates Ltd v Cradock & Others* (No.3) [1968] 2 All ER 1073.
89 *Per* Jonathon Parker J. in *Re Barings plc. (No. 5), Secretary of State for Trade and Industry v. Baker* [1999] 1 BCLC 433.
90 *In Re Tralee Beef and Lamb Limited (in liquidation)*, [2005] 1 ILRM 34.

Delegation

When it comes to the delegation by a director of some or all of their duties, Romer LJ. observed:

> In respect of all duties that, having regard to the exigencies of business and the articles of association, may properly be left to some other official, a director is, in the absence of grounds for suspicion, justified in trusting that official to perform such duties honestly.

On this basis directors may delegate to a fellow director who is skilled or competent in the manner required and whose previous conduct has given no grounds for suspicion As Lord Halsbury LC. stated in *Dovey v. Cory*[91]

> I cannot think that it can be expected of a director that he should be watching the inferior officers ... the business of life could not go on if people could not trust those who are put into a position of trust for the express purpose of attending to details of management.

However, while directors are entitled (subject to the articles of association of the company) to delegate particular functions to those below them in the management chain, and to trust their competence and integrity to a reasonable extent, the exercise of the power of delegation does not absolve a director from the duty to supervise the discharge of the delegated functions.[92]

While delegation is permissible, and advisable in certain circumstances, directors should not abdicate all management responsibilities, as *Dorchester v. Stebbing*, considered above, demonstrates.

In *Re Hunting Lodges Ltd*,[93] the wife of the executive director was appointed as the other director of the company, probably just to meet the minimum statutory requirements. The evidence showed that she had acted merely as a non-executive director and played no real role in the day-to-day management of the company. In an attempt to resist liability for fraudulent trading, she claimed that any business she did undertake was based on instructions from her husband. In holding her liable, Carroll J. held that a person who 'abdicates all responsibility is not to be lightly excused'.

In *Halley v. Nolan*[94] two directors, though formally appointed as directors, did little other than sign documents on the direction of another director. The court held that such a lack of independence in decision-making was not the responsible exercising of a director's function and a restriction order was granted against each of them. The case reaffirms yet again that those who accept formal appointment as directors of companies just to satisfy the statutory requirements, but act merely as 'puppets', do so at their peril.

---

91 [1901] 1 Ch 477.
92 See note 89.
93 [1985] ILRM 75.
94 Unreported, High Court, Finlay Geoghegan J., July 1, 2005.

Directors of group companies are often bound by decisions made by other companies in the group. Nonetheless, it is clear that they will not be exonerated from a finding of irresponsibility just because the structures of a particular group remove the decision-making function from them. In *O'Ferral v. Coughlan and Others*[95] the liquidator applied for an order of restriction under section 150 of the Companies Act 1990 against the respondent directors of the company on the grounds of their irresponsibility. The evidence showed that the operations of the company were financed as part of worldwide operations, the company was not in a position to operate independently and the financing of the Irish company was determined as part of group operations. Furthermore, while the directors were given financial information, it was in a consolidated form and did not identify the financial position of the company. In this regard the court held that by agreeing to act as directors of a corporate entity the directors had duties in respect of that entity. Despite their obligation to follow the policies of the entire group, the directors could not abdicate all their responsibilities. They remained under a duty to inform themselves about the affairs of the company, as distinct from any other part of the group, and to join with each other in supervising and controlling the affairs of the company. While the court acknowledged that their margin of discretion may have been small in terms of business decisions, this would not absolve them from their obligation to take decisions. On this basis, and given the fact that a complete abrogation of responsibility for the financial affairs of the company took place and the fact that proper books of accounts were not maintained, the court concluded that an order of restriction be made against the respondents.

As can be seen from these last two cases, negligence actions in their own right may not be a common occurrence when it comes to directors. However, where they are shown to have been in breach of their duty of care or competence they may be liable to be restricted under the provisions of the 1990 Act. Furthermore, in cases of gross negligence they may well face disqualification proceedings.[96]

Indemnifying Directors

It should be noted that the directors in *City Equitable* escaped liability by virtue of the company's articles of association. Section 200 of the Principal Act renders void any provisions in the company's articles that exempt company officers from liability. However, the company is permitted to purchase insurance for any of its officers in respect of any such liability.[97]

---

95 *In Re 360 Atlantic (Ireland) Ltd (in receivership and in liquidation)*, High Court, Finlay Geoghegan J., December 21, 2004.
96 Restriction and disqualification are discussed in Chapter 19.
97 Section 200(2) of the Principal Act.

CHAPTER NINETEEN

RESTRICTION AND DISQUALIFICATION OF DIRECTORS

Introduction

Prior to the introduction of Part VII of the 1990 Act, the practice whereby directors of insolvent companies could re-emerge with a similar business, but under a new corporate identity, went unregulated for the most part.[1] However, Chapter 1 of Part VII of the 1990 Act introduced new provisions designed to restrict or prevent such directors' further use of the statutory privileges of incorporation. These provisions were strengthened further by the the 2001 Act.

Restriction

Section 150(1) of the 1990 Act provides that a director of an insolvent company in liquidation or receivership,[2] who fails to satisfy the court as to his honesty and responsibility, will be restricted for a period of five years.[3] Shanley J. described the primary purpose of section 150 as:

> the protection of the public from persons who, by their conduct, have shown themselves unfit to hold the office of, and discharge the duties of, a director of a company and, in consequence, represent a danger to potential investors and traders dealing with such companies[4]

An application for a declaration of restriction may be made by a liquidator, receiver or the Director of Corporate Enforcement (the Director).[5] Since 2001, a liquidator of an insolvent company is obliged to make an application for a restriction order unless the Director of Corporate Enforcement has relieved the liquidator of such an obligation.[6]

Section 150 of the 1990 Act provides that the court shall make a declaration or restriction unless it is satisfied that the person concerned:

---

1 Section 184 of the Principal Act gave the court the power, on the application of the Attorney General, to restrain certain persons from acting as directors of or managing companies. This section was repealed by Part VII of the 1990 Act.
2 Section 154 of the 1990 Act applies the restriction provisions to directors of companies in receivership. However, the mandatory requirement imposed on liquidators to bring restriction applications, by virtue of section 56 of the 2001 Act, does not apply to receivers.
3 Section 150 of the 1990 Act.
4 *La Moselle Clothing Ltd v. Souhali* [1998] 2 ILRM 345.
5 Section 150(4B) of the 1990 Act.
6 Section 56 of the 2001 Act.

(a) acted honestly and responsibly in relation to the conduct of the affairs of the company and no other just and equitable reason exists for imposing the restriction;[7] or

(b) is a nominee of an institution providing credit facilities to the company, provided that personal guarantees from the directors have not been obtained for such facilities;[8] or

(c) is a nominee of a venture capital company which has purchased or subscribed for shares in the company.[9]

In the case of (a) above the onus is on the person concerned to satisfy the court that he acted 'honestly and responsibly' in relation to the conduct of the affairs of the company. The nominees of the financial institution or the venture capital company described above will not avoid a restriction order if it is proven that they did not act honestly and responsibly. However, in such cases the onus is on the applicant to show that the persons did not act honestly and responsibly.

To Whom does Section 150 Apply?

Directors: section 149 of the 1990 Act provides that the restriction provisions apply to a person who was a director or shadow director of an insolvent company at the date of, or within the twelve months prior to, the commencement of its winding up (or receivership). However, many companies are insolvent long before formal insolvency procedures such as receiverships or liquidations are commenced. If a company can carry on, albeit while insolvent, and some of the directors resign before the twelve-month period has kicked in, they will be exempt from the provisions even if they did not act honestly and responsibly during their tenure. It is quite common to see insolvent companies trading long after the insolvency of the company commenced, often in the belief, however unjustified, that they will trade out of their difficulties. Indeed in *Re Vehicle Imports Ltd*[10] the evidence showed that the company had actually been insolvent for about four years before formal insolvency procedures commenced. If any of the directors of that company had managed to resign (they did not) prior to the commencement of the twelve-month period they would have avoided the section 150 application. This is precisely what occurred in *Re Cavan Crystal Group Ltd*,[11] where Murphy J. held that one of the respondents could not be subjected to a restriction order because he had resigned as a director more than twelve months prior to the commencement of the receivership, even though it was clear from the evidence that the company was in 'acute' financial trouble at least three years

---

7 Section 150(2)(a) of the 1990 Act.
8 Section 150(2)(a) of the 1990 Act.
9 Section 150(2)(c) of the 1990 Act.
10 Unreported, High Court, Murphy J., February 23, 2000.
11 Unreported, High Court, Murphy J., April 26, 1996.

prior to the appointment of the receiver.

The restriction provisions also apply to shadow directors and *de facto* directors. A shadow director is 'a person in accordance with whose directions or instructions the directors of the company are accustomed to act'[12] and such persons are liable to be restricted under the provisions of the 1990 Act. In *Re Worldport Ltd (in liquidation)*[13] the High Court held that a corporate body could be a shadow director for the purposes of restriction applications under section 150. *De facto* directors are also liable to be restricted under section 150.[14]

The Honesty and Responsibility Requirement

Applications for restriction generally focus on the 'irresponsibility' rather than the 'honesty' of a director.[15] In determining what constituted the 'responsibility' of a director, Shanley J. in *La Moselle Clothing Ltd v. Souhali*[16] stated that the court should have regard to the following criteria, which necessarily overlap:

a   the extent to which the director has or has not complied with any obligation imposed on him by the Companies Acts 1963—90;

b   the extent to which his conduct could be regarded as so incompetent as to amount to irresponsibility;

c   the extent of the director's responsibility for the insolvency of the company;

d   the extent of the director's responsibility for the net deficiency in the assets of the company disclosed at the date of the winding up or thereafter; and

e   the extent to which the director, in his conduct of the affairs of the company, has displayed a lack of commercial probity or want of proper standards.

These criteria were approved by the Supreme Court in *Re Squash (Ireland) Ltd.*[17] It should be observed that the matters referred to by Shanley J. cannot be considered exhaustive. In *Kavanagh v. Delaney,*[18] Finlay Geoghegan J. suggested that the common law duties of care owed by directors should also be taken into account when considering the responsibility of directors. She endorsed the view that all directors, whether executive or non-executive, must take reasonable steps

---

12 Section 27(1) of the 1990 Act.
13 Unreported, High Court, O'Leary J., February 16, 2005. See also *Fyffes v. DCC plc & Others*, Unreported, High Court, Laffoy J., December 21, 2005. See Chapter 16.
14 See Chapter 16: *Gray v. McLoughlin*, Unreported, High Court, Finlay Geoghegan J., July 9, 2004.
15 In *Re Usit World plc*, Unreported, High Court, August 10, 2005 Peart J. suggested that dishonesty was more fundamental than irresponsibility as it goes to the core of a person's integrity.
16 [1998] 2 ILRM 345.
17 [2001] 3 IR 35.
18 [2005] ILRM 34.

to place themselves in a position to guide and monitor the management of the company[19] by informing themselves about the company's affairs and taking steps to join with their co-directors in supervising and controlling the company, particularly in difficult times.[20]

It is not uncommon to find that many of the criteria identified above arise in the same application. In *Kavanagh v. Cooke*[21] the liquidator applied for a restriction order against the respondent managing director of the company. The issues raised by the liquidator related to the non-filing of statutory accounts, failure to put in place appropriate financial management procedures, major discrepancies between the statement of affairs prepared by the directors and the actual realisable assets of the company, accumulated revenue debts, failure while trading to distinguish between the separate companies of which the respondent was a director, and the use of an insolvent company as a springboard to launch a related company. Having considered that there was no adequate defence to the matters raised or any further mitigating circumstances, MacMenamin J. granted the restriction order.

The wording of section 150 does not specify the limitation period on the 'honesty and responsibility' requirement. This matter has arisen in several cases relating to restriction. In *Re Gasco Ltd*[22] McCracken J. considered that the provisions applied only to directors who have behaved irresponsibly and dishonestly during the last twelve months of the life of the company, and that the actions of a director who is subject to a Section 150 application are to be looked at primarily in light of his actions during that period. These comments should not be read in isolation: McCracken J. later suggested that it is the twelve-month period prior to the winding up (or receivership) that should be the subject of 'particular scrutiny' as opposed to exclusive scrutiny. In this regard he stated:

> I think it is quite significant that no restrictions can attach to somebody who ceased to be a director of the company more than twelve months before the winding up. This seems to indicate that the primary aim of section 150 is to deal with directors who have behaved irresponsibly or dishonestly during the last twelve months of the life of the company, and that the actions of a director who is subject to section 150 are to be looked at primarily in the light of his actions during that period. This indeed has a considerable practical logic, as it is presumably intended to focus attention on the behaviour of the directors in the period leading up to the winding up, and to try to ensure that they deal responsibly with creditors when a company is in difficulties. In my view, therefore, there should be particular scrutiny of the actions of directors during the final months before winding up.

---

19 Citing with approval *Re Barings plc* [1999] 1 BCLC 433.
20 The Director of Corporate Enforcement has issued guidelines as to the factors he will take into account in relieving the liquidator of his obligation to bring restriction proceedings (Decision Notice D/2002/3).
21 *Re Cherby Ltd (in Liquidation)* [2006] 1 ILRM 191
22 Unreported, High Court, McCracken J., February 5, 2001.

In *Re Squash Ireland Ltd*[23] the Supreme Court held that the proper approach in any application was to examine the entire tenure of the directors. In this case the liquidator expressed concern at activities concerning the final months of the life of the company. While the Supreme Court acknowledged that there is always likely to be criticism of the director leading up to insolvency, in this particular case the directors' overall tenure going back sixteen years had shown them to be honest and responsible.

Delay in Proceedings

Since 2001, a liquidator of an insolvent company is obliged to bring restriction proceedings not earlier than three months and not later than five months after the date on which he has presented his report to the Director of Corporate Enforcement under section 56 of the 2001 Act.[24] Failure to do so renders the liquidator liable to an offence.[25] However, even if the liquidator fails to comply with this time period this does not prevent him — or indeed any other applicant permitted to bring an application under section 150 — from bringing proceedings against a director.[26]

However, unnecessary delay may deny an applicant his right to bring an application under section 150. In *Re Knocklofty House Hotel Ltd (in liquidation)*[27] *(ex tempore)*, the official liquidator of two related companies sought applications for restriction against these companies' directors. The companies had gone into liquidation in 1992 and 1993 respectively. The application for restriction was made in February 2004. The respondents argued that the application should be dismissed by reason of the delay in bringing the matter before the court. The court accepted that the relevant principles to be applied were:

1. Was the delay 'inordinate' and inexcusable'?
2. Whether the 'balance of justice' is in favour or against proceeding.

The court was satisfied that the delay was 'inordinate' and, although the liquidator pointed to various difficulties arising in the liquidation, the court was not satisfied that there was a sufficient excuse to justify an eleven-year delay. In considering whether the balance of justice favoured proceeding with the case the court noted that the respondents would have to satisfy the court that they acted honestly and responsibly in relation to the conduct of the affairs of the company for a period going back more than eleven years. The court further considered that

---

23 Unreported, Supreme Court, February 8, 2001.
24 Section 56(2) of the 2001 Act.
25 Section 56(3) of the 2001 Act.
26 *Coyle v. O'Brien*, Unreported, High Court, Finlay Geoghegan J., July 14, 2003.
27 *Ex tempore*, Unreported, High Court, Finlay Geoghegan J., April 5, 2005.

having regard to the respondents' right to earn a livelihood, there should come a time when they should be able to put behind them the consequences of an insolvent liquidation. The respondents had, for the previous five years, been involved as shareholders and directors of a limited company. They became so involved about seven years after the commencement of the liquidations of the companies to which the restriction application applies. The court considered that period sufficient and that the directors should be able to put the consequences of the liquidated companies behind them. The court concluded that the balance of interests was against proceeding with the application and it was dismissed.

The 'Just and Equitable' Ground

Even if the court is satisfied that the respondents acted honestly and responsibly it may still make an order for the restriction of the director if it considers that it is 'just and equitable' to do so. In *Fennell v. Carolan & Cosgrave*,[28] an order was sought by the liquidator to have the company directors restricted as a result of certain actions taken by them after the winding up had commenced. In the context of the post-liquidation period, Clarke J. referred to the judgment of Shanley J. in *La Moselle Clothing Ltd v. Souhali*[29] where he stated:

> Apart from satisfying the court that he as a director acted honestly and responsibly the director must also satisfy the court that there are no other reasons why it would be just and equitable to restrict him from acting as a director of a company. It is to be noted that acting honestly and responsibly relates to the conduct of the affairs of the company and arguably as such bears no relation to any period after the commencement of a winding up or receivership of the particular company where the person may not be involved any further in the conduct of the affairs of the company. That the director must satisfy the court that there is no other reason why it would be just and equitable to restrict the director, allows the court to take into account, in my view, any relevant conduct of the director after the commencement of the winding up or the receivership (for example, any failure to cooperate with the liquidator or receiver) in deciding whether or not to make an order under s.150(1) of the Companies Act, 1990.

In regard to the post-liquidation actions the liquidator raised various matters. First, the respondent directors had taken and kept in their possession for some months after the liquidation a forklift belonging to the company. Although they ultimately returned it, the court considered that directors have an obligation to be of assistance to a liquidator, and if their actions are such as to prevent a liquidator obtaining company assets for the purposes of discharging liabilities to creditors to the greatest extent possible, and as soon as possible, that would constitute a breach of obligation by the directors. The second matter raised by the liquidator related to the fact that the respondent directors had failed to co-operate with the

---

28 *Re CMC(Ireland) Limited (in voluntary liquidation)*, Unreported, High Court, March 4, 2005.
29 [1998] 2 ILRM 345.

liquidator and despite several attempts it was almost a year before the directors first met the liquidator. While the directors were under the impression that as they had resigned prior to the winding up they had no further obligations, the court was satisfied that their failure to co-operate with the liquidator was a matter that could be taken into account. This was particularly so if such failure placed a barrier in the way of the efficient conduct of the liquidation causing a protracted delay in the winding up, increased costs and consequently a diminution of the extent to which the creditors would be paid.

The final matter related to proceedings commenced by the liquidator seeking to recover monies owed to the company. The respondent directors had filed statements which appeared to be in favour of the defendants and against the interests of the company. The court acknowledged that a director is obliged to give evidence truthfully, irrespective of the consequences for the company. However, in this case the directors' evidence was at variance with the records of the company and the directors had not checked the records before making the statements. While the court accepted that there was no evidence of *male fides* on the part of the directors it considered that the obligations of directors in the course of a winding up should at least extend to exercising care when taking actions that could be detrimental to the interests of the company.

On the basis of the above the court was satisfied that the actions of the directors, at least taken cumulatively, amounted to a sufficient departure from the standards that could be expected from directors or former directors during a winding up to justify an order of restriction on a just and equitable basis and the directors were restricted.

Effect of Declaration

A declaration of restriction will operate to prevent a person from being a director or secretary or being involved in the formation or promotion of any company for a period of five years except where it is adequately capitalised.[30] In the case of private companies, this capital requirement is €63,487 in allotted paid-up share capital, and for public companies the greater amount of €317,435 is required.[31] Additionally, such companies will not enjoy the benefit of many of the capital maintenance exemptions under the Companies Acts.[32] Where the court makes a

---

30 Section 150(1) of the 1990 Act.

31 Section 150(3) of the 1990 Act.

32 The exceptions to the prohibition on a company providing financial assistance in connection with the purchase of its own shares, contained in section 60(2)—(11) of the Companies Act 1963 cannot be availed of; the restrictions that apply to allotments of shares, in public limited companies, other than in cash contained in Section 32 to 36 of the 1983 (Amendment) Act also apply to the company as if it were a public limited company; and the exceptions to the prohibition on a company making loans to directors and others contained in section 32 and section 37 of the 1990 Act cannot be availed of.

declaration of restriction the registrar of companies must be furnished with the particulars of the declaration.[33]

Court Relief

Section 152 allows for a person who has been restricted to apply to the court for relief from the restriction or from any order made in relation to him. The application may be made within twelve months of the restriction declaration. The court may grant such relief if it deems it just and equitable to do so. In contrast to section 150, the court is given a very broad discretion under section 152. The discretion is so broad that the court may accede to an application for relief in whole from the restrictions thereby imposed and, in effect, wholly negate the effect of the order under section 150. The only criterion stipulated in section 152 for the guidance of the court is that it should be 'just and equitable' to grant the relief.

The first application under section 152 arose in *Ferngara Associates Ltd; Robinson v. Forrest.*[34] The application was made by a director against a restriction order. Laffoy J. considered a number of mitigating factors: the applicant had allowed himself to be overpowered in management decisions by the managing director; the applicant had personally contributed in excess of £200,000 to discharge some of the creditors' claims; and the applicant had contended (which was undisputed) that he had acted responsibly since the winding up of the company. Interestingly, the court was also influenced by the fact that the livelihood of the director (together with the livelihoods of employees of another limited company of which he was a director) could be in jeopardy. Laffoy J. was satisfied that the applicant had learned an expensive lesson from his involvement in the company. The relief was granted under section 152 and the restriction order was lifted.

Partial relief may be granted in certain circumstances. In *Higgins v. Stafford*[35] the applicant sought relief under section 152 following a declaration of restriction made against him in 2004. It was submitted that the court should have regard to: the applicant's constitutional right to earn a livelihood; the absence of any finding of dishonesty regarding the applicant's conduct as a director; the applicant's conduct since the commencement of the winding up; and the hardship imposed on the applicant who was impecunious and could not meet the capital requirements imposed by section 150. The court considered that the fundamental purpose of section 150 is to protect the public from persons who in discharge of their duties as directors of companies have acted dishonestly or irresponsibly and no order for relief should be granted unless the court is satisfied that the public

---

33 Section 150(4) of the 1990 Act.
34 Unreported, High Court, Laffoy J., 11 February, 1999.
35 *Re Xnet Information Systems Ltd (in voluntary liquidation),* Unreported, High Court, O'Neill J., October 10, 2006.

will not be harmed by such an order. The court reviewed the matters that led to the restriction declaration and suggested that they were 'clearly not at the worst end of the scale of turpitude, but also, they are not at the other end either'. The court suggested that given the requirement under section 152(1) that the applicant must apply for relief within not more than one year, coupled with the relatively low capital threshold imposed by section 150(3), there was a suggestion that the Oireachtas intended the speedy rehabilitation of directors of whom declarations of restriction were made. Given the fact that the applicant had co-operated with the liquidator since the winding up, had been restricted for more than two years and had not just been unable to engage in trade through the medium of a limited liability company but had also to live with the stigma of the original declaration, the court was satisfied that relief should be granted in part. The court ordered that the restriction declaration should remain but subject to a lesser capital requirement in the amount of €7,500.

Register of Restricted Persons

The registrar of companies must keep a register of the particulars that have been notified to him under section 150.[36] At the expiry of five years from the date of the declaration the registrar must remove any particulars in relation to the person. Particulars of any relief granted under section 152 must also be maintained on the register, including any conditions imposed by the court in connection with partial relief. Where the court grants full relief the registrar shall remove any particulars of that person from the register.

Disqualification

Chapter 2 of Part VII of the 1990 Act widens considerably the grounds whereby a person may be disqualified by the court from acting as a director. The power to disqualify was described by Harmon J. in the English case of *Re Cladrose Ltd*[37] as follows:

> It is a power to be exercised to protect the public against those who display lack of commercial probity, 'rip-off' the public in colloquial terms, or otherwise shelter a totally rash and unjustified venture behind the shield of limited liability so that they themselves do not suffer when their rash venture fails, as was predictable, but leave the creditors at large to suffer.

A disqualification order is defined by section 159 of the 1990 Act as an order that the person against whom the order is made shall not be appointed or act as an auditor, director or other officer, receiver, liquidator or examiner or be in any way, whether directly or indirectly, concerned or take part in the promotion, formation or management of any company, or any society registered under the

---

36 Section 153(1) of the 1990 Act.
37 [1990] BCLC 204

Industrial and Provident Societies Acts 1893 to 1978. Unlike the restriction provisions, a person who has been disqualified can have no involvement in the promotion, formation or management of any company for the duration of the disqualification period regardless of the company's capitalisation. An application for a disqualification order can be made by the Director of Corporate Enforcement, the Director of Public Prosecutions, a member, creditor, officer, employee, receiver, liquidator or examiner of the company.

Automatic Disqualification

Section 160(1) of the 1990 Act makes provision for automatic disqualification of any person who is convicted on indictment of any indictable offence in relation to a company or involving fraud or dishonesty. Without anyone making application for a disqualification order, such a person is automatically deemed to be so subject for a period of five years from the date of conviction. Disqualification will be automatic in the following circumstances:

(a) where a person is convicted on indictment of any indictable offence in relation to the company or one involving fraud or dishonesty; or

(b) is convicted of acting while restricted except in the circumstances permitted by the 1990 Act; or

(c) is convicted of acting as auditor, officer, liquidator or examiner of, or in the formation, promotion or management of, any company while an undischarged bankrupt; or

(d) where a person is a director of a company and there has been a failure to notify the registrar, either at the time the memorandum and articles were being registered or when there was a change in the register of directors, that the person was disqualified in another jurisdiction, and details of same.

The effect of a disqualification order is that the person concerned is disqualified from acting as a director, auditor, officer, receiver, liquidator or examiner, or from being involved in the promotion, formation or management of a company for a period of five years or such other period as the court may direct.

Discretionary Disqualification

The court may also, at its own discretion and either on its own motion or on application, disqualify a person for such period as it deems fit where that person, while in the position of promoter, auditor, officer, receiver, liquidator or examiner of the company, has been guilty of any of the following:

(a) a person has been guilty, while a promoter, officer, auditor, receiver, liquidator or examiner of a company, of any fraud in relation to the company, its members or creditors; or

(b) a person has been guilty, while a promoter, officer, auditor, receiver, liquidator or examiner of a company, of any breach of his duty as such promoter, officer, auditor, receiver, liquidator or examiner; or

(c) a declaration has been granted under Section 297A of the 1963 Act (civil liability for fraudulent or reckless trading) in respect of a person;

(d) the conduct of any person as promoter, officer, auditor, receiver, liquidator or examiner of a company makes him unfit to be concerned in the management of a company; or

(e) in consequence of a report of inspectors appointed by the court or the Director of Corporate Enforcement under the Companies Acts the conduct of any person makes him unfit to be concerned in the management of a company; or

(f) a person has been persistently in default in relation to the relevant requirements (e.g. filing obligations) under the Companies Acts; or

(g) a person has been guilty of two or more offences under Section 202(10); or

(h) a person was a director at the time a company was struck off the register under section 12 of the 1982 Amendment Act and the company had not discharged all its debts;[38] or

(i) a person is disqualified under the law of another state.

To Whom does Section 160 Apply?

Unlike the restriction provisions, the scope of section 160 extends beyond directors and includes promoters, auditors, liquidators, receivers and examiners. Furthermore, 'officers' of a company are susceptible to disqualification on certain grounds. Section 159 of the 1990 Act states that an officer, 'in relation to any company, includes any director, shadow director or secretary of the company'. The insertion of the word 'includes' clearly denotes that the list is not exhaustive and is not limited to either the directors or the secretary of the company. The Irish courts have yet to decide what persons, other than directors or secretaries, will be considered an officer for the purposes of section 160.[39]

Other persons, even those not directly involved with the company, may also be disqualified where they have been found liable for breach of the fraudulent and reckless trading provisions of the Principal Act.[40] Any person who, following a report of inspectors appointed to investigate the affairs of the company, is

---

38 *Re Clawhammer Ltd; Director of Corporate Enforcement v. McDonnell and Endicott, Re Shinrone Food Market Ltd; Director of Corporate Enforcement v. Hoctor and Hoctor, Re Cautious Trading Ltd; Director of Corporate Enforcement v. Forristal and Forristal*, Unreported, High Court, Finlay Geoghegan J., March 15, 2005.

39 The matter was raised but undecided in *Director of Corporate Enforcement v. D'Arcy*, Unreported, High Court, Kelly J., October 26, 2005.

40 In *Re Hunting Lodges Ltd* [1985] ILRM 75, the purchaser of a pub owned by a company was held liable for fraudulent trading as he had received a 'kickback' of some of his purchase price for co-operating with the fraudulent transaction. See Chapter 18.

considered to be unfit to be involved in the management of a company.[41]

Concept of Unfitness and Mismanagement

The ground of 'unfitness' looks at the scope of directors' duties and the standard of care expected from a director. In *Re Lo-Line Electric Motors Ltd.*[42] Browne-Wilkinson VC. considered the matter of when directors are unfit to be concerned in the management of a company. In this regard he said:

> Ordinary commercial misjudgement is in itself not sufficient to justify disqualification. In the normal case the conduct complained of must display a lack of commercial probity, although I have no doubt that in an extreme case of gross negligence or total incompetence, disqualification could be appropriate.[43]

This passage was also quoted with approval by Murphy J. for the Supreme Court in the 2002 case of *Cahill v. Grimes*.[44] Here, the respondent had, without formal appointment, acted as a voluntary liquidator of the company. When an official liquidator was subsequently appointed, the respondent dumped the company's books, thus preventing the official liquidator perform his statutory function. The respondent claimed that his actions were motivated by trying to save the jobs of the employees of the company. The court considered that such actions were 'a very serious wrong' and showed a completely mistaken view as to the duties of a liquidator. The actions were such as to raise concerns about the propriety of the respondent being involved in the management of a company. Accordingly the Supreme Court upheld the decision of the High Court to disqualify the respondent.

In *Director of Corporate Enforcement v. D'Arcy*[45] the Director of Corporate Enforcement sought a disqualification order against the respondent. The application for disqualification arose following the completion of a report by court-appointed inspectors who investigated the affairs of National Irish Bank and National Irish Bank Financial Services Limited. There were several findings in the report regarding tax evasion and improper banking practices. In particular, the report concluded that bogus non-resident accounts had been opened and maintained in the bank's branches, enabling customers to evade tax through concealment of funds from the Revenue Commissioners. The inspectors concluded that the responsibility for the improper practices rested with senior management, including the respondent in this case. Mr D'Arcy had been head of the bank's Financial Advice and Services Division, but he was not a director of the bank or any of its subsidiary companies. The report concluded that the tax

---

41 *Director of Corporate Enforcement v. D'Arcy*, Unreported, High Court, Kelly J., October 26, 2005.
42 [1988] BCLC 698.
43 Approved by the Irish High Court in *Re Lynrowan Enterprises Ltd.*, Unreported, High Court, O'Neill J., July 31, 2002.
44 *Re CB Readymix Ltd.*, Unreported, Supreme Court, March 1, 2002.
45 Unreported, High Court, Kelly J., October 26, 2005

evasion scheme, promoted to customers by his financial services managers, was known to Mr D'Arcy for some six years and he did nothing to stop the practice. In considering whether the respondent was unfit to be involved with the management of a company the court considered the findings of inspectors, which were not disputed by the respondent; the role and responsibility of the respondent; and the 'special position' of trust on which the edifice of banking is built. On this basis the court held that there was a lack of commercial probity on the respondent's part and the order for disqualification was made.

As the decision of the courts is discretionary, mitigating factors may be taken into account. In *Re Dawson Print Group Limited*[46] a young director escaped disqualification, despite mismanagement, because the company was plagued with other problems such as bad luck, flooded premises, disastrous salesmen and family problems. In *Re Arctic Engineering Limited* (No. 2)[47] persistent defaults by a company accountant in terms of making and filing returns did not result in disqualification since there was no dishonesty.

Where the courts are not satisfied that the onus has been established to justify disqualification it may instead order that the person concerned is restricted.[48] In *Re Newcastle Timber Ltd,*[49] the liquidator demonstrated that the respondents had failed to make returns to the registrar of companies, they had traded whilst insolvent and they had paid trade creditors in priority to the Revenue Commissioners after the company had ceased trading. Nevertheless, the court accepted that while the directors had acted incompetently and irresponsibly they were not 'so much in breach of their duties that they are unfit to be concerned in the management of a company'. The court did, however, make a restriction order against the respondent directors.

Selective or Partial Disqualification

In *Re Majestic Recording Studios Ltd*[50] a director who had a disqualification order made against him was exempted in the case of one of his companies, which was paying its debts and keeping proper accounts, provided he had an independent chartered accountant as co-director of that company. One of the reasons for the court's exemption was that the company in question employed fifty-five people, whose jobs would have been placed in jeopardy had the director been disqualified.[51]

---

46 [1987] BCLC 601.
47 [1986] BCLC 341.
48 Section 160(9A) of the 1990 Act.
49 Unreported, High Court, McCracken J., October 16, 2001.
50 (1988) 4 BCC 519.
51 The position of employees was also averred to in *Re Dawson Print Group Limited* [1987] BCLC 601 and *Re Arctic Engineering Ltd.* (No.2) [1986] BCLC 253. In *Re Churchill (Plymouth) Hotel Ltd* [1988] BCLC 341 a director was found to be unfit but because of the lack of personal dishonesty and the fact that he controlled some eight other companies employing 80–90 people the court exercised its discretion and refused to grant a disqualification order.

The Irish courts have no great difficulty in making a partial disqualification order whereby a person is disqualified from some aspects of the management of a company. In *Cahill v. Grimes*, discussed above, the respondent had been disqualified from being concerned in the management of a company as a liquidator, receiver or examiner for a period of seven years and conditions were imposed on him limiting his right to act as auditor, director or secretary of a company during the same period. The Revenue Commissioners had submitted that section 160 was an 'all or nothing section' and that the court had no power to differentiate between the different offices or to impose conditions as to the terms on which any one or more of the offices might be exercised. The Supreme Court rejected this view and held that the wording of section 160(8) gave the court the power to grant relief 'either in whole or in part' on 'whatever terms and conditions it sees fit' which included a partial disqualification order in the manner in which the trial judge had so 'humanely' done.

The Period of Disqualification

Section 160(1) of the 1990 Act provides that in relation to automatic disqualification the person concerned shall be disqualified for a period of five years from the date of the conviction or for such other period as the court may order. In relation to discretionary disqualification under section 160(2) the court may made a disqualification order for such period as it sees fit. The courts have taken into account mitigating circumstances when exercising its discretion in this regard. In *Director of Corporate Enforcement v. D'Arcy,*[52] the court was of the opinion, based on the actions of the respondent, that the relevant disqualification period should be twelve years. However, the respondent had not contested the application, had already resigned from the companies of which he was a director and had indicated a willingness to give an undertaking in writing to the Director that he would not act as a director, promoter, officer or involve himself in any way in the formation or management of any company. In these circumstances the court was satisfied that this should be a mitigating factor and reduced the disqualification order by two years to ten years.

In *Re Clawhammer Ltd; Director of Corporate Enforcement v. McDonnell and Endicott,*[53] an application was taken by the Director of Corporate Enforcement on the grounds that the respondents had been directors of a company that had been struck from the register and was insolvent at such time. In fixing the period for disqualification the court acknowledged that the directors had paid most of the creditors of the company. Despite this the court was mindful that the directors had failed to submit certain annual returns or accounts, had paid trade creditors after the company ceased trading but had not discharged debts

---

52 Unreported, High Court, Kelly J., October 26, 2005
53 Unreported, High Court, Finlay Geoghegan J., March 15, 2005.

owing to the Revenue Commissioners, who may have ranked as preferential creditors in a winding up. The court considered that, given the circumstances, the lesser option of restriction might be warranted by the facts. However, the respondents indicated that, having regard to their circumstances, a declaration of restriction would be more onerous than an order for disqualification for a shorter period. Accordingly, the court made an order for the disqualification of the respondents for a period of one year.

Acting while Disqualified

A person who acts while disqualified is guilty of an offence.[54] Furthermore, his disqualification order will be extended for period of ten years. Where a person acts while disqualified the company shall be entitled to recover from him the consideration paid to him for an act done or service provided by him.[55] If a person acts while disqualified and the company concerned is wound up within twelve months of his so acting and the company is unable to pay its debts the court may order that the person concerned shall be personally liable for the debts of the company.

Notification to the Registrar

The court shall cause the registrar of companies to be furnished with particulars of all orders prescribed under section 160. The registrar shall keep a register of such particulars.

---

54 Section 161(1) of the 1990 Act.
55 Section 163(2) of the 1990 Act.

CHAPTER TWENTY

ACCOUNTS AND RETURNS

Introduction

In theory the statutory obligation to maintain a company's books of accounts and financial statements is a vital source of protection for those who deal with the company. However, given the non-compliance culture that existed in Ireland prior to 2001, whereby the annual returns and the accompanying financial information were not always up to date, in practice an accurate assessment of a company's financial position was not always ascertainable.

The new compliance regime in Ireland means that the value of these financial statements can now be considered an important tool for the assessment of a company for the purposes of investing or advancing credit.

After measures were implemented to ensure compliance with the existing statutory obligations, attention was then turned to reviewing the existing rules and, where necessary, introducing new measures to ensure the integrity of those financial statements. The role of the auditor, considered in the next chapter, came under particular scrutiny, as did the role of directors, who are under a statutory obligation to maintain the books of accounts and prepare the annual financial statements. This review culminated in the introduction of the Companies (Auditing and Accounting) Act 2003 (the 2003 Act), which introduced a number of new measures to improve the integrity of the financial accounts of a company and those who prepare and audit them.

The Companies Acts 1963–2006 require companies to prepare and maintain the following sets of financial information.

1. Proper books of account, which give a true and fair view of the state of affairs of the company and explain its transactions.
2. Annual accounts, which must be laid before the AGM and annexed to the annual return filed in the Companies Registration Office.

Books of Account

Section 202 of the Companies Act 1990 (the 1990 Act) requires a company to keep proper books of account. The books of account must be maintained on a 'continuous and consistent basis' and in such a manner that will enable the financial position of the company to be determined, at any time, with reasonable accuracy. They must also enable the directors to produce the statutory accounts and the auditors to audit the accounts accurately. The directors and auditors have a statutory right to inspect the books at all reasonable times, and although the members have no statutory right of inspection, the articles may provide otherwise.

Content of the Books

Section 202(3) of the Act requires the books of account to give a 'true and fair view' of the state of affairs of the company and explain its transactions. In particular, the books of account must contain the following:

(a) day-to-day entries of all monies received and expended and the matters in respect of which the receipt and expenditure takes place;
(b) a record of the assets and liabilities of the company;
(c) where the company's business involves dealing in goods, a record of all goods purchased and sold (except those sold for cash by way of ordinary retail trade) in such form as will identify the goods, the sellers, the buyers and the invoice relating thereto, together with a statement of stock held by the company at the end of each financial year and any records of stock-taking from which any such statement of stock has been or is to be prepared;
(d) if the company's business involves the provision of services, a record of the services provided and the invoices relating thereto.

Maintenance of the Books

The books of account must be kept for a period of six years from the date to which they relate, at either the company's registered office or such other place as the directors think fit. Where the books of account are kept at a place outside the State, accounts and returns relating to the business dealt with in the books of account must be sent to a place in the State at intervals not exceeding six months. These accounts and reports must be available for inspection by the directors at reasonable times and must be maintained in such a manner as to enable the company's balance sheet and profit and loss account to be prepared.

Criminal and Civil Sanctions

Failure to comply with the statutory requirement to maintain proper books of account may give rise to both criminal and civil liability. Section 202(10) of the 1990 Act makes it an offence for a company to contravene the requirements. By virtue of section 203 of the 1990 Act, if a company that is being wound up and is unable to pay its debts is shown to have failed in its obligation to keep proper books, every officer in default may be guilty of an offence if the court considers that the contravention contributed to or resulted in any of the following:

(a) the inability of the company to pay all its debts;
(b) a substantial uncertainty as to the assets and liabilities of the company;
(c) an impediment to the orderly winding up of the company.

An offence is punishable on summary conviction by a fine not exceeding £1,000 (€1,269) or imprisonment for a term not exceeding six months, or both.[1] Conviction on indictment is punishable by a fine not exceeding £10,000 (€12,697) or imprisonment for a term not exceeding five years, or both.

Where the circumstances that are described in section 203 exist, section 204 provides that a court may, on the application of the liquidator or any creditor or contributory of the company, declare that any one or more of the officers and former officers in default are personally liable for some or all of the debts of the company. In *Mehigan v. Duignan*[2] Shanley J. stated that before an officer could be held liable under section 204 the court had to be satisfied that the company had committed a criminal offence under section 202. It is a defence for every officer involved in proceedings under both section 203 and section 204 to prove:

(a) that he took all reasonable steps to secure compliance with the statutory requirements; or

(b) that he had reasonable grounds for believing, and he did believe, that a competent and reliable person, acting under the control and supervision of a director allocated with such responsibility, was charged with the duty to ensure that the section was complied with and was in a position to discharge that duty.

Any officer who is responsible for the destruction, hiding, concealment, mutilation or falsification of or the fraudulent parting with, alteration of or making of an omission in any book or document affecting or relating to the property or affairs of the company shall be guilty of an offence. The offence is punishable on summary conviction by a fine not exceeding £1,000 (€1,269) or by imprisonment for a term not exceeding twelve months, or both. Conviction on indictment is punishable by a fine not exceeding £10,000 (€12,697) or imprisonment for a term not exceeding five years, or both.[3]

A director who is guilty of failing to keep proper books of accounts or who interferes with them in the manner described in the preceding paragraph may also face a restriction or disqualification order if the company is wound up and is unable to pay its debts.[4]

Investigation by Auditors

The auditors are obliged, as part of their statutory duty, to investigate whether the company is keeping proper books of account. Where the auditors form the opinion that the books of account are not being kept in the manner required by

1 Section 203(1) of the 1990 Act.
2 [1997] 1 IR 340.
3 Section 243(1) of the 1990 Act.
4 See Chapter 19.

the Act, and the contravention is neither minor nor immaterial in nature, the auditors must serve a notice on the company stating their opinion to this effect.[5] Furthermore, they must, within seven days of serving this notice, notify the registrar of companies of the default. The registrar must notify the Director of Corporate Enforcement. Where the auditors file such a report they must, if requested by the Director, provide information and access to books and documents relating to the contravention.[6] Where the directors rectify the situation the auditors do not have to proceed with notification to the registrar.[7]

The Annual Accounts

Public and private limited companies are required to prepare annual accounts in accordance with the Companies (Amendment) Act, 1986 (the 1986 Amendment Act). Certain unlimited companies are also subject to the requirements of the 1986 Amendment Act in relation to preparing and filing accounts.[8] All other unlimited companies are exempt from the requirements of the 1986 Amendment Act and are governed by the less stringent requirements of section 149 of the Principal Act and the Sixth Schedule of that Act. Furthermore, even though unlimited private companies must prepare accounts they are exempt from the obligation to file accounts. All accounts must specify the accounting principles which are being observed, must follow a legislative format and must disclose certain information in the notes to the accounts.

Individual Accounts

Section 148 of the Principal Act requires the company directors to lay before the annual general meeting (the AGM) of the company a balance sheet and profit and loss account,[9] to which there must be annexed a copy of the directors' report and the auditors' report (where applicable). Where the company is a parent company that prepares group accounts and the notes of the company's individual balance sheet show the company's profit or loss for the financial year there is no requirement to lay the profit and loss account before the AGM.[10] The accounts must be signed by at least two directors and laid before the members in general meeting.[11] A resolution is normally proposed for the purpose of adopting or approving the accounts.

---

5 Section 194 of the 1990 Act.
6 Section 194(3A) of the 1990 Act.
7 Section194(2) of the 1990 Act.
8 Unlimited companies whose members are companies limited by shares or guarantee, or unlimited companies where the members are themselves unlimited companies but their members are companies limited by shares or guarantee.
9 An income and expenditure account will suffice in the case of a company which is not trading for profit.
10 Section 148(8) of the Principal Act. The requirements in relation to group accounts are discussed later in this chapter.
11 Section 156 of the Principal Act.

An individual company's accounts must be prepared in accordance with either section 149 of the Principal Act (Companies Act individual accounts), or in accordance with international financial reporting standards and section 149A of the Principal Act (IFRS accounts).[12]

Where Companies Acts individual accounts are prepared they generally[13] come within the ambit of the 1986 Amendment Act and the format and contents of the individual annual accounts set out in the Schedule to that Act must be complied with. The Schedule further requires that certain accounting principles be adhered to in the preparation of the accounts. In any case the accounts must show a 'true and fair view' of the state of affairs of the company even if this requires a departure from the Schedule's requirements or the provision of additional information by way of notes to the accounts.[14] Where a departure from the requirements of the Schedule is made, the directors must attach a note to the accounts giving details of and the reasons for the departures and their effect on the accounts. Certain companies are fully excluded from these requirements, and others are partially excluded.[15]

Exemptions for Small and Medium Private Companies

Although small and medium-sized private companies are not exempt from the 1986 requirements, they have been afforded some concessions.[16] Small private companies may lay before the AGM a short version of the profit and loss account and an abridged balance sheet. To qualify as a small company for the purpose of the concessions, at least two of the following three conditions must be satisfied in the relevant financial year:

(a) the balance sheet total does not exceed £1,500,000 (€1,900,000);
(b) the turnover does not exceed £3,000,000 (€3,810,000);
(c) the average number of employees does not exceed fifty.[17]

Medium-sized companies must lay before the AGM a full balance sheet, but they are permitted to lay before the AGM a short version of the profit and loss account. To qualify as a medium-sized company, at least two of the following three conditions must be satisfied in the relevant financial year:

---

12 Section 148(2) of the Principal Act.
13 Certain charitable companies not having a share capital and certain unlimited companies are exempt from the 1986 Amendment Act.
14 Section 3(1)(b) and section 4 of the 1986 Amendment Act.
15 Section 2 of the 1986 Act fully exempts from the requirements companies not trading for a profit and charitable companies. Licensed banks, insurance and assurance companies are partially excluded.
16 Section 8 of the 1986 Amendment Act.
17 Section 8(2) of the 1986 Amendment Act as amended.

(a) the balance sheet total does not exceed £6,000,000 (€7,620,000);
(b) the turnover does not exceed £12,000,000 (€15,240,000);
(c) the average number of employees does not exceed 250.

It is important to note that the concessions granted to small and medium private companies are subject to the overriding requirement that the accounts must give a 'true and fair view' of the state of affairs of the company. The fact that a company is entitled to an exemption on the basis of its size must be certified by its auditors.

IFRS Accounts

Where the directors of a company prepare IFRS accounts in accordance with European Communities (International Financial Reporting Standards and Miscellaneous Amendments) Regulations 2005 (IFRS)[18] they must state in the notes to those accounts that they have been prepared in accordance with IFRS.[19] Furthermore, section 149(1)(b) of the Principal Act requires that the directors ensure that the notes to such accounts include the following:

(a) details of directors' remuneration;[20]
(b) details of transactions between the company and its directors;[21]
(c) details of directors' interests in shares and debentures unless already disclosed in the directors' report;[22]
(d) details of group undertakings;[23]
(e) details of share capital and debentures;[24]
(f) restrictions on distributability of profits;[25]
(g) details of guarantees and other financial commitments;[26]
(h) details of financial assistance for the purchase of own shares;[27]
(i) details of staff numbers and remuneration;[28]
(j) details of shares and debentures held by subsidiary undertakings;[29] and
(k) details of remuneration of auditors.[30]

---

18 SI 116 of 2005.
19 Section 149(1)(a) of the Principal Act.
20 Section 191 of the Principal Act and para. 39(6) of the Schedule of the 1986 Amendment Act.
21 Sections 41–45 of the 1990 Act.
22 Section 63 of the 1990 Act unless it is disclosed in the directors' report.
23 Section 16 and 16A of the 1986 Amendment Act.
24 Paras. 26–28 of the Schedule to the 1986 Amendment Act.
25 Para. 32A of the Schedule to the 1986 Amendment Act.
26 Para. 36 of the Schedule to the 1986 Amendment Act.
27 Para 37(2) of the Schedule to the 1986 Amendment Act.
28 Para. 42 of the Schedule to the 1986 Amendment Act.
29 Para 46 of the Schedule to the 1986 Amendment Act.
30 Para. 39(5) of the Schedule to the 1986 Amendment Act.

Group Accounts

The legislative provisions governing group accounts are primarily governed by the European Communities (Companies: Group Accounts) Regulations 1992 (the GAR).[31] Regulation 5 of the GAR requires parent undertakings, which include, *inter alia*, both private and public limited companies, to prepare and lay before the annual general meeting audited group accounts detailing the state of affairs of the group. The required form, format and content of these consolidated accounts are specified in the regulations. However, exemptions are granted to small and medium-sized private companies,[32] certain subsidiary undertakings of an EC undertaking,[33] and certain unlimited companies.[34]

In general, a parent company's directors shall ensure that the individual accounts of the parent and the subsidiaries are all prepared using the same financial reporting framework, except to the extent that in their opinion there are good reasons for not doing so, and those reasons are disclosed in the individual accounts of the parent company.[35]

The GAR provides that the format and content of group accounts as set out in the Schedule to the 1986 Amendment Act will apply, with the appropriate modifications appropriate for consolidation. Where Companies Act group accounts are prepared they will comprise a consolidated balance sheet and consolidated profit and loss account, which must be in the form prescribed.[36] If the company's directors are of the opinion that it is better for the purpose of presenting the same or equivalent information about the state of affairs and profit or loss of the company and those subsidiaries and of so presenting that information that it may be readily appreciated by the company's members, the group accounts may be prepared in a different form and may consist of:

(a) more than one set of consolidated accounts dealing respectively with the company and one group of subsidiaries and with other groups of subsidiaries; or,
(b) individual group accounts dealing with each of the subsidiaries; or
(c) statements expanding the information about the subsidiaries in the company's own accounts; or
(c) any combination of those forms.[37]

---

31 SI 201/1992.
32 Regulation 7. The exemptions specifically apply to medium-sized companies but since small companies will also satisfy the criteria that apply to medium-sized companies, the exemptions also apply thereto.
33 Regulation 8. This exemption is not limited to private companies. Public companies not listed on a stock exchange may also avail of the exemption.
34 See note 8.
35 Section 150C(1) of the Principal Act.
36 Section 151(1) of the Principal Act.
37 Section 151(3) of the Principal Act.

Companies Act group accounts are not required to be prepared where the company, although a parent company, is also a subsidiary company of an Irish company.[38] Furthermore, Companies Act group accounts need not deal with a subsidiary of the company where the company's directors are of the opinion that it is impracticable or would be of no real value to the members of the company (in view of the insignificant amounts involved), or would involve expenses or delay out of proportion to the value to the members of the company, or the result would be misleading.[39] If the directors are of such an opinion about all the company's subsidiaries, group accounts shall not be required.

Generally speaking, Companies Act group accounts must be laid before the annual general meeting of the company and must give a fair view of the state of affairs, and the profit and loss, of the company and its subsidiaries.[40] The directors of a parent company must secure that, unless there is good reason against it, the financial year of each of its subsidiaries shall coincide with the company's own financial year.[41] The Minister may even permit the postponement of the submission of the accounts of a holding company or its subsidiary to the AGM, or may permit an extension of the annual return date, to allow the accounts or the annual return date of the holding company and its subsidiaries to coincide with each other.[42] Certain private companies which are also holding companies need not prepare group accounts provided the GAR does not apply.[43]

Where the company is trading on a regulated market of any EEA State, such as the ISEQ, the group accounts must be prepared in accordance with international financial reporting standards (the IFRS).[44] All other companies, both private and public, may opt to use the IFRS or may prepare their accounts in accordance with section 150A of the Principal Act (Companies Act group accounts). As with individual accounts, where the directors of a company prepare IFRS group accounts they must state in the notes to those accounts that they have been prepared in accordance with the IFRS.[45] Furthermore section 150(B)(2) of the Principal Act requires that the directors ensure that the notes to the accounts include the following:

---

38 Section 151(2)(a) of the Principal Act.
39 Section 151(2)(b) of the Principal Act.
40 Section 150(10) and Section 150A.
41 Section 153(1) of the Principal Act.
42 Section 153(2) of the Principal Act.
43 Regulation 5(5) of the GAR prohibits parent undertakings taking advantage of this exemption.
44 European Communities (International Financial Reporting Standards and Miscellaneous Amendments) Regulations 2005: SI 116 of 2005.
45 Section 150B(1) of the Principal Act.

(a) details of directors' remuneration;[46]
(b) details of transactions between the company and its directors;[47]
(c) details of directors' interests in shares and debentures unless already disclosed in the directors' report;[48]
(d) details of group undertakings;[49]
(e) details of staff numbers and remuneration;[50]
(f) details of share capital and debentures;[51]
(g) restrictions on distributability of profits;[52]
(h) details of guarantees and other financial commitments;[53]
(i) details of financial assistance for the purchase of own shares;[54]
(j) details of shares and debentures held by subsidiary undertakings;[55] and
(k) details of remuneration of auditors.[56]

Single-Member Companies

The requirement to lay the profit and loss account, balance sheet, directors' report and auditors' report before the AGM is deemed to be satisfied where these are sent to the sole member of the company.[57]

Directors' Reports

Section 158(1) of the Principal Act requires that a report by the directors on the state of the company's affairs must be annexed to the accounts laid before the annual general meeting. The directors' report must contain the following information:

(a) the amount, if any, the directors recommend by way of dividend;
(b) the amount, if any, they propose to carry to reserves;
(c) details of any change in the nature of the company's business or that of its subsidiaries;
(d) a list of the company's subsidiaries and companies in which it has a beneficial shareholding of more than 20 per cent of the voting shares,

---

46 Section 191 of the Principal Act and para. 16 of the Schedule to the GAR.
47 Sections 41–45 of the 1990 Act and para. 17 of the Schedule to the GAR.
48 Section 63 of the 1990 Act.
49 Subject to Regulation 36 of the GAR and paras. 18—22 of the Schedule to the GAR.
50 Para. 15 of the Schedule to the GAR.
51 Paras. 26–28 of the Schedule to the GAR.
52 Para. 32A of the Schedule to the 1986 Amendment Act.
53 Para. 36 of the Schedule to the 1986 Amendment Act.
54 Para. 37(2) of the Schedule to the 1986 Amendment Act.
55 Para. 46 of the Schedule to the 1986 Amendment Act.
56 Para. 39(5) of the Schedule to the 1986 Amendment Act.
57 This is because a single-member company is not required to hold an AGM.

including where these companies are incorporated and the nature of the business carried on by them;[58]

(e) a fair review of the development and performance of the business of the company and its position and that of its subsidiaries during the relevant financial year, together with a description of the principal risks and uncertainties they face;

(f) particulars of any important events which have occurred since the end of the financial year affecting the company and its subsidiaries;

(g) an indication of the likely future development, if any, in the business of the company and its subsidiaries;

(h) an indication of any research and development activities of the company and its subsidiaries;

(i) an indication of the existence of branches of the company or its subsidiaries;

(j) the financial risk management objectives and policies and the potential exposure of the company and the group to price risk, credit risk, liquidity risk and cash flow risk where the company or its subsidiaries have used financial instruments and where material for the assessment of the assets, liabilities, financial position and profit or loss of the company or the group;[59]

(k) details of the company's own shares acquired and, where acquired, details of those that were disposed of or cancelled during the relevant financial year, together with particulars of such transactions;

(l) details of directors' and secretaries' interests in the shares and debentures of the company, its subsidiaries, its holding company or subsidiaries of its holding company, provided that such information is not already given in the notes to the accounts;[60]

(m) a statement of the measures taken by directors to secure compliance with the requirements of section 202 of the Companies Act 1990, with regard to the keeping of proper books of account and the exact location of those books; and

(n) particulars of all donations exceeding £4,000 (€5,079) to political parties.[61]

---

58 This requirement does not apply to a company that is principally engaged in the acquisition and underwriting of shares or other securities of companies carrying on a trade or industry in the State and which holds a certificate of exemption from these requirements issued by the Minister. Furthermore, by virtue of the GAR this requirement does not apply to companies to which Regulation 37 of the GAR applies (parent companies preparing group accounts). However, Regulation 37 of the GAR imposes similar requirements in this regard.

59 Small and medium companies are exempt from this requirement.

60 This information can be contained in either the directors' report or the notes to the company's accounts.

61 Section 26 of the Electoral Act 1997.

Section 42 of the 2003 Act inserts a new subsection 205B into the 1990 Act. Under this subsection, the board of directors of all public limited companies must, and the board of large private companies may, establish an audit committee, and the directors are obliged to include in their report details of the audit committee's activities for the year. Where the board of a large private company does not establish an audit committee it must state this in its annual report and give the reasons for this decision. This provision has not yet commenced but is expected to come into force before the end of the year 2007.

Section 45 of the 2003 Act inserted a new subsection 205(E) into the 1990 Act. Under this subsection, the directors of all public companies and certain private companies must prepare a compliance statement relating to the company's policies and its internal procedures in respect of compliance with the companies obligations and its arrangements for implementing and reviewing the effectiveness of such policies and procedures. This compliance statement must be included in the directors' report. Section 45 of the 2003 Act has not yet been commenced. The Minister, following submissions by various parties and the recommendations of the Company Law Review Group has indicated that a legislative amendment will be made in this regard before the duty to prepare directors' compliance statements will be commenced.

The directors' report must be signed on behalf of the directors by two of the company's directors.[62] Failure to comply with the statutory requirements in respect of the annual accounts and the directors' report renders the directors liable for an offence punishable on summary conviction by a fine.

The Auditors' Report

Section 193(1) of the 1990 Act requires the auditors to make a report to the members on the accounts examined by them, and on every balance sheet and profit and loss account, and all group accounts, laid before the company in general meeting. The auditors' report must be read at the AGM of the company and must be open to inspection by any member.[63] The auditor's report must include:

(a) an introduction identifying the individual accounts and, where appropriate, the group accounts, that are the subject of the audit and the financial reporting framework that has been applied in their preparation; and
(b) a description of the scope of the audit identifying the auditing standards in accordance with which the audit was conducted.[64]

---

62 Section 158(2) of the Principal Act.
63 Section 193(2) of the 1990 Act.
64 Section 193(4) of the 1990 Act.

The auditors' report must also state clearly whether in the auditors' opinion the annual accounts have been properly prepared in accordance with the Companies Acts and, where applicable, Article 4 of the International Accounting Standards Regulation.[65] The report must also state:

(a) whether the auditors have obtained all the information and explanations that, to the best of their knowledge and belief, are necessary for the purposes of the audit;

(b) whether, in their opinion, proper books of accounts have been kept by the company;

(c) whether, in their opinion, proper returns adequate for their audit have been received from branches of the company not visited by them;

(d) whether the company's balance sheet and (unless it is framed as a consolidated profit and loss account) profit and loss account are in agreement with the books of account and returns;[66]

(e) whether the annual accounts give a 'true and fair view' in accordance with the relevant financial reporting framework of the state of affairs of the company or group and of the profit and loss of the company or the group;[67] and

(f) whether, in their opinion, there existed at the balance sheet date a financial situation that under section 40(1) of the Companies (Amendment) Act 1983 (i.e. a serious loss of capital) would require the convening of an extraordinary general meeting.[68]

In relation to any of these matters the report shall contain a statement or opinion which is either unqualified or shall include a reference to any matters to which the auditors wish to draw attention by way of emphasis without qualifying the report.[69] A statement or opinion is qualified if it is an adverse opinion or a disclaimer or opinion arising from a disagreement or a limitation in the scope of the work.[70] Where individual accounts of a parent undertaking are attached to the group accounts, the auditors' report on the group accounts may be combined with the report on the individual accounts. In addition to the above matters the report must also state:

---

65 Section 193(4A)(a) of the 1990 Act. The International Accounting Standards Regulation, as implemented in Ireland by European Communities (International Financial Reporting Standards and Miscellaneous Amendments) Regulations 2005 (IFRS): SI 116 of 2005

66 Section 193(4B) of the 1990 Act.

67 Section 193(4C)(i) of the 1990 Act.

68 Section 193(4C)(ii) of the 1990 Act.

69 Section 193(4D) of the 1990 Act.

70 Section 193(4E) of the 1990 Act.

(a) the particulars of any directors' salaries and payment involving directors that have not been disclosed in the notes to the accounts;[71]
(b) the particulars of certain contracts with the directors that have not been disclosed in the accounts or the notes to the accounts;[72]
(c) whether, in their opinion, the information given in the directors' report is consistent with the accounts prepared for that year.[73]

The auditors' report must be signed and dated by the auditors.[74]

Exemptions for Small Private Companies

Section 32 of the Companies (Amendment) (No.2) Act 1999 (the 1999 Amendment Act)[75] provides a mechanism by which certain companies, which meet certain conditions, may avail of an exemption from the requirement to have accounts audited. To qualify, a company must meet the criteria specified in section 32(3) of the 1999 (No.2) Act as follows:

(a) the company is one to which the 1986 Amendment Act applies;
(b) its turnover does not exceed €7,300,000;
(c) its balance sheet total does not exceed €3,650,000;
(d) the average number of employees does not exceed fifty;
(e) the company is not one specified in the Second Schedule of the 1999 Amendment Act with the exception of companies listed in paragraph 18 of this Schedule;[76]
(f) the company is not a parent or subsidiary company within the meaning of the European Communities (Companies: Group Accounts) Regulations 1992;
(g) the company is not the holder of a banking licence; and
(h) the company is a not an insurance company.

Before relying on any audit exemption, the directors must be of the opinion, and resolve formally, that the company satisfies the necessary criteria and will avail of the exemption.[77] A company cannot avail of an exemption unless the company's annual

71 Section 191(8) of the Principal Act and para. 39(6) of the Schedule of the 1986 Amendment Act.
72 Section 46 of the 1990 Act.
73 Section 15 of the 1986 Amendment Act.
74 Section 193(4D)(a) of the 1990 Act.
75 As amended by section 9 of the Investment Funds, Companies and Miscellaneous Provisions Act, 2006.
76 The Second Schedule of the 1999 Amendment Act lists companies that cannot avail of the exemption under section 32 and includes *inter alia* a member of the Stock Exchange, a stock exchange, an associated or related company of a member of the Stock Exchange or a stock exchange, an investment company or associate company, certain banks and financial institutions. Paragraph 18 of the Schedule lists certain non-life companies.
77 Section 32(1)(a) of the 1999 Amendment Act.

return is delivered to the registrar of companies in compliance with section 127 of the Principal Act or, if the annual return is not the first annual return, its previous annual return was also delivered to the registrar of companies in compliance with section 127 of the Principal Act.[78] This effectively means that if the company's annual return was delivered late in the current or previous year the company is not entitled to the audit exemption. A company cannot avail of the exemption if members holding at least 10 per cent of the voting rights request the company not to do so.[79]

Where the company avails of the exemption, its balance sheet must include a directors' statement to this effect, also confirming that the conditions for exemption have been satisfied, that no notice of objection has been received by members and that the obligations of the company to keep proper books of accounts has been satisfied. The statement must be immediately above the directors' signatures.[80]

Section 34 requires that the removal of an auditor, in a situation whereby the company is availing of the exemption, should be accompanied by a notice from the auditor to the company stating that there are no circumstances connected with the removal that should be brought to the attention of the members or creditors of the company. Where there are such circumstances, a statement of the same nature should be sent to the company, which must forward it to all members and creditors who are entitled to receive it. The registrar of companies must be given a copy of the auditor's notice. Where the criteria for exemption can no longer be satisfied, the directors must appoint an auditor as soon as is practicable.[81]

Rights of Members

Section 159(1) of the Principal Act provides that a copy of every balance sheet and every document required by law to be annexed thereto, which is to be laid before the AGM of a company, together with a copy of the directors' and auditors' report shall, not less than twenty-one days before the date of the meeting, be sent to every member of the company entitled to receive notices of general meetings and every holder of debentures of the company. Any member of a company and any debenture-holders of the company are entitled to be furnished on demand with a copy of the last balance sheet of the company and every document required by law to be annexed thereto together with copies of the directors' and auditors' reports.[82]

Role of the Supervisory Authority

Where the Supervisory Authority[83] believes that the accounts of public limited companies and certain large private limited companies limited by shares, which

---

78 Ibid., section 32A.
79 Ibid., section 33(1).
80 Ibid., section 33(4) and (5).
81 Ibid., section 35.
82 Section 159(4) of the Principal Act.
83 See Chapter 21.

have been sent to members under section 159(1) above or have been laid before the AGM or delivered to the registrar, do not comply with the statutory provisions they may give notice to the directors specifying the matters relating to the non-compliance.[84] The Supervisory Authority may give the directors at least thirty days to provide the Supervisory Authority with an explanation of the accounts or to prepare revised accounts to comply with the statutory requirements. Where the directors fail to explain the accounts or prepare revised accounts by the end of the specified period the Supervisory Authority may apply to the court for a declaration of non-compliance. If the court is satisfied that non-compliance has taken place it may order one or all of the following:

(a) require the directors to revise the accounts;
(b) give directions in regard to the auditing of the revised accounts, revision of the directors' report, the steps to be taken by the directors to bring the court order to the notice of persons likely to rely on the accounts and such matters as the court may think fit;
(c) require the directors to pay the costs incurred by the Supervisory Authority and any reasonable expenses incurred by the company in connection with the preparation of revised accounts.[85]

The registrar of companies must be given notice of any such proceedings and any court order.[86]

The Annual Return

With the exception of certain investment companies, all companies having a share capital are obliged, by virtue of section 125 of the Principal Act, to file a return on an annual basis with the registrar of companies in the prescribed form. The matters to be included in the annual return are set out in Companies Registration Office Form B1 as follows:

(a) the name of the company;
(b) the date to which the return is made;
(c) the financial year applicable;
(d) whether the company is claiming an audit exemption;
(e) the address of the registered office of the company;
(f) the address of the place where company registers are kept, if they are not kept at the registered office;
(g) details of political donations exceeding £4,000 (€5,079);

---

84 Section 26 of the 2003 Act. Section 26 has not yet come into force but is expected to do so by the end of 2007.
85 Section 26(8) of the 2003 Act.
86 Section 26(11) of the 2003 Act.

(h) details of the presenter of the annual return;
(i) details of all shares issued for cash and other consideration, any calls made, received or unpaid, any commissions paid or discounts given on shares or debentures and any shares forfeited;
(j) particulars of the total amount of indebtedness of the company secured by mortgages or charges that are required to be registered;
(k) a list of all persons, including their names and addresses, who on the fourteenth day after the company's AGM are members of the company, and of persons who have ceased to be members since the date of the last return. If the names are not in alphabetical order, the list must be accompanied by an index that will enable the name of any person contained therein to be easily found;
(l) details of the shares held by each of the existing members specifying the shares transferred since the date of the last return by existing members and persons who ceased to be members on the date of registration of the transfers;
(m) particulars of the directors and secretary that are required to be entered in the company's register of directors and secretary;
(n) the registered number of the company.

Section 7 of the 1986 Amendment Act provides that the following documents must be annexed to the annual return (except for the first annual return of a company):[87]

(a) a certified true copy of the balance sheet;
(b) a certified true copy of the profit and loss account;[88]
(c) a certified true copy of the directors' report;
(d) a certified copy of the auditors' report (where applicable).[89]

A director and secretary must certify that the accounts and reports are true copies of those laid before or to be laid before the AGM. Small and medium-sized private limited companies are exempt from some of the requirements in respect of the annual return.[90] Small companies are permitted to file an abridged balance sheet and are not required to annex copies of the profit and loss account and directors' report.

---

87 The first annual return must be made up to the date that is six months after the date of the company's incorporation. Annual accounts would not be available at that time and therefore the requirement to annex accounts only arises in respect of all subsequent annual returns.
88 The requirement to annex a certified copy of the profit and loss account shall not apply where the company is a parent undertaking and prepares group accounts and the notes to the company's individual balance sheet show the company's profit or loss for the financial year: Section 7(1A) of the 1986 Amendment Act.
89 Section 128(1) of the Principal Act and section 7(3) of the 1986 Amendment Act.
90 Section 8 of the 1986 Amendment Act.

Medium-sized companies are permitted to annex an abridged balance sheet (but the permitted omissions are fewer than in the case of small private companies) and a short form profit and loss account. Where small and medium-sized companies avail of these concessions, a special auditors' report must be annexed to the return. This report will contain the usual requirements of an auditors' report together with a statement that in the auditors' opinion the directors are entitled to annex abridged accounts and such accounts have been properly prepared. Unlimited private companies do not have to file accounts with their annual return, but are obliged to file an auditor's report.

A private company that is a subsidiary of another undertaking established in another EU member state is exempted from the requirement to annex accounts and reports to the annual return (imposed by section 7 of the 1986 Amendment Act), if certain conditions are fulfilled.[91] In this case, the following documents must be filed with the subsidiary company's annual return:[92]

(a) a notice stating that the company has availed of the exemption under section 17;
(b) a copy of an irrevocable guarantee by the parent undertaking of the liabilities of the subsidiary company's annual return;
(c) a notification by the company to the shareholders of the guarantee; and
(d) a declaration by the subsidiary that all the shareholders have declared their consent to the exemption, which must be signed by the secretary or a director.

Consolidated accounts of the parent undertaking drawn up in accordance with the requirements of the GAR and duly audited must be attached to the subsidiary undertaking's annual return.

Every company has an annual return date (ARD). Under section 127 of the Principal Act, the annual return shall be made up to a date which is not later than the company's ARD and delivered to the registrar of companies not later than twenty-eight days after the annual return date. The court or the registrar of companies may in certain circumstances extend the time for delivery. The registrar of companies will accept annual returns made before the company's ARD. Where the company files the annual return early it is given the option of retaining the same ARD for the subsequent year or moving the ARD to the anniversary of the earlier date for the next year.

If a company fails to comply with these requirements the annual return will be rejected by the registrar of companies. Furthermore, a breach of either section 125 or 127 renders the company and every officer in default, and any person in

---

91 Section 17 of the 1986 Amendment Act.
92 Section 17(1)(d) of the 1986 Amendment Act.

accordance with whose directions or instructions the directors of the company are accustomed to act, and to whose directions or omissions the default is attributable, guilty of an offence that may be prosecuted by the registrar of companies. The registrar of companies may strike a company off the register for failing to file one or more annual returns.[93]

---

93 See Chapter 3.

CHAPTER TWENTY-ONE

AUDITORS

Introduction

In general every company must have its financial statements audited on an annual basis. As mentioned in the previous chapter, certain companies are exempt from the requirement to have their accounts audited provided they comply with certain conditions. An auditor is an independent professional person qualified to perform a company's audit. An audit is essentially an examination by the auditors of the financial statements prepared by the company directors. This examination is necessary to enable the auditors report on whether those financial statements give a 'true and fair view' of the state of the company's affairs and its profit or loss and that the financial statements have been prepared in accordance with the Companies Acts and applicable accounting standards.

The role of auditors has come under much scrutiny in recent years, particularly in light of high-profile scandals in the late 1990s that centred upon poor and, in some instances, grossly negligent accountancy practices.[1] In Ireland, the report of the Review Group on Auditing[2] was published in 2000. The report made recommendations in relation to the following:

(a) the role of auditors in ensuring compliance with statutory provisions;
(b) the auditing of financial institutions;
(c) the regulation of the auditing and accountancy profession (an interim Irish Auditing and Accounting Supervisory Authority Board was established in 2001); and
(d) the creation of internal audit committees akin to the system which exists in the United States.

Many of the recommendations of the Review Group were introduced in the Companies (Audit and Accounting) Act 2003 (the 2003 Act). The Act provides, *inter alia*, for the establishment of the Irish Auditing and Accounting Supervisory Authority (the Supervisory Authority)[3] and improved measures to strengthen the regulation of auditors, including the introduction of audit committees, directors' compliance statements and additional obligations in respect of reporting obligations of auditors.

---

1 The collapse of Enron in the United States and the subsequent successful prosecution of Enron's auditors prompted a worldwide focus on accountancy practices and auditors' duties.
2 The Report of the Review Group on Auditing (Pn.8683)
3 Discussed later in this chapter.

Appointment of Auditors

The first auditors of the company may be appointed by the directors or, failing this, the company in general meeting. Thereafter, the company in general meeting must appoint an auditor to hold office from the conclusion of that meeting until the conclusion of the next such meeting.[4] A retiring auditor will automatically be re-appointed at the annual general meeting (the AGM) without the need for an authorising resolution unless any of the following occurs:

(a) he is not qualified for appointment; or
(b) a resolution has been passed at that meeting appointing somebody instead of him or providing expressly that he shall not be reappointed; or
(c) he has given notice in writing of his unwillingness to be reappointed;[5] or
(c) notice of a resolution to appoint a replacement has been given, but the proposed resolution cannot be passed by reason of the death, incapacity or disqualification of the replacement.[6]

Where the AGM fails to appoint an auditor, the company must notify the Minister within one week.[7] The Minister may then appoint a person to fill the vacancy. Failure to notify the Minister renders the company and every officer in default liable to a fine. Casual vacancies in the office of auditor may be filled by the directors or by the company in general meeting.[8]

The Companies Acts recognise the practice of appointing more than one person as auditor of a company. Section 160(9) of the Principal Act provides that where a firm is appointed as the auditors of a company, the partners for the time being of that firm, who are qualified to be auditors of a company, are deemed to be the company's auditors. Accordingly, any change in the partners of that firm during the relevant period will not constitute a change of auditors.

Qualifications for Appointment

Section 187(1) of the 1990 Act provides a list of persons who are qualified to be company auditors. These persons must be members of an accountancy body recognised by the Supervisory Authority and hold a valid practicing certificate from such a body, or hold an accountancy qualification that is in the opinion of the Supervisory Authority of an equivalent standard. Other individuals may have ministerial authorisation obtained prior to 3 February 1983 and be registered under the provisions of section 199(3) of the 1990 Act. Section 187(2) of the

---

4 Section 160(1) of the Principal Act.
5 Section 160(2) of the Principal Act.
6 Section 160(3) of the Principal Act.
7 Section 160(5A)(a).
8 Section 160(7) of the Principal Act.

1990 Act provides that none of the following persons shall be qualified for appointment as auditor of a company:

(a) an officer or servant of the company;
(b) a person who was an officer or servant of the company;
(c) a parent, spouse, brother, sister or child of an officer of the company;
(d) a person who is a partner of or in the employ of an officer of the company;
(e) a person who is disqualified, for any of the above reasons, for appointment as an auditor of any other body corporate which is a subsidiary or holding company of the company or is a subsidiary of the company's holding company, whether or not that body corporate is a company;
(f) a person who is disqualified, for any of the above reasons, for appointment as an auditor of any industrial or provident society which is a subsidiary or holding company of the company or a subsidiary of the company's holding company;
(g) a body corporate;
(h) a person in whose name a share in the company is registered, whether or not that person is the beneficial owner of the share.

Furthermore, a person is prohibited from acting as an auditor of any company if he has been subject to a disqualification order by the court under Part VII of the 1990 Act.[9] A person who acts as an auditor, or gives directions or instructions in relation to the conduct of an audit or works in any capacity in the conduct of an audit, while the subject of a disqualification order, will be guilty of an offence.

Auditors' Duties

Statutory Duties

First and foremost, auditors are required to make a report to the members on the individual accounts examined by them, and on every balance sheet and profit and loss or income statement, and all group accounts, laid before the company in general meeting during their tenure of office.[10] The auditors' report shall be read at the annual general meeting (AGM) of the company and shall be open to inspection by any member.[11] The content of this report was described in the previous chapter. In addition to the statutory report under section 193 auditors are also obliged to:

(a) report any failure to keep proper books of accounts;[12]
(b) carry out the audit with professional integrity;[13]

---

9 See Chapter 19.
10 Section 193(1) of the 1990 Act.
11 Section 193(2) of the 1990 Act.
12 Section 194 of the 1990 Act – see Chapter 20.
13 Section 193(6) of the 1990 Act.

(c) where, in the course of carrying out the audit, they have formed the opinion that there are reasonable grounds for believing that the company or an officer or agent of the company has committed an indictable offence under the Companies Acts[14], notify that opinion to the Director of Corporate Enforcement (the Director) and provide the Director with details of the grounds on which they have formed that opinion.[15] If requested by the Director the auditors must furnish the Director with such information in their possession or control relating to the matter as the Director may require and give the Director access to books and documents in their possession relating to the matter as the Director may require and give the Director access to facilities for the taking of copies of or extracts from those books and documents as the Director may require.[16]

(d) inform a designated officer of the company on becoming aware that the company is defrauding the Revenue Commissioners and require the company to rectify the situation. Where an auditor is not satisfied that remedial action has taken place to rectify the situation within six months, he must resign by giving notice to the designated officer of the company, and he must not act for the company for a period of three years. Failure to comply with this requirement renders the auditor liable on summary conviction to a fine not exceeding £1,000 (€1,270) and on indictment to a fine not exceeding £5,000 (€6,349) or two years' imprisonment, or to both.

(e) report to the gardaí any suspected offence by a director under the Criminal Justice (Theft and Fraud Offences) Act 2001.[17]

(f) make themselves familiar with the companies' articles of association;

Duty of Care and Skill

In addition to the statutory duties, auditors are under a common law duty to act honestly and with reasonable care and skill. The mere verification of the numerical accuracy of the accounts does not discharge this duty. The auditor must also ensure that omissions and untruths are not made and irregularities are investigated.[18] In *Re Thomas Gerrard & Sons Ltd*,[19] the managing director falsified accounts by including non-existent stock. As a result of the overstated profits, additional taxes were paid by the company and dividends were declared that otherwise would not have been. The auditors became suspicious when they discovered that invoices relating to the stock had been altered. Rather than investigate the matter they accepted the managing director's explanation. The

---

14 With the exception of indictable offences under section 125(2) or 127(12) of the Principal Act in relation to annual returns.
15 Section 194(5) of the 1990 Act.
16 Section 195(5A) of the 1990 Act.
17 Section 73 of the Criminal Justice (Theft and Fraud Offences) Act 2001.
18 *Fomento (Sterling Area) Ltd v Selsdon Fountain Pen Co.* [1958] 1 All ER 11.
19 [1967] 2 All ER 525.

auditors were held liable to the company for the amounts paid by way of dividends and excess taxes. In deciding whether an auditor has failed in his duties, the courts will take into account the standard statement of accountancy practices and auditing guidelines for the profession.[20]

To Whom is the Duty Owed?

Because auditors have a contractual relationship with the company, a duty of care is owed to the company. However, since the decision in *Hedley Byrne v. Heller Partners*,[21] it is clear that a person may also be liable for financial loss resulting from a negligent statement, even if there is no contractual relationship between the person making the statement and the person who relied upon it. In the absence of a contractual or statutory relationship, the plaintiff must demonstrate the following:

(a) there was a sufficient degree of proximity between the defendant and the plaintiff;
(b) the person who made the statement did so in a professional capacity, which makes it reasonably foreseeable that the plaintiff will rely on what he says;
(c) the plaintiff does rely on what was said and in doing so suffered a loss which was reasonably foreseeable.[22]

The principles laid down in *Hedley Byrne* are significant because in practice shareholders and prospective investors often rely on the audited accounts and auditors' statement. In *JEB Fasteners Ltd v. Marks, Bloom & Co.*,[23] the defendant firm had prepared an audited set of accounts that showed an over-inflated stock valuation. The auditors knew that the company, which was in financial difficulty, was seeking capital investments. The plaintiffs were shown the accounts and, although they were suspicious of the stock valuation, proceeded to purchase the company. When their investment subsequently failed they sued the auditors of the company for negligent misstatement. In applying the test laid down in *Hedley Byrne*, the court held that the defendants were negligent in preparing the accounts, and that they owed the plaintiffs a duty of care as they ought to have foreseen that outside investors would rely on the accounts. However, the court concluded that the plaintiffs would not have acted any differently had they known the true position of the accounts, because they were only interested in buying the company to obtain the services of two of its directors.

The judgment in *JEB Fasteners* was followed in the Irish case of *Kelly v. Haughey Boland & Co.*[24] The plaintiffs planned to purchase the company to

20 *Kelly v. Haughey, Boland & Co.* [1989] ILRM 373.
21 [1964] AC 465.
22 Ibid.
23 [1981] 3 All ER 289.
24 See note 20.

which the defendants were auditors. On this basis they were given a series of the company's audited accounts and, at a number of subsequent meetings, the company's auditors explained these accounts to them. Following the purchase the plaintiffs discovered a number of inaccuracies in the accounts and sued the auditors for negligent misstatement. It was held that the auditors were in breach of their duty of care to the plaintiffs. However, as the plaintiffs could not show a direct link between the negligence of the auditors and the loss they suffered, the action failed.

A much more restrictive approach was followed by the House of Lords in *Caparo Industries plc v. Dickman*.[25] In March 1984, the plaintiffs purchased a number of Fidelity shares in the open market. When the accounts of Fidelity, published in June of that year, revealed substantial profits the plaintiffs purchased further shares. By October they had purchased or received acceptances on enough of the issued shares to acquire the balance by way of compulsory purchase. The plaintiffs later claimed that their reliance on the 1984 accounts, which were inaccurate, had caused them a loss. The House of Lords decided that the relationship between a potential investor and the auditor of the company was not sufficiently proximate to satisfy the *Hedley Byrne* test, particularly as the auditors did not know of the plaintiffs' takeover plans for the company. The court also dismissed the plaintiffs' claim that the auditors owed a duty to existing shareholders who wished to buy more shares in the company. However, the auditors did not fare as well in *Morgan Crucible Co. plc v Hill Samuel Co. Ltd*.[26] During the course of a takeover bid, a profits forecast, supported by a letter from the auditors, was issued. As the auditors were aware of the proposed takeover and the purpose of the profits forecast, they were held to have owed a duty of care.

Rights of Auditors

In order to fulfil their statutory duties, auditors are conferred with the following rights.

(a) The right of access to the books, accounts and vouchers of the company.[27]
(b) The right to require from the officers and employees of the company such information and explanations as the auditors think necessary for the performance of their duties. Any person who fails to give such information, within two days of the request, or any person who knowingly or recklessly gives false information, will be guilty of an offence. However, it will be a defence to show that the request was complied with within a reasonable time.[28]

---

25 [1990] 2 AC 605.
26 [1991] Ch 295.
27 Section 193(3) of the 1990 Act.
28 Section 197 of the 1990 Act.

(c) The right to request information and explanations from either any of the company's subsidiary companies incorporated in the State or their auditors. If the subsidiary is incorporated outside the State, it is the duty of the holding company to obtain such information from the subsidiary. Failure to comply within five days with any such request for information renders the company or its auditor liable on summary conviction to a fine not exceeding £1,000 (€1,270) or on indictment to a fine not exceeding £10,000 (€12,697). It will be a defence to show that the request was complied with as soon as was reasonably possible.

(d) The right to attend any general meeting and to receive the same notices and communications relating to such meetings as the members. Auditors also have the right to be heard at such meetings on any matter that concerns them as auditors. Auditors may requisition an EGM of a company where the auditor gives reasons for his resignation in his written notice.[29] In the case of a single-member company, the auditor may even requisition an AGM.

Removal of Auditors

An auditor, other than the first auditor of the company, may be removed by an ordinary resolution of the company in general meeting.[30] Where a resolution proposes to remove or replace an auditor or fill a casual vacancy in the office of auditor, extended notice of the proposed resolution is required.[31] The auditor concerned must be sent a copy of the proposed resolution and must be given the right to make representations to the company and to request that such representations be notified to the members.[32] Where a request is made, the company must, unless it is too late to do so, circulate the members with a copy of the representations. Where the representations have not been circulated, the auditor may require them to be read out at the meeting at which it is proposed that he be removed. An application may be made to the court to prevent the auditor's right to make representations being abused.[33] The court may order that the representations need not be circulated or read out if it is satisfied that to do so would secure needless publicity for defamatory matters.

An auditor is also conferred with the following rights in the event that his removal or replacement is proposed:

(a) to attend the AGM at which, but for his removal, his term of office would have expired;
(b) to attend the general meeting at which it is proposed to fill the vacancy caused by his removal;

---

29 Section 186 of the 1990 Act.
30 Section 160(5) of the Principal Act.
31 Section 161(1)(a) and (b) of the Principal Act.
32 Section 161(3) of the Principal Act.
33 Section 161(4) of the Principal Act.

(c) to receive all notices and communications relating to the above meetings that a member is entitled to receive;
(d) to be heard at such a meeting on any part of the business of the meeting that concerns him as former auditor of the company.[34]

Where a resolution is passed removing an auditor the company must notify the registrar of companies within fourteen days of the meeting at which the resolution was passed.[35]

Where an auditor is being removed on the grounds that the company is exempt from having its accounts audited under section 34 of the 1999 Amendment Act the auditor must serve a notice on the company stating that there are no circumstances connected with the removal that should be brought to the attention of the members or creditors of the company or that there are such circumstances. Where there are such circumstances, a statement of the same nature should be sent to the company, which must forward it to all members and creditors who are entitled to receive it. The auditor must send the registrar of companies a copy of the notice.[36] Unless and until an auditor serves such a notice, any purported termination of his or her appointment as auditor to the company shall not have effect.[37]

Resignation of Auditors

An auditor is permitted to resign before the expiry of his term of appointment.[38] To effect such a resignation, the auditor must serve on the company a notice in writing containing a statement of the circumstances, if any, connected with his resignation, which he considers should be brought to the attention of members and creditors. Failure on the part of the auditor to state those circumstances, if any, constitutes an offence. Where a statement of such circumstances has been notified to the company, it must, within fourteen days of the notice being served, send a copy of the notice to every person entitled to receive copies of the annual accounts. Failure by the company to circulate the notice constitutes an offence.

Where those circumstances have been notified to the company, the auditor is also entitled to requisition a general meeting of the company for the purpose of considering these circumstances.[39] Where such a requisition has been made, the directors must convene a general meeting for a day not later than twenty-eight days after being served the resignation notice. The auditor is entitled to attend and be heard at such a meeting.

---

34 Section 161(2A) of the Principal Act.
35 Section 160(5A)(a)(ii) of the Principal Act.
36 Section 34(3)(a) of the 1999 Act.
36 Section 34(1)(ii) of the 1999 Act.
38 Section 185(1) of the 1990 Act.
39 Section 186 of the 1990 Act.

An auditor who has resigned is also entitled to attend and be heard at the AGM at which, but for his resignation, his term of office would have expired, and at any meeting at which it is proposed to fill the vacancy caused by his resignation. The registrar of companies must be notified of any resignation by the company's auditors within fourteen days of the notice to resign being served on the company.

Remuneration of Auditors

The remuneration and expenses of an auditor appointed by the directors or by the Minister is fixed by the person who appointed him.[40] Where the auditors are appointed by members, it is the AGM that fixes the remuneration or determines the manner in which it is to be fixed. In practice, the AGM usually delegates this power to the directors. Section 205D of the 1990 Act[41] requires companies, unless exempted, to disclose in the notes to their accounts details of the remuneration paid to the auditors. The note must specify the remuneration paid for audit work, audit re-work and non-audit work. This sub-section has not yet been brought into force but is expected to be by the end of 2007.

Investigation of Auditors

The Director of Corporate Enforcement (the Director) may enquire as to a person's qualifications to act as an auditor and, where that person is not qualified, can facilitate prosecution.[42] Where a disciplinary committee or tribunal of a body of accountants, recognised under section 187(1) of the 1990 Act, has reasonable grounds for believing that an indictable offence has been committed under the Companies Acts by any member of that body it must provide a report to the Director giving details of the alleged offence and furnish the Director with such information in relation to the matter as the Director may require.[43]

The Irish Auditing and Accounting Supervisory Authority.

The Irish Auditing and Accounting Supervisory Authority (The Supervisory Authority) was established under the 2003 Act. The principal objects of the Supervisory Authority are as follows —

1. to supervise how the prescribed accountancy bodies regulate and monitor their members;
2. to promote adherence to high professional standards in the auditing and accountancy profession;

---

40 Section 160(8) of the Principal Act.
41 Inserted by section 44 of the 2003 Act.
42 Section 187(12)(a) of the 1990 Act.
43 Section 192(6) of the 1990 Act.

3. to monitor whether the accounts of certain classes of companies and other undertakings comply with the Companies Acts and, where applicable, Article 4 of the IAS Regulation; and
4. to advise the Minister on auditing and accounting matters.[44]

The Authority's principal functions are set out in section 9 of the 2003 Act and include *inter alia* the following:

1. to grant recognition to bodies of accountants for the purposes of section 187 of the Companies Act 1990[45] and to attach such terms and conditions to such recognition;
2. to require changes to and approve the constitution and by-laws of each prescribed accountancy body including its investigation, disciplinary procedures and standards;
3. to conduct enquiries into whether a prescribed accountancy body has complied with the investigation and disciplinary procedures approved for that body and impose sanctions where there have been breaches of these procedures;
4. to undertake investigations into possible breaches of the standards of a prescribed accountancy body;
5. to supervise how each recognised accountancy body monitors its members and, where appropriate, to undertake a review of a member;
6. to co-operate with the recognised accountancy bodies and other interested parties in developing standards relating to the independence of auditors and to monitor the effectiveness of those standards;
7. to monitor the effectiveness of provisions of the Companies Acts relating to the independence of auditors;
8. to supervise the investigation and disciplinary procedures of each prescribed accountancy body;
9. to co-operate with the prescribed accountancy bodies and other interested parties in developing auditing and accounting standards and practice notes;
10. to review whether the accounts of certain companies and other undertakings comply with the Companies Acts and, where applicable, the IAS Regulation (i.e. IFRS);
11. to arrange for the regulation and supervision of individually authorised auditors by recognised accountancy bodies;
12 to perform the functions conferred on it in relation to the supervision of the transparency requirements of the Investment Funds, Companies and Miscellaneous Provisions Act 2006; and
13. to perform any other duties imposed on it by the Companies Acts.

---

44 Section 8 of the 2003 Act.
45 Recognition to bodies of accountants for audit purposes.

In order to carry out its statutory functions the Authority is vested with the power to do anything that appears to it to be requisite, advantageous or incidental to, or to facilitate, the performance of its functions.[46] The Authority is also given specific rights and powers, which include the following—

1. the right to apply to the High Court for an order compelling a prescribed accountancy body to comply with a rule adopted or guideline issued or a term or condition attached to its audit recognition;
2. the right to require access to prescribed bodies' records and to require explanations about the performance of their regulatory and monitoring duties;
3. the power to impose sanctions on prescribed accountancy bodies in circumstances where the Authority is not satisfied that their approved investigation and disciplinary procedures have been complied with;
4. the power to require a relevant person to attend before the Authority and the power to examine a relevant person on oath in the context of an investigation into a possible breach of the standards of a prescribed body;
5. the right to certify a refusal to co-operate with the Authority's investigations into a possible breach of the standards of a prescribed body to the High Court;
6. the power to impose sanctions on a member of a prescribed body where the member in question is found to have committed a breach of the body's standards;
7. where it is not satisfied that a company's financial statements are in compliance with the Companies Acts, the Authority may apply to the High Court for a declaration of non-compliance and for an appropriate order remedying the non-compliance.

---

46 Section 10 of the 2003 Act.

CHAPTER TWENTY-TWO

INVESTIGATION OF COMPANIES

Introduction

Under sections 165–173 of the Principal Act, the responsibility of appointing inspectors to investigate the affairs of companies was vested in the Minister. In practice, the power was seldom invoked due to both a reluctance on the part of successive Ministers to exercise their powers and to the limited circumstances in which the powers could be exercised. Part II of the Companies Act 1990 (the 1990 Act) repealed and replaced the 1963 provisions, and the power to order investigations was transferred to the High Court. The Minister was still given unilateral powers to appoint inspectors to investigate the *membership* of a company and these powers were exercised in a number of high-profile cases. Since the introduction of the Company Law Enforcement Act 2001, the Minister's powers in this regard have now been transferred to the Director of Corporate Enforcement (the Director).

Types of Investigations and Inquiries

1. Court Investigations

Under section 7(1) of the 1990 Act the High Court may appoint one or more inspectors to investigate the affairs of a company and to report thereon in a manner directed by the court. The order may be made on the application of any of the following:

(a) in the case of a company having a share capital, either at least 100 members, or members holding at least one-tenth of the paid-up share capital of the company;
(b) in the case of a company not having a share capital, not less than one-fifth in number of the members;
(c) the company itself;
(d) a director of a company;
(e) a creditor of a company.

An application to the High Court must be supported by such evidence as the court may require or as may be prescribed by way of ministerial regulation.[1] The court may also require applicants to put up security for the costs of the investigation which must be not less than €6,349 and must not exceed €317,435.[2] This security requirement may prove a deterrent for applicants with genuine grievances as well as vexatious applicants.

---

1 Section 7(2) (no such regulations have been introduced by the Minister in relation to company investigations).
2 Section 7(3).

Section 8(1) further empowers the court to order an investigation into the company's affairs on the application of the Director. However, the court must be satisfied that there are circumstances suggesting:

(a) that its affairs are being or have been conducted with the intent to defraud its creditors or the creditors of any other person or otherwise for a fraudulent or unlawful purpose or in an unlawful manner which is unfairly prejudicial to some part of its members, or that any actual or proposed act or omission of the company (including an act or omission on its behalf) is or would be so prejudicial, or that it was formed for a fraudulent or unlawful purpose; or
(b) that persons connected with its formation or the management of its affairs have in connection therewith been guilty of fraud, misfeasance or other misconduct towards it or towards its members; or
(c) that its members have not been given all the information relating to its affairs which they might reasonably expect.

A number of points arise in relation to (a) above. First, the reference to 'members' has, by virtue of section 8(2)(b), been extended to include not only those whose names appear on the register of members, but also those who acquired shares by operation of law, but who have not yet been registered or who have been refused registration as members. Accordingly, an apparent defect in previous legislation has been remedied by equating such persons with registered members for the purpose of the provision. Secondly, the importation of the English standard of conduct which is 'unfairly prejudicial' is unusual as it departs from the long-established statutory standard of 'oppressive' conduct which has heretofore been used in Ireland.[3] The manner in which the Irish courts will construe this new terminology remains to be seen.

It should be noted that the power to order an investigation under section 8 is exercisable with respect to a company notwithstanding that it is in the course of being wound up.[4]

The scope of an inspector's investigation and subsequent report on 'the affairs of the company' is a matter for the court. However, section 9 gives the inspector the power, subject to court approval, to extend his investigation into the affairs of a related company, where he considers it necessary for the purpose of his investigation.The definition of 'related company' has been extended beyond the normal statutory meaning (see Chapter 1) to include a company with which the investigated company has a 'commercial relationship'.

---

3 See Chapter 15.
4 Section 8(2)(a).

2. Section 14 Investigations by the Director

The Director may, under section 14 of the Act, appoint an inspector to investigate and report on the membership of any company for the purpose of determining the true persons who are or have been financially interested in the success or failure of the company, or who control or materially influence the policy of the company.

Grounds for a Section 14 Appointment

Before the Director can appoint an inspector, section 14(2) provides that he must be of the opinion that there are circumstances suggesting that the appointment is necessary:

(a) for the effective administration of the law relating to companies; or
(b) for the effective discharge by the Director of his functions under any enactment; or
(c) in the public interest.

Scope of a Section 14 Investigation

The scope of an investigation ordered by the Director is determined by the appointment itself,[5] and may include the investigation of any circumstances that suggest the existence of an arrangement or understanding which, though not legally binding, is, was or is likely to be observed in practice.[6] The far-reaching nature of the section 14 investigation can be seen in *Lyons and Others v. Curran*.[7] An inspector had been appointed to investigate and report on a number of companies involved in the highly publicised 'Greencore affair'. One of the companies named in the warrant of appointment was Gladebrook, which had purchased shares in a company called Sugar Distributors Holdings Ltd and at a substantial profit had resold them to Siúcra Éireann cpt. Gladebrook was partially owned by a foreign registered company, Talmino, and the inspector included this company in his investigation. The inspector's report later revealed that a director of Siúcra Éireann was the beneficial owner of Talmino. The applicants sought an order of *certiorari* quashing the report, on the grounds, *inter alia*, that:

(a) Talmino was not named in the warrant of appointment and therefore the inspector had no power to investigate its ownership;
(b) the inspector had not sought prior approval under section 9 to investigate a related company; and
(c) if the investigation of Talmino could proceed without the section 9 approval, this would render section 9 a superfluous provision in the Act.

Blayney J. rejected the applicants' contentions, stating that a correct construction of section 14 suggested that an inspector, appointed to investigate a

---

5 Section 14(3).
6 Section 14(4).
7 [1993] ILRM 375.

particular company, has the duty and power to investigate the membership of that company and to determine who are or have been financially interested in the success or failure of the company. He further observed that the statutory requirement to ascertain the *'true persons'* meant the real individuals who are financially interested and did not refer to a company. Where an inspector finds a company as shareholder in a company he is investigating, the court suggested that he must go further and seek to determine the persons who are the beneficial owners of that company. In relation to section 9, Blayney J. was satisfied that this section applied to a different category of cases, namely related companies, that as such had no bearing on the section 14 investigation in this case. Accordingly, the inspector was entitled to investigate a foreign company not included on his warrant in order to identify the persons who benefited from the dealings of the companies he was appointed to investigate.

3. Section 15 Inquiry by the Director

In certain circumstances the Director may inquire into the ownership of any shares or debentures of a company, without the appointment of inspectors. The grounds for ordering such an inquiry are the same as those for ordering an investigation under section 14. A person who is requested and fails to provide, or knowingly or recklessly provides false information to the Director in relation to any such inquiry is guilty of an offence.

4. Section 16 Restrictions on Shares

Where, in connection with an investigation or enquiry under sections 14 and 15, it appears to the Director that there is difficulty in finding out the relevant facts about any shares, the Director may, by notice in writing, direct that the shares be subject to the following restrictions:

(a) any transfer of those shares is void;
(b) no voting rights are exercisable in respect of those shares;
(c) no rights issue can be made to the holders of those shares; and
(d) no payment can be made to the shareholders of any sums due on the shares.[8]

Where shares are subject to a restriction any agreement to transfer the shares or, in the case of unissued shares, the right to be issued with the shares shall be void unless the Director makes a direction that the restriction be lifted.[9] The Director will only make such a direction if he is satisfied that the relevant facts about the shares have been disclosed to him.[10] Where the Director either restricts the shares or refuses to lift a restriction, the aggrieved person may apply to the

---

8 Section 16(1) and (2) of the 1990 Act.
9 Section 16(3) of the 1990 Act.
10 Section 16(6)(b) of the 1990 Act.

court to have the restriction lifted.[11] The Director or the court may lift the restriction, but only if satisfied that the relevant facts have been disclosed about the shares and the shares are being sold under a sale either approved by the court or the Director, as the case may be.[12]

In any case the court may, on the application of the Director or the company, having given notice to the Director, order the 'restricted' shares to be sold.[13] In granting an order for the sale of shares the court may lift the restrictions or continue them in so far as they relate to rights issues or payment entitlements acquired before the transfer. The court may also make such further orders relating to the sale of the shares as it thinks fit. Where the shares are sold on foot of a court order, the proceeds of sale shall be paid into court for the benefit of the persons beneficially interested in the shares, and those persons may apply to have the proceeds or a proportion thereof paid to them. Before ordering the payment to the interested person, the court may order that the costs of the application by the Director or the company shall be paid out of the proceeds of sale.

Any person who acts in breach of a restriction order or direction shall be guilty of an offence. Where shares are issued in contravention of the restriction, the company and any officer in default will also be guilty of an offence.

5. *Section 19 Order*

Section 19 also empowers the Director, or an officer authorised by the Director, to require the production of a company's books and papers for inspection. The section 19 order may be invoked against all companies formed or registered under the Companies Acts, unregistered companies, foreign companies carrying on business within the State, and all insurance companies.

Grounds for a Section 19 Order

The Director may make such an order if he is of the opinion that there are circumstances suggesting that:

(a) it is necessary to examine the books and documents of the body with a view to determining whether an inspector should be appointed; or
(b) the affairs of the company are being or have been conducted with intent to defraud its creditors, the creditors of any other person, the members or for any other fraudulent purpose; or
(c) the affairs are being conducted in a manner which is unfairly prejudicial to some of the members; or
(d) any actual or proposed act or omission or series of acts or omissions would be unfairly prejudicial to some of the members; or

---

11 Section 16(5) of the 1990 Act.
12 Section 16(6) of the 1990 Act.
13 Section 16(7) of the 1990 Act.

(e) any actual or proposed act or omission or series of acts or omissions are or are likely to be unlawful; or

(f) the body was formed for an unlawful or fraudulent purpose;

(g) the body may be in possession of books or documents containing information relating to the books or documents of a body which come within any of the above circumstances.

Where the Director requires the production of company books or documents he may also require the production of any books or documents from any other person who appears to be in possession of such books or documents, or copies of such books or documents.[14] Furthermore, the Director may require the production of other books and documents which may relate to any books or documents of the body.[15] As this power has far-reaching effect a number of constraints are imposed[16] on the exercise of this power, viz.:

(a) the Director must be of the opinion that there are reasonable grounds for believing that the books and documents are related to each other. Such grounds include (but are not limited to) where there is a relationship between the company and the person to whom an order of this type is proposed to be made, and a common origin of some or all of the information contained in the books and documents or similar considerations; and

(b) the Director formally notifies the person and states the grounds for his opinion and that the third party is given the opportunity to make submissions to the Director as to why he believes the Director's opinion is incorrect. The Director must have regard to those submissions, if any, before making a final decision as to whether or not to invoke the power. The Director does not have to issue any notice where he is of the opinion that it could result in the concealment, falsification, destruction or the disposal otherwise of the books or documents concerned;

(c) the person concerned need not comply with any such requirement to produce books and documents if such are privileged by any rule or law or enactment.

Where the Director requires the books or documents to be produced he may take copies or extracts from them, he may require that person or any past or present officer of the company or employee (including professional consultants) to provide explanations in relation to them and if the books or documents are not produced to require the person who was obliged to produce them to state the location of those books or documents.[17]

---

14 Section 19(3) of the 1990 Act.
15 Section 19(3)(b) of the 1990 Act.
16 By virtue of s.19(4) of the 1990 Act.
17 Section 19(5) of the 1990 Act.

Where the Director or a designated officer requests the production of books and documents a reasonable period of time must be given for compliance. In *Rogers v. George Maloney (Authorised Officer) and the Director of Corporate Enforcement*[18] the Director had appointed an authorised officer to whom he delegated certain investigative powers under section 19 of the Companies Act 1990. As part of the investigative process the authorised officer required the production of certain books and records of the company within three days. Given the extent of the documents required, the criminal penalty for concealment and the lack of any compelling reason for such a short period of time, the court considered that the demand was unreasonable.

Failure to comply with any of the requirements under section 19 by the company or any person may render the company or the relevant person guilty of an offence.[19] Any person who gives a false or misleading statement in relation to any explanation required may also be guilty of an offence. Any company or person who destroys, mutilates, falsifies or conceals any book or document may be similarly liable. Furthermore it is an offence for any person who knows or suspects that a Director is investigating, or may investigate, an offence under the Companies Acts to destroy or conceal any documentary evidence that may relate to that offence.[20]

The Director or a designated officer may apply to the District Court, and the judge, if satisfied that there are reasonable grounds for suspecting that any material information is to be found on any premises, may issue a search warrant.[21]

Powers of Inspectors

Section 10 confers a number of powers on the inspector in relation to the production of documents and evidence relevant to his investigation. Section 10(1) imposes a statutory duty on officers and agents of the company, under inspection or being investigated because of its related status, to produce books and documents of or relating to the company, or those of a related company which is being investigated, which are in their custody or power.[22] A document is within the power of a person if he has an enforceable legal right to obtain sight of it from the person who holds the document.[23] Furthermore, such persons are required to attend before inspectors when requested to do so, to be examined

---

18 Unreported, High Court, O'Leary J., December 21, 2005.
19 Section 19(6) of the 1990 Act.
20 Section 19A of the 1990 Act.
21 Section 20 of the 1990 Act.
22 In *Chestvale Properties Ltd and Hoddle Investments Ltd v. Glackin* [1993] 3 IR 35, the court held that an inspector was entitled to demand documents even when their ownership was vested in other companies.
23 *Bula Ltd v. Tara Mines Ltd* [1994] 1 ILRM 111. See also *Quigley v. Burke*, Unreported, Supreme Court, November 7, 1995.

under oath and to give inspectors all reasonable assistance in connection with the investigation. In this regard there is no obligation on the inspector to carry out all such enquiries in public.[24] For the purposes of this section the term 'officers' includes past and present officers and the term 'agents' includes the company's bankers, solicitors and those persons employed as auditors of the company. Inspectors are given the same powers in relation to third parties that are considered to be in possession of information concerning the affairs of the company or a related company. Where a person fails to produce books, documents or information as requested, and attend before the inspectors and answer any questions, the inspector may certify the refusal to the court, and the court may thereupon enquire into the case and, after hearing any witnesses and any statement offered in defence, make any order or direction it thinks fit.[25]

It is no defence to argue that compliance with an inspector's request to produce books or documents will breach an existing contractual agreement. In *Glackin v. Trustee Savings Banks*[26] it was held that a bank may not refuse to co-operate on the basis that to do so would breach the bank's duty of confidentiality towards its customer. According to Costello J. any such contractual arrangements are 'overridden' by the statutory duties imposed. Similarly, it would appear to be the case that a person may not refuse to answer a question which would be self-incriminating.[27] This clearly has implications, particularly as section 18 states that an answer given to an inspector exercising his section 10 powers can later be used in evidence against the person who gave such an answer. Even if the inspectors give some witnesses an assurance that their evidence will be used only to the extent necessary for completing their report, this assurance cannot be absolute and the court may order otherwise.[28] Nor is it a defence to a refusal to give evidence on oath that the information had already been submitted to the inspector by way of statutory declaration.[29]

Inspectors appointed by the court are empowered to require directors and connected persons to give details of their private bank accounts, whether held solely or jointly, within or outside the State. This power may be invoked if the inspector reasonably believes that accounts are being maintained which contain amounts that have not been disclosed to the company (when required to be so

---

24 *Re Redbreast Preserving Company (Ireland) Ltd*, 91 ILTR 12, and *Re Countyglen plc* [1995] 1 ILRM 213.
25 Section 10(6) of the 1990 Act.
26 [1993] 3 IR 55.
27 *Heaney v. Ireland* [1996] 1 IR 580, *Gilligan v. Criminal Assets Bureau* [1998] 3 IR 185, *R v. Harris* [1970] 2 All ER 746, but cf. *Saunders v. The United Kingdom* (43/1994/490/572).
28 *Re Ansbacher (Cayman) Ltd and Others*, Unreported, High Court, Finnegan P., May 25, 2004.
29 *Probets v. Glackin* [1993] 3 IR 134.

disclosed) or which are connected with any misconduct on the part of a director towards the company.

If at any stage during the course of an investigation the inspector is required to make a determination which may be damaging to a party, the principles of natural justice must be applied. The inspector is required to act reasonably,[30] the party concerned must be given an opportunity of being heard and fair procedures must be followed.[31]

Inspector's Report

Court-appointed inspectors may, and if so directed by the court shall, make interim reports to the court and on the conclusion of the investigation shall make a final report to the court.[32] An inspector may also, during the course of his investigation, inform the court of matters which tend to show that an offence has been committed.[33] The court shall furnish a copy of the report to the Director and may forward at its discretion a copy to any of the following:

(a) the company's registered office;
(b) any member of the company or other body corporate which is the subject of the report;
(c) any person whose conduct is referred to in the report;
(d) the auditors of that company or body corporate;
(e) the applicants for the investigation;
(f) any other person including an employee, creditor or other body corporate whose financial interests appear to the court to be affected by the matters dealt with in the report;
(g) the Central Bank, where the report relates to the affairs of a holder of a banking licence under section 9 of the Central Bank Act 1971.
(h) such other authorities as the court may direct.

The court may also cause the report to be printed and published but may direct that a part of the report be omitted from the printed or published form.

Having considered the inspector's report, the court may make such order as it deems fit.[34] It may make an order for the winding up of the company[35] irrespective of whether any other party requests that the company be wound up. In *Re National Irish Bank Ltd*[36] inspectors had been appointed by the High Court

---

30 *O'Keefe v. An Bord Pleanala* [1993] 1 IR 39.
31 *Re Pergamon Press Ltd* [1970] 3 All ER 589 and *Chestvale Properties Ltd v. Glackin* [1993] 3 IR 35.
32 Section 11(1) of the 1990 Act.
33 Section 11(2) of the 1990 Act.
34 Section 12(1) of the 1990 Act.
35 Section 12(1)(a) of the 1990 Act.
36 Unreported, High Court, Kelly J., July 23, 2004.

under section 8 to investigate the affairs of National Irish Bank (the bank) and National Irish Bank Financial Services Ltd (the company). The inspectors investigated the affairs and their final report was delivered to the court. The Director of Corporate Enforcement indicated that he did not intend petitioning the winding up of the bank and the company. The inspectors appointed to investigate the affairs did not consider it necessary that a winding-up order be made, and the bank and the company also opposed the making of a winding-up order.

Nevertheless, the court stated that the decision to wind up was exclusively a matter for the court. The court considered that in deciding whether to wind up the company it must carry out a 'balancing exercise' and in so doing may take account of the submissions of interested parties and the Financial Regulator, but must also identify for itself the aspects of the public interest that would be promoted by issuing a winding-up order.

As part of the balancing exercise, the court summarised the widespread improper practices carried out by the bank, the company and a number of senior bank personnel over a long period of time. On the other side of the balance, the court considered the contrite attitude of the bank, its commitment to ensuring a high level of governance and the financial costs associated with addressing the issues identified in the investigation. Furthermore, the court was of the view that an order to wind up would likely delay the repayment programme already agreed and have consequences for the bank's customers and the banking system. The court concluded that it would not be in the public interest to order the winding up of the company. Interestingly, the court observed that the cessation of improper practices was not in itself a ground for not winding up the company.

The court may also make an order for the purpose of remedying any disability suffered by any persons whose interests were adversely affected by the conduct of the affairs of the company, provided that when making such an order the court has regard for the interests of any other person who may be adversely affected by the order.[37] In *Re Ansbacher (Cayman) Ltd and Others*,[38] the Revenue Commissioners sought an order, under section 12 of the Companies Act 1990, for access to documents obtained by the inspectors in the course of their investigation but not included in the report or the appendices. The Revenue Commissioners submitted that as the inspectors' report had concluded that there was a conspiracy to defraud the Revenue, the information sought would be of assistance to the Revenue in its investigation of the Ansbacher account-holders. The Court made the order sought by the Revenue, but only in relation to those Ansbacher clients and those persons and companies found to have failed to co-operate with the inspectors in the enquiries, which group included individual members of the board of Ansbacher.

---

37 Section 12(1)(b) of the 1990 Act.
38 Unreported, High Court, Finnegan P., May 25, 2004.

It should be observed that once the inspectors have delivered their report and the court does not require any clarification on any matters relating to the report, the inspectors' statutory obligation is complete. *In Re National Irish Bank Ltd*[39] the Director of Corporate Enforcement sought orders under section 12 directing the inspectors to identify and disclose various documents considered by them in preparation of their final report. The Director sought these documents to assist him with applications for disqualification under section 160 of the 1990 Act against senior executives and directors of the bank named in the report. The High Court held that the statutory obligation on the inspectors to investigate the affairs of the company and then make a final report to the court did not envisage a continued obligation after the delivery of their final report.

Furthermore, the Director may, on the basis of the report, present a petition for the winding up of the company on the grounds that it is just and equitable to do so.[40]

Expenses of the Investigation

The expenses of an investigation ordered by the court will be defrayed in the first instance by the Minister for Justice, Equality and Law Reform. However, the court may direct that a body corporate dealt with in the report or the applicant for the investigation repay the Minister up to a maximum amount of £250,000 (€317,435). Similarly, any of the following parties may be ordered to repay all or part of the costs of the investigation:

(a) any person convicted of an indictable offence;
(b) any person ordered to pay damages or restore any property as a result of the investigation;
(c) any person who was awarded damages or to whom property was restored as a result of the investigation.

---

39 [2006] 2 ILRM 263.
40 Section 12(2).

CHAPTER TWENTY-THREE

REORGANISATION OF COMPANIES

Introduction

In certain circumstances companies may wish or be forced to undergo fundamental changes. This may involve the reorganisation of the capital structure, ownership or assets of the company or it may involve drastic changes in relation to the company that can prove terminal, not only for the company but also its underlying business and undertaking.

Whichever is the case, the law sets out certain procedures that must be followed, usually with some degree of independent supervision. In Chapters 25 and 26 the most drastic form of change in relation to a company — its winding up — is described in detail. The reorganisation of an insolvent company by way of a compromise and scheme of arrangement following the appointment of an examiner is discussed in Chapter 27. The following methods of reorganisation are discussed in this chapter:

(a) schemes of arrangement under sections 201–3 of the Principal Act;
(b) scheme of reconstruction under section 260 or 271 of the Principal Act; and
(c) amalgamations.

Schemes of Arrangement under Sections 201–3

Sections 201–3 of the Principal Act deal with a process of structured reorganisation that would involve the company in an arrangement[1] or compromise with its creditors, members or any class of them. This process may be engaged when a restructuring of the company's share capital is required or it may arise as part of the winding-up process. There is no requirement that the company is insolvent before the procedure can be invoked.[2]

Where a compromise or scheme of arrangement is proposed an application may be made to the court to call a meeting of the various classes of creditors or members.[3] The application may be made by the company, a creditor or member or, in the case of a company being wound up, by the liquidator.

---

1 Arrangement includes a reorganisation of the share capital of the company by the consolidation of different classes or by the division of shares into shares of different classes or by both these methods (section 201(7) of the Principal Act).
2 By contrast, a company must be insolvent before an examiner can be appointed and a scheme of arrangement put in place under the Companies (Amendment) Act, 1990 (see Chapter 27).
3 Section 201(1) of the Principal Act.

The application is made by way of special summons based on an affidavit, usually by a director, setting out in detail the terms of the scheme. On hearing the application the court is not concerned with the merits of, or giving its approval to, the scheme. Rather, if the court is satisfied that *prima facie* the proposal is suitable for consideration as a scheme of arrangement, it may then direct that a meeting of the various classes of creditors and members be held.

Where an application is made the court may, on such terms as it thinks just, stay all proceedings or restrain further proceedings against the company.[4] The purpose of this provision is to prevent any individual creditor from pre-empting any possible arrangement by getting a judgment in his favour.

1. Class Meetings

It is up to the company to decide on the different classes of creditors and members. Once this has been done the various meetings must be summoned. The information that must be provided with the notice of the meeting is set out in section 202 of the Principal Act as follows:

(a) a statement explaining the effect of the compromise or arrangement;
(b) details of any material interests of the directors and the effect thereon of the compromise and scheme in so far as it differs from the effect on the interests of other persons;
(c) a statement of the effect of the scheme on the rights of debenture holders where the compromise or arrangement affects the rights of the debenture holders.

Section 201(3) provides that a majority in number representing 75 per cent in value of the creditors or members or class of creditors or members present must vote in favour of the scheme before it will be sanctioned by the court. This means that each class must consent to the scheme. This aspect differs from the procedure for effecting a compromise or scheme of arrangement under the Companies (Amendment) Act 1990 (the 1990 Amendment Act), which requires that only one class of creditor need approve the scheme. In that instance, classes of creditors or members may be forced to accept a scheme. The difficulty with the section 201 procedure is that a class can effectively veto any compromise or scheme. This has proved to be a stumbling block for schemes of arrangement proposed for an insolvent company because the preferential or, indeed, the secured creditors are unlikely to approve a compromise to their claims when they enjoy a superior position in a liquidation situation.

As the company must decide on the different classes, great care should be taken in this regard. If within one class of shareholders or creditors there are

---

4 Section 201(2) of the Principal Act.

groups whose interests in the proposed scheme are clearly different, the court must be asked to order that separate meetings be called of each group. This is where the constitution of class meetings will differ from those held in the winding up of a company. Where a scheme does not distinguish each such group (to be consulted separately), the court will withhold its approval of the scheme on the ground that there has not been fair and proper consultation.

In *Re Hellenic and General Trust*,[5] a scheme of arrangement was agreed by the ordinary shareholders of Hellenic, the effect of which was that the shareholders would receive cash and ultimately the company would be taken over by a bank. When court approval for the scheme was sought, a minority shareholder objected on the grounds that the majority shareholder, who voted in favour of the scheme, was in fact a subsidiary of the company that would ultimately take control of Hellenic. If that majority shareholder had not constituted part of that class of shareholders, the dissentient shareholder would have had a sufficient shareholding to block the scheme. Despite the fact that all the shareholders belonged to the same class in terms of shares, the court refused to sanction the scheme. In rejecting the scheme the court concluded that where there are shareholders within the same shareholding class but who have different interests in the scheme being proposed, the class should be further divided and approval must be sought from the newly constituted classes.

The case is important for a number of reasons. First, it is clear that the constitution of the class meetings will not necessarily follow those held during the winding up of the company or indeed those held where a variation of shareholders' rights is being sought under section 78 of the Principal Act.[6] The difference between the section 201 procedure and these others is that the former requires the classes to be constituted depending on their interests, including their interests in the proposals, whereas the latter require the classes to be constituted in terms of the similarity in rights attaching to each category of shares. Second, the case demonstrates that if class approval is not obtained in the correct manner the entire scheme may be put in abeyance or may even founder completely.

However, it is not sufficient to claim that a class member has an ulterior motive for approving the scheme. In *Re Pye Ireland Ltd*,[7] an unsecured creditor, voting for a scheme of arrangement to defer payment of the company's debts, also happened to hold 25 per cent of the shares in the company. This creditor had an extra interest in voting for the scheme because the breathing space being granted to the company was advantageous and enabled it to develop its assets, which would ensure the benefit of the members as well as the creditors. The court held that inclusion of this creditor in the meeting did not render it improperly

---

5 [1976] 1 WLR 123.
6 See Chapter 8.
7 Unreported, High Court, Costello J., November 12, 1984.

constituted in the absence of proof that the others had been prejudiced by the inclusion. The meeting was accordingly declared to be valid.

2. Powers of the Court

Section 203 gives wide powers to the court to make orders facilitating the compromise or scheme of arrangement proposed for the purposes of reconstruction or amalgamation, but only where it is proposed to transfer all or any part of the company's undertaking or property to another company. In this regard the court may make provision for any of the following:

(a) the transfer of the whole or any part of the undertaking or property to the new company;
(b) the allotment or appropriation of any shares, debentures, policies or other interests by the transferee company to any person as provided in the scheme of arrangement;
(c) the continuation of any legal proceedings by or against the transferor company;
(d) the dissolution of the transferor company without winding up;
(e) the making of provision for any dissentients;
(f) any incidental, consequential and supplemental matters as are necessary to secure that the reconstruction or amalgamation shall be fully and effectively carried out.

The court has discretion to approve the scheme of arrangement or reject it. It will not sanction the scheme where the notices of the meetings contained insufficient information or where the authorising resolutions were improperly passed.[8] The court will also ensure that the scheme is one which an 'intelligent and honest man, a member of the class concerned and acting in respect of his interest, might reasonably approve'.[9] In *Re Colonia Insurance (Ireland) Ltd*,[10] a scheme of arrangement was proposed for a solvent company for the following reasons.

(a) The company was involved in the reinsurance of non-life business as part of an insurance group of companies.
(b) It had ceased writing business in December 2002 but continued to have liabilities in relation to business written prior to that date.
(c) These 'run-off liabilities' were likely to last far into the future and the scheme proposed to establish a mechanism to shorten the time involved in quantifying and paying these liabilities.

---

8 *Re Dorman Long and Company Ltd* [1934] 1 Ch 635.
9 Per Maugham J., ibid. at 655.
10 Unreported, High Court, Kelly J., March 15, 2005.

Before dealing with the scheme itself the court observed that the matters in which it had to be satisfied were as follows:

(a) sufficient steps were taken to notify the interested parties;
(b) the statutory requirements and directions of the court had been complied with;
(c) the classes of creditors were properly constituted;
(d) there was no evidence of coercion; and
(e) the scheme was such that an intelligent and honest man, a member of the class concerned, acting in respect of his interest might reasonably approve.

In relation to this last point Kelly J. considered the advantages of the scheme. The proposals provided for cost-effectiveness for the company and the claimants, a greater finality for the parties, a fair mechanism by which creditors would have a reasonable opportunity to assert their claim and have the value thereof adjudicated, early payment for the creditors and a monetary benefit. The court then turned to the disadvantages of the scheme, which were clearly set out by the company. The first concerned the potential failure of a scheme creditor to return his claim form by the due date, which would result in the claim being valued at nil. The second related to the fact that, in estimating the claims, there were circumstances whereby a scheme creditor could receive less, and perhaps more, in respect of their claims than they would have had if the claims matured in the normal way. The court accepted that there was some risk that a scheme creditor would receive less under the scheme, but it was satisfied that the advantages outweighed the disadvantages. Kelly J. was satisfied that an intelligent and honest man, a member of the class concerned and acting in respect of his interests, might reasonably approve the scheme. As creditors had approved the proposed scheme without dissent, the court exercised its power under section 201 and sanctioned the scheme.

If the scheme is sanctioned by the court it will be binding on all creditors, members, liquidators or contributors once an official copy has been delivered to the registrar of companies.

Section 201 schemes have not been commonly used in Ireland and there are few written decisions in relation to the section. This is probably due to the requirement to have court approval which may slow down the process somewhat. Since 1990 we have become more familiar with compromises and schemes of arrangements of insolvent companies under the court protection scheme of the 1990 Amendment Act. However, given recent changes to takeover legislation, it may well be that section 201 becomes a more popular method of reorganising a company. (See Amalgamations, below.)

Scheme of Reconstruction under Sections 260 or 271

Section 260 of the Principal Act permits only one type of reconstruction by which a company in voluntary liquidation sells its undertaking for shares in another company. Section 271 of the Act extends section 260 to a creditors' voluntary winding up. The procedure under section 260(1) is that when a company is proposed to be, or in the course of being, wound up voluntarily and the whole or part of its business or property is to be transferred to another company, the liquidator may, with the sanction of a special resolution, receive, in compensation for the transfer, shares in the transferee company for distribution among the members of the transferor company.

Section 260(2) provides that such sale or arrangement is binding on the members of the transferor company, and there is no provision whereby dissenting members may object. However, section 260(3) does allow a dissenting member to notify his dissent to the liquidator and request him either to abstain from carrying out the resolution or to purchase his interests. If the liquidator elects to purchase his shares, section 260(4) states that the purchase money must be paid before the company is dissolved and, unless otherwise provided for, shall be deemed to be part of the costs of the winding up.

The provisions of section 260 apply in exactly the same way in a creditors' winding up, except that section 271 prevents the liquidator from exercising his powers without the sanction of the court, or the committee of inspection.

Amalgamations

An amalgamation involves a reorganisation of a number of companies, by which all transfer their assets to one company that may have been formed solely for that purpose. In consideration for this transfer, shares in the transferee company will be allotted to the members of transferor companies in proportion to their original holdings. An amalgamation can take place by following the section 201 procedure outlined above, or it may take the form of a merger or takeover, whereby the companies are merged by consolidating their undertakings or by the acquisition of the controlling interests of both companies by a new company or by one company or the other company. The type of procedure followed may often depend on the relationship between the companies. Where, for example, an amalgamation is amicable, any method may be pursued. Where a proposed takeover is hostile, the acquiring company will first have to gain a controlling interest in the target company before it can pursue any further reorganisation. In practice, what occurs is that the acquiring company makes an offer to the shareholders of another company to buy their shares. Normally such an offer will be conditional on acceptance by a stated proportion of shareholders. By accepting the conditional offer the shareholders become bound to sell, but the offering company is not bound to buy until the condition is fulfilled. The reason for imposing the 'squeeze-out provisions' is to ensure that once a company has acquired this level it can compulsorily purchase the remaining minority shareholders' interests.

It should be noted that under recent legislative changes that implement the Takeovers Directive,[11] the 'squeeze-out' threshold is 90 per cent where the target company is a company listed on a regulated market. For all other companies, section 204 of the Principal Act requires the threshold to be 80 per cent. Given the increased threshold of 90 per cent for some companies it may be easier to opt for a section 201 scheme, which requires only a 75 per cent approval. Obviously, in the case of a hostile takeover bid the section 201 mechanism is unlikely to be a viable alternative given the requirement of approval from each class of member.

1. Compulsory Purchase under Section 204

In the case of companies not listed on a regulated exchange, section 204 provides that where a company makes an offer for all the shares of a target company and receives binding acceptances in respect of at least 80 per cent of the shares, the acquiring company is entitled to acquire the remaining shares in that company. The provision is designed to facilitate the completion of a takeover that has already been approved by the majority.

Section 204(1) provides that where the scheme, contract or offer involving the acquisition has become binding, or has been approved or accepted by the holders of 80 per cent of the relevant shares within four months after the publication of the scheme, contract or offer, the transferee company may, within six months following such publication, give notice to the dissenting shareholders that it intends to acquire their shares. When such notice is given the transferee company shall be entitled and bound to acquire those shares on the terms that under the scheme, contract or offer have become binding, approved and accepted.

A dissenting shareholder may apply to the court within one month of the notice being issued and the court may make such order as it thinks fit. The court will not sanction the compulsory takeover if full particulars have not been given to the shareholders,[12] or if there is any evidence of *male fides* on the part of the acquiring company or the assenting shareholders.[13] However, it is not sufficient for a dissenting shareholder to claim that the scheme is unfair to them. As Vaisey J. stated in *Re Sussex Brick Co.*:

---

11 Council Directive 2004/25/EC as implemented by the European Communities (Takeover Bids Directive 2004/25/EC) Regulations 2006.

12 *Securities Trust Ltd. v. Associated Properties Ltd and Others*, Unreported, High Court, McWilliams J., November 19, 1980.

13 *Re Bugle Press Ltd* [1961] Ch 270.

A scheme must be obviously unfair, patently unfair, unfair to the meanest intelligence. It cannot be said that no scheme can be effective to bind a dissenting shareholder unless it complies to the extent of 100 per cent, with the highest possible standard of fairness, equity and reason.[14]

This statement was approved by the Irish High Court in the case of *Walls v. Walls Holdings Ltd.*[15] Here, the applicant sought to prevent the respondent from acquiring his shares in two family-owned companies pursuant to the provisions of section 204(1). The two target companies, together with the respondent transferee company, had common shareholders who were all members of the Walls family. The applicant argued that the respondent was not an independent bidder in that its controlling shareholders and directors were the sole directors and, together with their children, the majority shareholders of the two companies subject to the takeover. The applicant further claimed that the respondent's offer was unfair on the grounds, *inter alia*, that the offer was at a substantial undervalue. Finally, the applicant submitted that the attempt to 'expropriate' the applicant's shares was made in contravention of his pre-emption rights under the company's articles of association.

In relation to the independence of the offeror, the court suggested that section 204 did not require that the holders of the four-fifths majority be independent or disinterested in the transferee company.[16] On the facts presented the court was satisfied that the majority shareholders had not exercised unjust influence or coercion.

With regard to the alleged unfairness of the scheme, the court stated that the onus was on the applicant to prove unfairness. While circumstances may justify reversing the onus[17] there were no such circumstances in the present case. In regard to the allegation that the sale was at an undervalue, the court was satisfied that the outcome of the offer was not a foregone conclusion and that as the applicant's shareholding in the respondent company would be increased, the court could not accept that the applicant had shown convincingly that the offer was unfair.

The final matter related to the breach of the pre-emption scheme provided for in the articles of association. The court accepted the respondent's contention that where there is a conflict between the articles of association and the provisions of the Act, the Act prevails. Furthermore, the discretion to deny the right to acquire under section 204 was vested in the court and not in a dissenting shareholder through reliance on the articles. Accordingly, the standard pre-emption rights did not intrude into the process to which section 204 applies. On this basis the court concluded that the offer was not unfair and refused to order the relief sought by the applicant.

---

14 [1961] Ch 289 at 291.
15 Unreported, High Court, Smyth J., November 5, 2004.
16 Re *Fitzwilton plc; Duggan v. Stoneworth Ltd.* [2000] 2 ILRM 263
17 Citing with approval Re *Bugle Press Ltd* [1961] Ch 270.

Section 204(1) is subject to 204(2), which provides that where the acquiring company is, at the date of publication of the offer, the beneficial owner of more than 20 per cent of the shares, the accepting shareholders must represent 75 per cent in number as well as 80 per cent value of the relevant shares.

The minority shareholder may also force the acquiring company to purchase his shares. Section 204(4) provides that if as a result of the scheme or offer the company holds 80 per cent of the target company's shares, then a dissenting holder may, within three months, require the transferee company to acquire his shares.

2. General Rules Regarding Takeovers and Mergers

Where any one of the above-mentioned methods of reorganisation is designed to effect a takeover or merger, a number of other legislative provisions will apply. Section 187 of the Principal Act declares unlawful any payments of compensation to a director for loss of office or as consideration for his retirement where a transfer of the whole or any part of the undertaking or property of a company occurs, unless details of these payments have been disclosed to and approved by the company in general meeting. Where such payments are received without satisfying these requirements the payments concerned shall be deemed to be received by the directors in trust for the company.

Directors are also under a duty to disclose payments to be made to them, whether in relation to compensation for loss of office or as consideration for or in connection with their retirement from office, in respect of any transfer of shares where such transfer results from:

(a) an offer made to the general body of shareholders; or
(b) an offer made by or on behalf of some other body corporate, with a view to the company becoming its subsidiary or a subsidiary of its holding company; or
(c) an offer made by or on behalf of an individual with a view to his obtaining the right to exercise or control the exercise of not less than one-third of the voting power at any general meeting of the company; or
(d) any other offer conditional on acceptance to a given extent.[18]

The director is obliged to take all reasonable steps to secure that the details of the proposed payments are included in or sent with any notice of the offer made for their shares which is given to any shareholders. The proposed payments must then be approved by a meeting of the holder of the shares to which the offer relates. In the event that the disclosure is not complied with and approval of the shareholders is not obtained, any sum received by the directors will be received in trust for any

---

18 Section 188 of the Principal Act.

persons who have sold their shares as a result of the offer made. These provisions do not apply in relation to payments made to a director for breach of his contract of service or in respect of pension payments for past services.

Section 60 of the Principal Act[19] prohibits companies from giving financial assistance for the purpose of, or in connection with, the acquisition of their shares. This provision is relevant in relation to takeovers or mergers where a target company is being acquired. The target company's assets cannot be used as security for any borrowings incurred by the transferee company for the purpose of buying the target company's shares. Similarly the target company cannot give guarantees for any such borrowings by the transferee company.

Acquisitions or disposals of any shares may be prohibited if they constitute market abuse (insider dealing or market manipulation) in the context of the Market Abuse Regulations and the Investment Funds Companies and Miscellaneous Provisions Act 2005.[20]

The Competition Act 2002 prohibits certain agreements (including mergers) where such will prevent, restrict or distort competition or which will give rise to an abuse of a dominant position. These agreements must be notified to the Irish Competition Authority, which will review the merger and make a determination. The Competition Authority may approve, approve subject to conditions or prohibit the proposed merger. Decisions may be appealed to the High Court. Under the EU Merger Regulation[21] proposed mergers involving certain worldwide or European Union-wide turnover criteria must be notified to the European Commission, which may investigate the proposed merger and make a determination.

Chapter 2 of Part IV of the 1990 Act provides, *inter alia*, that anyone[22] who acquires or disposes of shares in a public company that results in that person's interest going above or falling below five per cent of the voting shares of that company, must notify the company in writing of the amount of the holding and related particulars. Where a person already holds five per cent or more of the relevant shares they must disclose all future acquisitions that result in an increase of one per cent thereafter.

Where the public company is also listed on the Stock Exchange there is a further duty to notify the Stock Exchange where the percentage levels of a person's interest exceeds or falls below certain levels.[23]

---

19 See Chapter 10.
20 See Chapter 13.
21 Council Regulation 4064/89/EEC.
22 For the purposes of these provisions the relevant shares include: shares owned by the person's spouse or minor child; shares owned by a company that is, or whose board of directors is, accustomed to act in accordance with his directions or instructions or a company in which the person is entitled to exercise or control the exercise of one or more of the voting power at general meetings.
23 Section 91 of the Companies Act 1990.

The European Communities (Takeover Bids (Directive 2004/25/EC) Regulations came into effect on 20 May 2006, the due date for transposition of Directive 2004/25/EC on Takeover Bids. The Directive is one of the measures adopted under the EU Financial Services Action Plan (the FSAP) and provides for harmonised rules for the conduct of takeovers of companies traded on a regulated market in the EU, and equal protection for minority shareholders. The Directive sets down minimum standards and Member States may impose their own additional rules, which may be more stringent than those set by the Directive. The current rules for the supervision of takeovers in Ireland is provided for in the Takeover Panel Act 1997, and the Takeover Rules made pursuant to this Act. The Takeover Rules have been amended to reflect the requirements of the 2006 Regulations and provide *inter alia* for the following:

(a) the approach to be taken by an offeror to the offeree board before an announcement is made concerning the offer;
(b) the timing and contents of announcements;
(c) the obligation of the offeree board to obtain independent advice and to circulate it to the company's shareholders;
(d) the requirements where a director has a conflict of interest;
(e) restrictions on dealing in the securities of the offeree company during the relevant period;[24]
(f) restrictions on acquisitions of securities in the offeree company;
(g) the acquisition resulting on an obligation to make a formal bid;
(h) the consequences of certain dealings;
(i) the disclosure of certain dealings;
(j) the mandatory offer, its terms and conditions;
(k) provisions applicable to all offers;
(l) the conduct during the offer;
(m) the documents from the offeror and the offeree board;
(n) the forecast and valuations; and
(o) the timing and revision of offers.

The Substantial Acquisition Rules ('SARs') are also issued by the Irish Takeover Panel. The SARs impose various rules and restrictions on acquisitions of significant interests in public companies which must be complied with. A significant interest arises if:

(a) any voting securities are acquired by a person that confer an aggregate of 10 per cent or more of the voting rights of a company; and

---

24 The 'relevant period' is the period from the time at which a person first has reason to suppose that an offer, or an approach with a view to an offer being made, is contemplated to the time of the announcement of the offer or approach or the termination of discussions, whichever is the earliest.

(b) any voting securities acquired by a person, when aggregated with any existing voting securities already held by that person, gives that person 15 per cent or more, but less than 30 per cent, of the voting rights in the company; and

(c) in the case of a series of acquisitions of securities, all such acquisitions are made within a period of seven days.

The Listing Rules of the Irish Stock Exchange also include various requirements in respect of purchases of a specified percentage of the value of a listed company. These obligations primarily relate to disclosure and notification.

Takeovers and acquisitions of shares in certain industries such as banks, credit institutions and insurance companies are subject to additional legislation provisions regulating their particular industry.

CHAPTER TWENTY-FOUR

RECEIVERS

Introduction

The most common way for a debenture holder to realise his security is by appointing a receiver. The receiver will take control over the charged assets and by selling them and applying the proceeds will discharge the debt owing to the debenture holder.

A receiver may be appointed under the terms of a fixed or floating charge. However, where a debenture is secured only by a fixed charge or mortgage, the debenture holder will usually have a right to sell the asset without going through the expense of appointing a receiver. In Ireland the normal practice of lending institutions is to take the all-embracing fixed and floating charge over the entire assets and undertaking of the company. Where such a charge is being realised it will be necessary to appoint a receiver because the process may take quite a considerable period of time.

Appointment of a Receiver

A receiver can be appointed either by the debenture holder under the terms of the debenture or by the courts. The debenture or trust deed usually gives the debenture holders or their trustees the power to appoint a receiver in specified circumstances, usually described as events of default. Although a matter of negotiation between the company and the debenture holder, the debenture will usually incorporate the following events of default:

(a) the principal sum due has been unpaid for more than seven days;
(b) the company has failed to pay an instalment of the principal or interest;
(c) failure of any other covenant, condition, representation or warranty in the debenture;
(d) the levying of a distress or execution against the company;
(e) the appointment of a receiver over any of the company's assets;
(f) the disposal, without the sanction of the debenture holder, of a substantial part of the company's assets;
(g) the company is ceasing, has ceased to carry on business or is threatening to do so;
(h) there is a change in ownership of the company which is not acceptable to the debenture holder;
(i) there is a material adverse change in the business of the company, which in the opinion of the debenture holder would jeopardise the security.[1]

---

1 This 'catch-all' event of default has never been tested by the court, but is unlikely to survive judicial scrutiny unless it is exercised on reasonable grounds.

Court-appointed receivers are officers of the court and as such have their remuneration fixed by the court. Where appointed by the debenture holder, the receiver's remuneration will ordinarily be fixed by the terms of the debenture. However, a liquidator, member or creditor of a company may apply to the court under section 318 of the Principal Act to fix the remuneration of a receiver, even if the document under which the receiver has been appointed purports to fix the remuneration.[7]

A receiver appointed under a debenture may resign provided he has given one month's notice to the holders of floating charges over all or part of the company, the company itself or its liquidator, and the holders of all fixed charges over all or part of the property of the company.[8] When appointed by the court, a receiver can resign only with the consent of the court and subject to the terms laid down by the court.[9] Failure to comply with these notice provisions may cause the receiver to be liable to a fine.

The court may also, on cause shown, remove a receiver and appoint another.[10] Notice of such proceedings must be served on the receiver and the person who appointed him not less than seven days before the hearing. The receiver and the person who appointed him must be given an opportunity to appear and be heard at such proceedings.[11]

Receiver's Status

A receiver appointed by the court is an officer of the court and takes his instructions from the court. Where a receiver is appointed by the debenture holder he will be the agent of the debenture holder unless the contrary is specifically stated in the debenture. However, in normal circumstances the debenture will provide that the receiver is an agent of the company. This will have the effect of making the company and not the debenture holder responsible for any wrongful act on the part of the receiver. As the company's agent, the receiver may be bound by some of the company's obligations[12] and in other instances he may choose to repudiate those obligations.[13] The ability to repudiate existing contracts is considered later in this chapter.

Although the company is the receiver's principal, the relationship between the receiver and the company does not follow the normal agency rules. As Costello J.

---

7 *Re City Car Sales Ltd (in receivership & liquidation)* [1995] 1 ILRM 221.

8 Section 322C(1) of the Principal Act.

9 Section 322C(2) of the Principal Act.

10 Section 322A(1) of the Principal Act.

11 Section 322A(2) of the Principal Act.

12 In *Cretanor Maritime Co. Ltd v. Irish Marine Management Ltd* [1978] 3 All ER 164 it was held that the receiver was bound by a *Mareva* injunction, which the plaintiff had obtained against the defendant company. See also *Kilgobbin Mink and Stud Farm Ltd v. National Credit Company Ltd* [1980] IR 175.

13 *Ardmore Studios (Ireland) Ltd. v. Lynch* [1965] IR 1.

stated in *Irish Oil and Cake Mills Ltd v. Donnelly*,[14] 'the agency here is of course very different from the ordinary agency arising every day in commercial transactions'.

The difficulty in applying a strict agency relationship to the receiver and company lies in the fact that the receiver is appointed by the debenture holder and will always have the debenture holder's interests in mind. The company is therefore not in a position to instruct the receiver on the exercise of his powers and the carrying out of his duties, as would occur in a normal agency situation.[15] Neither can the company as principal dismiss the receiver. However, even where the debenture provides that the receiver is the agent of the company, the actions of the debenture holder may cause the court to infer an agency relationship between the debenture holder and the receiver. In *American Express International Banking v. Hurley*,[16] the facts of which are considered later in the chapter, the court held that the debenture holder, a bank, was liable in negligence to the guarantor of the company's debts because it had directed the receiver to sell the assets at an undervalue and thus had created a relationship of principal and agent between the bank and the receiver in this matter.

Effect of the Receiver's Appointment

The effect of the receiver's appointment is now considered under the following headings:

1. the company;
2. the directors;
3. the liquidator;
4. the examiner;
5. employees; and
6. publicity requirements.

1. The Company

The receiver must give notice of his appointment to the company although in reality the company will be aware that the receiver is appointed. The appointment of a receiver does not affect the legal status of the company. It continues its existence and its separate legal personality remains intact. However, once a receiver has been appointed, every invoice, order for goods or business letter issued by or on behalf of the company shall contain a statement that a receiver has been appointed.[17] Default by the company and any officer, liquidator or receiver of the company in complying with this provision may lead to a fine.[18]

---

14 Unreported, High Court, 27 March 1973.
15 Milman, *Receivers as Agents* 44 MLR 654.
16 [1986] BCLC 52.
17 Section 317(1) of the Principal Act.
18 Section 317(2) of the Principal Act.

Where the holder of a floating charge appoints a receiver over the whole or substantially the whole of the property of the company, a statement as to the affairs of the company must be submitted to the receiver within fourteen days of his appointment.[19] By virtue of section 320 of the Principal Act, this duty is imposed on the directors and secretary of the company or such person as may be specified by the receiver. The statement must include the following:

(a) particulars of the company's assets, debts and liabilities at the date of appointment of the receiver;
(b) names and addresses of the company's creditors;
(c) the securities held by those creditors;
(d) the dates when the securities were respectively given.

The statement of affairs must be verified by affidavit if the receiver has been appointed by the court, or by a statutory declaration where the receiver is appointed under a debenture. Default in complying with the statutory requirements to submit the statement of affairs may give rise to a criminal offence.[20] Where a statement is not submitted the court may, on the application of the receiver or any creditor of the company, make such order as it deems fit, including an order compelling the submission of a statement of affairs.[21]

The appointment of a receiver is an event which causes floating charges to crystallise and become fixed. Once this occurs the company may no longer deal with the assets charged without the receiver's consent.

2. The Directors

On his appointment the receiver assumes control over the assets which are the subject of the charge. Accordingly, the directors' powers in respect of those assets are suspended during the receivership. However, the directors remain in office and can exercise such powers which have not passed to the receiver. If a receiver is appointed over a specific asset only, the directors will retain their powers over all remaining assets and the management of the company. Where a receiver is appointed over all the assets and undertaking of the company, the directors' powers are substantially curtailed. However, their position is not completely usurped by the receiver, as they retain residual decision-making powers. In *Newhart Developments v. Co-operative Commercial Bank*,[22] a bank appointed a receiver under a debenture. The debenture gave the receiver numerous management powers including, *inter alia*, the power to bring legal proceedings in the name of the company. The company directors claimed that the bank was in breach of contract, but the receiver refused to begin proceedings for

19 Section 319(1)(b) of the Principal Act.
20 Section 320(5) of the Principal Act.
21 Section 320A of the Principal Act.
22 [1978] QB 814.

the company against the bank. He also sought to restrain the directors from themselves taking an action against the bank. In holding that the directors could continue the proceedings, the court was very much persuaded by two particular points. First, although the receiver was an agent of the company he was appointed and paid by the debenture holder. Accordingly, it was unlikely that he would take an action against the bank himself. Second, the directors had provided a personal indemnity for the costs of the litigation in the event that the action was unsuccessful. This latter point is of particular importance as the court will only permit the directors to exercise their residual powers where they do not impinge upon the debenture holder's security. It was the absence of such an indemnity that prevented the directors from suing in the company's name in *Tudor Grange Holdings Ltd v. Citibank NA.*[23]

The Irish courts have accepted the view that directors retain their power to institute proceedings in an appropriate case. In *Wymes v. Crowley*,[24] the directors sought to institute proceedings in the name of the company, alleging negligence against the receiver. The receiver attempted to resist the claim. The court held that the directors retained residual powers even where a receiver was appointed as a manager-receiver. These residual powers included the power to initiate litigation on the company's behalf. However, the court accepted the UK line of reasoning that the exercise of those powers was subject to one important limitation — it must not deprive the debenture holders of their security.[25]

3. The Liquidator

A receiver can still be appointed even if a liquidator is already in place. If the company goes into liquidation when the receiver is already in office, he ceases to be the agent of the company if appointed in that capacity. However, he will retain his powers in relation to the assets comprised in the charge.[26] The liquidator is entitled to receive any surplus that remains after the receiver has discharged his duties, but otherwise he cannot interfere with the receiver's exercise of his powers. However, the liquidator in a compulsory or creditor's voluntary winding up may apply to the court for an order directing that the receiver shall cease to act or act only in relation to certain assets.[27] In any case, where the liquidator is appointed by the court the receiver should seek the approval of the court before disposing of any assets.

Where a receiver is appointed under a charge which is subsequently invalidated under section 286 of the Principal Act,[28] he must vacate his office and

---

23 [1991] 4 All ER 1.
24 Unreported, High Court, February 27, 1987.
25 For a similar view see *Lascomme Ltd v. UDT* [1994] 1 ILRM 227.
26 *Sowman v. David Samuel Trust Ltd* [1978] 1 All ER 616.
27 Section 322B of the Principal Act.
28 See Chapter 26.

account to the liquidator forthwith. However, if the receiver has repaid the debenture holders before the charge is invalidated, the actions of the receiver cannot be retrospectively invalidated on that ground.

4. The Examiner

Where an examiner is appointed and a receiver is already in place, the court may make such order as it deems fit, including an order that:

(a) the receiver shall cease to act from the date specified by the court;
(b) the receiver act only in relation to certain assets as specified by the court;
(c) the receiver deliver to the examiner all books, papers and other records which are in his possession or control and which relate to the property or undertaking of the company;
(d) the receiver give to the examiner particulars of his dealings with the property or undertaking of the company.[29]

It should be noted that an examiner may not be appointed when a receiver stands appointed for more than three business days.[30] Furthermore, a receiver cannot be appointed if an examiner is already in place.[31]

5. Employees

The position of employees varies depending on the status of the receiver. At common law, the appointment of a receiver by the court operates to dismiss the employees automatically. However, the receiver may re-engage some or all of the employees if he considers it necessary. Where a receiver is appointed under a debenture there is no automatic dismissal and the position of employees will usually be a matter for the receiver. Where the debenture provides that the receiver is to be the agent of the company, all contracts of employment will usually remain in force. This is necessary in order to save the debenture holder the costs of redundancy payments which, as preferential payments, must be paid before the floating charge holder. However, there is nothing to prevent a receiver from dismissing employees where he considers it necessary, for example where the assets of the company are being sold on a piecemeal basis. Where the receiver decides to lay off workers, he is obliged to comply with many of the statutory requirements relating to labour law.[32]

6. Publicity

As soon as the receiver is appointed, the person who appointed him must, within seven days of the appointment, publish in the *CRO Gazette*, and in at least one

---

29 Section 6 of the Companies (Amendment) Act 1990.
30 Section 3(6) of the Companies (Amendment) Act 1990.
31 Section 5(2)(b) of the Companies (Amendment) Act 1990.
32 *Bolands Ltd (in receivership) v. Ward & Others* [1988] ILRM 382.

daily newspaper circulating in the district where the registered office of the company is situated, notice of his appointment.[33] Notice of his appointment must also be sent to the registrar of companies in the prescribed form.

Functions and Duties of a Receiver

The primary function of the receiver is to receive and realise the assets which are the subject of the security for the purpose of discharging the debt owed to the debenture holder together with the receiver's own expenses. If the receiver is able to discharge these debts, he vacates his office and the directors resume full control. The general responsibility of the receiver is to the debenture holder rather than to the company, even if he is formally an agent of the company. However, in carrying out his function the receiver may be under a duty to the company and those who may be affected by his actions, such as the company's guarantors. These duties are considered under the following headings:

1. to exercise care in disposing of company property;
2. to apply the proceeds of sale in the manner fixed by law;
3. to satisfy the notification requirements laid down in the Principal Act;
4. report any misconduct; and
5. to co-operate with the Director of Corporate Environment.

1. To Exercise Care in Disposing of the Company's Assets

It has been established by a long line of case-law that a receiver must exercise all reasonable care to obtain the best possible price for assets which are realised.[34] Provided he acts *bona fide* without negligence in the proper exercise of his powers, the company cannot recover compensation from him for his actions, even though those actions may not be in its long-term interests. However, if he acts negligently or on the improper instructions of the debenture holder he may be held personally liable.

This duty to obtain the best price possible for company assets is owed not only to the company but also to third parties, such as guarantors, who may be affected by the receiver's actions. In *American Express International Banking v. Hurley*,[35] the company's liability to the bank was secured by a charge over equipment and by a personal guarantee of Hurley, a director of the company. The equipment had been independently valued at £193,000. When the bank appointed a receiver, he sold the equipment for £34,500. The bank then sued

---

33 Section 107 of the Principal Act.
34 *McGowan v. Gannon* [1983] 1LRM 516, *Holohan v. Friends Provident and Century Life Office* [1966] IR 1, *Casey v. Irish Intercontinental Bank* [1979] IR 364 and *Standard Chartered Bank v. Walker* [1982] 3 All ER 938.
35 [1986] BCLC 52.

Hurley, on foot of his guarantee, for the balance of the company's liability. Hurley claimed that both the receiver and the bank as his principal were negligent in selling the equipment at an undervalue. The court held that the receiver owed a duty to Hurley to take reasonable care to realise the true value of the asset. Because the asset was sold at an undervalue, the receiver was in breach of his duty and was accordingly negligent.

The duty of the receiver to act without negligence was placed on a statutory footing by section 172 of the 1990 Act, which inserted a new section 316A into the Principal Act. This section provides that a receiver must, in selling the company's property, exercise reasonable care to obtain the best price reasonably obtainable for the property at the time of the sale. In determining the 'best price' the court is not concerned with perceived value. In *Re Bula Ltd*[36] a receiver was appointed by lender banks on foot of debentures, one of which was secured by a mortgage over certain lands, which included a mine. The receiver sought to dispose of the mine and retained international consultants to advise in this regard. Following advertisements, several parties expressed interest and discussions ensued. Only one offer materialised from these discussions and this consisted of an offer of £27.5 million by Tara Mines Ltd, a neighbouring mining company. The consultant advisers recommended that the sale proceed and the lending banks and shareholders also approved the sale. The receiver applied to the court pursuant to section 316A of the Principal Act for an order approving the sale of the lands and mine. The company, together with two of its directors, who were also guarantors of the company's indebtedness, opposed the application. They argued, *inter alia*, that the proposed sale was at a gross undervalue. They contended that the property, given its ore deposits and mineral reserves, was worth substantially more to the proposed buyer, which was a neighbouring mining company. The court accepted that the value to the proposed purchaser would be far greater than the value to any other potential bidders. However, the court held that the receiver's obligation under section 316(A) related to obtaining the 'best price' and the value to the purchaser was immaterial. As Murphy J. stated:

> Section 316A refers not to value nor cost but to price. The receiver, in selling the property of the company, which he is clearly entitled to do, must exercise all reasonable care to obtain the best price reasonably obtainable for the property at the time of sale.

On the basis that there was only one offer the court was satisfied that the receiver had obtained that best possible price and an order for the sale of the property was approved.

Section 316A does not impose an obligation on the receiver to delay a sale in order to receive a better price, presumably because it is probably impossible to

---

36 *Re Bula Ltd* [2002] 2 ILRM 513.

determine with foresight when would be the best time to sell. Indeed, both UK and Irish authorities have accepted that a receiver, in accepting the best price at the time of sale, is not obliged to delay for subsequent offers.[37]

In *Casey v. Irish Intercontinental Bank Ltd*,[38] an offer for assets, the subject matter of a floating charge, had been accepted by the mortgagee who considered that it was the best available price. After the contract for sale was completed, a further offer of a higher amount was made but rejected because of the original contract. An application was made to the court to have the original contract rescinded on the grounds that it did not obtain the best possible price. The Supreme Court rejected the application on the basis that a mortgagee who enters a contract for sale is only obliged to obtain the best price which all the circumstances and valuations show to be the best possible price at the date of the contract. That duty is discharged even where a higher price is offered at some time after the sale. However, where the mortgagee fails to consider alternative options available at the time, he will be in breach of his duty. In *Holohan v. Friends Provident and Century Life Office*,[39] the mortgagor successfully obtained an injunction restraining the mortgagee from selling a property without vacant possession, when he could have sold it for a higher price on the basis of vacant possession.

A receiver does not fulfil his statutory obligation to obtain the best possible price merely because he disposes of property at an auction. In *Tse Kwong Lam v. Wong Chit Sen*[40] a receiver was held liable to the mortgagor for disposing of the property to a sole bidder at an auction who also happened to be a major shareholder of the company. The court rejected the contention that a sale at a publicly advertised auction necessarily produces the best possible price. If a receiver has any doubt about the best price obtainable he should obtain an independent expert's opinion.[41] Indeed, the receiver may always apply to the court for directions in relation to any matter in connection with the performance of his duties.[42]

Where the receiver acts in breach of his obligations under section 316A, it will not be a defence to claim that he was acting as agent for the company.[43] Furthermore, where the receiver is in breach of his duty, he is not entitled to be indemnified by the company for any liability which may arise.[44] However, if a

---

37 *Bank of Cyprus (London) Ltd. v. Gill* [1980] 2 Lloyd's Reports 51; *Re Edenfell Holdings Ltd* [1999] 1 IR 443.
38 [1979] IR 364.
39 [1966] IR 1.
40 [1983] 1 WLR 1349.
41 See *Lambert Jones Estates Ltd v. Donnelly*, Unreported, High Court, O'Hanlon J., November 5, 1982.
42 Section 316 of the Principal Act as amended by section 171 of the 1990 Act .
43 Section 316A(2)(a) of the Principal Act.
44 Section 316A(2)(b) of the Principal Act.

receiver acts in breach of section 316A, a bona fide purchaser for value of such property obtains a good title to it.[45]

The duty of care owed by a receiver to the company is generally limited to the duty to obtain the best price available when disposing of assets. Even when a receiver is appointed as a receiver-manager, the duty of care does not extend to a duty to keep the company apprised of how the business of the company is going. In *Irish Oil and Cake Mills Ltd v. Donnelly*,[46] the company applied for a mandatory injunction ordering the receiver-manager to furnish accounts and information to the company. The company claimed, *inter alia*, that the receiver-manager owed a duty of care to the company and that this duty included the giving of such information. The court rejected the contention that the duty of care owed to the company to obtain the best possible price included a duty that a receiver is also obliged to furnish information concerning his trading activities. However, Costello J. suggested that each case would turn on its own facts and that in certain circumstances the receiver may be obliged to account to the company whose affairs he is managing.[47]

Although the receiver may be obliged to provide information to the company regarding the sale of the company's assets, this obligation does not appear to extend to providing such information to other parties including those who may be personally affected by the receiver's decision. This was made clear in *McGowan v. Gannon*,[48] where it was held that the receiver does not owe a duty to provide information to a guarantor of the company's debts.

The 1990 Act also introduced a new provision relating to the disposal of certain assets by the receiver. Where a receiver proposes to sell by private contract a 'non-cash' asset [49] of the company to anyone who is, or was in the three years prior to the date of the receiver's appointment, an officer of the company, he must give at least fourteen days' notice of his intention to do so to all the creditors of the company who are known to him.[50]

2. To Apply the Proceeds of Sale in the Manner Fixed by Law

The receiver is primarily concerned with discharging the debts owed to the debenture holder. Where he obtains a surplus to those requirements he will pay those amounts to the company. However, where a receiver is appointed by a debenture holder and realises assets subject to a floating charge, section 98 of the

---

45 *Re Ruby Property Co. Ltd et al. v Kilty & Another,* Unreported, McCracken J., December 11, 1995.
46 High Court, 27 March 1983.
47 High Court, 27 March 1983 at 13 citing with approval *Smiths Ltd v. Middleton* [1979] 3 All ER 942.
48 [1983] ILRM 516.
49 Defined as one not less than £1,000 (€1,270) in value, but that exceeds either £50,000 (€63,487) in value or 10 per cent of the company's net assets (section 29 of the 1990 Act).
50 Section 316A(3)(a) of the Principal Act.

Principal Act requires him to pay all preferential creditors before applying the proceeds to discharge the debts owed to the debenture holder.[51]

Section 98 has no application if a company is in the course of being wound up. However, the obligation to pay the preferential creditors continues if a liquidator is subsequently appointed before the receiver has complied with section 98. In *Re Eisc Teoranta*[52] a receiver had been appointed under a debenture, which was secured by a fixed charge over certain assets and a floating charge over other assets. The receiver realised all the assets charged and discharged the debts owing under the debenture out of the proceeds of the fixed charge. He was left in possession of the proceeds of the floating charge. Before he could apply those proceeds in payment of the preferential creditors, a liquidator was appointed. The liquidator requested that the receiver deliver the amounts realised under the floating charge. The receiver refused to comply with this request on the basis that he was under a statutory duty, by virtue of section 98, to discharge the preferential creditors out of the proceeds of the sale of the assets subject to the floating charge. The liquidator argued that section 98 did not apply once a liquidator was appointed. It was also argued that as no part of the assets subject to the floating charge had been used to discharge monies owed under the debenture, section 98 did not come into effect. Furthermore, once the surplus assets had been paid to the liquidator, section 285 of the Principal Act would apply, which gives priority to the preferential creditors in a liquidation. In reply to these arguments Lardner J. held as follows:

(a) the receiver's statutory duty to pay the preferential creditors out of the proceeds of the sale of assets subject to the floating charge was not terminated by the subsequent appointment of a liquidator;
(b) section 98 applied to a receiver once a claim for principal and interest had been made under a debenture – this claim existed at the time the receiver was appointed and it was irrelevant that the proceeds of the floating charge were surplus to requirements; and
(c) the fact that the preferential creditors would obtain a priority whether under section 98 or section 285 cannot be a factor in determining the statutory duty of a receiver.

The decision in *Re Eisc Teoranta* was approved in the High Court case of *Re Manning Furniture Ltd*.[53] Here the company had executed a debenture which was secured by a floating charge and other chattel mortgages in favour of ICC Bank plc. It had subsequently executed a legal charge in favour of the First National Building Society. A receiver was appointed and he discharged the bank's debt

---

51 For order of application of assets, see Chapter 26.
52 [1991] ILRM 760.
53 [1996] I ILRM 13.

from the proceeds of the sale of the assets subject to the chattel mortgages. However, he also took into his possession the assets which were subject to the floating charge, which gave him a surplus of £150,000. The receiver applied to the High Court for directions as to whether he was obliged to discharge the claims of the preferential creditors out of these surplus funds before paying the balance to the building society. The building society argued that the priority given by section 98 applied only in respect of debts due under the debenture and as no part of the assets which were subject to the floating charge were used in discharge of monies owed under the debenture, section 98 had no application. McCracken J. rejected this contention and held that the receiver must pay the preferential creditors out of any assets coming into his hands, irrespective of the fact that the proceeds of the floating charge were not used to discharge monies due under the debenture.

However, where a receiver does not realise or take into his possession the assets which are the subject of a floating charge and instead only realises the assets subject to a fixed charge it would seem that he is not obliged to pay the preferential creditors under section 98. In *United Bars Ltd v. Revenue Commissioners*[54] the receiver was appointed on foot of a debenture secured *inter alia* by a fixed and floating charge over certain of the company's assets. The receiver, having discharged the debenture holder's debt from the proceeds of assets which were subject to a fixed charge only, was left with a surplus. The question arose as to whether the receiver was obliged to pay that surplus to the preferential creditors or to the company. Murphy J., citing with approval the UK line of authority in this regard,[55] held that section 98 only applied to accounts coming into the hands of the receiver which were subject to a floating charge and not to assets which were the subject of a fixed charge. In his opinion, to interpret section 98 in such a way that the proceeds of the sale of assets subject to a fixed charge were to be made available to the preferential creditors, would confer on these creditors an unwarranted entitlement that they would not have in the event of a liquidation.[56] The court may make an order that section 98 should not apply if an examiner has been or may be appointed to the company. The court will not make such an order unless it would be likely to facilitate the survival of the company and the whole, or any part, of its undertaking as a going concern.[57]

3. Notification Requirements

Within two months from the receipt of the statement of affairs the receiver must send a copy of it, and any comments which he cares to make thereon, to:

---

54 [1991] 1 IR 396.
55 *Re GL Saunders Ltd (in liquidation)* [1986] 1 WLR 215 and *Re Lewis Merthyr Consolidated Collieries* [1939] 1 Ch 498.
56 [1991] 1 IR at 400.
57 Section 6A(1) of the 1990 Amendment Act.

(a) the registrar of companies;
(b) the company itself;
(c) the debenture holders or the trustees for the debenture holders;
(d) the court, where he is appointed by the court.[58]

Where a receiver of the whole, or substantially the whole, of the property of a company is appointed, he must also deliver to the registrar of companies the following information:

(a) an abstract showing the assets of the company of which he has taken possession since his appointment and their estimated value;
(b) the proceeds of sale of any such assets since his appointment;
(c) his receipts and payment during the period of six months from the date of his appointment; and
(d) an abstract at the end of every subsequent period of six months during which he continues to act as receiver.[59]

Where the receiver ceases to act as receiver of the property, the abstract shall be accompanied by a statement from the receiver declaring his opinion as to whether or not the company is solvent. The registrar shall, on receiving the statement, forward a copy of it to the Director of Corporate Enforcement.

4. To Report Misconduct

If it appears to a receiver that any past or present officer or member of the company has been guilty of an offence in relation to the company, he must report the matter to the DPP together with any information relating to the matter.[60] Where a receiver refers such a matter to the Director of Public Prosecutions, he must also furnish the same particulars to the Director of Corporate Enforcement. Where the DPP or Director considers that the case is one where a prosecution ought to be instituted, the receiver must give any assistance in connection with the prosecution that he is reasonably able to give. If the receiver fails to comply with his obligation to notify and furnish particulars to the DPP the court may direct that he does so.[61]

5. To Co-operate with the Director of Corporate Enforcement

The Director may, where he considers it necessary, request the production of a receiver's books for examination either in regard to a particular receivership or

---

58 Section 319 of the Principal Act.
59 Section 321 of the Principal Act.
60 Section 299 (2) of the Principal Act and section 179 of the Companies Act 1990.
61 Section 299(5) of the Principal Act.

to all receiverships undertaken by the receiver. The receiver must furnish such books, answer any questions concerning the content of the books and the conduct of a particular receivership, and give all assistance as the receiver is reasonably able to give. If the receiver defaults in complying with this statutory duty he is guilty of an offence.[62]

Receiver's Powers

Where a receiver is appointed by the court, his authority is vested in him by the court. A person who attempts to obstruct the receiver in the exercise of his powers may be held in contempt of court. Where a receiver is appointed by the debenture holder his powers are contractually determined by the terms of the debenture. Where the debenture is secured by a fixed and floating charge over the entire assets and undertaking of the company, it is usual to confer on the receiver the power to carry on the business of the company. Although such a receiver-manager has the power to manage the business of the company, it should be noted that these powers are conferred on him for the sole purpose of realising the security and not for rescuing the company. As Richardson J. observed in *First City Corporation Ltd v. Downsview Nominees Ltd*:

> While in practice receiverships are sometimes used to achieve a moratorium and rehabilitation of the company's business, that is legitimate only where it is an incident of the receiver's proper role. The receiver is there to enforce the security and only for that purpose to trade. He is not a white knight.[63]

The debenture will usually confer on the receiver many of the powers of the board of directors including, *inter alia*:

(a) the power to dispose of the company's assets and do such things as are incidental to that power;
(b) the power to carry on the business of the company;
(c) the power to borrow money and give security where necessary;
(d) the power to institute proceedings on behalf of the company.

It has already been noted that where a receiver is unsure about the exercise of a particular power, he may apply to the court for directions.[64] Furthermore, where a receiver is appointed by the debenture holder, section 316(1) of the Principal Act permits the following persons to apply to the court for directions as to the exercise of the receiver's powers:

(a) an officer of the company;
(b) a member of the company;

---

62 Section 323A of the Principal Act.
63 [1990] 3 NZLR 265.
64 Section 316(1) of the Principal Act.

(c) employees comprising at least half of those persons employed in a full-time capacity;

(d) a liquidator; and

(e) any contributory.

Receiver's Liability

Before a receiver is appointed he should ensure that the charge appointing him is valid.[65] If the charge is invalid, the receiver's appointment will be invalid and he will be liable in respect of any acts or omissions. However, the court may relieve him from such liability provided his acts or omissions would have been within his power if the debenture had been valid.[66] Where such relief is granted the court will hold the debenture holder liable for everything for which, but for the grant of relief, the receiver would have been liable.

The receiver is personally liable on contacts entered into on behalf of the company unless the contract provides otherwise. However, he has a right of indemnity against the company in respect of any liability which he incurs.[67] Where a receiver is conferred with management powers under a charge over the entire assets and undertaking of the company, he may transfer the business to a new company of which he becomes managing director rather than a receiver. This practice, called 'hiving-down', is a common means of avoiding personal liability. However, the receiver may be bound by the previous contracts of employment of the company's employees.[68]

The receiver is not personally liable on any other contracts entered into by the company prior to his appointment.[69] In *Ardmore Studios (Ireland) Ltd v. Lynch*,[70] a receiver was held not bound to an agreement entered into between the company and a trade union prior to his appointment. In respect of pre-appointment contracts, the receiver may repudiate them or agree to perform them. In *Re Thames Ironworks Co. Ltd*,[71] the receiver, on his appointment, discovered that the company had partly built ships which were to be completed before delivery. The contracts were unprofitable and the company was not in a financial position to complete them. The court gave leave to the receiver to repudiate the contracts. In

65 A charge may be invalid for lack of registration under section 99 of the Principal Act. Similarly, a charge may be avoided in a liquidation as a fraudulent preference under section 288 of the Principal Act. A floating charge may be invalidated under section 286 of the Principal Act during a liquidation.
66 Section 316(3) of the Principal Act.
67 Section 316 of the Principal Act.
68 European Communities (Protection of Employees on Transfer of Undertakings) Regulations 2003.
69 *Re Johnson & Co. (Builders) Ltd* [1955] 2 All ER 775.
70 [1965] IR 1.
71 [1912] WN 66.

rescinding a contract the receiver must exercise his powers *bona fide* and must not, without leave of the court, repudiate a contract in such a manner that it will have the effect of destroying the goodwill of the company's business.[72]

In exercising his right to dispose of assets, the receiver must be certain that the company actually owns the assets which are in its possession. It is often the case that many of the non-fixed assets of the company are subject to retention of title clauses. The effect of these clauses is that while assets are in the possession of the company, their ownership or title has been retained by the person that supplied them.[73] If a receiver sells assets that are owned by someone else he may be liable for the tort of conversion, and will in any case be obliged to account to the true owner.

---

72 *Re Newdigate Colliery* (1912) 1 Ch 468.
73 *Aluminium Industrie Vaasen BV v. Romalpa Aluminium Ltd* [1976] 2 All ER 552.

CHAPTER TWENTY-FIVE

THE LIQUIDATION PROCESS

Introduction

Liquidation is a winding-up process that ultimately leads to the demise of the company as its property is distributed for the benefit of its creditors and members. The liquidation process was summarised as follows:

> Once a winding-up order is made, the company is doomed to extinction. The winding-up process is the process of the administration of the assets of the company: their collection, realisation and distribution in discharge of the liabilities of the company to the creditors and of the entitlement of its contributories in accordance with the scheme of priorities in the Companies Acts.[1]

However, the life of the company is not formally terminated until either the company has been struck off the register by the registrar of companies or the court has dissolved it under section 249 of the Principal Act.[2] Until such time the corporate personality of the company remains intact. It should be noted that a liquidator cannot be appointed where an examiner stands appointed under the Companies (Amendment) Act 1990.[3]

Qualifications of a Liquidator

A liquidator is the person appointed to wind up the company. Although the Companies Acts do not prescribe specific qualifications for the position of liquidator, the following are prohibited from so acting:

(a) a body corporate;
(b) any person who is, or has been, an officer, servant or auditor of the company within the previous twelve months;
(c) any connected person, unless the court otherwise agrees;
(d) any partner of an officer or servant of the company;
(e) any person who has the above connections to any subsidiary of the company, the holding company and any subsidiary of the holding company;
(f) any person restricted or disqualified under the provisions of the 1990 Companies Act.[4]

---

1 *Per* Laffoy J. in *Re Greendale Developments Ltd* [1997] 3 IR 540 at 547.
2 See Chapter 2.
3 See Chapter 27.
4 Section 300 and 300A of the Principal Act.

Duties of a Liquidator

Once a liquidator is appointed he becomes a fiduciary and owes a fiduciary duty to the company. Accordingly he must act in good faith and not make any secret profits. His principal statutory duties can be summarised as follows:

(a) to take possession of the company's assets (including debtors) and to protect these assets.[5] In this regard the liquidator is given a number of powers to prevent the dissipation of company assets or to ensure their return;[6]

(b) to arrange a list of creditors and contributories[7] and to resolve all disputed claims. Where necessary the liquidator may request the court to adjudicate on any disputed claims;

(c) to realise the assets of the company and to apply the proceeds in payment of the company's debts and liabilities in accordance with the rules governing the priorities of payments;

(d) to distribute the surplus, if any, among the shareholders in accordance with the provisions of the Companies Acts and the company's own articles of association;

(e) to investigate the conduct of the company's affairs;

(f) to fulfil the various filing and notification requirements required by the Companies Acts;

(g) in the case of a compulsory winding up, to comply with any court direction to bring certain matters to the attention of the DPP or, in a voluntary winding up, to bring matters directly to the DPP;

(h) to provide to the Director of Corporate Enforcement (the Director) a report on matters relating to the liquidation in the event that the company is insolvent;[8]

(i) to apply to the court for a restriction order under section 150 of the 1990 Act against every director of an insolvent company, unless the Director relieves the liquidator of such an obligation;[9] and

(j) to communicate and co-operate with liquidators appointed in other EU jurisdictions where their appointment has an effect on the Irish company.[10]

Many of the duties relating to asset realisation and distribution are discussed further in the next chapter.

---

5 Section 229 of the Principal Act.

6 These powers are discussed later in this chapter and in Chapter 26.

7 A contributory is any person liable to contribute to the assets of the company in the event of its being wound up: section 208 of the Principal Act.

8 Section 56(1) of the 2001 Act. See Chapter 19.

9 Section 56(2) of the 2001 Act.

10 Article 31 of the Insolvency Regulation (Council Regulation (EC) 1346/2000) implemented in Ireland by SI 2002/333.

Types of Liquidation

There are essentially two types of liquidation — a voluntary winding up and a compulsory winding up. The objective of both is the same, namely the realisation and distribution of the company's assets. However, there are fundamental differences between the two types, the most notable being that the court has little or no role to play in a voluntary liquidation, whereas a compulsory liquidation is carried out by the court itself, which appoints an official liquidator to act on its behalf. Both types of liquidation are now considered further.

Compulsory Liquidations

A compulsory liquidation begins with the presentation of a petition to the High Court. Section 215 of the Principal Act provides that any of the following may present such a petition.

(a) The company — an authorising resolution must be approved by the shareholders. A general resolution will suffice if the company is insolvent; otherwise a special resolution is required.
(b) A creditor — this category also includes contingent or prospective creditors who must establish to the satisfaction of the court a *prima facie* case and provide such security for costs as the court may direct.
(c) A contributory — this category of applicant can only present a petition in certain circumstances, viz. where the number of members is reduced below the legal minimum or the contributory has been a registered member of the company or has held shares that have devolved through the death of a shareholder, for at least six months in the previous eighteen months.
(d) Any person entitled to bring an action under section 205 of the Principal Act.
(e) The Director on foot of a report by an inspector appointed by either the court or the Director.[11]

Other parties may also petition the court to have the company wound up,[12] and the court itself may make an order to wind up the company in certain circumstances.[13]

1. The Grounds for Presenting the Petition

The grounds for presenting a petition are specified in section 213 of the Principal Act and include the following:

---

11 Sections 8 and 14 of the 1990 Act.
12 Including the registrar of companies and a company receiver.
13 The court may order the winding up of a company without being requested to do so following a report by an inspector appointed under the 1990 Act or by an examiner appointed under the Companies (Amendment) Act 1990.

(a) the company has by special resolution resolved that the company be wound up by the court;
(b) the company does not commence its business within a year from its incorporation or suspends its business for a whole year;
(c) the number of members is reduced below the legal requirement for a company of its type;[14]
(d) the company is unable to pay its debts;
(e) the court is of the opinion that it is just and equitable to wind up the company;
(f) the court is satisfied that the company's affairs are being conducted, or the powers of the directors are being exercised, in a manner oppressive to any member or in disregard of his interests as a member, and that despite the existence of an alternative remedy, the circumstances warrant the winding up of the company.

The last three grounds have been the subject of most petitions, and are considered further below.

The Company Is Unable to Pay Its Debts

Section 214 of the Principal Act deems a company to have been unable to pay its debts if any of the following circumstances exist.

(a) A creditor is indebted in a sum exceeding £1,000 (€1,269) and that amount is unpaid after three weeks from the time a demand in writing has been made to the company. It should be observed that a creditor may not use the petition as a debt-collecting process, nor will the petition be successful if the claim against the company is *bona fide* disputed on reasonable grounds. This was made clear in *Re Pageboy Couriers Ltd*,[15] where the court rejected a petition because the petitioner's claim for unpaid director's fees was vehemently disputed by the company. The court accepted the view that until a person is established as a creditor he has no *locus standi* to present the petition, and to use the procedure as a means of deciding a disputed debt is an abuse of the court process.[16]
(b) An execution or other process issued on a judgment, decree or order of any court in favour of a creditor is unsatisfied. When the petitioner is relying on this ground he must be careful that a genuine attempt was made to obtain satisfaction of the judgment.[17]

---

14 Regulation 11 of the European Communities (Single-Member Private Limited Companies) Regulations 1994 (SI 275/1994) removes private companies limited by shares or by guarantee from the ambit of this subsection.
15 [1983] ILRM 510.
16 See also *Truck and Machinery Sales Limited v. Marubeni Komatzo Limited* [1996] 1 IR 12; *Coalport Building Co Ltd v. Castle Contracts (Ireland) Ltd*, Unreported, High Court, Laffoy J., January 19, 2004.
17 In *Re a Debtor* (No. 340 of 1992) [1994] 2 BCLC 171.

(c) It is proved to the satisfaction of the court that the company is unable to pay its debts and the court in its determinations has taken into account the contingent and prospective liabilities of the company. In this instance the creditor must demonstrate either that the company is unable to pay its debts as they fall due (the commercial insolvency test) or that the company's assets are less than its liabilities (the balance sheet insolvency test). If a creditor cannot satisfy either of these tests, any other evidence of actual or prospective insolvency may be produced.

The Just and Equitable Ground

The legislative provisions do not prescribe any preconditions that must be fulfilled before this ground can be invoked. The courts are loath to set any guidelines in this regard because to do so would have the effect of limiting their broad discretionary power. However, it is clear that the petitioner, to invoke the remedy, must come to court with clean hands.[18] Although each case will turn on its own facts, the following are examples of the circumstances in which the court has wound up a company on this ground.

(a) The Substratum of the Company has Failed

A company is used as a vehicle for obtaining certain objectives. Once these are achieved, and the *raison d'être* no longer exists, the company is usually liquidated voluntarily. Where the objectives have not or cannot be achieved and the company is not voluntarily liquidated it is open to an applicant, who will usually be a shareholder, to petition the court for the winding up of that company on the just and equitable ground. In *Re German Date Coffee Co.*,[19] the company had been formed for the sole purpose of manufacturing coffee from dates under a German patent. When this patent proved impossible to obtain, the company manufactured under a Swedish patent. A contributory successfully petitioned for a winding up order because the sole purpose of the company could not be achieved. It is important to note that where a company has several objects, failure to achieve one will not be a sufficient ground for a petition of this type. In *Re Metafile Ltd*[20] the company was incorporated with a broad range of objects but in practice it owned a factory premises which were used by a related company to conduct its business. The related company was wound up, the factory premises were sold by the company and the petitioner, a contributory of the company, petitioned that the company be wound up on the ground that there had been a failure of substratum. The company resisted the petition on the basis that the company wished to continue to trade with a view to initiating litigation against

---

18 *Re Vehicle Buildings and Insulations Ltd* [1986] ILRM 239.
19 [1882] 2 Ch D 169.
20 Unreported, High Court, Laffoy J., December 20, 2006.

the petitioner. The company acknowledged that it had not yet decided how it would proceed with the benefit of the proceeds of sale of the company's factory premises. The court held that the company was still empowered by the memorandum to carry out a number of businesses and that as the company had never indicated that it intended winding up after the sale of its main asset it was conceivable that it would trade again. Accordingly the court refused to wind up the company on the grounds that the substratum had failed.

(b) The Company was Formed for an Illegal or Fraudulent Purpose

A company cannot be formed to achieve an illegal purpose. In the unlikely event of such a company being registered, a petition for its winding up could be presented on the just and equitable ground. The same would apply where a company was set up for reasons which, although not illegal, were motivated by fraud. In *Re Shrinkpak Ltd*[21] a liquidator succeeded in having a company wound up on the ground that it was being used for the fraudulent purpose of diverting funds from another insolvent company.

(c) Deadlock in Management

Where it appears to the court that the relationship between the shareholders and directors has irretrievably broken down, it may order the winding up of a company, however profitable it appears to be. Such was the case in *Re Yenidje Tobacco Co.*,[22] where two sole traders had merged their businesses to form a company, of which they were the only shareholders and directors. The relationship between the two subsequently broke down and communications were non-existent except through the medium of the company secretary. Despite the fact that the company was successful, it was held that a winding up was justified. Similarly, in *Re Vehicle Buildings and Insulations Ltd*[23] a petition to wind up the company was presented on the grounds that it was just and equitable so to do. The petitioner and Mr H. were the only shareholders and directors of the company, each holding 50 per cent of the issued share capital. The petitioner alleged, *inter alia*, that there was a state of deadlock in the management of the business of the company and that it would be just and equitable to wind up the company. It was evident from the facts that a rift had developed between the parties. Both made allegations of serious wrongdoing against each other. Murphy J. found that there was no way in which such wrongdoings could be substantiated at a hearing to wind up the company. Nonetheless he was satisfied that irrespective of whether there was in fact any wrongdoing, the fact was that the shareholders/directors could not legally or practically administer the company without the co-operation of each other and that in practice neither party was able

---

21 Unreported, High Court, Barron J., December 20, 1989.
22 [1916] 2 Ch 426.
23 [1986] ILRM 239.

or willing to co-operate with the other. As the majority of creditors also supported the application to wind up the company he considered it an appropriate case in which to make an order for the winding up of the company on the grounds that it was just and equitable so to do.

(d) The 'Quasi-partnership' Relationship has Failed

Where the company is being operated in a manner similar to a partnership, and the relationship of trust and mutual confidence has broken down, the court may also make an order to wind up the company on the just and equitable ground. In *Re Murph's Restaurant Ltd*[24] the court made such an order when the relationship between the founding shareholders/directors had collapsed (see Chapter 15).

The Oppression of Minority Shareholders

Where the company's affairs are being conducted or the director's powers are being exercised in a manner oppressive to the applicant or to any other member, he can apply to court for an order under section 205 of the Principal Act, which deals with oppression of shareholders. Alternatively, a shareholder can apply under section 213(g) of the Principal Act for an order that the company be wound up. The court will usually only grant an order of this type where no other remedies are appropriate. This area of the law is considered in greater detail in Chapter 15.

2. The Hearing

When considering a petition the court may consider the views of other parties, particularly creditors.[25] At any time after the petition has been presented and before a winding up order has been made the court may, on the application of the company or any creditor or contributory, stay or restrain proceedings pending against the company.[26]

The court may also make an interim order appointing a provisional liquidator whose powers will be determined by the court.[27] A provisional liquidator will usually be appointed where it is necessary to protect the rights and interests of the company and its creditors. Once a provisional liquidator has been appointed, no action or proceeding can be taken against the company without the leave of the court.[28] The initial role of the provisional liquidator mirrors that of an official liquidator in that he must take into his custody or under his control all the property and things in action of which the company is or appears to be entitled.[29]

---

24 [1979] ILRM 141. See also *Re Westbourne Galleries* [1973] AC 360.
25 *Re R.W. Sharman* [1957] 1 All ER 737, *Re Bula Mines Limited*, Unreported, High Court, Costello J., July 18, 1986 and Supreme Court May 13, 1988.
26 Section 217 of the Principal Act.
27 Section 226 of the Principal Act.
28 Section 222 of the Principal Act.
29 Section 229 of the Principal Act.

Having heard the petition the court may dismiss it, adjourn it or make any other order as it sees fit, including a winding up order. A winding up order, if made, operates in favour of all the creditors and of all the contributories of the company in the same manner as if they had presented a joint petition.[30]

3. Notification and Filing Requirements

A copy of the winding up order must be delivered by the company, or by such other person as the court may direct, to the registrar of companies within twenty-one days.[31] The liquidator must also cause to have published in the *CRO Gazette* a notice of his appointment and deliver to the registrar of companies a copy of the court order appointing him.[32] The directors and secretary of the company, or such other person as the court may direct, must also, unless otherwise agreed by the court, file a statement of affairs of the company with the court. The statement must be filed within twenty-one days of the appointment of a provisional liquidator or the making of a winding up order, or such longer period as the court may agree.[33] Where any person defaults in complying with this requirement he shall be guilty of an offence and liable to a fine. The statement of affairs must be presented in the prescribed form, be verified by affidavit and show the following particulars:

(a) the company's assets, debts and liabilities;
(b) the names, residences and occupations of its creditors and the securities held by them respectively;
(c) the dates when the securities were respectively given; and
(d) such other information as may be prescribed or as the court may require.

4. Effect of the Winding Up Order

Once the court makes the order to wind up the company, the following takes effect:

(a) An official liquidator is appointed to wind up the company. The official liquidator shall receive such salary or remuneration as the court may direct.[34] The acts of the liquidator will be valid notwithstanding any defect later discovered in his appointment.[35]
(b) The order will take effect from the date the petition is presented. If a voluntary liquidation was already under way, the order takes effect from the date the authorising resolution for the voluntary liquidation was passed.[36]

---

30 Section 223 of the Principal Act.
31 Section 221 of the Principal Act.
32 Section 227(1) of the Principal Act.
33 Section 224 of the Principal Act.
34 Section 228(d) of the Principal Act.
35 Section 228(g) of the Principal Act.
36 Section 220 of the Principal Act. The significance of this is considered further in the next chapter.

(c) No proceedings may be continued or instituted against the company without the consent of the court.[37]

(d) Any disposition of the company's property and any transfer of its shares subsequent to the commencement of liquidation are void unless the court otherwise directs.[38]

(e) Any attachment, sequestration, distress or execution put in force against the property of the company after the commencement of the winding up shall be void.[39]

(f) Every invoice, business letter and order for goods which bears the name of the company must state that the company is in liquidation.[40]

(g) The employees of the company are automatically dismissed, but the liquidator may re-hire them if he so wishes.

(h) The directors' powers are assumed by the liquidator.

(i) Any floating charges crystallise.

(j) If a receiver has already been appointed he can no longer bind the company as its agent.

5. *Committee of Inspection*

If the court so orders, the liquidator shall summon a meeting of the creditors and contributories to decide whether or not to apply to the court for the appointment of a committee of inspection to assist him in carrying on the business.[41] The committee of inspection will be composed of creditors and contributories in such proportions as they agree or, failing agreement, in such proportion as the court will decide. The committee will meet on its own initiative or when called upon to do so by the liquidator. Decisions are made by a majority of the committee members, but the members cannot make a decision unless a majority is present at the meeting. A member of the committee of inspection may resign by notice to the liquidator and in specified circumstances his office becomes vacant.[42] Furthermore, a member of the committee may be removed by an ordinary resolution of the creditors or contributories, depending on which category he represents.

6. *Powers of the Liquidator in a Compulsory Liquidation*

Once appointed, the liquidator is obliged to take under his control all the property and things in action to which the liquidator is or appears to be entitled.[43] The court may also direct that the company's property shall vest in the liquidator by his

---

37 Section 222 of the Principal Act.
38 Section 218 of the Principal Act.
39 Section 219 of the Principal Act.
40 Section 303 of the Principal Act.
41 Section 232 of the Principal Act.
42 If a member becomes bankrupt or makes an arrangement with his creditors or is absent from five consecutive meetings of the committee without consent.
43 Section 229 of the Principal Act.

official name.[44] In order to fulfil his duties, section 231 of the Principal Act confers on the liquidator a number of powers, some exercisable at his discretion and others qualified in that they can only be exercised with the sanction of the court or the committee of inspection. The general powers of the liquidator are as follows:

(a) to sell any of the company's property — the liquidator shall not sell by private contract a non-cash asset to anyone who is, or was, in the three years prior to the date of the liquidator's appointment, an officer of the company, unless he has given at least fourteen days' notice of his intention to do so to all the creditors of the company;

(b) to execute all necessary documents on the company's behalf;

(c) to prove in bankruptcy against any contributory;

(d) to draw, accept, make and endorse any bill of exchange or promissory note on behalf of the company;

(e) to mortgage the company's assets;

(f) to take out letters of administration on any deceased contributory for the purpose of obtaining payment of any monies due by that contributory to the company;

(g) to give security for costs in the name of the company;

(h) to appoint agents to do such work as the liquidator is unable to do himself; and

(i) to do all other things necessary for the winding up.

The qualified powers include the following:

(a) to bring or defend any action in the company's name;

(b) to carry on the business of the company, if necessary for a beneficial winding up;

(c) to appoint a solicitor to assist him in his duties;

(d) to pay any class of creditors in full;

(e) to make any compromise or arrangement with creditors;

(f) to compromise claims against debtors.

7. Court Powers

The legislative provisions also empower the court to do any of the following.

(a) On the application of the liquidator or any creditor or contributory, annul the winding up order or stay any proceedings in relation to the winding up, on such terms and for such period as the court may deem fit.[45] Where such an application is made the court may, before making an order, require the liquidator to furnish to the court a report relating to any matters which are relevant. An office copy of any order to annul the winding up order or stay proceedings in relation to the winding up must be forwarded by the company,

---

44 Section 230 of the Principal Act.
45 Section 234(1) of the Principal Act.

or such other person as the court may direct, to the registrar of companies.[46]

(b) Settle a list of contributories and cause the assets of the company to be collected and applied in discharge of the company's liabilities.[47]

(c) Direct any contributory, trustee, receiver, banker, agent or officer of the company to pay such monies and deliver such property, books and papers, to which the company is *prima facie* entitled, to the liquidator.[48]

(d) Make calls on contributories.[49]

(e) Exclude claims by creditors not fixed within the period fixed by the court.[50]

(f) Make an order allowing for inspection of the company's books and papers following an application by a creditor or contributory or Director of Corporate Enforcement.[51]

(g) In the event that the assets of the company are insufficient to satisfy its liabilities, make an order that the costs, charges and expenses of the winding up be paid out of the assets of the company in such order of priority as the court thinks just.[52]

(h) Summon before it and examine, where necessary under oath, officers and any other person known or suspected to have in his possession any property of the company or supposed to be indebted to the company or any person whom the court deems capable of giving information relating to the affairs of the company and order them where appropriate to pay any indebtedness owed by them to the company or to deliver any money, property or books or papers in their possession which belong to the company.[53]

(i) Require the attendance of any officer at a meeting of creditors or contributories or at a meeting of the committee of inspection for the purpose of giving information in relation to the affairs of the company.[54]

(j) Order the arrest of, and the seizure of assets belonging to, any contributory director, shadow director, secretary or other officer of the company where there is evidence that such a person is about to quit the State or remove any of his property from the State.[55]

(k) Order the return of certain property or assets fraudulently transferred;

(l) Order that the company be dissolved where its affairs have been completely wound up.[56]

---

46 Section 234(4) of the Principal Act.
47 Section 235 of the Principal Act.
48 Section 236 of the Principal Act.
49 Section 238 of the Principal Act.
50 Section 241 of the Principal Act.
51 Section 243 of the Principal Act.
52 Section 244 of the Principal Act.
53 Sections 245 and 245A of the Principal Act.
54 Section 246 of the Principal Act.
55 Section 247 of the Principal Act.
56 Section 249 of the Principal Act.

8. Resignation and Removal of the Official Liquidator

A liquidator appointed by the court may resign or, on cause shown, be removed by the court.[57] A vacancy which arises as a result of the resignation or removal of an official liquidator shall be filled by the court.

Voluntary Liquidations

Section 251(1) of the Principal Act provides that a company may be wound up voluntarily in any of the following circumstances:

(a) when the period, if any, fixed by the articles of association for the duration of the company has expired;
(b) when the members resolve by special resolution that the company be wound up voluntarily;
(c) if the company in general meeting resolves that it cannot by reason of its liabilities continue in business and that it should be wound up voluntarily.

When a company has passed a resolution for voluntary winding-up, it shall within 14 days give notice of the resolution in the *CRO Gazette*.[58]

There are two types of voluntary liquidations; a members' voluntary winding up and a creditors' voluntary winding up. The most notable difference between the two is one of solvency. In a members' voluntary winding up the company must be solvent, while this is not the case in a creditors' voluntary winding up. Therefore where the company resolves that it cannot by reason of its liabilities continue in business and should therefore be wound up, the liquidation must proceed as a creditors' voluntary winding up liquidation. The differences between the two types of liquidation are now considered further.

1. Members' Voluntary Winding Up

Before a members' voluntary winding up proceeds the directors must, at a properly convened directors' meeting, make a statutory declaration of solvency.[59] In essence, this declaration is a sworn statement by the directors that in their opinion, following a full enquiry into the company's affairs, the company will be able to pay its debts within twelve months of the commencement of the winding up. A declaration of solvency will not have effect unless:

(a) it is made within the twenty-eight days immediately preceding the date of the passing of the resolution to wind the company up;[60]
(b) it is delivered to the registrar of companies within fifteen days of the delivery to the registrar of a copy of the resolution to wind the company up;[61]

---

57 Section 228(c) of the Principal Act.
58 Section 252(1) of the Principal Act.
59 Section 256(1) of the Principal Act.
60 Section 256(2)(a) of the Principal Act.
61 Ibid.

(c) it embodies a statement of the company's assets and liabilities at the latest date that is practicable and in any event at a date not more than three months before the making of the declaration;[62]
(d) it has attached to it a report, from an independent person who is qualified to be an auditor of the company, that states that in his opinion and to the best of his information the opinions of the directors in the declaration of solvency and the statement of the company's assets and liabilities are reasonable;
(e) a statement from the independent person is attached to the effect that he has given his written consent to the issue of the declaration with the report attached; and
(f) a copy of the declaration is attached to every notice of the general meeting at which it is intended to propose a resolution for voluntary winding up.

If, having made the declaration of solvency, it transpires that the company is not solvent the court may, on the application of the liquidator or any creditor or contributory of the company, declare that any director who was a party to the declaration without having reasonable grounds for his opinion shall be personally liable for any or all of the debts as the court may specify.[63] If the company's debts are not paid within twelve months after the commencement of the winding up, there is a presumption that the directors did not have reasonable grounds for their opinion.[64] This latter provision is intended to deter a director from making a declaration unless circumstances clearly suggest that the company is solvent. Once the declaration has been made, and the resolution of the company passed, notice of the resolution must be published in the *CRO Gazette* within fourteen days of its being passed.[65]

Once the company has completed the statutory formalities, it may appoint a liquidator to wind up the company. The liquidator must consent, in writing, to the appointment.[66] Once appointed, the liquidator must deliver to the registrar of companies a notice of his appointment and the registrar must forward a copy to the Director of Corporate Enforcement.[67] As the Director has a supervisory role in liquidations and a statutory decision-making role in insolvent liquidations this notification is essential.[68] The company in general meeting will determine the liquidator's remuneration.

2. Creditors' Voluntary Winding Up

Notwithstanding the fact that a members' voluntary winding up has commenced, it may still be converted into a creditors' winding up. Section 256(5) of the Principal

---

62 Section 256(2)(b) of the Principal Act.
63 Section 256(8) of the Principal Act.
64 Section 256(9) of the Principal Act.
65 Section 252(1) of the Principal Act.
66 Section 276A of the Principal Act.
67 Section 278 (1) of the Principal Act.
68 See Chapter 19.

Act provides that the court may make an order converting the liquidation into a creditors' winding up if, on the application of a creditor or creditors representing at least one-fifth in value and number of the creditors of the company, the court is of the opinion that the company is unlikely to pay its debts within twelve months. An application must be made within twenty-eight days after the authorising resolution to wind up the company has been advertised. In the event that the court makes such an order, a copy of the court order must be delivered to the registrar of companies by either the liquidator or the company itself.

Section 261 of the Principal Act provides that a liquidator is obliged to call a meeting of the creditors where, in a members' voluntary winding up, he is of the opinion that the company will not be able to pay its debts within the twelve months. The meeting must be called within fourteen days from the day he formed the opinion and it must be notified to the creditors and advertised in the *CRO Gazette* and two daily newspapers. At this creditors' meeting the liquidator must attend, preside and present a statement of affairs of the company. From this time onward the liquidation becomes a creditors' liquidation and the creditors can replace the liquidator with their own appointee.

Liquidations can also commence as a creditors' voluntary winding up, where the company has resolved that because of its liabilities it cannot continue and should be wound up voluntarily. Where this occurs the company must call a meeting of the creditors for the day or the day after the resolution for the voluntary winding up is to be proposed, with at least ten days' notice of meeting having been given to creditors.[69] The directors must present to the meeting a full statement of the company's affairs together with a list of creditors and the amounts owing to them. The creditors and the company at their respective meetings may nominate a person to be liquidator and if they nominate different persons, the person nominated by the creditors will be the liquidator, although an appeal can be made to the court to have this changed.[70] If the proposed liquidator has any connections with a creditor, that connection must be made known to the creditors' meeting. The court can appoint a voluntary liquidator where there is no other liquidator acting, and it can replace or remove one on cause shown.[71]

Where a liquidator has been appointed by the company and the creditors' meeting has not yet been held, the liquidator cannot exercise certain powers without the sanction of the court.[72] This provision is designed to prevent a 'friendly' liquidator from exercising his powers in a manner which might not be to the benefit of the company's creditors.

The creditors of a company have the power to appoint a committee of inspection which will consist of not more than five persons nominated by the creditors.[73] The

---

69 Section 266(1) of the Principal Act.
70 Section 267 of the Principal Act.
71 Section 277 of the Principal Act.
72 Section 131 of the 1990 Act.
73 Section 268 of the Principal Act.

company may also appoint three persons to the committee. However, the creditors may object to these appointees and the court may, on an application by the creditors, disqualify them from so acting.[74] The committee of inspection has considerably more powers than in a compulsory liquidation in that it may determine the remuneration of the liquidator, determine whether the liquidator should continue the business of the company, sanction the exercise of certain of the liquidator's powers and determine whether the powers of the directors should continue.[75]

3. Effects of the Appointment of a Voluntary Liquidator

The effects of the appointment of a voluntary liquidator are essentially the same as in a compulsory winding up. However, there are notable differences in that:

(a) while the directors' powers are assumed in a compulsory liquidation, the committee of inspection or the creditors can sanction the continuance of some or all of the directors' powers in a creditor's voluntary liquidation or the general meeting can sanction those powers in a members' voluntary winding up;

(b) a voluntary liquidation commences on the day the resolution is passed — it is not retrospective;

(c) the liquidator is not an officer of the court;

(d) there is no automatic stay of legal proceedings against the company;

(e) there is no automatic dismissal of the employees. However, the liquidator is unlikely to retain employees unless he is given the power to carry on the company's business;

(f) the company shall, from the commencement of the winding up, cease to carry on business except where it is necessary for the beneficial winding up of the company;

(g) any transfer of shares made after the commencement of the winding up without the sanction of the liquidator is void;

(h) any alteration in the status of the members of the company made after the commencement of the winding up is void.

4. Powers of Voluntary Liquidators

Section 276(1) of the Principal Act sets out the powers which can be exercised by a voluntary liquidator, which are similar to those of an official liquidator. However, unlike the official liquidator, he may exercise the following powers without the sanction of the court or committee of inspection:

(a) bring or defend any action or other legal proceedings in the name of and on behalf of the company;

---

74 Section 268(2) of the Principal Act.
75 Section 269 of the Principal Act.

(b) carry on the business of the company for the benefit of the winding up;

(c) appoint a solicitor to assist him in the performance of his duties;

(d) exercise the powers of the court in relation to settling lists of contributories, making calls and summoning general meetings;

(e) pay the debts of the company and adjust the list of contributories.

All other powers exercisable by the sanction of the court or the committee of inspection in relation to a compulsory liquidation must only be exercised by a liquidator in a member's voluntary winding up, with the sanction of the special resolution and, in the case of a creditors' voluntary winding up, with the sanction of the court or the committee of inspection.

5. Duties of the Liquidator

In addition to the normal duties of a liquidator, he is obliged to hold annual meetings of the company and creditors (in a creditors' voluntary winding up) until such time as the winding up is complete.[76] He must lay before each meeting an account of his acts and dealings during the preceding year. He must send a copy of this report to the registrar of companies within seven days.

6. Court Powers in Voluntary Winding up

The court's role in regard to voluntary liquidations is obviously less significant than in a compulsory winding up. However, the court has many of the powers similar to those in a compulsory winding up. It may, on the application of the Director of Corporate Enforcement, make an order for the inspection by the Director of any books and papers in the possession of a company, and the company and every officer and the liquidator shall co-operate with the Director in this regard.[77] The court may summon before it, for examination, any officer or person known or suspected to have in his possession any property of the company or supposed to be indebted to the company, or any person whom the court deems capable of giving information relating to the promotion, formation, trade, dealings, affairs or property of the company,[78] and order them where appropriate to pay any indebtedness owed by them to the company or to deliver any money, property, books or papers in their possession that belong to the company.[79] The court may order the arrest of, and seizure of assets belonging to, any contributory, director, shadow director, secretary or other officer of the company where there is evidence that the person is about to quit the State or

---

76 Sections 262 and 272 of the Principal Act.

77 Section 282A of the Principal Act.

78 Section 282B of the Principal Act.

79 Section 282C of the Principal Act.

remove any of his property from the State.[80] A liquidator may also apply to the court under section 280 of the Principal Act to determine any question arising in the winding up of a company or in the exercise of any of his powers. In relation to the determination the court may make such order as it thinks fit.[81]

7. Converting from Voluntary to Compulsory Liquidation

At any stage during the course of a voluntary winding up the court may be petitioned to wind up the company compulsorily. In such a case the petitioner must demonstrate that one of the grounds for such a winding up exists. It must also give good reason to the court as to why an order should be made converting the liquidation from a voluntary to a compulsory one. Of particular concern to the court will be the added costs involved where the liquidation is carried out by the court. This is of particular concern if the company's assets are already inadequate to cover the liabilities. In *Re Gilt Construction Ltd*,[82] a two-member company had agreed to be wound up. The members' choice of liquidator differed and the non-petitioning shareholder's choice was supported by the creditors. The petitioner argued that the other shareholder was manipulating the assets of the company for his own personal benefit. In considering the liquidator's skills, honesty and integrity, and the additional costs involved in a court-appointed liquidator, the court refused the order sought.

However, in *Re Hayes Homes Ltd*[83] the petitioner succeeded in having the liquidation converted. The company concerned was in voluntary liquidation. Over 90 per cent of its debt was owed to the Revenue Commissioners. The Revenue Commissioners had failed to get their nominee appointed as a liquidator at the creditors' meeting due to a technical error on their part in relation to the proxy they appointed. Accordingly, they petitioned the court to convert the liquidation into a compulsory one. The court considered a number of matters, including, *inter alia*: the fact that the petitioner was the only substantial creditor of the company; the company had transferred its only potentially realisable asset to an associate company without proper consideration; and the petitioner had undertaken to discharge the costs and expenses of the voluntary liquidation. The court exercised its discretion and granted the order to convert the liquidation from a voluntary to compulsory winding up.

8. Completion of Voluntary Winding Up

When the affairs of the company are fully wound up, the liquidator must present an account of the winding up — showing how it has been conducted and how the assets

---

80 Section 282D of the Principal Act.
81 Section 280(2) of the Principal Act.
82 [1994] 2 ILRM 456.
83 Unreported, High Court, O'Neill J., July 8, 2004.

of the company have been disposed of — to a general meeting of the company and a meeting of the creditors (in the case of a creditors' voluntary winding up). The liquidator must also send the registrar notification of his final report and three months after receipt by the registrar, the company is deemed to be dissolved.[84]

Supervision and Inspection by the Director of Corporate Enforcement

The Director of Corporate Enforcement may on his own motion, or where a complaint is made to him by a member, contributory or creditor of the company, request the liquidator to produce to the Director the liquidator's books for examination. The liquidator must comply with such a request and answer any questions of the Director concerning the content of the books. The liquidator must also give to the Director such assistance as he is reasonably able to give. If a liquidator fails to comply with these requirements he is guilty of an offence.[85] Where a liquidator is a member of a prescribed professional body[86] and a disciplinary committee or tribunal of such body finds that a member conducting a liquidation has not maintained appropriate records or if the body has reasonable grounds for believing that a liquidator has committed an indictable offence during the course of a liquidation the body shall report such matters to the Director.[87]

The Insolvency Regulation

The Insolvency Regulation,[88] which came into effect in May 2002, attempts to improve the efficiency and effectiveness of insolvency proceedings involving companies with cross-border dimensions. The key provision in the Regulation is that the courts of the member state in which the debtor's centre of main interests is situated shall have the jurisdiction to open insolvency proceedings. The centre of main interests is not defined, but there is a presumption (which may be rebutted) that it will be the place where the company has its registered office.

If the main insolvency proceedings are open in a particular member state the law of that particular member state — the *lex concursus* — will effectively apply to the insolvency proceedings in question. Matters such as the duties and powers of liquidators and the priority and ranking of claims will accordingly be determined by the laws of the member state where main proceedings are open. Proceedings subsequently initiated in another member state are considered 'secondary proceedings' for the purposes of the regulation. Liquidators in main proceedings and secondary proceedings must co-operate with each other.

---

84 Sections 263 and 273 of the Principal Act.
85 Section 57(1) of the 2001 Act.
86 SI 544/2002 provides a list of such bodies.
87 Section 58 of the 2001 Act.
88 Council Regulation 1346/2000.

CHAPTER TWENTY-SIX

ASSET REALISATION AND DISTRIBUTION

Introduction

As mentioned in the previous chapter, the liquidator's primary function is to gather in and realise the assets of the company and apply the proceeds in a manner prescribed by law. A liquidator is also obliged to investigate the affairs of the company, which may lead to the imposition of criminal and civil liability on the directors and other officers of the company. The liquidator's functions will be considered under the following headings:

1. asset realisation;
2. application of assets;

Asset Realisation

Once appointed, the liquidator will establish the extent of the company's assets and liabilities. He must take the company's property into his possession and he may apply to the court to have the title of the property vested in his name.[1] The liquidator may, subject to providing such indemnity as the court may direct, bring or defend in his name any action or legal proceedings relating to that property.

In carrying out his function, the liquidator will attempt to maximise the assets available for distribution and reduce the company's liabilities. Where a liquidator is selling property he must generally try to obtain the best possible price.[2] In any case the liquidator can apply to the court under section 280 of the Principal Act for directions in relation to any matters which may arise during the course of the liquidation. Where the liquidator has any doubt he would be advised to exercise his options under section 280, particularly as a liquidator may be liable for misfeasance.[3] As part of his asset realisation functions, the liquidator is conferred with what are often referred to as 'asset-swelling' powers, which have their origin in bankruptcy rules. The primary 'asset-swelling' measures are:

1. post-commencement dispositions;
2. disclaimer of onerous contracts under section 290 of the Principal Act;
3. fraudulent preference transactions under section 286 of the Principal Act;
4. avoidance of floating charges under section 288 of the Principal Act;
5. pooling and contributions orders under section 140 of the 1990 Act;

---

1 Section 230 of the Principal Act.
2 *Van Hool McArdle Ltd v. Rohan Industrial Estates Ltd & Anon* [1980] IR 137.
3 Section 298 of the Principal Act.

6. the return of assets which have been improperly transferred under section 139 of the 1990 Act;

7. applications to hold directors civilly liable for breach of their statutory duties or for any other wrong done to the company.

1. Post-commencement Dispositions

Section 218 of the Principal Act provides that in a winding up by the court, any disposition of the company's property and any transfer of shares or alteration in the status of the members of the company, which are made after the commencement of the winding up, will be void unless the court otherwise orders. Clarke J. summarised the purpose of section 218 as follows:

> It seems to me that the primary purpose of the section is to ensure, insofar as it may be possible, that the Company is 'frozen' as of the date of the presentation of the winding-up petition. Where it is sought to wind up a company on the basis of insolvency it will, save in the most exceptional cases, be the case that the company will end up being unable to pay all of its debts ... The Companies Acts provide an elaborate code for determining where the burden of not being paid should lie. The primary purpose of the section, it seems to me, is to ensure that the court has ample power to prevent any adjustment occurring subsequent to the presentation of the petition, which would disturb that elaborate balance.[4]

Prima facie, by virtue of section 218 all dispositions made after the winding up are void, but the court has the discretion to validate a disposition. Therefore what will constitute a disposition of property will, in the first instance, be a matter for the liquidator, subject to a right to challenge the decision in court. In *Re French's (Wine) Bar Ltd*[5] the company entered into a contract in October 1985 for the sale of its leasehold premises, goodwill, fixtures and fittings and its stock in trade. An order for the compulsory winding up of the company on a creditors' petition was made on 20 January 1986 on a petition presented on 5 December 1985. On 17 January 1986 the contract was completed, the lease was transferred to the purchaser and the proceeds of the sale were distributed to the company's bank. The court held that where, before the presentation of a winding-up petition, a company has entered into an unconditional contract for the sale of property that was specifically enforceable, the completion of the contract according to its terms after the petition has been presented would not constitute a post-commencement disposition.

As a compulsory winding up is deemed to commence on the date the petition to wind up the company is presented, transactions that are particularly vulnerable are those made between the date the petition is presented and the date the court orders the winding up. All transactions into and out of a company's bank account,

---

4 *Re Worldport Ireland Limited (in liquidation)*, Unreported, High Court, Clarke J., June 16, 2005
5 [1987] BCLC 499.

after the date of the presentation of the petition to wind up the company, are void unless subsequently validated by the court. Lodgements that have the effect of reducing a company's overdraft will be considered a disposition.[6] Payments out of a bank account will also be a disposition and the paying bank cannot rely on the defence that it has a contractual duty to carry out a customer's instructions once sufficient funds are in the account. In *Re Industrial Services Ltd*[7] the liquidator sought a motion against the bank under section 218 in regard to payments in and out of the company's bank account in the period between the date the petition for winding up was presented and the date the official liquidator was appointed. Kearns J. accepted that all post-commencement payments from a company's account in favour of third parties, whether the account is in credit or debit, involved a disposition in favour of the bank irrespective of the duty of the bank to carry out its customers' instructions. This leaves banks in an unfortunate position: if they allow dealings on the account they run the risk of having to make restitution to the liquidator if the petition is successful; alternatively the bank can freeze the customer's bank account and be sued for breach of contract by the customer if the petition is not successful.

In the United Kingdom, the courts have taken a different position to that adopted in Ireland. In *Hollicourt Contracts Ltd v. Bank of Ireland*[8] the Court of Appeal ruled that the bank was only an agent for its customer in making any transfer from the account and it was the ultimate recipient of the monies who should be considered the disponee for the purposes of the equivalent statutory provision. Pending a decision by the Supreme Court in relation to this matter the position in Ireland remains that where a bank makes a transfer from the customer's account after the date of the presentation of a petition for winding up it will be considered a disponee. Unless the courts subsequently validate the transfer the bank will be liable to return those amounts to a liquidator.

Once the disposition is declared void, the person who benefited from the disposition — the disponee — is obliged to make good the unlawful disposition. In some instances it may be that a number of parties will be considered a disponee for the purposes of a particular transaction.

In *Re Worldport Ireland Ltd (in liquidation)*,[9] the High Court had appointed a liquidator to the company on 13 May 2002. The petition to wind up the company had been presented on 15 April. On 22 April the company instructed its bank to transfer €256,044 to its parent company in the United States. The company's account was in credit and the bank complied with the transfer instruction. The liquidator of the company sought a declaration that a payment from the company's bank account was a void disposition. The liquidator primarily

---

6 *Re Gray's Inn Construction Ltd* [1980] 1 ALL ER 841.
7 [2001] 2 IR 118.
8 [2001] 2 WLR 290.
9 Unreported, High Court, Clarke J., June 16, 2005.

asserted that there was a disposition in favour of the parent company but it was also contended as a 'fall-back' position that there was a disposition either in favour of the bank or, alternatively, that on a proper construction of the transactions involved, the disposition was in favour of both the parent company and the bank.

Clarke J. examined the net effect of the transfer and concluded as follows.

(a) The bank's liability to the company was reduced, in that the balance standing to the credit of the customer was reduced by the sum of the payment.

(b) The third party received the sum out of monies held by the bank and that sum was paid on foot of obligations by the company to that third party. Accordingly, such obligations were, to the extent involved, either reduced or extinguished.

(c) The bank had less cash available to it as a result of the transfer but correspondingly it had a reduced set of obligations to the corporate customer as the amounts in the customer's account were reduced.

Having established the separate effects on each party, the court then sought to ascertain the parties that were disponees for the purposes of section 218. The court held that the bank was a disponee because of the reduction in the amount of the liability of the bank to repay what the company would have been entitled to demand. However, the court also held that the parent company could equally be a disponee as the company had discharged any obligation it may have had to the parent. Accordingly, both parties were held to be disponees within the meaning of section 218.

As mentioned above, the courts may validate a disposition that has fallen foul of section 218. Although the statutory provision does not give an indication of the matters that should be taken into account when validating an otherwise void disposition it would seem that the courts consider matters such as: whether the disposition would benefit the general body of creditors;[10] were the dispositions ones the liquidator would have made in the course of the winding up;[11] or were the dispositions made by a receiver carrying out his duties prior to the appointment of the liquidator.[12]

In *Re Clifton Place Garage Ltd*[13] a petition to wind up the company was presented on 30 November 1966. The company's bankers froze the company's account, leaving it without any means to carry on trading. It was a wholly-owned

---

10 *Re Industrial Services Company (Dublin) Ltd* (No. 2), Unreported, High Court, McCracken J., May 15, 2002; *Re Ashmark Ltd* (No. 1) [1990] ILRM 330; *Re McBirney & Co. Ltd*, Unreported, High Court, Murphy J., July 2, 1992.

11 *Re Industrial Services Co. (Dublin) Ltd (No. 2)* (ibid. note 10).

12 *Re McBirney and Co. Ltd* (ibid. note 10).

13 [1970] Ch 477.

subsidiary of another company, which had granted a secured debenture. On 24 December 1966, the debenture holders appointed a receiver and manager over the parent company. The receiver was given a misleadingly optimistic account of the company's position by its director, who was also the director of the parent company. On the basis of the information given him, the receiver believed that the company's shares constituted a valuable asset in his possession and that it would be in the best interests for it to continue trading while he sought a purchaser for its shares who would buy the company's assets and business as a going concern. He therefore arranged to open a special bank account with funds provided by the parent company out of which he would pay the company's current expenses — effectively trade creditors — to enable it to continue trading, and into which the company would pay its daily receipts from the business to reimburse those advances. As a result of these payments in and out of this special bank account, the receiver paid out more than he had received. The company was ordered to be wound up on 30 January 1967. The liquidator claimed from the receiver repayment of the amounts paid by the company into the special account on the ground that it was a disposition of the company's property made after the commencement of the winding up and was therefore void. The Court of Appeal held that the decision to validate was a matter of the judge's judicial discretion and should be determined on the facts of each case by what was just and equitable in all the circumstances. It was further suggested that regard should be had to the *bona fides* of the decision and any consequent detriment on the creditors. As the receiver had acted *bona fide* and the creditors would be unjustly enriched if the receiver had to repay the amounts sought by the liquidator the court was satisfied that the payments should be validated.

In *Industrial Services Co. (Dublin) Ltd (No.2)*[14] the court was asked to validate payments into and out of the company's bank account that had been declared void. An application was subsequently made to have these dispositions validated by the court. The court examined the payments in question and concluded that it would validate those made in the ordinary course of business in relation to current debts of the company. Such payments, according to the court, would probably have been made by the liquidator and could be said to be made for the benefit of the general body of creditors. The court refused to validate any payments made from the account that were not made in the ordinary course of business, many of which related to payments to the directors or persons connected with the directors.

2. Disclaimer of Onerous Contracts — Section 290 of the Principal Act

Section 290 of the Principal Act applies an age-old bankruptcy rule to companies by allowing a liquidator to disclaim any of the company's property which has

14 See note 10.

onerous obligations attaching to it. The object of the power is not to deny creditors their legal rights but rather to enable the liquidator to carry out his functions expeditiously without dragging out the liquidation process. The effect of the section is that a liquidator may discriminate against some creditors by disclaiming the company's obligations to them on the grounds that the performance would be unduly burdensome to the company. The liquidator has twelve months from the commencement of a liquidation to disclaim, provided he has leave from the court to do so. However, a creditor can force the liquidator to make a decision within a shorter period of time by making an application in writing to the liquidator asking him whether or not he intends to disclaim.[15] The liquidator must then respond within twenty-eight days, or such longer period as the court may allow. Failure to respond within this time frame has the effect of denying the liquidator the power to disclaim.

Practically speaking, almost any contract may be disclaimed, giving the liquidator wide scope. This is because section 290(1) of the Principal Act defines the property and interests capable of being disclaimed as consisting of:

> land of any tenure burdened with onerous covenants, of shares or stock in companies, of unprofitable contracts or any other property which is unsaleable or not readily saleable by reason of its binding the possessor thereof to the performance of any onerous act or to the repayment of any sum of money.

The principal issue that arises in relation to the disclaimer of onerous property relates to the position of third parties affected by the disclaimer. Section 190(3) of the Principal Act provides that:

> The disclaimer shall operate to determine, as from the date of disclaimer, the rights, interests and liabilities of the company, and the property of the company, in or in respect of the property disclaimed, but shall not, except so far as is necessary for the purpose of releasing the company and the property of the company from liability, affect the rights or liabilities of any other person.

The effect of a disclaimer on a third party can be seen in *Tempany v. Royal Liver Trustees Ltd.*[16] The liquidator disclaimed a lease because the rental was far in excess of the current market value and was therefore a drain on the company's resources. The defendant was the guarantor of the company's obligations under the lease and naturally opposed the application. The High Court held that it was not necessary to disclaim the guarantee to effect the disclaimer of the lease. It further held that the concern of the court was not the effect the disclaimer had on third parties but rather the effect it had on the interests of the company. If a claim is subsequently made against the guarantor, and he complies with his obligations under the guarantee, he will be entitled to join the ranks of the other company creditors in the winding up.

---

15 Section 290(5) of the Principal Act.
16 [1984] ILRM 273.

By virtue of section 290 any individual suffering loss as a result of the disclaimer shall be deemed to be a creditor of the company and may prove the amount as a debt in the winding up.[17]

The extent of a creditor's entitlement under a disclaimed contract has been the subject of much litigation. However, most cases have concerned bankruptcy rules, and as there are subtle distinctions between those and the insolvency rules of disclaimers, great care should be taken when such cases are being considered. In *Re Ranks Ireland Ltd*,[18] the contracts being disclaimed were telephone equipment leases. The terms of the lease provided that in the event of its repudiation a specified amount would become payable as damages. Murphy J. held that this was not the correct measure of damages in these circumstances, as that amount was only appropriate where the hirer had repudiated his contract. A repudiation, he said, was not the same as a disclaimer. Accordingly, the appropriate measure of damages was held to be the difference between the rent the company would have paid the lessor and the rent the lessor is likely to earn during the unexpired residue of the lease.

If a liquidator uses property which is later the subject of a 'disclaimer', that portion of the contractual amount payable during the period of usage must be paid by the liquidator. This principle has been established by case-law and is reflected in the rules of the Superior Court. In *Re GWI Ltd*,[19] Murphy J. held that:

> where a liquidator takes possession or remains in possession of leasehold property for the purposes of winding up, the rent of the premises ought to be regarded as a debt contracted for the purpose of winding up the company and ought therefore to be paid in full like any other debt or expense properly incurred by the liquidator for the same purpose.

In that case, the lessor had claimed the full amount of the lease for the period of liquidation on the basis that the liquidator enjoyed possession. In fact the liquidator was not in physical possession, but he had sublet it for an amount of £4,000. Murphy J. rejected the lessor's claim on the basis that he could have ordered the liquidator out for not paying the rent. He substituted the lessor's claim of £17,000 for the lesser amount of £4,000, representing what had been paid to the liquidator under the sub-lease.

3. *Fraudulent Preference under Section 286*

A number of statutory provisions exist to prevent a company, knowing that its financial situation is terminal, dissipating company assets that would otherwise be available for the general body of creditors. The reason for such provisions is to protect one of the core principles of insolvency law — that creditors of the

---

17 Section 290(9) of the Principal Act.
18 [1988] ILRM 751.
19 Unreported, High Court, Murphy J., November 10, 1987.

same class should be treated on a *pari passu* basis. Reference has already been made to the fact that post-winding up dispositions are void unless otherwise validated by the court.[20] In addition to these post-commencement dispositions, transactions that took place while the company was insolvent, but before the commencement of the winding up, can also be avoided.

Under the Principal Act, any transaction by a company which is intended to favour a creditor, and was entered into in the six months prior to a company going into liquidation at a time when the company was unable to pay its debts as they fell due, can be set aside for fraudulent preference.[21] In the case of a transaction between the company and connected person, the relevant time frame is twenty-four months. Furthermore, the statutory provisions now raise a presumption of fraudulent preference where transactions involve connected persons, related companies or a trustee or surety of any debt due to a connected person or a related company.[22] The section has a potentially wide application because the nature of the transactions likely to be impugned are not specified. It would seem that liquidators can challenge any transaction provided it meets the criteria of the section. In *Peat v. Gresham Trust*[23] it was held that the failure of a company to oppose an application to the court to extend the time for registering a charge was an action that could come within section 286.

Essentially, under section 286 the liquidator must prove that there was a dominant intention to prefer on the part of the company. This raises three difficulties. First, it is the 'intent' of the company itself that must be proven. As the company has no mind of its own, a liquidator must impute the intent of its agents to the whole company and this is difficult to do. In *Corran Construction v. Bank of Ireland Finance Ltd*,[24] the question arose as to whether the intention of a director could be imputed to the entire company. The defendant bank had taken a mortgage over certain of the company's land and some time later the bank discovered that the mortgage had not been registered in accordance with the Companies Act. The bank persuaded the director, who at that time was quite ill, to give a fresh charge. The evidence showed that the director appreciated the fact that the defendant would be secured in the event that the company did not repay its debt and that there was every chance, given the company's insolvency, that it could not meet the repayments. Despite this, the court held that the evidence was not sufficient to infer an intention on behalf of the company to prefer a creditor.[25]

---

20 Section 218 of the Principal Act.
21 Section 286 of the Principal Act.
22 Section 286(3) of the Principal Act as inserted by section 135 of the the 1990 Act.
23 [1934] AC 252.
24 [1976–7] ILRM 175.
25 See also *Kelleher v. Continental Irish Meats*, Unreported, High Court, Costello J., May 9, 1978.

The second difficulty lies in the fact that there will rarely be direct evidence of an intention to prefer. Therefore the court will be obliged to look at the surrounding circumstances in order to infer an intention. In *Station Motors v. AIB*,[26] the company had a large overdraft with the defendant bank which was guaranteed by the member-directors of the company, a husband and wife. The company became insolvent and the couple resolved that it should be wound up. Before this happened they caused certain payments to be made to the overdraft account which had the effect of reducing their exposure under the guarantee. The court held that the payments were a fraudulent preference designed to benefit the bank directly and the couple indirectly. In doing so Carroll J. considered the following points.

(a) Just because there is a preference, one cannot infer an intention to prefer. The liquidator has to positively prove that an intention to prefer existed at the time of the transaction and the onus rests on the liquidator to so prove.
(b) Where there is no evidence of an intention to prefer there is no legal principle precluding the court from drawing an inference of such an intention from the circumstances.
(c) The circumstances must demonstrate that the intention was a dominant one. It is not enough to say that a person benefited from an action which was motivated by another reason.
(d) Where the case involves directors and where they obtain an advantage from the transaction, the court may draw an inference from those transactions which must involve at the very least the taint of dishonesty.

As the payments were made to the company's current account after it was resolved to wind up the company, and those payments had the effect of reducing an overdraft which was personally secured by the directors, Carroll J. held that there was sufficient evidence to infer a fraudulent preference within the meaning of section 286.

The third difficulty arises because even when an intention to prefer is established it is further necessary to demonstrate that the intention was a 'dominant' one. In *Re FLE Holdings Ltd*,[27] a defective charge was registered. At the bank's request, the company executed a new charge and had it registered. The contention that the bank had been preferred was rejected on the grounds that the dominant intention was not to confer a preference on the bank, but to benefit the company by keeping on good terms with the bank.

---

26 [1985] IR 756.
27 [1967] 1 WLR 1409.

4. Avoidance of a Floating Charge under Section 288

Another statutory provision designed to protect the general body of creditors by preventing a reduction of an insolvent company's assets is section 288 of the Principal Act, as amended.[28] It provides that where a company is being wound up, a floating charge created in the twelve months prior to the commencement of the winding up shall, unless the company was solvent immediately after the time the charge was created, be invalid. Where a charge is created in favour of a connected person the relevant period is two years. Section 288 provides for exceptions where money was paid, or the price or value of goods or services sold or supplied, to the company at the time of or subsequently to the creation of and in consideration for the charge. As section 288 only applies in a winding up situation, if a chargee moves quickly to enforce his security before the company goes into liquidation he can retain the entire proceeds of realisation.[29]

Section 288 does not apply to fixed charges. However, in an appropriate case a fixed charge could be avoided under section 286 as a fraudulent preference.

A floating charge can only be invalidated if the company was at the time of giving the charge insolvent. The test of solvency to be applied was set out in *Re Creation Printing Co. Ltd*.[30] There, McWilliam J. held that where a company is unable to pay its debts as they fall due, it is insolvent irrespective of its balance sheet position.[31]

Section 288 will not apply to a charge that is given in consideration for, *inter alia,* money actually advanced or paid to the company either at the time the charge was created or later. The question of what constitutes 'at the time' the charge was created has given rise to litigation. In *Re Daniel Murphy Ltd*,[32] it was held that provided there was no delay in executing the charge and the transaction was not intended to deceive the creditors, a difference of thirty-five days between the time of advancing the cash and the taking of the charge could not be said to be unreasonable. The court will be concerned with the substance of any transaction that took place, and not simply its form. The test to be applied is whether the company indeed received funds in exchange for the security and whether the transaction benefited the company.[33] As Barron J. observed in *Smurfit Paribas Bank Ltd v. AAB Export Finance Ltd*:

> in order to treat payments made to the company before the execution of the charge as payments made at the time of the charge, the necessary elements to be established

---

28 Section 136 of the 1990 Act.
29 *Mace Builders (Glasgow) Ltd v. Lunn* [1987] BCLC 55.
30 [1978] ILRM 219.
31 This test was accepted on appeal by the Supreme Court [1981] IR 353.
32 [1964] IR 1.
33 *Re Destone Fabrics Ltd* [1941] Ch 319.

are; that an honest transaction has been put in place and there was a reasonable expedition in and about the preparation and execution of the charge.[34]

In that particular case, although the monies advanced were advanced on the basis that a company would grant a charge over its assets, the charge was not in fact duly executed until two years later. In Barron J.'s view such a protracted delay could not be justified and accordingly the floating charge was invalid.[35]

Section 289 of the Principal Act provides for additional circumstances whereby a floating charge may be avoided. Where a company is being wound up and it was within the previous twelve months indebted to an officer of the company and that debt was discharged wholly or partly by the company or any other person and the company had created a floating charge in favour of that officer within the twelve-month period, that charge is invalid to the extent of the repayment unless it can be shown that the company was solvent immediately after the creation of the charge. This provision prevents the avoidance of section 288 by the directors who arrange to have their loans repaid and then on the basis of fresh advances to the company obtain a floating charge.

5. Pooling and Contribution Orders

Section 140 of the 1990 Act has the effect of cutting across the veil of incorporation, as it applies to groups of companies, by empowering the liquidator to apply to the court for an order directing that a related company contribute to the assets of the company being wound up.

By virtue of section 141 of the 1990 Act, the liquidator may apply to the court for an order directing that the assets of a related company which is also being wound up be pooled between the creditors of both companies. (See Chapter 1 for the definition of related company.)

The main criterion for determining whether a contribution or pooling order should be made is that the court is of the opinion that it is 'just and equitable' to do so. The court in deciding this question must consider specific criteria regarding the relationship between the companies, the conduct of the related company towards the creditors of the company being wound up, and the extent to which the conduct of the related company contributed to the winding up of the other company. Furthermore, the court must, when considering making a contribution order, have regard to the effect of such an order on the creditors of the related company. When considering whether to make a pooling order the court must also have regard to the extent to which the businesses of both companies were intermingled.

---

34 [1991] 2 IR 19 at 30.
35 In the UK it has been held that the value must be provided contemporaneously with the creation of the charge: *Power v. Sharpe Investments Ltd* [1994] 1 BCLC 111.

6. Return of Improperly Transferred Assets

If on the application of the liquidator the court is satisfied that:

(a) any property of the company was disposed of by act or omission; and
(b) the effect of such disposal was to perpetrate a fraud on the company, its creditors or members;

the court may, if it considers it just and equitable to do so, order any person who appears to have the use, control or possession of the property or the proceeds of sale of that property to deliver the property or the proceeds to the liquidator on such terms as it sees fit.[36]

7. Application to have Officers Held Personally Liable for Debts of Company

Where a liquidator in the course of the winding up discovers evidence suggesting that either the directors' duties have been breached or a wrong has been done to the company, he may apply to the court for the appropriate declarations or orders. Many of these declarations can hold the directors responsible, in whole or part, for the debts of the company or order that the director account to the company for any loss suffered by the company or for any gain made by the directors. Many of these duties have been considered at length in previous chapters, including the following:

(a) the fiduciary duties of directors;[37]
(b) the duty of care and competence;[38]
(c) the duty to act *intra vires* the company;[39]
(d) the duty to maintain proper books of accounts;[40]
(e) the duty to take care when making a declaration of solvency in connection with the giving of financial assistance for the purchase of shares in the company;[41]
(f) statutory duties owed to the company's creditors under the fraudulent and reckless trading provisions of the Principal Act.[42]

The Application of Assets

Once the assets have been realised the liquidator must then apply the proceeds among the creditors of the company in accordance with the provisions of the

36 Section 139 of the Principal Act.
37 See Chapter 18.
38 Ibid.
39 See Chapter 17.
40 Section 202 of the 1990 Act: see Chapter 20.
41 Section 60(5) of the Principal Act: see Chapter 10.
42 See Chapter 18.

Companies Acts. If any surplus is available after these debts have been discharged, it will be distributed among the company's shareholders. Before any distributions will be made to creditors their claims must be proved.

1. Proving Claims

Section 283(1) of the Principal Act sets out those debts which may be proved in a winding up. All debts payable on a contingency, and all claims for damages against the company, whether present or future, certain or contingent, are admissible to proof against the company. The liquidator will advise the creditors of the company, in the form of an advertisement, as to where they should send their claims. When the claims are submitted the liquidator must then ascertain their validity. He will notify all claims to the High Court examiner who will adjudicate upon them. Irrespective of whether a claim is allowed or requires further proof, the liquidator must notify the relevant creditors. Where claims require further proof the examiner will fix a time for the creditors to attend and where necessary provide such information as the examiner or liquidator may require by way of affidavit. Any final adjudication must be certified by the examiner.

2. Order of Distribution of the Assets

Once the liquidator has established the valid claims he must apply the assets. There are detailed rules in the Companies Acts as well as the Bankruptcy Acts which determine the manner and priority in which the assets must be applied. If the company has sufficient assets to meet its liabilities there is unlikely to be a dispute regarding the application of assets. It is where the assets are insufficient that a jostling for pole position among creditors, attempting to maximise their recovery, will occur. As already mentioned, creditors must be treated equally on a *pari passu* basis.[43] However, there are a number of exceptions to the *pari passu* principle and in practice its application is more appropriate to classes of creditors. Accordingly, if there is any shortfall in the assets, which will usually be the situation in an insolvent winding up, all creditors in the same class must have the amount owing to them reduced on a *pro rata* basis. Class creditors may, for example, each receive fifty cent for every euro owing to them. While the amount may vary depending on the availability of assets the principle of equality remains, so that a class creditor cannot receive a greater amount than another creditor from a distribution to a particular class. Of course, a creditor may belong to a number of different classes with the result that his consolidated position, following a distribution to all classes, appears superior to that of other creditors. Once the classes of creditors and members have been established, the following rules generally apply regarding the distribution of assets.

---

43 See section 275 of the Principal Act.

Expenses of an Examiner

Where a company is wound up following a period of court protection, section 29(3) of the Companies (Amendment) Act 1990 provides that the remuneration, costs and expenses of the examiner shall be paid before any other claim, whether secured or unsecured.[44]

Costs of the Winding Up

When a liquidator is appointed he will require remuneration and will always incur expenses. A liquidation may necessarily be dragged out over a long period of time, and some have been known to last for years. Obviously a liquidator is not going to invest his time, energy and resources into a winding up if there is a risk that he will not get paid. It is for this reason that a priority position is given to the costs of a winding up. In the case of a voluntary winding up, section 281 of the Principal Act provides that all costs, charges and expenses properly incurred in the winding up, including the remuneration of the liquidator, shall be payable out of the assets of the company in priority to all other claims.

In the case of a compulsory winding up, section 244 of the Principal Act provides that the court may, where the assets are insufficient to satisfy the liabilities, make an order as to the payment from the assets of the costs, charges and expenses incurred in such order of priority as the court thinks just. This section is supplemented by the Rules of the Superior Court 1986[45] which provides for a priority for the fees and expenses incurred in preserving and realising the assets of the company, which includes the remuneration, costs and expenses the court may allow to a liquidator where the company had previously commenced to be wound up voluntarily. Furthermore, the remaining assets must then be applied to meet the costs of the petition, the costs incurred in making a statement of affairs, any remaining disbursements of the official liquidator, the costs of the solicitor for the official liquidator, the remuneration of the official liquidator and the out-of-pocket expenses, if any, of the committee of inspection.

Secured Creditors

Generally speaking, secured creditors[46] may opt out of the insolvency queue because they have the right to realise or otherwise deal with their security.[47] However, a secured creditor has a number of other options open to him. These are set out in paragraph 24 of the First Schedule to the Bankruptcy Act 1988, which provides that he may:

---

44 See Chapter 27.
45 Order 74, rule 128.
46 Defined by section 3 of the Bankruptcy Act 1988 as 'any creditor holding any mortgage, charge or lien on the debtor's estate or any part thereof as security for a debt due to him'.
47 Section 136(20) of the Bankruptcy Act 1988.

(a) realise the security and claim any shortfall;
(b) value the security and claim any shortfall;
(c) surrender the security and claim for the full debt.

It should be noted that not all secured creditors are entitled to realise their security in priority to other creditors. Holders of fixed charges over book debts may be subordinated to the claims of certain preferential creditors, namely VAT and PAYE.[48] Furthermore, all holders of floating charges are subordinated to the claims of preferential creditors.

Preferential Creditors

Legislation has ordained that certain creditors should obtain a priority position in the insolvency queue. Section 285 of the Principal Act confers preferential status on the following:

(a) all local rates and taxes due and payable within twelve months before the relevant date;
(b) taxes, including income tax and corporation taxes, assessed on the company up to the preceding 5 April, provided it does not exceed one year's liability;
(c) sums due in respect of PAYE deductions in the twelve months prior to the relevant date;
(d) wages and salaries of employees in respect of services rendered to the company during the four months preceding the relevant date up to a maximum of £2,500 (€3,174) in each case;
(e) accrued holiday remuneration for employees;
(f) except where the company is being wound up for the purposes of reconstruction or amalgamation –
  (i) national insurance and social welfare contributions for the twelve months before the relevant date;
  (ii) amounts due under workmen's compensation legislation and damages for injuries to employees except where covered by insurance;
(g) sums due under any scheme to employees absent owing to sickness and any sums due from the company under any superannuation scheme.

Where payments in respect of employees' wages, salaries and holiday pay are funded by another party such as a bank, it has the right of subrogation under section 285(6) of the Principal Act. Accordingly, it may step into the shoes of the preferential creditors to obtain a priority position.

In addition to the above-mentioned categories, employment legislation elevates the following payments to preferential status in a winding up situation:

---

48 Section 115 of the Principal Act as amended by section 174 of the Finance Act 1995, now section 1001 Taxes Consolidated Act 1997: see Chapter 11.

(a) any compensation payable by the company under the Unfair Dismissals Act 1977;[49]
(b) payments under the Redundancy Payments Act 1967;[50]
(c) amounts payable under the Minimum Notice and Terms of Employment Act 1973;[51]
(d) payments made by the Minister in respect of the company's obligations under any of the above.[52]

In the event that there are insufficient assets to meet the preferential payments, all preferential creditors will rank equally among themselves.[53] Preferential status will apply only to those debts which have been notified or have become known to the liquidator within six months of his advertisement for claims.

Floating Charges

Once the preferential creditors have been satisfied, the floating charge-holders are next in the insolvency queue. Where more than one floating charge is created over the same property and each is properly registered under section 99 of the Principal Act, the charge that was created first will rank first in terms of priority.

Unsecured Creditors

If and when the floating charge-holders have been paid in full, the next in line are the ordinary unsecured creditors. Unfortunately, in the case of most insolvent liquidations the unsecured creditors will not recover the full amount owing to them. Where there are insufficient assets available, the unsecured creditors must be treated on a *pari passu* basis. As mentioned earlier, section 283 of the Principal Act sets out the types of claim that may be proved but the section specifically excludes, unless the articles provide otherwise, dividends declared more than six years previously which have not been claimed.[54] The difficulty that arises in relation to applying assets among this class of creditors is that some of the claims may be contingent and therefore difficult to value. The usual practice is for the court to make an estimate of the value of the claim subject to a right to amend the claim at a later date, provided the amended claim does not interfere with distributions already made.[55]

---

49 Section 12.
50 Section 42.
51 Section 13.
52 Protection of Employees (Employer's Insolvency) Act 1984.
53 Section 285(7)(a) of the Principal Act.
54 Section 283(2) of the Principal Act.
55 For a detailed discussion of the rights of contingent creditors, see Lynch, Marshall and O'Ferrall, *Corporate Insolvency and Rescue* (Butterworths) 1996.

Members and Contributories

In the event that having satisfied all the creditors' claims assets are still available, they will be distributed among the members of the company according to their rights and interests in the company.[56] These rights and interests will usually be determined by the articles of association.[57]

Where members are also contributories of the company, adjustments of their rights may be necessary. In the case of a compulsory liquidation, the court has the power to settle the list of contributories and adjust their rights taking into account any sums due to them.[58] In the case of a voluntary liquidation, it is the liquidator that carries out this task.[59] Having made the appropriate adjustments, the court or the liquidator, as the case may be, will distribute any surplus among the contributories.

---

56 Section 275(1)(b) of the Principal Act.
57 See Chapter 5.
58 Section 242 of the Principal Act.
59 Section 276(2) of the Principal Act.

CHAPTER TWENTY-SEVEN

COURT PROTECTION

Introduction

Companies unable to pay their debts have traditionally been at the mercy of creditors who can appoint a receiver or cause a liquidator to be appointed. Such actions, however justifiable from the creditors' point of view, usually bring about the demise of the company. This situation was recognised as far back as 1897 when Lord McNaughten in *Salomon v. Salomon* exclaimed, 'Everybody knows that when there is a winding-up, debenture-holders generally step in and sweep off everything. And a great scandal that is.'[1]

For a number of years preceding 1990, demand existed in Ireland for a system to protect companies in financial difficulties from the predatory grasp of creditors whose actions could bring about the company's demise, sometimes prematurely. A new procedure was introduced by the Companies (Amendment) Act 1990 (the 1990 Amendment Act) designed to meet this need.

A company which is, *inter alia*, unable to pay its debts may be placed under the protection of the court for a period of time generally not exceeding seventy days.[2] The object of such protection is twofold. First, the company is 'immunised' from actions by creditors, and second, an examiner is appointed to investigate its affairs and make proposals for its survival through a compromise or scheme of arrangement (if possible), so as to keep the company, or part of it, alive as a going concern. McCarthy J. in *Re Atlantic Magnetics Ltd*[3] summarised the intention behind the legislation:

> ... its purpose is protection — protection of the company and consequently of its shareholders, workforce and creditors. It is clear that parliament intended that the fate of the company and those who depend upon it should not lie solely in the hands of one or more large creditors who can by appointing a receiver pursuant to a debenture effectively terminate its operation and secure as best they may the discharge of the monies due to them to the inevitable disadvantage of those less protected, the Act is to provide a breathing space albeit at the expense of some creditor or creditors.

The 1990 Amendment Act had been hurried into law to prevent the collapse of the Goodman Group of companies and the negative impact that such a collapse would have had on the Irish economy. The Act was fraught with

---

1 (1897) App Cas 22 HL.
2 This period may be extended by the court for an additional thirty days.
3 [1993] 2 IR 561.

difficulties and was perceived by lending institutions as anti-creditor in its approach. Indeed, the survival of a company under court protection usually had a disadvantageous effect on those creditors who would have had superior priority status in a receivership or liquidation scenario. A further criticism of the Act was that it did not give sufficient focus to viable companies.[4] Indeed, many of the companies that used the court protection procedure ultimately failed.

To deal with the perceived weaknesses of the court protection procedure, the 1999 Amendment Act introduced a number of amendments to the 1990 Amendment Act.

The Petition

The process of applying for court protection commences with the petition. All petitions are presented to the High Court, which may, if the liabilities of the company are less than IR£250,000 (€317,436), remit the matter to the relevant Circuit Court.

Section 3(1) of the Act lists those persons who may petition the court, and they are as follows:

Directors

In *Re Don Bluth Entertainment Ltd (No.1)*,[5] Murphy J. held that three of the five directors were entitled to present a petition on behalf of the directors, despite an objection from the other two directors. In that case a formal board resolution to appoint an examiner had been passed. However, where a meeting has not been properly convened and the resolution has not been formally passed the petition of the directors could be dismissed.[6]

The Company

The 1990 Amendment Act does not specify whether an ordinary or special resolution is required. However, in the above case Murphy J. accepted that, as the decision of the directors to petition for the appointment of an examiner was made pursuant to a properly convened board meeting, the directors were in fact acting on behalf of the company even though the petition was presented in the names of the directors.

The Creditors

Creditors include contingent and prospective creditors, and employees. Where an application is made by any one of these three categories, they are required to put

---

4 Report of the Company Law Review Group 1994.
5 Unreported, High Court, Murphy J., August 27, 1992.
6 *Re Aston Colour Print Ltd,* Unreported, High Court, Kelly J., February 21, 1997.

up such security for costs as the court considers reasonable until such time as a *prima facie* case for the appointment of an examiner has been established to the satisfaction of the court.

The Members

The legislation permits members to petition for the appointment where they hold at least one-tenth of the fully paid-up voting capital.

In the case of insurance companies, banks and companies supervised by the Central Bank, the petitioning parties vary from the Section 3(1) list.[7] In the case of insurance companies, only the Minister may present a petition. In the case of banks, only the Central Bank may do so and, in the case of all non-banks supervised by the Central Bank, only the Central Bank and those parties listed in section 3(1) may petition the court. However, where the company, its directors, creditors or members petition the court in such circumstances, they must give notice to the Central Bank, which will be entitled to be heard at any hearing relating to the petition.

Contents of the Petition

The petition, when presented, must nominate a person to be appointed as examiner[8] and it must be accompanied by a consent signed by the person nominated.[9] A person is only qualified to be an examiner if he is qualified to be a liquidator of the company. The report must also be accompanied by a report of an 'independent accountant' who is either the auditor of the company or who is qualified to be the auditor of the company.[10] The petition may be accompanied by a copy of the proposals for a compromise or scheme of arrangement (if they have been prepared) for submission to interested parties. Although there is no statutory bar on the independent accountant being nominated as the examiner, there may be circumstances where the court will not permit this to occur if the independent accountant's impartiality could be questioned.[11]

The Independent Accountant's Report

The report of the independent accountant shall comprise the following:

(a) details of the identity of the company directors, other officers and shadow directors;

---

7 Section 3(2) of the 1990 Amendment Act.
8 Section 3(3) ibid.
9 Section 3(4) ibid.
10 Section 3(3A) ibid.
11 *Re Wogan's (Drogheda) Ltd (No.3)* [1993] 1 IR 157; and *Re Tuskar Resources plc* [2001] 1 IR 668.

(b) details of other companies of which the directors are also directors;

(c) a statement of affairs of the company setting out the debts, assets, liabilities, and identity of all creditors and details of all securities held by them;

(d) a statement of opinion by the independent accountant as to whether any deficiency between the assets and liabilities of the company have been satisfactorily accounted for or, if not, whether there is evidence of a substantial disappearance of property that is not adequately accounted for;

(e) a statement of opinion by the independent accountant as to whether the company, and the whole or any part of its undertaking, would have a reasonable prospect of survival as a going concern and a statement of the conditions which he feels are essential to ensure such survival, whether as regards the internal management and controls of the company or otherwise;

(f) a statement of opinion as to whether the formulation, acceptance and confirmation of proposals for a compromise or scheme of arrangement with the company's creditors and members would offer a reasonable prospect of the survival of the company, and the whole or any part if its undertaking, as a going concern;

(g) his opinion as to whether an attempt to continue the whole or part of the undertaking of the company would be likely to be more advantageous to the members as a whole, and the creditors as a whole, than a winding up;

(h) his recommendations as to the course he thinks should be taken in relation to the company, including, if warranted, draft proposals for a compromise or scheme of arrangement;

(i) his opinion as whether the facts disclosed would warrant further inquiries with a view to proceedings under the fraudulent and reckless trading provisions of the Principal Act;

(j) details of the extent of the funding required to enable the company to continue trading during the period of protection and the sources of that funding;

(k) his recommendations as to which pre-petition liabilities should be paid;

(l) his opinion as to whether the work of the examiner would be assisted by a direction of the court extending the role and membership of the creditors committee; and

(m) any other matters he considers relevant.[12]

The requirement to present an independent accountant's report was introduced by the 1999 Amendment Act and meets some of the criticisms that had been levelled against the 1990 Amendment Act. Prior to the introduction of the 1999 Act, the High Court had very little to go on in terms of gleaning the financial position of the company and its future prospects. Furthermore, the examinership process had proven in many cases to be expensive in terms of the amount of

---

12 Section 3(3B) ibid.

expenses the examiner could certify in order to allow the company continue trading while the examiner was attempting to put together a rescue package. Such expenses would not necessarily have been anticipated at the petition stage. The courts are now in a better position to judge the overall financial state of the company, the funding required to allow it trade while under the court protection and the source of that funding.

Interim Protection Pending Independent Accountant's Report

Where there are exceptional circumstances outside the control of the petitioner that could not have been reasonably anticipated by him, the court may appoint an interim examiner for a period of ten days pending submission of the independent accountant's report.[13] What will constitute 'exceptional circumstances' remains to be seen: however, the legislation is clear about the fact that the mere appointment of a receiver will not itself constitute 'exceptional circumstances'.[14] Where the court makes an interim order of this nature and the petition has been presented by the members or the creditors of the company, the company directors must co-operate with the preparation of the independent accountant's report.

If the independent accountant's report is not presented within ten days, the company ceases to be under the protection of the court although a new petition may be presented under section 2.

Uberrima Fides

The court has stated on numerous occasions that all petitions must be made in the utmost good faith. In *Re Seluckwe Ltd*,[15] Costello J. held that there was evidence of a considerable lack of good faith on behalf of the petitioning directors and a lack of candour throughout the examination process. Nevertheless, he confirmed the proposals, subject to modification, on the grounds *inter alia* that the jobs of thirty employees were at stake. In *Re Wogan's Drogheda Ltd*[16] Costello J. said that the utmost good faith is required because the court must depend, to a considerable extent, on the truth of what it is told by the company. If such information is misleading, a potential injustice could arise in the making of a protection order, when the proper course is to wind up the company. He went on to say that in certain circumstances a serious lack of good faith could ultimately result in the examiner being discharged and the examiner's proposals being rejected.

This requirement of 'good faith' has now been codified into legislation. Section 4A provides that the court may decline to hear a petition if it appears that the

---

13 Section 3A.
14 Section 3(A)(3).
15 Unreported, High Court, Costello J., December 20, 1991.
16 Unreported, High Court, Costello J., May 7, 1992.

petitioner, or the independent accountant, has failed to disclose information material to the court in exercising its powers or has in any other way failed to exercise the utmost good faith. The amendment does not impose a statutory duty of good faith on the examiner himself. Presumably, under the authority of the High Court decision in the case of *Re Wogan's Drogheda*, such a requirement remains.

The Hearing

The court will not make an order either to dismiss a petition or to appoint an examiner without allowing each creditor an opportunity to be heard, if so desired.[17] All proceedings under the Act, whether at the hearing stage or later, may be held *in camera* if the court, in the interests of justice, considers that the interests of the company concerned, or its creditors as a whole, so require.

Section 3(6) provides that the court will not give hearing to a petition if a receiver stands appointed to the company for more than three days.

Appointing an Examiner

Although discretion is given to the court to decide whether or not to appoint the examiner, section 2(1) does lay down one positive and two negative criteria which must exist before the court has the power to use its discretion, namely that:

(a) the company is, or is likely, to be unable to pay its debts; and
(b) no resolution subsists for the winding up of the company; and
(c) no order has been made for the winding up of the company.

A company is deemed to be unable to pay its debts in any of the following circumstances:

(a) if it is unable to pay them as they fall due (the commercial solvency test);
(b) where the value of its liabilities exceeds its assets (the balance sheet solvency test); or
(c) where section 214(a) or (b) of the Principal Act applies to the company.[18]

In determining the company's insolvency, the court may also have regard to negotiations between the company and its creditors for the re-scheduling of the company's debts, from which it can be reasonably inferred that the company is likely to be unable to pay its debts.

---

17 Section 3B.
18 If a creditor, to whom the company is indebted in a sum exceeding £1,000 then due, has served on the company a formal demand in writing and the company has for three weeks thereafter neglected to pay the sum — section 214(a). If execution or other process issued on a judgment, decree or order of any court in favour of a creditor is returned unsatisfied in whole or in part — section 214(b).

Assuming that these conditions are satisfied, the court is guided further by the legislation. Section 2(2) provides that the court may make an order appointing an examiner if it considers that there is a 'reasonable prospect' of survival of the company, and the whole or any part of it, as a going concern. The requirement of a 'reasonable prospect' of survival was introduced by the 1999 Act and gives statutory support to the test laid down by Lardner J. in *Re Atlantic Magnetics Ltd*.[19]

The availability of the independent accountant's report, together with the onus of establishing a 'reasonable prospect' of survival, suggest that the onus on the petitioner will be more burdensome than heretofore. As McCracken J. stated in *Re Tuskar Resources*:[20]

> ... the new [requirement] prohibits the court from making an order unless it is satisfied there is a reasonable prospect of survival. If the court is to be 'satisfied' it must be satisfied on the evidence before it, which is in the first instance the evidence of the Petitioner. If that evidence does not satisfy the Court, the order cannot be made and in my view this is tantamount to saying that there is an onus of proof on the Petitioner at the initial stage to satisfy the court that there is a reasonable prospect of survival. For this reason the Court has to view the evidence in a different manner to that applicable prior to the 1999 Act.

The court will not appoint an examiner if the company cannot survive as a 'going concern'. In *Re Tuskar Resources*,[21] a petition was made to appoint an examiner to a holding company whose main asset was shares in a Nigerian company. The court held that such a holding could not constitute a 'going concern' and refused to allow an examiner to be appointed. Furthermore, the proposal to transfer the business of another company into the holding company was deemed to be outside the scope of the Act as it was introducing a new 'undertaking' to the company. This, said McCracken J., was more the job of a liquidator than that of an examiner whose purpose is to rescue an existing undertaking.

Notification Requirements

The petitioner must deliver a notice of the petition to the registrar of companies within three days of its presentation.[22]

Within three days of his appointment, the examiner must deliver to the registrar of companies a certified copy of the court order appointing him. He

---

19 [1993] 2 IR 561. The Company Law Review Group also recommended the adoption of the 'reasonable prospect' test.
20 [2001] 1 IR 668.
21 [2001] 1 IR 668.
22 Section 12(1) ibid.

must also advertise the fact of his appointment in two daily newspapers within the same time frame. Within twenty-one days, he must put similar notices in the *CRO Gazette*.

Every invoice, order for goods or business letter issued by or on behalf of the company, being a document on, or in which, the name of the company appears, must, immediately after the name, include the words: 'in examination (under the Companies (Amendment) Act 1990)'.

Effects of Court Protection

If the court appoints an examiner, the period of protection commences from the date of the presentation of the petition and ends on the expiry of seventy days, or such earlier date as the court may terminate the protection. However, under section 18(3), the time period may be extended by the court for a further thirty days, if the court is satisfied that the examiner can not report to the court within the initial seventy-day period. Under section 18(4), the court may grant a further extension to allow it consider the examiner's report. It has usually been only in the rarest circumstance that the court has had to invoke the latter sub-section. In the Goodman and Kentz examinerships, which involved a number of companies and complex negotiations with domestic and overseas creditors and investors, such extensions were permitted.

Section 5, as amended, lists many of the consequences of court protection which effectively suspend all actions by members and creditors (including contingent and prospective creditors) against the company. These consequences are as follows:

(a) a winding up of the company can not be initiated;
(b) a receiver can not be appointed, and if appointed within the three days prior to the appointment of an examiner, he must cease to act unless directed otherwise by the court;
(c) no attachment, execution, distress or sequestration can be enforced against the company's property or effects without the consent of the examiner;
(d) secured creditors cannot take steps to realise their security without the consent of the examiner. In *Re Holdair Ltd*[23], instructions from a lending institution to the company to lodge fixed charge receivables into a designated bank account during the court protection period was held to be an action prohibited by this section;
(e) no steps can be taken to repossess goods in the company's possession under any hire purchase agreement, including conditional sale and retention of title agreements;
(f) no relief under section 205 of the Principal Act can be granted by the court to members against the company concerning the conduct of the affairs of the

---

23 [1994] I IR 416.

company or the exercise of the powers of the director prior to the presentation of the petition;

(g) no guarantees by third parties on behalf of the company can be enforced; and

(h) no other proceedings can be commenced against the company except by leave of the court.

In addition to the above, no pre-petition debts can be paid by the company unless the report of the independent accountant contains a recommendation stating that such debts be paid and the court considers that a failure to do so would considerably reduce the prospects of the company, or the whole or any part of its undertaking, surviving as a going concern.[24]

As mentioned above, a guarantor of a company's debts is protected during the period of court protection. However, under section 25A of the 1990 Amendment Act, a company creditor can take legal action against the guarantor after the court protection has ended.

Creditor's Committee

An examiner may, and if directed by the court shall, appoint a Committee of Creditors to assist him in the performance of his functions.[25] Except as otherwise directed by the court, a committee appointed shall consist of not more than five members and shall include, where they are willing to serve, the holders of the three largest unsecured claims. The examiner should provide the committee with a copy of any proposals for a compromise or scheme of arrangement and the committee may express an opinion on the proposals on its own behalf, or on behalf of the creditors or classes of creditors represented thereon.

Receiver and Provisional Liquidator

If a receiver has been appointed not less than three days prior to the successful petition, the court may make any such order as it sees fit, including that the receiver shall cease to act, or act only in respect of certain assets, or that he must deliver all books, papers and other records relating to the goods or possessions in his control to the examiner, or to give the examiner full particulars of all his dealings with the property or undertaking of the company. If a provisional liquidator is already appointed, the court may make similar orders, including an order that the provisional liquidator is appointed the examiner. The court will only make an order in relation to a receiver or provisional liquidator if it is satisfied that there is a reasonable prospect of the survival of the company, and the whole or any part of its undertaking, as a going concern.

---

24 Section 5A.
25 Section 21.

Related Companies

Under section 4, the examiner may apply to the court for protection of any related company even when that company is not insolvent or near insolvent. The application must be grounded on the examiner's belief that court protection would facilitate the survival of the original company as a going concern. The protection period for related companies only commences from the date of the court order.

Powers of the Examiner

In order to carry out his statutory duties and functions, the examiner has extensive powers. Some of these are automatic from the date of his appointment and others are only available on application to the court. The examiner's discretionary powers are detailed to a large extent in sections 7 and 8, and include the following:

(a) all the powers and rights of an auditor;
(b) the power to convene, set the agenda for, and preside over meetings of the board of directors and general meetings;
(c) the right to be given reasonable notice of, to attend and be heard at, all board meetings and general meetings;
(d) the power to take whatever steps are necessary to halt, prevent or rectify the effects of any act, omission, course of conduct, decision or contract by any party in relation to the assets or liabilities of the company which, in the examiner's opinion, is or is likely to be detrimental to the company or any interested party. This power does not enable the examiner to repudiate a contract entered into prior to court protection. A provision in any contract preventing the company from borrowing or giving security can not be enforced if the examiner is under the opinion that, were it enforced, it would be likely to prejudice the survival of the company as a going concern. The examiner must serve notice on the parties concerned informing him of his opinion in this regard;
(e) to apply to the court to determine any question arising in the course of his office;
(f) in ascertaining the affairs of the company, an examiner has extensive investigative powers. These powers are supported by a corresponding statutory duty imposed on officers and agents of the company to produce, on the examiner's request, such books and documents including those relating to bank accounts held by directors or officers of the company.

Specific Powers

The Act also provides the examiner with specific powers which are subject to court approval. While each power in its own right appears necessary to enable the examiner to carry out his functions, when they are used together they can have a serious effect on secured creditors.

Directors' Powers

The appointment of an examiner does not affect directors' powers. They will continue to manage the business of the company unless the examiner applies to the court, under section 9, to have all or any of the directors' powers vested in him. One such power granted frequently to examiners is the directors' power to borrow on behalf of the company. In one case, the question arose as to whether the examiner's power of borrowing is subject to the same restrictions that apply to the directors' power. *In Re Holdair Ltd*[26] the examiner had applied for and obtained orders authorising him to borrow monies in order to facilitate the survival of the company as a going concern. Under the terms of a debenture, the directors of the company had been restricted from borrowing without the prior consent of the debenture holders. The court held that the examiner was not so restricted. Although Finlay CJ. felt that the examiner's borrowing was permitted under section 9, he decided the matter by reference to section 7(5) of the Act which enables an examiner to halt, prevent, or rectify, the effects of, *inter alia*, any contract that in his opinion is likely to be detrimental to the company.

Dealing with Property

Under section 11 of the Act, the examiner may apply to the court for leave to dispose of the company's property where he is of the opinion that such action would facilitate the survival of the company. Such property includes that which is subject to a floating or fixed charge, or goods that are in the possession of the company but are subject to a hire-purchase, conditional sale or retention of title agreement. However, the section provides for the proceeds of the sale of such property or goods to be applied towards discharging the amounts owed under the security. Furthermore, holders of fixed charges are protected even further because the court can ascertain the market value of the property subject to the charge and order that the difference between that amount and the actual proceeds will be paid to the fixed charge holder. This means that fixed charge holders will not suffer any adverse effect of a 'fire-sale' over the property charged.

The court will not permit the sale of the company's business and assets where the effect would be such that the company could no longer trade. In *Re Clare Textiles Ltd*,[27] the examiner had entered into conditional contracts for the sale of the company's premises, business, stock and machinery, which he stated would cause the company to cease trading and go into liquidation. Costello J. made it

---

26 [1994] 1 IR 416.
27 [1993] 2 IR 213.

clear that the function of the examinership was to facilitate (if possible) the survival of the company, or the whole or part of its undertaking, as a going concern and not act as liquidator, and on this basis the examiner had no power to enter into such contracts.

Certification of Expenses

One of the most controversial sections in the Act is section 10 which gives the examiner power to certify expenditure incurred during the period of court protection. Such expenditure must have been incurred in circumstances where, in the opinion of the examiner, the survival of the company would otherwise be seriously prejudiced. In addition, those liabilities of the company certified under section 10 will be treated as expenses incurred by the examiner for the purposes of section 29 of the 1990 Amendment Act. Accordingly, these 'certified expenses' will be payable in priority to all other claims (including a claim secured by a floating charge and claims by preferential creditors) with the exception of fixed security or pledges.

Section 10 does not require the examiner's certification to be approved by the court in advance. In *Re Don Bluth Entertainment Ltd*[28] it was contended by the examiner that section 10 conferred upon him a discretion that could not be reviewed by the court. He also argued that if it was reviewable, then this could only be done on the grounds that certification was carried out in bad faith, for an improper purpose, or that it was manifestly unreasonable. He went on to argue that if the court declined to sanction the expenses that had arisen, it would render null and void a decision properly made by the examiner and defeat the reasonable expectations of the creditors who dealt with the company in reliance of the statutory powers which the examiner purported to exercise. Murphy J. rejected this argument and went on to say:

> As the combined operation of ss. 10 and 29 of the Act of 1990 will frequently result in some creditors of a company being paid in full at the expense of the creditors who hold securities over the assets of the company or creditors who have enjoyed a statutory preference under section 285 of the Act of 1963 if the insolvency of the company in question had resulted in a liquidation rather than an Examinership, it is important that an Examiner should exercise great care and professional expertise in issuing certificates under section 10 aforesaid.

He went on to hold that expenses certified by the examiner in relation to the pre-petition and petition costs of the company were not expenses properly so called within the meaning of section 10. That provision, he said, did not confer any priority on the costs of petitioners and he added that it would seem to him: 'to be inappropriate to alter the scheme of the Act by the fortuitous event that a provisional or interim Examiner might be appointed.' For similar reasons the

---

28 [1994] 3 IR 141.

High Court also rejected pre-petition costs as certifiable expenses of the examiner in *Re Edenpark Construction Ltd*.[29]

Combined Powers

Prior to 1999, the exercise of combined powers by the examiner could have a detrimental effect on all the secured creditors of the company. In *Re Atlantic Magnetics Ltd*[30] the issue before the court was whether the examiner could use certain receivables — the subject of an existing fixed charge — to discharge the expenses of examination, including the borrowings of the examiner, during the protection process. The court was essentially asked to reconcile section 29 of the 1990 Amendment Act with section 11. Reading the sections together the court held that the examiner could apply the assets — the subject matter of a fixed charge — to pay his borrowings, effectively ignoring the charge. This position was reaffirmed by the Supreme Court in *Re Holdair Limited*.[31]

The implication of these judgments for secured creditors was severe. A lender who had provided borrowings to the company secured by the company's cash balances (back-to-back borrowing) would traditionally have been in the strongest position in the event of the company's insolvency. However, under the authority of the above cases an examiner could use such cash balances to meet the costs, expenses and remuneration of the examinership including those expenses certified by the examiner under section 10. Such an action by the examiner would put the secured creditor in an untenable position as his security would become ineffective. Even if there are no readily available assets such as cash, the examiner could borrow monies, as he did in the Atlantic Magnetics case, and certify the borrowings as expenses within the meaning of section 29. The lender to the examiner would therefore be paid before all other creditors, including those holding fixed charges.

The 1999 Amendment Act has rectified this position somewhat. Now, the remuneration costs and expenses of the examiner where sanctioned by the court, still take priority over all other claims, whether secured or unsecured.[32] However, expenses 'certified' by the examiner under section 10 are now treated differently from the other expenses of the examiner. While still maintaining a priority status in terms of other claims, including floating charges, the 'certified expenses' portion of the overall expenses of an examiner no longer have priority over fixed charges or pledges. Accordingly, an examiner cannot look to the assets secured by a fixed charge or a pledge to meet his 'certified expenses'. He can, however, use assets that are the subject of an existing floating charge.

---

29 [1994] 3 IR 126.
30 [1993] 2 IR 561.
31 [1994] 1 IR 416.
32 Section 29.

Hearing Concerning Irregularities

Under section 13A of the 1990 Act, the court may hold a hearing if irregularities in the report of the independent accountant are discovered. Creditors are entitled to attend and be heard at such sittings. Following a hearing of this kind, the court may make such orders as it deems fit, including, where appropriate, an order for the trial of any issue relating to the matter concerned.

Proposals for a Compromise or Scheme of Arrangement.

The examiner's primary duty is to formulate proposals for a compromise or scheme of arrangement.[33] In this regard, he has the power to convene and preside at meetings of members and creditors, to consider the proposals and report to the court within thirty-five days of his appointment or such longer period as the court may allow. At plenary meetings of members and creditors the examiner's proposals can be modified, but only with his consent.

The contents of the proposals for a compromise or scheme of arrangement are set out in section 22(1) of the Act. The proposals must:

(a) specify each class of the company's members and creditors;
(b) specify those classes of members and creditors whose interests or claims will not be impaired by the proposals together with those who will be impaired by the proposals;
(c) provide equal treatment for each claim or interest of a particular class unless the holder of a particular class or interest agrees to less favourable treatment;
(d) provide for the implementation of the proposals;
(e) specify whatever changes should be made in relation to the management or direction of the company where the examiner considers it necessary or desirable to do so in order to facilitate the survival of the company;
(f) specify any changes the examiner considers should be made to the memorandum or articles of the company with regard to the management or direction of the company;
(g) contain any other matters which the examiner considers appropriate;
(h) contain any such other matters as the court may direct.

A statement of the assets and liabilities of the company at the date of the proposals must be attached. There should also be attached a description of the estimated financial outcome of a winding-up for each class of members and creditors.

Proposals will be deemed to be accepted by a meeting of members if a majority of the votes cast are in favour of the resolution for the proposals. The

---

33 Section 18(1).

proposals are deemed to have been accepted by the creditors when a majority in number, representing a majority in value of the claims represented at the meeting, have voted in favour of the resolution for the proposals.[34]

If the proposals cannot be agreed by at least one class of creditors, the matter will return for consideration to the court which may direct that the company be wound up.

The Examiner's Report

The examiner is required to report back to the court within thirty-five days of his appointment. The contents of the report are set out in section 19 and include:

(a) the proposals, if any;
(b) any adopted modifications of the proposals;
(c) the outcome of each meeting;
(d) the committee of creditors' recommendations, if any;
(e) a statement of the company's assets and liabilities (including contingent and prospective creditors);
(f) a list of the officers of the company;
(g) the company's creditors, the amount owed to each of them and their priority status in an insolvency context (see Chapter 26, Asset Realisation and Distribution);
(h) the examiner's recommendations; and
(i) any such other matters as the examiner deems appropriate or the Court directs.

The examiner must deliver a copy of his report to the company on the same day as he delivers it to the court. Furthermore, the examiner must provide a copy of his report to any interested party upon a written application being made to him. The court may direct that parts of the report are omitted in the event that it is being provided to an interested party if it would otherwise prejudice the survival of the company, or the whole or any part of it, as a going concern.

The report shall be set down for consideration by the court as soon as possible thereafter. The company and any creditor or member whose claim or interest will be impaired if the proposals were implemented may appear at the hearing to consider the report. Section 22(5) defines an impaired creditor as one who receives less in payment of his claim than the full amount due at the date of presentation of the petition. In *Re Jetmara Teo Ltd*[35] Costello J. rejected a contention by the examiner that a lending institution which was to be repaid in full, although over a longer period of time than had been contractually agreed

---

34 Section 23.
35 [1992] I IR 147.

and without interest, was not an impaired creditor.[36] At such court hearings, any member or creditor whose rights are impaired may object to the proposals on the following grounds:

(a) there was a material irregularity at or in the plenary meetings of the creditors or members;
(b) that acceptance of the proposals was obtained by improper means;
(c) that the proposals were put forward for an improper purpose;
(d) that the proposals were unfairly prejudicial to the interests of the objector.

If any such objection is upheld, the court may order that the decision be set aside and that another plenary meeting be held. As a rule, the court may, as it thinks fit, confirm the proposals unconditionally, confirm them subject to modifications or reject them entirely.[37] However, it will not accept them in the following circumstances:

(a) unless at least one class of creditors whose interests or claims would be impaired by the implementation of the proposals has accepted the proposals; or
(b) where the sole or primary purpose of the proposals is the avoidance of the payment of taxes;[38] or
(c) where the court is not satisfied that the proposals are fair and equitable in relation to any class of impaired creditors that has not accepted the proposals;[39] or
(d) where the proposals are not unfairly prejudicial to any other interested party. In *Re Seluckwe Ltd*[40] Costello J. modified proposals which involved the release of two directors' personal guarantees. However, in *Re Antigen Holdings Ltd*[41] the court approved a scheme of arrangement where shareholders benefited from the scheme before all creditors had been paid off. Confirming the scheme on the ground that there was a high prospect of success, McCracken J. declared: 'disproportionately disadvantaged does not constitute unfairly prejudicial.'

Where the court confirms proposals, whether modified or not, they are binding on all members and creditors affected by the proposals, and also on the company. The court may make such orders as it deems fit for the implementation of the compromise or scheme of arrangement. The compromise or scheme of arrangement shall come into effect from a date fixed by the court which must be

---

36 See also *Re Antigen Holdings Ltd* [2001] 4 IR 600.
37 Section 25.
38 Section 24(3).
39 Section 24(4).
40 Unreported, High Court, Costello J., December 20, 1991.
41 [2001] 4 IR 600.

within twenty-one days from the date of confirmation. A copy of the confirmation order must be given to the registrar of companies and published in the *CRO Gazette* by the examiner within fourteen days of the order being granted.

If the company and any other interested party can show that the confirmation was procured by fraud, they can apply to the court within 180 days of the confirmation to have the decision revoked. If the court is satisfied that there was fraud, section 27 of the Act empowers it to revoke its confirmation or make such orders as it thinks fit. The court is directed by the Act to have regard for the interests of any *bona fide* purchaser for value of property who relied on the confirmation.

If the examiner's report is unfavourable to the extent that he does not believe that the company is capable of survival, he may apply to the court which may make such order as it deems fit including an order for the winding-up of the company.

Examiner's Costs Remuneration and Expenses

As already discussed, section 29 provides for the payment of the examiner's costs, remuneration and expenses before all other claims in the event of the liquidation of the company. We have seen where the court disapproved of certain certified expenses and a number of cases suggest that the court will do the same in relation to the examiner's costs and remuneration. In *Re Wogan's Drogheda Ltd* (No.3),[42] Costello J. refused to sanction the payment of the examiner's remuneration costs and expenses because he felt that the activities of the examiner were such as to abuse the court process. In *Re Clare Textiles Ltd,*[43] Murphy J. held that the examiner's remuneration and costs would only be paid up to the point when he ought to have ceased acting as an examiner. In addition, he refused to allow the examiner his remuneration for completion of his statutory report as it did not comply with the requirements of the legislation. In *Re Coombe Importers Ltd,*[44] Hamilton CJ. refused to sanction expenses that had been certified by the examiner, on the grounds that they were not a necessary expense of the examinership. In *Re Edenpark Construction Ltd,*[45] Murphy J. appproved only 80 per cent of the examiner's fee because it was clear from the information provided that the court protection ought to have been terminated some time prior to when it did.

Termination of Court Protection

The protection granted to a company ends either:

---

42 Unreported, High Court, Costello J., February 9, 1993.
43 [1993] 2 IR 213.
44 Unreported, Supreme Court, June 22, 1995.
45 [1994] 3 IR 126.

(a) on the coming into effect of the compromise or scheme of arrangement under the Act, or

(b) on such earlier date as the Court may direct.

Where a company ceases to be under the protection of the court, the appointment of the examiner shall terminate on the date of such cessation.[46]

---

46 Section 26.

TABLE A, COMPANIES ACT, 1963

[1963.] *Companies Act,* 1963 [*No.* 33.]

SCHEDULES

Sections, 2, 13,
16, 395.

FIRST SCHEDULE.

TABLE A, TÁBLA A, AND TABLES B, C, D AND E.

TABLE A.

PART I.

REGULATIONS FOR MANAGEMENT OF A COMPANY LIMITED BY
SHARES NOT BEÍNG A PRIVATE COMPANY.

Interpretation.

1. In these regulations:

"the Act" means the Companies Act, 1963 (No. 33 of 1963);

"the directors" means the directors for the time being of the
company or the directors present at a meeting of the board of
director and includes any person occupying the position of
director by whatever name called;

"the register" means the register of members to be kept as
required by section 116 of the Act;

"secretary" means any person appointed to perform the duties of
the secretary of the company;

"the office" means the registered office for the time being of the
company;

"the seal" means the common seal of the company.

Expressions referring to writing shall, unless the contrary
intention appears, be construed as including references to
printing, lithography, photography, and any other modes of
representing or reproducing words in a visible form.

Unless the contrary intention appears, words or expressions
contained in these regulations shall bear the same meaning as in
the Act or in any statutory modification thereof in force at the
date at which these regulations become binding on the company.

Share Capital and Variation of Rights.

2. Without prejudice to any special rights previously conferred on the holders of any existing shares or class of shares, any share in the company may be issued with such preferred, deferred or other special rights or such restrictions, whether in regard to dividend, voting, return of capital or otherwise, as the company may from time to time by ordinary resolution determine.

3. If at any time the share capital is divided into different classes of shares, the rights attached to any class may, whether or not the company is being wound up, be varied or abrogated with the consent in writing of the holders of three-fourths of the issued shares of that class, or with the sanction of a special resolution passed at a separate general meeting of the holders of the shares of the class.

4. The rights conferred upon the holders of the shares of any class issued with preferred or other right shall not, unless otherwise expressly provided by the terms of issue of the shares of that class, be deemed to be varied by the creation or issue of further shares ranking *pari passu* therewith.

5. Subject to the provisions of these regulations relating to new shares, the shares shall be at the disposal of the directors, and they may (subject to the provisions of the Companies Acts, 1963 to 1983) allot, grant options over or otherwise dispose of them to such persons, on such terms and conditions and at such times as they may consider to be in the best interests of the company and its shareholders, but so that no share shall be issued at a discount and so that in the case of shares offered to the public for subscription by a public limited company, the amount payable on application on each share shall not be less than one-quarter of the nominal amount of the share and the whole of any premium thereon.

6. The company may exercise the powers of paying commissions conferred by section 59 of the Act, provided that the rate per cent and the amount of the commission paid or agreed to be paid shall be disclosed in the manner required by that section, and the rate of the commission shall not exceed the rate of 10 per cent. of the price at which the shares in respect whereof the same is paid are issued or an amount equal to 10 per cent. of such price (as the case may be). Such commission may be satisfied by the payment of cash or the allotment of fully or

partly paid shares or partly in one way and partly in the other. The company may also, on any issue of shares, pay such brokerage as may be lawful.

7. Except as required by law, no person şhall be recognised by the company as holding any share upon any trust, and the company shall not be bound by or be compelled in any way to recognise (even when having notice thereof) any equitable, contingent, future or partial interest in any share or any interest in any fractional part of a share or (except only as by these regulations or by law otherwise provided) any other rights in respect of any share except an absolute right to the entirety thereof in the registered holder: this shall not preclude the company from requiring the members or a transferee of shares to furnish the company with information as to the beneficial ownership of any share when such information is reasonably required by the company.

8. Every person whose name is entered as a member in the register shall be entitled without payment to receive within 2 months after allotment or lodgement of a transfer (or within such other period as the conditions of issue shall provide) one certificate for all his shares or several certificates each for one or more of his shares upon payment of 12½ new pence for every certificate after the first or such less sum as the directors shall from time to time determine, so, however, that in respect of a share or shares held jointly by several persons the company shall not be bound to issue more than one certificate, and delivery of a certificate for a share to one of several joint holders shall be sufficient delivery to all such holders. Every certificate shall be under the seal or under the official seal kept by the company by virtue of section 3 of the Companies (Amendment) Act, 1977, and shall specify the shares to which it relates and the amount paid up thereon.

9. If a share certificate be defaced, lost or destroyed, it may be renewed on payment of 2s. 6d. or such less sum and on such terms (if any) as to evidence and indemnity and the payment of out-of-pocket expenses of the company of investigating evidence as the directors think fit.

10. The company shall not give, whether directly or indirectly, and whether by means of a loan, guarantee, the provision of security or otherwise, any financial assistance for the purpose of or in connection with a purchase or subscription made or to be

made by any person of or for any shares in the company or in its holding company, but this regulation shall not prohibit any transaction permitted by section 60 of the Act.

Lien.

11. The company shall have a first and paramount lien on every share (not being a fully paid share) for all moneys (whether immediately payable or not) called or payable at a fixed time in respect of that share; but the directors may at any time declare any share to be wholly or in part exempt from the provisions of this regulation. The company's lien on a share shall extend to all dividends payable thereon.

12. The company may sell, in such manner as the directors think fit, any shares on which the company has a lien, but no sale shall be made unless a sum in respect of which the lien exists is immediately payable, nor until the expiration of 14 days after a notice in writing, stating and demanding payment of such part of the amount in respect of which the lien exists as is immediately payable, has been given to the registered holder for the time being of the share, or the person entitled thereto by reason of his death or bankruptcy.

13. To give effect to any such sale, the directors may authorise some person to transfer the shares sold to the purchaser thereof. The purchaser shall be registered as the holder of the shares comprised in any such transfer, and he shall not be bound to see to the application of the purchase money, nor shall his title to the shares be affected by any irregularity or invalidity in the proceedings in reference to the sale.

14. The proceeds of the sale shall be received by the company and applied in payment of such part of the amount in respect of which the lien exists as is immediately payable, and the residue, if any, shall (subject to a like lien for sums not immediately payable as existed upon the shares before the sale) be paid to the person entitled to the shares at the date of the sale.

Calls on Shares.

15. The directors may from time to time make calls upon the members in respect of any moneys unpaid on their shares (whether on account of the nominal value of the shares or by way of premium) and not by the conditions of allotment thereof made

371

payable at fixed times, provided that no call shall exceed one-fourth of the nominal value of the share or be payable at less than one month from the date fixed for the payment of the last preceding call, and each member shall (subject to receiving at least 14 days' notice specifying the time or times and place of payment) pay to the company at the time or times and place so specified the amount called on his shares. A call may be revoked or postponed as the directors may determine.

16. A call shall be deemed to have been made at the time when the resolution of the directors authorising the call was passed and may be required to be paid by instalments.

17. The joint holders of a share shall be jointly and severally liable to pay all calls in respect thereof.

18. If a sum called in respect of a share is not paid before or on the day appointed for payment thereof, the person from whom the sum is due shall pay interest on the sum from the day appointed for payment thereof to the time of actual payment at such rate, not exceeding 5 per cent. per annum, as the directors may determine, but the directors shall be at liberty to waive payment of such interest wholly or in part.

19. Any sum which by the terms of issue of a share becomes payable on allotment or at any fixed date, whether on account of the nominal value of the share or by way of premium, shall, for the purpose of these regulations, be deemed to be a call duly made and payable on the date on which, by the terms of issue, the same becomes payable, and in case of non-payment all the relevant provisions of these regulations as to payment of interest and expenses, forfeiture or otherwise, shall apply as if such sum had become payable by virtue of a call duly made and notified.

20. The directors may, on the issue of shares, differentiate between the holders as to the amount of calls to be paid and the times of payment.

21. The directors may, if they think fit, receive from any member willing to advance the same, all or any part of the moneys uncalled and unpaid upon any shares held by him, and upon all or any of the moneys so advanced may (until the same would, but for such advance, become payable) pay interest at such rate not exceeding (unless the company in general meeting otherwise directs) 5 per cent. per annum, as may be agreed upon

between the directors and the member paying such sum in advance.

Transfer of Shares.

22. The instrument of transfer of any share shall be executed by or on behalf of the transferor and transferee, and the transferor shall be deemed to remain the holder of the share until the name of the transferee is entered in the register in respect thereof.

23. Subject to such of the restrictions of these regulations as may be applicable, any member may transfer all or any of his shares by instrument in writing in any usual or common form or any other form which the directors may approve.

24. The directors may decline to register the transfer of a share (not being a fully paid share) to a person of whom they do not approve, and they may also decline to register the transfer of a share on which the company has a lien. The directors may also decline to register any transfer of a share which, in their opinion, may imperil or prejudicially affect the status of the company in the State or which may imperil any tax concession or rebate to which the members of the company are entitled or which may involve the company in the payment of any additional stamp or other duties on any conveyance of any property made or to be made to the company.

25. The directors may also decline to recognise any instrument of transfer unless—

> *(a)* a fee of 2s. 6d. or such lesser sum as the directors may from time to time require, is paid to the company in respect thereof; and

> *(b)* the instrument of transfer is accompanied by the certificate of the shares to which it relates, and such other evidence as the directors may reasonably require to show the right of the transferor to make the transfer; and

> *(c)* the instrument of transfer is in respect of one class of share only.

26. If the directors refuse to register a transfer they shall, within 2 months after the date on which the transfer was lodged

with the company, send to the transferee notice of the refusal.

27. The registration of transfer may be suspended at such times and for such periods, not exceeding in the whole 30 days in each year, as the directors may from time to time determine.

28. The company shall be entitled to charge a fee not exceeding 2s 6d. on the registration of every probate, letters of administration, certificate of death or marriage, power of attorney, notice as to stock or other instrument.

Transmission of Shares.

29. In the case of the death of a member, the survivor or survivors where the deceased was a joint holder, and the personal representatives of the deceased where he was a sole holder, shall be the only persons recognised by the company as having any title to his interest in the shares; but nothing herein contained shall release the estate of a deceased joint holder from any liability in respect of any share which had been jointly held by him with other persons.

30. Any person becoming entitled to a share in consequence of the death or bankruptcy of a member may, upon such evidence being produced as may from time to time properly be required by the directors and subject as hereinafter provided, elect either to be registered himself as holder of the share or to have some person nominated by him registered as the transferee thereof, but the directors shall, in either case, have the same right to decline or suspend registration as they would have had in the case of a transfer of the share by that member before his death or bankruptcy, as the case may be.

31. If the person so becoming entitled elects to be registered himself, he shall deliver or send to the company a notice in writing signed by him stating that he so elects. If he elects to have another person registered, he shall testify his election by executing to that person a transfer of the share. All the limitations, restrictions and provisions of these regulations relating to the right to transfer and the registration of transfers of shares shall be applicable to any such notice or transfer as aforesaid as if the death or bankruptcy of the member had not occurred and the notice or transfer were a transfer signed by that member.

32. A person becoming entitled to a share by reason of the death or bankruptcy of the holder shall be entitled to the same dividends and other advantages to which he would be entitled if he were the registered holder of the share, except that he shall not, before being registered as a member in respect of the share, be entitled in respect of it to exercise any right conferred by membership in relation to meetings of the company, so, however, that the directors may at any time give notice requiring any such person to elect either to be registered himself or to transfer the share, and if the notice is not complied with within 90 days, the directors may thereupon withhold payment of all dividends, bonuses or other moneys payable in respect of the share until the requirements of the notice have been complied with.

Forfeiture of Shares.

33. If a member fails to pay any call or instalment of a call on the day appointed for payment thereof, the directors may, at any time thereafter during such time as any part of the call or instalment remains unpaid, serve a notice on him requiring payment of so much of the call or instalment as is unpaid together with any interest which may have accrued.

34. The notice shall name a further day (not earlier than the expiration of 14 days from the date of service of the notice) on or before which the payment required by the notice is to be made, and shall state that in the event of non-payment at or before the time appointed the shares in respect of which the call was made will be liable to be forfeited.

35. If the requirements of any such notice as aforesaid are not complied with, any share in respect of which the notice has been given may at any time thereafter, before the payment required by the notice has been made, be forfeited by a resolution of the directors to that effect.

36. A forfeited share may be sold or otherwise disposed of on such terms and in such manner as the directors think fit, and at any time before a sale or disposition the forfeiture may be cancelled on such terms as the directors think fit.

37. A person whose shares have been forfeited shall cease to be a member in respect of the forfeited shares, but shall, notwithstanding, remain liable to pay to the company all moneys which, at the date of forfeiture, were payable by him to the

company in respect of the shares, but his liability shall cease if and when the company shall have received payment in full of all such moneys in respect of the shares.

38. A statutory declaration that the declarant is a director or the secretary of the company, and that a share in the company has been duly forfeited on a date stated in the declaration, shall be conclusive evidence of the facts therein stated as against all persons claiming to be entitled to the share. The company may receive the consideration, if any, given for the share on any sale or disposition thereof and may execute a transfer of the share in favour of the person to whom the share is sold or disposed of and he shall thereupon be registered as the holder of the share, and shall not be bound to see to the application of the purchase money, if any, nor shall his title to the share be affected by any irregularity or invalidity in the proceedings in reference to the forfeiture, sale or disposal of the share.

39. The provisions of these regulations as to forfeiture shall apply in the case of nonpayment of any sum which, by the terms of issue of a share, becomes payable at a fixed time, whether on account of the nominal value of the share or by way of premium, as if the same had been payable by virtue of a call duly made and notified.

Conversion of Shares into Stock.

40. The company may by ordinary resolution convert any paid up shares into stock, and reconvert any stock into paid up shares of any denomination.

41. The holders of stock may transfer the same, or any part thereof, in the same manner, and subject to the same regulations, as and subject to which the shares from which the stock arose might previously to conversion have been transferred, or as near thereto as circumstances admit; and the directors may from time to time fix the minimum amount of stock transferable but so that such minimum shall not exceed the nominal amount of each share from which the stock arose.

42. The holders of stock shall, according to the amount of stock held by them, have the same rights, privileges and advantages in relation to dividends, voting at meetings of the company and other matters as if they held the shares from which the stock arose, but no such right, privilege or advantage (except

[1963.]   *Companies Act,* 1963   [*No.* **33.**]

participation in the dividends and profits of the company and in the assets on winding up) shall be conferred by an amount of stock which would not, if existing in shares, have conferred that right, privilege or advantage.

43. Such of the regulations of the company as are applicable to paid up shares shall apply to stock, and the words "share" and "shareholder" therein shall include "stock" and "stockholder".

Alteration of Capital.

44. The company may from time to time by ordinary resolution increase the share capital by such sum, to be divided into shares of such amount, as the resolution shall prescribe.

45. The company may by ordinary resolution—

> (*a*) consolidate and divide all or any of its share capital into shares of larger amount than its existing shares;

> (*b*) subdivide its existing shares, or any of them, into shares of smaller amount than is fixed by the memorandum of association subject, nevertheless, to section 68 (1) (*d*) of the Act;

> (*c*) cancel any shares which, at the date of the passing of the resolution, have not been taken or agreed to be taken by any person.

46. The company may by special resolution reduce its share capital, any capital redemption reserve fund or any share premium account in any manner and with and subject to any incident authorised, and consent required, by law.

General Meetings.

47. All general meetings of the company shall be held in the State.

48. (1) Subject to paragraph (2) of this regulation, the company shall in each year hold a general meeting as its annual general meeting in addition to any other meeting in that year, and shall specify the meeting as such in the notice calling it; and not more than 15 months shall elapse between the date of one annual general meeting of the company and that of the next.

(2) So long as the company holds its first annual general meeting within 18 months of its incorporation, it need not hold it in the year of its incorporation or in the year following. Subject to regulation 47, the annual general meeting shall be held at such time and place as the directors shall appoint.

49. All general meetings other than annual general meetings shall be called extraordinary general meetings.

50. The directors may, whenever they think fit, convene an extraordinary general meeting, and extraordinary general meetings shall also be convened on such requisition, or in default, may be convened by such requisitionists, as provided by section 132 of the Act. If at any time there are not within the State sufficient directors capable of acting to form a quorum, any director or any 2 members of the company may convene an extraordinary general meeting in the same manner as nearly as possible as that in which meetings may be convened by the directors.

Notice of General Meetings.

51. Subject to sections 133 and 141 of the Act, an annual general meeting and a meeting called for the passing of a special resolution shall be called by 21 days' notice in writing at the least, and a meeting of the company (other than an annual general meeting or a meeting for the passing of a special resolution) shall be called by 14 days' notice in writing at the least. The notice shall be exclusive of the day on which it is served or deemed to be served and of the day for which it is given, and shall specify the place, the day and the hour of the meeting, and in the case of special business, the general nature of that business, and shall be given, in manner hereinafter mentioned, to such persons as are, under the regulations of the company, entitled to receive such notices from the company.

52. The accidental omission to give notice of a meeting to, or the non-receipt of notice of a meeting by, any person entitled to receive notice shall not invalidate the proceedings at the meeting.

Proceedings at General Meetings.

53. All business shall be deemed special that is transacted at an extraordinary general meeting, and also all that is transacted at an annual general meeting, with the exception of declaring a

dividend, the consideration of the accounts, balance sheets and the reports of the directors and auditors, the election of directors in the place of those retiring, the re-appointment of the retiring auditors and the fixing of the remuneration of the auditors.

54. No business shall be transacted at any general meeting unless a quorum of members is present at the time when the meeting proceeds to business; save as herein otherwise provided, three members present in person shall be a quorum.

55. If within half an hour from the time appointed for the meeting a quorum is not present, the meeting, if convened upon the requisition of members, shall be dissolved; in any other case it shall stand adjourned to the same day in the next week, at the same time and place or to such other day and at such other time and place as the directors may determine, and if at the adjourned meeting a quorum is not present within half an hour from the time appointed for the meeting, the members present shall be a quorum.

56. The chairman, if any, of the board of directors shall preside as chairman at every general meeting of the company, or if there is no such chairman, or if he is not present within 15 minutes after the time appointed for the holding of the meeting or is unwilling to act, the directors present shall elect one of their number to be chairman of the meeting.

57. If at any meeting no director is willing to act as chairman or if no director is present within 15 minutes after the time appointed for holding the meeting, the members present shall choose one of their number to be chairman of the meeting.

58. The chairman may, with the consent of any meeting at which a quorum is present, and shall if so directed by the meeting, adjourn the meeting from time to time and from place to place, but no business shall be transacted at any adjourned meeting other than the business left unfinished at the meeting from which the adjournment took place. When a meeting is adjourned for 30 days or more, notice of the adjourned meeting shall be given as in the case of an original meeting. Save as aforesaid it shall not be necessary to give any notice of an adjournment or of the business to be transacted at an adjourned meeting.

59. At any general meeting a resolution put to the vote of the

meeting shall be decided on a show of hands unless a poll is (before or on the declaration of the result of the show of hands) demanded—

(a) by the chairman; or

(b) by at least three members present in person or by proxy; or

(c) by any member or members present in person or by proxy and representing not less than one-tenth of the total voting rights of all the members having the right to vote at the meeting; or

(d) by a member or members holding shares in the company conferring the right to vote at the meeting being shares on which an aggregate sum has been paid up equal to not less than one-tenth of the total sum paid up on all the shares conferring that right.

Unless a poll is so demanded, a declaration by the chairman that a resolution has, on a show of hands, been carried or carried unanimously, or by a particular majority, or lost, and an entry to that effect in the book containing the minutes of the proceedings of the company shall be conclusive evidence of the fact without proof of the number or proportion of the votes recorded in favour of or against such resolution.

The demand for a poll may be withdrawn.

60. Except as provided in regulation 62, if a poll is duly demanded it shall be taken in such manner as the chairman directs, and the result of the poll shall be deemed to be the resolution of the meeting at which the poll was demanded.

61. Where there is an equality of votes, whether on a show of hands or on a poll, the chairman of the meeting at which the show of hands takes place or at which the poll is demanded, shall be entitled to a second or casting vote.

62. A poll demanded on the election of a chairman or on a question of adjournment shall be taken forthwith. A poll demanded on any other question shall be taken at such time as the chairman of the meeting directs, and any business other than that on which a poll is demanded may be proceeded with pending the

taking of the poll.

Votes of Members.

63. Subject to any rights or restrictions for the time being attached to any class or classes of shares, on a show of hands every member present in person and ever proxy shall have one vote, so, however, that no individual shall have more than one vote, and on a poll every member shall have one vote for each share of which he is the holder.

64. Where there are joint holders, the vote of the senior who tenders a vote, whether in person or by proxy, shall be accepted to the exclusion of the votes of the other joint holders; and for this purpose, seniority shall be determined by the order in which the names stand in the register.

65. A member of unsound mind, or in respect of whom an order has been made by any court having jurisdiction in lunacy, may vote, whether on a show of hands or on a poll, by his committee, receiver, guardian or other person appointed by that court, and any such committee, receiver, guardian or other person may vote by proxy on a how of hands or on a poll.

66. No member shall be entitled to vote at any general meeting unless all calls or other sums immediately payable by him in respect of share in the company have been paid.

67. No objection shall be raised to the qualification of any voter except at the meeting or adjourned meeting at which the vote objected to is given or tendered, and every vote not disallowed at such meeting shall be valid for all purposes. Any such objection made in due time shall be referred to the chairman of the meeting, whose decision shall be final and conclusive.

68. Votes may be given either personally or by proxy.

69. The instrument appointing a proxy shall be in writing under the hand of the appointer or of his attorney duly authorised in writing, or, if the appointer is a body corporate either under seal or under the hand of an officer or attorney duly authorised. A proxy need not be a member of the company.

70. The instrument appointing a proxy and the power of attorney or other authority, if any, under which it is signed, or a

[1963.] *Companies Act, 1963* [*No.* **33.**]

notarially certified copy of that power or authority shall be deposited at the office or at such other place within the State as is specified for that purpose in the notice convening the meeting, not less than 48 hours before the time for holding the meeting or adjourned meeting at which the person named in the instrument proposes to vote, or, in the case of a poll, not less than 48 hours before the time appointed for the taking of the poll, and, in default, the instrument of proxy shall not be treated as valid.

71. An instrument appointing a proxy shall be in the following form or a form as near thereto as circumstances permit—

"

I/We of ....

Limited.

in the County of ....,being a

member/members of the above-named company hereby appoint ....

....

of ....

or failing him ....

of ....

as my/our proxy to vote for me/us on my/our behalf at the (annual or extra-ordinary, as the case may be) general meeting of the company to be held on the .... day of ...., 19 ...... and at any adjournment thereof.

Signed this ....day of ...., 19...........

This form is to be used *in favour of/against, the resolution.

Unless otherwise instructed the proxy will vote as he thinks fit.

*Strike out whichever is not desired."

72. The instrument appointing a proxy shall be deemed to confer authority to demand or join in demanding a poll.

73. A vote given in accordance with the terms of an instrument of proxy shall be valid notwithstanding the previous death or insanity of the principal or revocation of the proxy or of the authority under which the proxy was executed or the transfer of the share in respect of which the proxy is given, if no intimation in writing of such death, insanity, revocation or transfer as aforesaid is received by the company at the office before the commencement of the meeting or adjourned meeting at which the proxy is used.

[1963.] *Companies Act, 1963* [*No.* **33.**]

Bodies Corporate acting by Representatives at Meetings.

74. Any body corporate which is a member of the company may, by resolution of its directors or other governing body, authorise such person as it thinks fit to act as its representative at any meeting of the company or of any class of members of the company, and the person so authorised shall be entitled to exercise the same powers on behalf of the body corporate which he represents as that body corporate could exercise if it were an individual member of the company.

Directors.

75. The number of the directors and the names of the first directors shall be determined in writing by the subscribers of the memorandum of association or a majority of them.

76. The remuneration of the directors shall from time to time be determined by the company in general meeting. Such remuneration shall be deemed to accrue from day to day. The directors may also be paid all travelling, hotel and other expenses properly incurred by them in attending and returning from meetings of the directors or any committee of the directors or general meetings of the company or in connection with the business of the company.

77. The shareholding qualification for directors may be fixed by the company in general meeting and unless and until so fixed no qualification shall be required.

78. A director of the company may be or become a director or other officer of, or otherwise interested in, any company promoted by the company or in which the company may be interested as shareholder or otherwise, and no such director shall be accountable to the company for any remuneration or other benefits received by him as a director or officer of, or from his interest in, such other company unless the company otherwise directs.

Borrowing Powers.

79. The directors may exercise all the powers of the company to borrow money, and to mortgage or charge its undertaking, property and uncalled capital, or any part thereof, and subject to section 20 of the Companies (Amendment) Act, 1983 to issue

debentures, debenture stock and other securities, whether outright or as security for any debt, liability or obligation of the company or of any third party, so, however, that the amount for the time being remaining undischarged of moneys borrowed or secured by the directors, as aforesaid (apart from temporary loans obtained from the company's bankers in the ordinary course of business) shall not at any time, without the previous sanction of the company in general meeting, exceed the nominal amount of the share capital of the company for the time being issued, but nevertheless no lender or other person dealing with the company shall be concerned to see or inquire whether this limit is observed. No debt incurred or security given in excess of such limit shall be invalid or ineffectual except in the case of express notice to the lender or the recipient of the security at the time when the debt was incurred or security given that the limit hereby imposed had been or was thereby exceeded.

Powers and Duties of Directors.

80. The business of the company shall be managed by the directors, who may pay all expenses incurred in promoting and registering the company and may exercise all such powers of the company as are not, by the Companies Act 1963 to 1983 or by these regulations, required to be exercised by the company in general meeting, subject, nevertheless, to any of these regulations, to the provisions of the Act and to such directions, being not inconsistent with the aforesaid regulations or provisions, as may be given by the company in general meeting; but no direction given by the company in general meeting shall invalidate any prior act of the directors which would have been valid if that direction had not been given.

81. The directors may from time to time and at any time by power of attorney appoint any company, firm or person or body of persons, whether nominated directly or indirectly by the directors, to be the attorney or attorneys of the company for such purposes and with such powers, authorities and discretions (not exceeding those vested in or exercisable by the directors under these regulations) and for such period and subject to such conditions as they may think fit, and any such power of attorney may contain such provisions for the protection of persons dealing with any such attorney as the directors may think fit, and may also authorise any such attorney to delegate all or any of the powers, authorities and discretions vested in him.

82. The company may exercise the powers conferred by section 41 of the Act with regard to having an official seal for use abroad, and such powers shall be vested in the directors.

83. A director who is in any way, whether directly or indirectly, interested in a contract or proposed contract with the company shall declare the nature of his interest at a meeting of the directors in accordance with section 194 of the Act.

84. A director shall not vote in respect of any contract or arrangement in which he is so interested, and if he shall so vote, his vote shall not be counted, nor shall he be counted in the quorum present at the meeting but neither of these prohibitions shall apply to—

    (a) any arrangement for giving any director any security or indemnity in respect of money lent by him to or obligations undertaken by him for the benefit of the company; or

    (b) any arrangement for the giving by the company of any security to a third party in respect of a debt or obligation of the company for which the director himself has assumed responsibility in whole or in part under a guarantee or indemnity or by the deposit of a security; or

    (c) any contract by a director to subscribe for or underwrite shares or debentures of the company; or

    (d) any contract or arrangement with any other company in which he is interested only as an officer of such other company or as a holder of shares or other securities in such other company;

and these prohibitions may at any time be suspended or relaxed to any extent and either generally or in respect of any particular contract, arrangement or transaction by the company in general meeting.

85. A director may hold any other office or place of profit under the company (other than the office of auditor) in conjunction with his office of director for such period and on such terms as to remuneration and otherwise as the directors may determine, and no director or intending director shall be

[1963.]   *Companies Act*, 1963   [*No.* **33.**]

disqualified by his office from contracting with the company either with regard to his tenure of any such other office or place of profit or as vendor, purchaser or otherwise, nor shall any such contract or any contract or arrangement entered into by or on behalf of the company in which any director is in any way interested, be liable to be avoided, nor shall any director so contracting or being so interested be liable to account to the company for any profit realised by any such contract or arrangement by reason of such director holding that office or of the fiduciary relation thereby established.

86. A director, notwithstanding his interest, may be counted in the quorum present at any meeting whereat he or any other director is appointed to hold any such office or place of profit under the company or whereat the terms of any such appointment are arranged, and he may vote on any such appointment or arrangement other than his own appointment or the arrangement of the terms thereof.

87. Any director may act by himself or his firm in a professional capacity for the company, and he or his firm shall be entitled to remuneration for professional services as if he were not a director; but nothing herein contained shall authorise a director or his firm to act as auditor to the company.

88. All cheques, promissory notes, drafts, bills of exchange and other negotiable instruments and all receipts for moneys paid to the company shall be signed, drawn, accepted, endorsed or otherwise executed, as the case may be, by such person or persons and in such manner as the directors shall from time to time by resolution determine.

89. The directors shall cause minutes to be made in books provided for the purpose—

     (a) of all appointments of officers made by the directors;

     (b) of the names of the directors present at each meeting of the directors and of any committee of the directors;

     (c) of all resolutions and proceedings at all meetings of the company and of the directors and of committees of directors.

90. The directors on behalf of the company may pay a gratuity

or pension or allowance on retirement to any director who has held any other salaried office or place of profit with the company or to his widow or dependants, and may make contributions to any fund and pay premiums for the purchase or provision of any such gratuity, pension or allowance.

Disqualification of Directors.

91. The office of director shall be vacated if the director—

(a) ceases to be a director by virtue of section 180 of the Act; or

(b) is adjudged bankrupt in the State or in Northern Ireland or Great Britain or makes any arrangement or composition with his creditors generally; or

(c) becomes prohibited from being a director by reason of any order made under section 184 of the Act; or

(d) becomes of unsound mind; or

(e) resigns his office by notice in writing to the company; or

(f) is convicted of an indictable offence unless the directors otherwise determine; or

(g) is for more than 6 months absent without permission of the directors from meetings of the directors held during that period.

Rotation of Directors.

92. At the first annual general meeting of the company all the directors shall retire from office, and at the annual general meeting in every subsequent year, one-third of the directors for the time being, or, if their number is not three or a multiple of three, then the number nearest one-third shall retire from office.

93. The directors to retire in every year shall be those who have been longest in office since their last election but as between persons who became directors on the same day, those to retire shall (unless they otherwise agree among themselves) be determined by lot.

94. A retiring director shall be eligible for re-election.

95. The company, at the meeting at which a director retires in manner aforesaid, may fill the vacated office by electing a person thereto, and in default the retiring director shall, if offering himself for re-election, be deemed to have been re-elected, unless at such meeting it is expressly resolved not to fill such vacated office, or unless a resolution for the re-election of such director has been put to the meeting and lost.

96. No person other than a director retiring at the meeting shall, unless recommended by the directors, be eligible for election to the office of director at any general meeting unless not less than 3 nor more than 21 days before the day appointed for the meeting there shall have been left at the office notice in writing signed by a member duly qualified to attend and vote at the meeting for which such notice is given, of his intention to propose such person for election and also notice in writing signed by that person of his willingness to be elected.

97. The company may from time to time by ordinary resolution increase or reduce the number of directors and may also determine in what rotation the increased or reduced number is to go out of office.

98. The directors shall have power at any time and from time to time to appoint any person to be a director, either to fill a casual vacancy or as an addition to the existing directors, but so that the total number of directors shall not at any time exceed the number fixed in accordance with these regulations. Any director so appointed shall hold office only until the next following annual general meeting, and shall then be eligible for re-election but shall not be taken into account in determining the directors who are to retire by rotation at such meeting.

99. The company may, by ordinary resolution, of which extended notice has been given in accordance with section 142 of the Act, remove any director before the expiration of his period of office notwithstanding anything in these regulations or in any agreement between the company and such director. Such removal shall be without prejudice to any claim such director may have for damages for breach of any contract of service between him and the company.

100. The company may, by ordinary resolution, appoint

another person in place of a director removed from office under regulation 99 and without prejudice to the powers of the directors under regulation 98 the company in general meeting may appoint any person to be a director either to fill a casual vacancy or as an additional director. A person appointed in place of a director so removed or to fill such a vacancy shall be subject to retirement at the same time as if he had become a director on the day on which the director in whose place he is appointed was last elected a director.

Proceedings of Directors.

101. The directors may meet together for the despatch of business, adjourn and otherwise regulate their meetings as they think fit. Questions arising at any meeting shall be decided by a majority of votes. Where there is an equality of votes, the chairman shall have a second or casting vote. A director may, and the secretary on the requisition of a director shall, at any time summon a meeting of the directors. If the directors so resolve, it shall not be necessary to give notice of a meeting of director to any director who, being resident in the State, is for the time being absent from the State.

102. The quorum necessary for the transaction of the business of the directors may be fixed by the directors, and unless so fixed shall be two.

103. The continuing directors may act notwithstanding any vacancy in their number but, if and so long as their number is reduced below the number fixed by or pursuant to the regulations of the company as the necessary quorum of directors, the continuing directors or director may act for the purpose of increasing the number of directors to that number or of summoning a general meeting of the company but for no other purpose.

104. The directors may elect a chairman of their meetings and determine the period for which he is to hold office, but if no such chairman is elected, or, if at any meeting the chairman is not present within 5 minutes after the time appointed for holding the same, the directors present may choose one of their number to be chairman of the meeting.

105. The directors may delegate any of their powers to committees consisting of such member or members of the board

as they think fit; any committee so formed shall, in the exercise of the powers so delegated, conform to any regulations that may be imposed on it by the directors.

106. A committee may elect a chairman of its meetings; if no such chairman is elected, or if at any meeting the chairman is not present within 5 minutes after the time appointed for holding the same, the members present may choose one of their number to be chairman of the meeting.

107. A committee may meet and adjourn as it thinks proper. Questions arising at any meeting shall be determined by a majority of votes of the members present, and where there is an equality of votes, the chairman shall have a second or casting vote.

108. All acts done by any meeting of the directors or of a committee of directors or by any person acting as a director shall, notwithstanding that it be afterwards discovered that there was some defect in the appointment of any such director or person acting as aforesaid, or that they or any of them were disqualified, be as valid as if every such person had been duly appointed and was qualified to be a director.

109. A resolution in writing signed by all the directors for the time being entitled to receive notice of a meeting of the directors shall be as valid as if it had been passed at a meeting of the directors duly convened and held.

Managing Director.

110. The directors may from time to time appoint one or more of themselves to the office of managing director for such period and on such terms as to remuneration and otherwise as they think fit, and, subject to the terms of any agreement entered into in any particular case, may revoke such appointment. A director so appointed shall not, whilst holding that office, be subject to retirement by rotation or be taken into account in determining the rotation of retirement of directors but (without prejudice to any claim he may have for damages for breach of any contract of service between him and the company), his appointment shall be automatically determined if he ceases from any cause to be a director.

111. A managing director shall receive such remuneration

whether by way of salary, commission or participation in the profits, or partly in one way and partly in another, as the directors may determine.

112. The directors may entrust to and confer upon a managing director any of the powers exercisable by them upon such terms and conditions and with such restrictions as they may think fit, and either collaterally with or to the exclusion of their own powers, and may from time to time revoke, withdraw, alter or vary all or any of such powers.

Secretary.

113. Subject to section 3 of the Companies (Amendment) Act, 1982, the secretary shall be appointed by the directors for such term, at such remuneration and upon such conditions as they may think fit; and any secretary so appointed may be removed by them.

114. A provision of the Act or these regulations requiring or authorising a thing to be done by or to a director and the secretary shall not be satisfied by its being done by or to the same person acting both as director and as, or in place of, the secretary.

The Seal.

115. The seal shall be used only by the authority of the directors or of a committee of directors authorised by the directors in that behalf, and every instrument to which the seal shall be affixed shall be signed by a director and shall be countersigned by the secretary or by a second director or by some other person appointed by the directors for the purpose.

Dividends and Reserves.

116. The company in general meeting may declare dividends, but no dividend shall exceed the amount recommended by the directors.

117. The directors may from time to time pay to the members such interim dividends as appear to the directors to be justified by the profits of the company.

118. No dividend or interim dividend shall be paid otherwise than in accordance with the provisions of Part IV of the

Companies (Amendment) Act, 1983 which apply to the company.

119. The directors may, before recommending any dividend, set aside out of the profits of the company such sums as they think proper as a reserve or reserves which shall, at the discretion of the directors, be applicable for any purpose to which the profits of the company may be properly applied, and pending such application may, at the like discretion, either be employed in the business of the company or be invested in such investments as the directors may lawfully determine. The directors may also, without placing the same to reserve, carry forward any profits which they may think it prudent not to divide.

120. Subject to the rights of persons, if any, entitled to shares with special rights as to dividend, all dividends shall be declared and paid according to the amounts paid or credited as paid on the shares in respect whereof the dividend is paid, but no amount paid or credited as paid on a share in advance of calls shall be treated for the purposes of this regulation as paid on the share. All dividends shall be apportioned and paid proportionately to the amounts paid or credited as paid on the shares during any portion or portions of the period in respect of which the dividend is paid; but if any share is issued on terms providing that it shall rank for dividend as from a particular date, such share shall rank for dividend accordingly.

121. The directors may deduct from any dividend payable to any member all sums of money (if any) immediately payable by him to the company on account of calls or otherwise in relation to the shares of the company.

122. Any general meeting declaring a dividend or bonus may direct payment of such dividend or bonus wholly or partly by the distribution of specific assets and in particular of paid up shares, debentures or debenture stock of any other company or in any one or more of such ways, and the directors shall give effect to such resolution, and where any difficulty arise in regard to such distribution, the directors may settle the same as they think expedient, and in particular may issue fractional certificates and fix the value for distribution of such specific assets or any part thereof and may determine that cash payments shall be made to any members upon the footing of the value so fixed, in order to adjust the rights of all the parties, and may vest any such specific assets in trustees as may seem expedient to the directors.

123. Any dividend, interest or other money payable in cash in respect of any shares may be paid by cheque or warrant sent through the post directed to the registered address of the holder, or, where there are joint holders, to the registered address of that one of the joint holders who is first named on the register or to such person and to such address as the holder or joint holders may in writing direct. Every such cheque or warrant shall be made payable to the order of the person to whom it is sent. Any one of two or more joint holders may give effectual receipts for any dividends, bonuses or other moneys payable in respect of the shares held by them as joint holder.

124. No dividend shall bear interest against the company.

Accounts.

125. The directors shall cause proper books of account to be kept relating to—

    (a) all sums of money received and expended by the company and the matters in respect of which the receipt and expenditure takes place; and

    (b) all sale and purchases of goods by the company; and

    (c) the assets and liabilities of the company.

Proper books shall not be deemed to be kept if there are not kept such books of account as are necessary to give a true and fair view of the state of the company's affairs and to explain its transactions.

126. The books of account shall be kept at the office or, subject to section 147 of the Act, at such other place as the directors think fit, and shall at all reasonable times be open to the inspection of the directors.

127. The directors shall from time to time determine whether and to what extent and at what times and places and under what conditions or regulations the accounts and books of the company or any of them shall be open to the inspection of members, not being directors, and no member (not being a director) shall have any right of inspecting any account or book or document of the company except as conferred by statute or authorised by the directors or by the company in general meeting.

128. The directors shall from time to time, in accordance with sections 148, 150, 157 and 158 of the Act cause to be prepared and to be laid before the annual general meeting of the company such profit and loss accounts, balance sheets, group accounts and reports as are required by those sections to be prepared and laid before the annual general meeting of the company.

129. A copy of every balance sheet (including every document required by law to be annexed thereto) which is to be laid before the annual general meeting of the company together with a copy of the directors' report and auditors' report shall, not less than 21 days before the date of the annual general meeting be sent to every person entitled under the provisions of the Act to receive them.

Capitalisation of Profits.

130. The company in general meeting may upon the recommendation of the directors resolve that any sum for the time being standing to the credit of any of the company's reserves (including any capital redemption reserve fund or share premium account) or to the credit of profit and loss account be capitalised and applied on behalf of the members who would have been entitled to receive the same if the same had been distributed by way of dividend and in the same proportions either in or towards paying up amounts for the time being unpaid on any shares held by them respectively or in paying up in full unissued shares or debentures of the company of a nominal amount equal to the sum capitalised (such shares or debentures to be allotted and distributed credited as fully paid up to and amongst such holders in the proportions aforesaid) or partly in one way and partly in another, so however, that the only purpose for which sums standing to the credit of the capital redemption reserve fund or the share premium account shall be applied shall be those permitted by sections 62 and 64 of the Act.

130A. The company in general meeting may on the recommendation of the directors resolve that it is desirable to capitalise any part of the amount for the time being standing to the credit of any of the company's reserve accounts or to the credit of the profit and loss account which is not available for distribution by applying such sum in paying up in full unissued shares to be allotted as fully paid bonus shares to those members of the company who would have been entitled to that sum if it were distributed by way of dividend (and in the same proportions), and the directors shall give effect to such resolution.

131. Whenever such a resolution is passed in pursuance of regulation 130 or 130A, the directors shall make all appropriations and applications of the undivided profits resolved to be capitalised thereby and all allotments and issues of fully paid shares or debentures, if any, and generally shall do all acts and things required to give effect thereto with full power to the directors to make such provision as they shall think fit for the case of shares or debentures becoming distributable in fractions (and, in particular, without prejudice to the generality of the foregoing, to sell the shares or debentures represented by such fractions and distribute the net proceeds of such sale amongst the members otherwise entitled to such fractions in due proportions) and also to authorise any person to enter on behalf of all the members concerned into an agreement with the company providing for the allotment to them respectively credited as fully paid up of any further shares or debentures to which they may become entitled on such capitalisation or, as the case may require, for the payment up by the application thereto of their respective proportions of the profits resolved to be capitalised of the amounts remaining unpaid on their existing shares and any agreement made under such authority shall be effective and binding on all such members.

Audit.

132. Auditors shall be appointed and their duties regulated in accordance with sections 160 to 163 of the Act.

Notices.

133. A notice may be given by the company to any member either personally or by sending it by post to him to his registered address. Where a notice is sent by post, service of the notice shall be deemed to be effected by properly addressing, prepaying and posting a letter containing the notice, and to have been effected in the case of the notice of a meeting at the expiration of 24 hours after the letter containing the same is posted, and in any other case at the time at which the letter would be delivered in the ordinary course of post.

134. A notice may be given by the company to the joint holders of a share by giving the notice to the joint holder first named in the register in respect of the share.

135. A notice may be given by the company to the persons entitled to a share in consequence of the death or bankruptcy of a member by sending it through the post in a prepaid letter addressed to them by name or by the title of representatives of the deceased or Official Assignee in bankruptcy or by any like description at the address supplied for the purpose by the persons claiming to be so entitled, or (until such an address has been so supplied) by giving the notice in any manner in which the same might have been given if the death or bankruptcy had not occurred.

136. Notice of every general meeting shall be given in any manner hereinbefore authorised to—

(*a*) every member; and

(*b*) every person upon whom the ownership of a share devolves by reason of his being a personal representative or the Official Assignee in bankruptcy of a member, where the member but for his death or bankruptcy would be entitled to receive notice of the meeting; and

(*c*) the auditor for the time being of the company.

No other person shall be entitled to receive notices of general meetings.

Winding Up.

137. If the company is wound up, the liquidator may, with the sanction of a special resolution of the company and any other sanction required by the Act, divide among the members in specie or kind the whole or any part of the assets of the company (whether they shall consist of property of the same kind or not) and may, for such purpose, set such value as he deems fair upon any property to be divided as aforesaid and may determine how such division shall be carried out as between the members or different classes of members. The liquidator may, with the like sanction, vest the whole or any part of such assets in trustees upon such trusts for the benefit of the contributories as the liquidator, with the like sanction, shall think fit, but so that no member shall be compelled to accept any shares or other

securities whereon there is any liability.

Indemnity

138. Every director, managing director, agent, auditor, secretary and other officer for the time being of the company shall be indemnified out of the assets of the company against any liability incurred by him in defending any proceedings, whether civil or criminal, in relation to his acts while acting in such office, in which judgment is given in his favour or in which he is acquitted or in connection with any application under section 391 of the Act in which relief is granted to him by the court.

PART II.

REGULATIONS FOR THE MANAGEMENT OF A PRIVATE COMPANY LIMITED BY SHARES.

1. The regulations contained in Part I of Table A (with the exception of regulations 8, 24, 51, 54, 84 and 86) shall apply. *As amended 1977 S5 (4)*

2. The company is a private company and accordingly—

    (*a*) the right to transfer shares is restricted in the manner hereinafter prescribed;

    (*b*) the number of members of the company (exclusive of persons who are in the employment of the company and of persons who, having been formerly in the employment of the company, were while in such employment, and have continued after the determination of such employment to be, members of the company) is limited to fifty, so, however, that where two or more persons hold one or more shares in the company jointly, they shall, for the purpose of this regulation, be treated as a single member;

    (*c*) any invitation to the public to subscribe for any shares or debentures of the company is prohibited;

    (*d*) the company shall not have power to issue share warrants to bearer.

3. The directors may, in their absolute discretion, and without assigning any reason therefor, decline to register any transfer of any share, whether or not it is a fully paid share.

4. Subject to sections 133 and 141 of the Act, an annual general meeting and a meeting called for the passing of a special resolution shall be called by 21 days' notice in writing at the least and a meeting of the company (other than an annual general meeting or a meeting for the passing of a special resolution) shall be called by 7 days' notice in writing at the least. The notice shall be exclusive of the day on which it is served or deemed to be served and of the day for which it is given and shall specify the day, the place and the hour of the meeting and, in the case of special business, the general nature of that business and shall be given in manner authorised by these regulations to such persons as are under the regulations of the company entitled to receive such notices from the company.

5. No business shall be transacted at any general meeting unless a quorum of members is present at the time when the meeting proceeds to business; save as herein otherwise provided, two members present in person or by proxy shall be a quorum.

6. Subject to section 141 of the Act, a resolution in writing signed by all the members for the time being entitled to attend and vote on such resolution at a general meeting (or being bodies corporate by their duly authorised representatives) shall be as valid and effective for all purposes as if the resolution had been passed at a general meeting of the company duly convened and held, and if described as a special resolution shall be deemed to be a special resolution within the meaning of the Act.

7. A director may vote in respect of any contract, appointment or arrangement in which he is interested, and he shall be counted in the quorum present at the meeting.

8. The directors may exercise the voting powers conferred by the shares of any other company held or owned by the company in such manner in all respects as they think fit and in particular they may exercise the voting powers in favour of any resolution appointing the directors or any of them as directors or officers of such other company or providing for the payment of remuneration or pensions to the directors or officers of such other company. Any director of the company may vote in favour of the exercise of such voting rights, notwithstanding that he may be or may be about to become a director or officer of such other company, and as such or in any other manner is or may be interested in the exercise of such voting rights in manner aforesaid.

9. Any director may from time to time appoint any person who is approved by the majority of the directors to be an alternate or substitute director. The appointee, while he holds office as an alternate director, shall be entitled to notice of meetings of the directors and to attend and vote thereat as a director and shall not be entitled to be remunerated otherwise than out of the remuneration of the director appointing him. Any appointment under this regulation shall be effected by notice in writing given by the appointer to the secretary. Any appointment so made may be revoked at any time by the appointer or by a majority of the other directors or by the company in general meeting. Revocation by an appointer shall be effected by notice in writing given by the appointer to the secretary.

10. Every person whose name is entered as a member in the register shall be entitled without payment to receive within 2 months after allotment or lodgment of a transfer (or within such other period as the conditions of issue shall provide) one certificate for all his shares or several certificates each for one or more of his shares upon payment of 12½ new pence for every certificate after the first or such less sum as the directors shall from time to time determine, so, however, that in respect of a share or shares held jointly by several persons the company shall not be bound to issue more than one certificate, and delivery of a certificate for a share to one of several joint holders shall be sufficient delivery to all such holders. Every certificate shall be under the seal and shall specify the shares to which it relates and the amount paid up thereon. *Inserted by 1 S5 (5).*

Note:—Regulations 3, 4, 5 and 10 of this Part are alternative to regulations 24, 51, 54 and 8 respectively of Part I. Regulations 7 and 8 of this Part are alternative to regulations 84 and 86 of Part I. *As amended l 1977 S5 (6).*

Tábla A, Cuic and Cuid II h not been incl. here. They ar Irish languag. version of Tai A, Part I and II.

Index

ABUSE OF POWERS, 135, 150, 200, 207, 210. *see also* INSIDER DEALING; MARKET ABUSE
ABUSE OF PRIVILEGE, 17, 67
ACCESS TO THE COURTS, 62
ACCOUNTANCY BODIES, 265
  recognition, 273
  regulation and supervision, 7, 272–4. *see also* SUPERVISORY AUTHORITY
ACCOUNTANCY PROFESSION, 7, 272. *see also* AUDITORS
ACCOUNTS, 4, 5, 6, 7, 12, 246–63. *see also* ANNUAL ACCOUNTS; ANNUAL RETURNS
  accounting standards, 7, 9, 264
  AGM, to be laid before, 162, 249, 250
  audit committees, 7, 256, 264
  audit exemption thresholds, 7, 258–9
  auditor's duties, 267–9
  auditor's investigation, 248–9
  auditor's report, 256–9. *see also* AUDITORS' REPORT
  books of account, 246–9
  compliance statements, 256
  directors' obligations, 72
  directors' reports, 249, 254–6
  disclosure requirements, 221, 255
  filing obligation, 12, 72
  group of companies. *see* GROUP ACCOUNTS
  IAS Regulation, 9
  independent accountant's report, 352–4, 363
  individual accounts, 249–50
  inspection, 246–7
  members, rights of, 259
  offences, 262–3
  single-member companies, 254
  small and medium-sized private companies, 250–1, 252, 261–2
  Supervisory Authority, role of, 259–60, 272–4
  unlimited companies, 249
ACTING WHILE DISQUALIFIED, 245
ACTUAL AUTHORITY, 200–1
'ACTUALLY AWARE' TEST, 81–2
AER LINGUS, 10
AER RIANTA, 10
AGENCY, 63
  directors, 188, 201–3
  group of companies, 63, 64–7
  ostensible authority, 201–3
  piercing the corporate veil, 63, 64–5
  promoters, 30
  receivers, 300–1
  single economic entity test, 63, 65–7
AGM. *see* ANNUAL GENERAL MEETING (AGM)
AGRICULTURAL CREDIT COMPANY, 10
ALLOTMENT OF SHARES. *see* SHARE ISSUES

ALTERATION
  articles, 51–5, 84, 89
  authorised share capital, 47
  class rights, 48, 89–91, 113–14
  memorandum, clauses in, 46, 47, 48–9
  objects of company, 46–7, 75
  share capital, 47, 112–23. *see also* SHARE CAPITAL
ALTERNATE DIRECTORS, 193
AMALGAMATIONS, 291–7. *see also* MERGERS AND TAKEOVERS
  compulsory purchase (s. 204), 292–4
  directors' duties and liabilities, 294–5
  disclosure requirements, 294, 295
  distortion of competition, prohibition of, 295
  general rules, 294–7
  market abuse, prohibition of, 295
  Substantial Acquisition Rules (SARs), 296–7
  Takeover Rules, 296
ANCILLARY POWERS, 76, 78–9
ANNUAL ACCOUNTS, 246, 249–54
  adoption, 249
  AGM, to be laid before, 246, 249
  annual return, annexed to, 246
  auditors' report, 256–9
  directors' reports, 254–6
  exemptions, 12, 250–1
  format and contents, 250
  group of companies. *see* GROUP ACCOUNTS
  IFRS accounts, 251, 253–4
  individual accounts, 249–50
  legislative requirements, 249, 250
  rights of members, 259
  single-member companies, 254
  small and medium-sized private companies, 12, 250–1
  standards and principles, 251
  Supervisory Authority, 259–60
  'true and fair view,' 250, 257
  unlimited companies, 249
ANNUAL GENERAL MEETING (AGM), 161–2
  accounts and returns, 162, 249, 250, 253
  auditor, appointment of, 265
  auditors' report, 249, 256–8, 266
  business of, 162
  chairman, 167
  court order for, 161
  decision-making, 170–3
  direction to hold, 161
  Director of Corporate Enforcement, called by, 161
  directors' report, 162
  documents to be laid before, 162
  failure to hold, 161

form and content of notice, 165
location, 51, 161
minutes, 169
notice requirements, 163–6
notification of decisions, 170–1
ordinary business, 162, 165
ordinary resolutions, 170
proceedings, 166–73
profit and loss account, 162
proxies, 169
quorum, 166–7
shareholders' discretion, 171–2
single-member companies, 162
special business, 162, 165
special resolutions, 170
time for holding, 161
voting and polls, 168–9
ANNUAL REPORTS. *see* AUDITOR'S REPORT;
    DIRECTORS' REPORTS
ANNUAL RETURN DATE (ARD), 262
ANNUAL RETURNS, 35, 72, 246, 260–3
associated companies, 15
certification, 261
contents, 260
date for (ARD), 262
documentation, 261–2
exemptions, 12, 261–2
group companies, 13
members, list of, 261
non-compliance, penalties for, 262–3
offences, 262–3
rejection by registrar, 262
small and medium-sized private companies,
    12, 261–2
subsidiary undertakings, 262
APPLICATION OF ASSETS, 344–9. *see also* ASSET
    DISTRIBUTION
ARRANGEMENT, SCHEMES OF, 286–90
application for, 286–7
binding on approval, 290
class meetings, 287–9
court protection, proposals in, 363–4
discretion of court, 289
powers of the court, 289–90
stay of proceedings, 287
ARREST POWERS, 21, 325, 330–1
ARTICLES OF ASSOCIATION, 3, 33, 35, 50–8, 84
AGM, business of, 162
alteration, 37, 51–5, 84, 89, 90
assent principle, 52
bona fide test, 53–5, 90
contract, incorporation in 57
contractual nature, 56–8
court, alteration by, 55
deemed, 50
dividends, power to declare, 148–9
form, 50
informal alteration, 52
judicial construction, 50

listed companies, 51
memorandum, contrary to, 50, 55
minority protection, 54
model articles (Table A), 50. *see also* TABLE A
outsiders, and, 55, 56, 57
pre-emption rights, exclusion of, 97
private companies, 50
reference documentation, 36
restrictions on alteration, 53–5
section 25 contract, 56–8
share capital, alteration of, 51, 112
shareholders' rights, 86
transfer of shares, restrictions on, 137
variation of class rights, 89
voluntary registration, 50
weighted votes, 51
ASSENT PRINCIPLE, 52, 172–3
ASSET DISTRIBUTION, 344–9
costs of winding up, 346
dividends. *see* DIVIDENDS
expenses of examiner, 346
floating charge holders, 348
members and contributories, 349
order of distribution, 345–9
pari passu principle, 345, 348
preferential creditors, 347–8
proving claims, 345
secured creditors, 346–7
unsecured creditors, 348
ASSET REALISATION, 333–44
asset-swelling, 333–4
disclaimer of onerous contracts, 337–9
floating charge, avoidance of (s. 288), 342–3
fraudulent preference, 339–41
improperly transferred assets, return of, 344
liquidator's powers and functions, 333–44
personal liability declarations, 344
pooling and contribution orders, 343
post-commencement dispositions, 334–7
ASSETS, DISPOSAL OF
fixed charge, where, 125
fraud, perpetration of, 24
receiver's duty of care, 24, 305–8, 314
ASSETS, SEIZURE OF, 325, 330–1
ASSOCIATED COMPANIES, 14–15
annual accounts and returns, 15
qualifying capital interest, 14
ASSOCIATION CLAUSE, 48
AUDIT COMMITTEES, 7, 256, 264
AUDITED ACCOUNTS, 248, 256, 264. *see also*
    AUDITORS; AUDITORS' REPORT
exemptions, 6, 7, 12, 258–9, 260, 264, 271
AUDITORS, 4, 5, 7, 23, 264–74
account books, investigation of, 248–9
appointment, 265
disqualification, 240, 241, 266
duties, 23–4, 266–7
duty of care and skill, 267–9
firm of auditors, 265

fraud, notification of, 267
general meetings, rights in relation to, 270
information, requests for, 270
investigation of, 272
law reform, 264
legislation, 264
liability, 268
negligent statement, 268
offences, reporting of, 267
qualifications for appointment, 265–6, 272
regulation and supervision, 7, 264, 272, 273.
    see also SUPERVISORY AUTHORITY
removal of, 270–1
remuneration, 272
reporting duties, 267
reports. *see* AUDITORS' REPORT
resignation, 271–2
Review Group report (2000), 264
rights of, 269–70
role of, 264
statutory duties, 266–7
AUDITORS' REPORT, 24, 162, 256–9, 262, 264, 266
AGM, to be laid before, 256
annual return, annexed to, 249, 261
contents, 256–7
exemptions from audit, 7, 258–9, 260, 264, 271
inspection, open to, 256
statement or opinion, 257
'true and fair view,' 264
AUTHORISED SHARE CAPITAL, 111
clause, 47
AUTOMATED TRANSFERS, 141–2
AUTOMATIC CRYSTALLISATION CLAUSES, 130
AUTOMATIC DISQUALIFICATION, 240, 244

BAD FAITH *(MALA FIDES)*, 207–8
BANK OF IRELAND, 10
BANKS
acquisitions and takeovers, 297
court protection petitions, 352
BELL HOUSES CLAUSES, 77
BILLS OF EXCHANGE, 45, 70
BOARD MEETINGS, 195–7
chairman, 196
informal, 195–6
notification, 196
proceedings, 196
quorum, 196
voting, 196
BOARD OF DIRECTORS, 73, 188. *see also* BOARD
    MEETINGS
managing director, appointment of, 200
BONA FIDE. *see* GOOD FAITH
BONUS ISSUES, 91, 104
BOOK DEBTS
fixed charges over, 128–9
BOOKS OF ACCOUNT, 72, 246–9
auditors, investigation by, 248–9

content of, 247
criminal and civil sanctions, 247–8
inspection, rights of, 246–7
maintenance of, 246, 247
personal liability of officers, 248, 344
BORROWING POWERS, 78, 124
BRANCH DISCLOSURES, 36–7
BRANCHES, 255
BRITAIN, 1
BUBBLE ACT, 1720, 2
BUSINESS NAME. *see* NAME OF COMPANY
BUSINESS STATIONERY, 45, 192

CALLS, 1, 144–5
CAPACITY TO CONTRACT, 31, 62
CAPITAL, 12. *see also* FLOATING CHARGES; LOAN
    CAPITAL; SHARE CAPITAL
clause, 47
loss, 114
CAPITAL REDEMPTION RESERVE FUND, 118
CASE LAW, 8
CENTRAL BANK, 158, 352
CERTIFICATES
incorporation, 33, 34, 35, 45, 59
shares. *see* SHARE CERTIFICATES
trading, 13, 34–5
CHAIRMAN
board meetings, 196
shareholders' meetings, 167, 169
CHARGES, 124
book debts, over, 128–9
categories, 124
fixed, 125. *see also* FIXED CHARGES
floating, 125–31. *see also* FLOATING CHARGES
incorrect dating, 132
liquidation. *see* LIQUIDATION
mortgages over shares, 143–4
register of charges, 133
registration, 131–3
retention of title clauses, 128
satisfaction, 134
CHARITABLE COMPANIES, 11
CHARTERED CORPORATIONS, 2, 3, 9–10
CHARTERS, 1, 2, 3, 9
CHEQUES, 45, 70
CIVIL LIABILITY. *see also* LIABILITY
fraudulent trading, 222
insider dealing, 154–5
market abuse, 159
CLASS MEETINGS, 163
arrangement, scheme of, 287–9
CLASSES OF SHARES, 86–9
variation of class rights, 89–91
COMMENCEMENT OF BUSINESS
private company, 13, 34
public company, 34–5
COMMERCIAL RELATIONSHIP, 16
COMMITTEES OF INSPECTION, 323, 328–9
COMMON LAW, 8

COMPANIES. *see also* COMPANY LAW; DISSOLUTION
   OF COMPANIES; FORMATION OF COMPANIES;
   GROUP COMPANIES; INCORPORATION;
   INVESTIGATION OF COMPANIES; RECEIVERSHIP;
   REGISTRATION OF COMPANIES
   amalgamations. *see* AMALGAMATIONS;
      MERGERS AND TAKEOVERS
   associated, 14–15
   chartered corporations, 2, 3, 9–10
   conversion, 37–8, 39
   court protection. *see* COURT PROTECTION
   deed of settlement, 2
   development, 1–16
   directors and officers. *see* DIRECTORS;
      OFFICERS
   foreign, 36–7
   guarantee, limited by, 10, 11, 43
   Independence (1921), following, 3–4
   insolvency. *see* INSOLVENCY
   liability of members, 3, 10–11
   name of company. *see* NAME OF COMPANY
   registered, 10
   related, 15–16
   reorganisation. *see* REORGANISATION OF
      COMPANIES
   residency, 6, 69, 191
   shares, limited by, 10, 11, 42, 43
   statutory, 10
   types of, 9–16. *see also* PRIVATE COMPANIES;
      PUBLIC COMPANIES; SMALL AND MEDIUM-
      SIZED PRIVATE COMPANIES
   unlimited, 11
   winding up. *see* LIQUIDATION
COMPANIES REGISTRATION OFFICE (CRO), 22–3
COMPANY AUDITORS. *see* AUDITORS
COMPANY INSPECTORS. *see* INSPECTORS
COMPANY LAW, 2–9
   common law and equity, 8
   Companies Acts, 3–7, 3–8, 10, 84
   enforcement. *see* ENFORCEMENT AND
      COMPLIANCE
   European Union law, 8–9
   harmonisation, 9
   Joint Stock Companies Act 1844, 3
   law reform, 3–4, 25–6
   limited liability, 3, 17
   non-compliance, culture of, 6, 17, 18
   Principal Act (Companies Act 1963), 4
COMPANY LAW REFORM COMMITTEE
   Report (1958), 3–4
COMPANY LAW REVIEW GROUP, 6, 25
   functions of, 25–6
COMPANY NAME. *see* NAME OF COMPANY
COMPANY SECRETARY. *see* SECRETARIES
COMPANY SECURITIES. *see* DEBENTURES; SECURITIES;
   SHARES
COMPENSATION, 106–7, 154, 294, 348. *see also*
   DAMAGES
COMPETITION LAW, 295

COMPLIANCE AND ENFORCEMENT. *see* ENFORCEMENT
   AND COMPLIANCE
COMPLIANCE STATEMENTS, 256
COMPROMISE SCHEMES. *see* ARRANGEMENT,
   SCHEMES OF
COMPULSORY LIQUIDATIONS, 23, 317–26. *see also*
   LIQUIDATORS
   appointment of liquidator, 322
   arrest powers, 325
   commencement, 322, 334
   committees of inspection, 323
   conversion from voluntary liquidation, 331
   court powers, 324–5
   deadlock in management, 320–1
   dispositions of property, 323
   dissolution order, 39
   effect of orders, 322–3
   employees, and, 323
   entitlement to present petition, 317
   expenses, 346
   fraudulent purpose, formation of company for,
      320
   grounds, 317–18. *see also* JUST AND EQUITABLE
      GROUNDS (*BELOW*)
   hearings, 321–2
   illegal purpose, formation of company for,
      320
   inability to pay debts, 318–19
   inspection, order for, 325
   interim orders, 321
   just and equitable grounds, 69, 185–7,
      319–21
   notification and filing requirements, 322
   oppression of minority, 321
   post-commencement dispositions, 334–7
   powers of liquidator, 323–4
   provisional liquidator, 321
   quasi-partnership, failure of, 321
   realisation of assets. *see* ASSET REALISATION
   removal of liquidator, 326
   resignation of liquidator, 326
   seizure of assets, 325
   substratum, failure of, 46, 319–20
   transfers of shares, 323
   vesting of property, 323–4
   winding up order, 322–3
COMPULSORY PURCHASE (S. 204), 292–4
   independence of offeror, 293
   minority shareholder and, 292–3, 294
CONFLICTS OF INTEREST, 30, 211–13
CONNECTED PERSONS, 152
CONSIDERATION FOR SHARES, 98
   non-cash consideration, 12, 98–100
   share premium, 100–1
   undertaking for future services, 99
   valuation report, 99–100
CONSTITUTION OF IRELAND, 10n
CONSTITUTIONAL DOCUMENTS. *see* ARTICLES OF
   ASSOCIATION; MEMORANDUM OF ASSOCIATION

CONSTRUCTIVE NOTICE, 75, 203
    EU Regulations (1973), 206
    Turquand's Case, rule in, 203–6
CONTINGENT PURCHASE CONTRACTS, 116
CONTRACTS, 1
    articles of association, 56–8. *see also* ARTICLES
        OF ASSOCIATION
    capacity to contract. *see* CONTRACTUAL
        CAPACITY
    contingent purchase, 116
    directors, with, 194–5, 219–21
    disclaimers by liquidators, 337–9
    disclosure of interests, 28, 29, 217–18, 221
    employment. *see* CONTRACTS OF EMPLOYMENT
    enforcement, 75
    memorandum of association, 56–8. *see also*
        MEMORANDUM OF ASSOCIATION
    pre-incorporation, 30–2
    prohibited transactions, 219–21
    receiver's liability, 313–14
    rescission, 29, 109
    rights, enforcement of, 62
    section 25, 39, 56–8, 85. *see also* SECTION 25
        CONTRACT
    substantial property transactions, 217–18
    ultra vires transactions. *see* ULTRA VIRES
        DOCTRINE
CONTRACTS OF EMPLOYMENT
    compulsory liquidations, 323
    directors, 194–5
    receiverships, 304
    voluntary liquidations, 329
CONTRACTUAL CAPACITY, 31, 62, 75–83
    'actually aware' test, 81–2
    Bell Houses clauses, 77
    express and implied powers, 79–81
    'good faith' test, 83
    independent objects clauses, 76–7, 78
    judicial reaction, 76–81
    'lawfully and effectively' test, 82
    liability of directors, 82
    main object rule, 76, 77
    objects clause, and, 75–81
    objects v. powers, 77–9
    ostensible authority, 201–6
    pre-incorporation contracts, 30–2
    statutory reform, 81–3
    ultra vires rule, 75–82. *see also* ULTRA VIRES
        DOCTRINE
CONTRACTUAL OBLIGATIONS, 62
    avoidance of, 67–8
CONTRIBUTION ORDERS, 16, 343
CONTRIBUTORIES
    absconding, 21
    distribution of assets to, 349
CONVERSION OF COMPANIES, 37–8, 39, 47
CONVERTIBLE DEBENTURES, 92
CORPORATE DONATIONS, 255, 260
CORPORATE GOVERNANCE, 135, 188

CORPORATE PERSONALITY. *see* CORPORATE VEIL;
    SEPARATE LEGAL PERSONALITY
CORPORATE VEIL, 60–72
    agency relationships, 63, 64–5
    avoidance of legal obligations, 67–8
    failure to state company's name correctly, 70
    fraud, 68
    group companies, 71
    injustice, 68
    insufficient numbers, 70
    investigation of companies, 71
    liability of directors and officers, 71–2
    piercing, 63–72
    quasi-partnerships, 69
    related companies, 71
    residency, 69
    Salomon's case, 59–60, 61
    segregation of ownership, 62
    single economic entity test, 65–7
    statutory provisions, 69–72
CORPORATION TAX, 73
COURT INVESTIGATIONS, 275–6
    application requirements, 275
    Director of Corporate Enforcement,
        application by, 276
    expenses, 285
    inspector's powers, 281–3
    inspector's report, 283–5
    'related company,' definition of, 276
    scope, 276
    security for costs, 275
    winding up order, 283–4
    winding up petition, 285
COURT PROTECTION, 5, 350–67. *see also*
    EXAMINERS
    appointment of examiner, 355–6
    compromise proposals, 363–4
    confirmation of proposals, 365–6
    contents of petition, 352
    costs and expenses, 366
    creditors, application by, 351–2
    creditor's committee, 358
    criteria, 355–6
    dealing with property, 360–1
    Director of Corporate Enforcement,
        application by, 20
    directors, application by, 351
    effects of, 357–8
    entitlement to petition, 351–2
    examiner's report, 364–6
    'exceptional circumstances,' 354
    expenses, certification of, 361–2
    financial institutions, 352
    'going concern,' 356
    hearings, 355
    independent accountant's report, 352–4, 363
    interim orders, 354
    irregularities, 363
    legislation, 351

notification requirements, 356–7
objections to proposals, 365
petitions, 351–2
powers of examiner, 359–62
provisional liquidator, and, 358
purpose, 350
'reasonable prospect' of survival, 356
receivership, and, 358
related companies, 359
remuneration of examiner, 366
termination, 366–7
utmost good faith *(uberrima fides),* 354–5
winding up, application for, 366
CREDITORS. *see also* DEBENTURE HOLDERS
committees, 358
court protection, petitions for, 351–2
directors' duties to, 215–16, 222–5
distribution of assets to, 345–8
liquidation, petitions for. *see* CREDITORS'
VOLUNTARY WINDING UP
pari passu principle, 92, 340, 345, 348
preferential, 308–9, 347–8
schemes of arrangement. *see* ARRANGEMENT,
SCHEMES OF
secured, 124, 346–7
unsecured, 348
CREDITORS' VOLUNTARY WINDING UP, 327–9. *see*
also VOLUNTARY LIQUIDATIONS
committee of inspection, 328–9
liquidator appointed, where, 328
notification requirements, 328
reconstruction, scheme of (ss. 260, 271), 291
CRIMINAL LIABILITY
accounts, 72, 247–8
annual returns, 72, 262–3
companies, 62–3
directors and other officers, 72
disqualification of director, 240
fraudulent trading, 222
health and safety breaches, 72
market abuse, 155, 159
mens rea, 62–3
promoters, 30
prospectuses, mis-statements in, 108
service of documents, 63
CRO (COMPANIES REGISTRATION OFFICE), 22–3
CRO GAZETTE. see NOTIFICATION REQUIREMENTS
CRODISK SYSTEM, 36
CROSS-BORDER INSOLVENCY PROCEEDINGS, 9
CRYSTALLISATION OF FLOATING CHARGE, 126, 131,
302
automatic crystallisation clauses, 130

DAMAGES. *see also* COMPENSATION
deceit, 109
fraud, 109
insider dealing, 154–5, 159
market abuse, 159
minority shareholders, 176–8, 185

mis-statement in prospectus, 109
negligent misrepresentation, 109
DE FACTO DIRECTORS, 188–9
DE JURE DIRECTORS, 188
DEATH OF MEMBER, 142
DEBENTURE HOLDERS
receiver, appointment of, 298–9. *see also*
RECEIVERS
register of, 93
rights, 84, 91
shareholders and, difference between, 84
DEBENTURES, 84, 91–3, 124
automatic crystallisation clauses, 130
charges, 124–34. *see also* FIXED CHARGES;
FLOATING CHARGES
convertible, 92
crystallisation of floating charge, 126
debenture stock, 92
default, 298–9
interest, 84
issues, 92
legal nature, 91
ownership, investigation of, 21
pari passu clause, 92
redeemable, 92
register of, 93
section 15 inquiry, 278
series of, 92
single, 91–2
transfer, 92
trust deeds, 92
types, 91–2
DEBTS. *see also* CHARGES; CREDITORS; INSOLVENCY
book debts, 128–9
inability to pay, 318–19, 350, 355. *see also*
COURT PROTECTION; INSOLVENCY
liability to pay, 72
limited liability, 72
DECEIT, 109
DECISION-MAKING
directors, 195–7
informal, 172–3, 195–6
membership, 52, 170–3. *see also* SPECIAL
RESOLUTIONS
DECLARATIONS. *see also* STATUTORY DECLARATIONS
dividends, 148–9
restriction, 237–8
solvency, 326–7, 344
DEED OF SETTLEMENT COMPANIES, 2
DEFERRED SHARES, 89
DELAY
restriction proceedings, 235–6
DELEGATION
Director of Corporate Enforcement, 21
directors, 188, 200–1, 229–30
DEMATERIALISATION OF SHARES, 142
DERIVATIVE ACTIONS, 180–1
DILIGENCE, DUTY OF, 227–8
DIRECTOR OF CORPORATE ENFORCEMENT, 18–22

Acting Director, 18–19
AGM, direction to hold, 161
appointment, 18
arrest powers, 21
auditor, investigation of, 272
court investigation, application for, 276
court protection, application for, 20
delegation of powers, 21
disqualifications, 18
establishment of office, 6
fines, power to levy, 20
functions, 19–20
indemnification, 21
independence, 19
information, disclosure of, 21–2
injunctions, 20
investigative powers, 20–1, 71
liquidators, powers in relation to, 19, 20, 330, 332
officers of, 19, 20
powers of, 20–1
prosecution of summary offences, 20
receivers, powers in relation to, 19, 20, 311–12
removal of, 22
report to Minister, 21–2, 22, 23, 24
section 15 inquiry, 278
section 14 investigations, 277–8
section 19 order, 279–81
section 16 restrictions on shares, 278–9
Supervisory Authority, membership of, 19
supervisory powers, 20
term of office, 18
winding up petition, 285
DIRECTOR OF PUBLIC PROSECUTIONS (DPP), 23
insider dealing prosecutions, 155
receiver's referral to, 311
DIRECTORS, 5, 6, 7, 73, 188–99
allotment of shares, and, 94, 97
alternate directors, 193
annual reports. *see* DIRECTORS' REPORTS
annual return, details in, 261
appointment, 192–3
board, 73. *see also* BOARD MEETINGS
breach of duty, ratification of, 213
business letters, name on, 192
certification of annual return, 261
compensation on merger/takeover, 294
conflicts of interest, 211–13. *see also*
    DISCLOSURE REQUIREMENTS
contract of employment, 194–5
contracts, 195, 217–18, 221
criminal liability, 72
de facto directors, 188–9
de jure directors, 188
disclosure of interests, 216–18, 255. *see also*
    DISCLOSURE REQUIREMENTS
disqualification. *see* DISQUALIFICATION OF
    DIRECTORS

duties and liabilities. *see* DIRECTORS' DUTIES
    AND LIABILITIES
duty of care, 225–30
executive directors, 190, 200–1
fiduciary duties, 8, 150, 207–16, 344
fraudulent trading, 222–3
honesty and responsibility criteria, 232, 233–5
indemnification, 230
informal decisions, 195
insider dealing. *see* INSIDER DEALING; MARKET
    ABUSE
liabilities, 71–2. *see also* DIRECTORS' DUTIES
    AND LIABILITIES
loan transactions, 219–21
managing director, 200
meetings, 195–7. *see also* BOARD MEETINGS
minimum number of directorships, 191–2
misfeasance, 224–5
negligence, 225–30
non-executive, 190
number, 73
powers. *see* DIRECTORS' POWERS
prohibited transactions, 219–21
property transactions, and, 217–18
qualifications for office, 190–1
receiver's appointment, effect of, 302–3
reckless trading, 223–4
register of contracts, 195
register of directors, 198–9
register of interests, 217
removal from office, 193–4
remuneration, 194–5
reports. *see* DIRECTORS' REPORTS
residency, 33, 191
resignation, 193
restriction. *see* RESTRICTION OF DIRECTORS
retirement, 193
rotation of, 193–4
shadow directors, 189–90
share qualifications, 192
shares, interests in, 216–17, 255
solvency, declaration of, 326–7, 344
standard of care, 242
DIRECTORS' DUTIES AND LIABILITIES, 72, 207–30
annual reports, 254–6
books of account, 246, 248
breach of, 213, 344
Companies Acts, ensuring compliance with,
    221–2
company, duties owed to, 213–14
conflict of interest, duty to avoid, 211–13
creditors, duties owed to, 215–16, 222–5
criminal liability, 72
delegation of duties, 229–30
diligence, duty of, 227–8
disclosure of interests, 216–18
disqualification provision. *see*
    DISQUALIFICATION OF DIRECTORS
duty of care and competence, 225–30, 344

employees, duties owed to, 215
fettering of discretion, duty against, 209–11
fiduciary duties, 8, 150, 207–16, 344
fraudulent trading, 222–3
'honesty and responsibility' requirement, 232,
    233–5
indemnification, 230
individual shareholders, duties owed to,
    214–15
mergers and takeovers, in relation to, 294–5
misfeasance, 224–5
negligence, 225–30
non-cash assets, acquisition of, 218
personal liability, 71–2, 344
powers, proper exercise of, 208–10
prohibited transactions, 219–21
ratification of breach of duties by, 213
reckless trading, 223–4
restriction provisions. *see* RESTRICTION OF
    DIRECTORS
securing the assets of directors, 225
shares, disclosure of interests and dealings in,
    216–17
skill, 226–7
standard of care, 242
statutory duties and liabilities, 72, 216–25
substantial property transactions, disclosure of
    interests in, 217–18
ultra vires transactions, 82
to whom owed, 213–14
DIRECTORS' POWERS, 188, 200–6
abuse/misuse of, 135, 207, 208–9
actual authority, 200–1
calls, 144
collective, 195
court protection, and, 351, 360
delegation, 200–1
EU Regulations (1973), 206
executive directors, 200–1
exercise of, 208–10
good faith requirement, 137–8, 207–8. *see
    also* FIDUCIARY DUTIES
implied actual authority, 201
ostensible authority, 201–6
receivership, in, 302–3
registration of share transfers, refusal of,
    137–9
share transfers 137-139
specific powers, 200
Turquand's Case, rule in, 203–6
voluntary winding up, in, 329
DIRECTORS' REPORTS, 249, 254–6
annual returns, annexed to, 249, 261
audit committee's activities, details of, 256
compliance statements, 256
contents, 254–5
liability for non-compliance, 256
DISCLAIMERS OF CONTRACTS, 337–9
effect on third party, 338

extent of creditor's entitlement, 339
DISCLAIMERS OF LIABILITY
promoters, 32
DISCLOSURE REQUIREMENTS, 5, 6. *see also*
    AUDITORS' REPORT; DIRECTORS' REPORTS
amalgamations, 294, 295
contracts, interests in, 217–18, 221
directors, 216–18
market abuse provisions, 159
notice of meetings, 165
promoters, 28, 29, 30
shares, interests in, 6, 216–17
substantial property transactions, 217–18
DISCRETION, FETTERING OF, 209–11
DISHONESTY
restriction of directors, 232, 233–5, 238
DISPOSAL OF ASSETS
non-cash assets, 308
receiver's duty of care, 305–8, 314
DISPOSITIONS, POST-COMMENCEMENT, 334–7
DISQUALIFICATION OF DIRECTORS ETC, 5, 7, 231,
    239–45
acting while disqualified, 245
automatic disqualification, 240, 244
Director of Corporate Enforcement, powers
    of, 20
Director of Public Prosecutions, powers of,
    23
discretionary disqualification, 240–1
effect of order, 240
'mismanagement,' 242–3
notification to registrar, 245
ODCE Report 2005, 22
order, 239–40
period of disqualification, 244–5
power to disqualify, 239
promoters, 32, 240, 241
scope of application, 241–2
selective or partial, 243–4
striking off, following, 40
'unfitness,' 242–3
DISREGARDING MEMBERS' INTERESTS, 183–4
DISSOLUTION OF COMPANIES, 6, 39–41, 315
annual return, default in, 263
assets, vesting of, 39
court order, 39
liability, continuance of, 40
liquidation, on, 39
powers of Registrar, 23
restoration to register, 40–1
striking off by Registrar, 23, 39–41
transfer of files to Public Record Office, 40
void, 40
DISTRIBUTABLE PROFITS, 145–6
distributions, definition of, 146
profits, definition of, 145–6
realised profits, 146
DISTRIBUTION OF ASSETS. *see* ASSET DISTRIBUTION
DISTRIBUTIONS. *see* DIVIDENDS

DIVIDENDS, 84, 145–9
  arrears, 88
  declaration of, 148–9
  distributable profits, 145–6
  distributions, 145, 146–8
  general provisions, 147
  investment companies, 147
  non-cash assets, 149
  payments, 149
  preference shareholders, 86–8
  profits available for distribution, 145–6
  public limited companies, restrictions for 146-
    147
  scrip dividends, 149
  time limit for claims, 149
  unlawful distributions, 147–8
  unpaid, 149
DONATIONS TO POLITICAL PARTIES, 255, 260
DUTIES. see also FIDUCIARY DUTIES
  auditor, 266–9
  directors. see DIRECTORS' DUTIES AND
    LIABILITIES
  liquidators, 316, 330, 333
  receiver, 305–12
  voluntary liquidator, 330
DUTY OF CARE
  auditors, 267–9
  directors, 225–30, 344
  receiver, 305–8

EAST INDIA COMPANY, 1
EFFICIENT MARKET HYPOTHESIS, 150
EMPLOYEE SHARE SCHEMES, 104
EMPLOYEES
  compulsory winding up, and, 323
  directors' duties to, 215
  preferential creditors, as, 347–8
  receivership, and, 304
  voluntary winding up and, 329
ENFORCEMENT AND COMPLIANCE, 6, 7, 17–26
  arrest powers, 21, 325, 330–1
  auditors' duties, 23–4
  Companies Registration Office (CRO), 22–3
  Company Law Review Group, 25–6
  compliance statements, 7
  culture of non-compliance, 6, 17, 18
  Director of Corporate Enforcement, 6, 18–22.
    see also DIRECTOR OF CORPORATE
    ENFORCEMENT
  Director of Public Prosecutions (DPP), 23
  directors' duties, 221–2
  disqualifications. see DISQUALIFICATION OF
    DIRECTORS ETC
  examiners, role of, 24
  Financial Regulator, 25
  fines, 20, 22, 63, 70, 160, 222
  injunctions, 20
  inspectors, 23
  liquidators, role of, 20, 24

  market abuse provisions, 155, 159–60
  prosecutions. see PROSECUTION OF OFFENCES
  receivers, role of, 24
  reporting of offences, 20, 23–5
  restriction of directors. see RESTRICTION OF
    DIRECTORS
  seizure of assets, 325, 330–1
  Stock Exchange, role of, 25
  striking off. see DISSOLUTION OF COMPANIES
  supervisory and investigative powers of
    Director, 20–1
  Working Group report (1998), 17–18
EQUITABLE MORTGAGE
  shares, 144, 145
EQUITY, 8
EQUITY SECURITIES, 96–7, 101, 103, 106
EUROPEAN UNION, 8
  Financial Services Action Plan (FSAP), 9, 102
  legislation, 8–9
EXAMINERS. see also COURT PROTECTION
  appointment, 355–6
  certification of expenses, 361–2
  combined powers, 362
  compliance and enforcement role, 24
  compromise proposals, 363–4
  dealing with property, 360–1
  directors' powers, and, 360
  discretionary powers, 359
  disqualification, 240, 241
  expenses, 346, 366
  nomination of, 352
  powers, 359–62
  qualifications, 352
  receivership, and, 304
  remuneration, 366
  report, 364–6
  specific powers, 359–62
EXECUTIVE DIRECTORS, 190
  authority, 200–1
EXPRESS POWERS, 79–81
EXTRAORDINARY GENERAL MEETING (EGM), 114,
    162–3
  auditor, requisition by, 270
  procedure. see SHAREHOLDERS' MEETINGS
  requisitioning of, 163

FETTERING OF DISCRETION, DUTY AGAINST, 209–11
FIDUCIARY DUTIES, 8, 150, 207–16
  directors, 8, 150, 207–16. see also DIRECTORS'
    DUTIES AND LIABILITIES
  liquidators, 316
  promoters, 27–9
FINANCIAL ASSISTANCE FOR PURCHASING SHARES,
    120–3
  commercial reality test, 120
  exempted transactions, 122–3
  general prohibition, 120
  special resolution, 120–1
  statutory declaration of solvency, 122

Index

FINANCIAL INSTITUTIONS
  court protection, applications for, 352
  takeovers and acquisitions, 297
FINANCIAL INSTRUMENTS, 45, 70
FINANCIAL REGULATOR, 25, 104, 105, 106
  market abuse provisions, enforcement of, 158
FINANCIAL RISK MANAGEMENT OBJECTIVES, 255
FINANCIAL SERVICES ACTION PLAN (FSAP), 9, 102
FINANCIAL STATEMENTS. *see* ACCOUNTS; ANNUAL
    ACCOUNTS; ANNUAL RETURNS; AUDITED ACCOUNTS
FINES, 20, 22, 63, 70, 160, 222
FIXED CHARGES, 124, 125, 128, 298
  advantages of, 130–1
  book debts, over, 128–9
  disposal of charged asset, 125
  receivership, 310
FLOATING CHARGES, 73, 298
  advantages, 125
  book debts, 128
  crystallisation, 126, 130, 131, 302
  disadvantages, 130–1
  nature of, 125
  negative pledge clauses, 127
  primary security, as, 126–7
  receivership under, 308–9
  winding up situations, 342–3, 348
FLOTATIONS, 101, 110
FOREIGN COMPANIES
  registration, 36–7
FORGED TRANSFERS, 141
FORMATION OF COMPANIES, 9–10
  avoidance of legal obligations, 67–8
  commencement of business, 34–5
  expeditious registration, 36
  illegal or fraudulent purpose, for, 320
  notification of registration, 35
  pre-incorporation contracts, 30–2
  promoters, 27–32. *see also* PROMOTERS
  re-registration, 37–9
  registration, 32–4
  'sham' company, 68
  statutory declarations, 33
FOSS V. HARBOTTLE RULE, 8, 175–8
  exceptions, 178–81
  personal rights of shareholders, 176–8
FRAUD. *see also* FRAUDULENT TRADING
  accounts, 248
  corporate veil used for, 63, 68
  damages, 109
  disposal of assets, 24
  disqualification of directors etc, 240
  formation of company, 320
  minority, on, 179–80
FRAUDULENT PREFERENCES, 339–41
  intention to prefer, 341
FRAUDULENT TRADING, 4, 70, 222–3
  'knowingly' and 'with intent,' 222–3
  liability and sanctions, 70, 222
  single act, 223

FSAP (FINANCIAL SERVICES ACTION PLAN), 9
FUTURE DEVELOPMENT, 255

GARDA SIOCHANA, 19
GENERAL MEETINGS. *see* ANNUAL GENERAL MEETING
    (AGM); EXTRAORDINARY GENERAL MEETING
    (EGM); SHAREHOLDERS' MEETINGS
GLADSTONE, WILLIAM, 3n
GOOD FAITH. *see also* FIDUCIARY DUTIES
  alteration of articles, 53–5, 90
  alteration of objects, 46
  contractual capacity, 83
  court protection, petition for, 354–5
  directors' powers, exercise of, 137–8, 207–8
  promoters, 28
  reduction of share capital, 113
GOODMAN GROUP, 5, 350
GROUP ACCOUNTS, 13, 14, 71, 252–4
  AGM, to be laid before, 253
  annual accounts, 249, 252–4
  annual return date (ARD), 253
  annual returns, 262
  associated companies, 15
  Companies Act accounts, 252–3
  financial year, 253
  format and content, 252
  holding companies, 253
  IFRS accounts, 253–4
  regulations, 252, 262
  subsidiaries, 253
GROUP COMPANIES, 13–16
  agency relationship, 63, 64
  annual accounts. *see* GROUP ACCOUNTS
  associated companies, 14–15
  dominant influence, 14
  holding companies, 13, 15, 117
  participating interest, 14
  piercing the corporate veil, 63, 64–5
  related companies, 15–16
  single economic entity test, 63, 65–7
  subsidiary companies, 13–14, 117
GUARANTEE, COMPANY LIMITED BY, 10, 11, 12, 43,
    72

HEALTH AND SAFETY
  directors' liability, 72
HIGH COURT
  investigation of company, 275–6
HISTORY, 1–9
HOLDING COMPANIES, 13–14
  definition, 13
  subsidiary's acquisition of shares in, 117
HONESTY AND RESPONSIBILITY
  restriction of directors, 232, 233–5, 238

IAS REGULATION, 9
IFRS ACCOUNTS, 250, 251
  group accounts, 253–4
  notes, contents of, 251

ILLEGAL OBJECTS, 46, 320
IMPLIED POWERS, 79–81, 201
INCORPORATION, 2
  abuse of privilege, 17, 67
  board of directors, 73
  certificate of, 33, 34, 35, 59
  charter, by, 1, 9
  commencement of business, 34–5
  consequences of, 59–74
  CRODisk system, 36
  floating charge, 73
  foreign companies, 36–7
  legal status. *see* SEPARATE LEGAL PERSONALITY
  letters patent, by, 2–3, 9–10
  limited liability, 3, 17, 72
  memorandum. *see* MEMORANDUM OF
    ASSOCIATION
  notification requirements, 33, 35
  perpetual succession, 34, 72–3
  pre-incorporation contracts, 30–2
  privilege, 17, 67
  re-registration, 37–9
  registered office, 73–4
  registration, 3, 10, 32–4. *see also*
    REGISTRATION OF COMPANIES
  revocation of grant. *see* DISSOLUTION OF
    COMPANIES
  rights of company, 59
  Salomon's case, principles in, 59–60, 61
  segregation of ownership, 62
  separate legal personality, 59–72
  statutory companies, 10
  suing and being sued, 62–3
  tax concessions, 73
  transferable shares, 73
  veil of, 60–72
INDEMNIFICATION
  Director of Corporate Enforcement, 21
  directors, 230
  receiver, 313
INDEPENDENCE (1921), 3–4
INDEPENDENT ACCOUNTANT'S REPORT, 352–4, 363
INDEPENDENT OBJECTS CLAUSE, 76–7, 78
INDUSTRIAL CREDIT COMPANY, 10
INFORMAL RESOLUTIONS, 172–3, 195–6
INJUNCTIONS, 20, 82
INSIDE INFORMATION, 156–7
INSIDER DEALING, 5, 6, 9, 150–1, 295. *see also*
  MARKET ABUSE
  civil liability, 154–5
  Companies Act 1990 provisions, 151–5
  criminal liability, 155
  'dealing,' definition of, 151–2
  general prohibitions, 151–2, 156–8
  regulations, 151, 156–60
INSOLVENCY. *see also* COURT PROTECTION;
  LIQUIDATION; RECEIVERSHIP
  creditors, duty owed to, 222
  cross-border proceedings, 9

dividends owed, 88
EU Insolvency Regulation, 9, 332
fraudulent trading, 4, 80, 222–3
reckless trading, 223–4
restriction of directors. *see* RESTRICTION OF
  DIRECTORS
schemes of arrangement, 286, 287
INSPECTION. *see also* INSPECTORS; INVESTIGATION
  OF COMPANIES
  accounts, 246–7
  books and documents, 279, 280–1, 282–3
  committees of inspection, 323, 328–9
  register of members, 136
  section 19 orders, 279–81
INSPECTORS, 5, 16, 21, 23, 71. *see also*
  INVESTIGATION OF COMPANIES
  appointment, 5, 20, 21
  court investigations, 275–6
  powers of, 281–3
  report, 283–5
INTEREST PAYMENTS, 84
INTERESTS, DISCLOSURE OF. *see* DISCLOSURE
  REQUIREMENTS
INTERMEDIARIES, 101
INTERNATIONAL ACCOUNTING STANDARDS (IAS),
  9
INTERNATIONAL ACCOUNTING STANDARDS (IAS)
  REGULATION, 9
INTERNATIONAL FINANCIAL REPORTING STANDARDS,
  250, 251
INVESTIGATION OF COMPANIES, 6, 16, 23, 275–85
  court investigations, 275–6
  Director of Corporate Enforcement, powers
    of, 20–1
  expenses, 285
  inspectors' powers, 281–3. *see also*
    INSPECTORS
  inspectors' reports, 283–5
  production of books and documents, 279,
    280–1, 282–3
  related companies, 71
  section 15 inquiry, 278
  section 14 investigations, 277–8
  section 19 order, 279–81
  section 16 restrictions on shares, 278–9
  types of investigations, 275–81
  winding up order, 23, 283–4
  winding up petition, 285
INVESTMENT FUNDS LEGISLATION, 7
IRELAND'S INDEPENDENCE (1921), 3, 10
IRISH AUDITING AND ACCOUNTING SUPERVISORY
  AUTHORITY. *see* SUPERVISORY AUTHORITY
IRISH ENTERPRISE EXCHANGE (IEX), 103, 151
IRISH FINANCIAL SERVICES REGULATORY
  AUTHORITY. *see* FINANCIAL REGULATOR
IRISH FREE STATE, 10n
IRISH STOCK EXCHANGE. *see* STOCK EXCHANGE
IRISH TAKEOVER PANEL, 296
ISEQ, 151, 253

ISSUED SHARE CAPITAL, 111
ISSUING HOUSE, 101

JENKINS COMMITTEE (UK), 4n
JOINT STOCK COMPANIES, 1, 2, 3
JUST AND EQUITABLE GROUNDS
   restriction of directors, 236–7
   winding up order, 69, 185–7, 319–21

LAW SOCIETY OF IRELAND, 9
LAW TIMES, 17
'LAWFULLY AND EFFECTIVELY' TEST, 82
LEGAL MORTGAGES
   shares, over, 143–4
LEGAL OBLIGATIONS
   avoidance of, 67–8
LEGAL STATUS. *see* SEPARATE LEGAL PERSONALITY
LEGISLATION, 2–8. *see also* COMPANY LAW
LETTERS PATENT, 2–3, 9–10
LEX CONCURSUS, 332
LIABILITY. *see also* CIVIL LIABILITY; CRIMINAL
     LIABILITY; LIMITED LIABILITY
   auditors, 268
   cheques etc, dishonour of, 70
   clause, 47
   debts, 72
   Director of Corporate Enforcement, 21
   directors and other officers, 45, 71–2, 248,
     344. *see also* DIRECTORS' DUTIES AND
     LIABILITIES
   fraudulent or reckless trading, 70
   indemnification, 21, 230, 313
   liquidator's application against officers, 344
   members, 10–11, 85
   misdescription, 70
   promoters, 29–30, 32
   prospectuses, mis-statements in, 106–9
   receivers, 313–14
   unlawful dealing, 154–5
LIEN ON SHARES, 145
LIMITED COMPANIES
   conversion to or from, 38, 47
   guarantee, limited by, 10, 11, 43
   name of company, 43–4
   shares, limited by, 10, 11, 42, 43, 50
LIMITED LIABILITY, 1, 3, 10, 17, 72
   1855 Act, 3
   memorandum, clause in, 47
LIQUIDATION, 5, 126, 315–32
   application of assets. *see* ASSET DISTRIBUTION
   assets, realisation of. *see* ASSET REALISATION
   commencement of, 322, 329, 334
   committee of inspection, 323, 328–9
   compulsory, 317–26. *see also* COMPULSORY
     LIQUIDATIONS
   corporate personality, 315
   costs of winding up, 346
   court order, 322
   court powers, 324–5

cross-border dimensions, 332
Director of Corporate Enforcement, powers
   of, 332
disclaimer of onerous contracts, 337–9
dissolution of company, 39
duties and functions of liquidator. *see*
   LIQUIDATORS
effect of winding up order, 322–3
EU Insolvency Regulation, 332
fraudulent preference (s. 286), 339–41
grounds for, 317–21, 326, 327, 328
hearing, 321–2
High Court petition, 317
inspection, 330, 332
investigation, following, 283–4, 285
just and equitable reason, 185–7
member's petition, 185–7
notification and filing requirements, 322, 326,
   327, 328
post-commencement dispositions, 334–7
proving claims, 345
receivership, and, 303–4
related companies, 71
restriction of directors. *see* RESTRICTION OF
   DIRECTORS
statement of affairs, 322
supervision, 332
types of, 317
voluntary, 326–32. *see also* VOLUNTARY
   LIQUIDATIONS
LIQUIDATORS
   appointment, 315, 321, 322, 327, 328
   asset-swelling powers, 333–4
   assets, realisation of. *see* ASSET REALISATION
   disqualification, 240, 241, 315
   duties and functions, 316, 330, 333
   enforcement and compliance role, 20, 24
   fiduciary duties, 316
   misfeasance, 333
   official liquidator, 322. *see also* COMPULSORY
     LIQUIDATIONS
   powers of, 323–4, 329–30
   provisional, 321, 358
   qualifications, 315
   removal from office, 326
   remuneration, 322, 327, 329, 346
   reporting obligations, 20, 24
   resignation of, 326
   restriction of directors, obligation in relation
     to, 24, 231
   statutory duties, 330
   supervision of, 20
   vesting of property in, 323–4
   voluntary. *see* VOLUNTARY LIQUIDATIONS
LISTING RULES, 110, 297
LITIGATION, 62–3
LOAN CAPITAL, 111, 124. *see also* CHARGES;
   DEBENTURES; FIXED CHARGES; FLOATING
   CHARGES

LOAN TRANSACTIONS
  directors, with, 219–21
  shares as security, 143–4
LOCAL OFFERS, 103
LOSSES
  capital, 114
  realised, 146
  reflective, 177

MACNAGHTEN, LORD, 8
MAIN OBJECT RULE, 76, 77
MAINTENANCE OF SHARE CAPITAL, 111–23. *see also*
    SHARE CAPITAL
MALA FIDES. see BAD FAITH
MANAGEMENT, 200. *see also* DIRECTORS
  deadlock, 320
  delegation, 188
  mismanagement, 242–3
MANAGING DIRECTOR, 200
MARKET ABUSE, 7, 150–60
  acquisition or disposal of shares, 295
  civil liability, 154–5, 159
  companies, dealing by, 153
  competent authority, 158
  connected persons, 152
  criminal liability, 155, 159
  'dealing,' definition of, 151–2
  enforcement, 155, 158
  EU Directive, 9
  exemptions from prohibition, 154
  Financial Regulator, role of, 25, 158
  general prohibitions, 151–2, 156–8
  'inside information,' definition of, 156–7
  legislative framework, 151–60
  market insiders, 151
  'market manipulation,' 157–8
  market operators, obligations of, 159
  offences, 155, 159, 160
  others, dealing by, 153
  recommendations, 158
  regulations, 25, 151, 156–60
  'securities,' definition of, 152
  'tippees,' prohibition on, 152–3
MARKET MANIPULATION, 9, 150–1. *see also*
    MARKET ABUSE
  conduct constituting, 157–8
  definition, 157
MARKET OPERATORS
  obligations of, 159
MARKET PURCHASES, 116–17
MARKET VALUE OF SHARES, 98
MEDIUM-SIZED PRIVATE COMPANIES. *see* SMALL AND
    MEDIUM-SIZED PRIVATE COMPANIES
MEETINGS. *see* BOARD MEETINGS; SHAREHOLDERS'
    MEETINGS
MEMBERS' VOLUNTARY WINDING UP, 326–7. *see
    also* VOLUNTARY LIQUIDATIONS
  notification and filing requirements, 327
  solvency, declaration of, 326–7

statutory formalities, 326–7
MEMBERSHIP, 11–12, 96, 135–49. *see also*
    SHAREHOLDERS
  accounts and returns, rights in relation to, 259
  allotment of shares. *see* SHARE ISSUES
  annual return of members, 261
  assent principle, 52, 172–3
  asset distribution on winding up, 349
  calls, 144–5
  court protection, application for, 352
  death of member, 142
  decision-making, 170–2
  dividends, 145–9. *see also* DIVIDENDS
  index of members, 135
  insufficient number, 70
  investigation of, 21
  liability, 10–11, 85
  meetings. *see* SHAREHOLDERS' MEETINGS
  minimum number, 11–12, 70
  minority protection. *see* MINORITY PROTECTION
  private companies, 11–12
  public companies, 11
  register, 135–6. *see also* REGISTERS OF
    MEMBERS
  schemes of arrangement. *see* ARRANGEMENT,
    SCHEMES OF
  section 25 contract, 56–8
  share certificates, 142–3
  share warrants, 143
  single-member private limited companies, 12
  transfer of shares, 137–42. *see also* SHARE
    TRANSFERS
  transmission of shares, 142
  voluntary winding up. *see* MEMBERS'
    VOLUNTARY WINDING UP
MEMORANDUM OF ASSOCIATION, 3, 32, 35, 42–9
  'actually aware' test, 81–2
  articles contrary to, 50, 55
  association clause, 48
  authorised share capital clause, 47
  classes of shares, 86
  compulsory clauses, 42–8
  contractual capacity, and, 75–83. *see also*
    CONTRACTUAL CAPACITY
  contractual nature, 56–8
  display of company name, 45
  format, 42
  guarantee, company limited by, 43
  judicial construction, 50
  liability clause, 47
  name clause, 43–6
  non-compulsory clauses, 48–9
  objects clauses, 46–7, 62, 75. *see also* OBJECTS
    OF COMPANIES
  pre-emption rights, exclusion of, 97
  public limited company
    additional compulsory clause, 48
  reference memoranda, 36
  registration of, 42

Index

section 25 contract, 56–8
variation of class rights, 89
MENS REA, 62–3
MERGERS AND TAKEOVERS, 8, 291–2
  compensation payments, disclosure of, 294
  directors' duties and liabilities, 294–5
  disclosure requirements, 294, 295
  EU Directives, 292, 296
  financial institutions, 297
  general rules, 294–7
  'squeeze out provisions,' 292
  Substantial Acquisition Rules, 296–7
  Takeover Rules, 296
MINISTERIAL REGULATIONS, 8, 9
MINORITY PROTECTION, 4, 174–87
  abuse of powers by directors, 210
  alteration of articles, 53–4
  court's discretionary powers, 184–5
  derivative actions, 180–1
  disregarding members' interests, 183–4
  Foss v. Harbottle, rule in, 175–8
  fraud on the minority, 179–80
  oppressive conduct, 55, 182–3, 321
  reflective loss, 177–8
  rights of minority shareholders, 174–5
  section 205 action, 55, 181–5
  ultra vires transactions, 178
  winding up petition by member, 185–7
MINUTES OF MEETINGS, 169
MIS-STATEMENTS, 106–9
MISCONDUCT, REPORTING OF, 311
MISFEASANCE, 224–5
MISLEADING PROSPECTUSES, 109
MISMANAGEMENT, 242–3. *see also*
  DISQUALIFICATION OF DIRECTORS ETC
MORTGAGES. *see also* CHARGES
  shares, over, 143–4

NAME OF COMPANY
  change of, 44, 45–6
  display of, 45
  failure to state correctly, 70
  guidelines, 44
  limited/teoranta designation, 43, 70
  name clause in memorandum, 43–6
  passing off, 44
  plc/cpt designation, 70
  private companies, 43
  prohibitions, 44
  public limited companies, 43
  registered, 43–6
  reservation, 43
  trading name, 44
NATIONAL IRISH BANK LTD, 22
NEGATIVE PLEDGE CLAUSES, 127
NEGLIGENCE
  auditor, 268
  director's duty of care, 225–30
  misrepresentation, 109

promoters, 29–30, 32
receiver, 305, 306
NOMINAL VALUE OF SHARES, 98
NOMINEE SHAREHOLDINGS, 21
NON-CASH ASSETS
  acquisition of, 218
  disposal of, by receiver, 308
  restrictions on acquisition of, 218
NON-CASH CONSIDERATION
  share issues, 12, 98–100
NON-EXECUTIVE DIRECTORS, 190
NOTICE OF MEETINGS, 163–6
  AGM, 163–4
  disclosure of relevant information, 165
  form and content of, 165–6
  Table A requirements, 164
NOTIFICATION REQUIREMENTS
  CRO Gazette, 33, 35, 49, 94, 322, 326, 327
  Registrar, to. *see* REGISTRAR OF COMPANIES

OBJECTS OF COMPANIES, 46, 62
  alteration, 46–7, 75
  ancillary powers, 76, 78–9
  Bell Houses clauses, 77
  borrowing powers, 78, 124
  contractual capacity, and, 75–81
  express and implied powers, 79–81
  illegal, 46
  independent objects clauses, 76–7
  judicial interpretation, 76–81
  main object rule, 76, 77
  objects clauses, 46–7, 75
  objects v. powers, 77–9
  solvency requirement, 80
  substratum, failure of, 46
  ultra vires transactions, 46, 47, 75–82
ODCE REPORT 2005, 22, 23, 24. *see also*
  DIRECTOR OF CORPORATE ENFORCEMENT
OFF-MARKET PURCHASES, 115–16
OFFENCES. *see also* CRIMINAL LIABILITY; DIRECTOR OF
  CORPORATE ENFORCEMENT; ENFORCEMENT AND
  COMPLIANCE; FINES; PROSECUTION OF OFFENCES
  disqualification of directors etc, 240
  fraudulent trading, 222
  market abuse, 155, 159, 160
  reporting of, 20, 23–5, 155
OFFICERS, 188. *see also* DIRECTORS; SECRETARIES
  disqualification, 240, 241
  liability, 45, 71–2
OFFICIAL LIQUIDATORS. *see* COMPULSORY
  LIQUIDATIONS; LIQUIDATORS
OPPRESSIVE CONDUCT, 182–3, 321. *see also*
  MINORITY PROTECTION
ORDINARY RESOLUTIONS, 170
ORDINARY SHARES, 86, 91
OSTENSIBLE AUTHORITY OF DIRECTORS, 201–6
  constructive notice, 203–6
  EU Regulations (1973), 206
  Turquand's Case, rule in, 203–6

413

OWNERSHIP OF COMPANY
investigation of, 21
segregation of, 62

PARENT COMPANIES. *see also* GROUP COMPANIES;
HOLDING COMPANIES
agency relationship, 64–5
PARI PASSU PRINCIPLE, 92, 340, 345, 348
PARLIAMENTARY COMMITTEE ON JOINT STOCK
COMPANIES, 3n
PARTIAL DISQUALIFICATION, 243–4
PARTNERSHIPS, 1
quasi-partnerships, 63, 69, 321
PASSING OFF, 44
PERPETUAL SUCCESSION, 34, 72–3
PERSONAL LIABILITY. *see* CIVIL LIABILITY; CRIMINAL
LIABILITY; LIABILITY
PERSONAL RIGHTS
shareholders, 176–8
POLITICAL DONATIONS, 255, 260
POOLING ORDERS, 16, 343
POST-COMMENCEMENT DISPOSITIONS, 334–7
POWERS
director. *see* DIRECTORS' POWERS
examiner, 359–62
express and implied, 79–81
liquidator, 323–4, 329–30
objects and, 77–9
receiver, 312–13
PRE-EMPTION RIGHTS, 96–7
exclusion of, 97
PRE-INCORPORATION CONTRACTS, 30–2
disclaimer of liability, 32
payments under, 32
ratification, 31
PREFERENCE SHAREHOLDERS
dividend entitlements, 87–8
return of capital and surplus, 88
rights of, 86–9
voting rights, 88–9
PREFERENCE SHARES, 86–9
categories of, 91
PREFERENTIAL CREDITORS
receiver's duty towards, 308–9
winding up, priority in, 347–8
PRICE-SENSITIVE INFORMATION. *see* INSIDER
DEALING; MARKET ABUSE
PRIVATE COMPANIES. *see also* SMALL AND MEDIUM-
SIZED PRIVATE COMPANIES
accounts and returns, 12, 249–50
allotment of shares, 95, 98. *see also* SHARE
ISSUES
articles of association, 50. *see also* ARTICLES
OF ASSOCIATION
capital requirements, 12
commencement of business, 13, 34
conversion from public company, 37–8
conversion to public company, 37–8
definition, 11

membership requirements, 11–12
memorandum, 42
name clause, 43
public companies and, differences between,
11–13
share capital, 11, 12. *see also* SHARE CAPITAL
single-member companies, 11, 39
unlimited companies, 11, 12
PROFIT AND LOSS ACCOUNT, 162, 249, 252, 261.
see also ANNUAL ACCOUNTS
PROFITS
distribution, available for, 145–6
realised, 146
PROMISSORY NOTES, 45, 70
PROMOTERS, 2, 27–9, 27–32
agents, as, 30
breach of duties, remedies for, 29
conflicts of interest, 29, 30
definition, 27
disclaimer of liability, 32
disclosure of interests, 28, 29, 30
disqualification, 32, 240, 241
fiduciary duties, 27–9
good faith, duty of, 28
liabilities, 29–30, 32
pre-incorporation contracts, 30–2
preliminary expenses, 32
secret profits, 28, 29
statutory duties, 29–30
PROPER PURPOSE, USE OF POWERS FOR, 208–9
PROPERTY TRANSACTIONS
disclosure of interests, 217–18
PROSECUTION OF OFFENCES
Director of Corporate Enforcement, 19, 20, 22
Director of Public Prosecutions (DPP), 23
insider dealing, 155
mens rea, 62–3
PROSPECTUSES, 7, 9, 92, 101
allotment on foot of, 101, 109–10
annual information document, 106
application of rules, 103
approval, 105
breach of rules, 106
content, 105
criminal liability, 108
EU Directive, 9, 102
EU Regulations, 25
excluded offers, 103–4
Financial Regulator, role of, 25
format, 105
local offers, 103
mis-statements, liability for, 106–9
negligent misrepresentation, 109
passport, 106
'public offer,' 103
publication, 105–6
qualified investors, 103–4
regulated market, 103
regulatory framework, 102–3

remedies for mis-statements, 106–7, 109
rules, 102–10
summary, 105, 108
PROXIES, 169
PUBLIC COMPANIES, 4. *see also* PUBLIC LIMITED
    COMPANIES
allotment of shares, 95, 98, 99, 101–2. *see*
    also SHARE ISSUES
audit committees, 7
capital, 12
commencement of business, 13, 34–5
conversion from private company, 37–8
conversion to private company, 38
floating on Stock Exchange, 101
private companies and, differences between,
    11–13
share capital, 12. *see also* SHARE CAPITAL
trading certificate, 13, 34–5
PUBLIC LIMITED COMPANIES
additional memorandum clause, 48
definition, 11
dematerialisation of shares, 142
distributions, restrictions on, 146–7
memorandum of association. *see*
    MEMORANDUM OF ASSOCIATION
name clause, 43
undistributable reserves, 147
PUBLIC OFFER, 101, 102
definition, 103
prospectus rules, 102–10
PUBLIC RECORD OFFICE, 40
PURCHASE OF OWN SHARES, 114–17, 255
contingent purchase contracts, 116
exceptions to statutory prohibition, 115
market purchases, 116–17
off-market purchases, 115–16
statutory prohibition, 115
subsidiary, by, 117

QUALIFIED INVESTORS, 103–4
QUASI-PARTNERSHIPS, 63, 69, 321
QUORUM, 166–7, 196

RATIFICATION OF BREACH, 213
RE-REGISTRATION
cancellation of resolution, application for,
    38
capital requirements, 37–8
certificate of, 37
limited to unlimited company, 38
members' rights, 85n
private to single-member company, 39
single-member to private company, 39
special resolution, 37, 38
statutory declarations, 37
unlimited to limited company, 38
REALISATION OF ASSETS. *see* ASSET REALISATION
REALISED LOSSES, 146
REALISED PROFITS, 146

RECEIVERS, 5, 126, 298–314
agent of debenture holder, as, 300–1
appointment, 298–9, 313
breach of duty, 307–8
court-appointed, 299, 300
court officers, as, 300
Director of Corporate Enforcement, and, 20,
    311–12
disposal of assets, 305–8, 314
disqualification, 240, 241, 299
duties and functions, 24, 305–12
duty of care, 305–8, 314
effect of appointment, 301–5
employees, and, 304
enforcement and compliance role, 20, 24
general responsibility, 305
indemnity, right of, 313
invalid appointment, 313
liability, 313–14
misconduct, duty to report, 311
negligence, 305, 306
non-cash assets, disposal of, 308
personal liability, 313
powers, 312–13
preferential creditors, duty to, 308–9
proceeds of sale, application of, 308–10
removal, 300
remuneration, 300
resignation, 300
statement of affairs, 302
status, 300–1
supervision of, 20
RECEIVERSHIP. *see also* RECEIVERS
court protection, and, 358
crystallisation of floating charge, 302
directors, effect on, 302–3
directors' residual powers, 303
effect of, 301–2
examiner, and, 304
fixed charge, under, 310
floating charge, under, 308–9
liquidation, and, 303–4
notification requirements, 310–11
pre-appointment contracts, and, 313–14
publicity, 304–5
RECKLESS TRADING, 70, 223–4
liability, 70
objective test, 224
statutory requirements, 224
subjective test, 223–4
RECONSTRUCTION, SCHEMES OF, 291
procedure, 291
RECTIFICATION
register of members, 136
REDEEMABLE DEBENTURES, 92
REDEEMABLE SHARES, 91, 117. *see also*
    REDEMPTION OF SHARES
REDEMPTION OF SHARES, 117–20
cancellation on redemption, 118

conditions, 117–18
notification to the registrar, 119
premium, at, 118
section 89 validation, 119
Stock Exchange, duty to notify, 119–20
treasury shares, 118
REDUCTION OF SHARE CAPITAL, 112–14
court confirmation, 114
REDUNDANCY PAYMENTS, 348
REFERENCE MEMORANDA AND ARTICLES, 36
REFLECTIVE LOSS, 177–8
REGISTERED COMPANIES, 10
REGISTERED NAME. *see* NAME OF COMPANY
REGISTERED OFFICE, 73–4
REGISTERS
    charges, 133
    debentures, 93
    directors and secretaries, 198–9, 217
    directors' shareholdings, 4
    inspection, 74
    interests, 217
    members. *see* REGISTERS OF MEMBERS
    obligation to maintain, 72
    restricted persons, 239
REGISTERS OF MEMBERS, 135–6
    contents, 135
    errors or omissions, 136
    index, 135
    inspection, 136
    location, 135
    prima facie evidence, as, 136
    rectification, 136
    transferee, 137
    underlying arrangements, 136
REGISTRAR OF COMPANIES, 6
    establishment of office, 3
    name of company, and, 44
    notification requirements, 119, 170–1, 311
    striking off powers, 22–3, 39–40. *see also*
        DISSOLUTION OF COMPANIES
REGISTRATION OF CHARGES, 131–3
    form, 132
    offences, 133
    time limit, 131, 133
REGISTRATION OF COMPANIES, 3, 4, 10, 32–4
    certificate of incorporation, 33
    charges, 131–3
    CRODisk system, 36
    documentation, 32–3
    effect of, 34
    foreign companies, 36–7
    memorandum of association. *see*
        MEMORANDUM OF ASSOCIATION
    name clause, 43–6
    notification requirements, 33, 35
    re-registration, 37–9, 46
    reference memoranda and articles, 36
    registration number, 33
    residency requirement, 33

resolutions, 72
restoration to register, 40–1
statutory declarations, 33
striking off, 22–3, 39–41. *see also*
    DISSOLUTION OF COMPANIES
REGULATED MARKET, 103
    admission to, 102, 103, 106. *see also*
        PROSPECTUSES
RELATED COMPANIES
    court protection, application for, 359
    definition, 15–16
    investigation, 71
    pooling and contribution orders, 16, 343
    winding up, 71
REMOVAL FROM OFFICE
    auditor, 270–1
    director, 193–4
    Director of Corporate Enforcement, 22
    intention to propose, 164–5
    official liquidator, 326
    receiver, 300
REORGANISATION OF COMPANIES, 286–97
    amalgamations, 291–7
    schemes of arrangement, 286–90
    schemes of reconstruction, 291
REPRESENTATION
    ostensible authority, 201–3
RESCISSION, REMEDY OF, 29, 109
RESEARCH AND DEVELOPMENT, 255
RESIDENCY, 6, 33, 63, 69, 191
RESOLUTIONS. *see also* SHAREHOLDERS' MEETINGS
    authorised share capital, alteration of, 47
    notification of, 170–1
    ordinary, 170
    special, 170. *see also* SPECIAL RESOLUTIONS
RESTORATION TO REGISTER, 40–1
RESTRICTION OF DIRECTORS, 5, 7, 218, 220,
    231–9
    application for declaration, 231
    application of provisions, 232–3
    court relief, 238–9
    delay in proceedings, 235–6
    effect of declaration, 237–8
    'honesty and responsibility' requirement, 232,
        233–5
    'just and equitable' ground, 236–7
    limitation period, 234, 235
    liquidator's obligations, 24, 231
    onus of proof, 231–2
    partial relief, 238–9
    purpose of provision, 231
    register of restricted persons, 239
RETENTION OF TITLE CLAUSES, 128
REVIEW GROUP ON AUDITING, 7, 264
RIGHTS ISSUE, 102
ROYAL CHARTER, 10

SALOMON'S CASE, PRINCIPLES IN, 59–60, 61
SATISFACTION OF CHARGE, 134

SCHEMES OF ARRANGEMENT. *see* ARRANGEMENT, SCHEMES OF
SCHEMES OF RECONSTRUCTION. *see* RECONSTRUCTION, SCHEMES OF
SCRIP DIVIDENDS, 104, 149
SEAL OF COMPANY, 45
SECONDARY LEGISLATION, 8
SECRET PROFITS, 28, 29
SECRETARIES, 197–8
  authority, 197–8
  disqualification, 197
  functions and duties, 197
  qualifications, 197
  register details, 198–9\
  restricted persons, 197
SECTION 14 INVESTIGATION, 277–8
SECTION 15 INQUIRY, 278
SECTION 16 RESTRICTIONS, 278–9
SECTION 19 ORDERS, 279
  Directors' powers, 280
  grounds, 279–80
  production of books and documents, 280–1
SECTION 25 CONTRACT, 56, 85
  membership, applicable only to, 56–7
  memorandum and articles, 56–8
  termination, 39
SECTION 205 ACTION, 181–5. *see also* MINORITY PROTECTION
SECURED CREDITORS, 124
  definition, 346n
  winding up, options on, 346–7
SECURITIES, 84–93. *see also* DEBENTURES; SHARE ISSUES; SHARES
  definition, 152
  equity, 96–7
  insider dealing. *see* INSIDER DEALING; MARKET ABUSE
  public offer, 102–10. *see also* PROSPECTUSES
  regulated market, admitted to, 102, 103, 106
SEIZURE OF ASSETS, 325, 330–1
SEPARATE LEGAL PERSONALITY, 8, 59–60
  dissolution of company, 39
  Foss v. Harbottle, rule in, 175–6
  fraud or injustices, 68
  judicial recognition, 60
  piercing the corporate veil, 63–72
  Salomon's case, 59–60, 61
  segregation of ownership, 62
  suing and being sued, 62–3
  termination of, 39
  tests for, 63–72
  veil of incorporation, 60–2. *see also* CORPORATE VEIL
SERIES OF DEBENTURES, 92
SHADOW DIRECTORS, 189–90
  de facto directors, and, 190
  definition, 189
SHAM COMPANIES, 68

SHARE CAPITAL, 12, 111
  alteration, 51, 112–23
  articles of association and, 51, 112
  authorised, 111
  authorised share capital clause, 47
  financial assistance for purchasing shares, 120–3
  increase, 51, 112
  issued, 51, 111
  loss of capital, 114
  maintenance, 111–23
  minimum, 12
  private companies, 11, 12
  public companies, 12
  purchase by company of its own shares, 114–17
  redemption of shares, 117–20. *see also* REDEMPTION OF SHARES
  reduction, 51, 112–14
  related companies, 15
SHARE CERTIFICATES, 85, 95, 140, 142–3
  dematerialisation of shares, 142
  fraud, liability for, 143
  stolen, 141
  title, evidence of, 142–3
  transfer of shares, 140
SHARE ISSUES, 94–110
  allotment generally, 94–101
  authorisation, 94
  consideration, 98–100
  contract law, 95, 98–9
  discount, 98
  equity securities, 96–7
  intermediary, through, 101
  issuing house, 101
  letter of allotment, 95
  non-cash consideration, 12, 98–100
  non-compliance with statutory requirements, 96, 97
  pre-emption rights, 96–7
  process, 95–6
  prospectuses, 101, 102–10. *see also* PROSPECTUSES
  public, allotment to, 94, 101–2
  rights issue, 102
  tender, 102
  validation, 95
SHARE PREMIUM, 100–1
SHARE PRICES
  efficient market hypothesis, 150
SHARE QUALIFICATIONS
  directors, 192
SHARE TRANSFERS, 4, 137–42
  automated transfers, 141–2
  certification of transfer, 140
  dematerialisation of plc shares, 142
  forged transfers, 141
  instrument of transfer, 137
  procedure, 140–1

417

registration, directors' refusal of, 137–9
  restrictions on, 137
  stock transfer form, 140
SHARE WARRANTS, 143
SHAREHOLDERS, 135. *see also* MEMBERSHIP;
    SHAREHOLDERS' MEETINGS
  allotment process, 95–6. *see also* SHARE ISSUES
  debenture holders and, difference between, 84
  decision-making, 170–2. *see also* SPECIAL
      RESOLUTIONS
  directors' duties to, 214–15
  minority, protection of. *see* MINORITY
      PROTECTION
  ordinary, 86, 91
  personal rights, 176–8
  pre-emption rights, 96–7
  preference, 86–9, 91
  reflective loss, rule against, 177
  rights, 84–9, 176–8
  variation of class rights, 89–91
  voluntary winding up. *see* MEMBERS'
      VOLUNTARY WINDING UP
SHAREHOLDERS' MEETINGS, 135, 161–73
  adjournment, 167
  AGM, 161–2. *see also* ANNUAL GENERAL
      MEETING (AGM)
  assent principle, 172–3
  auditor's rights, 270
  chairman, 167
  class meetings, 163
  decision-making, 170–2
  discretion in decision-making, 171–2
  dissolution, 167
  extraordinary general meetings (EGM), 162–3
  informal decision-making, 172–3
  minutes, 169
  notice of meetings, 163–6
  notification of decisions, 170
  ordinary resolutions, 170
  procedure, 166–73
  proxies, 169
  quorum, 166–7
  removal of auditor, 270
  special resolutions, 170
  Table A requirements, 164, 165, 167, 169
  types of meeting, 161–3
  unanimous decisions, 170, 172
  voting and polls, 168–9
SHARES, 84–91
  allotment. *see* SHARE ISSUES
  annual return, 261
  bonus, 91
  calls, 144–5
  categories of, 91
  classes of, 86–9
  companies limited by, 10, 11, 12, 42, 43, 50,
      72
  deferred, 89
  dematerialisation, 142

disclosure of interests, 6, 216–17, 255
  dividends. *see* DIVIDENDS
  equitable mortgage, 144, 145
  financial assistance for purchasing, 120–3
  invalid issue, 95
  investigation of ownership, 21
  issue. *see* SHARE ISSUES
  legal mortgage, 143–4
  legal nature, 85
  lien on, 145
  loan, security for, 143–4
  market value, 98
  nominal value, 98
  ordinary, 86
  preference, 86–9
  prospectuses, 101, 102–10. *see also*
      PROSPECTUSES
  public, to, 101–2
  public companies, 95, 98, 99, 101–2
  purchase by company of its own shares,
      114–17, 255
  redeemable, 91
  redemption. *see* REDEMPTION OF SHARES
  registration of names, 95
  restrictions on, 278–9
  returns to registrar, 96
  rights issue, 102
  section 15 inquiry, 278
  section 16 restrictions, 278–9
  share premium, 100–1
  Stock Exchange requirements, 110
  tender, by, 102
  transfer of. *see* SHARE TRANSFERS
  transferability, 73, 137
  transmission, 142
  treasury, 91, 118
  variation of class rights, 89–91
SINGLE DEBENTURES, 91–2
SINGLE ECONOMIC ENTITY, 63, 65–7
SINGLE-MEMBER COMPANIES
  AGM, holding of, 162
  annual accounts, 254
  conversion, 39
  decisions of, 171
  general meetings, 166
  private limited companies, 11, 39
SKILL, DUTY OF
  auditors, 267–9
  directors, 226–7
SMALL AND MEDIUM-SIZED PRIVATE COMPANIES
  annual accounts, 12, 250–1, 252
  annual returns, 12, 261–2
  audit exemptions, 12, 258–9
  group accounts, 252
SOLVENCY, DECLARATIONS OF, 122, 326–7, 344
SOURCES OF LAW, 2–8. *see also* COMPANY LAW
  common law and equity, 8
SOUTH AMERICAN TRADING, 1–2
SOUTH SEA BUBBLE, 1–2

SOUTH SEA COMPANY, 1, 2
SPAIN, 1
SPECIAL RESOLUTIONS, 89, 116, 170
  alteration of articles, 51–2
  financial assistance for purchasing shares,
    120–1
  minority protection, 178–9
  non-compulsory clauses, alteration of, 48
  notification to Registrar, 170–1
  voluntary winding up petition, 326
STANDARD OF CARE
  directors, 242
STATE AID, 10
STATIONERY, 45, 192
STATUTORY COMPANIES, 10
STATUTORY CONTRACT. *see* SECTION 25 CONTRACT
STATUTORY DECLARATIONS, 33, 37, 43, 122, 326–7,
    344
STATUTORY DUTIES
  auditors, 266–7
  directors, 72, 216–25. *see also* DIRECTORS'
      DUTIES AND LIABILITIES
  liquidators, 330
  promoters, 29–30
  receivers, 305–12
STATUTORY INSTRUMENTS, 9
STOCK EXCHANGE, 9, 103, 153
  compliance and enforcement role, 25, 155
  flotations, 101, 110
  insider dealing, and, 153, 155
  listing rules, 110, 297
  market purchases, 116–17
  off-market purchases, 115–16
  redemption of shares, notification of, 119–20
STOP NOTICES, 136n
STRIKING OFF REGISTER, 22–3, 39–41. *see also*
      DISSOLUTION OF COMPANIES
  disqualification of directors, 40
  grounds, 39–40
  restoration, 40–1
SUBSIDIARY COMPANIES, 13–14, 15
  acquisition of shares in holding company,
    117
  agency relationship, 64–5
  annual return, 262
  deemed, 14
  definition, 13–14
  single economic entity, 65–7
SUBSTANTIAL ACQUISITION RULES (SARs), 296–7
SUBSTANTIAL INTEREST, UNDERTAKINGS OF. *see*
      ASSOCIATED COMPANIES
SUBSTANTIAL PROPERTY TRANSACTIONS
  disclosure of interests in, 217–18
SUBSTRATUM, FAILURE OF, 46, 319–20
SUPERVISORY AUTHORITY, 7, 19, 264
  Director of Corporate Enforcement and, 19
  establishment, 7
  functions, 273–4
  objects, 272–3

rights and powers, 274
  role, 259–60
SWORD BLADE COMPANY, 2

TABLE A, 50
  calls, 144
  chairman, 167
  directors' powers, 137–8, 200
  meetings, 162, 164, 167
  non-payment of calls, 144
  share capital, 112
  share transfers, 137
  variation of class rights, 89
TAKEOVERS. *see* MERGERS AND TAKEOVERS
TAXES
  concessions, 73
  priority in winding up, 347
TENDER FOR SHARES, 102
TIME LIMITS
  dividend claims, 149
  registration of charge, 131, 133
'TIPPERS', 152
TORTIOUS OBLIGATIONS, 62
TRADING CERTIFICATE, 13, 34–5
TRADING LOSSES, 114
TRADING NAME, 44
TRANSFER OF COMPANY. *see* AMALGAMATIONS;
      REORGANISATION OF COMPANIES
TRANSFER OF SHARES. *see* SHARE TRANSFERS
TRANSFERABLE SHARES, 73, 137
TRANSMISSION OF SHARES, 142
TRANSPARENCY DIRECTIVE, 7, 9
TREASURY SHARES, 91
  redemption of, 118
TRINITY COLLEGE DUBLIN, 9
TRUST DEEDS, DEBENTURE, 92
TURQUAND'S CASE, RULE IN, 203–6
TYPES OF COMPANY, 9–16

UBERRIMA FIDES
  court protection, petition for, 354–5
ULTRA VIRES DOCTRINE, 4, 8, 46, 47, 75, 85
  actually aware test, 81–2
  contractual capacity, and, 75–82. *see also*
      CONTRACTUAL CAPACITY
  enforcement of transactions, 81–2
  good faith, 83
  injunctions, 82
  lawfully and effectively test, 82
  liability of directors etc, 82
  members and debenture holders, rights of, 82
  minority protection, 178
  statutory reform, 81–3
UNANIMOUS DECISIONS, 170, 172
UNDERTAKINGS OF SUBSTANTIAL INTEREST. *see*
      ASSOCIATED COMPANIES
UNFAIR DISMISSALS COMPENSATION, 348
UNFITNESS, 242–3
UNINCORPORATED ASSOCIATIONS, 2

UNLAWFUL DEALING, LIABILITY FOR, 154–5. *see also* INSIDER DEALING
UNLAWFUL DISTRIBUTIONS, 147–8
UNLIMITED COMPANIES, 11, 12
    annual accounts, 249
    conversion, 38, 47
UNSECURED CREDITORS
    winding up, and, 348

VARIATION OF CLASS RIGHTS, 48, 89–91
    cancellation, application for, 89
    confirmation by court, 89–90
    good faith, 90
    procedure, 89
    reduction of share capital, 113–14
    unfairly prejudicial, 90
    what constitutes, 90
VEIL OF INCORPORATION. *see* CORPORATE VEIL
VOLUNTARY LIQUIDATIONS, 326–32
    arrest powers, 330–1
    circumstances when applicable, 326
    commencement, 329
    completion of, 331–2
    conversion to compulsory liquidation, 331
    costs of, 346
    court powers, 330–1
    creditors' voluntary winding up, 327–9
    directors' powers, 329
    dissolution of company, 39
    duties of liquidator, 330
    effects of appointment of liquidator, 329
    employees, and, 329
    inspection, order for, 330
    members' voluntary winding up, 326–7
    notification requirements, 326, 327
    powers of liquidator, 329–30
    reconstruction, scheme of (ss. 260, 271), 291
    seizure of assets, 330–1
    transfer of shares following, 329
    types of, 326
VOTING
    board meetings, 196
    preference shareholders, 88–9
    shareholders' meetings, 168–9

WINDING UP. *see* COMPULSORY LIQUIDATIONS; LIQUIDATION; LIQUIDATORS; VOLUNTARY LIQUIDATIONS
WORKING GROUP ON COMPANY LAW COMPLIANCE AND ENFORCEMENT, 6, 17–18